# Lights of Fortitude

Light and glory, greeting and praise be upon the Hands of His Cause, through whom the light of fortitude hath shone forth and the truth hath been established that the authority to choose rests with God, the Powerful, the Mighty, the Unconstrained, through whom the ocean of bounty hath surged and the fragrance of the gracious favours of God, the Lord of mankind, hath been diffused. We beseech Him – exalted is He – to shield them through the power of His hosts, to protect them through the potency of His dominion and to aid them through His indomitable strength which prevaileth over all created things. Sovereignty is God's, the Creator of the heavens and the Lord of the Kingdom of Names.

*Bahá'u'lláh*

The Hands of the Cause are such blessed souls that the evidence of their sanctity and spirituality will be felt in the hearts of people. Their influence must be such that the souls may be carried away by their goodly character, their pure motives, their justice and fairness, that individuals may be enamoured of their praiseworthy character and their virtuous attributes, and that people may turn their faces towards them for their qualities and resplendent signs. 'Hand of the Cause' is not a title which can be given to anybody. Neither is it a position to be handed down to whomsoever may desire it . . . The more any soul becomes self-effacing, the more confirmed will he be in the service of the Cause of God; and the more humble, the nearer will he be to Him.

*Attributed to 'Abdu'l-Bahá*

# Lights of Fortitude

Glimpses into the Lives
of the Hands of the Cause of God

by

Barron Deems Harper

GR

George Ronald
Oxford

George Ronald, Publisher
www.grbooks.com


Reprinted with revisions 2007, 2021

*A Cataloguing-in-Publication number
is available from the British Library*

ISBN 978-0-85398-413-9

# Contents

*List of Illustrations* ix
*Introduction by Donald R. Witzel* xiii
*Acknowledgements* xix
*Publisher's Note* xxii

I. Hands of the Cause Appointed by Bahá'u'lláh c. 1887 to 1892

Mullá 'Alí-Akbar-i-Shahmírzádí, Ḥájí Ákhúnd 3
Mírzá 'Alí-Muḥammad (Ibn-i-Aṣdaq) 8
Mírzá Muḥammad-Taqí (Ibn-i-Abhar) 12
Ḥájí Mírzá Ḥasan-i-Adíb 15

II. Hands of the Cause Mentioned by 'Abdu'l-Bahá, 1892 to 1921

Mullá Muḥammad-Riḍáy-i-Muḥammad-Ábádí 19
Muḥammad-i-Qá'iní, Nabíl-i-Akbar 25
Mullá Ṣádiq-i-Muqaddas-i-Khurásání (Ismu'lláhu'l-Aṣdaq) 29
Mírzá 'Alí-Muḥammad Varqá 38

III. Hands of the Cause Appointed Posthumously by Shoghi Effendi (date appointment announced in brackets)

Ḥájí Abu'l-Ḥasan-i-Ardikání (Amín-i-Iláhí, Ḥájí Amín) (July 1928) 47
'Abdu'l-Jalíl Bey Sa'ad (25 June 1942) 50
John Henry Hyde Dunn (26 April 1952) 53
John Ebenezer Esslemont (30 November 1925) 64
Louis George Gregory (5 August 1951) 75
Keith Ransom-Kehler (28 October 1933) 87
Muḥammad Taqí Iṣfahání (15 December 1946) 97
Martha Louise Root (2 October 1939) 99

Muṣṭafáy-i-Rúmí (14 July 1945) 109
Roy C. Wilhelm (23 December 1951) 115

IV. Hands of the Cause Appointed by Shoghi Effendi on 24 December 1951

Dorothy Beecher Baker 129
Amelia Engelder Collins 139
'Alí-Akbar Furútan 147
Ugo Giachery 158
Hermann Grossmann 175
Horace Hotchkiss Holley 184
Leroy C. Ioas 194
William Sutherland Maxwell 204
Charles Mason Remey 213
Ṭarázu'lláh Samandarí 229
George Townshend 238
Valíyu'lláh Varqá 249

V. Hands of the Cause Appointed by Shoghi Effendi on 29 February 1952

Shu'á'u'lláh 'Alá'í 255
Músá Banání 259
Clara Dunn 267
Zikrullah Khadem (Dhikru'lláh Khádim) 279
Adelbert Mühlschlegel 288
Siegfried Schopflocher 299
Corinne Knight True 306

VI. Hands of the Cause Appointed Individually by Shoghi Effendi (date appointment announced in brackets)

Amatu'l-Bahá Rúḥíyyih Khánum (Mary Sutherland Maxwell) (26 March 1952) 323
Jalál Kházeh (Jalál Kháḍih) (7 December 1953) 338
Paul Edmond Haney (19 March 1954) 344
Dr 'Alí Muḥammad Varqá (15 November 1955) 351
Agnes Baldwin Alexander (27 March 1957) 356

## VII. Hands of the Cause Appointed by Shoghi Effendi on 2 October 1957

Hasan Balyuzi (Ḥasan Muvaqqar Balyúzí) 367
Abu'l-Qásim Faizi (Abu'l-Qásim Fayḍí) 380
Harold Collis Featherstone 387
John Graham Ferraby 400
Raḥmatu'lláh Muhájir, *by Iran Furútan Muhájir* 405
Enoch Olinga 411
John Aldham Robarts 421
William Sears 440

Appendix I: Letter from the Universal House of Justice dated 26 November 2007 451

*Bibliography* 457
*References and Notes* 463
*Index* 487

# List of Illustrations

*Between pages 16 and 17*

Ḥájí Mullá 'Alí-Akbar-Shahmírzádí, Ḥájí Ákhúnd
Ḥájí Ákhúnd in chains and fetters
Ibn-i-Aṣdaq
Ḥájí Mírzá Muḥammad-Taqí, known as Ibn-i-Abhar
Ibn-i-Abhar
Ibn-i-Abhar in chains
Mírzá-i-Adíb
Mullá Muḥammad-i-Qá'iní, known as Nabíl-i-Akbar
Mírzá 'Alí-Muḥammad-i-Varqá with his son Rúḥu'lláh

*Between pages 126 and 127*

Ḥájí Abu'l-Ḥasan-i-Ardikání, surnamed Amín-i-Iláhí (Ḥájí Amín)
Mírzá Músá Khán, Ḥakím Báshí; Muḥammad Labíb; Hand of the Cause Ḥájí Amín
'Abdu'l Jalíl Bey Sa'ad
Hyde Dunn
Dr John Esslemont
Louis Gregory
Keith Ransom-Kehler
Muḥammad Taqíy-i-Iṣfahání
Martha Root
Martha Root with Sister Grace Challis
Martha Root, taken in Bombay in 1937
Siyyid Muṣṭafá Rúmí

Roy Wilhelm
Mrs Greenleaf, Hand of the Cause Roy Wilhelm and Mrs Agnes Parsons

*Between pages 252 and 253*

Amelia Collins
Dorothy Baker
Dorothy Baker speaking at a meeting in India
Dorothy Baker at Kanpur, India
'Alí-Akbar Furútan
'Alí-Akbar Furútan with Bahá'ís in Leicester, England
'Alí-Akbar Furútan with the Spiritual Assembly of Moscow, 1990
'Alí-Akbar Furútan at a youth conference in Sheffield, England
Dr Ugo Giachery
Dr Ugo Giachery views the construction of the Samoan Temple near Apia, 1982
Dr Ugo Giachery with children during the Finnish Bahá'í Summer School, 1985
Dr Hermann Grossmann
Dr Hermann Grossmann, Frankfurt, Germany, 1951
Horace Holley
Leroy Ioas
Leroy Ioas with Bahá'ís in Africa, 1953
Leroy Ioas with four African Bahá'ís who had invited Shoghi Effendi to Africa
Leroy Ioas visits Bahá'ís in Leicester, England
Sutherland Maxwell
May and Sutherland Maxwell
Charles Mason Remey
Ṭarázu'lláh Samandarí
George Townshend
Fourteen Hands of the Cause at the European Intercontinental Teaching Conference in Stockholm, 1953
Valíyu'lláh Varqá with 'Azízu'lláh Varqá, Ṭihrán, 1908
Valíyu'lláh Varqá

*Between pages 320 and 321*

General Shu'a'u'll'áh 'Alá'í
General 'Alá'í, with Shamsi Navidi, in London
Músá Banání
Clara Dunn
Zikrullah Khadem and his wife, Javidukht

Zikrullah Khadem at a pioneer institute, United States, 1985
Zikrullah Khadem
Zikrullah Khadem with Bahá'ís during the Caribbean Conference, Kings-ton, Jamaica, May 1971
Adelbert Mühlschlegel
Hands of the Cause Adelbert Mühlschlegel and Hasan Balyuzi
Siegfried Schopflocher
Hands of the Cause in Africa
Corinne True
Corinne True

*Between pages 364 and 365*

Agnes Alexander
Bahá'ís of Honolulu on the occasion of the visit of Charles Mason Remey and Howard Struven, December 1909
Paul Haney
Paul Haney with his wife, Margery
Corinne True and Paul Haney
Paul Haney with pioneers at the International Teaching Conference, Mérida, Mexico, February 1977
Amatu'l-Bahá and Paul Haney assist at the election of the first Universal House of Justice, 1963
Jalál Kházeh
Hands of the Cause William Sears, Zikrullah Khadem, 'Alí-Akbar Furútan, General Shu'a'u'll'áh 'Alá'í, Raḥmatu'lláh Muhájir, Ṭarázu'lláh Samandarí, Collis Featherstone, Abul-Qásim Faizi, Dr Hermann Grossmann, Jalál Kházeh at Bahjí
Amatu'l-Bahá Rúḥíyyih Khánum
Amatu'l-Bahá Rúḥíyyih Khánum with the first National Spiritual Assembly of the Andaman and Nicobar Islands
Amatu'l-Bahá with Princess Gcenaphi and Chief Johannes Diamini of Swaziland at the Master's House, March 1984
Amatu'l-Bahá with chiefs and sub-chiefs in Ishamba, Zaire, January 1972
Amatu'l-Bahá presents The Promise of World Peace to Pérez de Cúellar, Secretary-General of the United Nations, 1985
Amatu'l-Bahá Rúḥíyyih Khánum with the first National Spiritual Assembly of Romania, Riḍván 1991
Amatu'l-Bahá and Músá Banání at the laying of the foundation stone of the House of Worship at Kampala, Uganda, 26 January 1958
'Alí Muḥammad Varqá
'Alí Muḥammad Varqá at a conference for Deputies of Ḥuqúqu'lláh, Landegg Academy, August 1991

*Between pages 450 and 451*

Hasan Balyuzi
Hasan Balyuzi
Hasan Balyuzi and three of his five sons
Abu'l-Qásim Faizi speaks to Bahá'ís in London
Abu'l-Qásim Faizi
Abu'l-Qásim Faizi with member of the Universal House of Justice Hushmand Fatheazam
Collis Featherstone
Collis Featherstone with his wife, Madge, and Golbang in Thailand, 1988
John Ferraby
John Ferraby with his wife, Dorothy, and daughter, Brigitte
Dr Raḥmatu'lláh Muhájir
Dr Raḥmatu'lláh Muhájir
Enoch Olinga
Enoch Olinga looks on as a transcontinental telephone call is made between the Oceanic Conference of the South China Seas, Singapore, and the Continental Conference for West and central Africa, 1–3 January 1971
John Robarts
John Robarts with Counsellors at the Counsellors/Auxiliary Board Conference in Manitoba, Canada, 1984
William Sears
Hands of the Cause Zikrullah Khadem and William Sears

# Introduction

The Institution of the Hands of the Cause of God is mentioned by Bahá'u'lláh in the Kitáb-i-Aqdas (the Most Holy Book):

> Happy are ye, O ye the learned ones in Bahá. By the Lord! Ye are the billows of the Most Mighty Ocean, the stars of the firmament of Glory, the standards of triumph waving betwixt earth and heaven. Ye are the manifestations of steadfastness amidst men and the daysprings of Divine Utterance to all that dwell on earth. Well is it with him that turneth unto you, and woe betide the froward.[1]

In the Book of His Covenant Bahá'u'lláh wrote, 'Blessed are the rulers and the learned among the people of Bahá.'[2] Shoghi Effendi clarified this:

> In this holy cycle the 'learned' are, on the one hand, the Hands of the Cause of God, and, on the other, the teachers and diffusers of His Teachings who do not rank as Hands, but who have attained an eminent position in the teaching work.[3]

In His Will and Testament 'Abdu'l-Bahá states that:

> The obligations of the Hands of the Cause of God are to diffuse the Divine Fragrances, to edify the souls of men, to promote learning, to improve the character of all men and to be, at all times and under all conditions, sanctified and detached from earthly things. They must manifest the fear of God by their conduct, their manners, their deeds and their words.[4]

'Abdu'l-Bahá also mentions:

> . . . that the Hands of the Cause of God must be ever watchful and so soon as they find anyone beginning to oppose and protest against the Guardian of the Cause of God, cast him out from the congregation of the people of Bahá and in no wise accept any excuse from him. How often hath grievous error been disguised in the garb of truth, that it might sow the seeds of doubt in the hearts of men![5]

The true unity, harmony and absolute love of the friends, coupled with the prohibition of disunity, backbiting and dissension, are very important for the protection of the Cause of God. The two main functions of the Hands of the Cause of God are the protection and propagation of the Bahá'í Faith. Their lives have been dedicated to these primary purposes.

> The Hands of the Cause of God were individuals appointed by Bahá'u'lláh and charged with various duties, especially those of protecting and propagating His Faith. In *Memorials of the Faithful* 'Abdu'l-Bahá referred to other outstanding believers as Hands of the Cause, and in His Will and Testament He included a provision calling upon the Guardian of the Faith to appoint Hands of the Cause at his discretion. Shoghi Effendi first raised posthumously a number of the believers to the rank of Hands of the Cause, and during the latter years of his life appointed a total of 32 believers from all continents to this position.[6]

In October 1957 Shoghi Effendi named the Hands of the Cause the 'Chief Stewards of Bahá'u'lláh's embryonic World Commonwealth'.[7] After the passing of Shoghi Effendi on 4 November 1957 at approximately midpoint in his Ten Year World Crusade (1953–63), the Hands of the Faith met at the World Centre to elect 'from their own number nine persons that shall at all times be occupied in the important services in the work of the Guardian of the Cause of God'.[8] These 'Custodians' carried on the work initiated by Shoghi Effendi and triumphantly won the many goals of the World Crusade in the name of their beloved Guardian, finally establishing the institution of the Universal House of Justice at Riḍván 1963 at an election at the World Centre of the Faith during the first International Bahá'í Convention.

A few days later at the first World Congress held in London to celebrate the great victory of the Ten Year Plan, the Universal House of Justice was presented to the Bahá'í World for the first time. Its first message was read to the assembled believers, who heard this tribute to the Hands of the Cause:

> The paeans of joy and gratitude, of love and adoration which we now raise to the throne of Bahá'u'lláh would be inadequate, and the celebrations of this Most Great Jubilee in which, as promised by our beloved Guardian, we are now engaged, would be marred were no tribute paid at this time to the Hands of the Cause of God. For they share the victory with their beloved commander, he who raised them up and appointed them. They kept the ship on its course and brought it safe to port. The Universal House of Justice, with pride and love, recalls on this supreme occasion its profound admiration for the heroic work which they have accomplished. We do not wish to dwell on the appalling dangers which faced the infant Cause when it was suddenly deprived of our beloved Shoghi Effendi, but rather to acknowledge with all the love and gratitude of our hearts the reality of the sacrifice, the labour, the self-discipline, the superb stewardship of the Hands of the Cause of God. We can think of no more fitting words to express our tribute to these dearly loved and valiant souls than to recall the words of Bahá'u'lláh Himself: 'Light and glory, greeting and praise be upon the Hands of His Cause, through whom the light of fortitude hath shone forth, and the truth hath been established that the authority to choose rests with God, the Powerful, the Mighty, the Unconstrained, through whom the ocean of bounty hath surged and the fragrance of the gracious favours of God, the Lord of mankind, hath been diffused.'[9]

On 6 October 1963 the Universal House of Justice, 'after prayerful and careful study of the Holy Texts' and 'after prolonged consideration of the views of the Hands of the Cause residing in the Holy Land' announced 'that there is no way to appoint or to legislate to make it possible to appoint a second Guardian to succeed Shoghi Effendi'.[10] In November 1964 the Supreme Body announced that

> There is no way to appoint, or to legislate to make it possible to appoint, Hands of the Cause of God.
>
> Responsibility for decisions on matters of general policy affecting the Institution of the Hands of the Cause, which was formerly exercised by the beloved Guardian, now devolves upon the Universal House of Justice as the supreme and central institution of the Faith to which all must turn.[11]

In 1968 the Universal House of Justice established the Continental Boards of Counsellors with the view of extending into the future the Hands' functions of protection and propagation of the Faith. In 1973 the Supreme Body appointed the International Teaching Centre in the Holy Land, comprising four Hands of the Cause and three Counsellor members.

As the surviving representatives of the institution of Hands of the Cause pass away, it seems more important than ever to learn something of lives and services of these high-ranking, long-suffering officers of the Cause of God. Thus this book by Barron Harper is especially welcome at this time.

It was in the summer of 1987 that Barron awoke one morning with the idea to write a book on the Hands of the Cause. A Bahá'í since 1967, he had met Hands of the Cause Amatu'l-Bahá Rúḥíyyih Khánum, William Sears, 'Alí-Akbar Furútan, Enoch Olinga, John Robarts, Zikrullah Khadem and Ṭarázu'lláh Samandarí, all of whom had greatly inspired him. It occurred to him that little had been written about all 'these special people' and 'the project felt like something he could and wanted to do'. Thus he began the present work.

Mr Harper's professional background is in business. He holds a Masters degree in Accounting from North Texas State University. In 1986 he began his own accounting practice. In September 1992 he and his wife Nancy pioneered to Portugal, where he has taught principles of accounting, finance, management accounting and general accounting at private and public universities. In earlier years the family pioneered to Argentina.

Barron has served on seven local spiritual assemblies, regional teaching committees in Texas and Portugal and on the National Teaching Committee of Portugal. He has taught children's classes and at Bahá'í institutes and has lectured at colleges and clubs as well as on the radio and television. He has written several articles on the Faith and accounting.

Barron has been married since 1972 to Nancy, a professor of music at the University of Aveiro and an outstanding classical pianist. They have three children, Christopher, Leila and Eric.

Barron Harper's 'Glimpses' into the lives of Hands of the Cause are truly moving, as befits the station of these precious souls. In the words of the Universal House of Justice:

> The entire history of religion shows no comparable record of such strict self-discipline, such absolute loyalty, and such complete self-abnegation by the

leaders of a religion finding themselves suddenly deprived of their divinely inspired guide. The debt of gratitude which mankind for generations, nay, ages to come, owes to this handful of griefstricken, steadfast, heroic souls is beyond estimation.[12]

*Donald R. Witzel*

*Lights of Fortitude*

is dedicated to
my grandmother

*Mary Whatley Clarke*

historian, author, pioneer, philanthropist
whose unconditional love
nurtured me in my youth
and
sustains me in my years

and to my beloved father and mentor

*Ross Avery Harper*

who guided me to the blessed Cause of
Bahá'u'lláh

# Acknowledgements

Researching the life of any prominent person can be difficult, especially as the scholar must often sift through fragmentary and not always consistent sources in order to construct a reasonably accurate biography. To have prepared 50 brief biographies of the Hands of the Cause from scattered historical works, documents, news events, letters and recordings has been especially challenging, although greatly inspiring. When we consider, however, that in coming decades and centuries their lives will be further scrutinized, and portrayed in works the excellence of which we can but dimly foresee, then the truly humble nature of this work can be appreciated.

The problems confronting the Hands of the Cause, the uncertainties they encountered, the hardships they suffered and the courage they evinced in their sterling services to the Cause they so loved were by any standard formidable. For they were our Standard-bearers. Through their unshakeable faith, their unyielding perseverance and their astonishing devotion, they overcame many obstacles, released into the world tremendous transformative forces, and, in so doing, blazed a path of servitude the standard of which will surely inspire the followers of Bahá'u'lláh in every land who peruse their stories to strive to follow in their footsteps.

As work on their stories unfolded, I received help from many valued sources. In the early years those who encouraged, assisted and advised me were the Universal House of Justice, Hand of the Cause William Sears, member of the Universal House of Justice Hooper Dunbar, Dr Charles Berdjis, Steve Bosserman, Bill Dunning, Dr Betty Fisher, Ken Gretton, Conchita Ioas, Flore Kavelin, Mary Kuebler, Dr Michael Lemon, Shirley

Macias, Nancy Phillips, Dr Mihdi Samandari, Kambiz Victory, Kay Zinky, Lewis Walker at the National Bahá'í Archives in Wilmette, and other dear friends who sent me their personal reminiscences.

Later there were those who generously consented to read or review 27 of the biographies, inspiring me to complete the project: Hands of the Cause Amatu'l-Bahá Rúḥíyyih Khánum, 'Alí-Akbar Furútan and Dr 'Alí Muḥammad Varqá; Samihih Banání, Gloria Faizi, Madge Featherstone, Javidukht Khadem, Ursula Mühlschlegel, Marguerite Sears, Iran Furútan Muhájir, Audrey Robarts and Nina Robarts Tinnion (who provided historical works and tape recordings), Brigitte Ferraby Beales, Hartmut Grossmann, Charles Ioas, Louise Baker Matthias; member of the Universal House of Justice 'Alí Nakhjavání and former member David Hofman; and Dr Wilma Ellis, Dr Agnes Ghaznavi, Nell Golden, Claire Vreeland and Donald Witzel. The Universal House of Justice read the article on Charles Mason Remey and made helpful comments for its revision.

I must also acknowledge with profound gratitude the kind assistance and suggestions offered so spontaneously in the later stages of the book by Universal House of Justice members Hushmand Fatheazam and Adib Taherzadeh, and by Eunice Braun, Philip Hainsworth (on behalf of the National Spiritual Assembly of the United Kingdom), Dr Moojan Momen, Dr Said Jalali, Hilda Rodrigues, Dr Duane Troxel, H. Kaye Waterman, the National Spiritual Assembly of the United States, and the Department of the Secretariat at the Bahá'í World Centre. My thanks go also to Stephen Lambden, who provided me with brief biographies he had written for the *Encyclopedia Iranica* on Hands of the Cause Ibn-i-Abhar and Ibn-i-Aṣdaq.

Special affection to my wife, Dr Nancy Lee Harper, who offered her comments on many chapters and whose love for Dorothy Baker prompted her to prepare much of that biography; and to our daughter, Leila, whose proof-reading was invaluable.

Dr Wendi Momen, my editor and collaborator, became a close and dear friend through this work. She was a source of encouragement and support in the last stages of the book and her finishing touches brought a sparkle to the manuscript.

Finally I would like to thank Violette Nakhjavání for clarifying the late travel itinerary of Amatu'l-Bahá; as well as Erica Leith and Dr Khazeh Fananapazir for their selfless assistance, and Judith Oppenheimer, whose persistence made possible the republication of *Lights of Fortitude*. Special thanks also to Javidukht Khadem, Hartmut and Ursula Grossmann, and Marguerite Sears for their generous collaboration.

*Barron Deems Harper, Sr.*
Portugal, January 2006

# Publisher's Note

Some readers may ask whether this work includes all the Hands of the Cause. The Research Department at the Bahá'í World Centre addressed this issue in a letter to Dr Moojan Momen in 1991:

> The list in *The Bahá'í World*, vol. 14, contains the names of those believers whose appointment as Hands of the Cause is clearly supported by the evidence that was available at the time of the compilation of the list. In the case of the Hands nominated by Shoghi Effendi, for example, their appointment was accompanied by an official and public announcement to the Bahá'í world.
>
> With regard to whether other individuals might be identified as Hands of the Cause, it is interesting to note that Shoghi Effendi in a letter dated 19 April 1947, written on his behalf in response to a question about the references to Hands of the Cause contained in *God Passes By*, p. 195 and pp. 328–329, stated:
>
>> The Hands of the Cause, of Bahá'u'lláh's days, will be known to the friends by name when the history of the Cause in Persia and the Near East is written and available.
>
> In the view of the Research Department, the conditions set out above by the beloved Guardian have not, as yet, been met. Additional research will be needed to identify and confirm the name of any individual who may have been addressed by Bahá'u'lláh as a Hand of the Cause. Until such research is completed, it is preferable to use only those names listed in *The Bahá'í World*.
>
> As to the status of believers who might have been addressed by Shoghi Effendi as Hands of the Cause but whose names were not announced publicly to the friends, this, too, is a matter requiring additional research. For the present, the Universal House of Justice . . . has instructed that such names should not be included in the list of the Hands of the Cause.

# I

# Hands of the Cause Appointed by Bahá'u'lláh c. 1887–1892

# Mullá 'Alí-Akbar-i-Shahmírzádí, Ḥájí Ákhúnd 1842–1910

Mullá 'Alí-Akbar was born in the village of Shahmírzád in the province of Khurásán in about 1842. His father, Mullá 'Abbás, had become a Bábí in Karbilá but the defeat of the Bábís at Fort Shaykh Ṭabarsí in 1848 made him doubtful of the new religion and his adherence to it weakened. Thus, 'Alí-Akbar knew something of the Bábí Faith during his childhood, but was not a believer.

After 'Alí-Akbar married he went to Mashhad to continue his religious education. 'Abdu'l-Bahá writes that he

> . . . attended institutions of higher learning and laboured diligently, by day and night, until he became thoroughly conversant with the learning of the day, with secular studies, philosophy, and religious jurisprudence. He frequented the gatherings of philosophers, mystics, and Shaykhís, thoughtfully traversing those areas of knowledge, intuitive wisdom, and illumination; but he thirsted after the wellspring of truth, and hungered for the bread that comes down from Heaven. No matter how he strove to perfect himself in those regions of the mind, he was never satisfied; he never reached the goal of his desires; his lips stayed parched; he was confused, perplexed, and felt that he had wandered from his path. The reason was that in all those circles he had found no passion; no joy, no ecstasy; no faintest scent of love.[1]

Then, when he was about 19 years old, 'Alí-Akbar came across a copy of the Kitáb-i-Íqán. After discussions with Mullá Ṣádiq Muqaddas and others, he became a Bábí in 1861.

Soon after his conversion to the Faith, he laid all caution aside and taught the new religion openly and freely. He was successful in converting a 'multitude' of souls,[2] thus arousing the anger of fanatical theological students, who forced him to flee Mas͟hhad. Returning to his native village, he began once again to teach the Cause. However, enemies in S͟hahmírzád soon launched fierce attacks upon him and he was compelled to leave his wife and child and go to Ṭihrán. Soon after his arrival in the city he became known as a Bahá'í and his teaching efforts again evoked the wrath of the clergy.

In 1868 he was imprisoned at the instigation of Ḥájí Mullá 'Alíy-i-Kaní, one of the leading mujtahids of Ṭihrán. It is not known how long he remained in prison, but he was eventually freed through the intervention of Mírzá 'Isá, minister to the governor of Ṭihrán.

About this time Bahá'u'lláh sent instructions for Ḥájí Ák͟húnd and Siyyid Jamál Burújirdí to remove the remains of the Báb from their hiding-place in the shrine of Imám Zádih Ma'súm. Shortly after the remains were removed the shrine was rebuilt and, had they not been moved, they would certainly have been discovered. Ḥájí Ák͟húnd and Siyyid Jamál could not find a safe hiding-place so they set off for C͟has͟hmih-'Alí. Along the way they came across the Mosque of Más͟há'u'lláh, which was in a state of disrepair, and they buried the casket containing the sacred remains under bricks in a niche in the wall. The next day, however, they found that the hiding-place had been discovered, so they took the casket to Ṭihrán, secretly hurrying with it through the guarded gates of the city. Ḥájí Ák͟húnd rented a room in the house of one of the Bahá'ís, Mírzá Ḥasan Vazír, and for 15 months lived in the house as custodian of the Báb's remains. However, it soon became known that the remains of the Báb were in Mírzá Ḥasan Vazír's home and Bahá'ís began to arrive in large numbers to pay their respects. This was likely to alert the authorities to the whereabouts of the Báb's remains, so Ḥájí Ák͟húnd wrote to Bahá'u'lláh asking what to do. Bahá'u'lláh responded by sending Ḥájí S͟háh-Muḥammad Mans͟hádí to remove the remains to another location.

After this, Ḥájí Ák͟húnd lived in different Bahá'í homes in Ṭihrán and was soon a leading figure in the Bahá'í community. He became one of the main channels through which the Bahá'ís communicated with Bahá'u'lláh and received His replies. Over the years Ḥájí Ák͟húnd was able to lead his father back to the Faith, as well as convert his two brothers and four sisters.

Ḥájí Ák͟húnd also became well known to the authorities and a target of persecution. He was arrested several times and imprisoned on at least five or six occasions.[3] Altogether he spent about seven years 'bound in chains and fetters in the gloomy surroundings that were the Persian jails'.[4] 'Abdu'l-Bahá writes that whenever Ḥájí Ákhúnd heard of an outburst of persecution of the Bahá'ís, he would 'put on his turban, wrap himself in his 'abá' and await the arrival of the guards to arrest him.[5] He once explained that he believed one should anticipate the will of God and not run away from it.

In about 1870 Ḥájí Ákhúnd travelled to 'Akká to see Bahá'u'lláh. During his pilgrimage his wife died. On his return to Ṭihrán he married Fáṭimih Bagum, a descendant of one of the Safavid kings. At the time of his wedding, he is said to have been living in a 'dilapidated room' while 'his earthly possessions consisted of a sheepskin and a kettle'.[6] Only three days after the wedding Ḥájí Ákhúnd was imprisoned on the orders of Náyibu's-Salṭanih. Though he suffered greatly in prison, being kept in a small cell with a chain around his neck and stocks on his feet, he endured his imprisonment 'in a spirit of joy, of pride and of thankfulness to his Lord'.[7]

Ḥájí Ákhúnd was once advised by his fellow Hands to conceal himself from his enemies during the month of Muḥarram, when many people are particularly fanatical. He replied:

> It is true that in the Holy Tablets we are commanded to observe wisdom. By wisdom is not meant to be fearful or to have no reliance upon God. It means to act with thoroughness, and to conduct oneself with truthfulness, benevolence and patience; it means to sow the seeds of the teachings of God in the pure and goodly soil of the hearts. It does not mean fear or hiding.[8]

In 1887 Ḥájí Ákhúnd was arrested, together with a number of other Bahá'ís. After his release from prison he travelled once again to 'Akká, attaining the presence of Bahá'u'lláh for the second time in 1888. It was about this time that Bahá'u'lláh appointed him a Hand of the Cause.

Ḥájí Ákhúnd received numerous Tablets from Bahá'u'lláh, Tablets showering His blessings upon this radiant soul and condemning the actions of Ḥájí Ákhúnd's oppressors. In one Tablet Bahá'u'lláh states that the Supreme Concourse weeps over Ḥájí Ákhúnd's sufferings and urges him to be joyful for having endured hardships in the path of God. In another He writes that Ḥájí Ákhúnd should thank his Lord again and again for having received so much spiritual food and so many imperishable benefits. In yet another Bahá'u'lláh states that God had chosen Ḥájí Ákhúnd for service to His Faith, pointing out that the greatest service is that of uniting souls and causing them to love each other.

In April 1891 the Sháh, in an attempt to suppress the growing demand for constitutional reforms, ordered the arrest of a number of the leading reformers. Although they had no connection with the political agitation, Ḥájí Ákhúnd and Ḥájí Amín were arrested and kept in prison in Ṭihrán and Qazvín for two years. A photograph of the Hand of the Cause reached 'Abdu'l-Bahá:

> The photograph of this blessed individual, together with that of the great Amín, taken of them in their chains, will serve as an example to whoever has eyes to see. There they sit, these two distinguished men, hung with chains, shackled, yet composed, acquiescent, undisturbed.[9]

Indeed the spiritual qualities of Ḥájí Ákhúnd had already struck the Sháh. When he was imprisoned in Ṭihrán in 1882, the Sháh expressed his desire to meet his distinguished prisoner. Fearing to come face to face with Ḥájí Ákhúnd, the Sháh looked at him from behind a window. Impressed by Ḥájí Ákhúnd's dignity and bearing, the Sháh ordered his photographer to take a picture of him seated in chains and stocks.

While Ḥájí Ákhúnd and Ḥájí Amín were in prison Bahá'u'lláh revealed the Lawḥ-i-Dunyá (Tablet of the World), mentioning their names in the opening lines. In this Tablet is found the well-known prayer for the Hands of the Cause.

During this last imprisonment of Ḥájí Ákhúnd, Bahá'u'lláh passed away. When the Hand of the Cause was released in 1894 he departed for 'Akká. There he learned of Mírzá Muḥammad-'Alí's rebellion against 'Abdu'l-Bahá. Ḥájí Ákhúnd met with Mírzá Muḥammad-'Alí to persuade him to change his position but was unsuccessful in his attempt. When he returned to Ṭihrán he began to emphasize to the believers the importance of the Covenant and tried to forestall the activities of the Covenant-breakers.

In 1897 'Abdu'l-Bahá instructed the Hands of the Cause, who were at that time living in Ṭihrán, to begin consultations with prominent Bahá'ís in the city concerning the future organization of the community. These consultations resulted in the formation of the Central Spiritual Assembly in 1899. The Assembly consisted of the four Hands of the Cause and nine men elected by special electors appointed by the Hands. This body was the predecessor of both the Local Spiritual Assembly of Ṭihrán and the National Spiritual Assembly of Iran.

Ḥájí Ák͟húnd died in Ṭihrán on 4 March 1910 and was buried in the shrine of Imám Zádih Ma'súm. 'Abdu'l-Bahá paid this tribute to him:

> After the ascension of Bahá'u'lláh, Mullá 'Alí continued on, loyal to the Testament of the Light of the World, staunch in the Covenant which he served and heralded. During the lifetime of the Manifestation, his yearning made him hasten to Bahá'u'lláh, Who received him with grace and favour, and showered blessings upon him. He returned, then, to Írán, where he devoted all his time to serving the Cause. Openly at odds with his tyrannical oppressors, no matter how often they threatened him, he defied them. He was never vanquished. Whatever he had to say, he said. He was one of the Hands of the Cause of God, steadfast, unshakable, not to be moved.[10]

Ḥájí Ák͟húnd was named an Apostle of Bahá'u'lláh by Shoghi Effendi.

# Mírzá 'Alí-Muḥammad (Ibn-i-Aṣdaq)
# c. 1850–1928

Mírzá 'Alí-Muḥammad was born in Ma<u>sh</u>had, the youngest son of the Hand of the Cause Mullá Ṣádiq-i-Muqaddas-i-<u>Kh</u>urásání, who fought at <u>Sh</u>ay<u>kh</u> Ṭabarsí and was tortured with Quddús in <u>Sh</u>íráz. Mullá Ṣádiq-i-Muqaddas was given the title Ismu'lláhu'l-Aṣdaq by Bahá'u'lláh, and as his son showed many of his outstanding qualities, Mírzá 'Alí-Muḥammad became known as Ibn-i-Aṣdaq, son of Aṣdaq.

In 1861, while Ibn-i-Aṣdaq was still a young boy, he was taken by his father to Ba<u>gh</u>dád to see Bahá'u'lláh. The visit lasted two years and made a deep impression on him. During their stay in Ba<u>gh</u>dád Bahá'u'lláh revealed a prayer for Ibn-i-Aṣdaq: 'I ask Thee, O my God! to give him to drink of the milk of Thy bounty so that he may raise the standards of victory through Me, – a victory which is Thine – and arise to serve Thy Cause, when he groweth up, just as, when a youth, he hath arisen at Thy Command'.[1]

On their return to Iran Ibn-i-Aṣdaq and his father were arrested on the orders of the governor of <u>Kh</u>urásán. They and two other Bábís were chained and taken to Ṭihrán. The intention was to execute them, but the government ordered instead that they be imprisoned in the Síyáh-<u>Ch</u>ál. Here they remained, chained together, for 28 months.

Ibn-i-Aṣdaq fell ill while in prison but no doctor would treat a Bábí. Eventually the gaoler asked a Jewish doctor, Ḥakím Masíḥ, to tend to the boy. Ḥakím Masíḥ attended him for about two months, soon afterwards becoming a believer.

When Ibn-i-Aṣdaq and his father were released from the Síyáh-<u>Ch</u>ál they returned to Ma<u>sh</u>had. As he grew up Ibn-i-Aṣdaq often accompanied his father on teaching trips throughout Iran. While still a young man he married the niece of Mullá Ḥusayn Bu<u>sh</u>rú'í, the first to believe in the Báb, but she passed away without having any children. His second marriage was to a Qájár princess, a great-granddaughter of Fatḥ-'Alí Sháh, 'Udhrá Khánum, Ḍiyá'u'l-Ḥájiyyih, called by her family Ághá Ján. Already a Bahá'í, she was educated, talented and well versed in Persian poetry and literature. The couple had four daughters.

When he was about 30 years old Ibn-i-Aṣdaq sent a letter to Bahá'u-'lláh, asking Him to grant him the station of 'utter self-sacrifice', martyrdom.[2] In January 1880 Bahá'u'lláh replied to him through his amanuensis, Mírzá Áqá Ján:

> Thou didst beg the Supreme Lord . . . to bestow upon thee a station whereat in the path of His love thou wouldst give up everything: thy life, thy spirit, thy reputation, thine existence, all in all. All of these behests were submitted in the most sanctified, most exalted Presence of the Abhá Beauty. Thus did the Tongue of the Merciful speak in the Kingdom of Utterance: 'God willing, he shall be seen in utmost purity and saintliness, as befitteth the Day of God, and attain the station of the most great martyrdom. Today, the greatest of all deeds is service to the Cause. Souls that are well assured should with utmost discretion teach the Faith, so that the sweet fragrances of the Divine Garment will waft from all directions. This martyrdom is not confined to the destruction of life and the shedding of blood. A person enjoying the bounty of life may yet be recorded a martyr in the Book of the Sovereign Lord. Well is it with thee that thou hast wished to offer whatsoever is thine, and all that is of thee and with thee in My path.'[3]

Two years later, in 1882, Ibn-i-Aṣdaq again wrote to Bahá'u'lláh asking for martyrdom. This time Bahá'u'lláh, addressing him as Shahíd Ibn-i-Shahíd (martyr, son of the martyr) replied:

> We, verily, have ordained for him this exalted station, this high designation. Well it is with him that he attained this station prior to its appearance, and We accepted from him that which he intended in the path of God, the One, the Single, the All-Knowing, the All-Informed.[4]

On receiving this reply Ibn-i-Aṣdaq devoted the rest of his life to teaching the Bahá'í Faith and encouraging the Bahá'ís. He travelled extensively, visiting Bahá'í communities the length and breadth of the country, his wife's royal connections enabling him to teach the Bahá'í Faith among the members of the Iranian nobility as well as royalty. Ibn-i-Aṣdaq many times referred to 'hunting the lion rather than the fox'.[5] He and his wife moved from Mashhad to Ṭihrán, where a house was provided for them in one the best quarters of the city.

Bahá'u'lláh encouraged Ibn-i-Aṣdaq in his travels for the promotion of the Word and revealed in his honour a Tablet containing this well-known verse: 'The movement itself from place to place, when undertaken for the sake of God, hath always exerted, and can now exert, its influence in the world.'[6]

It was in a Tablet revealed by Bahá'u'lláh in April 1887, through His amanuensis, in honour of Ibn-i-Aṣdaq that the concept of 'Hand of the Cause' was first mentioned.[7] He calls upon His amanuensis, Mírzá Áqá Ján, to beseech 'the All-Abiding Lord to confirm the chosen ones, that is those souls who are Hands of the Cause, who are adorned with the robe of teaching, and have arisen to serve the Cause, to be enabled to exalt the Word of God'.[8]

In another Tablet written to Ibn-i-Aṣdaq, Bahá'u'lláh, having been informed by him that the Bahá'ís of Ṭihrán had arranged to observe the Mashriqu'l-Adhkár, wrote the prayer 'Blessed is the spot, and the house, and the place, and the city, and the heart, and the mountain, and the refuge, and the cave, and the valley, and the land, and the sea, and the island, and the meadow where mention of God hath been made, and His praise glorified.'[9]

After the passing of Bahá'u'lláh in 1892 'Abdu'l-Bahá encouraged Ibn-i-Aṣdaq to continue teaching prominent people. In addition to teaching them in Ṭihrán, he extended the range of his travels, visiting India, Burma and Russian Turkestan, always seeking out the notables of every city. In Marv he began preliminary work on the construction of a Mashriqu'l-Adhkár and founded a hospice and junior school. At home he initiated the establishment of teacher-training classes for Bahá'í women.

The early years of the ministry of 'Abdu'l-Bahá were plagued by the machinations of the Covenant-breakers. 'Abdu'l-Bahá called upon the Hands of the Cause to counter their activities. Ibn-i-Aṣdaq and the other Hands travelled throughout Iran explaining to the Bahá'ís the nature and power of the Covenant and confirming them in it. In 1899 'Abdu'l-Bahá also called upon the Hands to establish an elected Spiritual Assembly in Ṭihrán to administer the Faith. From this body evolved the National Spiritual Assembly of Iran.

In 1919 'Abdu'l-Bahá asked Ibn-i-Aṣdaq and Aḥmad Yazdání personally to deliver a Tablet to the Central Organization for a Durable Peace at the Hague. In the same year Ibn-i-Aṣdaq and other Hands of the Cause wrote a refutation of some of the statements made by Professor E. G. Browne about the Bahá'í Faith. Ibn-i-Aṣdaq also delivered to the Sháh the Risáliy-i-Siyásíyyih (Treatise on Politics) written by 'Abdu'l-Bahá during the lifetime of Bahá'u'lláh.

Ibn-i-Aṣdaq lived well into the 20th century, thus serving not only Bahá'u'lláh and 'Abdu'l-Bahá but Shoghi Effendi as well. He outlived his fellow Hands, passing away in Ṭihrán in 1928. Shoghi Effendi named him an Apostle of Bahá'u'lláh.

# Mírzá Muḥammad-Taqí (Ibn-i-Abhar)
## Mid-19th Century–1917

Bahá'u'lláh in one of His Tablets states that Ibn-i-Abhar 'was created to extol God and magnify His name, to teach His Cause and to serve Him'.[1] Born Mírzá Muḥammad-Taqí in Abhar, a village between Qazvín and Zanján, Iran, to Mírzá Ibráhím-i-Abharí, a cleric who became a believer in the Báb in the early days of His Faith, Ibn-i-Abhar was drawn to the Bahá'í revelation following the Declaration of Bahá'u'lláh. At a time when many Bábís were confused about the claims of Mírzá Yaḥyá, Mírzá Muḥammad-Taqí was advised by his father to study the Bayán in order to resolve his agitation. Mírzá Muḥammad-Taqí followed his father's advice and became a follower of Bahá'u'lláh in 1868. Bahá'u'lláh addressed Mírzá Muḥammad-Taqí as Ibn-i-Abhar, son of Abhar.

In 1874 Ibn-i-Abhar's father died by poison in Qazvín. Very traumatic times followed for Ibn-i-Abhar. His possessions were confiscated and he suffered many plots directed against him. Two years after the death of his father he wrote to Bahá'u'lláh asking whether martyrdom in the path of God or teaching His Cause was more praiseworthy. The Ancient Beauty indicated the latter and urged Ibn-i-Abhar to teach the Cause with wisdom. Years later 'Abdu'l-Bahá also pointed out to Ibn-i-Abhar the importance of wisdom in teaching, advising that the allegiance of certain eminent personages to the Faith not become common knowledge. Ibn-i-Abhar was successful in attracting several highly educated and influential people to the Cause.

Following the death of his father, Ibn-i-Abhar moved to Zanján, where he was able to convert many Bábís to the Cause of Bahá'u'lláh. His reinvigoration of the Bábí community in Zanján inevitably excited the jealousy of the divines, who then consigned him to 14 months and 15 days in prison. Though afflicted by dire hardships, he was resigned and patient throughout his ordeal.

In about 1886 Ibn-i-Abhar travelled to the Holy Land and attained the presence of Bahá'u'lláh. He was appointed a Hand of the Cause in the same year. He was directed by the Supreme Manifestation in a Tablet to 'pass through the cities, and even as a breeze that stirs at the break of dawn to shed upon whomsoever will turn to him the sweet savours of His loving-kindness and favours'.[2] For the rest of his life, Ibn-i-Abhar followed this injunction, his teaching activities contributing significantly to the expansion and consolidation of the Bahá'í community in Iran.

In 1891 Ibn-i-Abhar was wrongly accused of anti-government activities and was imprisoned in a dungeon in Ṭihrán. Incarcerated for about four years, he was subjected to much ill-treatment. His neck bore the chains which had once been placed upon the neck of Bahá'u'lláh. The food he was given was inadequate and had to be supplemented with supplies brought by two Bahá'í women. On various occasions he suffered the bastinado, the soles of his feet being beaten with rods. The believers were so grieved over this punishment that Ibn-i-Abhar wrote to them:

> Would it be fitting for He who is the Ruler of all the nations and the Lord of all creation to accept tribulations in order that mankind might be freed from the fetters of prejudice, liberated from attachments to this mortal world and disentangled from animalistic evil passions, while this insignificant being, who considers himself as one of His servants, be exempt from similar sufferings?
>
> I swear by God . . . that while my legs from knee to toe were in great pain, my soul was communing with my Beloved in the utmost joy, and my inner being was engaged in conversing with the loved ones of God . . . I did not pay any attention to the pain and suffering. For pain and bodily swellings will die down in a few days' time; only their mention will remain in this world but their bounty will last in the world of the spirit till eternity.[3]

This was just one of the letters written by Ibn-i-Abhar while in prison, many of them written in very small characters on the wrappers of sugar, tea and candles.

Bahá'u'lláh passed away while Ibn-i-Abhar was in prison. When he was released in 1895, he made the first of his eleven pilgrimages to the Holy Land, where he attained the presence of 'Abdu'l-Bahá.

During the ministry of 'Abdu'l-Bahá and until his death Ibn-i-Abhar travelled extensively, visiting 'Ishqábád, Iran, the Caucasus and India. He visited numerous Bahá'í communities, converted many persons to the Faith and met many prominent people. In 1897 he took part in the meeting of the Hands of the Cause which led to the formation of the Central Spiritual Assembly in Ṭihrán, the embryonic National Spiritual Assembly of Iran. He was accompanied on his trip to India in 1907 by two American believers, Hooper Harris and Harlan Ober.

After the ascension of Bahá'u'lláh, Ibn-i-Abhar was heartbroken. While still in prison he made a vow to devote his whole life to the service of the Cause. When he was freed he continued to uphold his vow to the point that he believed that to marry would break it. Even when the Master suggested to him that it was time he got married, Ibn-i-Abhar refused to do so. Eventually 'Abdu'l-Bahá told him to travel to Ṭihrán and marry Munírih Khánum, the daughter of Hand of the Cause Mullá 'Alí-Akbar. When he protested once again 'Abdu'l-Bahá said, 'My good man! I am the Centre of the Covenant; when I say you will not break your vow by marrying, you will not!'[4] Shortly afterwards Ibn-i-Abhar and Munírih Khánum were married.

The couple worked hard to promote the education of women in Iran and in 1909 served together on a special committee for the liberation of women. Ibn-i-Abhar helped to establish the Tarbíyat Bahá'í School for boys in Ṭihrán, while his wife later played a major role in establishing the girls' school.

A courageous and devoted Hand of the Cause, Ibn-i-Abhar is remembered in a Tablet of 'Abdu'l-Bahá revealed after the Master saw a photograph of him in chains:

> By chance I came across thy photograph. As I beheld thy person standing poised and in the utmost dignity with chains around thy neck, I was so affected that all sorrow was turned into joy and radiance, and I praised God that the world's Greatest Luminary hath nurtured and trained such servants who, while tied in chains and under the threat of the sword, shine forth in the utmost exultation and rapture.[5]

Shoghi Effendi designated Ibn-i-Abhar an Apostle of Bahá'u'lláh.

# Ḥájí Mírzá Ḥasan-i-Adíb
## 1848–1919

Ḥájí Mírzá Ḥasan-i-Adíb was born in Ṭalaqán, Iran, in September 1848. A distinguished and learned man, he ranked highly in literary circles as well as theological ones. He was given the title Adíbu'l-'Ulamá (litterateur of the clerics) for his literary accomplishments, which included poetry and writing books and articles for such works as the Námiy-i-Dánishvarán, which were published under the names of the Qájár princes who employed him. For a time he was the Imám-Jum'ih (Friday prayer leader) and a teacher at the Dáru'l-Funún, a school founded on western educational principles.

Mírzá Ḥasan-i-Adíb learned of the Bahá'í Faith through his close friend Shaykh Hádí Najmábádí and found that his own views were very much like those of the Bahá'ís. He conversed at length with Nabíl-i-Akbar and eventually came to recognize the station of Bahá'u'lláh. He became a Bahá'í in 1889 and soon afterwards Bahá'u'lláh designated him a Hand of the Cause. Unlike the other Hands appointed by Bahá'u'lláh, Mírzá Ḥasan never met Him.

Immediately he became a Bahá'í Mírzá Ḥasan-i-Adíb arose with an intensity of faith to promote the Cause of God. He was a great Bahá'í teacher and a source of strength to the believers. As soon as his new allegiance became known he was dismissed from his employment with the Qájárs. He turned his considerable talents to writing poems on the advent of Bahá'u'lláh and books on the history and proofs of the Faith.

Mírzá Ḥasan-i-Adíb participated in the gatherings of the Hands of the Cause in 1897 that led to the establishment of the Central Spiritual Assembly of Ṭihrán. Keenly interested in the education of Bahá'í youth, he played an important role in the founding and administration of the Tarbíyat Schools in Ṭihrán.

In 1903 Mírzá Ḥasan-i-Adíb went to Iṣfahán at the direction of 'Abdu'l-

Bahá. Just at this time the Mujtahid of Iṣfahán, Shaykh Muḥammad-Taqí, the Son of the Wolf, was fomenting trouble for the Bahá'ís in the city. As a result of his machinations a mob took to the streets, harassed the Bahá'ís, pillaged their homes and even killed a few. The arrival of Mírzá Ḥasan-i-Adíb inflamed an already volatile situation and the Hand of the Cause met with great sufferings. He was briefly imprisoned but was eventually able to leave the city and travel to Ábádih and Shíráz.

From Shíráz Mírzá Ḥasan-i-Adíb went on to Bombay and eventually to the Holy Land. His pilgrimage in the presence of 'Abdu'l-Bahá inspired him to continue his meritorious services to the Cause. He travelled at the behest of the Master to India and Burma in the company of the American Bahá'í Sidney Sprague. He eventually returned to Iran, where he passed away on 2 September 1919.

During his lifetime he was the recipient of many Tablets from both the Supreme Manifestation and His exalted Son. 'Abdu'l-Bahá revealed His tender love for this Hand of the Cause:

> He is God.
> O thou herald of the Covenant! The verses of thy poem, each like unto a shining and luminous pearl, were perused. These lines were in truth of the utmost grace, lustre, and brilliance. The cry and complaint to which thy remoteness hath given rise touched me beyond all conception. It moved me to the depths of heart and soul and filled me with perplexity. But what recourse have we? Thy presence here would be contrary to caution in these days. Verily thy lamentations have the most profound effect upon the hearts, and at this time thy presence is most needed in those lands. Be assured that, as soon as circumstances permit, thou shalt be summoned here without a moment's delay, for I am most eager to meet thee. I cherish the hope that this may soon be made possible. Upon thee be salutations and praise.[1]

Mírzá Ḥasan-i-Adíb was named an Apostle of Bahá'u'lláh by Shoghi Effendi.

Ḥájí Mullá ʻAlí-Akbar-Shahmírzádí, known as Ḥájí Ákhúnd

Ḥájí Ákhúnd in chains and fetters

Ibn-i-Aṣdaq

Ḥájí Mírzá Muḥammad-Taqí, known as Ibn-i-Abhar

Ibn-i-Abhar, *right*

Ibn-i-Abhar in chains

Mírzá-i-Adíb

Mullá Muḥammad-i-Qá'iní,
known as Nabíl-i-Akbar

Mírzá 'Alí-Muḥammad-i-Varqá, *right*,
with his son Rúḥu'lláh, who was martyred with him

# II

# Hands of the Cause Mentioned by 'Abdu'l-Bahá 1892–1921

# Mullá Muḥammad-Riḍáy-i-Muḥammad-Ábádí*
## c. 1814–1897

Mullá Muḥammad-Riḍá (Mullá Riḍá) of Muḥammadábád in Yazd was a fearless teacher of the Cause who was never at a loss for words. Whenever the opportunity arose, he would proclaim the Faith with unrestrained enthusiasm, with the result that he often antagonized fanatical elements among his listeners and brought on much suffering to himself and the friends in his company. Even when there was no opportunity to teach, he would speak out, much to the trepidation of those believers who were concerned for his safety. He is best known for his role in the debates between Bahá'í leaders and Qájár officials while in prison in Ṭihrán in 1882–3.

Unrivalled in speech, in his knowledge of the Qur'án and in Islamic law and tradition, Mullá Riḍá was educated to be a Muslim cleric and was known for his piety, eloquence and courage. He belonged to a well-known family, was tall in stature, imposing in bearing and remarkable in fortitude. He became a Bábí in the early years and became a follower of Bahá'u'lláh after reading the Qaṣídiy-i-Varqá'íyyih, of which he said, 'On the throne of these words I see the Promised One of the Bayán seated.'[1]

Mullá Riḍá was known as a gourmet who lived and ate well, and whose manners and tidiness were admirable. It was said that he would select a

---

* 'Abdu'l-Bahá referred to a few of the believers posthumously as being Hands of the Cause (*Memorials of the Faithful*, p. 5). Adib Taherzadeh points out that 'since there are one or two others by the same name [Shaykh-Riḍáy-i-Yazdí], it is not possible to identify him. However, some believe strongly that he is Mullá Muḥammad-i-Riḍáy-i-Muḥammad-Ábádí.' (Taherzadeh, *Revelation*, vol. 4, p. 286n.)

suckling lamb and raise the animal on sweets containing nuts and spices. At the appropriate time, he would invite guests to share in his feast.

Mullá Riḍá 'was a man of broad vision and great enterprise',[2] of 'peculiar conduct and of a trend of thought unusual by our standards'.[3] He believed that the organic unity of all substances would be established in the Bahá'í era and once said that 'if I were guided to discover this transmuting alchemy, I would build a town and erect in it a Mas͟hriqu'l-Ad͟hkár of crystal. Its central hall would be supported by ninety-five pillars and each of its 19 x 9-metre doors would be made of solid gold!'[4] He later came upon a lake in the vicinity of Kirmán where he proceeded to carry out his dream. Alone, he gathered together some five hundred digging tools and worked the land. The work went slowly owing to his advanced age. Then he was arrested, taken away, and the people from neighbouring villages seized his tools.

On one occasion Mullá Riḍá was detained in Yazd for Bahá'í activities. The governor ordered that he publicly suffer the bastinado at seven crossroads in a single day. At each crossroad he calmly removed his 'abá, turban and socks, putting them on the ground on top of a handkerchief. He would then lie down, cover his face with the hem of his garment and ask that the punishment proceed. Not once during any of these cruel beatings did he utter a word or indicate that he suffered any pain. At one point, his onlookers, baffled by his unusual calm, imagined he had collapsed. When his face was uncovered, however, he was found to be quietly cleaning his teeth.

Ḥájí Mírzá Ḥaydar-'Alí recalled that Mullá Riḍá used to tell fantastic stories to those gathered at the mosque. Once he proclaimed that the advent of the promised Qá'im, the Imám Mihdí, would occur in the year 1300 AH (1883). There was in those days an outstanding Bahá'í named Siyyid Mihdí towards whom the governor of Ṭihrán showed great respect. On one occasion this ruler picked up the siyyid's shoes and placed them at his feet as the siyyid prepared to leave the governor's room. Later, when the siyyid arrived in the capital, the believers went to welcome him. Ḥájí Mírzá Ḥaydar-'Alí told them, 'Go to Mullá Riḍá and tell him that his promised Mihdí is here now.' For a long time afterwards this was a joke among the Bahá'ís.[5]

In 1882–3 many Bahá'ís were arrested across Iran. Mullá Riḍá was detained in Ṭihrán and was called to appear at the court of Kámrán Mírzá, the son of Náṣiri'd-Dín S͟háh. Confronted by a gathering of eminent princes and prominent state officials, he fearlessly replied to every question and matter raised. During these interrogations, Prince Farhád Mírzá, an uncle of the Sháh, told Mullá Riḍá that he should not ignore certain established and reliable traditions, including the whereabouts of Jábulqá and Jábulsá, cities supposed to be the residence of the Hidden Imám. Mullá Riḍá retorted, 'Your Royal Highness! You yourself have written a book on geography. If such a city exists, a city which is claimed to have 70,000 gates, and according to others 100,000, please tell me in which part of the world you have placed it in your geography; show me where in your book you have referred to it and described it; then I shall accept all your arguments.' The prince was angered and demanded that Mullá Riḍá stop his arguing. Bahá'u'lláh, the prince claimed, had taken wine with him and was thus unworthy of the mullá's affections. Unruffled, Mullá Riḍá replied, 'Your Royal Highness is . . . well aware of the law of Islám: the testimony of a wrongdoer regarding another cannot be entertained. You yourself have here owned to drinking wine; therefore, your testimony regarding Bahá'u'lláh is inadmissible.' This brilliant response, a victory according to the Islamic rules of debate, resulted in the defeated prince storming out of the room.[6]

The purpose of the interrogation of Mullá Riḍá and the other Bahá'ís was to oppress the believers. Mírzá Abu'l-Faḍl relates:

> To carry out their [the country's leaders] corrupt and impossible designs they resorted to all kinds of means and intrigues . . . meetings were held for enquiry and argument in the governing circles. All manner of debate and proof-seeking was introduced. Evidently, with them, it is a canon of opposition to begin by resorting to that which they consider to be axioms of faith and belief. And when they receive irrefutable answers and find themselves unable to pose any proof, they turn to miracle-seeking and the supernatural. Having been worsted and brought to their knees in that arena as well, they resort to the last weapon of the transgressor and the evil-intentioned and that is slaying of the innocent and incarcerating the helpless.[7]

One night Prince Kámrán Mírzá invited Mullá Riḍá to dine with him. At the conclusion of the meal, he asked his guest whether he considered Bahá'u'lláh to be an Imám or a Prophet. The mullá replied that Bahá'u'lláh was a Manifestation of God whom all must recognize. To do otherwise, he said, would be to deny the Prophets who came before.

The next day the Bahá'í prisoners were once again interrogated. The prince asked Ḥájí Ákhúnd whether he considered Mullá Riḍá to be honest.

'He never lies,' came the reply.

The prince then accused the other Bahá'ís of lying. 'You have been telling me all along that in Bahá'u'lláh you witness the Return of Ḥusayn, whereas Mullá Muḥammad-Riḍá tells me that the Light of the Invisible Godhead is shining in the Person of Bahá'u'lláh.'

Amazed, Ḥájí Ákhúnd replied, 'Your Royal Highness! Mullá Muḥammad-Riḍá is the Ṣúfí of the Bábís, waxing extravagant.' Mullá Riḍá interrupted, saying, 'Your Royal Highness! You listen to me. What I have said is the truth. These are the samovar-centred Bahá'ís: when the samovar is boiling and they are seated somewhere safe and secure, they all say the same as I have told you. That is the belief of all; but now, at the time of testing, they draw a veil over it all and follow the dictates of circumspection.'[8] The prince had nothing else to say.

Thirteen years after his first imprisonment, Mullá Riḍá was caught up in the holocaust of persecutions launched against the Bahá'í community in the wake of the assassination of Náṣiri'd-Dín Sháh in 1896. At that time, he was in a mosque in Qum when a clergyman clamoured that the Bábís had murdered the king and ought to be crushed. Mullá Riḍá, who was among the crowd listening to the divine's raging, defended the believers, with the result that he was accused of being one himself. Without hesitation he admitted this was so. He was seized, sent to Ṭihrán and incarcerated in the notorious Síyáh-Chál.

Áqá Siyyid Asadu'lláh was a companion of Mullá Riḍá in the prison. He begged his friend to observe moderation when he spoke of the Bahá'í Faith and not to be so outspoken. Mullá Riḍá, however, paid no attention. Even in the prison he attracted 'new opportunities and spiritual powers which he grasped and exploited to the full, always disregarding the fact that such an indiscreet manner of public teaching in the presence of fanatical prisoners and authorities would entail fresh dangers and sufferings not only for himself but also for the rest of the friends who shared his dire fate'. When the incarcerated believers pointed out to Mullá Riḍá that confrontation with ignorant people only resulted in increased hostility, he 'contended that the Cause is great and therefore is bound to encounter great opposition and that those who try to defile its fair name through abuse and vituperation surely will never succeed in doing it any harm. What they actually do

. . . is to let everyone know how stupid they themselves are. Their foolish act resembles that of a man who tries vainly to spit on the sun.'[9]

Fearing reprisals if Mullá Riḍá continued to teach the Faith so boldly in the prison, the incarcerated friends approached their gaoler, Mashhadí 'Alí, and asked him to tell Mullá Riḍá not to speak publicly about the Cause. Mullá Riḍá ignored the directive and soon incurred the wrath of the gaoler. As punishment, he was taken to the prison yard and brutally flogged on his bare back. During this beating and in spite of the rigours of prison life, he showed no trace of pain; it was as if he had lost all sense of feeling. After the flogging, Siyyid Asadu'lláh tried to apply egg yolks to Mullá Riḍá's lacerated back in order to bring him some relief. But Mullá Riḍá rebuked him. 'Do you think that when they were punishing me, I was aware of what they were doing? O Siyyid! I was in the presence of the Blessed Perfection, speaking with Him!'[10]

One of the prisoners who witnessed the flogging was Ghulám-Riḍá Khán. He was impressed by Mullá Riḍá's amazing steadfastness and endurance. Deeply affected by what he had seen, he became a believer, testifying later that he received his light from the floggings: 'If instead hundreds of verses from the Qur'án had been recited to me or a thousand reasons adduced to convince me of the truth of this Message, none would have influenced me as did the unruffled calm which the old, stout-hearted Mullá Riḍá evinced under torture.'[11]

With the accession of Muẓaffari'd-Dín Sháh to the throne in 1896, attitudes towards the Bahá'ís began to change slightly. Five Bahá'í prisoners, among them Mullá Riḍá, were taken from the dungeon to the house of the Farrásh-Báshí (chief police officer), where they were to be liberated. Along the way, Mullá Riḍá collapsed, being old, feeble and much affected by his incarceration. Porters were called to carry him. Throughout the two-hour trek, he joked about the quality of his steed, the Bahá'í women in the watching crowds begging him to remain silent.

Finally the party reached their destination. They were about to be freed when a cleric and his theological students passed the house in which the prisoners were staying. Learning that the Bahá'ís were inside, the siyyid expressed a wish to see them. Most of the Bahá'ís refused, saying they were not well enough. However, Mullá Riḍá offered to meet the siyyid, despite the warnings of his brethren that he was putting himself in jeopardy. Within fifteen minutes of his entering the siyyid's room, a heated dispute erupted, the siyyid and the students being utterly confounded by the prisoner's proofs and arguments. The students began to beat Mullá Riḍá, who was heard shouting at the siyyid, 'You who could not prove the truth of the Faith of your forefathers, how dare you tell me to curse Ṣubḥ-i-Azal? You who do not know who [he] is and why he should be cursed, are trying to make me soil my tongue.' When Mullá Riḍá rejoined his anxious fellow believers, he expressed satisfaction at having defeated the siyyid. 'I put him in his place,' he commented.[12]

The siyyid, however, had the final word. He managed to have Mullá Riḍá sent back to the gaol. With no one to look after him there, he passed away within ten days of his reincarceration. The Pen of the Centre of the Covenant revealed the following in his exalted honour:

> He is God!
> Upon thee rest the most sublime salutations and the most wondrous praise, O thou glorious soul who hast, under chains and fetters, laid down thy life in the path of thy Lord! I bear witness that thou didst quaff from the wellspring of paradise and wert intoxicated with the choice wine proffered in the most sublime chalice, that thou didst attain unto the presence of the Most High, sought the shelter of His unsurpassing mercy, gained admittance into the Abhá Kingdom, ascended unto the highest heaven, rose to the loftiest station, entered within the heavenly abode, reposed in the gardens of delight, hearkened to the melodies of the birds of holiness singing upon the blessed Tree, and wert blest with the gift of reunion and granted life everlasting. Glorified then be His Most Exalted Name, He Who giveth and bestoweth, and Who hath ordained for thee this most gracious favour. Well is it with thee and with whosoever visiteth thy resting-place at dawn and eventide, in the daytime and the night season. This, verily, is but a token of the grace of thine incomparable Lord.[13]

# Muḥammad-i-Qá'iní, Nabíl-i-Akbar 1829–1892

Áqá Muḥammad-i-Qá'iní, also known as Fáḍil-i-Qá'iní (the Learned One of Qá'in) and surnamed Nabíl-i-Akbar, was born in the village of Naw-Firist on 29 March 1829. From a family of renowned clerics, he received a religious education. Following his studies under distinguished divines of Mashhad, he journeyed to Sabzivár, where for five years he studied under Ḥájí Mullá Hádí, the most eminent Persian philosopher of the time. In 1852 he set out for the holy shrines of Najaf and Karbilá to complete his education.

The persecution of the Bábís in Iran was then at its height and many were captured and martyred. When Áqá Muḥammad-i-Qá'iní arrived in Ṭihrán en route to Iraq he was arrested as a Bábí. His innocence was established and he was released but the incident left an impression on him and he determined to learn more. Later a Bábí from Qá'in asked him to comment on some of the writings of the Báb and Muḥammad-i-Qá'iní became a Bábí soon afterwards.

In Iraq Áqá Muḥammad-i-Qá'iní became a disciple of the mujtahid Shaykh Murtaḍáy-i-Anṣárí. 'He excelled', 'Abdu'l-Bahá says, 'not only in theology but in other branches of knowledge, such as the humanities, the philosophy of the Illuminati, the teachings of the mystics and of the Shaykhí School.'[1] Eventually 'he became the leading member of the mujtahid's company of disciples' and 'singled out from among them all, he alone was given the rank of mujtahid.'[2]

On his way back from the shrine cities Áqá Muḥammad-i-Qá'iní stopped in Baghdád, where he stayed for a time. Here he met Bahá'u'lláh, who had not yet made a public declaration of His mission. In the meetings of the Bábís, Áqá Muḥammad-i-Qá'iní would invariably take the most prominent position and address the audience. It was only after hearing Bahá'u'lláh's explanation of a certain point that Áqá Muḥammad-i-Qá'iní recognized Bahá'u'lláh's superior knowledge.

'Abdu'l-Bahá describes the esteem in which Áqá Muḥammad-i-Qá'iní afterwards held Bahá'u'lláh:

> One day, on the floor of the outer apartments reserved for the men, the honoured Nabíl was reverently kneeling in the presence of Bahá'u'lláh. At that moment Ḥájí Mírzá Ḥasan-'Amú, a trusted associate of the mujtahids of Karbilá, came in with Zaynu'l-'Ábidín Khán, the Fakhru'd-Dawlih. Observing how humbly and deferentially Nabíl was kneeling there, the Ḥájí was astonished.
>
> 'Sir,' he murmured, 'what are you doing in this place?'
>
> Nabíl answered, 'I came here for the same reason you did.'
>
> The two visitors could not recover from their surprise, for it was widely known that this personage was unique among mujtahids and was the most favoured disciple of the renowned Shaykh Murtaḍá.[3]

Following his recognition of the station of Bahá'u'lláh, Áqá Muḥammad-i-Qá'iní travelled to Khurásán, where the Amír of Qá'in showed him the utmost courtesy and respect. The Amír so admired Áqá Muḥammad-i-Qá'iní's eloquence and knowledge that he greatly valued the scholar's company. However, Áqá Muḥammad-i-Qá'iní taught the Cause with such fervour that many people in Qá'in became believers, arousing the jealousy of the clergy, who spread calumnies about him as far as Ṭihrán. These falsehoods much angered Náṣiri'd-Dín Sháh when he came to hear of them and the Amír, terrified of the Sháh's wrath, turned against Áqá Muḥammad-i-Qá'iní. Soon the whole city arose against him and he escaped to Ṭihrán.

'Abdu'l-Bahá describes his life as a fugitive:

> He was pursued by the watchmen; guards looked everywhere for him, asking after him in every street and alley, hunting him down to catch and torture him. Hiding, he would pass by them like the sigh of the oppressed, and rise to the hills; or again, like the tears of the wronged, he would slip down into the valleys. He could no longer wear the turban denoting his rank; he disguised

himself, putting on a layman's hat, so that they would fail to recognize him and would let him be.[4]

Despite this, Áqá Muḥammad continued to teach the Cause in secret. Eventually he was arrested and imprisoned in Bírjand. He was then sent to Mas͟hhad, where he was released; on his return to Qá'in he was arrested again and taken to Ṭihrán. In Ṭihrán the clergy plotted to kill him, and he had to flee once more.

Around 1874 Bahá'u'lláh asked Áqá Muḥammad to come to 'Akká. It was while he was on pilgrimage that Bahá'u'lláh revealed the Lawḥ-i-Ḥikmat (Tablet of Wisdom) in his honour.[5] In it Bahá'u'lláh 'reveals for him the secret of successfully teaching His Faith'.[6] These are the words of Bahá'u'lláh addressed to him:

> Teach thou the Cause of God with an utterance which will cause the bushes to be enkindled, and the call 'Verily, there is no God but Me, the Almighty, the Unconstrained' to be raised therefrom. Say: Human utterance is an essence which aspireth to exert its influence and needeth moderation. As to its influence, this is conditional upon refinement which in turn is dependent upon hearts which are detached and pure. As to its moderation, this hath to be combined with tact and wisdom as prescribed in the Holy Scriptures and Tablets.[7]

Bahá'u'lláh also bestowed upon Áqá Muḥammad-i-Qá'iní the title of Nabíl-i-Akbar. The name Nabíl means learned or noble.

Hájí Mírzá Haydar-'Alí described the effect of a talk he heard Nabíl deliver in Qazvín.

> One feature of his greatness was that no one could surpass his extraordinary power for expounding and elucidating matters. For instance, if he wished, he could prove that water was hot and dry and fire cold and wet, and no one was capable of arguing with him. Yet I have observed that even as the ocean of his utterance was surging and he was speaking with great vigour and conviction, he would, should someone point out a mistake he had made in his discourse, or should he himself become aware of it, immediately acknowledge his ignorance and confess his misjudgement.[8]

Nabíl-i-Akbar remained in 'Akká for a short time before Bahá'u'lláh instructed him to return to Iran to teach the Faith. He travelled to all parts of the country and was once again hunted by the authorities. Despite the danger, Nabíl-i-Akbar continued to teach the Faith wherever he travelled. 'In spite of his sufferings,' 'Abdu'l-Bahá says, 'he was never dispirited, rather his joy and ardour increased with every passing day'.[9]

Nabíl-i-Akbar was eventually arrested in Sabzivár but was allowed by the governor of the town to leave for 'Ishqábád. From there he and Mírzá Abu'l-Faḍl travelled to Bukhárá, where Nabíl-i-Akbar died on 6 July 1892.

'Abdu'l-Bahá named Nabíl-i-Akbar a Hand of the Cause and Shoghi Effendi designated him an Apostle of Bahá'u'lláh. Commenting on his life and rank, 'Abdu'l-Bahá wrote:

> A sign of guidance, he was, an emblem of the fear of God. For this Faith, he laid down his life, and in dying, triumphed. He passed by the world and its rewards; he closed his eyes to rank and wealth; he loosed himself from all such chains and fetters, and put every worldly thought aside. Of wide learning . . . he was . . . an accomplished man of letters and an orator without a peer. He had a great and universal mind.
>
> Praise be to God, at the end he was made the recipient of heavenly grace.[10]

# Mullá Ṣádiq-i-Muqaddas-i-Khurásání (Ismu'lláhu'l-Aṣdaq) c. 1800–1889

'Abdu'l-Bahá described Mullá Ṣádiq-i-Muqaddas-i-Khurásání as a 'blessed individual', 'accomplished', 'learned', a 'great scholar' and 'much honoured'.[1] 'As a teacher of the Faith,' He wrote, 'he spoke with such eloquence, such extraordinary power, that his hearers were won over with great ease.'[2] He taught cheerfully and responded gently and with good humour to those with whom he spoke, even when he encountered hostility. According to 'Abdu'l-Bahá, his method of teaching was 'excellent'.[3]

Mullá Ṣádiq was born in the city of Mashhad sometime around the beginning of the 19th century. By the 1830s he was in the holy city Karbilá and was a disciple of Ḥájí Siyyid Káẓim-i-Rashtí, the leader of the Shaykhís. He was renowned for his character, learning and eloquence and was given the rank of mujtahid in 1843 by Siyyid Káẓim. While in Karbilá he became a close friend of Mullá Ḥusayn and encountered the youthful Siyyid 'Alí-Muḥammad (the Báb), whose majesty deeply impressed him, praying tearfully at the Shrine of Imám Ḥusayn.

One day during this time in Karbilá Mullá Ṣádiq invited Siyyid 'Alí-Muḥammad to visit his house to attend a Rawḍih-Khání, a meeting devoted to the recital of the sufferings of the descendants of Muḥammad, particularly the Imám Ḥusayn. When Siyyid 'Alí-Muḥammad arrived at the meeting, Siyyid Káẓim and his disciples were already seated. Siyyid Káẓim immediately rose and asked Siyyid 'Alí-Muḥammad to take a seat higher in the room, astonishing those present at this mark of respect. A poem of Shaykh Aḥmad recounting the sufferings of the Imám Ḥusayn was then read by Mullá Ḥusayn. Siyyid 'Alí-Muḥammad wept so bitterly at this that everyone present was deeply moved.

In about 1841, at the behest of Siyyid Káẓim, Mullá Ṣádiq made his residence in Iṣfahán, where he was to prepare the people for the advent of the promised Qá'im. Soon after the declaration of the Báb in 1844, Mullá Ḥusayn travelled through Iṣfahán on his way to Ṭihrán to acquaint Bahá'u'lláh with the Báb's announcement. The Báb had told Mullá Ḥusayn that Mullá Ṣádiq would unhesitatingly embrace His Cause. Thus Mullá Ḥusayn spoke to his old friend and fellow disciple about the advent of the Báb without disclosing His identity, saying it was forbidden both to ask and divulge His name. Mullá Ṣádiq then asked Mullá Ḥusayn, 'Would it, then, be possible for me, even as the Letters of the Living, to seek independently the grace of the All-Merciful and, through prayer, to discover His identity?' 'The door of His grace is never closed before the face of him who seeks to find Him,' Mullá Ḥusayn responded. Mullá Ṣádiq later told the story of how he came to recognize the Báb:

> I immediately retired from his presence, and requested his host to allow me the privacy of a room in his house where, alone and undisturbed, I could commune with God. In the midst of my contemplation, I suddenly remembered the face of a Youth whom I had often observed while in Karbilá, standing in an attitude of prayer, with His face bathed in tears at the entrance of the shrine of the Imám Ḥusayn. That same countenance now reappeared before my eyes. In my vision I seemed to behold that same face, those same features, expressive of such joy as I could never describe. He smiled as He gazed at me. I went towards Him, ready to throw myself at His feet. I was bending towards the ground, when, lo! that radiant figure vanished from before me. Overpowered with joy and gladness, I ran out to meet Mullá Ḥusayn, who with transport received me and assured me that I had, at last, attained the object of my desire.[4]

Realizing that his vision was of the young Siyyid whom he had met in Karbilá some years before and whom he had greatly admired, Mullá Ṣádiq gave up his worldly station and arose immediately to promote His Cause. The morning after his vision he left Iṣfahán for Shíráz to meet the Báb. The journey took 12 days; at its end he was momentarily disappointed to find that the Báb, accompanied by Quddús, had left for Mecca to make his pilgrimage.

Mullá Ṣádiq, by now a Píshnamáz (a cleric who leads the congregation in prayer in a mosque), took up residence in Shíráz to await the return of the Báb. When the Báb returned to Iran, He sent Quddús to Shíráz with a Tablet instructing Mullá Ṣádiq to add to the call to prayer, 'I bear witness that He whose name is 'Alí-Qabl-i-Muḥammad [a reference to the Báb] is the servant of the Baqíyyatu'lláh [the Remnant of God, referring to Bahá'u'lláh]'.[5] As bidden, Mullá Ṣádiq proclaimed these words to the worshippers at the mosque, with the result that the divines accused him of heresy and called for his arrest, saying:

> Woe betide us, the guardians and protectors of the Faith of God! Behold, this man has hoisted the standard of heresy. Down with this infamous traitor! He has spoken blasphemy. Arrest him, for he is a disgrace to our Faith.[6]

Hearing this, the populace joined the clamour and soon the whole city was aroused. Ḥusayn Khán-i-Íravání, the governor of the province of Fárs, intervened and asked the cause of the commotion. He was told that Quddús was proclaiming the teachings of someone claiming a new divinely inspired revelation and that Mullá Ṣádiq was summoning the multitude to accept His message.

Ḥusayn Khán promptly ordered the arrest of the two Bábís. When he perused the copy of the Qayyúmu'l-Asmá' from which Mullá Ṣádiq had been reading to the congregation, the governor angrily asked about the Báb's words in the opening passage: 'Divest yourselves of the robe of sovereignty, for He who is the King in truth, hath been made manifest! The Kingdom is God's, the Most Exalted. Thus hath the Pen of the Most High decreed!'[7] Did this passage mean that Muḥammad Sháh was supposed to abdicate his throne and Ḥusayn Khán his own position, he demanded? Mullá Ṣádiq courageously replied:

> When once the truth of the Revelation announced by the Author of these words shall have been definitely established, the truth of whatsoever has fallen from His lips will likewise be vindicated. If these words be the Word of God, the abdication of Muḥammad Sháh and his like can matter but little. It can in no wise turn aside the Divine purpose, nor alter the sovereignty of the almighty and eternal King.[8]

The cruel governor was not at all pleased with this reply and, cursing Mullá Ṣádiq, ordered that he be scourged with a thousand lashes. An eye-witness to this savage punishment did not believe the mullá would survive even 50 strokes, as he was 'so advanced in age and frail in body'.[9] Each stroke of the lash was fiercely applied, yet Mullá Ṣádiq remained serene throughout his ordeal. He was even seen with his hand before his mouth, concealing a smile. Later asked by this same witness why he had covered his mouth with his hand, Mullá Ṣádiq commented that the first strokes were very painful but to the remainder he had become indifferent:

> I was wondering whether the strokes that followed were being actually applied to my own body. A feeling of joyous exultation had invaded my soul. I was trying to repress my feelings and to restrain my laughter. I can now realize how the almighty Deliverer is able . . . to turn pain into ease, and sorrow into gladness.[10]

Ḥusayn Khán also ordered that the beards of Mullá Ṣádiq, Quddús, as well as another Bábí, Mullá 'Alí-Akbar Ardistání, be burned, that each have a cord passed through an incision in his nose and that they be led through the city by this halter. 'Even in that condition', 'Abdu'l-Bahá remarked, 'composed and smiling, [Mullá Ṣádiq] kept on speaking to the people.'[11]

As the three were paraded through the bazaars, a merchant stopped them, wishing to increase their suffering. He placed a stout piece of timber between Quddús and Mullá Ṣádiq, one end of wood resting on one shoulder of each man, attached a measuring device and weighed 80 bales of sugar on the device as they stood in the heat of the day. Whenever they attempted to move their feet to readjust their load, their persecutors would lash them cruelly. Finally, covered with wounds and sores, the three were permitted to leave the city. Mullá Ṣádiq was thus among the first three believers to suffer persecution in the new Dispensation, this episode being but a prelude to the many sufferings he endured in his lifetime.

After leaving Shíráz Mullá Ṣádiq travelled to Yazd, proclaiming the Cause of the Báb along the way. He stayed in Yazd for two months, sending a herald to announce to the townspeople that he was the emissary of the Báb and would address them on Friday at a local mosque. A large crowd gathered on Friday to hear him. Mullá Ṣádiq ascended the pulpit and announced the coming of the promised One. At first no one raised any objections, but as Mullá Ṣádiq continued, the crowd became increasingly agitated and finally rushed the pulpit, intending to take his life. Only the intervention of Siyyid Ḥusayn, an influential divine who promised that he would investigate the matter, subdued the crowd.

Eventually Mullá Ṣádiq travelled to Khurásán, passing through Kirmán, where he suffered further afflictions. When he arrived at the camp of Mullá Ḥusayn, he joined the small band of Bábís who were proceeding, under the Black Standard, towards Mázindarán to assist Quddús, who was in Bárfurúsh. As the group travelled, more Bábís joined their ranks until they numbered about three hundred.

Near Bárfurúsh the Bábís encountered a multitude of armed townspeople, blocking their entry to the city. The crowd fired on the Bábís and several were slain, including a siyyid who had been one of Mullá Ḥusayn's constant supporters all the way from Mashhad. Unsheathing his sword, Mullá Ḥusayn spurred his horse into the crowd and pursued the assailant of his dead companion. Though his foe took refuge behind a tree and held aloft his musket as an added shield, Mullá Ḥusayn was able with a single stroke of his sword to cut through the trunk of the tree, the barrel of the musket and the body of the attacker. This amazing feat completely routed the enemy, who fled in terror.

In the next months Mullá Ḥusayn displayed marvellous swordsmanship and courage as he scattered the forces of a superior enemy who repeatedly attacked the Bábí stronghold at the fortress of Shaykh Ṭabarsí. The Bábís soon found themselves facing an army of twelve thousand men, who laid siege to the fortress, cutting off food and water, sniping at the Bábís, shelling the fort and mounting an occasional offensive. Again and again the defenders, lying exhausted within their fort, arose with amazing strength to repulse every attack.

Eventually Mullá Ḥusayn was struck by a bullet in the breast and carried back, mortally wounded, by two young companions to the fort. Mullá Ṣádiq and Mullá Mírzá Muḥammad-i-Furúghí recounted the amazing reunion between their slain leader and Quddús:

> We were among those who had remained in the fort with Quddús. As soon as Mullá Ḥusayn, who seemed to have lost consciousness, was brought in, we were ordered to retire . . . We were amazed a few moments later when we heard the voice of Mullá Ḥusayn replying to questions from Quddús. For two hours they continued to converse with each other. We were surprised to see Mírzá Muḥammad-Báqir so greatly agitated. 'I was watching Quddús,'

> he subsequently informed us, 'through a fissure in the door. As soon as he called his name, I saw Mullá Ḥusayn arise and seat himself, in his customary manner, on bended knees beside him. With bowed head and downcast eyes, he listened to every word that fell from the lips of Quddús, and answered his questions. "You have hastened the hour of your departure," I was able to hear Quddús remark, "and have abandoned me to the mercy of my foes. Please God, I will ere long join you and taste the sweetness of heaven's ineffable delights." I was able to gather the following words uttered by Mullá Ḥusayn: "May my life be a ransom for you. Are you well pleased with me?"'[12]

The death of Mullá Ḥusayn grieved the defenders, as well as the Báb, who declared in one of His Tablets of visitation that the 'very dust of the ground where the remains of Mullá Ḥusayn lie buried is endowed with such potency as to bring joy to the disconsolate and healing to the sick'.[13]

Under the leadership of Quddús, the Bábís at Shaykh Ṭabarsí continued their struggle against the government forces for several months. Eventually they were persuaded by their enemies to surrender, abandoning the fort and laying down their arms. As they left the encampment, the army set upon the Bábís, killing most of them. Quddús was taken to Bárfurúsh, where he was tortured and killed. Mullá Ṣádiq was among a handful of survivors.

'Abdu'l-Bahá, in describing the 'terrible ordeal' of the Bábís in Shaykh Ṭabarsí, remarked that Mullá Ṣádiq did not 'slacken under fire'.[14] Mullá Ṣádiq and a fellow survivor were handed over to Ḥusayn Khán, a prominent person in Mázindarán (not the governor of Fárs) whose father had been killed fighting the Bábís. His intention was to have Mullá Ṣádiq and his companion killed in the presence of his mother and sister, who were grieving the death of his father. As they made their way through the province of Mázindarán, Ḥusayn Khán stopped at every village, calling upon the local divines to examine his captives. When questioned, Mullá Ṣádiq responded politely with convincing evidence from the Qur'án and traditions. Impressed by Mullá Ṣádiq's learning and eloquence, no divine felt that he deserved death. Captivated by the serenity and certitude of Mullá Ṣádiq, Ḥusayn Khán decided to spare the Bábís' lives.

The captives remained, however, within the reach of the prince who had commanded the royal troops during the siege at Shaykh Ṭabarsí and who wanted the Bábís sent to Ṭihrán to be executed. A shepherd came to their aid, encouraging them to escape. Mullá Ṣádiq was at first unwilling to go as he was severely weakened from his recent privations. Nevertheless, he and his companion departed into the thick forests of Mázindarán and, after two weeks, reached Míyámí, where they rested before continuing on to Mashhad.

Mullá Ṣádiq lived in Mashhad for about 12 years. Among those he taught there about the religion of the Báb was Aḥmad-i-Yazdí, the recipient of the Tablet of Aḥmad. Gradually, however, life in Mashhad became impossible. In 1861 Mullá Ṣádiq journeyed with many friends to Baghdád, where he attained the presence of Bahá'u'lláh. He recognized the Manifestation's station even before His Declaration in the Garden of Riḍván in 1863 and for some 14 months remained in the city, near Bahá'u'lláh. He then directed his steps towards his native province of Khurásán, as bidden by Bahá'u'lláh.

In Khurásán, Mullá Ṣádiq was bitterly opposed on all sides. Although he met the opposition courageously, eventually the governor of Khurásán, Ḥisámu's-Salṭanih, an uncle of the Sháh, ordered his arrest and had him sent to Ṭihrán, where he was incarcerated in the Síyáh-Chál. Mullá Ṣádiq was forced by this cruel act to take with him his youngest son, Ibn-i-Aṣdaq, who was a child at the time. Chained together, they were kept in the dungeon for some two years and four months. Mullá Ṣádiq converted some of his fellow prisoners but the hardships of the prison caused the child to become seriously ill. No physician could at first be found willing to treat a Bábí patient. However a Jewish doctor, Ḥakím Masíḥ, was eventually contacted and readily assented.

For two months, he attended the child until he recovered. In the meantime, he learned about the Faith from Mullá Ṣádiq and soon became a believer, the first person of Jewish background to become a Bahá'í.[15]

Many prominent men visited Mullá Ṣádiq in prison and tried to persuade him to write a few lines to Náṣiri'd-Dín Sháh to obtain his release. The mullá, however, refused to make such an appeal. Then the Sháh suddenly decided to free him. Mullá Ṣádiq refused to leave the dungeon without his fellow prisoners. The Sháh was amazed but allowed the release of all but three prisoners.

After being released from prison, Mullá Ṣádiq came into contact with influential divines who had heard of his vast learning. They asked him many intricate questions and posed several problems. Although the divines were not well-disposed towards the Bahá'í Faith, the nature of Mullá Ṣádiq's replies was such that no one could challenge him. When Náṣiri'd-Dín Sháh learned of this, he rebuked Ḥisámu's-Salṭanih, his uncle, for having imprisoned such a man. He then ordered that Mullá Ṣádiq be given two horses and a gift of money. The Sháh's mother presented him with clothing befitting his rank. All of these royal gifts Mullá Ṣádiq returned to the Sháh, expressing his gratitude in a letter.

For the next nine years, Mullá Ṣádiq continuously promoted the Cause of God in Khurásán, Káshán, Iṣfahán and Yazd. He was instrumental in leading Ḥájí Mírzá Muḥammad-Riḍá, the future Vazír of Khurásán, to the Faith, as well as some of the Afnáns. He was constantly attacked and denounced by opponents of the Faith but 'spent every waking breath in calling the people to the Kingdom of God'.[16] Eventually, however, he became too frail to continue his work.

Enfeebled and exhausted, he yearned to make a second pilgrimage to the presence of Bahá'u'lláh. Before long, Bahá'u'lláh Himself summoned him to 'Akká, instructing him to bring another believer with him to take care of his needs. Mullá Ṣádiq remained in 'Akká for four months, at the end of which time Bahá'u'lláh revealed a Tablet for him, directing him to return home.

On his way home from 'Akká, Mullá Ṣádiq proclaimed to everyone the advent of the Day of God. When he reached Hamadán in 1889, he was physically exhausted but spiritually alive. For 12 days he never rested. On the twelfth day, he dressed in his best clothes and anointed himself with rose-water and perfume. An hour later he asked a companion to help him undress. The next moment, he spoke his last words, 'That is enough', and passed out of this world.[17]

Bahá'u'lláh gave Mullá Ṣádiq the title Ismu'lláhu'l-Aṣdaq (the Name of God the Most Truthful) and revealed many Tablets in his honour, among them the Lawḥ-i-Aḥbáb, in which:

> Bahá'u'lláh showers praises upon Ismu'lláhu'l-Aṣdaq in such profusion that it is not possible to describe them all. He refers to him as the one who recognized the Promised One as soon as he heard His call . . . It is clear from the utterances of Bahá'u'lláh in this and other Tablets that Bahá'u'lláh regarded him as one of His most devoted followers and a true believer in every sense of the word, one who would be worthy of emulation by all.[18]

The Centre of the Covenant has left us this tribute:

> He was like a surging sea, a falcon that soared high. His visage shone, his tongue was eloquent, his strength and steadfastness astounding. When he opened his lips to teach, the proofs would stream out; when he chanted or prayed, his eyes shed tears like a spring cloud. His face was luminous, his life spiritual, his knowledge both acquired and innate; and celestial was his ardour, his detachment from the world, his righteousness, his piety and fear of God.[19]

Many years later, 'Abdu'l-Bahá spoke of Mullá Ṣádiq, describing him as a Hand of the Cause and 'truly a servant of the Lord from the beginning of life till his last breath'.[20]

# Mírzá 'Alí-Muḥammad Varqá
# c. 1856–1896

O Thou! whence God's Beauty shineth, I know Thee.
Would my being, my soul Thy ransom be, I know Thee.
Shouldst Thou behind a hundred-thousand veils cover seek,
By God, O Thou, the Visage of God, I know Thee.
Shouldst Thou a King choose, or a Servant appear to be,
Apart – at the crest of each Station – apart, I know Thee.[1]

. . .

O Thou, the Root, Thou the Limb of Revelation,
In any garb, any garment, with any mantle, I know Thee.

*Varqá* [2]

Ḥájibu'd-Dawlih was enraged! Náṣiri'd-Dín Sháh had just been assassinated on the eve of his jubilee celebration. The brutal chief steward of the prison of Ṭihrán stormed the dungeon, where he terrified the startled prisoners, made fast their fetters, sent soldiers to nearby roof-tops and readied a row of executioners. Bent upon avenging the death of his sovereign, Ḥájibu'd-Dawlih then unchained the Bahá'ís, brought them out of the dungeon and ordered them in pairs down a corridor towards an inner chamber.

The first to pass through the corridor were Varqá and his twelve-year-old son, Rúḥu'lláh. Once inside the inner room, Ḥájibu'd-Dawlih confronted Varqá with the charge of killing the Sháh. When Varqá serenely replied that he was not aware of having done anything wrong, the bloodthirsty courtier plunged his dagger into the belly of this Apostle of Bahá'u'lláh.

'How are you?' Ḥájibu'd-Dawlih exultantly asked his victim. 'Feeling better than you,' was Varqá's dying reply. As the poet was being torn limb from limb, his blood flowing profusely in the room, Rúḥu'lláh, who had been compelled to witness the grisly slaughter, cried out, 'O dear father, father dear, take me, take me, take me with you.' Furious, Ḥájibu'd-Dawlih ordered his minions to bring a rope with which he might strangle the boy.[3]

* * *

The first of three members of an illustrious family to be designated a Hand of the Cause, Mírzá ʻAlí-Muḥammad Varqá is remembered for his boundless love for Bahá'u'lláh, his eloquence in teaching the Cause and his martyrdom with his son, Rúḥu'lláh. Using the title 'Varqá' (Dove) as his *nom de plume*, Mírzá ʻAlí-Muḥammad was both a talented poet and skilled in traditional Iranian medicine.

A native of Yazd, Varqá's story begins with his distinguished father, Ḥájí Mullá Mihdíy-i-Yazdí, from whom Varqá undoubtedly inherited some of his remarkable qualities and talents. Ḥájí Mullá Mihdí was a learned man and a bold and eloquent teacher of the Faith who became a Bábí when Vaḥíd taught the new religion openly in Yazd. He is remembered by ʻAbdu'l-Bahá as

> . . . an expert in the field of Muslim sacred traditions and an eloquent interpreter of orally transmitted texts . . . As a teacher of the Faith he was never at a loss for words, forgetting, as he taught, all restraint, pouring forth one upon another sacred traditions and texts . . . He was an eminent soul, with his heart fixed on the beauty of God. From the day he was first created and came into this world, he single-mindedly devoted all his efforts to acquiring grace for the day he should be born into the next.[4]

Ḥájí Mullá Mihdí taught the Bábí Faith to the point that he incurred the wrath of Shaykh Muḥammad-Ḥasan-i-Sabzivárí, a leading mujtahid in Yazd. One day Ḥájí Mullá Mihdí held a large meeting of over 200 Bábís. This so incensed the mujtahid that he summoned Ḥájí Mullá Mihdí to his office, ordered him to be brutally flogged in his presence and exiled him from Yazd. Ḥájí Mullá Mihdí, together with two of his three sons, Mírzá Ḥusayn and Mírzá ʻAlí-Muḥammad Varqá, left Yazd on foot. Varqá, the youngest son of Ḥájí Mullá Mihdí, was about 22 years old at the time.

The family travelled to Tabríz. Here Mírzá 'Abdu'lláh <u>Kh</u>án-i-Núrí, a prominent Bahá'í in the service of the Crown Prince, consulted Varqá over a medical problem. Mírzá 'Abdu'lláh <u>Kh</u>án and his wife had been unable to conceive a second child and the medicines they had tried so far were ineffective. Varqá prescribed a remedy and before long Mírzá 'Abdu'lláh <u>Kh</u>án's wife was expecting.

Mírzá 'Abdu'lláh <u>Kh</u>án was so grateful that he persuaded his wife to give their daughter to Varqá in marriage. The marriage produced four sons: 'Azízu'lláh, Rúḥu'lláh, Valíyu'lláh and Badí'u'lláh, who died in early childhood.

After the wedding Varqá, his father and brother travelled to the Holy Land. The journey was an arduous one, as described by 'Abdu'l-Bahá:

> [Ḥájí Mullá Mihdí] was imprisoned along his way; and as he crossed the deserts and climbed and descended the mountain slopes he endured terrible, uncounted hardships. But the light of faith shone from his brow and in his breast the longing was aflame, and thus he joyously, gladly passed over the frontiers until at last he came to Beirut. In that city, ill, restive, his patience gone, he spent some days. His yearning grew, and his agitation was such that weak and sick as he was, he could wait no more.
>
> He set out on foot for the house of Bahá'u'lláh. Because he lacked proper shoes for the journey, his feet were bruised and torn; his sickness worsened; he could hardly move, but still he went on; somehow he reached the village of Mazra'ih and here, close by the Mansion, he died.[5]

So lofty was Ḥájí Mullá Mihdí's station that Bahá'u'lláh revealed a Tablet of Visitation for him; once He stopped at his gravesite and revealed exalted verses in his honour.

After the passing of his father Varqá continued on to the Mansion of Mazra'ih and attained the presence of Bahá'u'lláh. This encounter Varqá had foreseen in a dream many years before as a child. In the dream he was playing with his dolls when God came and threw them into the fire, saying, 'O Varqá! Cast into fire idols of vain imaginings!'[6] Varqá had forgotten this dream until the Manifestation of God repeated these same words to him.

One day, as Varqá gazed in rapture at Bahá'u'lláh, he yearned that the Blessed Beauty might give him a sign of His station. A verse from the Qur'án suddenly came into his mind. Varqá then wished that Bahá'u'lláh would repeat this verse to confirm that this was indeed the sign he sought. Later that day Bahá'u'lláh did recite this very verse. Astonished,

Varqá silently wondered if His utterance was mere coincidence. At that instant, Bahá'u'lláh looked at him and said, 'Was this not sufficient proof for you?'[7] These and other experiences during this first pilgrimage transformed Varqá into a 'flame of fire, a tower of strength, a mine of knowledge and virtues'.[8]

Following his pilgrimage, Varqá journeyed to Tabríz where he rejoined his wife. For the next 12 years Tabríz was his home. From here he served the Cause courageously and eloquently, travelling throughout Á͟dhirbáyján to teach the Faith. The Crown Prince, Muẓaffari'd-Dín Mírzá, often asked Mírzá 'Abdu'lláh K͟hán to bring his son-in-law with him to Court that he might participate in the discussions of the learned men who gathered there from time to time.

Around 1882 Varqá decided to visit his only sister, Bíbí Ṭúbá, in his native Yazd, which lay within the domain of Mas'úd Mírzá, the Ẓillu's-Sulṭán. Soon after he entered the city, Varqá was arrested and detained in the city's prison for a whole year. From Yazd, he was carried fettered to Iṣfahán, where Mas'úd Mírzá lived. Eventually the Ẓillu's-Sulṭán came to admire Varqá's poetic talent and set him free, thinking some advantage to himself might be achieved.

Varqá made his second pilgrimage to the presence of Bahá'u'lláh about a year before Bahá'u'lláh's passing. He was accompanied by his sons 'Azízu'lláh and seven-year-old Rúḥu'lláh. During the course of this visit, Bahá'u'lláh spoke to Varqá about the station of 'Abdu'l-Bahá and His qualities. He also spoke of a phenomenon known as the Power of the Great Ether or the Most Great Elixir. Anyone possessing this power could do anything and could exert great influence on the world; for example, He said, Christ had this power and He revolutionized the world. Bahá'u'lláh pointed out that 'Abdu'l-Bahá also possessed this power, so the extent of His influence on the world of humanity would be immeasurable. These words of Bahá'u'lláh so excited Varqá that he fell prostrate at Bahá'u'lláh's feet and begged to be martyred in the path of the Master, a wish he was later granted.

When Varqá returned from 'Akká to Tabríz, his mother-in-law, never completely happy with the marriage of her daughter to a Bahá'í, was so hostile to him that he found no peace in his own home. Such was his mother-in-law's opposition that Varqá thought of divorcing his wife. His father-in-law dissuaded him from this course, advising him to travel throughout the province teaching the Faith instead. At the same time, Varqá's father-in-law fell out of favour with the Crown Prince, who determined to arrest him. Mírzá 'Abdu'lláh Khán quickly left Tabríz. His wife now planned to have Varqá killed. Her plan was unsuccessful but Varqá realized that the time had come for him to leave Tabríz for good. Taking 'Azízu'lláh and Rúḥu'lláh with him, Varqá went to Zanján. Valíyu'lláh and Badí'u'lláh were too young to travel and had to be left behind with their mother. Varqá and his wife, and Mírzá 'Abdu'lláh and his, were soon divorced.

In Zanján Varqá married Liqá'íyyih Khánum, a daughter of Ḥájí Ímán. Years later Varqá's first wife was brought to Ṭihrán by 'Azízu'lláh. There she declared her belief in Bahá'u'lláh and became a devoted Bahá'í.[9]

Following the ascension of Bahá'u'lláh, Varqá, together with 'Azízu'lláh and Rúḥu'lláh, made his third and final pilgrimage to the Holy Land. There the Master and the Greatest Holy Leaf showed particular admiration and love for Rúḥu'lláh. One day Bahíyyih Khánum asked Rúḥu'lláh how he taught the Faith. The boy answered that he looked into the eyes of the people to determine who had the capacity to receive the Message of Bahá'u'lláh. Khánum asked Rúḥu'lláh to look into the eyes of two sons of Bahá'u'lláh who later joined forces with Mírzá Muḥammad-'Alí, the Archbreaker of Bahá'u'lláh's Covenant. Rúḥu'lláh did so, sadly telling the Greatest Holy Leaf afterwards that their eyes were not worth looking into.[10]

In 1896 Varqá was compelled to leave Zanján and made plans to travel to Ṭihrán. He was anxious to follow 'Abdu'l-Bahá's instructions to take his Tablets and Bahá'í archives out of Zanján. He also wanted to see again Mírzá 'Abdu'lláh Khán, who now lived in the capital. While he acquired the necessary pack animals, Mírzá 'Azízu'lláh became impatient as the days passed and left for Ṭihrán on foot. Thus, when Varqá, Rúḥu'lláh and Ḥájí Ímán were later arrested on the road to Ṭihrán, on suspicion of hatching a plot against a local grandee, 'Azízu'lláh escaped sharing their fate.

Following their arrest, the three travellers were consigned to the gaol in Zanján. Miraculously, the pack animal carrying the Tablets and archival material was not stopped and it made its way to Qazvín, where its precious cargo reached trusted hands. The personal property of Varqá, however, including a watercolour painting of the Báb, was plundered.

Following his arrest, Varqá was questioned almost daily by the clerics of Zanján and its governor, 'Alá'u'd-Dawlih, in an attempt to persuade him to recant his faith and thereby secure his release. The questioning went on for 16 days. Eventually tiring of the endless arguments of the divines, the governor sent Varqá, his son and another Bahá'í, Mírzá Ḥusayn, to the capital for their fate to be decided.

Their journey on horseback to Ṭihrán was very difficult. Varqá and Mírzá Ḥusayn were chained and their feet heavily fettered; Varqá was made to ride on top of saddle-bags, which caused him much pain. The prisoners were harassed, maligned and maltreated. Two of the guards in particular vied with one another to make life difficult for the captives. When a sergeant-major remonstrated with one guardsman that his brutality resembled that of Azraq, a Syrian notorious in Islamic history for causing the suffering of the captive family of Imám Ḥusayn, the guard retorted, 'Not so, not so. It is these people who are the Azraqs of the present day. Now we must take our revenge. They think that they are the Imáms and we are the Syrians, while it is we who are the Imáms and they who are the Syrians.' Varqá was so pained by the guard's words that he said, 'May God judge between us. You have been very insolent.' Shortly afterwards, the guard was gripped by an unbearable pain in his stomach and died upon reaching Ṭihrán. Varqá was much saddened by this. 'I should not have put such an injunction upon him', he kept saying. 'We should not heap curses on our enemies, who are ignorant, but pray for them.'[11]

On their arrival in Ṭihrán, the Bahá'ís were imprisoned in a number of places and repeatedly interrogated. Finally they were moved to the government prison in the neighbourhood of Sabzih Maydán. Here they were kept in chains and stocks, abused, tortured and starved. Neither Varqá nor his son would leave the dungeon alive.

* * *

Ḥájí Ímán and Mírzá Ḥusayn waited anxiously in the corridor. They were next in line to meet death at the hands of the fiendish Ḥájibu'd-Dawlih. Voices could be heard from the other side of the partition separating them from the executioners' inner chamber. Directly a farrá<u>sh</u> appeared and fetched the instrument of bastinado. A little later a gaoler appeared carrying a bloody dagger which he proceeded to wash in a nearby pool. Still later an executioner appeared carrying Varqá's clothes.

As the two companions awaited their fate, Ḥájibu'd-Dawlih suddenly flung open the door to the chamber and fled in terror through the corridor, shouting, 'Take these two back to the gaol, I will deal with them tomorrow.'[12] Bewildered and benumbed, Ḥájí Ímán and Mírzá

Ḥusayn were returned to the dungeon. What, they asked themselves, had happened to Rúḥu'lláh? How had they escaped their turn with Ḥájibu'd-Dawlih?

Eventually the story was told. Having slain Varqá, Ḥájibu'd-Dawlih had turned to Rúḥu'lláh and said, 'Do not weep. I shall take you with myself, make you an allowance, obtain for you a post from the Sháh.'

'I do not want you. I do not want your allowance. I do not want any post that you might obtain for me. I want to join my father', sobbed Rúḥu'lláh.

Ḥájibu'd-Dawlih seized Rúḥu'lláh, placed his neck in the loop of the instrument used for the bastinado and strangled him to death. Dropping the senseless boy to the floor, the elated executioner ordered that the next two Bábís be brought in. But at that precise moment, the corpse of Rúḥu'lláh sprang up, falling to the ground a yard away. Panic-stricken, the murderous courtier fled the scene and did not return.

* * *

Mírzá 'Alí-Muḥammad Varqá was a passionate lover of both Bahá'u'lláh and 'Abdu'l-Bahá and a man of excellent qualities and achievements. He received in abundance the blessings and bounties of the Ancient Beauty. He was a hero who withstood the most difficult trials in the path of his Lord. He was truly a remarkable man who left for posterity in the example of his life a priceless and inspiring heritage and whose sons added lustre to his name and carried his light into the next century.

# III

# Hands of the Cause Appointed Posthumously by Shoghi Effendi

# Ḥájí Abu'l-Ḥasan-i-Ardikání (Amín-i-Iláhí, Ḥájí Amín) c. 1831–1928

When Ḥájí Amín travelled to London in 1912 to meet 'Abdu'l-Bahá, he was able to witness first hand the widespread homage paid to the Son of Bahá'u'lláh. Asked what he thought of 'Abdu'l-Bahá's ascendancy, he was lost in wonderment. No doubt he was remembering those days in 'Akká more than 40 years before, when he could only approach the Manifestation of God at a public bath, so fierce was the oppression of the Bahá'ís. Then he had been advised to show no sign that he recognized Bahá'u'lláh; now crowds of people sought out His Son.

Born in the village of Ardikán near Yazd, Ḥájí Abu'l-Ḥasan was raised and became a staunch Muslim. As was the custom, his parents arranged his marriage when he was 17 years old, to the daughter of a local merchant. At the merchant's insistence and contrary to custom, he took up his residence in the home of his bride rather than that of his father. This arrangement put Ḥájí Abu'l-Ḥasan into close contact with his wife's six brothers, who were all Bábís. Ḥájí Abu'l-Ḥasan was persuaded to investigate the Bábí religion and, following lengthy discussions, he embraced the Cause of the Báb shortly after His martyrdom. He then taught his wife, who also became a Bábí.

When Ḥájí Abu'l-Ḥasan learned that Bahá'u'lláh had made His Declaration, he immediately recognized His station and became a Bahá'í. He underwent a remarkable spiritual transformation, dedicating his whole life to the Manifestation. He became utterly self-sacrificing, detached from worldly things and completely dedicated to his Lord. He travelled throughout Persia, visiting the homes of virtually all the Bábís and telling them about the coming of Bahá'u'lláh. He lavished such love and encouragement upon the believers that they longed for his visits. Welcomed as a loving family member wherever he went, he was known as one who genuinely cared for the well-being and spiritual development of all.

Ḥájí Abu'l-Ḥasan eventually became a devoted assistant to the first Trustee of the Ḥuqúqu'lláh, Ḥájí Sháh-Muḥammad Manshádí, Amínu'l-Bayán, and the two travelled together to collect the Ḥuqúqu'lláh on behalf of Bahá'u'lláh. Ḥájí Sháh-Muḥammad soon came to rely on Ḥájí Abu'l-Ḥasan, who travelled around the country earning his living by trading and writing letters for those who could not write. Ḥájí Abu'l-Ḥasan was thus able to call on the Bahá'ís, deliver the Tablets of Bahá'u'lláh to them and collect the Ḥuqúqu'lláh, as well as any letters the believers wished to send to Bahá'u'lláh. Bahá'u'lláh gave both men the title 'Amín' (trusted one).

Soon after Bahá'u'lláh arrived in 'Akká, Ḥájí Amín and Ḥájí Sháh-Muḥammad were able to enter the city, disguised as Arab merchants. Sending word to Bahá'u'lláh that they were present in the city, He permitted them to see Him in the public baths. Thus Ḥájí Abu'l-Ḥasan was the first Bahá'í from outside 'Akká to meet Bahá'u'lláh within the city walls. However, when Bahá'u'lláh appeared at the bath Ḥájí Amín was so overcome by emotion that he fell to the floor, severely injuring his head, and had to be carried out bleeding.

Around 1880 Ḥájí Sháh-Muḥammad and Ḥájí Amín were caught up in a massacre by Kurds in which Ḥájí Sháh-Muḥammad was killed. Though wounded in the leg, Ḥájí Amín survived and was appointed Trustee of the Ḥuqúqu'lláh by Bahá'u'lláh. As Trustee, Ḥájí Amín gave everything he had to the Cause. By word and deed, he strove to convey to the believers that a person's 'most meritorious achievement in life is to offer up everything he has – his time, his labours, his substance and even his life – in the path of God'.[1]

Ḥájí Amín realized the transforming effects of sacrifice and this prompted him to give everything he had to the Cause of God. Through the example he set, the believers themselves sacrificed more readily. As Trustee of the Ḥuqúq, he well understood how the contributions of the believers benefited both the Cause and themselves:

> Beseech ye God that He may enable everyone to discharge the obligation of Ḥuqúq, inasmuch as the progress and promotion of the Cause of God depend

> on material means. If His faithful servants could realize how meritorious are benevolent deeds in these days, they would all arise to do that which is meet and seemly.[2]

There are many heartwarming stories that reflect upon the sacrifices of Ḥájí Amín. He disliked extravagance as diminishing the ability of the believers to support the Cause of God. When invited to meals, he would often insist on eating only one dish of the simplest food and would ask that a little water be added to account for his share, a recipe that became renowned among the Persians as 'the soup of Ḥájí Amín'.

In 1891 Ḥájí Amín was arrested on the orders of Náṣiri'd-Dín Sháh and his son Kámrán Mírzá. For three years he was imprisoned in Ṭihrán and Qazvín with Hand of the Cause Ḥájí Akhúnd. The two were photographed in chains for the Sháh to see. Such was their resignation and calm that 'Abdu'l-Bahá, gazing at their picture, rejoiced in His heart and placed the photograph in the hallway of His house opposite His room.

On his release from prison after the passing of Bahá'u'lláh, Ḥájí Amín continued to travel, visiting 'Abdu'l-Bahá in 'Akká and Haifa many times. 'Abdu'l-Bahá, in appreciation of his services, named one of the doors of the Shrine of the Báb for him.

Towards the end of his life Ḥájí Amín lived in Ṭihrán, where he died in 1928. Upon his passing Shoghi Effendi conferred upon him the rank of Hand of the Cause, mentioned him among those he named Apostles of Bahá'u'lláh and notified the Persian Bahá'í community:

> The distressing news of the ascension of his honour Amín-i-Iláhí has caused the utmost grief, sadness, and sorrow. That distinguished and precious soul was engaged, over the course of many years and with extraordinary enthusiasm and determination, in serving the sacred Threshold. Not for a moment did he find rest; not for a minute did he seek repose. In constancy and faithfulness he was a shining example to the righteous disciples and companions of God, and in self-abnegation, high-mindedness, and purity of heart and motive, he was the standard to which the loved ones of the Lord aspired. He was a dynamic Hand of the Cause of the unseen Beauty in that sacred land, and was accounted amongst the chosen and the favoured ones of God. His station is among the loftiest that may be, and the passage of ages and centuries will never efface the record of his splendid services.[3]

# 'Abdu'l-Jalíl Bey Sa'ad
## ?–1942

The Egyptian Hand of the Cause 'Abdu'l-Jalíl Bey Sa'ad was noted for his courage, determination and self-sacrifice. Taught by the great Bahá'í scholar Mírzá Abu'l-Faḍl, who was sent to Egypt by 'Abdu'l-Bahá in 1895, he profoundly loved the Faith of Bahá'u'lláh and sought every means to serve his Lord.

'Abdu'l-Jalíl Bey Sa'ad was an imposing man, quite tall and something over 200 pounds in weight. He was always well dressed, particularly at Bahá'í functions, usually wearing a beautiful red fez. A judge in the civil courts, he wrote inspiring articles on the subject of religious freedom when the constitutional laws of Iran were being formulated in 1923. Maintaining that all religions should be treated with equal freedom, he succeeded in persuading the legislators to accept this principle.

In 1929 the believers in Egypt were in great difficulties owing to the passage in the Muslim Court four years before of a verdict against the Bahá'ís of Kom El Sa'ayda. 'Abdu'l-Jalíl Bey Sa'ad was able to improve conditions gradually through negotiations with the prime minister and other high-ranking officials.

Five years later, in 1934, the Declaration of Trust of the National Spiritual Assembly of the Bahá'ís of Egypt needed to be legalized. The Mixed Tribunal, however, refused to deal with the matter on the grounds that the document was of a religious nature and beyond the bounds of its jurisdiction. 'Abdu'l-Jalíl Bey Sa'ad persistently supported the claims of the Bahá'ís to the Prosecutor General, eventually overcoming all resistance and gaining the legal recognition of this instrument which later would facilitate transactions between the believers and the government of Egypt.

At the same time Shaykh el Kharashi attacked the Bahá'ís in a series of articles entitled 'The Bahá'í Faith Is a Pleasing Illusion'. 'Abdu'l-Jalíl Bey Sa'ad, in defence of the Faith, published a series of 14 articles entitled 'The Bahá'í Faith Is an Everlasting Truth'. With such zeal and detail did he defend the Cause that the Shaykh was utterly defeated.

As a result, the fanatics appealed to authorities, demanding to know why a judge in a Muslim country was able to promote religious teachings determined to be contrary to the Muslim religion. When the Minister of Justice, to whom the Muslims appealed, requested 'Abdu'l-Jalíl Bey Sa'ad to cease writing his articles, the zealous Bahá'í retorted, 'If your Excellency wishes me to cease defending my belief, then the other side should also cease attacking it.'[1] The question of religious freedom was referred back to the House of Parliament, where the Minister stated that although freedom of religion was accepted in Egypt, nevertheless both sides had been required to stop the publication of articles.

Meanwhile, 'Abdu'l-Jalíl Bey Sa'ad was sent to a remote part of upper Egypt where the Muslims thought he would be effectively isolated and therefore unable to pursue his Bahá'í activities. However, despite his isolation, he was able to proclaim more loudly the Cause of God. Taking advantage of the opportunity, he translated *The Dawn-Breakers* into Arabic, thus giving the Bahá'ís in the Arabic-speaking countries the means to study this significant history of the Faith. The translation was published in 1941 but owing to the war, was referred to the Publicity Section of the Government. The Muslim authorities who reviewed it denounced it as being against Islam. The book was banned and the entire print-run gathered for destruction.

Undaunted by this turn of events, 'Abdu'l-Jalíl Bey Sa'ad worked tirelessly until he overcame the opposition, obtained the release of his work and received the permission of the authorities to distribute it throughout Egypt. His success over seemingly hopeless circumstances was proof of the Guardian's words, 'To try, to persevere, is to ensure ultimate and complete victory.'[2]

In 1941 'Abdu'l-Jalíl Bey Sa'ad again used the Declaration of Trust, to induce the Ministry of Civil Defence to grant permission to build a Ḥaẓíratu'l-Quds in Cairo. Determined to see its completion, he involved himself personally in the work, locating a site and supervising the construction. During this period he became ill, perhaps as a result of working so hard in the intense heat. On 25 May 1942 he died suddenly following an operation.

In a letter to India written on his behalf, Shoghi Effendi stated:

> The passing of 'Abdu'l-Jalíl Beg Saad [sic] was a great loss to the Faith in Egypt, and the Guardian was pleased to hear that his co-workers in India held memorial meetings for him. Such occasions constitute eloquent testimonials to the profound love that binds Bahá'ís to each other, whoever and wherever they may be.[3]

'Abdu'l-Jalíl Bey Sa'ad was remembered by Shoghi Effendi in a cable to the National Spiritual Assembly of the United States and Canada of 25 June 1942:

> 'ABDU'L-JALÍL BEY SA'AD ABU'L-FAḌL'S MOST RENOWNED DISCIPLE FOREMOST CHAMPION FAITH EGYPT, OUTSTANDING BAHÁ'Í ADMINISTRATOR BRILLIANT AUTHOR, INDEFATIGABLE TEACHER ASCENDED ABHÁ KINGDOM LOSS IRREPARABLE HEARTS GRIEF-STRICKEN. ADVISE HOLD BEFITTING MEMORIAL GATHERING TEMPLE TO ASSOCIATE AMERICAN BELIEVERS UNIVERSAL MOURNING DISTINGUISHED HAND CAUSE BAHÁ'U'LLÁH.[4]

# John Henry Hyde Dunn
# c. 1855* –1941

John Henry Hyde Dunn was born in London, England, learned of the Faith of Bahá'u'lláh in Seattle, Washington, and, together with his beloved Clara, established the Cause of God in the Australian sub-continent. Called Australia's 'spiritual conqueror'[1] by Shoghi Effendi, he is praised in *God Passes By* as 'the great-hearted and heroic Hyde Dunn' who arose at an advanced age with his wife, settled as a pioneer in Australia and carried 'the Message to no less than seven hundred towns throughout that Commonwealth'.[2]

The son of a consulting chemist, he was, as a child, once bounced on the knee of Charles Dickens. As a young man, he worked as a salesman in England and France before emigrating with his first wife, Fanny, to the United States. He apparently adopted the name 'Hyde', which was his mother's maiden name, while in his youth.

In 1905 Hyde chanced to be in a small tinsmith shop where he overheard a Bahá'í, Ward Fitzgerald, remark to the shop's owner Bahá'u'lláh's statement, 'Let not a man glory in this, that he loves his country; let him rather glory in this, that he loves his kind.' Hyde later recalled how hearing this famous utterance of Bahá'u'lláh from one who had recently visited 'Akká and 'Abdu'l-Bahá touched his hungry, searching heart:

> The words reached me with dynamic force, its truth and power crystallized in my heart – a new consciousness awakened, man's attitude to humanity made clear and the significance and love of the Christ-life unfolded. That one glorious utterance magnetized my whole being, appealed as a new note, sent

* Several different dates are given for John Hyde Dunn's birth; the one on his tombstone reads 5 March 1855.

> forth from God to His wandering creatures – a Message from the Supreme to the sons of men.[3]

Hyde Dunn accepted the Faith immediately and soon he and Ward Fitzgerald were travelling together to conduct business and spread the teachings. Practising strict economy, Hyde taught the Cause even when he wasn't working – travelling, for instance, to Walla Walla, Washington to hold Bahá'í meetings during a brief period of unemployment. His practice of thrift in daily living would enable him, more than once, to contribute to the support of the Faith as well as to help others when they found themselves in straitened circumstances.

It was on this trip to Walla Walla in about 1907 that Hyde visited a medical centre and met Clara Davis. He invited her to a Bahá'í meeting. She was struck by the distinguished English gentleman's countenance, saying, some years later, that she had '. . . never seen a man that looked just like him, that had something new in his face, a new light that I didn't know in any other human face I'd ever met'.[4] Hearing Hyde Dunn's message, she was sure it was from God.

Clara learned that neither Hyde nor Ward had any money at this time. Attending a talk they gave at a hall the following Sunday, she was astonished when Mr Fitzgerald asked Mr Dunn to take up a collection. 'Poor Father (Dunn) nearly fainted. He didn't want to take up any collection for giving the Bahá'í message.'[5] Clara paid their fare to Seattle.

In 1911 Lua Getsinger was giving a series of lectures in San Francisco. Hyde Dunn, a travelling salesman, went there as often as he could to learn from the 'mother teacher of the West'. He became friends with Thornton Chase, Helen Goodall and Ella Cooper during this period.

The following year 'Abdu'l-Bahá made His historic eight-month trip to America. While He was visiting the eastern United States, many Bahá'ís in California wondered whether He would come west. Some sent Him telegrams, beseeching Him to visit them. But 'Abdu'l-Bahá's strength was already taxed and the journey would be long and tiring. When He was in New York, He said He would not come to the west unless the love of the friends attracted Him. Hyde Dunn, Willard Hatch and another believer stayed up all night, praying that He would come. The next morning, they received a telegram from Him announcing the date of His arrival there. When He arrived in California, He told the friends several times, 'Your love drew Me to you.'[6]

When Hyde heard that 'Abdu'l-Bahá was coming to San Francisco, he set out to meet Him. He did not care whether he lost his job or what happened to him. In order to be near the Master, he took up residence in a hotel near the house where 'Abdu'l-Bahá was to stay. When 'Abdu'l-Bahá arrived in a cab at this house, Hyde was standing across the street in order to catch a glimpse of Him. When Clara arrived on 'Abdu'l-Bahá's final evening in California, she found Hyde 'nearly out of his head with joy and excitement'.[7] Indeed, the Master's penetrating glance and life-giving words imbued Hyde Dunn with the power of universal love, inspiring him to devote his remaining years to the establishment and growth of the Cause in California and in the world's smallest continent.

The next morning, a group of about two hundred people gathered to say farewell to 'Abdu'l-Bahá. He had a large bottle of rose water from which He anointed everybody. Clara instinctively held out her hands, feeling she was to serve. He anointed both her hands. Mr Dunn He anointed on the head.

In 1916 Hyde Dunn's wife Fanny died. She had been unable to embrace certain aspects of the Faith, and had, perhaps as a consequence, stood in the way of Hyde using their home to advance the Cause of God. Nevertheless, through his loving devotion, her 'end was glorious: It was Bahá'í'.[8]

Sixteen months later, on the anniversary of the Martyrdom of the Báb, Hyde and Clara were married in San Jose, California. Their home became a gathering place for black and white, rich and poor, religious and irreligious, native and foreigner.

In 1919 Hyde and Clara Dunn were on holiday in Santa Cruz, California when they received the Tablets of the Divine Plan. Hyde recalled how they made their decision to respond to 'Abdu'l-Bahá's stirring appeal for pioneers:

> It was all very simple – a wave that came into our lives possessing us and satisfying every desire to serve our beloved Cause, the Cause of Bahá'u'lláh and His Glorious Covenant. Mother was reading 'Abdu'l-Bahá's . . . call to the United States and Canada, and His appeal was so penetrating and thrilling, it pierced our hearts. In one part He said, 'If I could only go in poverty and barefooted, and raise the call of Yá-Bahá'u'l-Abhá, but that is not now possible.' Mother looked up and said, 'Shall we go, Father?' 'Yes,' was my reply, and no further discussion took place. We returned to San Francisco, and after a

> few months my resignation (to my firm) was sent, everything given up, and arrangements made for our prompt sailing.[9]

They arrived at Sydney, Australia on 10 April 1920 on board the SS *Sonoma*. On the way they spent two months in Honolulu serving the Cause of God and made a short stop in Samoa. Aboard ship Clara met the manager of the firm that she had represented in America some years before and he offered her a job in the Australian branch of his company. She accepted this fortuitous offer straightaway, as Hyde had become ill and was unable to work.

Hyde Dunn later recalled that 'at the end of September, while laying the cloth for dinner, a voice, a mental voice, said to me, "Now is the time for you to write to the firm in Melbourne, regarding a position."'[10]

> The mail that night carried a letter to a good firm in Melbourne . . . to whom I felt able to give good service. By return post a reply arrived (which read) 'Your application is most opportune . . .' (Thus) a good position was obtained which ultimately took me over the whole of Australia . . . and to New Zealand with the Bahá'í Message. . . . Praise be to God!
>
> Mother was able to surrender her position and God made it possible for me to earn enough to travel all over the continent, taking Mother to the capital cities.[11]

Thus Hyde began to work for the Bacchus Marsh Milk Company (soon after acquired by Nestlé's Milk). For the first two and a half years they were in New South Wales. They lived in a rented cottage in Sydney where Clara stayed during the week while Hyde travelled to the country towns. Clara would meet people and invite them to meetings at the weekends, at which Hyde would speak. During this time 'interest in the Cause continually increased and people . . . came at all times to see us. There was no breathing space at all. It was an incessant plowing ahead.'[12]

Despite their hard work, it was two years before the first person enrolled as a Bahá'í. Hyde recalled that auspicious event:

> I was at Lismore [498 kilometers north of Sydney] on business and had gathered round me a few business men and we were discussing the world problems and the twelve Bahá'í principles for their solution . . . but they were all very sceptical . . . So one of them suggested that they would invite Mr Whitaker. His

> friends brought him along in great triumph. He asked me one question and one question only – which they all thought would flaw the Bahá'í Faith and Revelation . . . He asked me, 'Can you tell me what love is?' My reply was, 'Yes. The whole Law and Power of the great universe is formulated love in action.' He then said, 'Is that what love is?' He never asked me another question.[13]

Oswald Whitaker became a Bahá'í late in 1922 and was a loving and faithful friend to Father Dunn. He later guided a study group in Sydney. In 1934 he was elected to the first National Spiritual Assembly of the Bahá'ís of Australia and New Zealand.

Near the end of 1922 Father and Mother Dunn went on holiday to New Zealand to teach the Faith. There they met the country's only Bahá'í, Margaret Stevenson, who had become a Bahá'í in 1913 through reading an article about the Faith in *The Christian Commonwealth*. During their visit, Hyde and Clara spoke of the Cause in homes, churches and at a Higher Thought Centre. Sarah Blundell, in whose home the first Bahá'í meeting in New Zealand was held during this time, soon accepted the Faith. Clara remained for a time in New Zealand to help establish a study group while Hyde returned to Australia. Margaret Stevenson later said that the Faith began to spread in Auckland from the time of the Dunn's visit. Shoghi Effendi, in a letter written in mid-1923 to an individual believer, praised the work of the Dunns in New Zealand:

> He [conveys] to you his high estimation for the beauty of the faith of the New Zealand friends, and deep appreciation towards the splendid services of our dear Mr and Mrs Dunn, who are so wonderfully blessed and assisted by the power of the Holy Ghost.[14]

After two and a half years in New South Wales Hyde was promoted and 'the whole of the continent was given me to work in.'[15] The Dunns first went to Melbourne, staying in the state of Victoria for six months. Through Hyde's business connections the Dunns eventually visited every state in Australia.

It was in Melbourne that Effie Baker, one of Australia's first colour photographers, heard of the Bahá'í Faith through Hyde and became a Bahá'í. Her photographic record of historic sites in Iran associated with the Faith, taken some years later at great sacrifice, is preserved in *The Dawn-Breakers*.

In 1923 the Dunns established themselves in Adelaide in South Australia. Within seven weeks of their arrival, they hosted a Feast which 135 people attended. Near the end of the year, Percy and Maysie Almond accepted the Faith at a meeting at which Hyde was speaking.

After several months the Dunns left Adelaide for Western Australia, where they established study classes. The distinguished teacher Honor Kempton met them in Perth. She had journeyed from Hong Kong to Melbourne for 23 days over stormy seas and then taken a five-day train journey to Perth. She recorded in her diary for July 1924:

> Mr and Mrs Dunn are in Perth. Such a welcome! It is heaven. My room filled with the most exquisite bouquets, fifteen friends brought them, a bottle of perfume, an exquisite rosary necklace . . . I have the parlour in a beautiful home. Reporters came, friends came. At night Clara Dunn massaged my back . . . Such wonderful souls in Australia. It seems like a miracle all Mr and Mrs Dunn have accomplished. No need to ask what kind of teachers they are . . . one only needs to look at their confirmed radiant Bahá'í children.[16]

When Martha Root arrived in Melbourne in 1924 she received an elaborate welcome from the Bahá'ís, who sent dozens of bouquets, baskets of fruit and various gifts. She also received a railway ticket from the Dunns, asking that she join them in Perth.

Martha described Clara and Hyde Dunn as 'two Bahá'ís, with beautiful grey hair and sweet young faces . . . filled with Light and Love'.[17] Clara, who had a 'wonderful magnetic healing power in her hands',[18] massaged Martha's back to ease her nagging pain and, with Effie Baker, 'set about restoring [Martha's] physical well-being'.[19]

Martha spent five hectic and triumphant months in Australia and New Zealand, claiming that the unselfish work of the Dunns, their exemplary lives and the foundation they laid were responsible for any success she had in spreading the Bahá'í teachings. Nevertheless, Father Dunn confided in Martha that he wished he could do something for Australia. Mother Dunn felt that she had failed, and wept. Martha, whose praise of the work of the Dunns was boundless and whose admiration was infinite, said of them: 'It is in sweet humbleness like this that the spiritual gardens of Bahá'í souls have come into their first exquisite bloom in this fair land of the Southern Cross.'[20]

The same year, Shoghi Effendi wrote to the Dunns:

> What an encouragement and what an inspiration to be revived every now and then with a fresh breeze wafting from far away Australia and laden with the perfume of your love and devotion for His Sacred Cause. A thousand times well done, my dearly beloved ones! Your warmth, your perseverance, your confidence, your faith, will, I am certain, establish our precious Cause in the very heart of that continent which in future will ring with the Greatest Name and extol the glorious self-sacrificing labours of you who are the pioneers of His Cause in those far away regions. Your reward will be unexpectedly great and your efforts will be richly recompensed by 'Abdu'l-Bahá Himself in the world to come.[21]

Before year's end, Hyde and Clara left Western Australia for a visit to Tasmania. Establishing themselves at a flat in Hobart, they held fireside meetings and enrolled Miss Gretta Lamprill, who would be elected to the National Spiritual Assembly in 1942 and serve as its secretary for several years. The Dunns went on to make extended visits to several cities in Australia, returning to Sydney in 1925.

The exciting events of these early years must have inspired Father Dunn to voice these sentiments:

> How strange things happen – and how wonderfully does God act and guide His plans into our lives with the bounty of life, so that we can serve Him . . . He has no limit, if we will but listen and be sincere in act and motive . . . O beloved ones of Bahá'u'lláh (!) make firm your steps and secure every opportunity to serve with a new consciousness of love and service, and so justify our being Bahá'ís.[22]

Following the establishment of the first Local Spiritual Assembly in Melbourne, in December 1923, the Faith advanced steadily under the Dunns' loving and tender care in succeeding years. As the Dunns continued their extensive travels in Australia and New Zealand, Local Spiritual Assemblies were raised up, outstanding Bahá'í teachers such as Keith Ransom-Kehler and Fred Schopflocher visited, a Bahá'í quarterly newsletter was established and a Bahá'í summer school founded. The first National Spiritual Assembly of the Bahá'ís of Australia and New Zealand was formed in 1934. Both Hyde and Clara Dunn were asked to address the inaugural convention. As Hyde 'rose to his feet every heart felt a throb of joy and thankfulness that these two chosen instruments, who had brought understanding and peace to so many of those present, were there to guide and inspire them to greater heights of achievement in His path.'[23]

In the evening of his life, Hyde's health began to decline. In 1935 the Guardian, through his secretary, wrote:

> Regarding dear Mr Hyde Dunn's health; Shoghi Effendi is grieved beyond words to learn that he is growing so weak physically. Will you kindly assure him, as well as Mrs Dunn, of his supplications for the amelioration of his health and for the complete restoration of his forces.[24]

However, a year later Hyde was well enough to write an article for the first issue of the Bahá'í Quarterly:

> Our appeal to the Bahá'í world would be to follow the call and desire of our beloved Guardian to read and study the 'Divine Plan' given in 1917 by 'Abdu'l-Bahá, the Centre of God's Covenant, so that Bahá'ís will re-awaken to the ever increasing demand of Bahá'u'lláh to spread His revelation and teach the people.[25]

Writing about how the Tablets of the Divine Plan inspired the Dunns to pioneer to Australia, Hyde continued:

> Our storehouse was filled in abundance with the realities of His outpourings and our faith steadfast in its purpose. This was our whole stock. Praise be to God He caused confirmation to follow us. It was not of us that the message spread, but by His guidance and bounty. O, beloved sisters and brothers in Bahá, this great PIONEER service is still waiting and calling for recruits. Perchance some of you might respond, for the field of endeavour is still wide open and is expecting YOU. Territories and islands of the sea offer great fields for confirmation to those who will join the Divine Service of Brotherhood. It is YOU they are longingly asking for.[26]

Describing the role of pioneers, Hyde went on to say:

> Pioneers must be strong and ready to face all the hardships that may appear on their path. These are as naught compared with the delights of loving response and the confirmation that follow. The readiness to accept any vicis-

situdes is an essential of service to God. The service awakens the consciousness within us of our real rank and station in the world of humanity – the rank and station ordained for the release of perfections and virtues. Thus does God become visible in this world of creation – this is the station of the human soul. With dearest love in His sweet Name . . .[27]

The Fitzners, early believers who knew the Dunns, described Hyde Dunn giving 'everyone a joyous welcome. He always had a sweet smile on his dear face . . . [His] manner was at all times kind and gentle. He always had a good answer for enquirers. He had great patience . . . [He] was always well dressed (with a neat bow tie), spotlessly clean and tidy and of handsome appearance. He had snow white hair . . . He always wore immaculately laundered shirts.'[28]

Six days before he passed away, Father Dunn attended 'the Healing Meeting at the Centre on Tuesday afternoon, February 11th, and was his usual bright, informative self.'[30] Upon arriving home, however, he became unconscious for a brief time. He revived, but three days later he became unconscious again and did not regain consciousness. He passed away following the weekend on Monday morning, 17 February 1941. The National Spiritual Assembly of the Bahá'ís of Australia and New Zealand paid him this remarkable tribute:

The history of the Bahá'í Cause in Australia and New Zealand during the last twenty years is bound up with the life and work of Mr John Henry Hyde Dunn. Mr and Mrs Dunn together responded to the call of 'Abdu'l-Bahá to the American believers for workers in other fields. It was to these countries, Australia and New Zealand, they travelled, and the story of their joint pioneer work is known and appreciated throughout the length and breadth of these dominions. Alone and unknown, with no material prestige whatsoever they raised the call of the New Day in all the capital cities of Australia, and in Auckland, New Zealand. Carefully and lovingly they nurtured the Faith. In the first few years no fewer than five local Spiritual Assemblies were established . . . [and] a number of groups. In 1934 Father's heart was rejoiced to see the further flowering of his labour when the National Spiritual Assembly came into being.

All hearts were turned in loving sympathy to Mother Dunn when the news was sent to the believers of Father's passing to the Abhá Kingdom on February 17th, 1941. The threads binding him to earth had been wearing thinner and his hold on life becoming lighter for some time, thus preparing us for the severe blow of separation. Though conscious of our irreparable loss, grief for one so full of years and honour and who lived to accomplish so much would be misplaced. Let us rather thank God for the privilege vouchsafed us and future generations who are destined to inherit the fruit of his glorious labours. To the sincere seeker he was a finger post on the spiritual highway.

Absolutely and completely confirmed, he was a brilliant example of one in whom the confirmations of the spirit had become a living force, vitalizing every thought and action. Bahá'u'lláh, as the embodiment of Reality, was the spring from which he drew his ever-increasing supply of spiritual sustenance. It was not alone the great message of which he was the bearer that arrested attention but in addition, the unearthly light that suffused his whole personality when giving the message, endowing him with a quality which set him on a spiritual plane to which others were blindly groping, a height reached only through surrender of personal will and ambition. The only recompense he sought was the joy of being used in the service of Bahá'u'lláh. Every contingency he accepted as an opportunity he must seize for the furtherance of his supreme task – spreading the Message, sowing the seed which was to fructify into the world order envisaged by Bahá'u'lláh. From this task he never swerved, never lost heart, however hard the ground, or poor the soil, or meagre the apparent harvest. His faith in the ultimate triumph of the Beloved's Cause was firm as a rock that no buffetings of indifference or adversity in the path could move.

This steadfast soul-satisfying faith coupled with his kindly graciousness and understanding heart contributed in no small degree to his unique attractive personality. But it was his dauntless faith in the power inherent in the Cause he proclaimed that enabled him to light a flame in these distant lands that can never be extinguished. Let us all unite in praise and thanksgiving to God for the privilege, vouchsafed to us of this generation, of personal friendship with dear Father Dunn. May we be moved to emulate his complete consecration.[30]

Four days after he passed away, Shoghi Effendi sent the following cable:

I SHARE SORROW LOSS, PARTICIPATE REJOICINGS TRIUMPH BELOVED FATHER DUNN. MAGNIFICENT CAREER VETERAN WARRIOR FAITH OF BAHÁ'U'LLÁH REFLECTS THE PUREST LUSTRE WORLD HISTORIC MISSION CONFERRED

> AMERICAN COMMUNITY BY 'ABDU'L-BAHÁ. TO THREE HEROINES WHOSE DUST REPOSES HEART PERSIA, PACIFIC ISLAND AND SOUTHERN EXTREMITY AMERICAN CONTINENT,[31] A FOURTH WITNESS IN FAR-OFF AUSTRALIA NOW ADDED, ATTESTING FIRST VITAL SPARKS FAR-FLUNG SPIRITUAL DOMINION AMERICAN BELIEVERS COMMISSIONED ESTABLISH. MOVED CONGRATULATE THEM RESPLENDENT SUCCESSES PLAN DESTINED ENCIRCLE ENTIRE GLOBE. ADVISE HOLD NATIONAL MEMORIAL GATHERING MASHRIQU'L-ADHKAR BEFITTING THE RANK AUSTRALIA'S SPIRITUAL CONQUEROR.[32]

On 27 April 1952 the National Spiritual Assembly of Australia and New Zealand received a message from Shoghi Effendi: 'HYDE DUNN REGARDED HAND.'[33]

# John Ebenezer Esslemont
# 1874–1925

Born into a distinguished family of Aberdeenshire, Scotland on 19 May 1874, John Esslemont was a brilliant man who accomplished much in his brief lifetime of 51 years. He was the fourth child of John E. Esslemont, a successful merchant, and Margaret Davidson. His elder brother, William, was a solicitor while his younger brother, Peter, was a tea merchant and writer. John's uncle, Peter Esslemont, became Lord Provost of the City of Aberdeen and was a Member of Parliament, while one cousin, George, also became a Member of Parliament and another, James, became a member of the Land Court of Scotland.

John was educated at Ferryhill School and Robert Gordon College, Aberdeen. In 1898 he graduated from Aberdeen University with honourable distinctions in the degrees of Bachelor of Medicine and Surgery, 'having won a medal in clinical surgery and having been *proxime accessit* for the James Anderson Gold Medal and Prize in clinical medicine in his final year'.[1] As the first winner of the Phillips Research Scholarship, he spent the last half of 1899 at the Universities of Berne and Strasbourg, where he wrote and published a research paper on pharmacology. At the end of the year he returned to Aberdeen, where he was assistant to the Regius Professor in Materia Medica and continued his research. John was a man of diverse interests. He was fluent in Esperanto, French, Spanish and German and later learned Persian and Arabic. He loved music and had a good tenor voice. He was particularly interested in the treatment of tuberculosis – which he had contracted during his college days – and developed a sophisticated plan for its elimination. He took an active interest in proposals to set up a national health service. He investigated many kinds of religious beliefs and occult systems before becoming a Bahá'í.

In 1901 he became attracted to his sister's music teacher, who was an accomplished pianist, and they became engaged. The couple married in Australia in December 1902, settling first in Wollongong, New South Wales. John then took a post at Ararat Hospital and became District Surgeon and Health Officer to Alexander County. The marriage was not, however, a happy one, although John never spoke of this publicly, and the couple had no children. In 1903 John left Australia and returned to Aberdeenshire for the summer.

With the approach of winter in Scotland, John left for South Africa, where he hoped the climate would be more salubrious to his health. He remained in South Africa for five years, working as Medical Officer at a government hospital in Durban and later as District Surgeon at Kroonstad. He also published two papers on his medical observations there.

In 1908 he returned to Britain where he became the Resident Medical Officer of the Home Sanatorium, Southbourne, Bournemouth, one of many institutions of the day established for the treatment of pulmonary tuberculosis. In searching out treatments for the disease, Dr Esslemont was, perhaps not surprisingly, in the forefront of applying new techniques. At the time, tuberculosis was extremely widespread: in Britain, one in seven adults died of the disease.

John Esslemont worked long hours at the Home Sanatorium. Being a firm believer in maintaining the morale of his patients, he organized social events for them and often stayed up late into the night to care for a dying patient.

While others in the medical profession hotly debated with the government proposals for a national health insurance scheme, in 1912 John and other eminent health professionals set up the State Medical Service Association, which envisioned the introduction of a complete national health service. John was a member of the executive committee and wrote the first article to be printed in the Association's journal, *The Medical World*. The Association compiled statistics and useful information which it presented to the Consultative Council on Medical and Allied Services and produced a far-sighted document, the recommendations of which became the foundation of the British National Health Service.

It was through his work with the State Medical Service Association that John learned of the Bahá'í Faith. Katherine Parker, the wife of the secretary of the Association, had met 'Abdu'l-Bahá when He was in

London. Although she was not a believer, she mentioned the Faith in a conversation with John in December 1914. Esslemont was interested and asked for the loan of a few booklets. He was greatly impressed with the Bahá'í teachings. 'I was', he later wrote, 'at once struck by their comprehensiveness, power and beauty. They impressed me as meeting the great needs of the modern world more fully and satisfactorily than any other presentation of religion which I had come across.'[2]

Within a few months he had read many Bahá'í books and was so enamoured of the Faith that in March 1915 he kept the Fast and gave a talk on the religion to over 30 people at the Bournemouth Lodge of the Theosophical Society. At the same time he struck up a lifelong correspondence with Dr Luṭfu'lláh Ḥakím, writing to him on 14 March 1915:

> The Bahá'í Teachings have filled me with new hope for the world. Just as the 'miracle of Spring' is taking place in the material world today, so I hope it will prove that a similar 'miracle of Spring' is coming in the spiritual and social world, and that Bahá'u'lláh will accomplish for the world of humanity what the material sun is doing for the flowers and trees.[3]

John was immediately immersed in the work of the Cause. In March and April 1915 a London believer, Florence George, arrived in Bournemouth to help John establish a Bahá'í group in the town. Together they taught the Faith, speaking to various groups and organizations and at centres of adult education. When in 1916 he heard the appeal for funds for the building of the House of Worship in America, John made a generous contribution to it and worked to raise subscriptions from various friends in Britain. Convinced of the need for an international language, he worked to promote the use of Esperanto and through his knowledge of it was able to communicate with Bahá'ís across the world. In 1916 he and Dr Ḥakím translated the Hidden Words into Esperanto.

John's love for the Faith and his devotion to it were expressed in a letter written in 1916:

> There is no limit to what the human spirit can achieve in the strength of Divine Inspiration. The germ of the Divine Nature is in every man; only most of us are not manifesting it. Instead, we are smothering it. It is like a plant, which needs sun and rain for its growth, the Sun and Rain of the Divine Love and Bounty. We have the power either to open our hearts to that Love and

> Bounty or to reject them. Only by turning our attention and interest away from the world and turning them to God can we grow in spirit. Such turning means attending to the reality and inner significance of things instead of to the outward appearance. It means that our interest in and love for everything in all God's universe should vastly increase, but that we should regard all outward appearances but as the garments of the inner realities, as dawning places for the Glory of God. Oh! may people all over the world soon turn to God, as revealed in Bahá'u'lláh, with humble and contrite hearts, begging for His forgiveness and blessing and imploring His mercy and bounty! Then shall His Kingdom come in men's hearts and the whole world become one home and all mankind one family.[4]

As early as October 1916 John had begun to write a book on the Bahá'í Faith, and although progress on it was very slow owing to his work in the Sanatorium, by May 1918 he had completed about half of it. About the time he was writing the chapter on health and healing, he wrote to Dr Ḥakím of his interest in the Bahá'í perspective on the subject:

> I made a special study of the Bahá'í teachings with regard to healing . . . It seems to me that if we have the right sort of faith, we ought to have the power of healing – that if we could realize sufficiently the Presence, the Power and the Love of God, we should receive healing for our sickness, bodily as well as mental, and be able to help others, by spiritual means to get rid of their sickness.[5]

In July 1918 Ethel Rosenberg, one of the very early English Bahá'ís, travelled to Bournemouth for a visit. While there she read the draft chapters of Esslemont's book and thought that one of the chapters in particular might serve as a pamphlet. Her suggestion was taken up and a 31-page booklet entitled 'What is a Bahá'í' was published by the Malvina Press in West Kensington in 1919.[6]

One of the people John met in Bournemouth was Major Wellesley Tudor Pole, who was able to visit 'Abdu'l-Bahá in Haifa on 19 November 1918. He must have spoken well of Esslemont's services to the Faith, for Shoghi Effendi immediately wrote to John:

> My dear spiritual brother,
>
> . . . Captain Tudor Pole . . . mentioned your name to the Beloved and mentioned your untiring services in the Cause. How gratified the Beloved was to

hear that. He prayed for you and asked His Heavenly Father for confirmation and help.[7]

This was the beginning of a warm friendship between the two men, rare for the future Guardian, whose responsibilities would leave him little time for close ties.

In January 1919 John received a Tablet from 'Abdu'l-Bahá asking him to submit a copy of his book for the Master's review. John responded by forwarding the first nine chapters to the Master and memorized the Tablet, hoping to translate 'Abdu'l-Bahá's words into his life:

> Verily have I chanted thy verses of praise to God, inasmuch as He hath illumined thine eyes with the light of guidance, the light of the oneness of the world of humanity; so much so that thy heart overflowed with the love of God, and thy spirit was attracted by the fragrance of God, and I supplicate divine Providence that thou mayest become a torch to that gathering, so that the light of knowledge might shine out from thee, that thou mayest be confirmed to act in accordance with the significances of the 'Hidden Words' and strengthened by God under all circumstances . . .
>
> I pray the Lord to support thee in the service of all humankind, irrespective of race or religion. Nay rather, thou shouldst deal with all according to the teachings of Bahá'u'lláh, which are like unto life in this Glorious Age.[8]

John hoped to go to the Holy Land with Dr Ḥakím when he travelled there in July 1919, but 'Abdu'l-Bahá asked Esslemont to bring his completed manuscript with him and it was not yet ready. Eventually he left for Haifa in October 1919, going overland through Paris and Rome to Bari, across from Naples, to take the ship to Alexandria. At Bari he met Corinne and Edna True, who were also en route to Haifa, and they spent several days together, taking wonderful walks and discussing world affairs. Edna later wrote that she found Dr Esslemont's companionship to be 'stimulating' and 'delightful'.[9] The Trues were the first western pilgrims to arrive in Haifa after the World War.

Dr Esslemont, who took a later steamer from Bari, arrived in Haifa on 5 November but, owing to quarantine regulations, did not meet 'Abdu'l-Bahá until 6 November. He succumbed to illness soon after his arrival and was thus unable to attend many of 'Abdu'l-Bahá's talks. John was very disappointed since 'Abdu'l-Bahá was the most important source of material for his book and meeting Him the primary reason for his journey. However Dr Ḥakím came to John's room every day to tell him what 'Abdu'l-Bahá had said and John was sometimes well enough to sit with the pilgrims when they gathered at 'Abdu'l-Bahá's table.

'Abdu'l-Bahá once visited John in his room during his illness. When John asked the Master to pray for his health, 'Abdu'l-Bahá replied:

> I will be happy to pray for you. The prayer will be spiritual treatment. I will pray for your spiritual health. That is essential . . . I have suffered here much, and you must have a portion and suffer a little too.[10]

The American pilgrims left Haifa on 27 November. John recovered shortly afterwards and was able to visit with the Iranian pilgrims, take Persian lessons and give Esperanto classes. Every evening he and the other pilgrims ate at the table of 'Abdu'l-Bahá, after which the Master spoke on the history and teachings of the Faith. John also assisted Shoghi Effendi and Dr Ḥakím in the translation of 'Abdu'l-Bahá's Tablet to the Hague.

'Abdu'l-Bahá discussed Esslemont's book with him several times and made suggestions for its improvement. As John had gathered so much new information, the book required much revision. It was decided that John should return to England to work on the manuscript and he left Haifa on 23 January 1920.

John finished working on the book in June and in August sent all the chapters to Dr Ḥakím so that he could translate them into Persian for 'Abdu'l-Bahá's review. Upon completing his book, John set about studying Persian, spending two hours every day learning the language. It was John's longing to study the Bahá'í teachings more fully in their original languages that prompted him to learn Persian and Arabic. In September Shoghi Effendi came to Bournemouth and visited him for a few days at the Sanatorium.

A Bahá'í Council had been set up in England many years before to administer the affairs of the Bahá'ís on a national level but it had not met since 1916. In His final interview with John in Haifa, 'Abdu'l-Bahá had told Esslemont to re-establish the Council:

> We know there are very few in England now, there is no need for any election. Let the present ones go on and introduce a few more whom the friends wish. Then let them work together. I want you to be in it too.[11]

Thus a 'preliminary meeting was held on 22 October 1920',[12] attended, among others, by Dr Esslemont, Ethel Rosenberg and Florence George. The Council met formally for the first time in five years on 7 December 1920, a meeting which John described in a letter to Dr Ḥakím as 'very harmonious':

> I think we all felt that it marked the beginning of a new era in the history of the Cause in this country. The meeting was arranged in accordance with the advice given by 'Abdu'l-Bahá through me that the old members of the council who were still able to act should add to their numbers a few new ones whom the friends approved and they should then work together.[13]

John was appointed by the Council to collect and forward contributions for the House of Worship in the United States.

In addition to this and his work at the Sanatorium, John was engaged in a number of other activities. He continued his studies in Persian, was involved in promoting the study and use of Esperanto, was secretary of the local League of Nations Union, organized local Bahá'í events and in January 1921 began negotiations with the Swarthmore Press for the publication of his book.

In November 1921 'Abdu'l-Bahá suddenly passed away, grieving the entire Bahá'í world. Although He had begun to review John's book, only chapters 1, 2, 5 and part of chapter 3 had been corrected by the time of His death. John wrote immediately to Shoghi Effendi, who was at this time studying in Oxford:

> Dearest Shoghi,
>
> It was indeed a 'bolt from the blue' when I got Tudor Pole's wire this morning . . . It must be very hard for you, away from your family and even away from all Bahá'í friends. What will you do now? I suppose you will go back to Haifa as soon as possible. Meantime you are most welcome to come here for a few days . . . Just send me a wire . . . and I shall have a room ready for you . . . If I can be of any help to you in any way I shall be so glad. I can well imagine how heart-broken you must feel and how you must long to be at home and what a terrible blank you must feel in your life . . . Christ was closer to His loved ones after His ascension than before, and so I pray it may be with the beloved and ourselves. We must do our part to shoulder the responsibility of the Cause and His Spirit and Power will be with us and in us.[14]

John went immediately to London, where he found Shoghi Effendi in bed prostrate with grief and unable to eat, sleep or think. John took him back to Bournemouth while preparations were made for his to travel back to Haifa. John wrote to Dr Ḥakím:

> At times he was very sad and overcome with grief, but on the whole he kept up very bravely, and gradually the conviction that although the bodily presence was removed, the Spirit of the Beloved was as near, as powerful and as accessible to us as ever, seemed to revive his strength and hope.[15]

Shoghi Effendi left London for Haifa on 16 December, learning on his arrival of his appointment in the Will and Testament of 'Abdu'l-Bahá as Guardian of the Bahá'í Faith. Ethel Rosenberg, who had arrived in Haifa just after 'Abdu'l-Bahá's passing, received instructions from the new Guardian to call an election for a spiritual assembly that would reach beyond the confines of London. On her return to Britain, the election was held in May 1922 for the 'Spiritual Assembly of London', also known as the All-England Bahá'í Council. There were ten elected members plus two appointed by Shoghi Effendi, Edward Hall representing Manchester and John Esslemont Bournemouth. Owing to illness John missed the first meeting, on 17 June, but he was elected vice-chairman. He wrote to Dr Ḥakím, 'I do hope that the appointment of this new Council will mark the beginning of a new and more prosperous era for the Bahá'í Movement in this country.'[16] On 11 April 1923 the Bournemouth Bahá'ís formed their first Local Spiritual Assembly, electing John their chairman.

Shoghi Effendi carried on the work begun by 'Abdu'l-Bahá of reviewing John's book, although this was delayed by his absence from the Holy Land. Early in 1923 he sent several suggestions, saying, 'Your book, I am sure, is the finest presentation that has so far been given of the Cause and I am confident that it will arouse immense interest.'[17] *Bahá'u'lláh and the New Era* was finally published early in September 1923 by George Allen and Unwin.

On 20 April 1923 John left Bournemouth and returned to Aberdeen. Intending it to be a time for relaxation, Esslemont busied himself once again with his Persian studies and read histories of the Faith in Persian. In November he travelled south, speaking at a Unitarian Church in Manchester and returning to Bournemouth in December. In 1924 he visited Stokenchurch in Buckinghamshire and it was from there that he wrote his first letter to Dr Ḥakím in Persian. Near the end of May he completed a pamphlet entitled 'Bahá'u'lláh and His Message', which was published two months later. At the same time he busied himself arranging for the publication of the American edition of his book, which eventually appeared in October 1924. In June 1924, however, his breathing deteriorated again, forcing him to rest for over three months at Torphins and in Aberdeenshire.

The Guardian had written to the London Bahá'ís in January 1923 expressing his need for a 'competent assistant in my translation work'[18] but no one had responded to the appeal. Advised to leave Scotland before the onset of winter, John received an invitation from the Guardian to come to Haifa, which he gladly accepted. He arrived in the Holy Land on 21 November 1924.

John immediately began Persian lessons. In November he helped the Guardian translate the Tablet of Aḥmad and by December he was reading and translating extracts from Nabíl's Narrative. In February 1925 he assisted Shoghi Effendi to translate the Hidden Words and other passages from the writings of Bahá'u'lláh. Concerned with the burden of work placed on the young Guardian, John was anxious to be of whatever service he could. When the Guardian asked him to make Haifa his home, John quickly agreed. By February 1925 he was acting as Shoghi Effendi's English-language secretary. Shortly afterwards, however, his health deteriorated again. An attack of pleurisy, a complication of his tuberculosis, put him in hospital for more than two weeks in March.

During his illness, Martha Root came to Haifa as a pilgrim. She and Dr Esslemont spent time together studying Esperanto. She found his book to be an excellent teaching tool and she believed him to be a great scholar. Remembering their time together, Martha later wrote:

> Everything he did bore the mark of extreme efficiency . . . In our Esperanto work he was not satisfied with just any word, but sometimes we would discuss a dozen words and search for their exact meanings in several dictionaries to find the word that would most brilliantly express the spirit of each thought.[19]

One day as he lay seriously ill in bed, Martha told John, 'If you do not do anything, you are still doing much work every day, for your book is spreading the Bahá'í message in every land.'[20] Like John, Martha was concerned with how much work Shoghi Effendi had to do:

> Dr Esslemont helps him a great deal, but Dr has been very ill, he came out of the hospital to his room last week and could walk out a little each day. Then he had a relapse and is now in bed. His health is very frail but he is so precious to the Cause with his writing, his Persian, his help in translating. Please let us pray for him strength to serve longer.[21]

Following his release from the hospital, it was decided that John should spend some time recuperating in the Black Forest in Germany. While there he worked with his hostess on a revision of the German translation of his book.

Near the end of September he returned to Haifa but was still not very well and often spent several days at a time in bed. Early in November he suffered a relapse and was again confined to bed. At about midnight on 21 November, exactly one year after his arrival in Haifa, he suffered a stroke. Shoghi Effendi sat up with him the whole night. The next day, John suffered a second stroke and then a third, to which he succumbed at about 7 o'clock on the evening of 22 November.

On 23 November Shoghi Effendi cabled the Bahá'ís in London: 'BELOVED ESSLEMONT PASSED AWAY. COMMUNICATE FRIENDS AND FAMILY DISTRESSING NEWS. URGE BELIEVERS DEDICATE SPECIAL DAY FOR UNIVERSAL PRAYER AND REMEMBRANCE.'[22]

John Esslemont's body was dressed and wrapped in white silk cloth and perfumed by attar of roses. On John's finger Shoghi Effendi placed his own Bahá'í ring, which he had worn for many years. John was buried at the foot of Mount Carmel, next to the grave of Vakílu'd-Dawlih, the cousin of the Báb and the chief builder of the House of Worship at 'Ishqábád.

On John Esslemont's passing, Shoghi Effendi wrote:

> It is with feelings of overwhelming sorrow that I communicate to you the news of yet another loss which the Almighty, in His inscrutable wisdom, has chosen to inflict upon our beloved Cause. On the 22nd of November, 1925 – that memorable and sacred day in which the Bahá'ís of the Orient celebrated the twin Festivals of the Declaration of the Báb and the Birthday of 'Abdu'l-Bahá, Dr John E. Esslemont passed on to the Abhá Kingdom. His end was as swift as it was unexpected. Suffering from the effects of a chronic and insidious disease, he fell at last a victim to the inevitable complications that ensued, the fatal course of which neither the efforts of vigilant physicians nor the devoted cares of His many friends could possibly deflect.

> He bore his sufferings with admirable fortitude, with calm resignation and courage. Though convinced that his ailments would never henceforth forsake him, yet many a time he revealed a burning desire that the friends residing in the Holy Land should, while visiting the Shrines, implore the All-Merciful to prolong his days that he may bring to a fuller completion his humble share of service to the Threshold of Bahá'u'lláh. To this noble request all hearts warmly responded. But this was not to be. His close association with my work in Haifa, in which I had placed fondest hopes, was suddenly cut short . . . The Cause he loved so well, he served even unto his last day with exemplary faith and unstinted devotion. His tenacity of faith, his high integrity, his self-effacement, his industry and painstaking labours were traits of character the noble qualities of which will live and live forever after him. To me personally he was the warmest of friends, a trusted counsellor, an indefatigable collaborator, a loveable companion.
>
> With tearful eyes I supplicate at the Threshold of Bahá'u'lláh . . . in my ardent prayers, for the fuller unfolding in the realms beyond of a soul that has already achieved so high a spiritual standing in this world. For by the beauty of his character, by his knowledge of the Cause, by the conspicuous achievements of his book, he has immortalized his name and by sheer merit deserves to rank as one of the Hands of the Cause of God.[23]

John Esslemont's *Bahá'u'lláh and the New Era* became one of the most widely used textbooks on the Bahá'í Faith. Shoghi Effendi referred to it as 'an abiding monument to his pure intention' which would 'alone, inspire generations yet unborn to tread the path of truth and service as steadfastly and as unostentatiously as was trodden by its beloved author'.[24] It has been revised and brought up to date many times and has been translated into over 60 languages. It remains one of the best-known books on the teachings of Bahá'u'lláh.

# Louis George Gregory
# 1874–1951

> All the Bahá'ís had gathered for the Nineteen Day Feast. It was being held some eight or nine blocks from our house. Apparently, after the Feast a Local Spiritual Assembly meeting had been called. Mr Gregory was our guest at the time, so rather than keep him there I was asked by my mother to guide him to our home. I was no more than eight years old and accepted the responsibility with great dignity. The night was dark and so was Mr Gregory. I remember to this day one glance in which I looked up at him. My gaze was held for a moment on the beauty and peace of his face, but most of all, it was the shimmering radiance that was so remarkable, that seemed to be part of him. I was so amazed that in such darkness and also in the darkness of his colouring that there could be so much light. I was unable to take my eyes off of his face.[1]

Louis George Gregory, an African-American, was born on 6 June 1874, eleven years after Abraham Lincoln declared an end to slavery in the United States in his historic Emancipation Proclamation. A native of Charleston, South Carolina, Louis belonged to the first generation of his race to be born free in America. His father died of tuberculosis when Louis was five years old and the young boy was brought up by his mother and maternal grandmother – until 1865 both slaves on the Darlington plantation of George Washington Dargan.

Louis's grandmother was a formidable woman who, although illiterate, schooled him in dignity, courage and laughter. Of wholly African blood, she was Chancellor Dargan's slave wife and Louis's mother was their daughter. Although Dargan died in 1859, Louis would think without bitterness of his white forebears as distinguished for their work in religion and education and for their ready acquiescence to the end of slavery.

In the decades immediately following the Civil War the vast majority of African-Americans suffered privations, being denied the economic advantages afforded whites. Louis's family, however, was especially impoverished following the deaths of his father and his black grandfather, who was shot by the Ku Klux Klan. It was his grandmother who gave the family stability during this period of intense hardship.

While Louis was still in his childhood, his mother married George Gregory, who became a real father to Louis. He had been born free around 1842. He was something of a property owner, and brought into the marriage an appreciation of literature and music. Louis added to the lessons of his grandmother and mother those of his stepfather about self-respect, resourcefulness and a desire to learn. In later years George Gregory would apprentice Louis to a tailor and pay for his first year at college.

During the Reconstruction that followed the Civil War African-Americans could vote in elections, live in integrated neighbourhoods, hold government office and receive redress for grievances through the courts. However, following the withdrawal of Union troops in 1877, economic dependence, widespread illiteracy and white supremacy effectively denied them the rights gained during Reconstruction. Soon African-Americans found themselves denied basic human rights – the vote, public accommodation, quality education, ownership of property, service on juries, even citizenship and the protection of the law.

Now an oppressed and segregated people, African-Americans were often attacked, and their property seized, in riots initiated primarily by whites in order to terrorize blacks into submission. Between 1884 and 1900 more than two-and-a-half thousand lynchings of African-Americans occurred, mostly in the South. In 1915 membership in the Ku Klux Klan expanded rapidly as violence spread over the whole country. The year 1919 became known for the 'Red Summer', when about 25 race riots occurred in American cities in the second half of the year. Acts of terrorism took place in both the South and the North.

It was under these conditions that Louis, sensitive to the sufferings of his people, completed his education and became one of the few highly educated men of his race at the time. He attended primary school in Charleston, being among the first generation of African-Americans to have a right to education. Louis continued his education at Avery

Institute in Charleston, graduating in 1891, and then went on to Fisk University in Nashville, Tennessee where, after his first year, he paid his tuition through scholarships and earned extra money by tailoring and working as a waiter. When he received his bachelor's degree in 1896, he was among only two thousand African-Americans out of perhaps nine million to have graduated from a university or college. After teaching at Avery Institute for a few years, he enrolled at Howard University to study law, graduating with his LL.B. degree in 1902.

After being admitted to the bar, Louis went into partnership in Washington DC with another young lawyer. In 1906 he took a position in the Treasury Department. Living in the nation's capital, he witnessed the forces affecting African-Americans. Louis's views at this time were 'radical' and he favoured agitation to remove the wrongs suffered by his people.[2] He was deeply influenced by W. E. B. DuBois and the Niagara Movement, which demanded suffrage for all men, equal civil rights, equal opportunity, free compulsory education, access to high schools and colleges, elimination of racial discrimination, fair on-the-job treatment and the abolition of Jim Crow laws – laws designed to segregate African-Americans in public places.

In 1907 one of Louis's few white friends encouraged him to attend a Bahá'í meeting. Louis went out of friendship – not because he wished to go – and met Pauline Hannen, who introduced the evening's speaker, Lua Getsinger. Mrs Getsinger persuasively recounted the history of the Bahá'í Faith and the persecutions and martyrdoms of the early Bahá'ís of Persia. Intrigued, Louis began to study the Faith. Every Sunday evening for the next 18 months he went to the home of Joseph and Pauline Hannen to learn about the new religion. 'The light they unfolded', he later wrote, 'was so wonderful that for about a year we sat in dumb amazement, listening to their patient, loving talks, not knowing whether to advance or retreat, yet held by supernal power.'[3] In June 1909 Louis Gregory became a Bahá'í.

From the outset, Louis was confronted by segregation within the Washington Bahá'í community. Although directed by 'Abdu'l-Bahá to hold interracial meetings, the community remained for some years separated into three camps. The first camp, to which the Hannens, Lua Getsinger and Louis belonged, openly supported and participated in integrated meetings. The second favoured segregation, since racial mixing was so unnatural in those times. The third preferred that each believer be allowed to choose between integrated or segregated meetings.

Louis, who was cultivated, articulate, educated and distinguished, was something of an enigma in the community. He helped bring about an attitudinal change among the early believers by quietly but uncompromisingly forcing them to confront the issue of racial prejudice, no doubt drawing inspiration from 'Abdu'l-Bahá, who had written him within five months of his enrolment:

> I hope that thou mayest become . . . the means whereby the white and coloured people shall close their eyes to racial differences and behold the reality of humanity, and that is the universal unity which is the oneness of the kingdom of the human race, the basic harmony of the world and the appearance of the bounty of the Almighty . . . Rely as much as thou canst upon the True One, and be thou resigned to the Will of God, so that like unto a candle thou mayest be enkindled in the world of humanity and like unto a star thou mayest shine and gleam from the Horizon of Reality and become the cause of the guidance of both races.[4]

Louis, who was then 35 years old, committed his full time to realizing 'Abdu'l-Bahá's hope. Calling himself a 'racial amity worker', he travelled, wrote, lectured and taught in the cause of racial unity for the next 40 years.

Louis made his first teaching trip in 1910. He visited eight Southern cities, including Charleston; Richmond, Virginia; and Macon, Georgia, thus launching a career that made him the most widely travelled Bahá'í teacher in the United States during his lifetime. He became a spokesman for the Cause of God to his own people and a standard-bearer for the cause of race unity to all people. Over the years he travelled frequently to the South, often for months at a time, and in every city found people who accepted the message of Bahá'u'lláh. He became a familiar visitor at black colleges and secondary schools in the South and often lectured at Fisk University and at the Tuskogee Institute. He kept in close touch with leading black intellectuals of the time and interested George Washington Carver in the Faith.

In 1911 Louis made a pilgrimage to the Holy Land. His visit coincided with that of Louisa Mathew, a British believer who had already won admiration for her devotion to the Faith. During Louis's first meeting with 'Abdu'l-Bahá, the Master raised the question of conflict between the races in the United States. He told Louis that the races must be united in a literal sense, through intermarriage. Intermarriage, He said, effaces racial differences and produces strong offspring, and He asked Louis to use his influence to encourage the races to intermarry.

While Louis was on pilgrimage 'Abdu'l-Bahá wrote to Charles Mason Remey, a white Bahá'í in Washington DC:

> As both races are under the protection of the All-Knowing God, therefore the lamps of unity must be lighted in such a manner in these meetings that no distinction be perceived between the white and coloured. Colours are phenomenal; but the realities of men are Essence. When there exists unity of the Essence what power has the phenomenal? When the Light of Reality is shining what power has the darkness of the unreal?
>
> If it be possible, gather together these two races, black and white, into one assembly and put such love into their hearts that they shall not only unite but even intermarry. Be sure that the result of this will abolish differences and disputes between black and white. Moreover by the will of God, may it be so. This is a great service to the world of humanity.[5]

Knowing full well the dangers awaiting both races if racial prejudice were allowed to flourish, 'Abdu'l-Bahá repeatedly warned that 'enmity will be increased day by day, and the final result will be hardship and may end in bloodshed . . . Until these prejudices are entirely removed from the people of the world, the realm of humanity will not find rest. Nay, rather, discord and bloodshed will be increased day by day, and the foundation of the prosperity of the world of man will be destroyed.'[6] If not checked, He wrote, 'the antagonism between the Coloured and the White, in America, will give rise to great calamities'.[7] A quarter of a century later Shoghi Effendi would describe racial prejudice as 'the most vital and challenging issue confronting the Bahá'í community'.[8]

Louis, transformed by his pilgrimage, left the Holy Land and went, at the request of 'Abdu'l-Bahá, to Germany. On his return home he immediately resumed his teaching activities, travelling to Green Acre in Maine in the summer of 1911.

'Abdu'l-Bahá arrived for his eight-month journey across America in April 1912. Almost immediately, He confronted the racial issue and challenged the practice of social segregation. On 23 April a luncheon was held in His honour at the home of Ali-Kuli Khan, the Iranian chargé d'affaires in Washington DC. Several prominent members of Washington society attended. 'Abdu'l-Bahá had invited Louis to come to the Khans' for an interview before the luncheon. When luncheon was announced, Louis waited for an opportunity to leave the house:

> All were seated when suddenly 'Abdu'l-Bahá stood up, looked all around, and then said to the Mírzá Khan, Where is Mr Gregory? Bring Mr Gregory! There was nothing for Mírzá Khan to do but find Mr Gregory . . . Finally Mr Gregory came into the room with Mírzá Khan. 'Abdu'l-Bahá . . . had by this time rearranged the place setting and made room for Mr Gregory, giving him the seat of honour at His right. He stated He was very pleased to have Mr Gregory there, and then, in the most natural way as if nothing unusual had happened, proceeded to give a talk on the oneness of mankind.[9]

Louisa Mathew was one of the small number of Western Bahá'ís who travelled with 'Abdu'l-Bahá to America on the SS *Cedric*. On boarding the ship at Naples, she received the first intimation that 'Abdu'l-Bahá had plans for her. Asking her to walk on deck with Him, He told her He had 'planted a seed' in her heart. She later wrote

> In this country Abdul Baha first revealed to me symbolically, through a white flower which He told me to give Mr Gregory & by looking at me in a peculiar way conveyed his meaning to me, that He wished me to marry Mr Gregory. Curiously after this love began to grow in my heart & the desire for the marriage whereas before I only liked Mr Gregory as a friend.[10]

With increasing directness, 'Abdu'l-Bahá conveyed to Louis and Louisa His desire to see them marry. Intermarriage was illegal in several American states and stigmatized everywhere, and despite 'Abdu'l-Bahá's assertions that it would help overcome prejudice, most Bahá'ís found intermarriage hard to accept. Obeying 'Abdu'l-Bahá's instruction that they use wisdom and discretion so as not to attract sensational newspaper reports, Louis Gregory and Louisa Mathew were married in a quiet ceremony in New York on 27 September 1912. 'Abdu'l-Bahá described this first marriage between a black and a white Bahá'í as 'an introduction to the accomplishment of fellowship between the races'.[11]

The couple experienced many obstacles in their marriage. They could not always travel together and were often denied a place to live. They could not travel together in the South, where Louis undertook so much of his teaching work. Their union was seen by many as a crime and even many Bahá'ís felt awkward in their presence. Louis recalled the 'vile reproaches' which came to him from both races for taking a step he never regretted. With his charming sense of humour, he said of those years that his friends were 'none too many'.

While Louis and Louisa were often separated by teaching work and circumstances, they enjoyed each other's company, felt encouraged by each other's accomplishments and were wholly devoted to each other. Louis would speak of his joy at being with his wife, of her devotion and of her self-forgetfulness. Louisa offered Louis encouragement, concern and sacrifice. Together they endured financial hardships cheerfully in the shared belief that the world was in transition and that building a new world order was more important than trying to salvage temporary security from the old one. Louis once confided to a friend, 'It is our hope that our enforced separation along the line of service to the Divine Cause will mercifully bring to us eternal reunion in the worlds of God.'[12] 'During the years', he later commented, 'we have had but one spirit, one purpose and one purse.'[13]

If the Gregorys suffered misunderstandings and hostility as an interracial couple in an era of deeply entrenched racial prejudice, Louis also suffered many indignities in his travels. On a visit to see Dr Ugo Giachery and his wife in New York City, Louis had to take the service elevator to their apartment, much to the chagrin of Dr Giachery. On another occasion he was denied accommodation in a Pullman car, although he had purchased a ticket; when he refused to move to the Jim Crow car, he was arrested and spent the night in a Kentucky jail. Invited to lecture at a college, he was afterwards given no hospitality by the students and abandoned at a train station. Despite these indignities, Louis never showed anger, impatience or resentment. On the other hand, he could be quite formidable when defending principle.

In 1916 the first of 'Abdu'l-Bahá's Tablets of the Divine Plan arrived in the United States. 'Abdu'l-Bahá particularly called for teachers to establish the Faith in the Southern states, where so few Bahá'ís lived. Louis immediately responded. By 31 October he had already spoken to five thousand people throughout the South.

Despite numerous difficulties, frequent rebukes and other obstacles, Louis visited cities and towns throughout the South, where he reached many thousands of both races with the message of Bahá'u'lláh. In 1917 he and Louisa sold their homes to provide funds for Louis's travels. When he was not lecturing in centres of learning, public halls, churches, clubs, organizations or private homes during his travels, he might be found visiting a sick believer, holding a fireside, writing a newspaper article, assisting in the formation of a Local Spiritual Assembly or planning a race amity meeting.

In November 1921 'Abdu'l-Bahá passed away and the Bahá'í world was thrown into confusion. Many western Bahá'ís did not understand the station of the Guardian and found it difficult to transfer their loyalty from 'Abdu'l-Bahá to Shoghi Effendi. Louis, however, had no difficulty in doing so:

> His attitude toward the Guardian revealed from the beginning the quality that Bahá'ís term firmness in the Covenant of Bahá'u'lláh, a loyalty to the central figures and institutions of the Faith so unshakable that it prevents disunity and eventual schism.[14]

Under the Guardian, Louis continued to travel and teach the Cause. Miriam Haney commented on his success as a teacher in 1922:

> I do not think we have had anything that approached it in any way in the 24 years or since 1895 when the Cause first started in this country . . . because it is the first time that any teacher so marvellously illumined as Mr Gregory has been able to reach thousand[s] and thousands of people, coloured and white. This is why we must consider it a very remarkable spiritual work.[15]

Harlan Ober wrote:

> It is probable that no individual teacher in the Faith has travelled more extensively throughout the United States than Mr Gregory. Living in the utmost simplicity, sacrificing at every turn, he spoke in schools, colleges, churches, forums, conferences and with individuals throughout the land. With a marvellous blending of humility and courage, of tenderness and adamantine firmness and steadfastness, he met high and low, rich and poor, educated and ignorant, and gave to them the cup of the Water of Life.[16]

While Louis took the message of Bahá'u'lláh to the people of the South in America, Louisa went to Eastern Europe to teach the Cause. The Gregorys continued to spend their summers together, however, except for the period 1933–6, when Louisa remained to Belgrade to establish a Bahá'í community there. This prompted speculation in some quarters about the vitality of the marriage, but it was only their dedication and service to the Faith of Bahá'u'lláh that kept the Gregorys apart.

Not only was Louis a remarkable teacher of the Faith, he was an able administrator as well. In 1912 he was elected both to the Washington Working Committee and to the Executive Board of Bahá'í Temple Unity, serving on the Board again in 1918. When the National Spiritual Assembly of the United States and Canada was established, he served on the body for a total of 14 years on three separate occasions, from 1922 to 1924, from 1927 to 1932 and from 1939 to 1946. Until 1946, when Elsie Austin was elected to the National Spiritual Assembly, he was the only African-American to serve on it. He helped draft the by-laws of the National Spiritual Assembly, the model for all National Assembly charters. He attended virtually every national Bahá'í convention from 1911 until his retirement, often as convention secretary, reporter or speaker.

Louis's gift as a Bahá'í speaker was recognized early in his Bahá'í life, when he addressed the National Convention of the Bahá'í Temple Unity in 1912, establishing himself as one of the finest Bahá'í speakers of the era, with his musical tone of voice and personal magnetism. Over the years he spoke on a diversity of subjects, including 'The Reality of Humanity', 'The Feast of Riḍván', 'A Demonstration of Divinity and Inspiration', 'The Interdependence of Individuals, Nations and Races', 'The New Educational System of Bahá'u'lláh', 'The Underlying Unity of All Religions', and 'The Power of the Holy Spirit'. He also wrote for *Star of the West*, *World Order Magazine* and *The Bahá'í World*.

Louis's main subject, however, was the cause of race unity. He addressed the issue head on, as 'Abdu'l-Bahá had done. He expounded, for instance, on the intelligence of the dark skinned races, on the greatness of earlier black civilizations, on the accomplishments of educated blacks, and on their potential for achievement. He argued that racial colours arose from climatic conditions and that therefore distinctions based on them were insignificant. He elaborated on the power of Bahá'u'lláh to bring about racial unity. He wrote a tribute to the outstanding black educator George W. Henderson of Henderson Business College and also wrote an extensive historical review of race amity in America. Whenever progress was made in improving race relations, however small, Louis readily acknowledged it.

An example of Louis's writing and his passion for racial harmony is found in this article published in 1933:

> The power of the Prophet brings new birth. The new teachings of the new day are adequate for unity in all race relations. This work is one of the most needed and the most inviting for human service. Justice to our fellow beings clarifies our own vision. The ignorant can and must be taught. The heedless must be attracted and even the 'dead' must be revived! People born in an atmosphere of prejudice are not hopeless. Such conditions yield to spiritual training.[17]

In 1920 Mrs Agnes Parsons, a Washington DC Bahá'í, went on pilgrimage. 'Abdu'l-Bahá instructed her to arrange a conference in Washington for racial amity. A socially prominent, wealthy white woman, Mrs Parsons, who rarely ventured outside her own social circle, was an unlikely advocate of such a controversial programme. Nevertheless, she took up the challenge and in May 1921 convened the first of many race amity conventions. The conference brought together capable and intelligent leaders of both races, the Congress of the United States also being represented. Louis, in his report on the conference in *The Bahá'í World*, remarked, 'It is reliably stated that the President of the United States, the late Mr Harding, upon reading the press reports which were so friendly and widespread said, "Thank God for that convention!"'[18] A message from 'Abdu'l-Bahá revealed the real importance of such gatherings:

> Say to this convention that never since the beginning of time has one more important been held. This convention stands for the oneness of humanity. It will become the cause of the removal of hostilities between the races. It will be the cause of the enlightenment of America. It will, if wisely managed and continued, check the deadly struggle between these races which otherwise will inevitably break out.[19]

Louis actively supported this and later conventions. Although he assumed a relatively minor role at the outset and deferred to Mrs Parsons, Louis nevertheless influenced the tenor of the meetings. He urged the adoption of the Bahá'í perspective and recommended that the gatherings be held regularly. He understood the influence of speakers who were able to convey the power of love, the importance of involving prominent people of both races in the programme and the need for extensive publicity.

Four race amity conferences were held between May 1921 and October 1924 and then enthusiasm for them waned. Louis was concerned that the Bahá'ís of Washington DC would neglect their racial amity work, so he continued to promote them as a way to bring the races together. But Louis was not naive. He knew how matters stood between the races, writing:

> The two races little understand each other. Apprehensions, imaginations, prejudices, resentments, fears, hatreds destroy confidence in each other's good intentions and create a wall of separation which is generally thought impassable.
>
> The danger of the situation is extremely grave. This city which is a nation's pride has already been disgraced by rioting and lawlessness on the part of mobs, during which shots were fired even within a block of the White House, and scenes of like [nature] are continually threatened. The feelings of many people are bitter and intense. Such feelings are the augury of no good. Wherever in the world today there is hatred of class for class, nation for nation, race for race, tragedy lurks. Its outbreak may be delayed, but unless sentiments are changed it cannot be prevented. [20]

Louis suggested how to promote race amity conferences:

> The structure of an amity conference is a group of harmonious and willing workers. These must strive wisely to enlarge their circle by conveying their hopes and ideals to others. The social and welfare workers who are found in every community are often those most likely to respond to an appeal for this humanitarian service, bringing their noblest treasures of heart and mind. How the psychology of suffering masses may be affected by the knowledge that somewhere in the world there is a group of people who believe in translating high thoughts into action is something to ponder. That which is, is affected by that which ought to be. The real is influenced by the ideal. Ideals must be cherished and spread.[21]

Louis G. Gregory was the mainspring behind Bahá'í race amity work for over 35 years and kept the issue alive and at the forefront of the Bahá'ís' attention. While the interest of the Bahá'ís in the cause of race relations ebbed and flowed over the years, Louis continued to promote it, writing reports on race amity activities in America, praising signs of a new spirit of dedication among the believers when they appeared, acting as a facilitator or speaker at amity meetings, travelling with different white believers to the South, hosting several annual banquets in honour of the National Association for the Advancement of Colored People and attending race unity conferences at Green Acre. He also endorsed a remarkable statement on race entitled *The Divine Call to Race Amity*.

In 1937, at the outset of the first Seven Year Plan, the Gregorys travelled to Haiti for three months. Later that year their paths diverged again, as Louisa briefly returned to Belgrade and Louis went back to the South to establish Bahá'í communities in Alabama. The imminence of the war and her own failing health brought Louisa back to America. She lived in Eliot, Maine, while Louis continued to travel until 1946.

In 1939 Louis was re-elected to the National Spiritual Assembly, serving again as recording secretary. He was appointed, together with Amelia Collins and Dorothy Baker, to the Committee on Assembly Development, which helped Local Spiritual Assemblies function more effectively. He was a member of the Race Unity Committee for several years, for two of which he served as its secretary. In the 1940s Louis was a member of the Green Acre school committee and he served on the editorial committees of both *The Bahá'í World* and *Bahá'í News*.

In 1946 Louis fell ill for a time. Although he claimed to be as fit and well as ever, Louisa was now over 80 and very frail. In 1947 Louis retired to his cottage near Green Acre, where he and Louisa enjoyed a quiet life in a community where their interracial marriage caused little comment. Since he was no longer travelling, he had more time to write to the many people he had met on his journeys.

In December 1948 Louis suffered a stroke. Although he was expected to live only a few days, he improved almost immediately and was allowed home, where he caught up with his correspondence, puttered around the house, gardened a little and – what he cherished most – hosted firesides and study classes until the very end of his life.

Louis Gregory passed away on 30 July 1951. Six days later Shoghi Effendi cabled:

> PROFOUNDLY DEPLORE GRIEVOUS LOSS DEARLY BELOVED, NOBLE-MINDED, GOLDEN-HEARTED LOUIS GREGORY, PRIDE EXAMPLE NEGRO ADHERENTS FAITH, KEENLY FEEL LOSS ONE SO LOVED, ADMIRED TRUSTED 'ABDU'L-BAHÁ. DESERVES RANK FIRST HAND CAUSE HIS RACE. RISING BAHÁ'Í GENERATION AFRICAN CONTINENT WILL GLORY HIS MEMORY EMULATE HIS EXAMPLE. ADVISE HOLD MEMORIAL GATHERING TEMPLE TOKEN RECOGNITION UNIQUE POSITION, OUTSTANDING SERVICES.[22]

# Keith Ransom-Kehler
## 1876–1933

The resting place of Keith Ransom-Kehler lies near the graves of Mírzá Muḥammad-Ḥasan and his brother, Mírzá Muḥammad-Ḥusayn, in the vicinity of Iṣfahán, Iran. The two illustrious brothers were martyred in 1879. Designated by Bahá'u'lláh the King of Martyrs and the Beloved of Martyrs respectively, the brothers were celebrated for their generosity, trustworthiness, kindliness and piety. Keith too was beloved for her generosity, loyalty, sincerity and virtue. Separated in death by a half century, Mírzá Ḥasan and Keith confronted the forces of darkness with unshakeable resolve. The virtuous example of their lives was felt by the common people, challenged by the authorities and feared by the ruling class in the land of Bahá'u'lláh's birth. The passing of each was mentioned as a tragic loss by the head of the Faith of their time.

Keith was born Nannie Keith Bean on 14 February 1876 in Dayton, Kentucky. She attended a private school in Cincinnati and later graduated from Vassar. She undertook post-graduate work at the Universities of Michigan, Arizona and Chicago and was eventually awarded an MA degree. She taught French at Albion College, and later headed the department of English Literature.

In 1903 Keith married Ralph (Guy) Ransom and went with him to Paris, where he studied art for a few years. When Keith was 32 years old, her husband died of tuberculosis. In order to support her daughter, Julia, Keith took an intensive course in design and then became head of the interior decoration section of the Carson, Pirie, Scott department store in Chicago. In 1910 she married James Kehler, a former colleague from Albion College and now an advertising executive from New York. His death in 1923 was a great and lasting sorrow to her. Sometime near the time of Jim Kehler's passing she wrote to May Maxwell, 'Pray for me, May, it is my only refuge . . . Through this bitter storm of trial in which every attribute of light is obscure or withdrawn, you still stand, a dazzling presence on the further shore toward which I struggle . . .'[1]

From 1918 to 1922 Keith was leader of the Liberal Religious Fellowship in Chicago and Chief Counsellor for the Home Beautiful Service. She was involved in Hull House settlement work, prison reform at Sing Sing, and fruit and chicken farm operations. Her work on Municipal Ownership was incorporated in a report of the Federal Bureau of Labour and Statistics. She published articles and gave lectures on psychology, comparative religions and interior decorating, with titles such as 'The Divine Adventure – Why be Unhappy?' 'Psychology of Human Relations', 'Making the Most of Ourselves', 'Child Guidance', 'Is Universal Brotherhood Possible?' 'Life's Essential Purpose', 'What is Permanent?' 'Crime and its Remedy', 'A Journey of the Soul', 'Making Houses Homes', 'The Beautiful Necessity' and 'Interior Decorating'.[2]

Although Keith met 'Abdu'l-Bahá in London on 13 September 1911, nearly ten years passed until she became a believer in May 1921. She was elected to the Local Spiritual Assembly of Chicago and served as its secretary. A part of Chicago's elite society, Keith gave up her social life when she became Bahá'í, although she retained her sense of beauty and elegance. When she was in Iran in 1933 she impressed the young Zikrullah Khadem as 'the most stylish woman he had ever met':

> She had a beautiful and elegant mink coat cut in the latest fashion. Her dresses were so exquisite they would attract the attention of onlookers. Yet they were also very dignified and tasteful . . . She was stunning.[3]

In about 1925 Keith began to rise to prominence within the Bahá'í community. Trained as a Christian minister, she turned her talents to the service of the Bahá'í Faith, chairing meetings, travelling and teaching. Several of her articles appeared in the early *Bahá'í World* volumes. In the winter of 1926 she made the first of her two pilgrimages to the Holy Land. She was deeply touched by the suffering of the Guardian and wrote about him to the 18th Annual National Convention:

> . . . this youth under thirty, labouring day and night for us, sacrificing every human desire and tendency to further our efforts . . . with no more personal

> life than a graven image, no more thought of self than a breeze or a flower, just a hollow reed for the divine melody. Any one of us is ready to die for him, but can we conscientiously number ourselves among those who are willing to live for him?[4]

When she returned to the United States in the spring of 1926 Keith encouraged the Bahá'ís of New York City to lease a larger centre and to initiate a teaching programme. From this point on, Keith never rested; her only permanent address was the Vassar Club in New York City. In 1929 she travelled to the West Indies and in 1930 began the extensive world tour to promote the Bahá'í Faith from which she never returned. Leaving Chicago, she visited every Local Assembly en route to the Pacific coast. From there she sailed to Japan, China, New Zealand, Australia and India. She spent a year visiting Bahá'í communities in the Orient, strengthening and encouraging the friends and giving public talks on the Faith. In Shanghai she carried out an intensive programme of teaching which included radio addresses, public lectures and interviews with prominent educators and officials.

In Japan Keith joined Agnes Alexander in her teaching activities, and afterwards she travelled to Australia, where she passed through Brisbane, Sydney and Melbourne. In Adelaide she held her audiences in rapt attention with her inspired public lectures, radio talks and private interviews.

In the early part of 1932 Keith arrived in the Indian subcontinent, travelling to Rangoon, Mandalay, Myamo, Kanjangaon, Calcutta, Benares, Lucknow, Agra, Delhi, Aligarh, Amritsar, Lahore, Karachi, Bombay, Poona, Hyderabad and Bolepur. She spoke many times to Bahá'í and non-Bahá'í audiences, covering such subjects as 'The Spiritual Basis of Citizenship', 'The Great Message of Bahá'u'lláh', 'The Bahá'í Teachings: They make a person a better follower of his own religion', 'Is Universal Brotherhood Possible?' and 'The Bahá'í Solution of World Problems'.[5]

While she was in India in 1932, Keith received a cable from Shoghi Effendi asking her to come to Haifa and prepare herself for a special journey to Iran. Taken wholly by surprise at this development, Keith travelled to the Holy Land at once. Shoghi Effendi's secretary wrote to the American National Spiritual Assembly: 'Mrs Keith Ransom-Kehler is now with us in Haifa and in a few days will start for Persia. She rendered wonderful services in both Australia and India, and Shoghi Effendi trusts that she will do the same in Persia.'[6]

Shoghi Effendi entrusted to Keith a delicate mission: she was to try to convince the Sháh to permit the publication and distribution of Bahá'í books in Iran. Shoghi Effendi had hoped that the new Pahlavi dynasty in Iran 'would speedily usher in a new phase in the development of Bahá'u'lláh's Faith in that country' and had written to the American National Assembly advising it to seek permission to print Bahá'í books in Iran and to establish a Publishing Trust.[7] When this was refused, the Guardian had written again to the American Assembly, urging it to communicate with the Iranian government once again and to point out the moral value of Bahá'í literature. When this attempt also failed, the Guardian wrote once again:

> URGE ADDRESS PROMPTLY WRITTEN PETITION ON BEHALF AMERICAN BELIEVERS TO SHAH INTRODUCING RANSOM-KEHLER AS CHOSEN REPRESENTATIVE EMPOWERED APPEAL FOR ENTRY BAHÁ'Í LITERATURE PERSIA. STRESS WIDESPREAD APPRECIATION INTERNAL REFORMS AND SPIRITUAL TIES BINDING BOTH COUNTRIES EMPHASIZE HIGH TRIBUTE PAID IN BAHÁ'Í WRITINGS TO ISLAM AND THEIR MORAL VALUE TO PERSIA. MAIL PETITION PERSIAN NATIONAL ASSEMBLY.[8]

In response, the National Spiritual Assembly of the United States and Canada sent a petition to the Sháh:

> Mrs Keith Ransom-Kehler, an American citizen, a member of the Bahá'í community of this country, and a distinguished student of the teachings and history of the Bahá'í Faith, can, with your Majesty's gracious permission, amplify and supplement the statements made by this Assembly in the written petition addressed to your Majesty under date of January 12, 1932 . . . The appointment of a representative to journey to Ṭihrán for the purpose of presenting in person the petition of this Assembly will make it evident to your Majesty how profoundly the American Bahá'ís are moved by their inability to communicate fully with their fellow-religionists in Persia by reason of the Postal regulations still prohibiting the entry of Bahá'í books and magazines published in the United States and Canada.[9]

While Keith was in Haifa the Guardian briefed her thoroughly on the situation and prepared her for her task. Soon after arriving in Iran, on 20 August 1932, Keith cabled the United States: 'Mission successful.'[10]

A fuller report was received by the American National Spiritual Assembly shortly afterwards:

> On August 15 I saw His Highness Taymur Tash and received from him the direct, unqualified assurance that Bahá'í literature would be admitted freely into Persia and permitted to circulate.[11]

Keith also received assurances that her own books might be sent to Iran for her personal use while in the country.

Overjoyed, the American National Spiritual Assembly cabled the Court Minister at Ṭihrán:

> On behalf American Bahá'ís we express abiding gratitude for removal ban on entry Bahá'í literature into Persia. This noble action of His Imperial Majesty's Government has profoundly impressed Bahá'ís of the United States and Canada who have already felt strong attachment to Bahá'u'lláh's native land. We wish to assure your Highness of our sympathy for his Imperial Majesty, our great interest in the progress and welfare of his Empire and our desire to assist in enhancing its prestige throughout the world.[12]

When tested, however, the assurances of the Iranian Court Minister proved hollow. When Keith's Bahá'í books were shipped from Beirut to Iran, they were confiscated. The Governor General of Á<u>dh</u>irbáyján refused to receive Keith. Police orders were issued forcing meetings arranged in her honour by the local Bahá'ís to be abandoned.

Undaunted, Keith arranged an interview with the Secretary for American affairs at the Foreign Office, who explained why Bahá'í literature could not circulate in Iran: it was contrary to the constitution of Persia to recognize any religion founded after Islam; it was contrary to the constitution to permit the circulation of literature opposed to Islam; and the circulation of Bahá'í literature might cause internal disorders and effect suffering to the Bahá'ís themselves.

Keith responded to these lines of reasoning in a letter to the <u>Sh</u>áh himself dated 25 February 1933:

> In my report to America I shall be constrained to admit that I must have misunderstood completely the purpose and intent of the interpreter, for exhaustive investigation reveals no reference in the Constitution of Persia to the status of religions founded later than Islám.
>
> Since every Bahá'í before he can so designate himself must accept the validity of the Prophet Muḥammad . . . and since this attitude is inculcated

> through Bahá'í literature, the point of excluding it because it is opposed to Islám will, I fear, be incomprehensible . . . I shall await your Majesty's authority to submit the result of my conversation with the Foreign Office, herein set forth, to the proper Bahá'í centres throughout the world; for I have no desire, a second time, to find myself mistaken as to your Majesty's intention.[13]

Keith received no reply to this appeal. She continued to petition the government, writing to every cabinet minister appealing for justice, championing the principles of Bahá'í loyalty to government and reiterating the sanctity of Islam. In letters to the Sh͟áh she courageously reminded him of his support of religious freedom, referred to his lofty accomplishments, mentioned the loyalty of the rank and file of believers to his government, explained that Bahá'í literature supported Islam, and deplored a recent desecration of 'Abdu'l-Bahá's photograph by government officials. The Minister of Education replied, saying that all inhabitants of Iran, regardless of nationality or conviction, enjoyed tranquillity and security under the rule of the Sh͟áh. However, he added, new publications considered contrary to the official religion of the country could not be permitted.

Keith became worn down by the constant round of meetings with suave but hypocritical officials and her health weakened. Nevertheless she was able to encourage the Iranian Bahá'ís, who dearly loved her. Several meetings were held in the Ḥaẓíratu'l-Quds of Tabríz, where large numbers of Bahá'í men and women met the international teacher. She visited Mílán, where the believers felt Keith fulfilled the prophecy of Bahá'u'lláh and 'Abdu'l-Bahá that brothers and sisters from the West would help promote the Cause in Iran. In Ṭihrán she was received by thousands of believers and impressed everyone. Zikrullah Khadem recalled:

> She taught me so much! I learned about generosity and the appreciation of human dignity. When we went to the bazaar, she would seek out the vendors who were especially honest and hard-working and would reward them with large purchases or generous tips. She would take some of these people gifts during their holidays. Our trips to the bazaar were usually for this purpose. When she noticed those in need of love and compassion, she would visit them more frequently. People would cluster around her, drawn by her sincerity and love, and would appreciate her in the most lavish ways. They would ask God's blessings for her and shower praise on her. They would thank God for her presence among them. Oh how they loved her.[14]

Keith herself reflected on her mission, in a letter to the American National Spiritual Assembly of March 1933:

> How strange the ways of God, that I, a poor, feeble, old woman from the West, should be pleading for liberty and justice in the land of Bahá'u'lláh . . .[15]

Meanwhile the American National Spiritual Assembly passed a resolution which it presented to the Iranian Minister at Washington in July 1933:

> It seems desirable to inform your Excellency that the Twenty-Fifth Annual Convention of the Bahá'ís of the United States and Canada adopted unanimously the following resolution:
>
> Resolved, that the delegates of the Twenty-Fifth Annual Convention representing sixty communities of the United States and Canada, realizing the burdens of oppression still laid upon their brethren of Persia, recommend and urge the National Spiritual Assembly to take immediate action to bring about the cessation of the reported maltreatment of our Bahá'í brethren, to secure the entry of Bahá'í literature and to restore the constitutional provision for the printing and circulation of Bahá'í literature within Persia;
>
> And be it further resolved, that the delegates pledge the support of the local Bahá'í communities to the National Spiritual Assembly in its effort to carry out the terms of this appeal.[16]

On 26 July 1933 the American National Spiritual Assembly sent to Keith a summary of actions it had taken on matters affecting the Iranian believers and asked that she communicate this information to the Iranian government and report back the results. On 10 September, Keith cabled the National Spiritual Assembly: 'Petition unanswered.'[17]

Exhausted and disappointed by her failed efforts, Keith wrote:

> I have fallen, though I never faltered. Months of effort with nothing accomplished is the record that confronts me. If anyone in future should be interested in this thwarted adventure of mine, he alone can say whether near or far from the seemingly impregnable heights of complaisance and indifference, my tired old body fell. The smoke and din of battle are to-day too dense for me to ascertain whether I moved forward or was slain in my tracks.[18]

Despite her weakened condition, Keith remained intensely active, refusing to rest. From Ṭihrán she travelled to Qum, Árán, Káshán and finally to Iṣfahán, where she visited the believers, met local officials, taught the Faith and saw the Bahá'í holy places. Her schedule was hectic with meetings, the press of hundreds of people and public presentations.

On 10 October, Keith fell ill with chills and fever. Over the next few days her condition worsened. On 13 October she requested a cable be sent to the Guardian begging for his prayers. She was then diagnosed as having smallpox. Her condition ebbed and flowed until, on 22 October, she suddenly lost the power of speech. Some hours later, she was able, with difficulty, to repeat, 'Yá Bahá'u'l-Abhá' and 'Alláh-u-Abhá'. The following day, she passed away.

On 28 October, the Guardian sent the following cable to the Iranian believers:

> The intrepid defender and illustrious herald of God's Cause has risen triumphant from depths of darkness to her heavenly home; her magnificent deeds were hidden from the negligent in that land; the Supreme Concourse knew her worth; she possesses the rank of martyrdom and is one of the Hands of the Cause. The entire Ṭihrán Assembly will surely in conjunction with delegates from Shíráz, Kirmán, Ábádih, Yazd and the southern ports go on pilgrimage in my stead to her venerated grave.[19]

The National Spiritual Assembly of Iran wrote:

> Our dear Keith spent approximately sixteen months in Persia; she entered the country from the western frontier, visiting the friends of Kirmansh！áh, Hamadán and Qazvín, after staying some time in Ṭihrán and recovering from sickness she travelled to Adhirbáyján where the friends derived great profit from her eloquent teaching; she then made another journey through the East and North, and the friends of Khurásán and Mázindarán and Gílán had the bounty of her presence, her fluent speech, her spiritual life. Everywhere the friends paid her due honour, sending representatives ahead to welcome her into their cities, escorting her for some distance when she left. They felt themselves fortunate in being with her, and thanked God that the power of His word had raised out of the old beliefs such shining, devoted souls for the service of His Cause, the salvation of all the world; they prayed for the success of her important mission in this land.

During her sojourn in Ṭihrán, Keith strained every nerve to fulfil the instructions of the Guardian. Her tireless effort, her refusal to rest, were an example in sacrifice, and recalled the impassioned deeds of our Heroic Age. On seven occasions she composed and sent to His Majesty lengthy petitions in which she clearly proved the necessity of lifting the ban on Bahá'í literature, and asked the removal of existing restrictions on Bahá'í activity. She left no phase of her task undone; in her meetings with distinguished officials she spoke with power and convincing authority, informing them of the Bahá'í principles and of the greatness of Bahá'u'lláh's Cause throughout East and West, she gave countless talks to audiences of Bahá'ís and non-Bahá'ís, setting forth in inspiring words the reality of religion and the teachings of the new Manifestation; all who heard her recognized the breadth of her knowledge, the value of the Bahá'í Faith and its superiority to other ways of life. Her talks addressed to Bahá'ís kept us continually mindful of the main issues confronting us at this time. In the face of trials and difficulties besetting the Cause in our country she stood firm, and at all times turned in lowliness and prayer to Bahá'u'lláh and begged for confirmation. Her spiritual qualities, the beauty of her nature drew people to her, and awakened those who could comprehend her station; she was an example of a true Bahá'í.[20]

On 30 October 1933 Shoghi Effendi sent the following cable:

KEITH'S PRECIOUS LIFE OFFERED UP SACRIFICE BELOVED CAUSE IN BAHÁ'U'LLÁH'S NATIVE LAND. ON PERSIAN SOIL FOR PERSIA'S SAKE SHE ENCOUNTERED CHALLENGED AND FOUGHT FORCES OF DARKNESS WITH HIGH DISTINCTION, INDOMITABLE WILL, UNSWERVING EXEMPLARY LOYALTY. MASS OF HER HELPLESS PERSIAN BRETHREN MOURN SUDDEN LOSS THEIR VALIANT EMANCIPATOR. AMERICAN BELIEVERS GRATEFUL AND PROUD MEMORY THEIR FIRST AND DISTINGUISHED MARTYR. SORROW-STRICKEN I LAMENT EARTHLY SEPARATION INVALUABLE COLLABORATOR UNFAILING COUNSELLOR ESTEEMED AND FAITHFUL FRIEND. URGE LOCAL ASSEMBLIES BEFITTINGLY ORGANIZE MEMORIAL GATHERINGS IN MEMORY ONE WHOSE INTERNATIONAL SERVICES ENTITLE HER EMINENT RANK AMONG HANDS OF CAUSE OF BAHÁ'U'LLÁH.[21]

On 3 November Shoghi Effendi sent this message: 'Instructed Iṣfahán Assembly to inter Keith in the vicinity of the grave of Sulṭánu'sh-Shuhadá, surnamed by Bahá'u'lláh "King of Martyrs"'.[22] Thus was Keith Ransom-Kehler buried in the heart of the country she served so well.

Although she was disappointed at what she felt was a failed mission, Keith left a poignant reminder of the value of service to the Cause:

> Nothing in the world is meaningless, suffering least of all. Sacrifice with its attendant agony is a germ, an organism. Man cannot blight its fruition as he can the seeds of earth. Once sown it blooms, I think forever, in the sweet fields of eternity. Mine will be a very modest flower, perhaps like the single, tiny forget-me-not, watered by the blood of Quddús that I plucked in the Sabz-i-Maydán of Bárfurúsh; should it ever catch the eye, may one who seems to be struggling in vain garner it in the name of Shoghi Effendi and cherish it for his dear remembrance.[23]

# Muḥammad Taqí Iṣfahání
## c. 1860–1946

The details of the life of Muḥammad Taqí are difficult to reconstruct. He was born near Iṣfahán, in Sidih, a village with an active Bábí, and later Bahá'í, community of distinguished teachers and poets. It was probably through one of these Bahá'ís that Muḥammad Taqí became a Bahá'í himself.

In about 1875 he was arrested along with other prominent Bahá'ís, beaten and sent to prison in Iṣfahán. It is said that he left Iran to settle in Egypt in 1878, stopping in 'Akká along the way.[1] However, he was in Iran in March 1879 when the King and Beloved of Martyrs were killed,[2] so it is likely that he returned to Iran after this journey and left that country permanently somewhat later. He visited the Holy Land four times during the lifetime of Bahá'u'lláh, the last occasion being in 1891, and many times during the ministry of 'Abdu'l-Bahá. It is suggested that it was during his second pilgrimage that Bahá'u'lláh advised him to settle permanently in Egypt.[3] Muḥammad Taqí's last pilgrimage in the time of 'Abdu'l-Bahá was made in February 1919.

'Abdu'l-Bahá was often in Egypt between 1910 and 1913. While there, He was frequently with Muḥammad Taqí and visited his home, which was the centre of many Bahá'í activities. It was in this home that Mírzá Abu'l-Faḍl Gulpáygání lived the last year of his life, before his death in 1914 and where Lua Getsinger passed away in 1916.

Muḥammad Taqí was devastated by the passing of 'Abdu'l-Bahá in 1921 and felt that the very spirit of life had left the world. He immediately travelled to Haifa, remaining for 40 days, and was present when the Will and Testament of 'Abdu'l-Bahá, naming Shoghi Effendi the Guardian of the Bahá'í Faith, was read. Fearing that the youthful Shoghi Effendi would be vulnerable to the attacks of the Covenant-breakers at such a sensitive time in the history of the Cause, Muḥammad Taqí began to write a defence of the Bahá'í Faith. When he had written several volumes, he realized that Shoghi Effendi was capable of defending the Faith himself, and so locked away his own work.

In 1925 a Covenant-breaking group headed by an Egyptian named Fá'iq began to attack the institutions of the Faith, creating a crisis in the Egyptian Bahá'í community. Muḥammad Taqí was among the main opponents of this group.

Muḥammad Taqí was elected to the first National Spiritual Assembly of Egypt when it was established in December 1924. He was a member of the Publishing Committee and undertook both the translation and the publication of Bahá'í literature. As well as writing articles about the Faith, he translated such works as the Kitáb-i-Íqán and *Some Answered Questions* into Arabic.

Muḥammad Taqí had memorized most of the general Tablets of Bahá'u'lláh and 'Abdu'l-Bahá and could recount most of the historical events of the Cause. He was kind and hospitable, remarkably steadfast, and long suffering. His wife, whose name is not recorded, predeceased him, while his eldest son, 'Abdu'l-Ḥusayn, a member of the early Swiss Bahá'í community, died in 1922.

Muḥammad Taqí died 'with a smile of peace'[4] on 13 December 1946 at his home in Cairo and was buried in the Bahá'í cemetery. Memorial services were held in several Bahá'í centres and Shoghi Effendi sent a cable posthumously naming him a Hand of the Cause:

> HEARTS GRIEF STRICKEN PASSING BELOVED, OUTSTANDING, STEADFAST PROMOTER FAITH, MUḤAMMAD TAQÍ IṢFAHÁNÍ. LONG RECORD HIS MAGNIFICENT, EXEMPLARY SERVICES IMPERISHABLE DESERVES RANK HANDS CAUSE GOD. ADVISE HOLD BEFITTING MEMORIAL GATHERINGS EGYPTIAN CENTRES. CONTRIBUTION TWO HUNDRED POUNDS CONSTRUCTION GRAVE.[5]

# Martha Louise Root
# 1872–1939

Martha Root was 47 years of age the year she embraced the challenge of the Tablets of the Divine Plan. It is said that after their unveiling at the Annual Bahá'í Convention in 1919, Martha was found packing her bags and booking passage for South America. True or not, she was, according to Shoghi Effendi, the first to respond to 'Abdu'l-Bahá's stirring call to take the Faith to all the corners of the earth.

Martha was an unlikely heroine of the Cause of God. Plain, almost homely in appearance, she was modest in stature and suffered from poor health and limited means. Yet her going forth was like that of Badí', who, in the time of Bahá'u'lláh, volunteered to deliver his Lord's Tablet to the Sháh of Persia, knowing that he would give up his life in doing so.[1] Possessed of dauntless faith and a deep love of God, Martha became an 'exemplary advocate of the Bahá'í Faith',[2] the 'peerless herald of the Cause',[3] the 'archetype of Bahá'í itinerant teachers',[4] the 'Leading Ambassadress' of Bahá'u'lláh's Faith, 'the foremost Hand raised by Bahá'u'lláh since 'Abdu'l-Bahá's passing'[5] and established a record described by Shoghi Effendi as 'the nearest approach to the example set by 'Abdu'l-Bahá Himself to His disciples in the course of His journeys throughout the West'.[6]

Martha was born in Richwood, Ohio, and raised in Cambridge Springs (Cambridgeboro before 1898), Pennsylvania, during the Victorian era. Her parents, Timothy T. and Nancy Hart Root, were devout communicants of the Baptist church, congenial, fun-loving and close-knit. Mattie, as Martha was called, loved her mother but felt a particular bond with her father. T. T., as he was generally known, was a successful entrepreneur who had a dairy farm, a marble works, a cheese factory, a lumber business and a house building enterprise. A deacon at the local church, T. T. deeply impressed Mattie as a man of wisdom, generosity and morality. He was a man of few words, a peace-maker in the community and detached from worldly cares. Mattie told a friend that she could live in perfect harmony with her father.[7]

Mattie, unlike her mother, had no inclination towards domestic work. Instead, she preferred books and writing. Always reaching out beyond the limits of her known world, Martha visited Niagara Falls at 14 and Europe at 17. Then, unusual for a young woman of her time, she begged to be allowed to attend college.

She attended Oberlin College in Ohio from 1889 until 1894, studying languages, literature, psychology, mathematics and the Bible. In 1893 she became a member of Ælioian, one of the oldest literary societies for women students. She should have graduated from Oberlin in 1895, but by then she had moved on to the University of Chicago, where she pursued further studies and published a few literary essays. She was awarded her baccalaureate degree from Chicago in June 1895.

In the years that followed her graduation, Martha taught school and served as school principal in Union City, Pennsylvania. Realizing that this work did not satisfy her, she developed a series of dramatic lectures based on the works of Shakespeare which she presented to clubs, schools and churches in Philadelphia and New York.

In 1900, her literary talent established, Martha began work as a journalist for the *Pittsburg Chronicle Telegraph*.[8] Later the same year, she worked with the *Pittsburg Dispatch* and the *Pittsburg Press*, thus launching her newspaper career. In June 1901 Martha moved to the *Index of Pittsburg Life*, a weekly magazine. As these were the days when people were fascinated with the lives of the rich and with their playthings, particularly the new automobiles, Martha wrote on such subjects as the Hunt Club and other social events; but she specialized in writing about cars. Her first such article was on 'stables' for automobiles and she followed this with essays on every aspect of the car, from rubber for its tyres to road conditions. She sailed to France in 1902 as automobile editor for the *Index*, while in 1903 she went to the British Isles on the SS *Cedric* to cover automobile racing in Ireland.

Immersed in her career as a journalist, Martha chanced to hear about the Bahá'í Faith at Child's Restaurant in Pittsburgh, where she went in 1908 to cover an interdenominational missionary convention. Some of the delegates were sitting in the crowded restaurant, debating the plight of the heathen of the world, when Roy Wilhelm, who happened to be seated next to Martha, commented that he had just returned from the East where he had met members of other religions who actively prayed for and promoted the brotherhood of man. This comment appealed to Martha, who was at the time the Society and Religious Editor of the *Pittsburg Post*. She gave her card to Mr Wilhelm, who began to send her Bahá'í books. These at first she disregarded, sending them to Theosophists and others interested in religious matters. Eventually, however, she began to read some of them and gradually her interest in the Cause grew. Being an investigative reporter and interested in having all the facts, she travelled to New York, Washington and Chicago to meet Bahá'ís and discuss with them the new revelation. Among the Bahá'ís she met was Thornton Chase, the first American believer. She was taken to see him at Kimball's Restaurant in Chicago, where he and other Bahá'ís were accustomed to gather and discuss the Faith. Martha spoke with Mr Chase for several hours and later said that he paved the way for her acceptance of the religion. Three months later, in January 1909, Martha became a Bahá'í in Pittsburgh.

Later the same year, Martha published a long article in the *Pittsburg Post* in which she set out the history and teachings of the Faith, quoting Bahá'u'lláh's well-known words to Professor E. G. Browne, 'We desire but the good of the world and the happiness of the nations'.[9]

When 'Abdu'l-Bahá arrived in America in 1912, Martha followed Him around New York City, Washington and Chicago as both reporter and believer. She was profoundly affected by everything about Him – His words, manner, spirituality and message. She had two personal interviews with Him. At the first, in Pittsburgh, 'Abdu'l-Bahá presented Martha with a white rose which, perhaps not surprisingly, became her favourite flower. He anointed her with attar of rose and rested her head against His shoulder.

Martha had developed a deep mistrust of doctors as a result of an accident in 1896, when she was 24. She had been seriously injured when she was thrown from her bicycle after it hit a stone as she coasted downhill. The operation that followed rendered her incapable of bearing children. This event caused her to refuse medical assistance, even when she was in severe physical need.

Now, in her meeting with 'Abdu'l-Bahá, Martha told Him that she had discovered a lump or two in her breast but was unwilling to see a doctor.

'Abdu'l-Bahá suggested she use alum (aluminium sulphate) to shrink the lumps. As He did not tell her how to use it, Martha dissolved the compound in water and drank it rather than rubbing it into the affected area. In any case, the growths were in remission for a number of years.

One meeting with 'Abdu'l-Bahá in New York City made a deep impression on Martha. 'Abdu'l-Bahá was accompanied that evening by Valíyu'lláh Varqá, son of Hand of the Cause Mírzá 'Alí-Muḥammad Varqá who had been martyred in 1896 together with his 12-year-old son Rúḥu'lláh. 'Abdu'l-Bahá told the story of these two steadfast believers, asking Valíyu'lláh to sit near Him. So moving was this story that 'Abdu'l-Bahá retired to His room weeping. Twenty years later Martha wrote her own account of the Varqá family, 'White Roses of Persia'.

In 1915 Martha embarked on the first of her eight extensive journeys. Her purpose was to see how the Bahá'í Faith affected people in other countries. Departing from New York City on 30 January, in the middle of the First World War, she travelled through Italy, Greece, Spain, Sardinia, Egypt, India, Burma, Japan and Hawaii before returning to the United States via San Francisco. She had intended to visit 'Abdu'l-Bahá and the resting places of the Báb and Bahá'u'lláh in the Holy Land, but was unable to do so owing to the war. In Japan she met and became fast friends with Agnes Alexander. Together these two irrepressible women proclaimed the Cause through the Japanese press.

On 7 November 1918, two years after the passing of her mother and four days before the Armistice marking the end of the First World War was signed, Martha wrote to 'Abdu'l-Bahá of her yearning to travel the world to teach the Cause of God. He replied with these soul-stirring words:

> Today the promulgation of the ideal principles of His Holiness Bahá'u'lláh, which are manifestly recorded in the Books, is the spirit of this age and the cause of the realization of assistance and confirmation. Assuredly whenever thou holdest fast to it, in whatever enterprise thou mayest engage, thou shalt find the doors of might and power flung open to thy face. My hope from the blessings of His Holiness Bahá'u'lláh is that thou mayest become self-sacrificing in His path, that thou mayest forget rest and composure and like unto a swift-flying bird, thou mayest cover long distances and in whatever land thou tarriest thou mayest reproduce the melody of the Kingdom and engage in songs and music in the best of tunes . . .
>
> As ears are awaiting the summons for Universal Peace, it is therefore advis-

> able for thee to travel . . . to the different parts of the globe and roar like unto a lion in the Kingdom of God. Wide-reaching consequences thou shalt witness and extraordinary confirmations shall be exhibited unto thee.[10]

At the 11th Annual Bahá'í Convention, held in New York City in April 1919, all 14 Tablets of the Divine Plan were presented. Five of these Tablets had reached America in 1916 and Martha was familiar with at least some of them; but at the time of their first reading she had been unable to respond to them, as her mother had recently passed away and she needed to look after her father. Now, however, she could feel the power of the Tablets' message and was overwhelmed by a sense of urgency. Uncertain and anxious lest her decision to leave her ageing father be wrong, she nonetheless booked passage for South America on a ship scheduled to sail on 21 June 1919.

The ship, delayed by a strike, actually sailed a month later. Within two days of sailing, Martha made a presentation about the Bahá'í Faith to the passengers, captain, purser and several officers. She had to hold on to a pillar as she spoke, as the ship pitched and rolled alarmingly.

The ship made various stops along the Brazilian coast and Martha took advantage of these to proclaim the Bahá'í teachings and distribute copies of the blue booklets 'Big Ben' and 'Little Ben' produced by Roy Wilhelm in 1917. Her main goals, however, were Bahia and Panama, places mentioned by 'Abdu'l-Bahá in the Tablets of the Divine Plan. Both seemed impossible to reach, yet in both cases Martha found a way.

Martha had to take a second ship from Pernambuco to Bahia, where she disembarked with her many pieces of luggage (most of which contained Bahá'í literature) into the yellow fever-ridden city and was immediately engulfed by a violent rainstorm. In Bahia she put Bahá'í books in the local library, gave out literature and put articles in the newspapers. She was warned that she might be stranded in the city for months, but she was able to leave, as planned, after six days.

By the time Martha reached Argentina almost all the Bahá'í literature she had carried with her was gone, such was the extent of her teaching. Everywhere she went Martha contacted the newspapers, gave lectures and spoke to groups such as the Theosophists and Esperantists, as well as to people from all walks of life. She had, she felt, achieved her first goal. Now she had to get to Panama.

Martha's solution was to cross the Andes on mule-back over a perilous ancient trail 10,400 feet above sea level. At the end of the journey, during which she wore 'three suits of woollen underwear, two sweaters, two coats and a steamer rug'[11] to keep from freezing to death, she gave Bahá'í literature to her guides and to the customs officials, then boarded a train to Valparaiso with its tropical climate.

The varying climates and the punishing schedule of activities Martha set for herself made her ill, but still she pressed on. She took a ship sailing up the west coast of South America, came down with a very bad case of influenza, but still managed to tell people in every port about Bahá'u'lláh. By now she had given away all her Bahá'í books and pamphlets and had spent $50, a large sum in 1919, on the South American newspapers and magazines that carried her articles. These, too, she had given away.

The ship reached Panama on 25 October 1919 – Martha had attained her second goal. As elsewhere, virtually every group and association, every newspaper and magazine became a vehicle for Martha's proclamation of the Faith.

From Panama Martha travelled to Cuba, spending only one day and two nights in Havana – enough time for her to give lectures and make useful contacts.

On her travels Martha carried with her, as well as mountains of Bahá'í literature, photographs of the kings and rulers whom Bahá'u'lláh had addressed a half century before and pictures of 'Abdu'l-Bahá for publication in the newspapers she contacted. She maintained that her articles had a better chance of being published if they came with pictures.

Martha was on a short trip to Mexico and Guatemala when 'Abdu'l-Bahá passed away in November 1921. Looking back on the trip, she recalled that the night of 27 November and the day of 28 November had been the most dangerous for her.

The reins of the Faith passed to 'Abdu'l-Bahá's grandson Shoghi Effendi. In her book *The Priceless Pearl*, Rúḥíyyih Khánum tells of the sufferings of Shoghi Effendi, the unfaithfulness of his family, the inertia of the believers and the burdens of his work sometimes driving him to the brink of despair. He went through these 'ordeals by fire', for he 'seemed to fairly burn with suffering', and then 'some rain from heaven, in the form of good news, would shower upon him and help to revive him'.[12] Martha Root often brought him these showers with news of her teaching activity.

After her father passed away in 1922, Martha was able to begin her travels around the world in earnest. Shoghi Effendi would write, appealing to her, 'I hunger for every minute detail of your triumphal advance in the field of service'; 'write me fully and frequently for I yearn to hear of your activities and of every detail of your achievements';[13] 'Your letters . . . have given me strength, joy and encouragement at a time when I felt depressed, tired and disheartened'.[14]

Martha had a lot to write about. In an almost unbroken period of travel extending for nearly 25 years, she circled the globe four times, travelling to the Far East and Australia from 1923 to 1925; the Holy Land and Europe between 1925 and 1929; the Middle East, India and the Far East from 1929 to 1931; to the Balkans, Scandinavia and North America from 1932 to 1937; and the Far East, India, Australia and New Zealand from 1937 to 1939. She visited China and Japan four times and India three times. Throughout these tours, she fearlessly took the Message of Bahá'u'lláh to kings, queens, princes, princesses, presidents, ministers, statesmen, professors, newspapermen, clergymen, poets, artists and a vast number of people in all walks of life. She attended religious congresses, peace societies, Esperanto associations, socialist congresses, Theosophical societies and women's clubs.

Martha lectured at over 400 universities and colleges. She visited all but two German universities twice, as well as nearly 100 educational establishments in China. She published innumerable articles in newspapers and magazines in practically every country she visited. She delivered numerous broadcasts. She placed unnumbered books in private and state libraries and supervised the translation and publication of Dr Esslemont's book *Bahá'u'lláh and the New Era* in a significant number of languages. She presented Bahá'í books to people of prominence and visited the historic sites associated with the Faith in Iran and Adrianople. She unfailingly assisted the administrators of the Faith in all countries where institutions had been erected or were being established.

In addition to her letters to the Guardian and to fellow Bahá'ís, such as Roy Wilhelm, Martha wrote a book on the life of Ṭáhirih, published in 1938. She also wrote prolifically about her travels and the Cause of God. In the early *Bahá'í World* volumes one can find essays by Martha about the Bahá'í presence at various Esperanto congresses and universities in North America, Germany and northern India. She wrote about some of the personalities she met on her travels: King Faisal of Iraq, Prince Paul and Princess Olga of Yugoslavia, King Haakon of Norway, President

Eduard Benes of Czechoslovakia and Queen Marie of Romania. She wrote about the greatness of the Bahá'í movement, Leo Tolstoy and the Bahá'í Faith, Ṭáhirih's message to the modern world, Russia's cultural contribution to the Bahá'í Faith and her visit to Adrianople.

Not surprisingly, Shoghi Effendi, as early as 1926, wrote of Martha, 'In her case we have verily witnessed in an unmistakable manner what the power of dauntless faith, when coupled with sublimity of character, can achieve, what forces it can release, to what heights it can rise.'[15]

Beginning in 1926, Martha had eight audiences with Queen Marie of Romania over an 11-year period, starting with her first interview in January of that year, and ending with their meeting in February 1936. Granddaughter of Queen Victoria of England, one of the sovereigns addressed by Bahá'u'lláh, Queen Marie became, through Martha, the first monarch to embrace the Faith of Bahá'u'lláh and to champion His Cause. Shoghi Effendi considered the Queen's acceptance and defence of the Faith astonishing and highly significant to the progress of the Cause. He was filled with joyous admiration and gratitude.

In May 1937 Martha set out from San Francisco on her final world encircling journey. She visited Japan, China, the Philippines, India, Australia and New Zealand before heading for home, where she hoped to assist in the first Seven Year Plan. When the Japanese bombed Shanghai in August 1937, Martha escaped on an American ship to Manila, where she experienced a typhoon and the worst earthquake in a century. By the time she arrived in Honolulu on 7 June 1939 she was so ill and exhausted that she had to be assisted as she disembarked from her ship. Two days after her arrival she wrote to her friend Roy Wilhelm:

> I screamed with the pain in my neck, terribly inflamed muscles. I thought I would pass. I came to these friends and everything is being done for me . . . the first night they sent for their doctor. I was in such pain, it was hard to swallow. I could not lift my head.[16]

Eventually Martha reluctantly agreed to see a Dr Molyneux but refused to tell him the real nature of her illness. Winning her confidence, Dr Molyneux persuaded her to have X-rays taken. They showed disseminated cancer of the breast arising from two lumps in her breast – tumours of more than 20 years' standing.

Over the next months Martha's condition gradually worsened. She died at the age of 67 years on 28 September 1939 and was buried in the Nuuanu cemetery in Honolulu.

Seriously ill himself with a fever of 104°F when the news of Martha's passing came,[17] Shoghi Effendi struggled to sit up in his bed and pen the following:

> MARTHA'S UNNUMBERED ADMIRERS THROUGHOUT BAHÁ'Í WORLD LAMENT WITH ME EARTHLY EXTINCTION HER HEROIC LIFE. CONCOURSE ON HIGH ACCLAIM HER ELEVATION RIGHTFUL POSITION GALAXY BAHÁ'Í IMMORTALS. POSTERITY WILL ESTABLISH HER AS FOREMOST HAND WHICH 'ABDU'L-BAHÁ'S WILL HAS RAISED UP FIRST BAHÁ'Í CENTURY. PRESENT GENERATION HER FELLOW-BELIEVERS RECOGNIZE HER FIRST FINEST FRUIT FORMATIVE AGE FAITH BAHÁ'U'LLÁH HAS YET PRODUCED. ADVISE HOLD BEFITTING MEMORIAL GATHERING TEMPLE HONOUR ONE WHOSE ACTS SHED IMPERISHABLE LUSTRE AMERICAN BAHÁ'Í COMMUNITY. IMPELLED SHARE WITH NATIONAL ASSEMBLY EXPENSES ERECTION MONUMENT SYMBOLIC SPOT MEETING-PLACE EAST WEST TO BOTH WHICH SHE UNSPARINGLY DEDICATED FULL FORCE MIGHTY ENERGIES.[18]

Martha once asked herself, while musing upon the life of Ṭáhirih, 'was Ṭáhirih great enough instantly to say, "O God, I give my life to establish this Faith among mankind!" or did she, too, need to be trained by the Infinite God to long to give her life as a martyr to serve this new universal Revelation?'[19] That Martha fulfilled her own longing is demonstrated by her services to the Cause. For what other explanation can there be for the work of a soul whose outstanding and historic accomplishments mostly occurred after her fiftieth birthday?

Yet if you had asked her about establishing the Cause of God, she would have simply replied, 'If you want to give the Message to anyone, love them, and if you love them, they will listen'. She felt that 'we live in moments, not in years'. And so she made every meeting an occasion. 'Give something always,' she would say, 'if only a flower, some candy, or fruit. Pray that they will accept from you the Greater Gift.'[20]

Such was her humility. Shoghi Effendi best described her in *God Passes By*:

> Neither age nor ill-health, neither the paucity of literature which hampered her early efforts, nor the meagre resources which imposed an added bur-

den on her labours, neither the extremities of the climates to which she was exposed, nor the political disturbances which she encountered in the course of her journeys, could damp the zeal or deflect the purpose of this spiritually dynamic and saintly woman. Single-handed and, on more than one occasion, in extremely perilous circumstances, she continued to call, in clarion tones, men of diverse creeds, colour and classes to the Message of Bahá'u'lláh, until, while in spite of a deadly and painful disease, the onslaught of which she endured with heroic fortitude, she hastened homeward to help in the recently launched Seven Year Plan, she was stricken down on her way, in far off Honolulu. There in that symbolic spot between the Eastern and Western Hemispheres, in both of which she had laboured so mightily, she died, on September 28, 1939, and brought to its close a life which may well be regarded as the fairest fruit as yet yielded by the Formative Age of the Dispensation of Bahá'u'lláh.[21]

# Muṣṭafáy-i-Rúmí
## c. 1846–1945

Sulaymán Khán was an untiring, devoted and renowned travel teacher who, dressed as a dervish, roamed the Ottoman territory in order to attract souls to the Cause of God. It happened that a few members of the Afnán family had established themselves in Bombay and had set up a printing press on which the first volumes of Bahá'í writings were published. Realizing the Indians were receptive to the Faith, they petitioned Bahá'u'lláh to send a Bahá'í teacher of knowledge and experience to assist them. Their petition coincided with Sulaymán Khán's second pilgrimage to 'Akká. Bahá'u'lláh instructed him to go to India.

After reaching Bombay, Sulaymán Khán, who was popularly known as Jamál Effendi, travelled throughout India, teaching the Bahá'í Faith. Owing to his dignified bearing and dress, he was perceived as a man of culture and thought. He showed the people genuine friendship and love. His talks were attractive and his manner of listening admirable. People of diverse backgrounds sought enlightenment from him. Thus he attracted many people to the Cause.

In Madras, Jamál Effendi encountered a young man, Siyyid Muṣṭafáy-i-Rúmí. The siyyid belonged to a noble family from Baghdád and had come to Madras to help his aged father in his business. Rúmí was proficient in a number of languages, including Arabic, Persian, Turkish, Gujarati, Bengali, Urdu and English. He was engaged in the rice trade until 1876, when he suffered heavy losses and decided to return to Iraq. He was in the last stages of preparing to leave India when he attended a gathering of men discussing various philosophical and religious questions and was at once attracted by the eloquent talk and courtly manners of Jamál Effendi.

Rúmí was very attached to Islam and carefully observed its religious rites. As soon as he became acquainted with Jamál Effendi, he was attracted to his commanding personality and did not wish to leave his side.

When Jamál Effendi was called back to Rampur in northern India, Muṣṭafá Rúmí decided to forgo his own plans and follow his mentor. Jamál Effendi spent several months teaching in northern India, with Rúmí as his constant companion. The pair eventually made their way to Calcutta. It was while they were there, near the end of 1877, that Rúmí became a Bahá'í. Up to this time it had been the personality of Jamál Effendi that had held his devotion.

In Calcutta Rúmí and Jamál Effendi were visited by two Bahá'ís who were on their way to Iran. The conversation turned to the Russo-Turkish war and the prophecies of Bahá'u'lláh about Turkey. Jamál Effendi then asked Rúmí to chant Bahá'u'lláh's Lawḥ-i-Ra'ís for their guests. The reading of this Tablet had a tremendous impact on Rúmí. Afterwards he sat spellbound as the men discussed the significance of Bahá'u'lláh's mission. Although he had heard many discourses by Jamál Effendi, this seems to have been the first time Rúmí understood the full impact of the Revelation. He immediately declared his belief in Bahá'u'lláh. Shortly afterwards Jamál Effendi wrote to Bahá'u'lláh stating that Rúmí was a new believer, and Bahá'u'lláh sent a Tablet to Rúmí in reply.

In May 1878 Jamál Effendi and Rúmí sailed for Burma, where there was already one young Persian Bahá'í, Ḥájí Siyyid Mihdí. In time, a number of people became Bahá'ís through the efforts of these three believers. Early in 1879 Jamál Effendi and Rúmí, together with a number of the new believers, travelled to Mandalay, where they taught primarily among the Muslims. About 200 people became Bahá'ís in the ensuing months and in late 1880 the two Bahá'í teachers left Mandalay for Rangoon. The next year they returned to encourage the Bahá'í community, and later went to India.

In India they visited a number of cities, including Madras, where Rúmí was able to meet his aged father. After India the two teachers embarked on an extended journey through south-east Asia, sailing first for Singapore, then to Java, Bali and Celebes, and then back through Siam and Malaya to Rangoon. At Rangoon, Jamál Effendi and Rúmí parted, Rúmí remaining in Burma and Jamál Effendi going back to India.

In Rangoon Rúmí married into a prosperous Indo-Burmese family of traders and joined his brothers-in-law in their business activities. The communities of Rangoon and Mandalay continued to grow slowly, Bahá'u'lláh sending the Bahá'ís there numerous Tablets through Rúmí.

At the end of the 19th century the Bahá'ís of Burma made a beautiful marble sarcophagus to hold the remains of the Báb, Musṭafá Rúmí being one of three believers who helped to pay for it. In 1899 Rúmí, together with a few others, carried the sarcophagus to the Holy Land as a gift to 'Abdu'l-Bahá, who welcomed them graciously. Another ten years would pass, however, before the Master was at last able, on Naw-Rúz 1909, to transfer the sarcophagus to the mausoleum on Mount Carmel, where the wooden casket containing the Báb's remains was laid within it and the sarcophagus interred in the Shrine.

During these years Rúmí could devote only part of his time to the Faith, as his work and family required most of his attention. In 1910, however, his business failed and shortly afterwards his wife died. He therefore determined to devote his full time to the service of the Cause.

In 1911 an All-India Conference of Religions was held in Allahabad, for which Rúmí wrote a thesis on the history and teachings of the Faith. His work explained how differences among the various warring communities of India could not be overcome so long as religion and politics continued to influence the affairs of the antagonists. Although Rúmí was unable to attend the conference himself, a young Bahá'í of Hindu background, Narayan Rao Sethji (Vakil) read the thesis on his behalf and it was distributed widely among the audience.

As well as establishing the Bahá'í communities of Rangoon and Mandalay, Rúmí was also responsible for raising up the Bahá'í community of Daidanaw, a village in the township of Kungyangoon. How this came about is an interesting story. One of the Bahá'ís of Rangoon stood surety for the headman of Daidanaw when he became involved in a legal problem and no one else would help him. The elders of the village were so impressed that they asked the Bahá'í to what Faith he belonged. Learning that he was a Bahá'í, they wished to know more and were brought to Rúmí, who was so convincing in his presentation that the entire village of some 800 people embraced the Cause. Desiring to help these new Bahá'ís, Rúmí then obtained financial aid from the Rangoon believers and started a school in the village. In later years the Guardian strongly encouraged the Daidanaw community to maintain its school, sending 30 pounds through the care of Musṭafá Rúmí for its upkeep.[1]

A staunch defender of the Covenant, Siyyid Muṣṭafá Rúmí effectively countered the efforts of the Covenant-breakers to spread their propaganda in India following the ascension of Bahá'u'lláh. In 1921, when 'Abdu'l-Bahá passed away, he again defeated those faithless souls by teaching the friends to adhere to the provisions of 'Abdu'l-Bahá's Will and Testament.

Muṣṭafá Rúmí was loved by 'Abdu'l-Bahá and received many Tablets from Him. He visited the Holy Land twice during the lifetime of 'Abdu'l-Bahá and once after His passing. After 'Abdu'l-Bahá's ascension Rúmí served the Guardian fervently.

Siyyid Muṣṭafá Rúmí was a scholar who knew the religious books of the Jews, Christians, Muslims and Buddhists. His methods of teaching were very successful. He was able to present the teachings of these great religions in light of the Bahá'í message in a convincing manner. When people accepted the Cause, Rúmí was then able to help them to form administrative groups, laying the foundation of many spiritual assemblies. One of Rúmí's greatest strengths was his ability to consolidate new Bahá'í communities as well as to raise them up.

Rúmí also translated many books into Burmese, including the Hidden Words, the Kitáb-i-Íqán, *Some Answered Questions* and *Bahá'í Prayers*. He compiled in Urdu *The True Criterion* (*Almayarus-Sahih*), supervised the translation into Urdu of *Maoála-i-Sayyáh* and wrote *Lessons in Religion* in Burmese.

In the early 1930s Rúmí was elected to the National Spiritual Assembly of India and Burma and served on it for several years. In later years he made his home in Daidanaw. During the Second World War many of the Bahá'ís of Rangoon and Mandalay took refuge in the village. It was a time of intense nationalistic fervour and people of foreign backgrounds were in particular danger. The Bahá'ís asked Rúmí to escape from the village as he was in great risk of his life but he refused, referring to his advanced age and his determination not to leave the place he had chosen to serve.

On 13 March 1945 the village was attacked by a mob of three thousand people who surrounded it in order to purge it from all foreign influence. The Bahá'í school, the Ḥaẓíratu'l-Quds and many Bahá'í homes were burned to the ground and property was looted. Most tragically, however, 11 Bahá'ís were killed in the attack, among them Siyyid Muṣṭafá Rúmí. The mob burned his home, beheaded him and chopped his body to pieces. Later the Bahá'ís gathered his body and buried him in front of the

Bahá'í centre. On 14 July 1945 the Guardian sent a cable to the Bahá'ís of India and Burma elevating Rúmí to the rank of Hand of the Cause:

> HEARTS GRIEF STRICKEN PASSING SUPREME CONCOURSE DISTINGUISHED PIONEER FAITH BAHA'U'LLAH DEARLY BELOVED STAUNCH HIGH MINDED NOBLE SOUL SIYYID MUSTAFA. LONG RECORD HIS SUPERB SERVICES BOTH TEACHING ADMINISTRATIVE FIELDS SHED LUSTRE ON BOTH HEROIC AND FORMATIVE AGES BAHA'I DISPENSATION. HIS MAGNIFICENT ACHIEVEMENTS FULLY ENTITLE HIM JOIN RANKS HANDS CAUSE BAHA'U'LLAH. HIS RESTING PLACE SHOULD BE REGARDED FOREMOST SHRINE COMMUNITY BURMESE BELIEVERS. ADVISE HOLDING MEMORIAL GATHERINGS THROUGHOUT INDIA HONOUR HIS IMPERISHABLE MEMORY. URGE INDIAN BURMESE BAHA'IS PARTICIPATE CONSTRUCTION TOMB. CABLING THREE HUNDRED POUNDS MY PERSONAL CONTRIBUTION SO PRAISEWORTHY PURPOSE.[2]

In August 1945 the Guardian, through his secretary, again wrote to the Indian Bahá'ís:

> He was deeply grieved to hear of the death of our very dear and esteemed Bahá'í brother, Siyyid Mustafa. He was truly an example of steadfast devotion and one of the outstanding pioneers the Faith produced during the first century of its existence. He was also very sad to hear of the ruin of the Bahá'í Ḥaẓíratu'l-Quds and the plight of the Bahá'ís in general.[3]

The Guardian wrote again in December of the same year:

> He was very sad to read of the sufferings of the beloved Burmese friends, of the death of that bright star of the Faith, Siyyid Mustafa, and of the murder of many other of the friends![4]

Rúmí's devotion and selflessness set an example for Bahá'ís everywhere. In 1948, in a letter to the National Spiritual Assembly of Australia and New Zealand encouraging it to persevere in its efforts to teach the Faith, the Guardian focused attention on Siyyid Muṣṭafá Rúmí's accomplishments in Burma:

> We can truly say that this Cause is a cause that enables people to achieve the impossible! For the Bahá'ís, everywhere, for the most part, are people with

no great distinguishments of either wealth or fame, and yet once they make the effort and go forth in the name of Bahá'u'lláh to spread His Faith, they become, each one, as efficacious as a host! Witness what Mustafa Roumie accomplished in Burma . . . It is the quality of devotion and self-sacrifice that brings rewards in the service of this Faith rather than means, ability or financial backing.[5]

# Roy C. Wilhelm
# 1875–1951

Roy Wilhelm was a man of habit. He would wear dark conservative suits, take the train to Wall Street, buy the *Herald Tribune*, work in the office, return home by train, purchase flowers for his mother, change into a dinner jacket at home, and put on his slippers for another evening's relaxation. A wealthy and respected entrepreneur in the coffee business, in 1900 he had moved to New York, where he half-heartedly attended Bahá'í meetings with his parents when they visited him. One evening, however, the routine of his life was for ever altered:

> He was sitting on his bed, changing his shoes, when the room was suddenly transformed. The walls were whitewashed, and there was a divan. Standing next to Roy was a majestic figure with a long black beard, dressed in what appeared to be an oriental gown. The figure approached Roy, taking off His ring and placing it on Roy's finger and removing Roy's ring and placing it on His finger.[1]

Roy was transfixed by the apparition. A practical man not prone to visions or psychic experiences, he was unable to reconcile what he had seen with who he considered himself to be.

He decided to tell no one about the experience. After all, his 'practical' friends would never understand. And his mother, a confirmed Bahá'í since the earliest days of the Cause in America, would certainly renew her efforts to draw him into the Faith.

Roy Wilhelm was born in Zanesville, Ohio, on 17 September 1875. His maternal grandmother believed that the promised day was near and counselled those close to her to watch out for this event. Roy's parents, although church members, held unorthodox views. When Roy was about 15 his mother, Laurie, became dissatisfied with Christian doctrine and began to investigate other religious teachings and philosophies. Like her mother, she became convinced that the 'Great Day' was near.

Around 1898 Laurie received from a friend some Bahá'í pamphlets, selections from the Hidden Words and a letter about the Bahá'í Faith. As soon as she read these, Laurie accepted the Bahá'í teachings. Anxious to share the good news with her son, she sent him a photograph of 'Abdu'l-Bahá and a short newspaper article about Him. Neither impressed Roy, who returned the newspaper clipping to his mother with the words 'Strange if true' written in the margin.[2]

As time passed and her knowledge of the Cause deepened, Mrs Wilhelm increasingly spent her free hours teaching and corresponding with believers and seekers in various parts of the world. When she visited her son in New York, she took him to Bahá'í meetings, but Roy was simply not convinced that the Bahá'í Faith offered a lifestyle suited to his temperament. He tolerated his mother's beliefs but he was satisfied with his life just as it was.

In 1907 Laurie Wilhelm received permission to go to the Holy Land to see 'Abdu'l-Bahá. She asked her son to accompany her. Roy, unwilling for his mother to travel so far alone, agreed. Thus, in April 1907 Roy and Laurie travelled to 'Akká and the home of the Master.

When they reached their destination, Roy found himself suddenly, strongly and warmly embraced by 'Abdu'l-Bahá. 'Welcome! Very welcome!' 'Abdu'l-Bahá said on their arrival. 'I have been waiting for your coming. It is with God's help that you have reached 'Akká . . . You represent all the American believers . . . Thank God that you came.'[3] Recovering from the shock of finding himself hugged by another man, Roy felt his reservations vanish as he relaxed into the welcoming atmosphere of 'Abdu'l-Bahá's home.

Some time during the Wilhelms' six-day stay at the prison house, 'Abdu'l-Bahá urged Roy to visit Bahjí. On the way, one of the Persian believers took him to a small white house in which Bahá'u'lláh used to stay when He visited the Garden of Riḍván. As he entered the house, Roy found himself in the room he had seen in his vision. Shaken, he quickly left the house, realizing he had to share his secret with 'Abdu'l-Bahá.

'You had a spiritual experience,' 'Abdu'l-Bahá told Roy. 'Bahá'u'lláh had wedded you to His Faith.'[4] From that moment Roy Wilhelm was a Bahá'í.

During this pilgrimage of mother and son, 'Abdu'l-Bahá intimated the future greatness of the Bahá'í Revelation in these words:

> When Christ passed away, He had eleven disciples. The greatest among them was Peter and he denied Christ three times, but when Bahá'u'lláh departed He had a hundred thousand believers who were calling out Yá-Bahá'u'l-Abhá while they were under swords and daggers, and in these late years many men and women in Yazd were killed by inches without uttering a single cry or complaint, but rather called out the Greatest Name. From these incidents we may judge the future of this Revelation.[5]

Roy was intensely affected by his pilgrimage in 'Akká and subsequently wrote of it in a booklet entitled 'Knock, and it shall be opened unto you'. On the front cover he put a photograph he had taken of 'Abdu'l-Bahá's doorway.[6] In his article for *The Bahá'í World*, 'Two Glimpses of 'Abdu'l-Bahá',[7] Roy recalled that pilgrimage as demonstrating the power of love and harmony.

In the article, he recounts seeing within the house of 'Abdu'l-Bahá Jews, Christians, Muslims, Zoroastrians and Hindus living together in perfect unity. He remembers how the members of 'Abdu'l-Bahá's household sacrificed their lives for one another and mentions sitting beside the Master, who put His arm around him while holding his mother's hand in His own. He witnessed 'Abdu'l-Bahá's famed generosity towards the poor of 'Akká and saw prominent people of various backgrounds and systems approach and consult the Master. He remembers the little birds flying into the rooms at the prison house and a believer who had waited 22 years to come to the Holy Land. Among the Bahá'ís he met was the 'Angel of Carmel', Ḥájí Mírzá Ḥaydar-'Alí, who had been exiled and imprisoned for 12 years for his belief in the new Revelation.

In 1908 Roy had a chance encounter with Martha Root at a restaurant in Pittsburgh and introduced her to the Faith, for ever altering Bahá'í history. Roy and Thornton Chase were Martha's mentors. Not only had they both met 'Abdu'l-Bahá, they were highly successful in the world of business, maintaining their competitive advantages

> through integrity and ethical practices, and without seeking to manipulate or denigrate others in their fields. They were industrious and managed to incorporate a high level of business activity with work for the Bahá'í Faith.[8]

Some months after Roy's first encounter with Martha, the Wilhelms transferred their business from the mid-west to New York and moved into a house in West Englewood, New Jersey. This house, with its nearby evergreen grove, surrounding hills and open space, would be the scene of many Bahá'í activities in years to come. Meetings were regularly held there and in a few other homes nearby in an effort to attract converts, but it was several years before a group was permanently established, causing Roy to recall a comment of 'Abdu'l-Bahá 'that it required a great expenditure of effort to accomplish even small things in this world'.[9]

In 1909 Roy was one of the nine members elected to the Executive Board of the Bahá'í Temple Unity. Except for a year of illness, he served on the Board and it successor, the National Spiritual Assembly of the United States and Canada, until 1946, acting as treasurer for many years. He won the admiration of fellow National Assembly member Horace Holley for his years of service:

> No other American believer has achieved a comparable record. As treasurer, the integrity of his character and the simple, direct humanness of his exposition of financial matters brought about a rapid development of the Bahá'í fund as an organic institution of the community.[10]

In 1912 'Abdu'l-Bahá came to America. At His behest, a unity feast was held in the grounds of the Wilhelm home in West Englewood on 29 June 1912 for the Bahá'ís of the New York area. Among the 250 people present were Martha Root, Lua Getsinger, Grace Robarts, Ali Kuli Khan, Marjorie Morten, Juliet Thompson and Grace Krug. 'Abdu'l-Bahá addressed the gathering, saying:

> This is a delightful gathering; you have come here with sincere intentions, and the purpose of all present is the attainment of the virtues of God . . . This is a new Day, and this hour is a new Hour in which we have come together. Surely the Sun of Reality with its full effulgence will illumine us, and the darkness of disagreements will disappear . . . Such gatherings as this have no equal or likeness in the world of mankind, where people are drawn together by physical motives or in furtherance of material interests, for this meeting is a prototype of that inner and complete spiritual association in the eternal world of being.
>
> . . . Hundreds of thousands of meetings shall be held to commemorate this

occasion, and the very words I speak to you today shall be repeated in them for ages to come.[11]

Juliet Thompson described in her diary what was for her the highlight of the feast:

> To me the most beautiful scene of all came later, when the Master returned to us after dark. About fifty or sixty people had lingered, unable to tear themselves from Him. The Master sat in a chair on the top step of the porch, some of us surrounding Him . . . Below us, all over the lawn, on each side of the path, sat the others, the light summer skirts of the women spread out on the grass, tapers in their hands (to keep off mosquitoes). In the dark, in their filmy dresses, they looked like great moths and the burning tips of the tapers they waved like fireflies darting about.
>
> Then the Master spoke again to us. I was standing behind Him, close to Him, and before He began He turned and gave me a long, profound look. . . .
>
> Before He had finished He rose from His chair and started down the path still talking, passing between the dim figures on the grass with their lighted tapers, talking till He reached the road.[12]

Out of the darkness, Juliet heard Him call back, 'Peace be with you'. 'May I always remember, and *hear the Voice*,' she wrote.[13]

This occasion marks the 'only public Memorial which the American Bahá'ís are permitted to construct in reverent observance of 'Abdu'l-Bahá's visit'.[14] This memorable 'Souvenir Picnic', as it came to be known, is still commemorated every year.

One day while He was in New York, 'Abdu'l-Bahá asked Roy to come to the Hotel Ansonia, where He was staying:

> Roy left immediately. When he entered the presence of 'Abdu'l-Bahá, he noticed a number of friends, including several Persians, seated around the room. The Master had Roy sit in the middle of the room, and began to talk to him about the importance of obedience, in a reprimanding manner, waving His finger at Roy. Most other people would have whimpered and cowered, or stomped out of the room; but Roy didn't flinch. He was puzzled, but never questioned the Master.[15]

Later Roy learned that the Master's lecture was intended to reach a

Persian believer present in the room who was tending towards Covenant-breaking.

While 'Abdu'l-Bahá was in America, Martha Root submitted, through Roy Wilhelm, an outline for a world teaching trip she hoped to undertake. Roy spoke about the proposal to 'Abdu'l-Bahá, who reluctantly agreed that Martha could go, so long as she could continue to receive her salary. However, He really wanted her to remain in Pittsburgh. Reporting back to Martha, Roy expressed 'Abdu'l-Bahá's concern for her safety and the hardships she would be likely to suffer. The closeness between them enabled him to offer his own advice:

> I think too, Martha, it is a mistake to strain too hard to *create conditions*. I believe in trying to be in shape to grasp opportunities *when* they come and then to lay low for the arrival of the when, and I doubt if your whenly for this big jaunt has yet arrived, though I some how feel in my bloomin' bones that it *will come*.[16]

Martha took the advice of 'Abdu'l-Bahá and Roy and postponed her proposed tour and, although she must have been disappointed, she joined Roy and his parents the following year for a month-long motoring and camping trip through New England. Each one had a particular, if not peculiar, responsibility for the tour: Roy was chief engineer; his father was in charge of the commissary; Laurie was the 'poet–cook'; and Martha was the pilot. The trip was a success, deepening the attachment of the Wilhelms and Martha to one another and creating much happiness. Roy and Martha afterwards wrote an article about the adventure which appeared in *Collier's*, a popular weekly magazine.

Roy was keenly aware of the shortage of Bahá'í literature. In the years preceding the establishment of the Bahá'í Publishing Trust, he could often be seen in his unheated office after midnight making copies of the latest Tablets from the Master. He made hundreds of such copies and had them circulated throughout the American Bahá'í community. Roy had injured his back at the age of 16 when he jumped from the window of a barn onto a pitchfork concealed in a wagonload of hay. Such tedious work must have exacerbated the often severe pain he suffered to such a degree that he sometimes had to work standing up.

At the ninth Annual Bahá'í Convention, held in Boston in April 1917, two small blue teaching booklets were displayed, one less than two inches square and the other slightly larger. Dubbed 'Little Ben' and 'Big Ben', these booklets had been prepared by Roy as small gifts for the Bahá'ís who attended the Riḍván feast before the convention, but became extremely popular. The first edition of 15,000 copies was quickly sold. Another 75,000 copies were printed and soon used up also. Translated into several languages, they became Martha Root's primary teaching aids when she began her world travels. 'Abdu'l-Bahá was so delighted with these booklets that He requested 100 copies of each to be sent to Him, 'for they are exceedingly praiseworthy'.[17]

Always looking for a way to spread the message of Bahá'u'lláh, Roy not only produced his teaching booklets but even included quotations from the Bahá'í writings in his business advertisements in trade journals. Moreover, in his public talks he was able to introduce serious subjects in an amusing way and seemed to inspire affection and confidence in those who knew him. He used the opportunities afforded by his business trips across the country to teach the Cause to any willing listener. He frequently visited the Bahá'ís, who greatly looked forward to his arrival, and gave lectures.

Around the time he was serving on the Local Spiritual Assembly of New York City in 1920, Roy persuaded Curtis Kelsey, a young electrician, to go to the Holy Land to design and install electrical lighting systems at the Shrines of the Báb and Bahá'u'lláh and at the home of 'Abdu'l-Bahá. Roy had been deeply moved by the words of the Báb revealed during His incarceration in the fortress of Mákú:

> How veiled are ye, O My creatures . . . who, without any right have consigned Him [the Báb] unto a mountain [Mákú], not one of whose inhabitants is worthy of mention . . . In His presence, which is My presence, there is not at night even a lighted lamp! And yet, in places [of worship] which in varying degrees reach out unto Him, unnumbered lamps are shining! All that is on earth hath been created for Him, and all partake with delight of His benefits, and yet they are so veiled from Him as to refuse Him even a lamp![18]

Roy had written to 'Abdu'l-Bahá asking permission to send a lighting plant to illumine the Shrine of the Báb and had received a cable from Him saying that three plants were required. Within a few weeks, Roy had sent the generators to Haifa. Now someone was needed to install them. A year after the equipment had been delivered, Curtis arrived in the Holy Land to install it, his passage having been paid through the sale of a beloved car, some unexpected money from his father and a gift of $500 from Roy. Thus it was that Curtis Kelsey found himself in the Holy Land during the last months of 'Abdu'l-Bahá's life.

Throughout His ministry 'Abdu'l-Bahá had been plagued by those who wished to undermine the Faith, to create divisions and draw others away from the Centre of the Covenant. Much of 'Abdu'l-Bahá's energy was used to maintain the unity of the Faith and to urge the Bahá'ís to remain faithful to the Covenant.

'Abdu'l-Bahá often advised Roy and others in whom He had confidence to guard the community against the machinations of Covenant-breakers. For example, in the summer of 1920 He wrote to Roy:

> thou and all the friends should encourage the souls (people) to become firm in attachment to the Testament and Covenant, for the power of the Covenant brings together and makes them united and harmonious; otherwise every ambitious soul arises to bring about their separation, in order to draw a few souls around himself.[19]

'Abdu'l-Bahá trusted Roy implicitly and, as His life drew to a close, He cabled Roy on 8 November 1921, 'HOW IS SITUATION AND HEALTH FRIENDS?' Roy replied the very next day: 'Chicago, Washington, Philadelphia agitating violation centring Fernald, Dyer, Watson. New York, Boston refused join, standing solidly constructive policy.'[20] No doubt Roy's unhesitating frankness on this occasion, in revealing the true situation of these Bahá'í communities, was one reason for the Master's confidence in him.

On 12 November 'Abdu'l-Bahá responded to Roy's report:

> HE WHO SITS WITH LEPER CATCHES LEPROSY. HE WHO IS WITH CHRIST SHUNS PHARISEES AND ABHORS JUDAS ISCARIOT. CERTAINLY SHUN VIOLATORS. INFORM GOODALL, TRUE AND PARSONS TELEGRAPHICALLY.[21]

Later the same day 'Abdu'l-Bahá sent a second message to Roy: 'I IMPLORE HEALTH FROM DIVINE BOUNTY.'[22] These were the last messages from 'Abdu'l-Bahá received by the American Bahá'ís. The next cable Roy received from the Holy Land, dated 28 November 1921, was from the Greatest Holy Leaf, informing him of 'Abdu'l-Bahá's ascension.

Four months later, Shoghi Effendi, despite his own distress, summoned to Haifa a group of prominent Bahá'ís to consult on the future of the Cause. This group included Mountfort Mills, Mason Remey and Roy Wilhelm from America; Laura and Hippolyte Dreyfus-Barney from France; Consul and Alice Schwarz from Germany; Major Tudor Pole, Lady Blomfield and Ethel Rosenberg from England; and Emogene Hoagg, who was living in Haifa at the time. Other believers came later.

Some Bahá'ís and members of 'Abdu'l-Bahá's family felt that Shoghi Effendi's youth implied a lack of maturity to discharge the affairs of the Cause but he quickly and effectively assumed the reins of leadership. Ethel Rosenberg was to help the British Bahá'ís establish their first National Spiritual Assembly upon her return home. Shoghi Effendi charged the American and German representatives with the responsibility of establishing Bahá'í administrative bodies in their respective countries, telling Roy and Mountfort Mills to convey to the forthcoming American convention that the Executive Board of the Bahá'í Temple Unity was to have a legislative function and was to guide all national affairs rather than merely implement decisions and recommendations of the annual convention.[23] The conversion of the Bahá'í Temple Unity into the National Spiritual Assembly of the Bahá'ís of the United States and Canada took three years: Shoghi Effendi recognized the body as the National Assembly in 1925.

The loss of 'Abdu'l-Bahá was keenly felt by many believers in the fledgling American Bahá'í community. In New York some Bahá'ís, wishing to create disunity, began to circulate rumours against Roy and Mountfort Mills, both members of the Local Spiritual Assembly. Roy, unable to stop the rumours, felt frustrated. However, one night 'Abdu'l-Bahá appeared to him in a dream:

> In the dream, Roy was sitting beside the Master in His high buckboard wagon, with 'Abdu'l-Bahá handling the reins. It was so real that Roy could feel the heat of the Master's body. While driving, 'Abdu'l-Bahá turned, facing Roy squarely, smiling and saying, 'But you would still have Me.' When Roy awoke, that gnawing feeling of having been abused, having been treated unjustly had vanished.[24]

Near the end of August 1922 Martha Root was once again with the Wilhelms, travelling with them from Green Acre in Maine to 'The Cabin' in New Jersey, the Wilhelm home which had been remodelled and turned over to the Bahá'ís of West Englewood. As Martha left the Bahá'í gathering at 'The Cabin' for home, Roy's father had a stroke and lapsed into unconsciousness. He died in late October. Martha's own father closely followed J. O. Wilhelm, passing away on 3 November 1922.

As Martha travelled the world, Roy often sent her money and the two corresponded regularly. Martha always repaid Roy, no matter what the amount. In 1925 she wrote to him about a small sum for which he was refusing to be reimbursed:

> My cousin Sidney has just written me about that $90 . . . I want you to take it and I will write you and Sidney a joint letter from Geneva . . . I shall never feel I can write you for anything if you do not take the money – and I know you are doing far too much for me. I do not want you to go 'broke' and all worried about money affairs. Shoghi told me about the lights you sent . . . and . . . told me about the land . . . You are an ideal Bahá'í, Roy, and I want you to be careful and not give more than you can. I don't want you to be harassed about finances . . . What you have done for me has helped me so much that I could go forward without stopping one day.[25]

In 1928 she wrote: 'Roy, you have been so good to me. I can never thank you for all you are to me, but Bahá'u'lláh knows how deeply I appreciate you! May Bahá'u'lláh bless you always.'[26] The next year, while Martha was on a teaching tour of Germany, Roy sent her $100 just as her own money was running out. Later the same year she found the tea he sent to her as she travelled across Europe to Constantinople indispensable to her well-being. In 1932, as Martha was about to leave America yet again, Roy wrote to her:

> Well, dear Martha, away you go . . . we'd like to keep you here with us – but you well know that the bee which hugs the hive doesn't gather the honey – so we're glad to speed you towards your work – in God's care.
>
> . . . don't run yourself too close nor too fast. Unduly squeezing may retard the highest efficiency which, in view of so very few workers, is of first import. 'Wilhelmite' is thus far a spring in which Bahá'u'lláh deposits as fast – even faster – than the Water is withdrawn . . . Keep me informed at all times as to your financial outlook say for sixty to ninety days ahead of you.[27]

Roy owned a beautiful retreat in the Maine hills which he called 'Evergreen Camp'. A small working farm, it boasted 500 maple trees and

19 goats. Here Martha rested for two months in 1936 before setting off on an extensive lecture tour of the American eastern seaboard and her final world teaching trip. Some years later, Roy penned this tribute to her:

> Martha was a unique. She seemed to have been born for her special work. I doubt if there is another who has brought attention to the Faith to so many tens of thousands over so many corners of the earth. I sometimes think my chief reason for being born was to get Martha started.[28]

Another Bahá'í Roy supported in his teaching work was Louis Gregory, with whom he formed a close friendship. For example, in 1919 Roy gave Louis $19, which Louis used on books and pamphlets to give away.[29]

Roy's mother died in 1937, following a stroke. In her obituary Roy, greatly grieved at her passing, wrote, 'It is indeed comforting to now have the assurance of the Guardian that Mother is making a near approach to the Beloved'.[30]

Roy retired from Bahá'í administrative work in 1946, at the age of 71, due to serious illness. He had served the Bahá'í community continuously, except for one year of illness, for 37 years.

Roy received many Tablets from 'Abdu'l-Bahá, these few selections from which illuminate 'the essential worth of this man, and his service as a steadfast pillar of a new and worldwide Faith':

> Verily thou art serving in every respect; thou art striving more than thine energy permits, and thou art rendering self-sacrifice. I am pleased with thee to the utmost.

> Thou art self-sacrificing in service to the Kingdom. Even a minute thou dost not neglect. Thy heart is overflowing with the love of God. Be thou assured that thou wilt receive great Confirmations.

> The sight of your portrait brought joy to My heart, because it is luminous and celestial.

> I am extremely pleased with you because you are a true Bahá'í. Your house is My house: there is no difference whatsoever between yours and Mine.[31]

Roy passed away in Lovel, Maine, on 20 December 1951. Even after his death he continued to serve the Faith. In 1953 Shoghi Effendi was able, after 30 years of effort, to acquire property of over 23,000 square metres within the precincts of the Shrine of the Báb, thanks to the estate bequeathed to the Faith by Roy Wilhelm.

On Roy's passing Shoghi Effendi elevated him to the rank of Hand of the Cause in a cable sent to the American believers:

> HEART FILLED SORROW LOSS GREATLY PRIZED, MUCH LOVED, HIGHLY ADMIRED HERALD BAHÁ'U'LLÁH'S COVENANT, ROY WILHELM. DISTINGUISHED CAREER ENRICHED ANNALS CONCLUDING YEARS HEROIC OPENING YEARS FORMATIVE AGE FAITH. STERLING QUALITIES ENDEARED HIM HIS BELOVED MASTER, 'ABDU'L-BAHÁ. HIS SAINTLINESS, INDOMITABLE FAITH, OUTSTANDING SERVICES LOCAL, NATIONAL, INTERNATIONAL, EXEMPLARY DEVOTION, QUALIFY HIM JOIN RANKS HANDS CAUSE, INSURE HIM EVERLASTING REWARD ABHÁ KINGDOM. ADVISE HOLD MEMORIAL GATHERING TEMPLE BEFITTING HIS UNFORGETTABLE SERVICES LOFTY RANK.[32]

Ḥájí Abu'l-Ḥasan-i-Ardikání, surnamed Amín-i-Iláhí (Ḥájí Amín)

*Left to right*: Mírzá Músá Khán, Ḥakím Báshí; Muḥammad Labíb; Hand of the Cause Ḥájí Amín

‘Abdu’l Jalíl Bey Sa‘ad

Hyde Dunn

Dr John Esslemont

Louis Gregory

Keith Ransom-Kehler

Muḥammad Taqíy-i-Iṣfahání

Martha Root

Martha Root with Sister Grace Challis, *centre*

Martha Root,
taken in Bombay in 1937

Siyyid Muṣṭafá Rúmí

*Left to right*: Mrs Greenleaf, Hand of the Cause Roy Wilhelm and
Mrs Agnes Parsons at Dubin, New Hampshire (USA) in about 1934

# IV

# Hands of the Cause Appointed by Shoghi Effendi on 24 December 1951

CABLEGRAM, 24 DECEMBER 1951

... HOUR NOW RIPE TO TAKE LONG INEVITABLY DEFERRED STEP IN CONFORMITY WITH PROVISIONS OF 'ABDU'L-BAHÁ'S TESTAMENT IN CONJUNCTION WITH SIX ABOVE-MENTIONED STEPS THROUGH APPOINTMENT OF FIRST CONTINGENT OF HANDS OF CAUSE OF GOD, TWELVE IN NUMBER, EQUALLY ALLOCATED HOLY LAND, ASIATIC, AMERICAN, EUROPEAN CONTINENTS. INITIAL STEP NOW TAKEN REGARDED AS PREPARATORY FULL DEVELOPMENT OF INSTITUTION PROVIDED IN 'ABDU'L-BAHÁ'S WILL, PARALLELED PRELIMINARY MEASURE FORMATION INTERNATIONAL COUNCIL DESTINED TO CULMINATE IN EMERGENCE OF UNIVERSAL HOUSE OF JUSTICE. NASCENT INSTITUTION FORGING FRESH LINKS BINDING RISING WORLD CENTRE OF FAITH TO CONSOLIDATING WORLD COMMUNITY OF FOLLOWERS OF MOST GREAT NAME, PAVING WAY TO ADOPTION SUPPLEMENTARY MEASURES CALCULATED REINFORCE FOUNDATIONS STRUCTURE OF THE BAHÁ'Í ADMINISTRATIVE ORDER.

NOMINATED HANDS COMPRISE, HOLY LAND, SUTHERLAND MAXWELL, MASON REMEY, AMELIA COLLINS, PRESIDENT, VICE-PRESIDENT, INTER-NATIONAL BAHÁ'Í COUNCIL; CRADLE FAITH, VALÍYU'LLÁH VARQÁ, ṬARÁẒU'LLÁH SAMANDARÍ, ALÍ-AKBAR FURÚTAN; AMERICAN CONTINENT, HORACE HOLLEY, DOROTHY BAKER, LEROY IOAS; EUROPEAN CONTINENT, GEORGE TOWNSHEND, HERMANN GROSSMANN, UGO GIACHERY. NINE ELEVATED TO RANK OF HAND IN THREE CONTINENTS OUTSIDE HOLY LAND ADVISED REMAIN PRESENT POSTS AND CONTINUE DISCHARGE VITAL ADMINISTRATIVE, TEACHING DUTIES PENDING ASSIGNMENT OF SPECIFIC FUNCTIONS AS NEED ARISES. URGE ALL NINE ATTEND AS MY REPRESENTATIVES ALL FOUR FORTHCOMING INTERCONTINENTAL CONFERENCES AS WELL AS DISCHARGE WHATEVER RESPONSIBILITIES INCUMBENT UPON THEM AT THAT TIME AS ELECTED REPRESENTATIVES OF NATIONAL BAHÁ'Í COMMUNITIES.

COMMUNICATE TEXT OF ANNOUNCEMENT TO ALL NATIONAL ASSEMBLIES.

- SHOGHI

# Dorothy Beecher Baker
# 1898–1954

The life of Dorothy Beecher Baker is an example to all who struggle upon this earth. Her capacity was gradually increased as she was spiritually transformed. She became the embodiment of these words attributed to 'Abdu'l-Bahá: 'Faith is like the rain: at first it comes in drops, then it falls in torrents.'[1]

The starting point of spiritual growth has variously been described as rebirth, resurrection and renewal. Bahá'u'lláh refers to this awakening as the birth of the spirit of faith.[2] This birth comes through recognition of the Manifestation of God for the age and obedience to His teachings. Reaching this station is the very purpose for which humankind was created.

For Dorothy, this spiritual awakening came when she met 'Abdu'l-Bahá in 1912. Taken by her grandmother, Mother Beecher – as she was called by the Bahá'ís – to visit the Master in New York City, Dorothy later said that she acquired in that hour 'a passion for all people'.[3] Several days later she wrote to 'Abdu'l-Bahá and begged to serve Him and the Cause of His Father. He replied to her letter, offering tender encouragement while charging her grandmother to train Dorothy as His own daughter.

Born on 21 December 1898 in Newark, New Jersey, to Henry and Luella Beecher, Dorothy could trace her paternal family to Henry Ward Beecher, a liberal clergyman eloquent on the subjects of prohibition and the abolition of slavery, and to Harriet Beecher Stowe, author of *Uncle Tom's Cabin*. Dorothy's grandmother, Ellen Tuller Beecher, was active in movements concerned with women's rights. Both of Dorothy's parents were well educated: Henry Beecher was a Harvard Law School graduate while Luella was a graduate of the Women's Homeopathic College of Medicine and Surgery.

Dorothy attended Northfield Seminary for Young Ladies and Montclair Normal School and in 1919 began a career in teaching. In 1920 she met Frank Baker, a widower nine years her senior with two young children, Conrad and Sally (Sara); they married on 21 June 1921. The children, who both respected and resented Dorothy, eventually accepted her as a replacement for their deceased mother, thanks to Dorothy's determination to make her marriage succeed. She gave up her career in teaching to provide a stable and loving home for the children. In May 1922 Dorothy and Frank had a daughter, Louise.

In 1923 the family moved to Buffalo, New York, which was more central to Frank's job as general manager of ten bakeries for the National Biscuit Company. Although Dorothy was an able wife and mother, she often felt lonely when Frank was away on business trips. One day she met a woman psychic who insisted on telling Dorothy the future of her children. Asked about Sally, the fortune teller replied that Sally's destiny was different but beautiful. She also told Dorothy to train well the child she was carrying. As she believed she was not pregnant, Dorothy dismissed the psychic's predictions. Some weeks later, a doctor confirmed that Dorothy could expect her second child in seven months. William was born in November 1923.

Buffalo had a Bahá'í community. Although Dorothy was not yet a public speaker, she enjoyed telling Bahá'í stories to the children and hosting weekly firesides. She was elected to the Local Spiritual Assembly – her first administrative Bahá'í experience. She considered herself a Bahá'í but she still tended to mix Bahá'í ideas with current thinking on such subjects as astrology and numerology.

In 1926 Dr Ali Kuli Khan, a noted Bahá'í scholar and diplomat, visited Buffalo and gave a talk on the Seven Valleys. Dorothy decided to take Conrad and Sally. During the lecture, Sally lifted her head, tears streaming down her cheeks. Later that night when Dorothy tucked her into bed, Sally said, 'I just want you to know, no matter what, that I'm a Bahá'í.'[4]

A few weeks later, during a shopping trip with Dorothy, Sally seemed unusually tired. A medical examination revealed she had leukaemia. The doctor's prognosis stunned the family: Sally had only one week, or perhaps a little more, to live. A few days later she died. Frank crumbled.

Having lost his mother to typhoid and his first wife to pneumonia, he was ill-prepared to accept Sally's death. Several nights after Sally's passing, however, Dorothy saw a brilliant light streaming in through the bedroom window. Down that path of light danced Sally with garlands of flowers in her hair and carrying two wicker baskets. She exclaimed, 'Oh Muzz, I'm so happy! Look, I have all the wildflowers I want!' She looked at her father sleeping in the bed. 'Tell him I'm happy, Muzz. Tell him how happy I am.' And off she danced up the path of light.[5]

Frank decided to move away from the place of so much suffering and set out to find a bakery for sale some distance from Buffalo. Eventually he decided to build a bakery in Lima, Ohio. To Dorothy, Ohio was 'out west' and Lima was not even near civilization. Nevertheless, in 1927 the family moved into a spacious house at 615 W. Elm. It had originally been owned by a Mr and Mrs Barnard who had placed a large 'B' on the glass front door. In later years Dorothy maintained that the 'B' stood for 'Baker' and 'Bahá'u'lláh'.[6]

Frank's bakery – 'Frank Baker Bread Company – Makers of Plezol Bread' – thrived. Mother Beecher, at the age of 88, came to live with the Bakers. Her wish was to see Dorothy become active in the Bahá'í Faith, for up to now it had merely been her 'other life'.[7]

Dorothy and Mother Beecher began studying the Holy Writings for an hour a day. They frequently said the Tablet of Aḥmad for 19 consecutive days for the resolution of problems, a habit Dorothy would follow the rest of her life.

Early in 1929, Dorothy, emotionally tired from years of hardship but seemingly physically well, went for a routine medical check-up. Fully expecting a good report, she learned that she had a spot on her lung, indicating tuberculosis. Shocked and worried for Frank's peace of mind, Dorothy told no one. When she found a lump in her breast a few days later, she did not even tell her doctor.

Convinced that this was to be her last spring, Dorothy decided to attend the annual Bahá'í Convention in Chicago. She hoped that at the Bahá'í House of Worship she would receive some indication that her life had been worthwhile or that she would be spared. After three days of the Convention she had received no sign and, weeping hopelessly, slipped out by a side door to go for a walk along Lake Michigan. Though no one knew of her illness, Albert Vail, a long-time friend of the family, followed her. 'Dorothy, are you willing to leave this world without rendering some great service to the Cause?' he asked. Feeling like a drowning person fighting her way back to life, Dorothy went to the spot where 'Abdu'l-Bahá had laid the cornerstone for the Mother Temple. She later wrote: 'The few minutes at the shrine will never be forgotten. How my throat ached. What those moments taught me cannot be put into words. I think my heart was laid at the Master's feet there.'[8]

When she returned home, Dorothy wrote her first letter to Shoghi Effendi, asking for his advice. She told him of her desire to write children's stories about the history of the Bahá'í Cause, as there was so little literature for children. The Guardian replied that a comprehensive compilation was being made in Persia that would serve her purposes well and that he would pray for her at the Holy Shrines that she might render distinct services to the Cause.

As her strength began to return, Dorothy suffered another set-back. One September evening she opened a can of salmon for dinner. Thinking it smelled strange, she tasted a very small amount before discarding the rest. A few hours later she was struck down by ptomaine poisoning and remained unconscious through the night, the doctor holding out no hope of her survival.

But Dorothy did survive and discovered in herself a passionate will to live and to serve the Cause of God. Challenging herself to learn the writings, use the prayers and practise meditation, she underwent another transformation of the spirit.

In 1931 Dorothy spoke at the first Louhelen Summer School near Davison, Michigan. She and Frank became more active in the Bahá'í community, although they maintained their membership of the Ohio Synod Lutheran Church. Unlike many other businesses, Frank's bakery flourished during the Depression – everyone needed bread.

In 1932 Mother Beecher had a fall, slipped into a coma and died ten days later. She was praised by the Guardian for her services to the Cause – and she had fulfilled her promise to 'Abdu'l-Bahá to train Dorothy well.

Shortly after Mother Beecher's death, one of Frank's employees asked him if he knew anything about an organization called Unity. Frank said he didn't but that his wife could tell him about the Bahá'í Faith, which taught the unity of humanity and of religion. Dorothy spent every spare moment preparing a talk for that first Sunday evening meeting. By February 1933 the first Lima Bahá'í group was formed with 18 members. Two study classes had to be established to meet the growing demands. By now Dorothy was spending 20 to 40 hours a week studying the teachings and preparing for these classes. Soon there were 29 active believers in Lima.

The success of the Bahá'í community seemed to threaten the local clergy, who began to stir up trouble. Dorothy asked the Guardian for his prayers. On 15 April 1934 a secretary wrote on his behalf:

> The forces of opposition which the clergy of Lima have used and are still using in order to counteract the continued advancement of the Faith of God will assuredly be vanquished. Their hatred, instead of quenching the flame of faith in the hearts of the faithful, will serve to intensify it. The believers should, therefore, be confident, and encouraged by such an assurance; they should redouble their efforts for the extension of the Cause . . .[9]

In November 1935 Dorothy wrote to the Guardian asking permission to go on pilgrimage. She felt that she had enough of her own money to afford the rather expensive trip. While Shoghi Effendi extended a hearty welcome to her, he suggested that she contribute part of her money to the National Fund, which at the time was in deficit. Dorothy promptly donated $2,000 to the Fund, and postponed, for the foreseeable future, her plans for pilgrimage. Four times more she would be disappointed in her desire to go on pilgrimage. Despite these disappointments, Dorothy obeyed and spent her energies on serving the Faith.

In the middle of the 1930s Dorothy expanded her work for the Faith to include public talks in nearby cities such as Cleveland, Milwaukee, Dayton and Pittsburgh. Her success in lecturing and teaching began to bring her national fame. Her star rapidly rising, in 1936 she lectured at Green Acre Bahá'í school. Louis Gregory, who would later refer to Dorothy as 'the foremost Bahá'í of the western world',[10] spoke to her following her class.

'That was a very good course, Dorothy,' he said. 'You thought so too, didn't you? Remember, the moment you begin to think it is Dorothy Baker who is accomplishing this work, that moment your service to Bahá'u'lláh ends.'[11] Horrified, Dorothy realized the truth. She resolved never again to give a talk unless she first asked God to strike her dumb rather than let her speak from herself.

In 1937 Dorothy was elected to the National Spiritual Assembly of the United States and Canada. By 1939 she had given dozens of talks on the Faith and was spending much time on its administration.

The early 1940s were filled with many Bahá'í activities for Dorothy. Not only did she serve on the Local and National Spiritual Assemblies but also on six national committees, including the Inter-America Committee, designed to spread the Bahá'í teachings into the southern hemisphere, and the National Race Unity Committee, which was one of her primary interests. She gave hundreds of talks on the Bahá'í Faith and began to speak about the Bahá'í teachings at college and university campuses across the country. Shoghi Effendi wrote to her in 1941 and 1942 encouraging her to do as much of this type of work as possible. She seemed able to inspire a vision of the essential unity of humankind, even during the years of war and racial prejudice. By 1952 she had spoken at 140 colleges.

Those who heard Dorothy speak were often deeply moved. Before she spoke she prayed at length, using the Tablet of Aḥmad. Although she studied diligently, she sought to speak from the heart and was recognized as one of the outstanding Bahá'í speakers of her generation.

In the mid-1940s Dorothy travelled to Mexico, Colombia, Venezuela, Peru and various other places in South and Central America in order to teach the Cause of God and to help the Bahá'í communities overcome their problems. Dorothy taught herself Spanish and although she was not wholly fluent, she had an unusual capacity for reaching the Latin people. They loved her spirituality and enthusiasm. To them, she was a great teacher.

In 1947 Dorothy wrote to the Guardian asking how she should allocate her time. Do not, he replied, 'over-tax your strength, but rather save it for your essential work on the NSA and in such important fields as Europe'.[12]

In 1948 Louise left to pioneer in Portugal and Dorothy flew to Europe, visiting England, Ireland, Scotland, Norway, Sweden, Denmark, the Netherlands, Belgium, Luxembourg, France, Switzerland, Italy, Spain and Portugal. She wrote in her report:

> Europe is frustrated and often sceptical, living in fear and believing in nothing. But Europe is groping too, and in search of a soul, and the part of her that finds it will go to almost any length to keep it. The new believers are the eyes of Europe; they alone can look ahead. To them the Cause is the difference between everything and nothing.[13]

In 1950 Dorothy represented the National Spiritual Assembly of the United States and Canada and the Inter-America Committee at the Fourth

International Teaching Congress of South America in Lima, Peru – the last of its kind before the formation of the National Spiritual Assembly of South America in 1951. Altogether, during the years between 1943 and 1952 Dorothy visited 16 Central and South American countries.

Dorothy was a successful teacher of the Faith wherever she travelled. She wrote to a friend:

> I have only two rules to give you. One is this: Look not to the creatures. Let your heart be supremely attached to our Beloved; then you can serve all of His children with detachment and joy, and never fail any of them, no matter what they do. When people make mistakes, you are only witnessing moments that are hook-ups between states of consciousness. It does not matter. The second rule is this: Make a joyous thing of the little services, because you can never tell which is little and which is big in God's sight. Bahá'u'lláh said: A single deed done in My Name is equal to the deeds of a hundred thousand years; nay, I ask pardon of God for this limitation, for such a deed is without limited reward. So when you speak His Holy Name, rejoice, be quiet in your heart, and know that this is a Very Great Occasion, an occasion of pure joy. He verily is the Lord of Hosts, and will assist you at all times.[14]

Dorothy relied utterly on the power of divine assistance. When asked how she remained so calm and confident, Dorothy invariably answered that 'only prayer could bring security'.[15] Prayer alone, however, was not enough to overcome difficulties. In a radio script Dorothy outlined how to face challenges:

> Three steps may be followed to achieve the desired results. First, be quiet; meditate on the problem from all angles, and turn to God with a sense of listening. If possible, use one of the beautiful prayers of Bahá'u'lláh for guidance. The second step is to take hold of a definite conclusion with the full help of reason, facts, and, above all, the sense of being assisted by God. Sometimes this step comes in a clear flash; sometimes not. I have often arisen from a prayer for guidance without a sense of having achieved the answer, only to find that every door opened for the right fulfilment. The third step is to proceed courageously, knowing that it is answered. Banish all fear or anxiety and walk confidently; act as if the desired results have already been accomplished. If you fail to do this, your prayer is perhaps like a beautiful child still-born and therefore of no avail to this world.[16]

By the end of the 1940s all of Frank and Dorothy's children were married; by 1951 they all had children of their own. In December of that year Edna True called Dorothy from the National Centre and read her a cable from Shoghi Effendi:

> HOUR NOW RIPE TAKE LONG INEVITABLY DEFERRED STEP CONFORMITY PROVISIONS 'ABDU'L-BAHÁ'S TESTAMENT CONJUNCTION WITH SIX ABOVE-MENTIONED STEPS THROUGH APPOINTMENT FIRST CONTINGENT HANDS CAUSE GOD TWELVE IN NUMBER . . .[17]

Dorothy was stunned when Edna read out her name; she thought Edna must have made a mistake. When the news was confirmed, she lost her voice for three days.

In 1953, at the request of Shoghi Effendi, Dorothy attended all four Intercontinental Teaching Conferences commemorating the inauguration of the Bahá'í Dispensation. In February 1953, on her way to the first Conference, in Kampala, Dorothy was at last able to make her pilgrimage to the Holy Land and to meet Shoghi Effendi. On so many occasions before her plans had been postponed for various reasons: the needs of the Fund, the need of her presence in Europe as a travel teacher, the persecution of the Bahá'ís in Lima, which limited her finances, and the war which made travel to Palestine impossible. Now she had seven nights to pray at the Shrines and to learn from Shoghi Effendi.

In August 1953, a few months after the launching of the Ten Year Crusade, Dorothy returned home briefly from her travels. She and Frank cabled the Guardian: 'OFFER SETTLE ISLAND CARIBBEAN AFTER INDIA. AWAIT DECISION REVERED GUARDIAN.' On 7 August Shoghi Effendi replied: 'HEARTILY APPROVE LOVING PRAYERS ACCOMPANYING YOU SHOGHI.[18] Four other members of the National Spiritual Assembly of the United States resigned that year to pioneer.

Before the Bakers could leave for Grenada, Dorothy had to attend the last Intercontinental Teaching Conference in New Delhi in October 1953. At the end of the event she was about to depart for home when the Guardian cabled that she and two other Hands should remain in India for another month. While Dorothy travelled across India, Frank made preparations to leave for Grenada. Then he received another letter from Dorothy: the Guardian had asked her to stay on yet another month.

Dorothy had a hectic schedule in India. By the end of November she had visited more than a dozen towns, giving as many as six talks in each. Every hour of every day was filled and Dorothy was quite exhausted and weak by the end of her stay.

According to Hand of the Cause Dr Muhájir, 'The Guardian told Dorothy Baker to go to India and discover why we could not teach the masses there. She went to several villages and then said, "This is the heart of India. Mass teaching will start in these villages."'[19] Afterwards Shirin Boman went to the villages where Dorothy had taught the Faith and 'whole villages became Bahá'í', one after the other.[20]

In Delhi Dorothy's luggage was stolen, so she travelled to Karachi with only the clothes she wore. On 9 January 1954 she spoke to the Bahá'ís of Karachi, calling for at least nine to pioneer. Twenty people arose in response. Yearning to offer these prospective pioneers something, Dorothy said to them, 'I wish I had something, but I have nothing to give you as a gift. All I can offer you is my life.'[21]

That evening, Dorothy travelled to the airport for her flight home. It seemed as though her departure would be delayed, as the papers needed to board the plane had not been delivered. At the last moment, a Bahá'í came running in, waving the papers over his head. Dorothy safely boarded. The plane made stops in Beirut and then in Rome where Dorothy mailed her final reports to the Guardian. At 9:31 on the morning of 10 January, the Comet lifted off for London, its final destination. Somewhere over the sea near the island of Elba, the plane exploded in mid air. All the passengers were killed. A few days later a handbag belonging to a passenger was found on the beach. Inside it was a Bahá'í pamphlet.

Three days following Dorothy's passing the Guardian cabled:

> HEARTS GRIEVED LAMENTABLE, UNTIMELY PASSING DOROTHY BAKER, DISTINGUISHED HAND CAUSE, ELOQUENT EXPONENT ITS TEACHINGS, INDEFATIGABLE SUPPORTER ITS INSTITUTIONS, VALIANT DEFENDER ITS PRECEPTS. LONG RECORD OUTSTANDING SERVICE ENRICHED ANNALS CONCLUDING YEARS HEROIC OPENING EPOCH FORMATIVE AGE BAHÁ'Í DISPENSATION. FERVENTLY PRAYING PROGRESS SOUL ABHÁ KINGDOM. ASSURE RELATIVES PROFOUND LOVING SYMPATHY. NOBLE SPIRIT REAPING BOUNTIFUL REWARD. ADVISE HOLD MEMORIAL GATHERING TEMPLE BEFITTING HER RANK IMPERISHABLE SERVICES. . .[22]

A month later Shoghi Effendi wrote to Hand of the Cause Hermann Grossmann:

The sudden passing of dear Dorothy Baker is indeed a great loss to the Faith, and leaves a sad gap in the ranks of the Hands of the Cause. She was exemplary in so many ways . . .[23]

# Amelia Engelder Collins
## 1873–1962

Shoghi Effendi called her the 'outstanding benefactress of the Faith'[1] for contributing so much to the Cause she loved so well. She was directly responsible for purchases of properties for the Faith in Africa, Europe, Australia, Persia, Central and South America, Geyserville, California and on Mount Carmel. Beyond her outstanding generosity, Amelia Collins, whose purity of heart and motive and whose sincerity and humility endeared her to the Master and the Guardian, was the first Hand of the Cause to be so designated by Shoghi Effendi in her lifetime.

Born in Pittsburgh, Pennsylvania, the seventh of the 14 children of Catherine Groff, an American, and Conrad Engelder, a German who had gone to the United States at an early age, Milly, as she was known, was raised, as a Lutheran, to appreciate those qualities of frugality and obedience so valued by the Central Figures of the Faith. As a young woman, she married a successful businessman, Thomas H. Collins, who had mining interests in Calumet, Michigan and Bisbee, Arizona.

Milly heard of the Bahá'í Faith from Nellie Stevison French and became a Bahá'í in 1919. She was encouraged by her Bahá'í friends to write a letter to the Master to ask for 'confirmation and strength'.[2] She reluctantly penned the letter, but afterwards spent an uneasy night. In the morning, when she opened the curtains of her room and saw the sun shining in, she asked herself whether the sun in all its grandeur needed a letter. She then tore up her note, confident that the spirit of the Master would understand. He did not, she was convinced, need to be bothered by her unworthy requests.

Shortly afterwards a Tablet from 'Abdu'l-Bahá arrived, the contents of which Milly kept secret for some time – she would only say that 'Abdu'l-

Bahá had addressed her as 'lady of the kingdom'.

After 'Abdu'l-Bahá's passing in 1921, Milly's earnest desire was to please her beloved Guardian. 'Out of the immense treasury of all the Writings', she wrote, 'I memorized one sentence and did my utmost to follow that one injunction. It served as a lamp of guidance, shedding light on the dark and obscure paths of my life. That phrase is from the Will and Testament of the Master, where He says that the friends should make Shoghi Effendi happy. Whatever step I took in my life, any vote cast in the Assemblies, any trip taken, even any thought, I would first ask myself whether my vote, words, trip or thought would make him happy. When I was sure, then I would take action without fear.'[3] In some ways Milly, who had no children, came to regard Shoghi Effendi as her own son, while continuing to honour him with all the reverence due his station.

Early in 1923, Milly made her first pilgrimage to Haifa, accompanied by her husband, Tom, who was not a Bahá'í. Milly often spoke of the great and loving kindness shown by Shoghi Effendi to her husband:

> The beloved Guardian had advised me always to be as kind and loving to my husband as possible. I tried always to follow this advice. Nor did I ever disobey Tom. For his sake I stopped having meetings in my home and even going to meetings. As time passed, gradually his heart changed and he allowed me to attend meetings and to hold Nineteen Day Feasts in our own home. But he never became a Bahá'í in this world.[4]

Tom Collins, for his part, admired Shoghi Effendi. Milly wrote:

> My husband was not a Bahá'í, but after two or three days of my pilgrimage he became so enthralled with love for the Guardian that one day, while looking at the new and uncompleted building of the Western Pilgrim House, he became angry and exclaimed, 'How can the Bahá'ís see an unfinished building every day in front of the Guardian's eyes? You [Milly] will see that the building is brought to completion.'[5]

When Tom passed away suddenly on board ship in 1937 while on a trip to Europe, Shoghi Effendi sent Milly words of comfort:

> GREATLY DISTRESSED SUDDEN PASSING BELOVED HUSBAND. HEART OVERFLOWING TENDEREST SYMPATHY. OFFERING SPECIAL PRAYERS. ADVISING

> GEYSERVILLE SUMMER SCHOOL HOLD BEFITTING MEMORIAL GATHERING RECOGNITION GENEROUS SUPPORT THEIR INSTITUTION. MAY BELOVED AID HIM ATTAIN GOAL HE WAS STEADILY APPROACHING CLOSING YEARS OF HIS LIFE.[6]

Shortly afterwards, when Milly was on her second pilgrimage, the Guardian said to her, 'Your husband is in the presence of the Master and is proud of your services.'[7]

Before Amelia Collins met Shoghi Effendi she yearned to know something of the next world, and believed the Guardian could enlighten her. She also longed to learn from him truths about prayer and the purification of one's heart and soul. During her first pilgrimage, Shoghi Effendi gave her some papers to study. Thinking them to be the answers to her questions, she was greatly disappointed to discover that they concerned the World Order of Bahá'u'lláh and its establishment. When the Guardian asked her the following day what her thoughts on the documents were, Milly answered frankly that she did not understand one thing. Later in the day Shoghi Effendi and Milly took a walk and the Guardian elucidated his theme with infinite patience. Milly still hoped that he would yet disclose the mysteries of prayer and the world beyond, but the Guardian simply explained to her the administrative principles of the Faith.

When she returned to the United States, she went directly to the National Convention, arriving just in time to hear the chairman read the very letter she had studied in the Holy Land. Called to speak before the delegates, Milly was able to draw on the Guardian's explanations to her to help the Bahá'ís appreciate his intention and to resolve misunderstandings.

Milly rendered so many services to the Cause that only a few of them can be touched upon here. In 1924, one year before its official recognition by Shoghi Effendi, she was elected to the National Spiritual Assembly of the Bahá'ís of the United States and Canada. She served on that body until 1933 and again from 1938 until she was called by the Guardian to the Holy Land in 1951. She was a member of various committees, including the National Teaching, Assembly Development and Inter-America committees. While on a cruise to Iceland in 1924 she introduced to the Faith Hólmfridur Arnadóttir, who made the first translation of Bahá'í literature into Icelandic.

In 1926 Milly sent a large sum of money to the Holy Land so that Shoghi

Effendi could develop the Bahá'í properties there. Later her contributions helped to embellish the area surrounding the Shrine of Bahá'u'lláh and to furnish the International Archives Building.

In 1936 Milly and Tom erected a large meeting hall, known as Collins Hall, at the Bahá'í summer school at Geyserville, California; the next year they donated a fully equipped dormitory for 50 people. Milly also purchased property for the Bahá'í summer school at Davison, Michigan.

Milly was the first to contribute to the Bahíyyih Khánum Fund for the erection of the Mother Temple of the West, and she also made substantial contributions to the Temple Fund of Persia. She made gifts of property near the Wilmette Temple and made possible the purchase of 19 temple sites in Latin America, Europe and Asia. She donated the entire sum for the purchase of many national Ḥaẓíratu'l-Quds and endowments on five continents.

In 1934 Milly paid for the first publication of Bahá'í literature in Amharic. Later she defrayed the cost of publishing four volumes of *The Bahá'í World.*

Milly travelled extensively for the Faith, particularly after Tom passed away. Between 1937 and 1953 she visited virtually every Bahá'í centre in the United States and Canada to help the Bahá'ís deepen in their Faith, and she went on many missions for Shoghi Effendi. For example, in 1942, at the behest of the Guardian, Milly travelled to Argentina to help the Bahá'ís erect a fitting monument to May Maxwell, who had passed away there and was buried in the Quilmes Cemetery in Buenos Aires.

Milly was among the first to teach native Americans, her work resulting in the formation, in Macy, Nebraska, of the first Indian Local Spiritual Assembly.

On 22 November 1946 the Guardian sent a cable to Milly:

> YOUR MAGNIFICENT INTERNATIONAL SERVICES EXEMPLARY DEVOTION AND NOW THIS SIGNAL SERVICE IMPEL ME INFORM YOU YOUR ELEVATION RANK HAND CAUSE BAHÁ'U'LLÁH. YOU ARE FIRST BE TOLD THIS HONOUR IN LIFETIME. AS TO TIME ANNOUNCEMENT LEAVE IT MY DISCRETION.[8]

It was not until 24 December 1951 that the Guardian publicly announced her appointment, along with that of 11 others.

In November 1950 the Guardian decided to create the International Bahá'í Council and Milly received a cable from Shoghi Effendi inviting her to the Holy Land to serve on it. In January 1951 he announced his decision to the Bahá'í world, and in March of the same year wrote to the Bahá'ís of East and West:

> Greatly welcome assistance of the newly-formed International Council, particularly its President, Mason Remey, and its Vice-President, Amelia Collins, through contact with authorities designed to spread the fame, consolidate the foundations and widen the scope of influence emanating from the twin spiritual, administrative World Centres permanently fixed in the Holy Land constituting the midmost heart of the entire planet.[9]

Although Shoghi Effendi referred to Amelia Collins as the 'outstanding benefactress of the Faith', it should never be thought that his kindness and devotion to her was for the material good she could do for the Cause. Indeed, in January 1947 the Guardian wrote to Milly, 'The high rank you now occupy [as a Hand of the Cause] . . . has been conferred solely in recognition of the manifold services you have already rendered, and is, by no means, intended to be a stimulus or encouragement in the final path of service.'[10] The many letters he wrote to her over the years reflect his appreciation of her manifold services. In 1926 he wrote, 'My dear and precious fellow-worker: Your steadfastness in service, your selflessness and devotion to the work you are engaged in greatly encourage me and inspire me in my work. Your many services, past and present, will ever be remembered with praise, gladness, and gratitude.'[11] And again, 'I never cease praying for you from the bottom of my heart and wish you success in the glorious work that lies before you.'[12]

When Milly sent her contribution for the erection of the superstructure of the Báb's Shrine in 1944, Shoghi Effendi responded through his secretary, 'He wants you to know that this is the first contribution he has received for this glorious undertaking, and he is not surprised that it should come from you!'[13] In another instance both the Guardian's and Milly's contributions were received at the same time; Shoghi Effendi cabled her: 'OUR RECENT CONTRIBUTIONS TEACHING CAMPAIGN SYNCHRONIZED EVIDENCE OUR HEARTS ATTUNED NOBLE CAUSE.'[14]

One of the evidences of Milly's generosity is the Collins Gate at the head of the path leading to the Shrine of Bahá'u'lláh. Milly, from childhood, had always wanted a gate. When she was small, she had built a tiny house for her dolls and tried to make a gate across the entrance. Later, when she and her husband built a house in New England, Tom asked her about a gate, but she did not want to spend the money at the time. When Milly embraced the Faith she forgot about her gate, along with other worldly things. Many years later, when Milly was serving in Haifa, she offered the Guardian a contribution for his personal needs. Some time after this she received a letter from Shoghi Effendi and a photograph of a very large and imposing gate. The Guardian had purchased the gate with the money Milly had offered him. This gate became known as the Collins Gate.

In spite of her wealth, Milly lived simply, and often in one room. She would alter last year's dress to make it more fashionable, rather than purchase a new one. The luxuries she denied herself were often viewed as necessities by others. Simplicity, sweetness of character, purity of motive and instant obedience characterized her life. Milly never made mention of her contributions to the Faith; indeed, many of them were not known by the Hands of the Cause until after the passing of Shoghi Effendi, when the minutes of the National Spiritual Assemblies were read. She wanted her contributions to be kept confidential. She would say, 'Just send the money; don't mention my name.'[15]

In later years Milly suffered greatly with arthritis. With the Guardian's permission, it was often her habit to return to the desert heat of Arizona each summer to recuperate and to attend to her affairs. The day after she arrived back in the Holy Land from one such journey in 1957, she received the news of the passing of Shoghi Effendi in London.

The very next morning Milly left Haifa for England, carrying rose petals from the threshold of the Shrine of the Báb. 'Don't be sad,' Shoghi Effendi had said to her just before he left for London in June 1957. Now she assisted Rúḥíyyih Khánum with the funeral arrangements and gave her the love and support the Guardian's widow so needed in her hour of tragedy and shock. The rose petals were spread over the body of Shoghi Effendi before he was buried.

Perhaps Milly, as she accompanied her fellow Hand during those sorrow-laden days in London, recalled how Shoghi Effendi had once removed his scarf and placed it around her neck when she was ailing in bed. How the warmth of that action and wrap had cheered her and speeded her recovery.

After the passing of Shoghi Effendi, Milly, one of the nine Hands resident in the Holy Land, continued, despite her advanced age, to serve the

Faith. In 1958 she attended the Intercontinental Conference in Frankfurt as the representative of the Guardian, and in November 1960 she laid the cornerstone of the European House of Worship in Germany. She attended every one of the annual Conclaves of the Hands of the Cause, even though her health was failing and she was in constant pain. So frail was she at her final Conclave in 1961 that she had to be carried upstairs to the meeting in a chair. Even then she spoke with 'great conviction and strength' and recited a prayer in the Shrine of Bahá'u'lláh 'every word of which took wings to the Abhá Kingdom'.[16] After this Milly was completely bedridden.

On her deathbed, Milly asked Hand of the Cause Mr Faizi to chant for her, as he had done so often in the past. When he had finished he translated for her, saying, 'It was one of the prayers of the Master in which He recommends that we open our eyes and behold the grandeur and beauty of the Abhá Kingdom . . . When man's soul spreads its wings and gets ready for the eternal flight, he sees some signs of the majesty of God's creation and the immensity of the world beyond.'[17]

On 1 January 1962 Amelia Collins passed away in the arms of her beloved Rúḥíyyih Khánum. The next day, Milly's body was laid to rest in the Bahá'í cemetery, next to the Afnán who had built the 'Ishqábád Temple.

Milly was eighty-eight years of age at the time of her death. Her life was indeed the embodiment of 'Abdu'l-Bahá's words written to her in 1919:

> from the bounties of His Holiness Bahá'u'lláh, My hope is that thou mayest daily advance in the Kingdom, that thou mayest become a heavenly soul, confirmed by the breaths of the Holy Spirit, and may erect a structure that shall eternally remain firm and unshakable.[18]

On her passing the Hands of the Cause in the Holy Land cabled the Bahá'í world:

> WITH DEEPEST REGRET SHARE NEWS BAHA'I WORLD PASSING DEARLY LOVED HAND CAUSE OUTSTANDING BENEFACTRESS FAITH AMELIA COLLINS. UNFAILING SUPPORT LOVE DEVOTION BELOVED GUARDIAN DARKEST PERIOD HIS LIFE BROUGHT HER UNIQUE BOUNTY HIS DEEP AFFECTION ESTEEM CONFIDENCE AND HONOUR DIRECT ASSOCIATION WORK WORLD CENTRE. SIGNAL SERVICES EVERY FIELD BAHA'I ACTIVITY UNFORGETTABLE. PURCHASE SITE FUTURE MASHRIQU'L-ADHKAR MOUNT CARMEL GENEROUS GIFTS HASTENING CON-

STRUCTION MOTHER TEMPLES FOUR CONTINENTS ACQUISITION NATIONAL HAZIRATU'L-QUDS ENDOWMENTS CONSTANT SUPPORT HOMEFRONTS WORLD-WIDE TEACHING ENTERPRISES AMONG HER MUNIFICENT DONATIONS. URGE NATIONAL ASSEMBLIES HOLD MEMORIAL GATHERINGS PARTICULARLY TEMPLES COMMEMORATE HER SHINING EXAMPLE CEASELESS SERVICES MAINTAINED UNTIL LAST BREATH.[19]

# 'Alí-Akbar Furútan
# 1905–2003

The Hand of the Cause of God 'Alí-Akbar Furútan was born in Sabzivár, in the province of Khurásán, Iran on 29 April 1905. His father, Karbalá'í Muḥammad-'Alíy-i-Sabzivárí, was a well-known Bahá'í and openly taught the Faith. He suffered great persecution from the townspeople and from his mother and wife, who were fanatical Muslims. This unpleasant situation continued until Muḥammad-'Alí's wife accepted the Cause through a dream about 'Abdu'l-Bahá, when her son was about four years old. Muḥammad-'Alí's mother also became a believer.

Mr Furútan spent his childhood years in Sabzivár and studied in a *maktab* (traditional school), learning reading and writing and studying the Qur'án. In 1904 the persecution of the Bahá'ís of Sabzivár grew intense and Muḥammad-'Alí was condemned to death. Only the intervention of the leading mujtahid of the city, a relative, prevented his execution. By 1914 the persecutions had reached such a level that Muḥammad-'Alí determined to leave the city. His wife had a dream of the Master, who instructed the family to pioneer to 'Ishqábád. Thus the whole family left Sabzivár for Russia.

The Bahá'ís of 'Ishqábád owned two schools in the vicinity of the Mashriqu'l-Adhkár, one for boys and the other for girls. Mr Furútan started his studies at the school for boys, and, upon the completion of his elementary education, was asked by the school committee to teach the first grade when he was only 14 years old. He was engaged in this service for three years and then transferred to a Russian secondary school.

Mr Furútan was very active in the Bahá'í community of 'Ishqábád. While still in secondary school he was appointed to the National Youth Committee, was elected its secretary, and founded a news sheet for the youth. He was also the director of the Maḥmúdiyyih Bahá'í library. He began to lecture at Bahá'í meetings while still a youth.

In the summer of 1923 Mr Furútan was instructed by the Local Spiritual Assembly of 'Ishqábád to go on a trip to Baku, where he participated in some very successful teaching activities for three months.

In 1925, after completing his high school studies, Mr Furútan was appointed principal of the two Bahá'í schools and the two Bahá'í kindergartens in 'Ishqábád. He won a scholarship to the University of Moscow, where in 1926 he furthered his studies in education and child psychology.

In his first year at the University of Moscow, he received a letter from the Teaching Committee of 'Ishqábád suggesting that he leave his studies and continue his teaching activities. He was deeply disturbed by this letter, as it presented him with a decision he could not make alone. He consulted with the Local Spiritual Assembly of Moscow and was advised to write to the Guardian and ask for his guidance. He received a reply dated 16 November 1926:

> Your letter was received by the Guardian of the Cause of God . . . and brought much joy to his heart. He spoke of you and praised God that you . . . are assisted by divine confirmations in your education, that you intend to complete it and wish to diffuse the heavenly fragrances, to serve the Faith, and to teach the Cause of God. This intention attracts the confirmations of the One true God and the favours of the Kingdom of eternity. Therefore, he cherishes the hope that you will eventually attain the goal of your desire . . .
>
> Teaching the Cause of God is possible under all circumstances, even through trade and commerce and through proper conduct, as it is said that goodly deeds and a praiseworthy character are in themselves the teachers of the Cause. Therefore, any individual, in whatever profession he may be engaged if he conduct himself in a praiseworthy manner and exemplify the human perfections, he will himself become the sign of the propagation of the Word of God and will hoist the banner of the glory of the Cause of God.
>
> Concerning the determination of your duty, the Guardian stated that you should in no way be disturbed and distressed. If in all circumstances you resort and cling to the cord of consultation you will be confirmed in all your efforts. In all cases, you should refer to the Spiritual Assembly and act according to the wishes and approval of its respected and elected members.
>
> Whatever the result of the consultation of the Spiritual Assembly may be,

that is the correct course of action and will meet with the good pleasure of the Lord . . .

The beloved Guardian also remembered your parents and prayed for them.

Shoghi Effendi wrote in his own hand in the margin of this letter:

O spiritual Friend:
This servant in this illumined spot prays at the Sacred Threshold from the depths of his heart for your peace of mind, prosperity and success, so that you may excel in divine knowledge and material learning.[1]

Mr Furútan then consulted with the Local Spiritual Assembly, which decided unanimously that he should continue his studies.

In 1928 Mr Furútan was elected a member of the Local Spiritual Assembly of Moscow. He also taught Bahá'í classes for children and youth and gave Persian lessons.

While he was in Russia Mr Furútan began the travels which would characterize his life. For example, in the summer of 1927 he went on a travel teaching trip to the Caucasus, where he visited many friends and seekers in Baku, Gandzha and Tiflis. He visited the resting places of Leo Tolstoy in Yasnaya Polyana, of Tchaikovsky in Leningrad (St Petersburg) and of Ivan Sergeevich Turgenev, a well-known Russian writer. He also went sight-seeing in Nizhni-Novgorod and Astrakan and journeyed to Arkhangelsk to observe the schools in that region as part of his academic studies.

Mr Furútan completed his studies in the field of child psychology in 1930. His thesis, 'On the method of Shapushnikov and his book *The Live Voice for Children*', was published in the official journal of the Ministry of Education of the Soviet Union in the same year. Despite his academic excellence, Mr Furútan was expelled from the Soviet Union for his involvement in Bahá'í activities. Returning to Iran via 'Ishqábád, he wrote to Shoghi Effendi giving a comprehensive account of the Bahá'í activities in Russia, including the details of his exile. In May 1930 the Guardian replied in a letter written on his behalf:

Your detailed report containing the news of Bahá'í activities in Russia, reached the eminent presence of the Guardian . . . The report was comprehensive and complete, and was acceptable in his sight. He expressed his favour and grace,

> and praised and admired your spirituality, radiance, perseverance, and devotion. It is certain that the manifestation of these divine sentiments . . . will increase your spiritual strength, will further your devotion, will bring joy and happiness to your heart and soul, and that the afflictions and sorrows which you have encountered will be removed and forgotten.

To this the Guardian appended a marginal note in his own hand:

> O spiritual friend:
> Be not disturbed and saddened by the current difficulties, the present situation in that region will not last for ever. What will remain and persist will be the institutions which the friends have established in that land. Patience and endurance are needed. He will indeed aid the weak through the power of His might, and help His loved ones with the exalted angels of His most glorious Kingdom.
>
> For the present you should remain in Persia, and engage in the activities of the Cause in that country. It is my hope that in the days to come you will also be enabled to render great and outstanding services in the countries of Russia.[2]

In April 1930 Mr Furútan attended the Bahá'í convention in Ṭihrán. The delegates decided that he should either stay in Ṭihrán and become an employee of the government or go to the province of Adhirbáyján as a travelling teacher. He chose the latter. A few days later he left for Tabríz, and on arrival there began to hold firesides, children's classes and classes for Bahá'í women.

In 1931 Mr Furútan married 'Aṭá'íyyih (Ataieh) Khánum, who was from a prominent Bahá'í family. Later that same year Effie Baker arrived in Adhirbáyján, on the instructions of the Guardian, to photograph its historic sites for *The Dawn-Breakers.* Mr Furútan and his wife accompanied her to Saysán, a small village near Tabríz. They discovered that, despite its large Bahá'í community, Saysán did not have a Bahá'í school. The Furútans sought the permission of the Guardian to move to the village to establish a school. He approved their plans, showering them with loving encouragement and appreciation.

Mr Furútan and his wife were making the necessary preparations for their move to Saysán when Mr Furútan received a telegram from the Local Spiritual Assembly of Ṭihrán, asking him to come to the capital immediately. Despite the harsh winter and the difficult road conditions, he managed to get to Ṭihrán to meet with the Assembly. The Assembly told him that he had been appointed principal of the Tarbíyat school for boys. Mr Furútan explained that the Guardian had already approved his plans to go to Saysán and the Assembly therefore postponed the appointment.

With the assistance of the Local Spiritual Assembly of Saysán and the village Bahá'ís, the building of the school was soon completed, and close to 700 boys and girls began their education. At the end of the first academic year Mr Furútan sent a report to the Guardian, who replied through his secretary:

> Your comprehensive and refreshing report . . . on the condition of the Bahá'ís of Saysán . . . and [their] activities, was received . . . and brought much joy and happiness to his heart . . . It is hoped that in the future . . . you will succeed in rendering greater services, and will perform more glorious feats . . . Please God that you may also be confirmed and honoured to render international services.[3]

In 1934 the first National Spiritual Assembly of Iran was elected. Mr Furútan, attending the Convention as a delegate from A<u>dh</u>irbáyján, was elected to the Assembly. He served as its secretary for 24 years.

In the same year, on the instructions of Shoghi Effendi, Mr Furútan took up the position of principal of the Tarbíyat School, replacing Mr 'Azízu'lláh Miṣbáh, a well-known scholar and writer. When the school refused to remain open on a Bahá'í holy day in December 1934, the Ministry of Education closed it and all other Bahá'í schools in the country permanently.

Early in 1941 Mr Furútan, accompanied by his wife, mother and eight-year-old daughter, made his first pilgrimage to the Holy Land, where he spent 23 delightful days. Shoghi Effendi said to him, 'You are the secretary of both the National and Local Spiritual Assemblies. The affairs of the National Spiritual Assembly are conducted in a very organized manner, and I testify to your work. Your services are now local and national, and they will be international in the future.'[4]

During the next ten years Mr Furútan undertook a number of activities in addition to his services as secretary of the National Assembly. In 1946 he was invited by the Iranian Radio and Broadcasting Service to give a series of lectures on child psychology and education. The programme was cancelled after six months, at the instigation of the mullás, although in later years the text of the talks was published, with the permission of the Ministry of Education, as *Majmú'ih Risálát Tarbíyatí* (Essays on Education). In 1950 Mr Furútan wrote an article for the *Bahá'í News* commemorating the 100th anniversary of the Martyrdom of the Báb. And always he encouraged the believers, visiting numerous communities.

In December 1951 Mr Furútan was appointed a Hand of the Cause of God. This marked, he later wrote, a 'momentous transformation' in his 'spiritual life'.[5] One of his first tasks was to encourage the Iranian Bahá'ís to contribute towards the cost of the building of the Shrine of the Báb.

In 1953, at the beginning of the Ten Year Crusade, Mr Furútan embarked on the international services Shoghi Effendi had foreseen for him. He attended all the Intercontinental Teaching Conferences – at Kampala, Chicago, Stockholm and New Delhi. Among the highlights of these travels was the dedication of the Mother Temple of the West in Wilmette. At the end of the New Delhi Conference Shoghi Effendi instructed him to journey to Australia and New Zealand. He spent one year travelling, visiting 16 countries in Australasia, North America and Europe. This journey was one of his longest travel teaching trips.

In 1954 he went on a second pilgrimage to the Holy Land. On the instructions of Shoghi Effendi, he returned to Iran and visited all the major towns and Bahá'í centres in the country.

In 1955 a wave of severe persecution of the Bahá'ís began in Iran, resulting in the seizure of the Ḥaẓíratu'l-Quds of Ṭihrán, anti-Bahá'í disturbances across the country and the killing of seven Bahá'ís in Hurmuzak. Mr Furútan, acting on behalf of the National Spiritual Assembly of Iran, sent many petitions to the government in an attempt to halt the persecution.

In 1956, on the instructions of Shoghi Effendi, Mr Furútan travelled to Turkey to visit and encourage the Bahá'ís. In 1957 he set out for Indonesia to represent the Guardian at the Convention in Jakarta which was to elect the first Regional Spiritual Assembly of South-East Asia, one of 16 new National and Regional Spiritual Assemblies to be formed in 1956 and 1957.

On the morning of 5 November 1957 Mr Furútan received a cable from Amatu'l-Bahá Rúḥíyyih Khánum which, he later wrote, 'violently shook the core of my being and benumbed me':[6] the Guardian had passed away in London the day before. In need of consolation himself, Mr Furútan did not attend the Guardian's funeral, but rather remained in Ṭihrán, at the request of the National Spiritual Assembly of Iran, to support the friends and to attend the many memorial gatherings.

Anxious about the future of the Cause at this precarious time, when Bahá'u'lláh's Faith seemed unshepherded, Mr Furútan read and re-read the Guardian's messages of June and October 1957 and took comfort from them:

> The security of our precious Faith, the preservation of the spiritual health of the Bahá'í communities, the vitality of the Faith of its individual members, . . . the fulfilment of its ultimate destiny, all are directly dependent upon the befitting discharge of the weighty responsibilities now resting upon the members of these two institutions [the Hands of the Cause of God and the National Spiritual Assemblies].[7]

> This latest addition [the appointment of another contingent of Hands of the Cause] to the band of the high-ranking officers of a fast evolving World Administrative Order . . . calls for, in view of the recent assumption by them of their sacred responsibility as protectors of the Faith, the appointment by these same Hands, in each continent separately, of an additional Auxiliary Board, equal in membership to the existing one, and charged with the specific duty of watching over the security of the Faith.[8]

On 18 November 1957 Mr Furútan joined his fellow Hands in Haifa for their first Conclave. He was among the nine Hands appointed to serve at the Bahá'í World Centre. Thus, he and his wife left Ṭihrán to settle in Haifa.

The following year the Hands of the Cause made the decision that the Universal House of Justice would be elected in 1963. Over the next few years Mr Furútan visited Turkey, participated in the ceremony to lay the foundation stone of the Mother Temple of Europe, attended the first National Conventions of Brazil and Uruguay, and visited various communities in the British Isles. Following the election of the Universal House of Justice, Mr Furútan stayed in Haifa, serving as one of the Hands of the Cause resident in the Holy Land.

In 1965 Mr Furútan was asked by the Universal House of Justice to visit Turkey and Iran to encourage the Bahá'ís to fulfil the goals of the Nine Year Plan. Later he passed through India, where he visited important centres and met with the country's Vice-President and the Minister of Education.

In 1967 six Intercontinental Conferences were held in different parts of the world in honour of the centenary of Bahá'u'lláh's proclamation to the kings and rulers. The Universal House of Justice appointed Mr Furútan to represent it at the Conference in Kampala. Before leaving for Uganda Mr Furútan, with the other five Hands representing the Universal House of Justice at the Conferences, prayed together at the Holy Shrines, then departed for Turkey, where they offered prayers at the House of Bahá'u'lláh in Edirne before dispersing to their different destinations.

In Kampala, 450 Bahá'ís from 24 nations gathered to commemorate the proclamation of Bahá'u'lláh to the kings and rulers of the world. Mr Furútan spoke of the arduous life of Bahá'u'lláh in Adrianople. He urged the Bahá'ís to be united and to obey the Law of God so that the victory might be won for Bahá'u'lláh. After the Conference he and Enoch Olinga were interviewed for six minutes on national television, watched by more than half a million people.

In 1968 Mr Furútan attended the Palermo Conference, held to commemorate the centenary of Bahá'u'lláh's arrival in the Holy Land. More than 2,300 Bahá'ís from 67 countries attended the Conference. In the closing session, describing Bahá'u'lláh's incarceration in the Most Great Prison, Mr Furútan said:

> Here Bahá'u'lláh was condemned to perpetual imprisonment to break His will and end His influence; He responded by renewed proclamation. Here He revealed many of His most important Writings including the *Kitáb-i-Aqdas*, and here the flame of His light burned most brightly.
>
> Sulṭán 'Abdu'l-'Azíz is dead and forgotten, while thousands of Bahá'ís have gathered to celebrate the victory of his Victim. 'Chains did not prevent this Cause; imprisonment did not become a barrier . . . From the beginning of the world never before has the Cause of God been proclaimed so openly.' We too must thrive and proclaim in the face of adversity.[9]

In 1969 and 1970 Mr Furútan made extensive travels in the United States, Canada, Alaska and Hawaii. Stopping at numerous cities and visiting many Bahá'í schools, he spoke on a variety of topics, including religious and racial prejudice. Of racism he said:

> The friends are well aware that racial prejudices have for many long years disturbed the peace and tranquillity of mankind, and have stained the earth

> with the blood of people in different countries. One race says, 'We are white', another, 'We are black', the third, 'We are red', the fourth, 'We are brown', and the fifth asserts that it is yellow. They have fought with each other and destroyed each other's homes only because of difference in the superficial colour of their skins, which is due to nothing but the effect of the rays of the sun. Even at the present time the flames of this destructive fire have not been extinguished. Blessed are we, the people of Bahá, that we follow this supreme utterance of Bahá'u'lláh: 'O well-beloved ones! The tabernacle of unity hath been raised; regard ye not one another as strangers. Ye are the fruits of one tree, and the leaves of one branch.'[10]

Elsewhere he spoke of the bounty of recognizing Bahá'u'lláh, saying that we do not yet realize our good fortune. While we cannot realize the glory and majesty of Bahá'u'lláh, we can strive to obey Him and to teach His Cause. He said that the believers are few in number, but what matters more than quantity is quality. We must teach, he said, according to the example set by 'Abdu'l-Bahá, which is to provide the healing message of Bahá'u'lláh according to the needs and beliefs of our listeners. Otherwise, the remedy we offer is like a prescription without an examination. Assistance from the Supreme Concourse, he concluded, will come through our prayers, devotion and willingness to serve.

Mr Furútan's travels in subsequent years were extensive and, as the Guardian had hoped, truly international in scope. His most cherished trip was his return in April 1990 to the Soviet Union, where, following the collapse of Communism, Mr Furútan was able to return to many of the scenes of his youth, as the Guardian had promised. On this journey he visited the Bahá'ís in eight cities across four Republics from the south to the north and attended the Convention for the re-election of the Local Spiritual Assembly of Moscow, which had lapsed more than 50 years before. In 1991 he again visited Moscow, to represent the Universal House of Justice at the election of the National Spiritual Assembly of the Soviet Union. In 1992 he travelled to Tallin and Budapest to represent the Universal House of Justice at the first National Conventions of the Baltic Republics and of Hungary.

Mr Furútan spoke five languages and published many works on child education. Among his books are *Principles of Education*, *Scientific Essays*, *A Glimpse of History* and *The Story of My Heart*. His popular book *Mothers, Fathers and Children* is a translation of Essays on Education and in 1991 was published in Russian. He also compiled *Stories of Bahá'u'lláh*.

Asked to comment on those philosophies which suggest that one's circumstances, good or bad, are the outcome of one's expectations or fears, Mr Furútan wrote:

> According to the rules of psychology, a person's beliefs and thoughts form the principal foundation of his behaviour and conduct – meaning that his outward actions are the manifestations of his beliefs. Therefore, it is incumbent upon every believer to learn that which the Manifestation of God has urged him to do, and that which He has forbidden. To understand and realize this objective I have always pondered on two verses from the Kitáb-i-Aqdas – both when I was a young student at the University of Moscow surrounded by atheists and agnostics, and now that I have entered old age.
>
> The two verses are these:
>
> > Recite ye the verses of God every morn and eventide. Whoso faileth to recite them hath not been faithful to the Covenant of God and His Testament, and whoso turneth away from these holy verses in this Day is of those who throughout eternity have turned away from God . . . (*Kitáb-i-Aqdas*, para. 149)
>
> > Read ye the Tablets that ye may know what hath been purposed in the Books of God, the All-Glorious, the Ever-Bounteous. (*Kitáb-i-Aqdas*, para. 36)
>
> I always mention this in gatherings with the Bahá'ís, and especially I point this out to the youth, that we must act according to these blessed instructions so that we may not be diverted from the straight path, and do not become entangled in undesirable philosophies.[11]

Throughout his life Mr Furútan strove to serve the Bahá'í community. During the final years of his life he followed a demanding programme of activities at the World Centre, including regular meetings with the pilgrims. He passed away on the Day of the Covenant (26 November) 2003 at the Pilgrim Reception Centre in Haifa, and was buried in the Bahá'í cemetery in Haifa.

The Universal House of Justice announced his passing in the following message:

> With profound feelings of loss, we announce the passing, yesterday evening, on the Day of the Covenant, of the dearly loved Hand of the Cause of God

'Alí-Akbar Furútan. Having addressed the assembled pilgrims as was his practice, he paused to exchange a few words with some of the Russian-speaking friends; then, as he was leaving the room, his heart failed. He had fulfilled his longing to serve the Cause to his last breath.

Born in Sabzivar, Iran, on 29 April 1905, 'Alí-Akbar Furútan moved with his family to 'Ishqabad in what was then Russian Turkestan, and, through his years of school and university, he took an active part in the work of the Bahá'í communities of 'Ishqabad, Baku, Moscow, and other parts of Russia. In 1930 he was expelled from the Soviet Union for his involvement in Bahá'í activities and, from that time on, played an ever more significant role in the work and administration of the Iranian Bahá'í community. In December 1951 he was among the first to be appointed by Shoghi Effendi as Hands of the Cause of God. Following the passing of the Guardian, he was one of the nine Hands of the Cause selected, at their first Conclave, to serve as Custodians in the Holy Land. For the remaining forty-six years of his life he laboured strenuously at the World Centre, undertaking journeys throughout the world, assisting, advising, and enthusing the friends and their national and local institutions. The journeys culminated in 1990 and 1991 with visits to the newly re-emerging Bahá'í communities of the countries of the Soviet Union.

'Alí-Akbar Furútan's single-minded devotion to the Faith and its Guardian, the vital role he played in the establishment of the Administrative Order in Iran, his contribution to the spiritual and material education of children, his services as a Hand of the Cause of God, and his unswerving support of the Universal House of Justice together constitute an imperishable record of service in the annals of the Cause. His penetrating mind, his loving concern, and his sparkling humour are ineffaceable memories in the hearts of the thousands of believers with whom he spoke.

While praying in the Holy Shrines for the progress of 'Alí-Akbar Furútan's illumined soul in the Abhá Kingdom, we supplicate Bahá'u'lláh to bless likewise the fruition of the seeds he sowed in this world.

We extend our loving sympathy to his daughters, Írán Muhájir and Parvín Furútan, to his granddaughters, and to all other members of his family.

We advise friends in all lands to commemorate his passing and to hold memorial services in his honour in all Mashriqu'l-Adhkárs.[12]

# Ugo Giachery
# 1896–1989

Ugo Giachery was a native of Palermo, Sicily. He was born on 13 May, four years before the turn of the century. As a child he experienced the influence of the Church in that Catholic country, and late in life he still recalled childhood memories of the nativity scene at Christmas time: 'the crib of the infant Jesus . . . surrounded by clay angels and awed figures of men and animals, trees and flowers and burning candles, and the music of a mechanical carillon, repeating a seraphic tune over and over again.'[1]

An aristocrat in the literal sense of the word, Ugo Giachery as a youth developed an appreciation for gardening from the gardeners on his family's estate in Sicily. His knowledge of this avocation would, years later, delight the Guardian of the Bahá'í Faith when the two men together developed ideas for the gardens at the Bahá'í World Centre. As the climate and flora of the Giachery estate were similar to those of the Holy Land, Dr Giachery was particularly able to appreciate what the Guardian envisaged for those gardens.

During his youth Dr Giachery studied English, a language he described as offering freedom of expression and influencing the course of his life. In his teens, an English teacher whom he greatly admired urged him to read Shakespeare, Byron and Shelley. As a result, he said, his partiality for the language was inflamed.

Ugo Giachery once described his education as being based mainly on Greek and Roman culture, and recalled how, in his childhood, a learned tutor fascinated him with tales of Greek mythology. He earned three degrees: two from the Royal Technical Institute of Palermo, and the other, his doctorate in chemistry, from Palermo's Royal University. As a young man he also served in the King of Italy's Grenadier Guards.

For some years Dr Giachery taught chemistry at university level and undertook research in the field of inorganic chemistry and metallurgy. He was also interested in foreign banking and the tourist trade. For two decades he worked to develop tourist travel to all continents. His hobby was archaeology, on which he lectured extensively.

It was while he was working at a tourist agency in Italy that Dr Giachery met two Bahá'ís, Mrs Loulie Mathews and her daughter Wanden. Together they travelled to the United States in September 1924.

While in the United States Dr Giachery met his beloved wife, Angeline Westergren, through mutual friends. A native of Sweden and related to its royal family, Angeline had been educated in her home country and in England. She particularly enjoyed mathematics, liberal arts, literature and poetry. As a small child she studied music and became an accomplished violinist. While in Boston in the early 1920s she was introduced to the Bahá'í Faith. She immediately embraced it wholeheartedly and sincerely, and served it with remarkable fervour. She spent much time with those early believers who had been in the presence of 'Abdu'l-Bahá and took accurate notes of their experiences.

Ugo Giachery was absolutely devoted to Angeline. They married in New York City on 24 February 1926. Either shortly before or shortly after his marriage, Dr Giachery became a Bahá'í.

The Giacherys settled in New York. Dr Giachery wrote that Angeline arranged music recitals in order to attract influential people to the Cause. She would open her home to seekers and conquer hearts with her 'melodious eloquence'.[2] Dr Giachery himself was an active Bahá'í from the first, serving as chairman of the New York State Teaching Committee and treasurer of the New York City Local Spiritual Assembly.

As early as 1924 Ugo Giachery became acquainted with the Guardian's lofty spiritual stature through his letters written in majestic English. Revealing his own passion for the language, Dr Giachery described Shoghi Effendi's writings:

> When Shoghi Effendi's first messages appeared, followed soon by his translations of the Sacred Writings, it was clear that a new style came into bloom, a new standard was set, and a perfect balance was achieved between the poetic and flowery Eastern languages of the original texts and the rationalistic Western idioms. I vividly remember spending long hours reading and living

> every word, feeling the joy of being part of some reality which reflected an unseen world as yet unknown to most human beings.[3]

> As a writer Shoghi Effendi achieved a degree of brilliancy that cannot be equalled. He dealt with an intangible subject in a way no other writer can ever approach . . . His pen penetrated the most remote by-ways of human feelings, bringing tears to the eyes and gripping the heart with a variety of new emotions. Moreover, in his translations, his use of the English language reached the highest form of epic. Because his life had been interwoven with sacrifice, suffering and renunciation, his mind became a pure channel for the spirit; he could translate in ample rhythms, in masterly phrases, the mysteries of the subconscious in a flow of inspiration which poured forth from divine sources.[4]

Dr Giachery himself struggled to translate the major sacred writings of the Faith into Italian. He felt that translating is an art requiring knowledge, imagination and mastery of the two languages in order to retain the style, form and character of the original text. This is particularly difficult in cases where the two languages have different grammatical structures or lack some corresponding words. He thus first turned to a somewhat easier task. In 1946, with Angeline's help, he translated Esslemont's *Bahá'u'lláh and the New Era* into Italian.

In 1946 Shoghi Effendi launched North America's second Seven Year Plan, making the expansion of the Bahá'í Faith in Europe its major goal. The Giacherys decided to sell their home in New York and to settle in Rome as pioneers, sailing to Europe in February 1947.

Angeline particularly was distressed by the conditions they found in Rome, so recently occupied by the Allied forces. The misery and destruction in Italy was widespread and there were many cold and hungry children living on the streets. The Giacherys were, however, greatly cheered by an encouraging cable from the Guardian: 'SUPPLICATING ABUNDANT BLESSINGS NOBLE MISSION.'[5] At Riḍván 1948 the first Local Spiritual Assembly of Rome was elected. Shoghi Effendi requested a photograph of the Assembly, arranged for its framing, and placed it at the head of his bed in the room he occupied when staying overnight in the Mansion of Bahjí.

Through what he calls a 'fortunate coincidence'[6] Dr Giachery began a working relationship with Shoghi Effendi almost immediately after his arrival in Italy. Although he was 'practically unknown'[7] to the Guardian, Shoghi Effendi charged him with the responsibility of securing carved marble and other materials for the outer structure of the Shrine of the Báb, then just beginning its construction. Thus began a nine-year association during which Dr Giachery worked closely with Shoghi Effendi on this and other projects. 'The greatest gift received from the Omnipotent, during my lifetime', he wrote years later,

> was the privilege of being closely associated with Shoghi Effendi for a number of years. No words will ever be able to describe the depth of my devotion and of my abiding love for him, nor the transformation I underwent under the influence of his warm and tender affection; an influence that changed my character, my outlook on life, my habits, and opened my eyes to the unending vista of new aspirations and horizons.[8]

The site for the Shrine of the Báb had been selected by Bahá'u'lláh and pointed out by Him to His eldest son on the occasion of one of His visits to Mount Carmel in the evening of His life. In 1899 the mangled remains of the Báb and His fellow martyr, Mírzá Muḥammad-'Alíy-i-Zunúzí, Anís, reached 'Akká via a circuitous route from Iran, having survived 50 lunar years of dangerous and uncertain concealment. The same year, 'Abdu'l-Bahá laid the foundation stone of the edifice which would house the Báb's remains and the construction of which He would oversee during the next ten years.

During those years, 'Abdu'l-Bahá was delayed by Covenant-breakers, resisted by government bureaucrats and hampered by circumstances in His efforts to complete the historic charge of His beloved Father, causing Him to cry out, 'Every stone of that building, every stone of the road leading to it, I have with infinite tears and at tremendous cost, raised and placed in position.'[9] At last, at Naw-Rúz in the year 1909, He was able, with His own hands, to lay the wooden casket containing the sacred remains into its marble sarcophagus.

Shoghi Effendi, who as a youth of 12 witnessed this moving event, wrote years later:

> When all was finished, and the earthly remains of the Martyr-Prophet of Shíráz were, at long last, safely deposited for their everlasting rest in the bosom of God's holy mountain, 'Abdu'l-Bahá, Who had cast aside His turban, removed

> His shoes and thrown off His cloak, bent low over the still open sarcophagus, His silver hair waving about His head and His face transfigured and luminous, rested His forehead on the border of the wooden casket, and, sobbing aloud, wept with such a weeping that all those who were present wept with Him.[10]

Several years passed before Shoghi Effendi felt the time propitious to erect a fitting superstructure over the original edifice in accordance with 'Abdu'l-Bahá's instructions. In 1915 'Abdu'l-Bahá said to a pilgrim, 'The Shrine of the Báb will be built in the most beautiful and majestic style.'[11] In 1928 Shoghi Effendi began to excavate the rock behind the Shrine and then built three extra rooms onto the original six rooms completed by the Master. In the centre of the square building rested the body of the Báb. He envisaged that around the building would be erected a majestic arcade. In 1942 Shoghi Effendi asked Sutherland Maxwell to design the arcade and dome. Two years later a scale model was completed and the American Bahá'í community was notified of the Guardian's intention to complete the Shrine as soon as circumstances permitted.

Shoghi Effendi charged William Sutherland Maxwell with the task of locating appropriate materials and craftsmen to build the Shrine. Unable to place any contracts in Palestine, owing to the war of independence then raging, Mr Maxwell went to Italy in hopes of contracting with a firm in Carrara for granite columns for the arcade. In a letter to Ugo Giachery dated 6 April 1948, the Guardian, through Rúḥíyyih Khánum, asked that he assist Mr Maxwell in dealing with Italian companies.

Dr Giachery, who felt that an act of Providence had placed him in Italy at this time of need, met Mr Maxwell some ten days later. Together they were able to locate the best marble for the arcade and to place the necessary contracts. A close relationship was established between Mr Maxwell, acting for the Guardian, and the contracting firm's architects and technical experts. Dr Giachery's role 'was to act as personal representative of the Guardian for selection of material, supervision of its artistic carving, for the packing and shipment of the finished work, for its insurance, and as the clearing agency for the voluminous mail and exchange of technical data.'[12]

Over the next five years Ugo Giachery's contribution to the work on the Shrine was prodigious, but the difficulties he faced were formidable. The cessation of the British Mandate in 1948 had provoked a mass exodus of nearly all Palestinian artisans, and the Guardian looked to Italy to supply both materials and craftsmen. In Italy, however, public services were virtually non-existent; railways were severely damaged; rolling-stock had been destroyed or confiscated; shipping was at a standstill; millions of the male population were still prisoners of war in nearly every continent; Rome was still occupied by Allied forces; the reparation indemnities being paid to the Allied Powers were staggering; and food, electricity and water were either rationed or unavailable. Naturally, the nation's industrial power was geared to reconstructing the country and not to foreign projects. Such was the demand for building materials within Italy itself that they were almost impossible to obtain for export and every item – including cement, steel, lumber, nails, wire, pipes, paint, switches and mouldings – required a licence issued by the Ministry of Industry and Commerce. The lengthy procedures needed to obtain these licences, and the approval of the Ministries of Foreign Trade and Finance, occupied many hours during which Dr Giachery waited in various offices all over Rome and filled out large numbers of forms.[13] Shipping space was virtually unavailable, waters were still mined, and shipping was often confiscated off the shores of Israel by hostile warships.

In Italy's shattered economy Ugo Giachery searched for quarries which met Sutherland Maxwell's requirements and whose accesses had not been blown up by the retreating enemy. He meticulously translated the discussions held in English and Italian, transcribed drawings and plans, and accurately communicated a myriad of technical details and terms to the World Centre at a time when the means of communication with the Holy Land were uncertain. As well as being faced with all these difficulties, he was regularly harassed by the police for being a Bahá'í.

Unexpected crises occurred as well. A drought in 1949 limited industrial electric power to three working days each week, curtailing workers' use of the great pneumatic drills, chisels and cutting saws. The partner of a key contracting firm unexpectedly died. Steamers did not arrive as scheduled, keeping cargo destined for the Holy Land on a wharf for days and days. An earthquake forced the evacuation of an entire seaside town, leaving no one to load a ship. The captain of another ship was alarmed by a plane as cargo was being unloaded in Haifa, and returned hastily to Italy with half the cargo still on board. A fire broke out on another steamer. From still another ship, a lighter with a full load of stone went to the bottom of the sea in the port of Haifa. Later, William S. Maxwell, the architect, passed away, in 1952.

In spite of such formidable obstacles, Dr Giachery oversaw to a successful conclusion the work carried on by scores of men and artisans who quarried tons of marble and granite and carved columns, pilasters, capitals, star panels, arcade arches and walls, monumental corners, cornices and parapet panels for shipment in what has been described as the largest prefabricated building ever to be moved from the European continent to any other point in the world. Seventeen different steamers were required over a period of 19 months to ship nearly 800 tons of finished material in 1,800 wooden cases. During this period 4,587 finished pieces were transported from Italy to Mount Carmel.[14]

Owing to unstable political and economic conditions in the Holy Land, the Guardian's original plan had been to complete only the arcade of the Shrine, in time for the 100th anniversary of the martyrdom of the Báb in 1950. However, the beauty of the arcade as it unfolded on Mount Carmel moved him to undertake the completion of the entire superstructure. Therefore, on the first day of September 1950 he sent a cable to Dr Giachery asking for an estimate of the cost and time to complete the octagon. A contract was eventually signed in Rome, on 21 October, for the Chiampo marble from which the octagon would be carved.

Once the work of cutting and carving the stone began it was determined that the original inner Shrine would not support the octagon, drum and dome, the combined weight of which was estimated at 1,000 tons. Ugo Giachery was called upon to supply 100,000 pounds of cement and eight huge Manesmann pipes – hollow steel columns 15 feet high and 1 foot wide – so that eight huge piers could be sunk through the original Shrine into the bedrock. After many difficulties arising from Italian government regulations, Dr Giachery was eventually able to send this material to Haifa on two ships in April 1951.

Meanwhile, Shoghi Effendi asked Dr Giachery for further estimates to complete the drum and dome, and to conclude contracts for a beautiful wrought-iron balustrade for the octagon, iron window frames, stained glass windows, an oak door with wrought-iron grille, 12,000 tiles of over 50 variations in size for the dome, gold to cover the tiles, and, to embellish the terraces outside the Shrine, lamp-posts and artistic wrought-iron gates. Total tonnage from Italy had now risen to 1,600 tons.[15]

Many years later Ugo Giachery commented about the five-year period in which the superstructure of the Shrine of the Báb was constructed, during which he was somehow able to overcome so many obstacles in order to carry out Shoghi Effendi's instructions and deadlines:

I still wonder how it was possible to obtain all that was needed and in such large quantities. I can only say that I was wholly confident in the power that emanated from the World Centre of the Faith; I knew that if the Guardian asked for something, nine-tenths of the problem had been solved . . . I never informed him of the obstacles, the labour and the heartaches involved to obtain licences, nor of the many hours of work required each day, month after month for nearly five years. I had had to move fast from Ministry to Ministry, from committees to individual officials, all scattered in different parts of Rome, waiting long hours in antechambers, filling out forms, even paying dues in advance so that the applications could be considered. I am sure the Guardian knew well my anxiety and cares and pains.[16]

The Guardian did indeed know of Dr Giachery's dedication to his task and of the difficulties he faced in carrying it out. While Ugo Giachery was on pilgrimage in 1952, Shoghi Effendi told him and those sitting at the dining table:

The service you have rendered is not sufficiently appreciated today, but it will be fully appreciated in the future . . . you worked for so long all alone; and no one appreciates this more than I, myself. When you are alone, you have such a big weight to carry. Single-handed, you have rendered an historic service to the Cause.[17]

Dr Giachery, who was embarrassed by Shoghi Effendi's words of praise and gratitude, wrote that the Guardian 'was always ready to give comfort, verbally or in writing, to encourage, to praise and to stimulate to such a degree that one felt the urge to place at his disposal life, time and possessions within the range of one's capacity'.[18]

Ugo Giachery's 'love for the Guardian . . . blossomed into a tenacious unbounded devotion'[19] and he felt 'a mysterious, unbreakable bond' that 'influenced and guided' him 'in all the manifold activities' Shoghi Effendi called upon him to perform.[20] He learned from the Guardian an attribute which brought about victories within amazingly short periods of time:

Perseverance was one of Shoghi Effendi's most noble qualities, and taught me many a lesson. I learned much from him in pursuing and accomplishing any given task. It is part of human nature to give up when attempts fail at the beginning; only a few persist in an endeavour when beset with obstacles of all

> sorts. His instructions to me, always to go or appeal to the highest authorities, to seek always the best, to accomplish things in the shortest time possible, and to persevere under all circumstances, became my second nature while I was privileged to work for the Cause under his personal guidance. In nearly every letter I received from him over a period of many years, the word 'persevere' is repeated. It had the power of a talisman for me . . .
>
> Were I to relate all the difficulties, some nearly insurmountable, that I met during the years of supervising production of the carved marble and other material needed to construct the Báb's Shrine and the International Archives, I should have to write at much greater length. In nearly every case I did not trouble the Guardian with these obstacles. Clad with the armour of perseverance, in the certainty that his prayers were following me . . . I knew that the impossible could be accomplished.[21]

Reflecting on the challenge of arranging shipping in 1948, when few ships were available and the space on those was inadequate, Dr Giachery described the essential quality behind perseverance. 'Only faith', he wrote, 'could have removed the difficulties.' 'If frustration or despair', he added, 'had taken hold of me, even for one brief instant, this whole chain of prodigious events would have been interrupted. Under the most distressing circumstances we never doubted, feeling confident that a propitious solution would soon be at hand. This was the lesson I had learned in working with Shoghi Effendi.'[22]

Thus not only did Dr Giachery have faith, which enabled him to accomplish so many difficult things, and devotion to the Bahá'í Faith, he was also totally loyal to the Guardian, with whom he had a profound relationship. His vision of the future made him ambitious for the progress of the Faith, but he was not ambitious for himself. In fact, he warned Bahá'ís that personal ambition can destroy an individual.[23]

Convinced of the ultimate triumph of the Faith of Bahá'u'lláh, Shoghi Effendi said one evening to Dr Giachery and the other pilgrims, 'If I should be influenced by the chaotic condition which exists in the world, I would remain passive and accomplish nothing.' Ugo Giachery felt that this unbounded faith of Shoghi Effendi in the victory of the Cause 'provided him with the power to accomplish things which by human standards would be considered extremely difficult, even impossible'.[24]

Dr Giachery was the recipient of several dozens of letters from the Guardian providing guidance, encouragement, praise and gratitude.

Then, in December 1951, Shoghi Effendi cabled the Bahá'í world that Ugo Giachery had been appointed among the first contingent of the Hands of the Cause. A few months later, in March 1952, Dr Giachery was appointed to the International Bahá'í Council. He was further honoured when Shoghi Effendi announced, in a cable to the Intercontinental Conference in New Delhi, that he had named the door on the western side of the Shrine of the Báb 'Báb-i-Giachery'.

> MOVED REQUEST ATTENDANTS CONFERENCE HOLD BEFITTING MEMORIAL GATHERING PAY TRIBUTE HAND CAUSE, SUTHERLAND MAXWELL, IMMORTAL ARCHITECT ARCADE SUPERSTRUCTURE SHRINE. FEEL MOREOVER ACKNOWLEDGEMENT BE MADE SAME GATHERING UNFLAGGING LABOURS VIGILANCE HAND CAUSE UGO GIACHERY, NEGOTIATING CONTRACTS, INSPECTING DESPATCHING ALL MATERIALS REQUIRED CONSTRUCTION EDIFICE, AS WELL AS ASSIDUOUS, CONSTANT CARE HAND CAUSE, LEROY IOAS, SUPERVISING CONSTRUCTION BOTH DRUM DOME. TO TWO DOORS SHRINE RECENTLY NAMED AFTER FIRST TWO AFOREMENTIONED HANDS, OCTAGON DOOR, NOW ADDED, HENCEFORTH ASSOCIATED THIRD HAND WHO CONTRIBUTED RAISING STATELY, SACRED STRUCTURE.[25]

In February 1952 Ugo Giachery made his first pilgrimage. In Shoghi Effendi's presence, he was filled with a sensation of continuity and safety, of contingent matters becoming unimportant, of obstacles within himself being levelled. He felt a sense of new-found freedom and perspective. Over a period of weeks he felt that he was being enlightened on every subject the mind could conceive, by the Guardian, whose spiritual perception was astonishing and whose knowledge was immense.

The following month, Shoghi Effendi indicated that he wanted Ugo Giachery's services to continue beyond the completion of the Shrine of the Báb. This news brought Dr Giachery much inner happiness, as he wished only to help lighten Shoghi Effendi's burdens. Charging Dr Giachery with the purchase of such items as pedestals, marble blocks, columns and bird baths for the beautification of the gardens at the World Centre, Shoghi Effendi told Ugo Giachery that a great Shrine of untold magnificence would be built in future decades for the Supreme Manifestation. The present requirement was merely to embellish the Shrine of Bahá'u'lláh.[26]

Thus, near the end of April 1952 Shoghi Effendi began to make dramatic improvements to the grounds surrounding the Shrine at Bahjí.

Dr Giachery was astonished by the changes made in so short a time under the Guardian's masterful direction. Within one week of intense labour the gardens at Bahjí were transformed from a 'sea of sand' into a 'garden and paradise of incomparable beauty'.[27] Later, Ugo Giachery received a sketch from Shoghi Effendi for a new door to the Shrine of Bahá'u'lláh, with a request to have a scale drawing made and to get estimates for the work. This task was accomplished over several months. Shoghi Effendi, pleased by the door's 'simplicity, perfect execution and highly decorative beauty', sent a cable to Dr Giachery thanking him for his work, a message that brought 'much cheer' to his heart.[28]

During this same period, however, Shoghi Effendi was under attack by Covenant-breakers, who sought to prevent him from moving forward with his plans to beautify the grounds at Bahjí by taking legal proceedings against him and calling him as a witness in a court case. As this unsettling period unfolded, Shoghi Effendi shared with Ugo Giachery the history of the perfidious conduct of the Covenant-breakers. Agonized by the visible suffering of the Guardian over this latest attack, Dr Giachery

> became conscious that the Divine Covenant was assailed with vehemence by ruthless, satanic people, and that while the mass of believers throughout the world were unaware of this grave danger, he, Shoghi Effendi, single and alone, was its defender, protected only by the armour and shield of his faith in God and His Covenant.[29]

As Ugo Giachery listened, Shoghi Effendi

> went into the details of the provocations, the fiendish machinations, the defiant and open hostility, backed at times by, and in alliance with, sworn external enemies of the Cause for the express purpose of destroying the Divine Covenant, a spiritual madness which had contaminated almost all the surviving members of the family of Bahá'u'lláh.[30]

Dr Giachery had to prevent himself from taking Shoghi Effendi in his arms, he so wished to shield the Guardian from further suffering and assure him that there were thousands of believers who were ready to shed their blood for him. Later, Ugo Giachery was one of three representatives the Guardian sent to Jerusalem to make representations to the Prime Minister that the court case concerning Bahjí was a purely religious matter. This appeal was successful and the matter was removed from the civil courts. Thus Dr Giachery helped prevent further machinations of the Covenant-breakers.[31]

In July 1953 Dr Giachery travelled to Stockholm to attend the Intercontinental Conference as the Guardian's special representative 'honoured by direct association with the newly-initiated enterprises at the world centre of the Faith'.[32] He carried with him a reproduction of a small portrait of the Báb to show to the Bahá'ís gathered at the historic conference, and the message from Shoghi Effendi elucidating the character and purpose of the ten-year World Crusade and rallying the participants to prosecute the tasks that lay ahead.

A few months later, in October, Ugo Giachery travelled to the Intercontinental Conference in New Delhi bearing a pen and ink drawing of the future International Archives building to display to the participants. Over the next four years he worked on the construction of that building, undertaking many of the same tasks he had performed for the superstructure of the Shrine of the Báb. Describing the magnitude of this project, he wrote:

> It took seventeen ships to carry the total of one thousand tons of carved marble for the Archives building from Italy to Haifa. Other ships were used to transport structural steel, cement, floor and roof tiles, lumber, stained and clear glass, small and large iron window-frames, varnish and paint for the interior, chandeliers, electric and other wires, the main and the vestibule bronze doors, the oak balustrades and plinth for the balconies, lamp-posts and many other items, such as chain-lifts, nails, drain-pipes. The one-third section of every column weighed two tons; each capital and the six anthemia, one ton each. The roof tiles weighed forty tons and were packed in 7,200 cardboard boxes with the additional use of 25,000 metres of gummed paper in strips.[33]

For several years, Shoghi Effendi had envisioned the building of a Mashriqu'l-Adhkár on Mount Carmel in fulfilment of one of 'Abdu'l-Bahá's longings. A drawing was completed in May 1952, from which a wooden model was made in Rome. The model was placed on view at the 1953 Chicago Intercontinental Conference and subsequently placed in the main hall of the Mansion of Bahjí, awaiting the day when the Temple could be erected. Shoghi Effendi planned to place a marker in the middle of the land set aside for the Mashriqu'l-Adhkár and asked Ugo Giachery for his ideas as to what would be suitable. Dr Giachery suggested an obelisk such as the Romans had used to celebrate great events. The Guardian liked this idea and asked Ugo Giachery to supervise its construction. Over the next few months the obelisk was made in Italy and Dr Giachery shipped over 20 tons of marble to the Holy Land. Troubles with neighbouring countries prevented the erection of the obelisk until 1971, for security reasons.

On the occasion of their pilgrimage in December 1954, Dr Giachery and Angeline were invited to accompany Shoghi Effendi to the Temple site on Mount Carmel. There they prayed together and visualized the future House of Worship. On 25 December, following a succession of memorable days at the World Centre, the Giacherys left Shoghi Effendi's presence for the last time.

On 4 November 1957, Ugo Giachery's reason and strength were shattered by a telephone call in the early afternoon from Amatu'l-Bahá Rúḥíyyih Khánum, informing him that the Guardian had died. He managed to get a plane from Rome to London immediately, joining Rúḥíyyih Khánum, Hasan Balyuzi and John Ferraby at the Ḥaẓíratu'l-Quds. In the succeeding days, he helped to select the cemetery, a burial plot and an appropriate coffin. Together with Rúḥíyyih Khánum and Hasan Balyuzi he officially registered Shoghi Effendi's death. The attar of rose given to Dr Giachery by Shoghi Effendi some time before was used to anoint the Guardian's body and a Bahá'í ringstone he carried in his pocket was placed in the Guardian's mouth. He and his fellow Hands kept vigil by the casket. At the funeral service, Dr Giachery felt his heart pounding to the breaking point.[34]

Rúḥíyyih Khánum decided that the most fitting memorial for the resting place of Shoghi Effendi was a marble column. Dr Giachery was called upon to supervise the preparation of the marble and other materials needed for the monument. Meanwhile, Rúḥíyyih Khánum purchased a Dover-stone balustrade to enclose the plot where the monument would be erected, as well as stone urns and a wrought-iron monumental gate for the entrance. In October 1958 she supervised the erection of the sepulchre.

In 1957 Ugo Giachery was already 60 years old. Nine years of serving the Guardian and of close collaboration with the Sign of God on earth had suddenly come to an end. A modest man, he was reluctant to mention his own sterling services, choosing instead to fix his eyes upon the Guardian whom he loved so dearly: the Guardian who, as well as calling upon him to assist in projects at the World Centre, had asked him to assist in the selection of a site for the first Italian Mashriqu'l-Adhkár, to represent him at the Intercontinental Conferences in Stockholm and in New Delhi in 1953, to go to Iran following those conferences in order to encourage assemblies and individuals in the goals of the World Crusade, to take steps aimed at forming the first National Spiritual Assembly of the Bahá'ís of Italy and Switzerland, to receive contributions to the European Continental Bahá'í Fund, to take up chairmanship of the International Appeal Committee to the United Nations in connection with the persecution of the Faith in Iran in 1955, and to represent him at the convention of the Iberian Peninsula in 1957. As remarkable as were these services and little as Ugo Giachery could have anticipated in 1957, he still had another 32 years of work for the Cause of God to lay at the feet of Shoghi Effendi.

In May 1958 Dr Giachery represented the Guardian at the Intercontinental Conference in Chicago and exhibited the portraits of Bahá'u'lláh and the Báb to the participants. In July that same year he attended the Intercontinental Conference in Frankfurt and in the following year visited Bahá'í centres in the Iberian Peninsula, Panama, Mexico, British Honduras, Haiti, the Dominican Republic, Jamaica, Cuba, Puerto Rico and the Virgin Islands. In 1960 he visited the same countries as well as Nicaragua, Guatemala, Costa Rica and the United States. He represented the World Centre at the National Conventions of Haiti and Venezuela in 1961 and of Italy and Switzerland in 1962.[35] He was a member of the International Bahá'í Council until 1961, served as chairman of the National Spiritual Assembly of Italy and Switzerland from 1953 to 1964, and was chairman of both the Local Spiritual Assembly of Rome and the National Teaching Committee of Italy during these years.

When the Giacherys returned to America and settled in California in 1964, Ugo Giachery was able to travel often to Central America and the Caribbean region. He also travelled in Europe, Indonesia, Australia, New Zealand and the Pacific area. He represented the World Centre at the Conventions of the Leeward, Windward and Virgin Islands, of Belize, and of Australia in 1967.

It was during his journey to the Pacific in 1967 that Dr Giachery travelled to Samoa and presented *The Proclamation of Bahá'u'lláh* to His Highness Malietoa Tanumafili II on 27 October. The discussions between the two men led the Malietoa to investigate the Bahá'í Faith further and eventually to accept it. Dr Giachery returned to Samoa in 1968 to confirm the Malietoa's allegiance to the Cause. In audiences on 16 January and 11

February His Highness declared his belief in Bahá'u'lláh and Dr Giachery informed the Universal House of Justice, although the public announcement was not made until March 1973.[36]

On 9 April 1968, at the request of the Universal House of Justice, Dr Giachery presented *The Proclamation of Bahá'u'lláh* to the Vatican through Cardinal Paolo Morella in the Vatican City. In August of that year he represented the Universal House of Justice at the Oceanic Conference in Palermo, Sicily.

The author of many articles on the Bahá'í Faith in English and Italian, Dr Giachery wrote a remarkable essay entitled 'One God, One Truth, One People' comparing the 1963 Peace Encyclical of Pope John XXIII with the teachings of Bahá'u'lláh and demonstrating how the Encyclical parallels the principles of peace enunciated by the Founder of the Bahá'í Faith.[37]

Meanwhile Angeline, having painfully detached herself from her friends in Italy in 1964, initiated intensive teaching activities, including several firesides each week and teaching trips that took her to Arizona, Oregon, Washington and Yukon Territory. A large cabin used as a Bahá'í school, located north of Whitehorse and capable of holding 40 students, was named in her honour. In Alaska she won the affection of the Indians, the elders of one tribe bestowing upon her the title 'Princess of Tlingit Eagle Tribe'. She loved the peoples of the Arctic regions of the planet and visited northern countries from Finland to Alaska.

In 1969 Ugo and Angeline Giachery settled in the Principality of Monaco and Dr Giachery's activities centred around 15 European and Near Eastern countries. Each year he attended several European summer schools, usually accompanied by Angeline. In 1975 he visited Iran and in 1976 he accompanied the Malietoa on a pilgrimage to the resting place of Shoghi Effendi in London. In the same year some 130 Bahá'ís heard him speak on the Tablets of the Divine Plan at Lake Garda, and he also attended the National Teaching Conference in France. He presented the Bahá'í teachings to Franz Joseph II, Prince of Liechtenstein and he represented the Universal House of Justice at the international conference in Helsinki.

In 1975 the Universal House of Justice announced that work would soon begin on the construction of its seat on Mount Carmel. Dr Giachery was once again involved in the work he had at one time undertaken for Shoghi Effendi. In June 1981 he accompanied Count Paolo Marzotto, president of the firm in Chiampo, Italy, that had undertaken the marble work, and some of the marble workers, to Haifa to view the completed building.

In 1980 Angeline became frail, sorrowing that she could no longer travel and see the believers. During her illness 'Dr Giachery was extremely devoted to (her) care and many people surrounding him in Monaco were deeply moved by his total devotion and tenderness toward (her)'.[38] Her end came suddenly, on 23 April 1980. She was buried near Monaco in Cap d'Ail Cemetery, facing the Mediterranean Sea. Her inconsolable husband designed her sepulchre. Following her passing, he penned these poetic words:

> The solemn beauty of her native land, bejewelled by thousands of rivers and lakes, and dotted with serenely tranquil and majestic forests, impressed itself upon her gentle spirit and found reflection in her stainless character. Highly sensitive to the divine intelligence and exquisite harmony that rule the universe, she found perfection in all created things. The inner happiness which suffused her being was crowned by her peerless love for the Creator.[39]

Dr Giachery travelled three more times to Samoa. On 31 December 1980 he was received by His Highness the Malietoa Tanumafili II in audience. In September 1982 Dr Giachery visited Samoa after representing the Universal House of Justice at the Canberra international conference. His travels were much restricted after this, owing to his age and infirmity. However, he greatly wished once again to visit his friend in Samoa and thus he travelled back to the South Pacific in 1989.

Arriving on 16 April, Dr Giachery was formally greeted by His Highness Malietoa Tanumafili II, who walked the long distance to the plane and placed a garland of flowers around Ugo Giachery's neck. Dr Giachery was then ushered into the royal limousine.

During the next three months he saw His Highness often and was officially received at Vailima. He attended several services at the House of Worship and spoke to the believers publicly and privately. He was, however, in pain. Planning to return to his home in Europe, he experienced a sudden change in his physical condition. He was admitted to hospital, where he passed away on the evening of 5 July.

His funeral service was attended by His Highness Malietoa Tanumafili II, the Prime Minister, four Ministers of Cabinet, four Counsellors, five Auxiliary Board members, representatives of six national communities of the Pacific, and over 200 believers from many parts of the country. The Counsellor, Mr 'Alá'í, eloquently spoke of Dr Giachery's unique relationship with the growth of the Cause in Samoa. Prayers in Italian, Persian, English, Maori, Tongan, Fijian and Samoan were read. He was interred on the mountainside at Tiapapata, Apia, overlooking the Pacific Ocean.

The Universal House of Justice sent this message in memory of his remarkable life:

> DEEPLY GRIEVED LOSS VALIANT, INDEFATIGABLE, DEARLY LOVED DISTINGUISHED HAND CAUSE DR UGO GIACHERY. HIS PASSING IN COURSE HISTORIC VISIT SAMOA ADDS FRESH LAURELS TO CROWN ALREADY WON DURING MINISTRY BELOVED GUARDIAN, AND REINFORCES SPIRITUAL DISTINCTION VAST PACIFIC REGION, ALREADY BLESSED BY INTERMENT FOUR OTHER HANDS.
>
> HIS MAGNIFICENT ACCOMPLISHMENTS AS MEMBER AT LARGE OF INTERNATIONAL BAHÁ'Í COUNCIL IN CONNECTION RAISING SUPERSTRUCTURE SHRINE OF THE BÁB, WHICH PROMPTED GUARDIAN TO NAME ONE OF THE DOORS OF THAT NOBLE EDIFICE AFTER HIM, HIS PAINSTAKING EFFORTS IN PROMOTING ON THE LOCAL, NATIONAL AND INTERNATIONAL LEVELS, PARAMOUNT INTERESTS OF THE FAITH, HIS NOTABLE ACHIEVEMENT IN ESTABLISHMENT ITALO-SWISS NATIONAL SPIRITUAL ASSEMBLY ON EVE LAUNCHING TEN YEAR CRUSADE, HIS OUTSTANDING QUALITIES OF ZEAL, FIDELITY, DETERMINATION AND PERSEVERANCE, WHICH CHARACTERIZED IMPERISHABLE RECORD HIS ARDUOUS LABOURS – ALL COMBINE TO RICHLY ADORN ANNALS FAITH OVER PERIOD HIS SUPERB, ASSIDUOUS EXERTIONS, AND UNDOUBTEDLY ASSURE HIM BOUNTIFUL REWARD IN KINGDOM ON HIGH.
>
> ADVISE ALL NATIONAL SPIRITUAL ASSEMBLIES HOLD BEFITTING MEMORIAL GATHERINGS HIS NAME, PARTICULARLY IN MASHRIQU'L-ADHKÁRS IN RECOGNITION HIS UNIQUE POSITION, SPLENDID SERVICES.[40]

# Hermann Grossmann
# 1899–1968

In the first decades of the 20th century, under Kaiser Wilhelm II, the Germans were class conscious, respectful of monarchy, meticulous record-keepers and strictly proscribed by hundreds of petty regulations. They were steeped in tradition, confident of the superiority of the German race and restless for military adventure. When war inevitably broke out in 1914, Germany was the second largest industrial nation in the world, close behind the United States.

As a German, Hermann Grossmann suffered through two world wars, first as a soldier in the First World War and later as a Bahá'í in the Second World War. Born in Rosario, Argentina and raised by loving and tolerant parents, during the first ten years of his life Hermann was exposed in the city of his birth to peoples of different races and convictions who lived together in friendship and freedom. Following his family's return to Germany, he found the contentious and intolerant attitudes in the imperialistic Reich to be in sharp contrast to his early experiences in Argentina.

A sensitive young man, Hermann rejected the rigid thinking of his countrymen. His service in the German army in France during the final two years of the First World War was a shattering experience. He returned to his home weary, disappointed and despairing. As the broken German nation struggled against anarchy, upheaval and rampant inflation, Hermann searched for answers to the suffering. Was humanity destined to endure misery, hatred and destruction? If God created humankind for love and sent successive divine Beings to illumine the earth, perhaps it was time for another Messenger to come?

While American Bahá'ís Harlan and Grace Ober were on pilgrimage in the Holy Land in 1920, 'Abdu'l-Bahá asked them to travel to Germany. They accepted an invitation to speak on the Bahá'í Faith to the Theosophical Society in Leipzig in July of that year. Hermann was a student at the University of Leipzig and decided to attend the meeting. Arriving late, he saw a radiant woman proclaiming to the audience that all people are the leaves of one tree and the flowers of one garden. The young man was immediately attracted to the message and accepted the new Revelation instantaneously.

As was the custom, Hermann wrote a letter to 'Abdu'l-Bahá accepting the Faith and enthusiastically expressing his deep gratitude for having been allowed to find the divine truth, and his desire to serve the Bahá'í Cause. 'Abdu'l-Bahá replied on 9 December 1920:

> O thou who hast been guided by the Light of Guidance!
>
> Thy letter has been received. It indicated that thou hast turned thy face toward the Abhá Kingdom. Yield thee thanks unto God that thou hast been enabled to rend the veils asunder, to gaze on the beauty of the Sun of Reality, and to walk in the path of the Kingdom. Thou shouldst be eternally obliged and thankful to those who were the cause of thy guidance, inasmuch as they conferred heavenly life upon thee and enabled thee to be admitted into this resplendent Kingdom. Upon thee rest the Glory of the Most Glorious.[1]

From that time on Hermann devoted his life to studying the Bahá'í writings and to serving the Cause.

Lina Benke became a Bahá'í the same night as Hermann, and shortly afterwards her husband also accepted the Faith. Soon the Benkes and Hermann were regularly visiting Alma Knobloch, who was then living in Leipzig. Miss Knobloch had become a Bahá'í in 1903 and had settled in Germany in 1907 at the request of 'Abdu'l-Bahá to establish the Faith in that country. Alma was therefore able to nurture Hermann and the Benkes in the Faith and help them deepen their understanding of its teachings.

Before long Hermann returned to Hamburg. To his great joy, his mother and sister accepted his new Faith. Hermann began immediately to serve the Cause. He received a doctorate from the University of Hamburg in 1923 for his thesis on the use of leather substitutes in the shoe industry and began work as an associate manager of Koch and Company, a firm that produced leather substitutes and cardboard products.

During some practical training at a factory in Pirmasens, Hermann met Anna Hartmuth, and they married in 1924. The couple lived first in Hamburg, then moved to Weinheim and eventually, in 1933, Hermann built a house in Neckargemünd for his own family, and another one for his parents and sister. The Grossmann home became the focal point for Bahá'í activity and people of diverse backgrounds and rank were made welcome in it. In 1925 Hermann and Anna became parents of a daughter, Susanne Bahíyyih, and five years later they had a son, Hartmut Harlan.

In the 1920s Hermann, together with another young Bahá'í, took on the publication of a monthly magazine in Esperanto called *La Nova Tago* (The New Day). Often published only with great effort and sacrifice on Hermann's part, the magazine achieved worldwide circulation. Shoghi Effendi delighted in the publication:

> It has given me the greatest pleasure to receive the first issues of the *Bahá'í Esperanto Gazette*, and to learn of the splendid start you have made along a path which I am certain will lead you ultimately to glorious and abiding success.[2]

Hermann was especially interested in themes relating to the harmony of science and religion, and to humanity's need to find unity in its diversity, and these he emphasized particularly when he spoke to Bahá'í youth. He compiled texts on these themes, thinking they would be useful in a future Bahá'í university. He also produced a number of major writings which were based on these compilations: *The Economic Question and Its Solution According to the Bahá'í Teachings*, *The Dawn of a New Age*, *A Change-over to Unity* and *What is the Bahá'í Religion?* His intention to establish an Institute for Religion and Science won the approval and encouragement of the Guardian.

Hermann was elected to the National Spiritual Assembly of Germany and Austria within a few years of its establishment in 1922, probably in 1924, and helped put the institution on a sound footing.

In the 1930s, with the Guardian's encouragement, the European Bahá'ís began to hold summer schools on the Faith. For a few days or a week, the believers met to deepen their knowledge of the teachings through lectures, discussion and fellowship. Hermann often taught at the 'Häusle' (Little House) near Esslingen.

Hermann gave particular attention to the education of Bahá'í children and while in Hamburg held regular children's classes. He published many pamphlets and lessons, as well as an illustrated magazine called *Das Rosengärtlein* (The Little Rose Garden). In several towns in Germany Little Rose Garden groups were founded to teach Bahá'í children.

In 1935 Hermann wrote to the Guardian about his recent translation of The Seven Valleys into German. Shoghi Effendi replied through his secretary:

> He wishes me to congratulate you most heartily for this great service you have been able to render the Cause, and which no doubt will serve to enrich the record of the manifold contributions you have, during the last few years, so brilliantly made towards the spread of the Faith throughout Germany.[3]

The Guardian added in his own hand:

> Dear and valued co-worker:
>
> I am so eager to learn that your health is fully restored, for I believe your services are a most valuable asset to the Faith you serve in these troublous days. I welcome your efficient and unrelaxing cooperation, in spite of the obstacles which face you, in so many fields of Bahá'í activity. I am confident that as a result of your strenuous endeavours the administrative institutions in your land will be further consolidated and extended and the cause of teaching receive an added impetus.[4]

In 1937 Hermann, his wife and sister went on pilgrimage. For nine days they basked in the presence of Shoghi Effendi. In his conversations with the pilgrims, the Guardian again and again expounded on the nature of the embryonic Administrative Order of the Cause. Hermann yearned to find ways to increase the awareness of the believers of the importance of the emerging World Order of Bahá'u'lláh.

Hermann carried with him on pilgrimage the original Tablet he had received in 1920 from 'Abdu'l-Bahá and offered it as a gift to Shoghi Effendi. Warmly accepting the document, the Guardian asked Hermann whether he was aware of the Tablet's significance. Hermann, after some thought, replied that the words 'Thou shouldst be eternally obliged and grateful to those who were the cause of thy guidance' were of special importance. Shoghi Effendi, however, said that he felt the most significant passage was 'thou hast been enabled to rend the veils asunder . . . and to walk in the Path of the Kingdom'.[5] In a letter dated 14 October 2000,

Hartmut Grossmann wrote: 'My father said that Shoghi Effendi had told him that these words of the Tablet had moved him to appoint Hermann a Hand of the Cause of God.'

On one occasion Shoghi Effendi asked Hermann if he might one day wish to return to South America. Hermann answered that he had taken a long time to settle in Germany but was now happy there. The Guardian then smiled and said that perhaps one day Hermann would be glad to go back to Latin America. Many years later, when the Hands of the Cause asked Hermann to go to South America to help the friends complete the goals of the Ten Year Crusade, he was to remember that conversation.

Hermann returned from pilgrimage with his love for Shoghi Effendi at the very core of his being. The animating purpose of his life was now to bring happiness to his beloved, and he resolved to spread the Bahá'í teachings more energetically than ever.

However, Hermann's resolve was undermined only a month after his return from pilgrimage. On 21 May 1937 the Faith and its administrative institutions were banned by special order of the Reichsführer SS and chief of the German secret police (Gestapo) Heinrich Himmler. The announcement of the ban was published in all the German newspapers in June. Efforts to obtain an annulment of the edict were fruitless. Bahá'í homes all over the country were raided and Bahá'í books, letters, documents and other materials relating to the Faith, among them the stock of *La Nova Tago*, were confiscated and destroyed. The Bahá'ís were forbidden to gather and numbers of believers were detained, intimidated, imprisoned or deported, and some perished. Hermann was particularly persecuted, as he steadfastly refused to become a member of the National Socialist Party.

In one night Hermann lost most of his very valuable Bahá'í library and archives, including nearly all the records relating to the development of the Faith in Germany, which he had gathered at the cost of great effort over 20 years. Of this period, Hermann said, 'If I did not think that it was a sacrifice for Bahá'u'lláh, I could not bear the loss'.[6] In 1943 another wave of persecutions centred on Bahá'ís in the Heidelberg area and Hermann was arrested and fined. He lost further valuable Bahá'í documents, although a small part of the archives survived, and Hermann succeeded in obtaining permission to donate them to the library of the University of Heidelberg.

The persecution of the Bahá'ís of Germany was widespread. In 1939

Marta Brauns-Forel, a former member of the then forbidden National Spiritual Assembly, had her books and correspondence confiscated and was herself detained and rudely cross-examined for four hours. Paul Köhler, who had multigraphed one of Bahá'u'lláh's prayers, was imprisoned for 99 days. Hermann's wife, Anna, also a former member of the National Spiritual Assembly, was questioned by the Gestapo for having 'kept suspicious relations' with another former member of the Assembly.[7] Hermann's sister, Elsa Maria Grossmann, was questioned by a member of the Gestapo who menacingly waved a pistol at her while her books, private correspondence and various effects were confiscated. She was arrested without being charged and spent nine days in a prison cell.

In May 1944 public judicial proceedings were taken against seven believers and friends of the Cause – among them Anna Grossmann – who were questioned before the Sondergericht of Darmstadt, falsely charged with 'having continued the organization of the dissolved and prohibited Bahá'í sect'.[8]

Although Hermann Grossmann was at the centre of much Bahá'í work in Germany, he was fortuitously overlooked by the Gestapo and was therefore free to 'fight for the Cause of Bahá'u'lláh at the Centre of the Geheime Staatspolizei of Karlsruhe as well as before the tribunals of Darmstadt and Heidelberg where he succeeded in being admitted as a witness for the seven defendants'.[9] Pleading the non-political character of the Faith, Hermann asked that the ban against it be lifted, stating that the accusation that the Faith was hostile to the state entirely disregarded the attitude of Bahá'ís in Germany and throughout the world. Asked about the international character of the Faith, Hermann replied that the Cause stood for a universal order which does not exclude national order. Nevertheless, in 1944 he was accused of having been active in leading the 'forbidden Bahá'í Sect' and was subsequently heavily fined.

After the war the German Bahá'ís set about rebuilding their shattered community. On 14 August 1945 the American Army of Occupation issued a permit to the Bahá'ís in the Western zones enabling them to resume practice of their religion. Hermann received permission to visit the Bahá'ís in the Heidelberg area and in the region of Baden-Württemberg, to reorganize the communities, hold meetings and print Bahá'í materials. Immediately he set out to produce Bahá'í pamphlets, study materials and excerpts from the Bahá'í writings and he translated, compiled and edited a number of small booklets to support the teaching work. The little literature he had managed to salvage was mimeographed and bound in hard cover. The Grossmann home in Neckargemünd had survived destruction and again became a focal point of Bahá'í activity.

Pleased with their efforts, the Guardian wrote to the German Bahá'ís on 30 December 1945:

> My heart is filled with joy, pride and gratitude as I witness, thru the receipt of your most welcome letter, the evidences of the protection of the Almighty and of the vitality of the faith of the long-suffering German believers, who have laboured so devotedly and valiantly during so long and crucial a period and who as a community have survived the greatest ordeal in the history of their Faith in that land. My prayers during these years of danger, of stress, of suspense and anxiety have ever surrounded them, and I rejoice to learn of their safety, their unity, their zeal, and their determination to arise and resume the great and historic work they are destined to carry to a triumphant conclusion in the years that lie ahead . . . I am appealing to various Bahá'í communities in East and West to lend their assistance in whatever manner possible to the arduous task of reconstruction that now faces the German believers . . . Please assure them all of my great love, of my profound admiration, of my bright hopes for their future, of my heartfelt gratitude for their perseverance and of my fervent prayers for their future success.[10]

In January 1946 the first edition of *Bahá'í Nachrichten*, of which Hermann was the editor, was issued. The National Spiritual Assembly was re-established on 6 April 1946, 150 Bahá'ís gathering in a refurbished bomb-damaged room in Stuttgart to hear the news of the reconstruction of the German Bahá'í community. Hermann, who was chairman of the Convention, gave an eloquent talk on activities in Heidelberg and Neckargemünd. In a second talk he underlined the importance of the teaching work and how only a supreme effort could attract the masses from their disillusionment and waywardness. Hermann was not only elected to the National Spiritual Assembly but was also elected its chairman.

Hermann was among the first contingent of living Hands of the Cause named by Shoghi Effendi on 24 December 1951. As one of his tasks as a Hand of the Cause was to protect the Bahá'í community from those who broke the Covenant, Hermann devoted himself to a study of the nature of Divine Covenants in religious history. A result of his research was the publication in 1956 of his short book *God's Covenant in Revealed Religions*. That same year he also wrote *The Bahá'í Believer and the Bahá'í Community*.

In July 1953 Hermann attended the Intercontinental Conference in Stockholm, Sweden. When the fierce persecutions of the believers in Iran began in 1955, he became a member of the International Appeal Committee to the United Nations. He attended the first National Convention of the Benelux Countries in April 1957 as the representative of Shoghi Effendi.

In the spring of 1957 Hermann and Anna made their second pilgrimage to the Holy Land. For the pilgrim who had pondered so much on the World Order of Bahá'u'lláh, Shoghi Effendi traced its gradual unfoldment. He discussed with them the design of the Mother Temple to be constructed near Frankfurt, the plans for which the Grossmanns had brought on behalf of the National Assembly.

After Shoghi Effendi's passing only a few months later, the Hands of the Cause met for their first Conclave. Hermann's contributions to the discussions were highly valued. In 1959 the Hands of the Cause asked him to return to South America to help the believers complete their Ten Year Crusade goals.

Hermann left for South America early in 1959 and travelled around the entire continent and into the countries of the interior. However, his health suffered from the high altitudes of the Altiplano and he contracted typhoid fever, forcing him to postpone further travels.

South America at this time had only two National Spiritual Assemblies, each responsible for five countries. Hermann's enthusiastic reports to the Hands of the Cause of the development of the Faith in Latin America inspired them to work towards the establishment of ten new Assemblies at Riḍván 1961.

In January 1960 Hermann returned to South America together with his wife, Anna, for his longest visit to the region. For over seven months he travelled throughout the continent, helping the Bahá'ís create the conditions necessary for the election of their National Spiritual Assemblies. In 1961 he again returned to witness the birth of these national institutions, calling on them to carry the teachings of Bahá'u'lláh to the indigenous peoples.

Hermann's last journey in South America was in 1962. One of the lasting services that he rendered was to protect the Cause in South

America from attacks against the Covenant from both within and without the Faith, thus saving several communities from being seriously affected. Exhausted from his extensive travels across the continent, he returned to Germany in October for much-needed rest. Although he was able to attend the election of the Universal House of Justice and the World Congress in London in 1963, his travels after this became shorter and less frequent. In 1965 he wrote *What is the Bahá'í Religion?*

Hermann was present at the International conference in Frankfurt in October 1967 with fellow Hands of the Cause John Ferraby, Adelbert Mühlschlegel and Paul Haney, but his health permitted him to attend only one day. Nine months later, on 7 July 1968, he passed away and was laid to rest in the cemetery of Neckargemünd facing the beautiful and peaceful Neckar valley. His funeral service was remembered in these words:

> Now up on the slope [his] soul seemed free from all suffering and it was as if the heart of him would beat once more whose entire life was dedicated to the establishment of the Faith of God in the heart of Europe, in Latin America and in the whole of mankind. He truly was the Establisher of the Faith in these lands, a great educator, a scholar and a true brother. As we looked upon the roses, the snow-white lilies in their prayerlike beauty, upon the crimson-red of the carnations and the last gifts of the Bahá'í institutions . . . we realized that our beloved Hand of the Cause was now freed to exercise his influence as never before and in a way more powerful than all the perishable things of this world.[11]

The Universal House of Justice cabled the Bahá'í world:

> DEEPLY REGRET ANNOUNCE PASSING HAND CAUSE HERMANN GROSSMANN GREATLY ADMIRED BELOVED GUARDIAN. HIS GRIEVOUS LOSS DEPRIVES COMPANY HANDS CAUSE OUTSTANDING COLLABORATOR AND BAHÁ'Í WORLD COMMUNITY STAUNCH DEFENDER PROMOTER FAITH. HIS COURAGEOUS LOYALTY DURING CHALLENGING YEARS TESTS PERSECUTIONS GERMANY OUTSTANDING SERVICES SOUTH AMERICA IMMORTALIZED ANNALS FAITH. INVITE ALL NATIONAL SPIRITUAL ASSEMBLIES HOLD MEMORIAL GATHERINGS BEFITTING HIS EXALTED RANK EXEMPLARY SERVICES. REQUEST THOSE RESPONSIBLE MOTHER TEMPLES ARRANGE SERVICES AUDITORIUM.[12]

# Horace Hotchkiss Holley
## 1887–1960

Horace Hotchkiss Holley[1] was a complex, spiritual man who possessed an inner strength, a remarkable intellect and an untiring devotion. A member of the American National Spiritual Assembly, he served as that body's secretary for 34 years of his 36-year tenure. He wrote a prodigious number of works for the Faith during his half century as a follower of Bahá'u'lláh and earned the admiration of the Guardian for his sterling qualities and remarkable industriousness.

Born on 7 April 1887 in Torrington, Connecticut of Puritan stock and springing from a race of determined, self-reliant and taciturn people, Horace counted among his New England ancestors noted educators and congregationalist ministers. His parents were affluent, but when Horace was a child his father suffered a nervous breakdown, and died in 1896. When Horace was 14 he entered Lawrenceville, a private school in New Jersey, where he showed an interest in literature and began to write poetry. He left Lawrenceville in 1906 and went on to study literature at Williams College in Williamstown, Massachusetts, where he was a member of the Phi Delta Theta Fraternity and the Gargoyle Society.

Upon leaving college in 1909, Horace set out for Europe with the intention of spending the summer there and returning to Williams to complete his education. On the outward voyage, however, he met Bertha Herbert, a young artist who, in 1907, had introduced Lady Blomfield to the Bahá'í Faith while at a reception in Paris.[2] A tall, graceful girl with shining dark eyes and a glowing face,[3] Bertha lent Horace a book to read, *Abbas Effendi, His Life and Teachings* by Myron Phelps.

The 22-year-old Horace was impressed with the wisdom, universality of spirit and love expressed in 'Abdu'l-Bahá. 'Without knowing what it meant,' he later wrote, 'I had become a Bahá'í.'[4]

An inheritance enabled Horace to remain in Europe, studying and travelling. He and Bertha were married in October 1909 in Paris and moved to Italy, where their first daughter, Hertha, was born. They were living in Siena when they heard in late August 1911 of the arrival of 'Abdu'l-Bahá at Thonon-les-Bains, France. As they had hoped to make their pilgrimage to the Holy Land, they took the opportunity to meet the Master at Lake Leman.

The family arrived at Thonon-les-Bains on the afternoon of 29 August. Horace felt that if he could see 'Abdu'l-Bahá from a distance he would be satisfied:

> I saw among them a stately old man, robed in a cream-coloured gown, his white hair and beard shining in the sun. He displayed a beauty of stature, an inevitable harmony of attitude and dress I had never seen nor thought of in men. Without having ever visualized the Master, I knew that this was He. My whole body underwent a shock. My heart leaped, my knees weakened, a thrill of acute, receptive feeling flowed from head to foot . . . From sheer happiness I wanted to cry – it seemed the most suitable form of self-expression at my command . . . I yielded to a feeling of reverence which contained more than the solution of intellectual or moral problems. To look upon so wonderful a human being, to respond utterly to the charm of His presence – this brought me continual happiness . . . I was content to remain in the background.[5]

'Abdu'l-Bahá gave each of those present a Bahá'í ringstone as a gift. As Horace and Bertha were preparing to leave, Horace asked 'Abdu'l-Bahá to hold the ring in His hands as a blessing for his infant daughter to whom he wished to give the ring. Horace published an account of this visit later that year under the title *A Pilgrim to Thonon*.[6]

In 1912 Horace and Bertha moved to Paris and set up home. Bertha ran a successful designing business and Horace founded and directed the Ashur Gallery of Modern Art. Horace again had the privilege of meeting the Master and hearing many of His talks when 'Abdu'l-Bahá visited Paris during the first half of 1913. It was in 1913, while he was living in Paris, that Horace published his first books of verse and his first general work on the Bahá'í Faith, *Bahaism: The Modern Social Religion*,[7] which focuses on the social teachings of the Faith. Horace sent a copy of his Bahá'í book to 'Abdu'l-Bahá, who, in September 1913, sent to Horace from Ramleh,

Egypt, the first of the two Tablets He wrote to him:

> . . . thy aim is to render service to the Kingdom of Abhá and to promote the teachings of Bahá'u'lláh. Although the glory and greatness of this service is not known at present, in future ages it will assume the greatest importance and will attract the attention of learned men.[8]

After the outbreak of the First World War the Holleys were among those who fled from Paris, going first to London and then to New York, where they stayed with the Kinneys, a well-known Bahá'í family. The Holleys eventually established themselves in Greenwich Village and associated with the rather Bohemian literary and artistic society there, moving in much the same circles as they had in Paris. Their second daughter, Marcia, was born in 1916. Horace continued to write, publishing more verse and plays. He produced a further book on the Bahá'í Faith, *The Social Principle*, which was published in 1915.[9]

In New York the Holleys' marriage gradually deteriorated. Their private income did not stretch as far in New York as it had in Europe and the money they received from Horace's writing and Bertha's artistic endeavours did not make up the difference. Horace became an advertising copy-writer to supplement his income, working with the Iron Age Publishing Company from 1918 to 1920. The Holleys' difficulties were not only financial: their marriage had been under strain for some time and the circles in which they moved did not contribute to its stability. Horace apparently wrote of his anguish to 'Abdu'l-Bahá, because in His second Tablet to him, the Master wrote, 'All that thou hast written was a cry from the depths of a sincere heart.'[10]

In 1919 the Holleys divorced, but their difficulties continued. Not only were there financial problems, but their daughter Hertha went through repeated and worsening periods of mental disturbance, which were very costly for all the family, both financially and emotionally.

Later in 1919 Horace married Doris Pascal, whom he had first met in Paris. Together they served the Faith for 41 years.

In 1921 Horace left Iron Age Publishing to take up a position as chief of the copy department at the Redfield Advertising Agency, where he worked until 1925. He published his third book on the Faith in 1921, *Bahai, the Spirit of the Age*, in which he presented the Bahá'í Faith from the view-point of a number of different religious traditions and philosophies.[11]

From his arrival in New York, Horace was active in the Bahá'í community, and in the early 1920s he became increasingly occupied with service to the Faith. In 1921 he edited the first comprehensive English compilation of the Bahá'í writings, *Bahá'í Scriptures*, which was later revised by him and published as *Bahá'í World Faith*. In 1923 he was elected to the National Spiritual Assembly of the United States and Canada, and served as its secretary from 1924 to 1930 and from 1932 to 1959. He contributed articles to *Star of the West*, conceived and edited *Bahá'í News*, suggested the idea for a Bahá'í yearbook, which became *The Bahá'í World*, and was the moving force behind the Bahá'í Publishing Committee. He also served as editor of *World Unity Magazine* and worked with the World Unity Foundation.

In this early period of the Faith the Bahá'ís were not required to dissociate themselves from their church affiliations and Horace was an active member of St Mark's Episcopal Church in New York, which, under its rector Dr William Norman Guthrie, had developed an association with the Bahá'í community in the years before the First World War. Holley served as Junior Warden of the vestry from 1928 to 1933, writing the church's publicity materials, acting as part-time manager of its rental apartment buildings and spearheading its fund-raising efforts. He left the church in 1933, along with many Bahá'ís and others, in consequence of a disagreement between the vestry and the rector over church finances.

Shoghi Effendi highly valued Horace's work for the Faith. He wrote in the mid-1920s:

> Your personal contribution to so many aspects and phases of the Movement, performed so diligently, so effectively and so thoroughly are truly a source of joy and inspiration to me.[12]

The Guardian desperately needed capable Bahá'ís to work with him in Haifa. After the passing of John Esslemont in November 1925, Shoghi Effendi wrote to Horace in May 1926:

> I have often felt the extreme desirability of having a collaborator like you working by my side here in Haifa. The loss of Dr Esslemont is keenly felt by me and my hope is that the conditions here and abroad will enable me to establish this work in Haifa upon a more systematic basis. I am waiting for a favourable time.[13]

Shoghi Effendi realized, however, that Horace was needed in the United States, writing in June 1926 to two of Horace's friends:

> Horace of course is the ideal man, but he mustn't leave his position at the present time.[14]

Horace never did go to Haifa to work with Shoghi Effendi. In 1925 he became the full-time secretary of the National Spiritual Assembly, giving up his independent career to serve the Faith. Despite the criticism of some of his fellow believers and his own discomfort at having to be supported by the Bahá'í funds, Horace accepted the position in order to devote to the Faith the time it deserved. Shoghi Effendi, well aware of the circumstances of Horace's position, wrote to the National Spiritual Assembly:

> I rejoice to learn that ways and means have been found to enable the National Secretary, who discharges in such an exemplary manner the manifold and exacting duties of a highly responsible position, to devote all his time to the pursuit of so meritorious a task. I am fully conscious of the privations and sacrifice which the choice of this arduous work must involve for him.[15]

With a full-time secretary now in place to serve the National Spiritual Assembly that was primarily responsible for the execution of 'Abdu'l-Bahá's Divine Plan, Shoghi Effendi was able to initiate the process of developing more fully the Bahá'í Administrative Order. Horace not only grasped Shoghi Effendi's instructions and interpretations of the Bahá'í teachings but also delighted in the Guardian's breadth of vision. Described by the Guardian as 'the foremost exponent of Bahá'í administration in the world',[16] Horace would play a supreme and historic role during the early Formative Age in the unfoldment of the Bahá'í Administrative Order, a role which was greatly prized by Shoghi Effendi:

> Your ready pen, your brilliant mind, your marvellous vigour and organizing ability, above all your unwavering loyalty are assets that I greatly value and for which I am deeply grateful.[17]

> I wish to re-assure you of my keen appreciation of your continuous efforts for the consolidation of the work of the Cause throughout America.[18]

ASSURE YOU MY EVER DEEPENING ADMIRATION YOUR UNRIVALLED SERVICES.[19]

Horace Holley was a master of correct Bahá'í procedure and a scholar of the Bahá'í teachings. He, together with the Bahá'í lawyer Mountfort Mills, was largely responsible for drafting the Declaration of Trust and By-laws which were adopted by the National Spiritual Assembly of the United States and Canada in April 1927 and which became the pattern for all such legal instruments of the Faith in other national Bahá'í communities.

Horace served on the editorial board of *The Bahá'í World* and wrote much of the material for the publication. He wrote the statement 'Aims and Purposes of the Bahá'í Faith', which appeared at or near the beginning of every volume from 3 to 13, and wrote every 'International Survey of Current Bahá'í Activities' – a historical record of the growth of the Cause and an interpretation of current events – from volumes 2 to 11. The Survey was a key article and Shoghi Effendi felt no other Bahá'í was qualified to produce it. The Guardian placed much importance on the publication of *The Bahá'í World*, which he believed was suitable for the public, scholars and libraries and an important instrument for 'removing the malicious misrepresentations and unfortunate misunderstandings that have so long and so grievously clouded the luminous Faith of Bahá'u'lláh'.[20] An invaluable source of information for Bahá'í historians, the Survey covered such topics as the persecution of the Cause in Iran, Germany, Russia and Turkestan; the establishment, re-establishment and incorporation of administrative bodies; the activities of travelling teachers; progress in the construction of the Wilmette Temple; the establishment, dedication and preservation of Bahá'í shrines, schools and historical sites; the increase in the number of translations and publications of Bahá'í works; the extension of Bahá'í endowments; statistics pertaining to the growth of assemblies, communities and localities; annual reports of National Spiritual Assemblies; activities of Bahá'í summer schools; teacher training and youth activities; and the growth and development of the Faith generally around the world. While Shoghi Effendi collected much of the data himself, Horace was the one who wrote and edited the material. 'Detailed letter mailed for International Survey confident your masterly treatment collected data,' the Guardian cabled Horace.[21]

In addition to this and his administrative work, Horace prepared study guides to the Kitáb-i-Íqán and *God Passes By* and wrote the introductions to *Bahá'í World Faith*, *The World Order of Bahá'u'lláh*, The Secret of Divine Civilization, *Foundations of World Unity*, *The Reality of Man*, *Messages to the Bahá'í World* and *Bahá'í Administration*. He wrote memorial articles for *The Bahá'í World* on the lives of Mountfort Mills, George Latimer and Roy Wilhelm. As secretary of the National Spiritual Assembly he wrote letters to Reza Sháh Pahlaví and President Harry S. Truman. His own works include 'The World Economy of Bahá'u'lláh', 'The Spiritual Basis of World Peace', 'Religion and World Order', 'The Bahá'í Principle of Civilization', 'The Human Situation', 'The Bahá'í Faith and Labour', 'The Root of Struggle', 'Challenge to Chaos', 'Communion with the Infinite' and 'Our Covenant with 'Abdu'l-Bahá'. He also wrote an introductory book on the Bahá'í Faith, *Religion for Mankind*, which was published in 1956 and in which some of the above articles are to be found.[22]

Horace also gave the titles to the Guardian's general letters to America, such as *The Promised Day is Come* and 'The Dispensation of Bahá'u'lláh', as well as suggesting the subtitles found in these texts.

With such a prodigious output, little wonder that Shoghi Effendi wrote to Horace:

> I greatly value, as you already know, your presentation of the various aspects of the Cause, for whose expansion, consolidation and defence you have, during so many years, laboured so indefatigably and served with such distinction.[23]

Over the years Horace established a kind of camaraderie with the Guardian based on their common burden of work:

> He is always happy to hear from you, as he has a great deal of sympathy for what he fully realizes must be your continually overworked state. Hard-pressed for time as he himself constantly is, he well knows what it means! . . . he hopes you yourself are keeping in very good health and not overdoing? – Though he knows from long experience that it is almost impossible not to overdo when the work of the Cause keeps piling up![24]

In the late 1930s Shoghi Effendi wished that the national headquarters of the Bahá'í Faith in the United States be moved from New York to Wilmette so that the spiritual and administrative headquarters could be together. This meant the Holleys had to leave their home in New York to live in a small mid-western town where they would be constantly interrupted by visitors. The Guardian understood Horace's feelings about this and cabled him: 'AWARE, PROFOUNDLY APPRECIATE SACRIFICE PERSONAL CONVENIENCE INVOLVED TRANSFERENCE TEMPLE VICINITY DEEPEST LOVE.'[25]

Having made the move to Wilmette in 1939, Horace became deeply involved in the activities of the local Bahá'í community, as well as serving on national committees. He conducted study classes on such subjects as Bahá'í administration, personal transformation and world peace, gave many public lectures, hosted Nineteen Day Feasts, participated in various symposia, became a member of the Rotary Club and both founded and chaired for many years the Wilmette Historical Commission. During the war he served as an air-raid warden. In the summer he frequently gave courses at Green Acre, where he and Doris had a cottage.

Not surprisingly, Horace did 'overdo' and eventually his health weakened. In 1944 he suffered a heart attack and was hospitalized for some time. From that year on he had recurring bouts of ill health, both because of his heart and later because of a nerve condition that caused him to be in almost constant pain. He also had problems with his eyesight. The Guardian was concerned and sent Horace several letters expressing his hope for a speedy recovery:

> . . . my prayer to the Almighty is to give you all the strength you need to enable you to win still greater victories in the course of your historic labours for the establishment of His Faith and the consolidation of its nascent Institutions. Be happy, rest assured, and persevere. Your true and grateful brother.[26]

Despite his weakened state, Horace represented the outgoing National Spiritual Assembly of the United States and Canada at the Convention held in Montreal in 1948 to elect the separate National Spiritual Assembly of Canada. In 1951, together with Dorothy Baker, he represented the United States National Assembly at the Convention in Panama City to elect the National Spiritual Assembly of Central America.

It was perhaps his ill health that caused Horace's mystic nature tore-emerge. His poem entitled 'God Most Glorious!' appeared in volume 12 of *The Bahá'í World*:

Beyond the sweep of farthest star
Beneath the beauty of the rose
His tokens shine remotely far
His glory stands ineffably close.
(Radiant the heart of him who knows.)

No longer weak as creed outworn
No longer dim as hope denied
His will proclaims celestial morn
Within the dungeon of our pride.
(His power no people can deride.)

A scourge He gives each bitter fear
He arms for death each sullen hate.
His lovers know that He is here
Destroying sin in man and state
(The world is witness to its fate.)

His glory seizes East and West
Confounding nation, sect and clan
A fiery crucible to test
The soul committed unto man.
(The goal of life since time began.)

He builds upon our ruined age
A kingdom righteous, firm and sure.
Behold! Our ancient heritage
Summons the meek, awaits the pure.
(His peace forever will endure.)[27]

In 24 December 1951 Horace received a cable from the Guardian appointing him one of the three Hands of the Cause in America along with Dorothy Baker and Leroy Ioas. While maintaining his position as secretary of the National Spiritual Assembly of the United States, Horace now had a new set of responsibilities. In 1953 he attended the four Intercontinental Conferences called by Shoghi Effendi in Kampala, Stockholm, Chicago and New Delhi. At the year's end, after three decades of collaboration by correspondence, Horace finally met the

Guardian when he went on pilgrimage in December.

In 1957, as Shoghi Effendi's personal representative, Horace attended the Convention in Lima, Peru, at which the first National Assembly for the northern countries of South America was elected. Horace was ill in hospital when Shoghi Effendi passed away in November 1957 and was unable to attend the funeral in London. Although constant pain in his legs and a weakened heart left him almost an invalid, he was present later that month at the first Conclave of the Hands of the Cause at Bahjí, writing the first draft of the Proclamation of the Hands which established the authority of the Custodians for the next six years.

At the 1959 Conclave his fellow Hands elected him one of the Hands of the Cause resident in the Holy Land. He returned to the United States to put his affairs in order and to resign from the National Spiritual Assembly. He arrived in the Holy Land on the last day of 1959. By now virtually an invalid, Horace attended the meetings of his fellow Hands, listening attentively but saving his ebbing strength until he was required to express an opinion. Signifying agreement when necessary through moving his head or waving his hand, Horace made contributions to those meetings that were of inestimable help, particularly during the defection of Mason Remey, when he was able to offer valued, mature and wise advice.[28]

On the evening of 12 July 1960 Horace Holley collapsed and died immediately. A beautiful service was held in the hall of the Master's home. Less than 24 hours after his passing, he was laid to rest in the Bahá'í cemetery, near the graves of Dr Esslemont and Ḥájí Mírzá Muḥammad-Taqí, the Afnán who built the 'Ishqábád Temple. Recalling Horace's many years of outstanding service and devotion, the honours he had so plentifully received from Shoghi Effendi and the invaluable help he had rendered as a Hand of the Cause, the Custodians cabled the Bahá'í world:

> GRIEVED ANNOUNCE PASSING HAIFA MUCH-LOVED DISTINGUISHED HAND CAUSE GOD HORACE HOLLEY OUTSTANDING CHAMPION FAITH SINCE DAYS MASTER PRAISED BY BELOVED GUARDIAN FOR UNIQUE CONTRIBUTION DEVELOPMENT ADMINISTRATIVE ORDER. HIS INDEFATIGABLE SERVICES PROTECTION TEACHING ADMINISTRATIVE FIELDS CULMINATING SERVICE HOLY LAND INSPIRING EXAMPLE PRESENT FUTURE GENERATIONS BAHA'IS. SHARE ABOVE MESSAGE HANDS ALL NATIONAL ASSEMBLIES. URGE HOLD MEMORIAL GATHERINGS TEMPLE LOCAL COMMUNITIES UNITED STATES.[29]

# Leroy C. Ioas
# 1896–1965

Leroy Ioas, known as 'the Guardian's Hercules', was praised by Shoghi Effendi for his 'tireless vigilance, self sacrifice, and devotion to the Cause in all its multiple fields of activity', his 'prodigious labours' and his 'stupendous efforts'.[1]

Diligently serving the Bahá'í Faith for over a half century, Leroy was also a successful businessman in the railroad industry, working chiefly for Southern Pacific. Over the 40 years he worked for the railroads, he rose from a minor post to become Passenger Traffic Manager for the company in the eastern United States. He was 'a practical man, of outstanding attainment in business, shrewd, determined, hard-working, content only with success . . . discerning, undeviating, trustful'.[2]

Leroy, one of ten children, was born to Charles and Maria Ioas, both German immigrants, on 15 February 1896 in Wilmington, Illinois. Charles Ioas, a lawyer and certified public accountant from a Lutheran background, had come to the United States from Munich in 1880. Maria Ioas, a photographer, was a Catholic. The Ioases joined the Methodist church and shared an interest in the subject of Christ's return: when Charles was a child his mother had told him that he might live to see Christ come again.

Eventually Charles and Maria Ioas came into contact with the Bahá'í Faith and attended classes given by Paul Dealy of Chicago. In the 12th lesson they learned about Bahá'u'lláh. Maria later told her daughter:

> [When we were told] that God in His love and mercy for mankind had again manifested His Spirit on earth in a human temple in Bahá'u'lláh, there was a stillness in that room – it seemed as if everyone's breath had stopped; it seemed as if it was too much for our hearts to bear.[3]

Charles and Maria became Bahá'ís in July 1898.

As a youth, Leroy was already known for his remarkable spiritual perception. When he was 16 'Abdu'l-Bahá came to America. Leroy immediately took the Master for his guide in life. One day the youth led his father to Him through a crowded hotel lobby, finding the Master outside the side entrance to the hotel as a moth finds a lamp. Leroy was present when 'Abdu'l-Bahá laid the cornerstone of the House of Worship in Wilmette and later, as a young man, he taught Bahá'í classes on its grounds.

In 1919 Leroy married Sylvia Kuhlman and the couple settled in San Francisco, where they would reside for the next 27 years. Upon his arrival, Leroy sent a letter to 'Abdu'l-Bahá asking 'that this faltering one may be quickened through that Divine Power, and thereby render some service which may be conducive to the happiness of the heart of 'Abdu'l-Bahá'.[4]

The Ioases began teaching in San Francisco by inviting people to their home for a social evening. Several people were introduced to the Faith in this way. About a year and a half after Leroy arrived in the city he was elected to the Local Spiritual Assembly. A few months later, Bahá'ís everywhere were crushed by the passing of 'Abdu'l-Bahá. Leroy's response was to take on more of the responsibilities of the Cause. He became a member of several local Bahá'í committees and was appointed corresponding secretary of the Assembly. In 1923 he began to chair public meetings, and not long afterwards became the speaker at these meetings himself.

The Ioases' first daughter, Mary Lorraine, was born in 1920. Leroy asked a Bahá'í who was going on pilgrimage to request that 'Abdu'l-Bahá give the baby a Persian name. Some time later Leroy received a small piece of paper with the name 'Farrukh' ('very joyous') pencilled on it. From that time on, Mary was known by this name.

A second daughter, Anita, was born to the Ioases in 1921, and the family moved for a few years to Burlingame, south of San Francisco. In 1925 Ella Goodall Cooper made available to the Bahá'ís a large Victorian house in San Francisco which they used as their Bahá'í centre. Because the house needed to be occupied for insurance purposes, the Ioas family moved in and kept the centre open for the regular Wednesday meetings, firesides, study classes, Assembly meetings, committee meetings, holy day commemorations and Nineteen Day Feasts.

In 1926 the great Bahá'í teacher Orcella Rexford came to San Francisco on a lecture tour. After such a tour Orcella would arrange for the local Bahá'ís to organize study classes for those interested. Thus Leroy soon found himself conducting classes for 100 people in Oakland, an hour and a half ferry ride away. Although the classes were extremely successful – out of them came a Bahá'í community of 35 members – Leroy was disappointed that no other Bahá'ís came forward to help in the teaching work and he found the situation 'extremely discouraging'.[5] The Ioases were very hospitable and their home seemed always to be open for meetings, social evenings, youth gatherings and study classes. At the same time Leroy became chairman of the Spiritual Assembly and a member of the Western States Teaching Committee. The stress caused by the burden of all these activities affected his health and he resolved to change the situation. After a period of reflection, he felt the solution lay in reaching the country's leaders with information about the Faith, finding a way to develop teachers for the Faith and creating a teaching plan that would unify all the individual efforts so as to have more effect. Accustomed to figuring out the steps necessary for solving problems, Leroy proposed three different teaching plans:

> One was to establish in this liberal western area very large unity conferences . . . Another was the revised teaching plan which ultimately found its consummation in the first Seven Year Plan . . . The third was to find a place where people could gather for a period of one or two weeks for the dual purpose of deepening their understanding of the Faith and preparing them for public teaching.[6]

The projects that sprang from these ideas greatly influenced the growth of the Bahá'í Faith in North America and in the Bahá'í world as a whole.

In 1912 'Abdu'l-Bahá had been moved by the unity of the believers gathered in San Francisco to bid Him farewell and had expressed His hope that their 'amity' would 'lead to spirituality in the world' and enlighten all humankind.[7] Leroy remembered these words and set about arranging an amity conference as a means of implementing his first idea.

When Leroy first mooted the suggestion the Assembly did not take it up, but when he presented it for a second time the Assembly appointed him to investigate the possibilities. As his preliminary investigations showed a positive response to the idea, the Assembly appointed Ella Goodall Cooper and Kathryn Frankland to help him. Leroy took a year's holiday to work on the conference, the three Bahá'ís winning the support of Dr David Starr Jordan, Chancellor Emeritus of Stanford University, Rabbi Rudolf I. Coffee of Temple Sinai and other civic and religious leaders. Dr Jordan served as the honorary chairman.

The Conference for World Unity took place from 20 to 22 March 1925 in San Francisco. Deemed to be highly successful, the event was reported to Shoghi Effendi, who congratulated the committee on the high tenor of the conference, saying he hoped it would 'prove a starting point for further important developments'.[8] The National Assembly took up the idea and in the next two years a series of World Unity Conferences was sponsored by the Bahá'ís in 16 cities of the United States and Canada.

Dr Jordan was so impressed with young Leroy's qualities that he offered him a scholarship to Stanford. Alas, Leroy could not accept the kind and generous offer of a chance to secure a college education. The needs of his growing family and his Bahá'í responsibilities were, he felt, already too demanding.

Leroy began to search for a way to implement his other proposals: to bring people together for their serious study of the teachings and to create a teaching plan. He discussed his ideas with John and Louise Bosch, who had decided to dedicate their property at Geyserville, California, to Bahá'í service. On 1 August 1925 some 100 believers from nine communities gathered at Geyserville for the Nineteen Day Feast and to celebrate John Bosch's 70th birthday. There they discussed a unified teaching plan and resolved to meet each year. Afterwards, the National Spiritual Assembly appointed Leroy, John Bosch and George Latimer to work towards the establishment of a permanent Bahá'í school. Geyserville was selected as a venue for the school and the first session was held in 1927. Leroy took two days off work to speak at this initial session. So successful was the school that 12 years later the Guardian wrote through his secretary that 'the unique contribution which the Geyserville Summer School has made . . . has been to teach the friends and inspire them to live up to the high standard which the Teachings inculcate, and thus teach the Cause through the power of example'.[9]

Leroy's teaching work carried him into the San Joaquin Valley, southern California and Arizona. He was also deeply involved with activities in the San Francisco area, including the library and reading room which the Assembly had opened in the late 1920s and the Inter-Racial Amity Committee inaugurated by the Bahá'ís.

In 1932 Leroy was elected to the National Spiritual Assembly. Shoghi Effendi greeted the election of this youngest member with a 'deep sense of satisfaction' and looked forward to Leroy's 'advice and executive ability' to 'lend a fresh impetus . . . to the work that the Assembly has arisen to accomplish'.[10]

Upon his election to the National Assembly Leroy was immediately appointed to the National Teaching Committee, serving as its chairman for 14 years. It was during this period that Shoghi Effendi was leading the Bahá'í community towards the fulfilment of its mission under the Divine Plan. In 1935 Leroy submitted to the Guardian the committee's plan for establishing the Cause in 12 states where as yet no Bahá'í lived. Shoghi Effendi gladly endorsed the plan. At the next Convention, in April 1936, the Guardian focused the attention of the American Bahá'í community on establishing the Cause in every state within the American Republic and every Republic in the American continent, launching the first Seven Year Plan to meet this great challenge.

By the end of the Plan, spiritual assemblies had been established in 34 North American states and Canadian provinces where no assemblies had existed before. The number of localities where Bahá'ís lived had trebled. All the Latin American goals were achieved. These were years of work, anxiety and stress for the members of the National Teaching Committee and the National Spiritual Assembly, the more so for Leroy, who served on both bodies. Shoghi Effendi much admired Leroy's work on the 'all-important National Teaching Committee', acclaiming its work as 'truly stupendous, highly meritorious and magnificent in all its aspects'.[11] To Sylvia, Shoghi Effendi wrote that 'without the steady faith and tireless devotion' which Leroy had 'brought to bear on the teaching work of North America, the Plan might not have gone ahead as smoothly to victory as it did'.[12]

In 1946 Sylvia and Leroy left San Francisco for Chicago, where Leroy had been transferred by his employer after a promotion. A trustee of the House of Worship for 14 years, Leroy was now in a position to devote more energy to the work at a time when the inner ornamentation and landscaping of the Temple were being completed. Eighteen months after his arrival, he was appointed a member of the five-strong delegation attending the United Nations Conference on Human Rights in Geneva as representatives of the Bahá'í International Community. He also participated in the first European Teaching Conference in the same city and visited Bahá'í communities in the ten European goal countries. The next year he was appointed to the European Teaching Committee. In 1950 he was elected treasurer of the National Spiritual Assembly.

During the years that Leroy was assuming increasing responsibilities within the Faith of God, he was also active socially. In San Francisco he was a member of the Commonwealth, Kiwanis and Cosmos Clubs and was also the first white member in San Francisco of the National Association for the Advancement of Colored People. In Chicago he was a member of the Rotary, Skal and Union League Clubs and served on an executive committee of the American Association of Passenger Traffic Officers.

In the spring of 1951 Amelia Collins was sent to the United States by the Guardian to confer with the National Spiritual Assembly concerning events in Haifa. While in Chicago, she talked at length with Leroy about conditions in the Holy Land and the cares of the Guardian. Her news affected Leroy almost as much as had the passing of the Master nearly 30 years before. In October of that year Shoghi Effendi sent Leroy a letter in which he expressed through his secretary the hope that 'a time will come when you can devote more time to the work, and internationally as well as nationally'.[13]

In December 1951 Leroy was named a Hand of the Cause. Two months later, on 12 February, he received a message written on behalf of the Guardian:

> . . . what he needs, I might almost say desperately, is a capable, devoted believer to come and really take the work in hand here, relieve him of constant strain and details, and act as the secretary-general of the International Bahá'í Council. If you accept to do this it will be rendering him and the Faith an invaluable service.[14]

Leroy had a 'terrifically hard' decision to make – 'the most difficult decision I have had to make in my entire Bahá'í life', he wrote to Paul Haney[15] – but cabled the Guardian:

> LETTER JUST RECEIVED. SYLVIA AND I DEEPLY MOVED PRIVILEGE SERVE BELOVED GUARDIAN. IF SATISFACTORY I WILL ARRIVE MARCH TENTH. DEVOTED LOVE.

The Guardian's immediate cabled reply to Leroy was: 'WELCOME. LOVE. SHOGHI.'[16]

Few understood Leroy's sudden and unexpected decision to resign from his business and positions of responsibility at the National Bahá'í Centre; many colleagues and friends throughout the United States were stunned. His business associates respected his decision as one of courage and principle – for Leroy had never concealed his allegiance to the Bahá'í Faith – while Bahá'ís and Bahá'í institutions inundated him with messages of respect and praise. Leroy's long years of service had profoundly affected the American Bahá'ís and he would be sorely missed.

Three weeks later, on 17 March, Leroy arrived in Haifa. After a few days he settled into his new job as Secretary-General of the year-old International Bahá'í Council and soon became the Guardian's assistant secretary as well. He was one of four Hands of the Cause the Guardian asked to live in the Holy Land and, under the Guardian's direction, he was soon shouldering enormous duties: strengthening ties between the Council and the civil authorities of the fledgling State of Israel; negotiating the purchase of properties on Mount Carmel and near the Shrine of Bahá'u'lláh; establishing branches of four National Spiritual Assemblies in Israel to hold the title to these properties; vigorously defending the Faith against Covenant-breakers who sought to oppose the Guardian's plans; supervising the building of the drum and dome of the Shrine of the Báb; and overseeing, between 1955 and 1957, the construction of the International Archives building. When the Shrine of the Báb was completed in October 1953, Shoghi Effendi honoured Leroy by naming the octagon door of the Shrine after him.

Leroy accomplished all his tasks in spite of the 'austerities of a new State, the conditions of labour, the interminable procedures of officialdom, the excessive burdens which they strove to carry, and even their own inexperience for the tasks assigned'.[17] In order to foster relations with business and civic leaders, Leroy joined various clubs and societies, just as he had in America. His first public talk in the Holy Land was to the Haifa Rotary Club only six months after he had arrived, and this led to further invitations to speak at Rotary Clubs around the country. Later, and much to Shoghi Effendi's satisfaction, Leroy spoke about world peace to the Rotary Club in Jerusalem.

So much work, however, caused Leroy's health to decline. By October 1953 his heart was already weakened and he required long periods of rest, which he sought annually in America or Europe. Despite his poor health, however, Leroy continued to serve the Guardian, sharing in the voluminous correspondence, now increased with the launching of the Ten Year Crusade in 1953, and travelling across four continents to visit Bahá'í communities.

Leroy represented Shoghi Effendi at the first Intercontinental Conference, held in Kampala in 1953, reading the Guardian's message and displaying the maps of the Crusade's objectives. He was present in 1955 at the dedication of the British Ḥaẓíratu'l-Quds in London. He was sent by the Guardian to Frankfurt, Germany, in 1956 to consult with the National Spiritual Assembly about its important work of erecting the first European Temple. In 1958 he attended the Intercontinental Conferences in Jakarta–Singapore and Wilmette.

Perhaps the most important service Leroy rendered the Guardian was his effort to secure for the Faith the properties around the Shrine of Bahá'u'lláh which had been for 60 years in the hands of the Covenant-breakers. By June 1957 the Guardian was able to cable the Bahá'í world that the 'victory' over the Covenant-breakers had been won. By September they and all their belongings had been removed from the precincts of the Shrine. This service, Shoghi Effendi told Leroy, was 'gold'.[18] Shortly afterwards, Shoghi Effendi passed away in London, to the devastation of the Bahá'í world.

On Shoghi Effendi's death, Leroy remained in Haifa to take care of all the necessary formalities while the other Hands of the Cause travelled to London for the Guardian's funeral. Leroy notified the Israeli government that Shoghi Effendi had passed away and placed guards at the Holy Places and at the Guardian's home before departing for London himself, arriving on the morning of the funeral. He carried with him items requested by Rúḥíyyih Khánum: a small rug from the Shrine of Bahá'u'lláh to place under the casket in the burial vault and a blue and gold brocade covering to spread over the coffin.

Leroy returned to Haifa the night after Shoghi Effendi's funeral. Within a few days all of the Hands of the Cause except Corinne True arrived to discuss the future of the Faith. On 15 November the four Hands of the Cause resident in the Holy Land – Rúḥíyyih Khánum, Amelia Collins, Charles Mason Remey and Leroy Ioas – accompanied by Ugo Giachery, entered the apartment of the Guardian and sealed his safe and desk. The keys to Shoghi Effendi's safe were placed in a sealed envelope in Leroy's safe. Four days later, on the morning of 19 November, nine representatives of the Hands of the Cause, including Leroy, entered the Guardian's apartment, broke the seals and examined the contents of his safe and desk. At the end of their thorough search they reported to the other Hands: the Guardian had left no will. Following guidance in the Will and Testament of 'Abdu'l-Bahá, the Hands chose from among their number nine Hands of the Cause to serve on their behalf in the Holy Land, pending the election of the Universal House of Justice. Leroy was among the nine elected to act as 'Custodians'.

Leroy's work in the Holy Land following the death of Shoghi Effendi further sapped his declining health. Although advised by his doctors to rest for the sake of his heart, he maintained a fairly busy schedule during the next five and a half years, travelling more widely than ever before for the Cause. In 1960 he travelled to the United States to attend the wedding of his daughter Anita. This joyous event was followed closely, in April 1960, by the unexpected death of Leroy's elder daughter, Farrukh, who was in her 40th year. While in the United States Leroy attended the Annual Bahá'í Convention, visited the Geyserville summer school and travelled to various Bahá'í communities. The next year he was in Switzerland, where he visited the country's 12 Local Spiritual Assemblies. In 1962 he made a tour of Europe which included visits to Finland, Sweden, Denmark, Luxembourg and Germany.

In April 1963 the Universal House of Justice was elected and the Custodians handed over the administration of the Faith to it, the Hands retaining their primary responsibilities of protection and propagation of the Cause. Shortly after the election, the first Bahá'í World Congress was convened in London. Leroy contracted pneumonia at the opening of the Congress and had to rest in Germany for some months afterwards.

In October 1963 Leroy attended the meeting of the Hands with the Universal House of Justice, then left for the United States, where it was intended he should convalesce. Instead, he embarked on his last great teaching trip, which took him through the south and west of the country. Though physically frail and suffering from chronic bronchitis as well as a weak heart, he inspired the believers in general, and the youth in particular, to embrace the challenges of the Nine Year Plan. Returning to Wilmette in April 1964, he represented the Hands in the Holy Land at the Annual Convention that launched the Plan.

Exhausted at the end of this tour, Leroy rested until October, and then returned to the Holy Land. He passed away nine months later, on 22 July

1965, after some weeks in hospital. He was 69 years old. He was buried in the Bahá'í Cemetery at the foot of Mount Carmel. He was remembered in memorial services at the House of Worship in Wilmette, at Geyserville school and in Bahá'í communities around the world. A sequoia grove at Geyserville was named in his memory and in later years a similar grove at the Bosch school in California received his name.

On his passing the Universal House of Justice cabled the Bahá'í world:

> GRIEVE ANNOUNCE PASSING OUTSTANDING HAND CAUSE LEROY IOAS. HIS LONG SERVICE BAHÁ'Í COMMUNITY UNITED STATES CROWNED ELEVATION RANK HAND FAITH PAVING WAY HISTORIC DISTINGUISHED SERVICES HOLY LAND. APPOINTMENT FIRST SECRETARY GENERAL INTERNATIONAL BAHÁ'Í COUNCIL PERSONAL REPRESENTATIVE GUARDIAN FAITH TWO INTERCONTINENTAL CONFERENCES ASSOCIATION HIS NAME BY BELOVED GUARDIAN OCTAGON DOOR BÁB'S SHRINE TRIBUTE SUPERVISORY WORK DRUM DOME THAT HOLY SEPULCHRE NOTABLE PART ERECTION INTERNATIONAL ARCHIVES BUILDING ALL ENSURE HIS NAME IMMORTAL ANNALS FAITH. LAID TO REST BAHÁ'Í CEMETERY CLOSE FELLOW HANDS ADVISE HOLD BEFITTING MEMORIAL SERVICES.[19]

## William Sutherland Maxwell

R.C.A., F.R.I.B.A., F.R.A.I.C.

## 1874–1952

Mount Carmel, which means 'the vineyard of God', is one of the most historic landmarks in the Middle East; the ancient great civilizations of biblical times flowed about its foot for generations. Today, occupying a central position on its slopes, there stands a stately golden-domed edifice visited by tens of thousands of people. This is the famous 'Bahá'í Shrine' where the Báb, the forerunner of the Founder of the Bahá'í Faith, is buried. The Guardian of the Bahá'í Faith, Shoghi Effendi, in a cable addressed to the Bahá'ís of the world, described the Tomb of the Báb as 'QUEEN CARMEL ENTHRONED GOD'S MOUNTAIN CROWNED GLOWING GOLD ROBED SHIMMERING WHITE GIRDLED EMERALD GREEN ENCHANTING EVERY EYE FROM AIR SEA PLAIN HILL.'[1] The imposing superstructure of this Tomb was designed by the eminent Canadian architect William Sutherland Maxwell.

William Sutherland Maxwell was born in Montreal, Canada on 14 November 1874. Following high school, he worked in the architectural office of his older brother, Edward, in Montreal and by 1895 was furthering his training in the large architectural firm of Winslow and Wetherell in Boston. His extraordinary talent for drawing and design eventually led him to Paris, where he was admitted to the atelier of the well-known architect Paschal, a leading architect closely associated with the École des Beaux Arts. Following his academic experiences there, he returned to Canada, where he joined his brother in his architectural practice.

Before the First World War, the firm of Edward and W. S. Maxwell was one of the foremost and largest in Canada. The Maxwell brothers turned out many Canadian landmarks, such as the Parliament Building in Regina, the Palliser Hotel in Calgary, and the Museum of Fine Arts, the Church of the Messiah and the Nurses' Wing of the Royal Victoria Hospital in Montreal. The knowledge, ability and acumen of the older brother, combined with the talent for proportion and design of the younger Sutherland, were a winning combination which led to their having the biggest architectural office in Canada at that period.

In 1902 William Sutherland Maxwell married May Ellis Bolles, whom he had met when in Paris through her brother, Randolph Bolles, also a student of architecture at the École des Beaux Arts. Following their marriage in London, they returned to live in Montreal. Seven years later the couple travelled together on pilgrimage to the Bahá'í holy places in Haifa and 'Akká. Though exposed for nearly a decade to the Bahá'í Faith through his wife – the beloved handmaid of 'Abdu'l-Bahá – Sutherland felt that God could be worshipped directly rather than through any intermediary. Upon meeting 'Abdu'l-Bahá, Sutherland was taught by Him that whatever image man may form of God is his own imagination and that an intermediary is necessary to make a connection between the Infinite Essence and man's finite condition. It is the role of what we call a Manifestation of God to bring into this finite world that otherwise Unknowable Essence – God.

From that encounter with 'Abdu'l-Bahá, the seed of faith germinated in Sutherland. The 'oriental cult' to which Mrs Maxwell belonged appeared very strange to the mainly French Canadian Catholic population of Montreal; Sutherland, however, risking the censure of the uninformed, did not hesitate to accept Bahá'u'lláh and support Bahá'í activities. Thus the home of Sutherland and May Maxwell – today a Bahá'í historic property – became the centre of Bahá'í activity in Canada at that time. Sutherland served for decades as a member, and often as chairman, of the Montreal Bahá'í Local Spiritual Assembly. In the teaching work he was May's silent but willing partner. During those early years, he became known as a man whose nature was described as 'all goodness'.[2] It was said, for instance, that he never approached another person except in a spirit of friendliness, courtesy and graciousness. He also had remarkably sound judgement.

In 1912 'Abdu'l-Bahá visited Montreal, spending the first three days of His brief visit there in the home of the Maxwells. At this time He was undoubtedly introduced to His hosts' infant daughter, Mary Sutherland

Maxwell. During the couple's pilgrimage three years previously 'Abdu'l-Bahá had promised to pray that May and Sutherland might have a child.

Sutherland was a gifted artist. He had 'an encyclopedic knowledge of all the arts, and a creative capacity for bringing new things into being'.[3] The firm of Edward and W. S. Maxwell designed, for instance, the lines of the 17-storey Chateau Frontenac, including many details of the interior, ranging from wrought-iron railings to furniture, grilles, lamps, ceilings and elevator interiors, such details often being designed by Sutherland, who could draw, paint, model and carve with great ability.

Inevitably Sutherland's achievements won him many honours: he became a Fellow of the Royal Institute of British Architects; a Fellow and later President of the Royal Architectural Institute of Canada; an Academician of the Royal Canadian Academy; a member and President of the Province of Quebec Association of Architects; and a founding member of the Pen and Pencil Club as well as the Arts Club in Montreal. As Sutherland approached the evening of his life, these enviable honours would be eclipsed by such honours as only God can bestow upon a man of goodly character, integrity and talent.

Most of William Sutherland Maxwell's mature years were taken up by the demands of his profession. Except for attending some Annual Bahá'í Conventions, visiting Green Acre Bahá'í School and serving on the Montreal Local Assembly, Sutherland had not distinguished himself in the forefront of Bahá'í teaching work.

In his 60s, two events occurred that dramatically changed his life. The first came in 1937, in the form of a cable requesting him to be present at the marriage of his daughter, his only child, to the Guardian of the Bahá'í Faith. His wife and daughter were already in Haifa, following a two-year stay in France, Belgium and Germany. The second happened in 1940, when May arose and won the crown of martyrdom. Frail in health but nonetheless yearning to be more worthy of her beloved daughter, at the age of 70 she embarked on a teaching trip to Argentina, where, upon her arrival in Buenos Aires, she suffered a fatal heart attack on 1 March 1940. After her death, Shoghi Effendi invited Sutherland to transfer his residence to Haifa, which he did, leaving Montreal in May of that year. Upon arriving in Haifa, he moved into the Western Pilgrim House. From then until his death, the man known mostly as 'May Maxwell's husband' was to become intimately involved with his beloved son-in-law in a variety of projects, including the erection of the superstructure of the Shrine of the Báb.

To Sutherland, this change of residence from a life of predictable calm in Canada to the World Centre of the Bahá'í Faith in the Middle East must surely have been challenging. He was in proximity not only to the upheavals of two successive conflicts – one involving the world at large and the other the emerging State of Israel – but also to the historic developments taking place on Mount Carmel.

Through his nobility of character, devotion to the Cause and love for the Guardian, Sutherland enjoyed an intimacy with Shoghi Effendi which few ever achieved. The Guardian, who, in the 1940s, was increasingly preoccupied with his work and, at the same time, afflicted by crises within his own family, warmly bestowed his affections on Sutherland Maxwell.

As Sutherland brought new sketches to Shoghi Effendi in the privacy of his bedroom, the Guardian sometimes invited him to sit close to his bed so they could go over the work together. When the Guardian enthusiastically rubbed attar of rose perfume on Sutherland, the pure-hearted older man, unused to eastern customs, would react with a peculiar mixture of consternation and joy.

In the midst of such intimate moments, one of the crowning glories of Sutherland Maxwell's life moved inexorably forward. Two years after his arrival in the Holy Land, he was asked by the Guardian to make a design for the superstructure of the Shrine of the Báb. In providing Sutherland with cursory indications of how the Shrine should ultimately appear, Shoghi Effendi described the edifice as requiring a dome and an arcade and explained that the building must be neither purely western nor eastern in style and should not appear as a mosque or church. Sutherland was left to conceive his own design.

In 1891 Bahá'u'lláh had designated to 'Abdu'l-Bahá the site for the Tomb of His Herald. Seven years later, the Master instructed Mírzá Asadu'lláh Iṣfahání to transport with the utmost care the remains of the Báb from Iran to the Holy Land. Meanwhile 'Abdu'l-Bahá, 'with infinite tears and at tremendous cost',[4] erected a simple six-room edifice to contain the Báb's remains and built the road leading to it. In 1909 He was able to inter the remains of the Martyr-Herald within the building, in a marble sarcophagus provided by the Bahá'ís of Burma.

Unable Himself to accomplish any further progress on the Shrine, 'Abdu'l-Bahá had expressed His concept of the finished structure: the building would have nine rooms and be surrounded by an arcade and surmounted by a dome. These thoughts of his beloved Grandfather were never far removed from Shoghi Effendi's mind. But, until the 1940s, he lacked both the architect and the money to add anything more than the three additional rooms to the original structure.

By 1944 Sutherland Maxwell had developed, in close collaboration with Shoghi Effendi, the design and model for the superstructure. This model was unveiled in the Eastern Pilgrim House, near the Shrine of the Báb, on 23 May 1944, the 100th anniversary of the Declaration of the Báb, before a group of Bahá'í visitors from various countries. The Guardian joyfully announced to the Bahá'í world two days later the following:

> ANNOUNCE FRIENDS JOYFUL TIDINGS HUNDREDTH ANNIVERSARY DECLARATION MISSION MARTYRED HERALD FAITH SIGNALIZED BY HISTORIC DECISION COMPLETE STRUCTURE HIS SEPULCHRE ERECTED BY 'ABDU'L-BAHÁ ON SITE CHOSEN BY BAHÁ'U'LLÁH. RECENTLY DESIGNED MODEL DOME UNVEILED PRESENCE ASSEMBLED BELIEVERS. PRAYING EARLY REMOVAL OBSTACLES CONSUMMATION STUPENDOUS PLAN CONCEIVED BY FOUNDER FAITH AND HOPES CHERISHED BY CENTRE HIS COVENANT.[5]

In a letter to the Haifa Local Building and Town Planning Commission in 1947, Shoghi Effendi described his plan to complete a building of great beauty, sending along drawings of the completed structure portraying in some detail the future golden-domed Shrine. 'The Architect of this monumental building', Shoghi Effendi concluded his letter, 'is Mr W. S. Maxwell, F.R.I.B.A., F.R.A.I.C., R.C.A., the well-known Canadian architect . . . I feel the beauty of his design for the completion of the Báb's Tomb will add greatly to the appearance of our city and be an added attraction for visitors.'[6]

In 1948 Sutherland and his beloved family experienced the perils associated with the Jewish War of Independence. During that war, travel and communications were limited or entirely cut off. Gunfire raged in the environs of the Bahá'í World Centre. Arabs fled before opposing forces.

Amidst these upheavals, the Guardian was inspired to send Sutherland on a mission to Italy, where he would join Dr Ugo Giachery. There the two men began a collaboration for the building of the superstructure of the Shrine of the Báb. Mr Maxwell was charged by Shoghi Effendi to search for proper material and craftsmanship for carrying out his designs for the Shrine. His departure from Haifa, however, caused Rúḥíyyih Khánum grave concern for her father's safety. To reach the airport, Mr Maxwell and his travelling companion, Ben Weeden, had to travel in an armour-plated taxi. Departing from Lydda (now Ben Gurion) Airport on 16 April 1948 on one of the last planes to get out, they were not heard from for some time. Unable to communicate that they had reached their destination safely, Sutherland could not know that his daughter and beloved Guardian feared for his life.

Dr Giachery met their plane at Rome's Ciampino Airport. Though the entire Italian nation was suffering from the great destruction wrought by the Second World War, Mr Maxwell's stay in Rome brought much joy to Dr and Mrs Giachery. Staying at the Hotel Savoia for lack of apartments, the Giacherys were delighted with Mr Maxwell's grace, humour and boundless love for the Guardian. During the month of his absence from Haifa, Sutherland was able, with the assistance of Dr Giachery, to conclude the necessary contracts; he returned to Haifa on 15 May and assured the Guardian that the erection of the superstructure was a certainty.

In 1948 construction of the superstructure of the Shrine of the Báb began, in spite of the tremendous difficulties imposed within the emerging State of Israel following the ravages of the world war. Gradually the colonnade and arcade, the octagon, the drum with its 18 lancet windows honouring the Letters of the Living, and at last, the crown and dome with its golden tiles, appeared.

Completed in 1953, this wondrous Shrine and the significance of the site of the Báb's sacred remains which it enfolds had been placed in proper perspective by Shoghi Effendi in a letter written by him in March 1951:

> His sacred remains constitute the heart and centre of what may be regarded as nine concentric circles, paralleling thereby, and adding further emphasis to the central position accorded by the Founder of our Faith to One 'from Whom God hath caused to proceed the Knowledge of all that was and shall be', 'the Primal Point from which have been generated all created things'.
>
> The outermost circle in this vast system, the visible counterpart of the pivotal position conferred on the Herald of our Faith, is none other than the entire planet. Within the heart of this planet lies the 'Most Holy Land', acclaimed by 'Abdu'l-Bahá as 'the Nest of the Prophets' and which must be regarded as the centre of the world and the Qiblih of the nations. Within this Most Holy Land rises the Mountain of God of immemorial sanctity, the Vineyard of the Lord, the Retreat of Elijah, Whose Return the Báb Himself symbolizes. Reposing on the breast of this holy mountain are the extensive properties permanently dedicated to, and constituting the sacred precincts

> of, the Báb's holy Sepulchre. In the midst of these properties, recognized as the international endowments of the Faith, is situated the most holy court, an enclosure comprising gardens and terraces which at once embellish, and lend a peculiar charm to, these sacred precincts. Embosomed in these lovely and verdant surroundings stands in all its exquisite beauty the mausoleum of the Báb, the shell designed to preserve and adorn the original structure raised by 'Abdu'l-Bahá to be the Tomb of the Martyr-Herald of our Faith. Within this shell is enshrined that Pearl of Great Price, the holy of holies, those chambers which constitute the tomb itself, and which were constructed by 'Abdu'l-Bahá. Within the heart of this holy of holies is the tabernacle, the vault wherein reposes the most holy casket. Within this vault rests the alabaster sarcophagus in which is deposited that inestimable jewel, the Báb's holy dust. So precious is this dust that the very earth surrounding the edifice enshrining this dust has been extolled by the Centre of Bahá'u'lláh's Covenant, in one of His Tablets in which He named the five doors belonging to the six chambers which He originally erected after five of the believers associated with the construction of the Shrine, as being endowed with such potency as to have inspired Him in bestowing these names, whilst the Tomb itself housing this dust He acclaimed as the spot round which the Concourse on high circle in adoration.[7]

Many times Dr Giachery asked himself whether any other architect could have rivalled Mr Maxwell in the conception and design of the superstructure. Writing of Sutherland's completed work Dr Giachery stated:

> The whole edifice displays a great variety of architectural and artistic gems, products of the inventiveness and refined taste of Mr Maxwell; Shoghi Effendi highly valued and admired every expression of such taste, which manifested itself in the ornamental details abounding throughout the edifice. Nearly every stone shows the gracefulness of the Maxwell artistic talent; in some instances the delicacy of the design is like a beautiful piece of embroidery or hand-made jewellery. It would require much space and time to enter into the details of all the motifs which beautify every frieze, festoon, moulding, garland, arabesque, finial, leaf, flower, rosette and chaplet, with which the appearance of every component piece of marble, or granite, or iron-work, or glass, is enriched.[8]

While the crowning glory of his design was being built, Sutherland, in the winter of 1949–50, became desperately ill. The 75-year-old architect was unable to consciously recognize surroundings or family, and his condition was deemed hopeless by local doctors. Shoghi Effendi, determined that Sutherland should not die, sent Mr Maxwell, accompanied by his daughter Rúḥíyyih Khánum and a trained nurse, to Switzerland, where he made a remarkable recovery and regained all his faculties.

But he was frail. Besieged by repeated gall bladder attacks and requiring a special diet of fresh food, he would deteriorate and then improve, collapse and then recover. Longing to see his beloved homeland, with Shoghi Effendi's approval he journeyed in 1951, with his devoted nurse, to Montreal where, less than a year later, he died on 25 March 1952.

On 24 December 1951, three months before his passing, Shoghi Effendi had appointed Sutherland Maxwell a Hand of the Cause. Humble and profoundly touched upon receiving the news of this great honour, he said, 'I did not do it all alone; there were so many others who helped.'[9]

Rúḥíyyih Khánum, following her attendance at the 1953 Bahá'í Intercontinental Conference in Chicago, travelled to her father's grave site. There she fulfilled Shoghi Effendi's wish that she sprinkle some attar of rose he had given her on Sutherland's grave and place on his resting-place flowers taken from the Shrine of the Báb. When she returned to Haifa bearing photographs of her visit to her beloved father's grave, Shoghi Effendi looked at them for a long time and kept them for himself.

To the Bahá'í world, on the day after Sutherland Maxwell's passing, Shoghi Effendi, whose grief was intense, cabled:

> WITH SORROWFUL HEART ANNOUNCE THROUGH NATIONAL ASSEMBLIES HAND CAUSE BAHÁ'U'LLÁH HIGHLY ESTEEMED DEARLY BELOVED SUTHERLAND MAXWELL GATHERED GLORY ABHÁ KINGDOM. SAINTLY LIFE EXTENDING WELLNIGH FOURSCORE YEARS ENRICHED COURSE 'ABDU'L-BAHÁ'S MINISTRY SERVICES DOMINION CANADA ENNOBLED FORMATIVE AGE FAITH DECADE SERVICES HOLY LAND DURING DARKEST DAYS MY LIFE DOUBLY HONOURED THROUGH ASSOCIATION CROWN MARTYRDOM WON MAY MAXWELL INCOMPARABLE HONOUR BESTOWED HIS DAUGHTER ATTAINED CONSUMMATION THROUGH HIS APPOINTMENT ARCHITECT ARCADE SUPERSTRUCTURE BÁB'S SEPULCHRE AS WELL AS ELEVATION FRONT RANK HANDS CAUSE GOD. ADVISE ALL NATIONAL ASSEMBLIES HOLD BEFITTING MEMORIAL GATHERINGS PARTICULARLY MASHRIQU'L-ADHKÁR WILMETTE ḤAẒÍRATU'L-QUDS ṬIHRÁN. INSTRUCTED HANDS CAUSE UNITED STATES CANADA HORACE HOLLEY FRED SCHOPFLOCHER ATTEND MY REPRESENTATIVES FUNERAL MONTREAL. MOVED

> NAME AFTER HIM SOUTHERN DOOR BÁB'S TOMB TRIBUTE HIS UNIQUE SERVICES SECOND HOLIEST SHRINE BAHÁ'Í WORLD. MANTLE HAND CAUSE NOW FALLS SHOULDERS HIS DISTINGUISHED DAUGHTER AMATU'L-BAHÁ RÚḤÍYYIH WHO ALREADY RENDERED STILL RENDERING MANIFOLD NO LESS MERITORIOUS SELF-SACRIFICING SERVICES WORLD CENTRE FAITH BAHÁ'U'LLÁH.[10]

At the conclusion of the Holy Year marking the centenary of the birth of Bahá'u'lláh's mission, Shoghi Effendi, on 7 October 1953, cabled to the fourth and final Intercontinental Teaching Conference of that special year, held in New Delhi, the following message announcing the completion of the superstructure of the Shrine of the Báb:

> OVERJOYED SHARE FOLLOWING . . . ANNOUNCEMENT . . . FIVE YEAR OLD THREE QUARTER MILLION DOLLAR ENTERPRISE CONSTITUTING FINAL STAGE INITIAL EPOCH EVOLUTION PROCESS INITIATED OVER SIXTY YEARS AGO FOUNDER FAITH HEART MOUNTAIN GOD CONSUMMATED . . . STEADILY SWELLING THRONG VISITORS FAR NEAR MANY DAYS EXCEEDING THOUSAND FLOCKING GATES LEADING INNER SANCTUARY MAJESTIC MAUSOLEUM PAYING HOMAGE QUEEN CARMEL ENTHRONED GOD'S MOUNTAIN CROWNED GLOWING GOLD ROBED SHIMMERING WHITE GIRDLED EMERALD GREEN ENCHANTING EVERY EYE FROM AIR SEA PLAIN HILL. MOVED REQUEST ATTENDANTS CONFERENCE HOLD BEFITTING MEMORIAL GATHERING PAY TRIBUTE HAND CAUSE SUTHERLAND MAXWELL IMMORTAL ARCHITECT ARCADE SUPERSTRUCTURE SHRINE.[11]

# Charles Mason Remey
# 1874–1974

Charles Mason Remey was born into a prominent family in Burlington, Iowa, on 15 May 1874 and lived most of his childhood in Washington DC. He studied at Cornell University from 1893 to 1896 but did not take a degree. In 1896 he went to Paris, where he studied architecture at the Sorbonne until 1903.

Raised an Episcopalian, as a young man Remey was a satisfied and conservative Christian. His religious interests broadened after he read James Freeman Clarke's *Ten Great Religions* and took a course on Buddhism at Cornell. He was also influenced by the turn-of-the-century intellectual atmosphere of Paris.

Through Randolph Bolles, who was a fellow student in one of his architecture classes, he became slightly acquainted with May Bolles at a party hosted by Phoebe Hearst. When he learned that Miss Bolles had unusual religious beliefs, he contacted her. May, in response to Mason Remey's enquiry, gave him Ibráhím Khayru'lláh's twelve lessons[1] in the autumn of 1899. Remey noted:

> These lessons were interspersed with prayer and I joined with her in this spiritual exercise with great anticipation of what was to follow.[2]

Although the lessons were meant to be kept secret, Mason Remey shared each one with his room-mate, Herbert Hopper, who was to follow Remey into the Cause. On the morning of 31 December 1899, May unveiled to Remey the 'pith' of the lessons – information about Bahá'u'lláh and 'Abdu'l-Bahá. Mason Remey later wrote:

> I believed the moment that I was told, and I found myself in the highest ecstasy. I arrived at my rooms, my mind in a whirl; I was in the seventh heaven. I don't remember just how I got home . . .[3]

Thus Charles Mason Remey became the third Bahá'í in Paris.

The intense love which May Bolles had for 'Abdu'l-Bahá attracted more believers to the Faith in Paris. These included Laura Barney, Hippolyte Dreyfus, Marion Jack and the Englishman Thomas Breakwell. When Breakwell passed away, it was Mason Remey who wrote to 'Abdu'l-Bahá about the funeral service held for him by the Paris Bahá'ís, enclosing with his letter a few flowers from the grave. In response Remey received 'Abdu'l-Bahá's beautiful eulogy to Thomas Breakwell, revealed before He had been advised of the young man's passing.[4]

The Bahá'ís of this period held many misconceptions about the Faith and the station of 'Abdu'l-Bahá. There was little in print about the Cause and much of the information came only from Khayru'lláh and those few who had been able to make the pilgrimage to 'Akká. When the western Bahá'ís learned that much of Khayru'lláh's teaching was inaccurate, the resulting doctrinal crisis sorely tested the faith of many believers. After Khayru'lláh defected in 1900 and allied himself with the Covenant-breakers in the Holy Land, hundreds of Bahá'ís left the Cause.

Slowly, guidance began to arrive from the Holy Land. 'Abdu'l-Bahá sent Iranian teachers to deepen the Americans and wrote many Tablets to the western believers. Returning pilgrims also helped to increase the knowledge of the Bahá'ís, who gradually acquired a rudimentary understanding of their Faith. Remey, who became one of America's most knowledgeable and active believers, reflected on his own elementary knowledge, as evidenced by a talk he gave at Green Acre in the early years of the century:

> I myself would have gladly varied my talk and brought in things and thoughts that would add a little variety to what I used to tell people but I just didn't know much about the Baha'i Faith and I was loath to add to my meagre store of tellable materials anything that I was not sure of. I, like many of the other early believers, knew but little of the teachings, but one thing we did know was that 'the Lord had come' and of this we were very sure indeed and this we reiterated over and over again . . . eventually little by little we added other knowledge of the teachings to this.[5]

As awareness of Bahá'í moral and social teachings gradually spread during the early years of the 20th century, Khayru'lláh's emphasis on biblical prophecy gave way to literature on social reform, which broadened the understanding of the Bahá'ís and enabled them to attract others to the Cause. *Bahá'í Revelation*, written by Thornton Chase, was an outstanding work on spiritual development. Anton Haddad's translation of the Kitáb-i-Aqdas and various Tablets of Bahá'u'lláh promoted the understanding and spread of Bahá'í social teachings on the American continent. Soon Mason Remey began to write pamphlets about the Bahá'í Faith, which he published privately and financed himself. In February 1905 his first pamphlet, *Unity: The Revelation of Bahá'u'lláh*, was published.[6]

Over the years Remey produced a large quantity of Bahá'í literature, including more pamphlets, several books, a compilation on the Covenant, a 56-volume set of his personal archives entitled *Bahá'í Reminiscences, Diary, Letters and Other Documents*, and a 119-volume set called *Reminiscences and Letters*. William Collins's *Bibliography of English-Language Works on the Bábí and Bahá'í Faiths 1844–1985* lists over 55 separate works by Remey.[7]

In June 1906 'Abdu'l-Bahá wrote to the Bahai Publishing Society emphasizing the importance of forming an Assembly in Washington and establishing ties between it and the Assemblies in Chicago and New York. Thornton Chase, on behalf of the Chicago House of Spirituality, wrote to Mason Remey asking whether the believers in Washington contemplated organizing themselves. Remey replied:

> we here are not an organized Assemblage, and have not the status as such, as have you in Chicago, or the Believers in New York . . . It will probably be a long time before we have an organized Assembly . . . by that I mean that I feel that the Cause in Washington will have to pass through stages of development before this will come.[8]

Nevertheless, just six months after writing this letter, Remey, an excellent organizer, was able to persuade the Washington Bahá'ís to form a consultative body, and an assembly of nine individuals was established on 14 March 1907. It called itself the 'Working Committee', and its members soon received a Tablet from 'Abdu'l-Bahá encouraging them to be steadfast and to persevere.

'Abdu'l-Bahá also wrote to Mason Remey praising him and his services to the Cause: 'Indeed thou hast served in Washington with no will save the will of God in view and thou hast made me happy and attained my pleasure.' In this same Tablet 'Abdu'l-Bahá revealed these tender words: 'That face of thine which attracts the hearts is far more beautiful and better than this rose, for with that beauty is accompanied illumination.'[9]

Like many Bahá'ís of the time, Mason Remey corresponded with 'Abdu'l-Bahá on matters concerning the Cause and on personal queries, receiving in response Tablets conveying the Master's guidance, enlightenment and encouragement. Many believers wrote to 'Abdu'l-Bahá seeking clarification of the teachings and of the stations of Bahá'u'lláh and the Master. To one such question Remey received this celebrated reply:

> Regarding the station of this servant: My station is Abdul-Baha, my name is Abdul-Baha, my qualification is Abdul-Baha, my praise is Abdul-Baha, my title is Abdul-Baha.[10]

In the Tablet cited above, in which 'Abdu'l-Bahá addressed Mason Remey as 'O thou who art firm in the Covenant!' the Master outlined the seven qualifications of the divinely enlightened soul: Knowledge, Faith, Steadfastness, Truthfulness, Uprightness, Fidelity and Evanescence or Humility. 'Truthfulness', 'Abdu'l-Bahá wrote to Remey, 'is the foundation of all the virtues of the world of humanity. Without truthfulness, progress and success in all the worlds of God are impossible for a soul.' By humility, He wrote, He meant that 'man must become evanescent in God. Must forget his own selfish conditions that he may thus arise to the station of sacrifice . . . When he attains to this station, the confirmations of the Holy Spirit will surely reach him, and man with this power can withstand all who inhabit the earth.'[11]

In a Tablet to Mason Remey as yet untranslated, 'Abdu'l-Bahá advised the young man to travel to all the cities of the United States, including Honolulu, to call all the friends to firmness in the Covenant, to gladden all with its spirit and to guide everyone to spread the Teachings.[12] As Remey possessed considerable financial means – he had inherited a fortune – he was able to fulfil 'Abdu'l-Bahá's hope. Between 1906 and 1911 he travelled across the United States, emphasizing the need for firmness in the Covenant and promoting the creation of local Bahá'í Assemblies. He became so well known for his position on the Covenant that many years later, in 1918, he was appointed to a 'Committee of Investigation' in Chicago to look into possible Covenant-breaking.

In 1907 and 1908 Mason Remey made pilgrimages to the Holy Land, where he visited 'Abdu'l-Bahá, and began his travels for the Faith. In 1907 he travelled to Western Europe and in 1908 he combined his pilgrimage with journeys to England, Germany, Turkestan and Iran. In 'Akká 'Abdu'l-Bahá spoke of the urgent need of uniting the western and eastern believers. In Constantinople Mason Remey was joined by Sydney Sprague and the two travellers journeyed to Odessa, Baku and 'Ishqábád, where they received a stupendous welcome. Remey was able to visit and examine the Temple and its dependencies, and later prepared the first western written account of the Mashriqu'l-Adhkár of 'Ishqábád and the most complete description available in English.[13] Commenting on the importance of building a Temple in Chicago, Remey wrote:

> The rearing of this temple in the East has been a great source of strength to the people there, for through thus expressing their unity the Bahais have become stronger and more united than ever before. Now in America the Bahais are arising to build a Mashrak-el-Azcar. Who can estimate the effect which will be produced by this building? It will be the cause of great strength and unity among the believers of the Occident . . . The erection of a temple in the West will strengthen the Holy Cause in the East more than anything which could happen in this country . . . Throughout the Bahai world the eyes of all are expectingly turned toward this country.[14]

In Iran, Remey and Sprague were warmly greeted, and they held many private meetings in the capital. Their visit, as 'Abdu'l-Bahá had desired, reinforced ties binding the American and Iranian Bahá'í communities. Remey was particularly impressed by the attitude of the Persian Bahá'ís towards women, especially with regard to their education, training and freedom.

In November 1909 Mason Remey and Howard Struven left California on the first 'around the world' Bahá'í teaching trip. Over a period of seven months they visited the Hawaiian Islands, Japan, China, Burma, India and 'Akká. In Hawaii, the Honolulu Bahá'ís were inspired by the visitors to hold their first public meeting. They also decided to establish a community with elected officers. In Japan, Remey was so impressed by the qualities of the Japanese that he wrote to the Chicago House of Spirituality saying that prominent educated Japanese were receptive to the Faith and that thousands of Bahá'í teachers were needed. Remey and Struven were possibly the first western Bahá'ís to visit China. Remey wrote to the Washington DC Bahá'ís about the excellent business opportunities in Japan and China, which could facilitate the settlement of young men from America. In Burma, Remey and Struven visited the Bahá'ís in Rangoon, Mandalay and Daidanaw, where 400 or 500 people had become Bahá'ís since 1907. Remey's letters home emphasized the importance of education in this part of the world. The two men visited various communities in India and spoke at Theosophical lodges and colleges. From India the two travellers sailed to 'Akká. 'Abdu'l-Bahá told them to encourage the Bahá'ís, particularly women teachers, to go to India.

When he returned to the United States in mid-June 1910, Mason Remey wrote about his trip in *Bahai News*, emphasizing in his article that the love and unity of the oriental believers and the initiative and activity of the American Bahá'ís should be combined so that good works might be launched. Remey's interest in establishing ties of unity between the East and the West involved him in the work of the Persian-American Educational Society, of which he became an honorary vice-president. Sponsored by the Washington DC Bahá'í community, the Society was established in 1910 to assist in the educational and economic development of Iran.

In 1911 Mason Remey travelled to England to hear 'Abdu'l-Bahá's first public address in the West, delivered at the City Temple in London. In 1914 he and George Latimer travelled to Europe at the bidding of 'Abdu'l-Bahá, crossing military lines to teach the Faith in France, England and Germany before sailing to 'Akká for a two-week stay. In a Tablet to Agnes Alexander around this time 'Abdu'l-Bahá praised Remey: 'In reality that youth is the son of the Kingdom and the herald of the appearance of Bahá'u'lláh.'[15]

On 8 August 1910 Remey, who had kept in touch with his mentor from Paris, went with Juliet Thompson to the Hahnemann hospital in New York City, where May Maxwell gave birth to her daughter Mary, later to become Amatu'l-Bahá Rúḥíyyih Khánum. Sutherland Maxwell arrived later from Montreal, where the couple had resided since their marriage in 1902.[16]

As a prominent early believer and as an architect, Mason Remey played an important role in the building of the Wilmette Temple. When the Washington DC Bahá'ís wrote to the Centre of the Covenant in 1906, seeking His permission to build their own Temple, 'Abdu'l-Bahá, in oral instructions to Mason Remey, urged them to support the work in Chicago. Following a visit to Chicago in late December 1907, Remey recommended that the Washington community send out circular letters to Bahá'ís across the country proposing the establishment in every local

Bahá'í community of 'temple branches' of a national Temple organization, with the Chicago House of Spirituality as the national coordinating body. Washington sent out three circular letters, with the result that many Bahá'í communities established Temple committees and, consequently, their first Bahá'í organizations.

In his travels around the United States Mason Remey was able to obtain a national perspective of the Cause which many Bahá'ís lacked. He well understood the need for a higher level of cohesion among the Bahá'ís and believed that regular communication among them would assist this end. As interest in the construction of a Bahá'í Temple for North America increased, the necessity of a medium for the circulation of news became paramount. Mason Remey observed:

> At present, no systematic arrangement has been devised for keeping the various assemblies informed of the progress of the Temple work. If people's interest is to be kept up, they must be in regular and constant communication with the centre. Now Mrs True and others are writing hundreds of letters – long hand – and expending energy and time and only reaching a limited number of people. An organ is needed to hold the Believers in communication. The Temple work needs this more than anything else.[17]

Although Corinne True resisted the idea of a monthly magazine in Chicago, through the influence of the Washington community a publication was soon launched. In March 1910 the magazine *Bahai News* first appeared. A year later, the name was changed to *Star of the West*.

At the first Annual Bahá'í Convention of the American believers, held on 20 and 21 March 1909 in Chicago, the Baha'i Temple Unity was established as a national organization, comprising representatives of various Bahá'í communities in North America. Nine individuals were appointed to serve on the Executive Board, among them Charles Mason Remey. The first national Bahá'í institution in the world, the Board published Bahá'í literature, coordinated teaching activities across the continent, assisted isolated believers and oversaw the work of the Temple project. Mason Remey served on the body from 1909 to 1910, from 1911 to 1912, from 1918 to 1920 and from 1921 to 1924.

After the formation of the Baha'i Temple Unity, slow progress was made towards the building of the House of Worship. Although land had been purchased in Wilmette, a suburb of Chicago, as early as 1908, the foundation stone was not laid until 1912, when 'Abdu'l-Bahá visited America. For the next eight years the Executive Board of the Baha'i Temple Unity worked to raise the money necessary to begin the project. Meanwhile, architects were invited to submit drawings for the proposed building. Eventually, at the Annual Bahá'í Convention in 1920, a final decision on the design was to be made. Although at least 15 designs were on display, only three architects were present: Sutherland Maxwell, Louis Bourgeois and Charles Mason Remey.[18] Each of the architects was allowed 20 minutes to explain his concept. Mason Remey 'recounted the long years he had spent preparing nine designs, each based on a different style of architecture. Although he displayed all nine, he recommended only one for the delegates' consideration – a design in an Indian style, presented as a landscaped model – because he felt its size and cost were reasonable.'[19] Remey's design was estimated to cost less than $600,000, compared to Bourgeois's $1,500,000. After much discussion an informal vote was taken:

> The announcement was a clear majority for the Bourgeois model. Then it was that Mr Remey, the only other architect at this time present, arose to the sublime height of self-effacement. He expressed the opinion that[20] 'nothing would please Abdul Baha more, in this present deliberation, than if we could make it a unanimous vote for Mr Bourgeois's model.'[21]

Thunderous applause followed, the delegates rising to their feet to mark their agreement with the motion. 'Abdu'l-Bahá, in a Tablet to Corinne True, praised Mason Remey for his action.

Certain aspects of the Bourgeois design had been influenced by Remey's work. Designs prepared and published by Remey in 1917 had helped Bourgeois solve architectural problems of the first floor. Later, Mason Remey suggested certain modifications to the design to make it more durable and less expensive. He also recommended that the design be submitted for review by a board of architects and civil engineers experienced in large building projects, a plan with which Shoghi Effendi agreed.

In March 1922 Mason Remey was among the small group of veteran believers from the West and the East invited to Haifa by Shoghi Effendi to consult on the development of the Faith following the ascension of 'Abdu'l-Bahá. Shoghi Effendi was perceived by some believers to be immature and inexperienced and certain family members, some older Bahá'ís and even the Governor of Haifa believed he should form the Universal House of

Justice immediately. Having concluded that the formation of the Supreme Body would be premature at that time, Shoghi Effendi instructed his visitors to return to their home countries to work towards the establishment of local and national Bahá'í administrative institutions. While Mason Remey was in Haifa Shoghi Effendi discussed with him plans for the construction of a tomb for 'Abdu'l-Bahá, the site of the future Bahá'í Temple on Mount Carmel and a general landscaping plan for the Bahá'í properties.

Between 1922 and 1950, when he was called to the World Centre by Shoghi Effendi, Charles Mason Remey rendered many services to the Bahá'í Cause. He was a member of the Mashriqu'l-Adhkár Building Committee, which oversaw the building work of the Temple. In 1925 he made a preliminary design for a monumental domed superstructure for the Shrine of the Báb. The next year he made signs for and distributed programmes at the Amity Convention in Philadelphia. In the 1930s he served on national Bahá'í committees, participated in teaching work under the direction of the National Teaching Committee and served for several years on the Regional Teaching Committee of the states of Maryland, Delaware, Virginia and West Virginia.

At a memorial meeting conducted for the late Queen Marie of Romania at the National Cathedral in Washington DC on 25 July 1938, the American Bahá'í Community was represented by a floral tribute, thanks to the initiative and thoughtfulness of Mason Remey. In 1939 Remey designed the memorial to Martha Root in the form of a tablet on which were inscribed the Greatest Name, words of Bahá'u'lláh about teaching and the words of Shoghi Effendi conferring on her a high spiritual station. In May 1948 Mason Remey was a member of the five-strong Bahá'í delegation representing the Bahá'í International Community at the United Nations Conference on Human Rights in Geneva.

During this period Remey also continued to travel for the Faith. In 1943, 1944 and 1947 he visited the American south, and in 1946 the American mid-west. Between 1946 and 1947 he went to cities in Brazil, Colombia, Chile, Cuba, Panama and Peru. From 1947 to 1949 he travelled several times to Europe.

In November 1950 Shoghi Effendi sent cables to Luṭfu'lláh Ḥakím, Jessie and Ethel Revell, Amelia Collins and Mason Remey inviting them to Haifa. One afternoon when they gathered at the Western Pilgrim House with Rúḥíyyih Khánum and Gladys and Ben Weeden, the Guardian announced his intention to constitute from this group the International

Bahá'í Council. In a cable dated 9 January 1951 Shoghi Effendi officially announced his decision to the National Spiritual Assemblies of the East and the West:

> Proclaim National Assemblies of East and West weighty epoch-making decision of formation of first International Bahá'í Council, forerunner of supreme administrative institution destined to emerge in fullness of time within precincts beneath shadow of World Spiritual Centre of Faith already established in twin cities of 'Akká and Haifa . . . Nascent Institution now created is invested with threefold function: first, to forge link with authorities of newly emerged State; second, to assist me to discharge responsibilities involved in erection of mighty superstructure of the Báb's Holy Shrine; third, to conduct negotiations related to matters of personal status with civil authorities. To these will be added further functions in course of evolution of this first embryonic International Institution marking . . . its transformation into duly elected body, its efflorescence into Universal House of Justice, and its final fruition through erection of manifold auxiliary institutions constituting the World Administrative Centre destined to arise and function and remain permanently established in close neighbourhood of Twin Holy Shrines.[22]

The reaction of those assembled in the Western Pilgrim House was recorded by Rúḥíyyih Khánum: 'we were all overcome by the unprecedented nature of this step he was taking and the infinite bounty it conferred upon those present as well as the entire Bahá'í world.'[23] Shoghi Effendi appointed Remey the president of the Council.

Parallel with this step was the development of the institution of the Hands of the Cause. On 24 December 1951 Shoghi Effendi cabled the Bahá'í world:

> Hour now ripe to take long inevitably deferred step in conformity with provisions of 'Abdu'l-Bahá's Testament in conjunction with six above-mentioned steps through appointment of first contingent of Hands of Cause of God, twelve in number, equally allocated Holy Land, Asiatic, American, European continents. Initial step now taken regarded as preparatory full development of institution provided in 'Abdu'l-Bahá's Will, paralleled preliminary measure formation International Council destined to culminate in emergence of Universal House of Justice.[24]

Among the 12 names mentioned by Shoghi Effendi was that of Charles Mason Remey.

On 8 March 1952 Shoghi Effendi announced the enlargement of the International Bahá'í Council, which now comprised Amatu'l-Bahá Rúḥíyyih Khánum, liaison between the Guardian and the Council; Charles Mason Remey, president; Amelia Collins, vice-president; Ugo Giachery, member-at-large; Leroy Ioas, secretary-general; Jessie Revell, treasurer; Ethel Revell, Western assistant secretary; and Luṭfu'lláh Ḥakím, Eastern assistant secretary. In May 1955 the membership was increased to nine through the appointment of Sylvia Ioas.

The Council relieved Shoghi Effendi of many burdensome tasks and he was particularly grateful to Mason Remey and Amelia Collins for their work:

> Greatly welcome assistance of the newly-formed International Council, particularly its President, Mason Remey, and its Vice-President, Amelia Collins, through contact with authorities designed to spread the fame, consolidate the foundations and widen the scope of influence emanating from the twin spiritual, administrative World Centres.[25]

In 1952 Shoghi Effendi asked Mason Remey to prepare a design for the International Bahá'í Archives building, using the proportions of the Parthenon in Athens. Although Remey designed the building, it was Shoghi Effendi 'who set the design . . . to such an extent that its architect would invariably state it was Shoghi Effendi's design, not his'.[26] In effect, Shoghi Effendi directed the architect's hand, refining the drawings during many evenings at the Pilgrim House, until the proposed building achieved a more perfect proportion. Shoghi Effendi had a preliminary drawing of the building displayed at the Intercontinental Conference in New Delhi in October 1953.

Shoghi Effendi also approved Mason Remey's designs for the Houses of Worship built in Kampala and Sydney and for the projected House of Worship in Iran. Mason Remey also designed the House of Worship that is to be built on Mount Carmel – a promise made to him by 'Abdu'l-Bahá – and offered many suggestions for the design of the Shrine of the Báb.

The Guardian requested the Hands of the Cause to attend the Intercontinental Conferences called in 1953 to launch the Ten Year Crusade. Mason Remey represented Shoghi Effendi at the New Delhi Conference and attended those in Kampala, Wilmette and Stockholm. Shoghi Effendi called for a further five Intercontinental Conferences at the midway point of the Plan, in 1958, and again appointed Hands of the Cause to represent him. Mason Remey was asked to be his representative at the conference in Sydney. Before these conferences could be held, Shoghi Effendi passed away in London, on 4 November 1957.

Mason Remey went immediately to England. On the evening of 8 November a meeting of those Hands of the Cause then in London planned the programme for the funeral. The next day the funeral cortège of some 60 motor cars set out from the London Ḥaẓíratu'l-Quds for the Great Northern Cemetery. Mason Remey accompanied Rúḥíyyih Khánum and Amelia Collins in the first car.[27]

On 15 November Rúḥíyyih Khánum, Mason Remey, Amelia Collins, Ugo Giachery and Leroy Ioas entered the Guardian's apartment in Haifa and sealed with tape and wax the safe where he kept important documents. The keys of the safe were then placed in an envelope, which was sealed, signed by the five Hands of the Cause and placed in the safe of Leroy Ioas. The drawers of Shoghi Effendi's desk were also sealed and the seals countersigned.

Four days later, on 19 November, these same five Hands, together with Hands of the Cause Hasan Balyuzi, Horace Holley, Músá Banání, and 'Alí Muḥammad Varqá entered the Guardian's apartment. After ascertaining that the seals were intact, they searched Shoghi Effendi's safe and desk. 'After a thorough search the nine Hands signed a document testifying that no Will or Testament of any nature whatsoever executed by Shoghi Effendi had been found. This information was then reported to the entire body of the Hands assembled in the Mansion of Bahá'u'lláh in Bahjí, adjoining His tomb.'[28]

On 25 November 1957 Mason Remey and his fellow Hands of the Cause issued a 'Unanimous Proclamation of the 27 Hands of the Cause of God' stating that Shoghi Effendi had passed away 'without having appointed his successor'.[29] The Hands also issued a 'Proclamation' addressed to the Bahá'ís of East and West, signed in person by all the Hands of the Cause except Corinne True, who signed by affidavit on 30 November, her frail health having prevented her attendance. The 'Proclamation' announced that 'Shoghi Effendi had left no Will and Testament. It was likewise certified that the beloved Guardian had left no heir.'[30]

> The Aghṣán (branches) one and all are either dead or have been declared violators of the Covenant by the Guardian for their faithlessness to the Master's Will and Testament and their hostility to him named first Guardian in that sacred document.[31]

On the same date Charles Mason Remey was among nine Hands nominated in accordance with 'Abdu'l-Bahá's Will and Testament to serve the interests of the Faith at the World Centre. Known as 'the Hands of the Cause residing in the Holy Land' or, legally, as 'the Custodians of the Bahá'í World Faith', they guided the worldwide Bahá'í community through the next five and a half years to the election of the Universal House of Justice in 1963. Just before he passed away Shoghi Effendi, in October 1957, had written to the Bahá'í world identifying the Hands of the Cause as the 'Chief Stewards of Bahá'u'lláh's embryonic World Commonwealth, who have been invested by the unerring Pen of the Centre of His Covenant with the dual function of guarding over the security, and of insuring the propagation, of His Father's Faith'.[32] This, together with the provisions of the Will and Testament of 'Abdu'l-Bahá, ensured the loyalty and support of the Bahá'ís throughout the world.

Following their historic Proclamation, the Custodians shared with the various National and Regional Assemblies copies of documents relating to the establishment of the Custodianship. All these Assemblies sent letters of recognition of the Custodians to the World Centre, enabling the Custodians to safeguard the properties of the Faith and to take legal responsibility for the affairs of the Cause. The support of these Bahá'í institutions made it possible for the Custodians to lead the international activities of the Cause.

In 1958 the Intercontinental Conferences called by the Guardian convened. The Hands of the Cause appointed by Shoghi Effendi to act as his special representatives to the conferences in Kampala, Sydney and Frankfurt were entrusted with

> a portion of the blessed earth from the inmost Shrine of Bahá'u'lláh, a lock of His precious Hair, and a reproduction of His Portrait, to be exhibited by them to the assembled friends at these Conferences. Two of these representatives will be instructed to deposit, on my behalf, the blessed earth in the foundations of the two Temples to be erected in the African and Australian continents.[33]

Mason Remey represented the Guardian at the conference in Sydney in March 1958. He presented the message from the Hands in the Holy Land and, in a profoundly moving ceremony at the Ḥaẓíratu'l-Quds, anointed the believers with attar of rose as they viewed the precious relics sent by Shoghi Effendi. On the second day of the conference, Mason Remey and Clara Dunn placed the sacred earth from the Most Holy Shrine and plaster from the Báb's cell at Máh-Kú in the foundations of the House of Worship, in a position which would be directly under the centre of the dome. Later, in May 1958, Mason Remey attended the Intercontinental Conference in Wilmette.

At the third Conclave of the Hands, held at Bahjí in October and November 1959, the Hands of the Cause decided to call for the election at Riḍván 1961 of the International Bahá'í Council, originally appointed by Shoghi Effendi in 1951. In their message of 4 November 1959 they stated:

> The embryonic institution established and so highly extolled by the beloved Guardian will thus enter its final stage preceding the election of the Universal House of Justice.[34]

Mason Remey's name was not among those of the Hands of the Cause who signed this letter. On 5 November 1959 the Custodians cabled that Mason Remey was unable to serve as a Custodian:

> ANNOUNCE ALL NATIONAL ASSEMBLIES SELECTION HORACE HOLLEY JOHN FERRABY MEMBERS BODY NINE HANDS HOLY LAND REPLACING MASON REMEY HASAN BALYUZI BOTH UNABLE SERVE PERMANENT CAPACITY.[35]

Returning to Washington from the Holy Land, the ageing Mason Remey, despite his many services, extending over almost six decades, now moved away from the Cause. In April 1960, now in his eighty-sixth year, Charles Mason Remey suddenly issued a proclamation declaring himself to be the second Guardian. 'This extraordinary and sudden display of unexpected pride and conceit'[36] on the part of a Hand of the Cause much loved by 'Abdu'l-Bahá and distinguished in the Cause of God added to the heart-breaking responsibilities of his colleagues. Why he made such a claim in light of the clear guidance of the Will and Testament of 'Abdu'l-Bahá is baffling. Rúḥíyyih Khánum commented on his enigmatic behaviour:

> The death of Shoghi Effendi had really been like an arrow shot into our hearts. Each one [Hand of the Cause] struggled with his bereavement in his own way. One of us, Mason Remey, one of the oldest and most distinguished, solved his personal dilemma by concluding that the Bahá'í Faith could not go on without a Guardian and that undoubtedly Shoghi Effendi's successor was himself.[37]

Initially Mason Remey's fellow Hands regarded his preposterous claim as 'EVIDENCE CONDITION PROFOUND EMOTIONAL DISTURBANCE' from which they hoped he would soon recover.[38] Later, however, they reluctantly concluded that his defection from the Bahá'í teachings was 'a persistent and well-thought-out campaign',[39] as he followed his original proclamation with other statements, including 'The Question of the Guardianship' and his first 'Encyclical' to the Bahá'í world. In this latter document Mason Remey referred to all the Hands of the Cause as violators and called upon the Bahá'ís to turn to him for guidance.

Very few Bahá'ís responded to Mason Remey's call. The Custodians cabled the Continental Hands and all National Spiritual Assemblies on 28 April asking them to repudiate Remey's claims. By 10 May 1960, 29 responses had been received at the World Centre from National Spiritual Assemblies and National Conventions around the world, each pledging loyalty to the Custodians and rejecting Remey's assertions completely. By the end of May this number had risen to 35. A meeting of the International Bahá'í Council on 27 April similarly rejected Remey's claims. Only the National Spiritual Assembly of France voted to recognize the claim, first eight and later only five of its members upholding Mason Remey's assertions. The National Spiritual Assembly was dissolved and a new election was called. On 15 June the Custodians were able to write to the Continental Hands that 'It seems only about fifteen believers throughout the world have accepted Mason Remey's claim, of whom about ten are in France and five in the United States.'[40]

After an agonizing period of consultation by post, the Hands of the Cause cabled all National Spiritual Assemblies on 26 July:

> ENTIRE BODY HANDS OBEDIENT PROVISIONS WILL TESTAMENT CENTRE COVENANT COMMUNICATIONS BELOVED GUARDIAN ENJOINING THEM PROTECT HOLY CAUSE ATTACKS ENEMIES WITHIN WITHOUT ANNOUNCE BAHA'I WORLD MASON REMEY COVENANT BREAKER EXPELLED FAITH. ACTION FOLLOWS LONG PERIOD PATIENCE FORBEARANCE OPPORTUNITY GIVEN HIM WITHDRAW SHAME-

> FUL PRETENSION SACRED STATION GUARDIANSHIP CONSTITUTING HERETICAL CLAIM CONTRARY EXPLICIT PROVISIONS WILL MASTER. DESPITE UNIVERSAL REPUDIATION DENUNCIATION BY ALL HANDS INTERNATIONAL BAHA'I COUNCIL ALL NATIONAL ASSEMBLIES REMEY CONTINUING AGITATE UNFOUNDED CLAIM ACTIVELY SEEKING CREATE DIVISION RANKS FAITHFUL SOW SEEDS DOUBT HEARTS BELIEVERS UNDERMINE ACTIVITIES INSTITUTION HANDS CHIEF STEWARDS DEDICATED FULFILMENT BELOVED GUARDIAN'S TEN YEAR PLAN. ACCORDANCE INJUNCTION WILL TESTAMENT ABDU'L-BAHA CALL UPON FRIENDS EVERYWHERE SHUN REMEY AND ANYONE ASSOCIATING WITH HIM OR ACTIVELY SUPPORTING HIS CLAIMS. CONFIDENT COMMUNITY MOST GREAT NAME UNITED WHOLEHEARTED CONDEMNATION THIS LATEST ILL-FATED ATTEMPT DISRUPT GOD'S HOLY CAUSE WILL EMERGE TRIUMPHANT STRENGTHENED GALVANIZED ISSUE FORTH WIN REMAINING GOALS GLORIOUS WORLD ENCIRCLING CRUSADE.[41]

A small number of believers in Europe, the United States and elsewhere who accepted Remey's claim were also expelled from the Faith. Some of the more prominent Remey followers later provoked a series of conflicts among themselves that hopelessly divided his supporters.

The disaffection of Charles Mason Remey was a bitter and tragic experience for those Hands who had known and loved him for much of their lives. His defection added to the burdens of the Chief Stewards and saddened their hearts. Indefatigable in their role of safeguarding the security of the Faith worldwide as the Remey drama unfolded and played itself out, the Hands of the Cause of God were lauded by the Universal House of Justice in its first message of 30 April 1963, which acknowledged the 'sacrifice, the labour, the self-discipline, the superb stewardship'[42] of the Hands during such a critical time in the history of the Faith.

Charles Mason Remey died a few months short of his 100th birthday, on 4 February 1974. On 5 April 1974 the Universal House of Justice informed the Bahá'í world:

> CHARLES MASON REMEY WHOSE ARROGANT ATTEMPT USURP GUARDIANSHIP AFTER PASSING SHOGHI EFFENDI LED TO HIS EXPULSION FROM RANKS FAITHFUL HAS DIED IN FLORENCE ITALY IN HUNDREDTH YEAR OF HIS LIFE BURIED WITHOUT RELIGIOUS RITES ABANDONED BY ERSTWHILE FOLLOWERS. HISTORY THIS PITIABLE DEFECTION BY ONE WHO HAD RECEIVED GREAT HONOURS FROM BOTH MASTER AND GUARDIAN CONSTITUTES YET ANOTHER EXAMPLE FUTILITY ALL ATTEMPTS UNDERMINE IMPREGNABLE COVENANT CAUSE BAHÁ'U'LLÁH.[43]

# Ṭarázu'lláh Samandarí
## 1874–1968

Ṭarázu'lláh Samandarí came from an illustrious family. His great-grandfather Ḥájí Rasúl was a pious man; a Shaykhí, he encountered the Báb many times in the Shrine of the Imám Ḥusayn around 1841 and was greatly attracted to Him. Ṭarázu'lláh's grandfather was a well-known and highly respected merchant of Qazvín who recognized the Cause of God from the earliest times. His father was the Apostle of Bahá'u'lláh Shaykh Muḥammad Káẓim-i-Samandar.

Ṭarázu'lláh Samandarí was born in Qazvín, Iran, on 16 October 1875 and was raised by his parents and a grandmother who had been one of the companions of Ṭáhirih. Bahá'u'lláh gave the infant the name Ṭarázu'lláh, which means the 'ornament of God'. Ṭarázu'lláh was addressed as 'Ṭaráz Effendi' by Bahá'u'lláh, 'Mírzá Ṭaráz' by 'Abdu'l-Bahá and 'Jináb-i-Samandarí' by Shoghi Effendi. A few months after Ṭarázu'lláh's birth, his mother's paternal uncle and his wife had a baby girl named Ṭarázíyyih. Twenty-one years later the two 'Ṭarázes' married.

'Abdu'l-Bahá revealed prayers for Ṭarázu'lláh, including this supplication:

> Gladden his bosom with the light of Thy knowledge and loose his tongue through the vitalizing breaths of Thy celestial might. Enable him to intone the verses of divine unity in the assemblies . . . Grant him the joy of gazing upon the resplendent light of Thy mercy in the mystic Paradise and enable him to reveal the evidences of Thy grace amongst Thy servants by the manifestation in his luminous temple of the signs of Thy bounty.[1]

Ṭarázu'lláh's father had living with the family the distinguished scholar and accomplished calligrapher Mullá 'Alí, known as 'Jináb-i-Mu'allim', who had been introduced to the Bahá'í Faith by Samandar. He was put in charge of the education of Ṭarázu'lláh, his brothers and his cousins and Ṭarázu'lláh received much of his education from him. Jináb-i-Mu'allim was praised by Bahá'u'lláh as the first teacher to put into practice Bahá'í principles of education. Under his tutelage, the young Ṭarázu'lláh learned Persian and Arabic grammar, rudimentary bookkeeping and calligraphy. The boy showed great aptitude for calligraphy and would copy prayers and Tablets in his beautiful handwriting:

> gradually I developed a strong love for inscribing the scriptures. At the age of twelve I invariably got up four hours before dawn and occupied myself with copying the holy scriptures. I felt extremely joyful and not at all tired. Later on, even while travelling on the road, in a train, in a ship, or during stoppages, I was busy copying the holy writings.[2]

Ṭarázu'lláh later became an outstanding master of the art and one of the most distinguished calligraphers in Iran. He became well versed in the Bahá'í writings from copying many volumes of scriptures. Thus, although he lacked formal training, he was revered as a highly educated man who could always refer to relevant texts when needed. His craft enabled him to become familiar, to a unique degree, with the penmanship of the Báb, Bahá'u'lláh, 'Abdu'l-Bahá and their various amanuenses; in later years he would use this skill to identify innumerable Tablets.

When Ṭarázu'lláh was 13 he joined his father's office and learned the skills of trade. He studied hard but he longed to attain the presence of Bahá'u'lláh. When he was 16 he had the opportunity to go on pilgrimage, and in early November 1891, together with his maternal aunt, his sister and a few friends, he left for the Holy Land. He later described his meeting with Bahá'u'lláh:

> On the third day of arrival in 'Akká, I was summoned and had the honour of being in His presence in the House of 'Abbúd. He was seated on a chair and bade me to be seated. A servant served tea, but I was absolutely unable to drink. I was so overwhelmed by His grandeur and might that I was unable to look at His peerless countenance and beauty . . . Again I attained His presence in the Mansion as He was revealing holy verses. There was no one else there except the amanuensis. Since that embodiment of might and majesty was

walking while revealing and chanting the verses, I managed to have a proper look at His face which reflected a divine grandeur and sovereignty. While revealing verses, His holy face was illumined; sometimes He gestured with His hand and gazed at the sea. The amanuensis was writing at great speed; the floor was covered with pages and pages of Tablets; perhaps the equivalent of one-fifth of the Qur'án was revealed during those few hours. The words were flowing out of His holy mouth, at times in chanting and at other times with great majesty.[3]

Ṭarázu'lláh remained in 'Akká for seven months and was in the Holy Land when Bahá'u'lláh passed away in May 1892. He told many stories of this pilgrimage throughout his life. For example, on the first day of Riḍván, he and three other believers were sitting on the floor facing Bahá'u'lláh, who was sitting on a chair. Bahá'u'lláh began to chant the Tablet of Sulṭán. 'The spiritual experience', Ṭarázu'lláh said, 'the ecstasy, is beyond description.'[4]

On Naw-Rúz Bahá'u'lláh had sent the youth a gift of clothes – a robe, a shirt, a cummerbund and socks. Later that day He received guests in the Garden of Junaynih and the 16-year-old Ṭarázu'lláh again found himself in the presence of Bahá'u'lláh. Bahá'u'lláh revealed some verses, a banquet was served and the poets Nabíl and 'Andalíb composed poems for the occasion. Ṭarázu'lláh later described the garden as 'the throne of the highest heaven'.[5] Afterwards Ṭarázu'lláh and a few others accompanied Bahá'u'lláh back to Bahjí. 'It would take me days to tell you about my seven months in His presence seventy-two years ago,' Ṭarázu'lláh Samandarí said to the Bahá'ís gathered in the Albert Hall in London in 1963.[6]

While he was in the Holy Land, Ṭarázu'lláh learned the true station of the Most Great Branch. One day, after he had been ill for many days and unable to enter the presence of Bahá'u'lláh, Ṭarázu'lláh begged for an audience with Him. When this was granted, Bahá'u'lláh remarked to the youth that he had complained of not seeing Him for two weeks. Had he not seen 'Abdu'l-Bahá? 'Yes, my Lord, every evening and every morning,' Ṭarázu'lláh replied. 'Then why did you complain that you did not have the reward of pilgrimage?' Bahá'u'lláh asked.[7]

Nine months before His ascension, Bahá'u'lláh had expressed His desire to leave this world. During the final months of His life He never spoke openly about His approaching end, but to those believers who came into His presence the close of His earthly life became increasingly apparent. Fifty days after Naw-Rúz in 1892 He contracted a persistent fever, which weakened Him. His loved ones were thrown into agony, despair and turmoil. Six days before His passing, He summoned for a final audience those believers who were present in the Mansion.

Ṭarázu'lláh, who was among those summoned, left this account of his final meeting with Bahá'u'lláh:

> It was the tenth or eleventh day of His illness; just before sunset the word came that He had given permission that all who were in the Mansion – permanent residents, pilgrims, servants – everybody could go and meet Him and so I entered His presence. His bed was spread in the middle of the room, on the floor, and He was leaning against two or three pillows. He was extremely weak and His voice was feeble. After some words of kindness in greeting, He uttered some words denoting separation and leave-taking. He counselled us to love and unity and quoted sentences from the Kitáb-i-Aqdas [with regard to His ascension]. It can be imagined how we all felt after hearing those words. 'Andalíb, overtaken by grief and with tears flowing, exclaimed, 'O, Bahá! O, Bahá!' He gave us permission to leave. Immersed in sorrow and with hearts consumed with grief, we prostrated ourselves at His feet, circumambulated Him, and left the room.[8]

Mr Samandarí recalled the verse Bahá'u'lláh repeated that day from the Most Holy Book:

> Be not dismayed, O peoples of the world, when the daystar of My beauty is set, and the heaven of My tabernacle is concealed from your eyes. Arise to further My Cause, and to exalt My Word amongst men. We are with you at all times, and shall strengthen you through the power of truth. We are truly almighty. Whoso hath recognized Me will arise and serve Me with such determination that the powers of earth and heaven shall be unable to defeat his purpose.[9]

At this final meeting Bahá'u'lláh stressed the importance of firmness in the Covenant, and with good reason. The violation of the Covenant by 'Abdu'l-Bahá's brothers following closely upon the passing of Bahá'u'lláh directly affected Ṭarázu'lláh. His sister Thurayyá was married to the 'vacillating Mírzá Ḍíyá'u'lláh',[10] the third son of Bahá'u'lláh, who joined the ranks of the Covenant-breakers. After her husband's death in 1898 she was kept in the Mansion of Bahjí against her will; when her father came to take her home, he was attacked and beaten on the order of Mírzá Muḥammad-'Alí and thrown out of Bahjí.[11]

The ninth day after Bahá'u'lláh's passing, His Book of the Covenant, the Kitáb-i-'Ahd, was unsealed and read before a group of nine men chosen from His family. In the afternoon it was read a second time, at the Shrine of Bahá'u'lláh before an assemblage of family and Bahá'ís, including Ṭarázu'lláh Samandarí. After the document was read 'Abdu'l-Bahá asked the pilgrims to relate all they had witnessed to the Iranian Bahá'ís when they returned home. A month after Bahá'u'lláh's passing Ṭarázu'lláh left for Iran, travelling by mule through Turkey to avoid an area infected by cholera.

Ṭarázu'lláh Samandarí made his second pilgrimage in 1898, staying in 'Akká for four months, and his third pilgrimage in 1904. During Mr Samandarí's 40-day visit 'Abdu'l-Bahá showed him a long scroll inscribed with the names of American Bahá'ís who had pledged their allegiance to the Master. 'Abdu'l-Bahá asked Ṭarázu'lláh to take the scroll to Iran and Turkestan, show it to the Bahá'ís and encourage them to arise and dedicate themselves to the service of the Cause.

When Mr Samandarí returned to Iran he met with 'Alí-Akbar Rafsanjání, who was to be his travelling companion, and together the two men set out in about October 1904 to accomplish the mission set them by 'Abdu'l-Bahá. For the next five years they journeyed by mule, donkey, carriage and on foot to many remote villages in Iran and Turkestan. It was a dangerous time for Bahá'ís in Iran, owing to the political instability of the country. Mr Samandarí and his companion were in Fars when the martyrdom of 18 believers took place in Nayríz. He and Mr Rafsanjání helped care for those who fled the persecutions. 'Abdu'l-Bahá was extremely pleased by the success of the two travellers and encouraged other believers to follow in their footsteps.

It was around 1895 that Mr Samandarí married his cousin Ṭarázíyyih. While her husband was away on his lengthy journey she received a Tablet from 'Abdu'l-Bahá 'praying that this temporary separation would be the cause of eternal reunion'.[12]

Towards the end of 1909 'Abdu'l-Bahá invited Mr Samandarí and Mr Rafsanjání to the Holy Land. While they were there 'Abdu'l-Bahá told them that their services 'would never be effaced from the hearts and memories of the friends who had met them'.[13]

After his long journey Ṭarázu'lláh found himself in poor health and he was advised to return to Qazvín, where he resided for the next 17 years and carried on his trade. During this time he actively taught the Faith, corresponded with many Bahá'í centres, served as secretary of the Spiritual Assembly and produced a Bahá'í newsletter. The young Guardian, Shoghi Effendi, asked him to copy and verify the authenticity of various Tablets received by the Bahá'ís of Iran. This last task resulted in an 18-volume compilation of the priceless documents.

About six years after the ascension of 'Abdu'l-Bahá the Spiritual Assembly of Ṭihrán asked Mr Samandarí to undertake a teaching trip to Adhirbáyján. With the encouragement of Shoghi Effendi, who called him a 'strong pillar' and an example of 'obedience and dedication',[14] Mr Samandarí left for Tabríz in February 1928, together with his wife and two sons. After this he never again had a settled home, spending the next 40 years travelling and teaching the Faith. At the beginning of the journey he started his diaries, which he wrote daily and which are now deposited in the International Archives in Haifa.

In 1933, at the request of the Central Spiritual Assembly of Ṭihrán, Mr Samandarí interrupted his travelling for a few months to manage the Bahá'í national office in Ṭihrán, but the Guardian soon asked him to resume his journeys. After the death of their eldest son in 1940, the Samandarís were invited to Haifa, where they spent 50 days. During this pilgrimage the Guardian told Mr Samandarí, 'The first cycle of your services has come to an end; now is the beginning of the second cycle.'[15] His special mission was to encourage the Bahá'ís to pioneer to the countries around Iran. When he returned home, Mr Samandarí consulted with the National Spiritual Assembly and a pioneer committee was formed.

In 1945 Mr Samandarí was asked to go to Shíráz to protect the Faith from Covenant-breakers. He remained there for some seven years. During this period his wife died, on 7 November 1947, at her pioneer post in Zanján. Mr Samandarí had not seen her for three years.

On 24 December 1951 Mr Samandarí was among the 12 believers appointed Hands of the Cause of God by Shoghi Effendi. At the request of the Guardian he attended all four Intercontinental Conferences in 1953 and visited many centres in Europe and America. In 1957 he represented Shoghi Effendi at the inaugural Convention of the National Spiritual Assembly of Arabia.

In November 1957 came the shocking news of the passing of Shoghi Effendi. Mr Samandarí travelled to London to attend the funeral and then on to Haifa for the first Conclave of the Hands of the Cause. He attended every subsequent Conclave and was able, during these visits to the Holy Land, to identify many Tablets. He travelled widely during the custodianship of the Hands, visiting, among other places, Egypt, Uganda and Somalia in 1958; Turkey in 1960 and 1962; and the Indian subcontinent in 1959 and 1962. He attended the Intercontinental conferences in Kampala in January 1958 and Jakarta–Singapore in September. He also attended the first convention of the National Spiritual Assembly of Burma in 1959.

Ṭarázu'lláh Samandarí was of small but erect stature. His movements were quick, his gait rapid, his eyes penetrating, his hair dark, his hands sensitive and his speech powerful. An early riser, he rested only to regain his strength and to prepare himself to serve others. He maintained a dignity, courtesy and kindness which attracted and inspired generations of youth to embark on paths of service.

He also had a keen sense of humour. Once he was in the Philippines with Hand of the Cause Dr Muhájir, who had been asked by the Universal House of Justice to visit a particularly difficult country for the protection of the Cause.

> He went to Mr Samandarí and gently told him, 'Samandaríján, today I have received an invitation to go to . . . As it is on your way I want to write to them that they will have the bounty of your visit instead of mine.' Mr Samandarí roared with laughter. 'You young people think you can put something over on this old man? Whenever I am asked to go there . . . I literally weep. I think they should again have the bounty of your visit this time.'[16]

Out of his love for Raḥmat Muhájir, Mr Samandarí went to that country.

In 1967 Mr Samandarí travelled to Edirne with other Hands of the Cause to pray at the House of Bahá'u'lláh before attending the Intercontinental conference in Wilmette in October as the representative of the Universal House of Justice. Although he was now 92 years old, he travelled in the cold winter months to Alaska, Canada and many cities in the United States. Despite weakness and fever, he was interviewed by many American newspapers. The *Los Angeles Times* reported: 'Aged Persian likens self to Apostle Peter: There is only one difference, he asserts; Apostle "heard the Son, I saw the Father"'.[17]

On his travels in the United States Mr Samandarí spoke of the tests and calamities that would befall the world and of the importance of steadfastness. He emphasized the staunch faith of the disciples of Christ, whose example 'Abdu'l-Bahá had asked the Bahá'ís, in His Will and Testament, to follow.

One group of believers was particularly unsettled by his remarks about coming calamities and asked him whether the believers would be protected. He firmly replied, 'The Faith will be protected.'[18]

The Faith of God, he said, progresses through tests and calamities. This has always been the way of God. Christ endured great calamities and pressures for three years, sacrificing comfort and finally his life. His disciples likewise abandoned rest and tranquillity to spread Christianity until one by one they laid down their lives. The Báb suffered for seven years for the sake of the Cause of His Successor and for humankind. The Letters of the Living behaved exactly as the disciples had, sacrificing their all for the Cause of God.

On another occasion, Mr Samandarí told his listeners that steadfastness was found in the blood of the martyrs of Iran and in the endurance of men, women and children who remained at their pioneering posts regardless of the difficulties. Steadfastness, he said, is a strength that brings victories to the Cause of God and is a quality born of love for Bahá'u'lláh and His wondrous Faith.

Following nearly a year of extensive travel, Ṭarázu'lláh Samandarí returned to the Holy Land in August 1968 to attend the commemoration of the centenary of Bahá'u'lláh's arrival on those shores. As soon as Mr Samandarí arrived, however, his health deteriorated and he had to be hospitalized. Although he could not attend the observances, he survived to witness the 100th anniversary of Bahá'u'lláh's sojourn in the Holy Land. He passed away on 2 September 1968.

Nearly a thousand Bahá'ís attending the commemoration events escorted Mr Samandarí's coffin from the House of 'Abdu'l-Bahá to the Bahá'í cemetery at the foot of Mount Carmel. He was buried next to Ḥájí Mírzá Ḥaydar-'Alí, a wish he had often expressed. 'The funeral was one of the largest and most impressive since the time of the Master.'[19]

Thus was laid to rest the only Hand of the Cause of God to serve the Faith during the ministries of Bahá'u'lláh, 'Abdu'l-Bahá, Shoghi Effendi, the Custodians and the Universal House of Justice; one who long ago was the recipient of these immortal words of the Guardian:

> The brilliant, the continuous and sincere services of that chosen one of the Lord of all beings are engraved on my heart and inscribed in permanent characters in the records of the Abhá Kingdom; the passage of ages and centuries cannot efface them.[20]

On 3 September the Universal House of Justice cabled the Bahá'í world:

> WITH SORROWFUL HEARTS ANNOUNCE PASSING HAND CAUSE GOD SHIELD HIS FAITH DEARLY LOVED TARAZULLAH SAMANDARI NINETY-THIRD YEAR HIS LIFE ON MORROW COMMEMORATION CENTENARY BAHAULLAHS ARRIVAL HOLY LAND. FAITHFUL TO LAST BREATH INSTRUCTIONS HIS LORD HIS MASTER HIS GUARDIAN HE CONTINUED SELFLESS DEVOTED SERVICE UNABATED UNTIL FALLING ILL DURING RECENT TEACHING MISSION. UNMINDFUL ILLNESS HE PROCEEDED HOLY LAND PARTICIPATE CENTENARY. EVER REMEMBERED HEARTS BELIEVERS EAST WEST TO WHOSE LANDS HE TRAVELLED BEARING MESSAGE HIS LORD WHOSE COMMUNITIES HE FAITHFULLY SERVED THIS PRECIOUS REMNANT HEROIC AGE WHO ATTAINED PRESENCE BLESSED BEAUTY YEAR HIS ASCENSION NOW LAID REST FOOT MOUNTAIN GOD AMIDST THRONG BELIEVERS ASSEMBLED VICINITY VERY SPOT BAHAULLAH FIRST TROD THESE SACRED SHORES. REQUEST ALL NATIONAL ASSEMBLIES HOLD MEMORIAL SERVICES INCLUDING FOUR MOTHER TEMPLES BAHAI WORLD BEFITTING LONG LIFE DEDICATED EXEMPLARY SERVICE LORD HOSTS BY ONE ASSURED CENTRE COVENANT LOVING WELCOME PRESENCE BAHAULLAH ABHA KINGDOM. EXTEND LOVING SYMPATHY ASSURANCE PRAYERS MEMBERS DISTINGUISHED FAMILY.[21]

# George Townshend
## 1876–1957

Sometime Canon of St Patrick's Cathedral, Dublin, and Archdeacon of Clonfert, George Townshend was born on 14 June 1876 into a large and prosperous Anglo-Irish family. His father, Charles Uniacke Townshend, was twice married and sired 14 children. A successful businessman, philanthropist, Justice of the Peace and administrator in late 19th-century Dublin, Charles initiated a hospital project for the poor, founded a highly successful Land Agency, and, as Secretary and Vice-President of the Royal Dublin Society, made a very great contribution to the raising of farming standards in Ireland. He was the first employer of George Bernard Shaw.

The first child of Charles's second marriage, to Anna Maria Roberts, George had an idyllic childhood and became a good horseman. When he was ten he was sent to school in England, first to Wynyards School in Watford and then to Uppingham, a famous public school in Rutland, to which he won a scholarship and where he distinguished himself in literature and sports. As a result of these achievements, he was made a prefect and was elected to The Union Society and the Committee of Games.

Between 1895 and 1899, George attended Oxford University as an exhibitioner at Hertford College, reading classics and English. He achieved no particular scholastic distinction, receiving thirds in Mods and Greats. He did, however, continue to excel in sports, so that when he graduated with his modest BA he had a number of cups for athletics but no plans for a career. In later years he confided to his daughter, Una, that he 'just didn't work', his main interest being athletics.[1]

George spent the next four years at odds with himself. David Hofman writes that he lived at home to please his mother, and was articled to a law firm in Dublin. At some time during these four years he became a leader writer for *The Irish Times*. At the end of this time he earned a degree in law, and was called to the Bar in October 1903. Although he continued to pay his dues to the legal Society until 1920, he never argued a case and expressed to his father his distaste for the field. Charles Uniacke immediately offered him the opportunity to travel anywhere in the world for two years, and so George, at the age of 27, abandoned his fledgling law career for the Rocky Mountains of America.

He spent the next two years as a nomad, footloose and content with his meanderings. Lacking a permanent address, he spent his days in solitude, in contemplation and in the saddle. Wandering about in the majesty of that region, he worked as a logger when his funds ran out, fought a forest fire, visited Yellowstone Park and, occasionally, deliberately got himself lost.

One day he came across a copy of the Bhagavad-Gita. This holy book prompted him to focus on spiritual matters, which led, in turn, to his decision to devote himself to the search for the knowledge of God. Reborn, George found that he now had a purpose in life. Unsure about how he should proceed, he decided, after some thought, to enter the Church. He became a deacon in 1905 and was ordained as a priest in the Episcopal Church of America at Salt Lake City the following year. He was placed in charge of the Mission to the Mormons and Indians at St Mary's in Provo, Utah from 1904 to 1909.

Later, at the University Extension Department at the University of the South in Sewanee, Tennessee, George became Assistant-Director and in 1912 was appointed Assistant-Professor of English. In 1910 he met Nellie Jennings Roche, the great-great-granddaughter of General James Robertson, who had founded the city of Nashville. Within three years they were engaged to be married. George set out in July 1913 for Ireland to make the necessary arrangements.

Meanwhile, Nellie became convinced that George had 'a definite spiritual destiny' incompatible with marriage to her.[2] So, soon after George arrived in Ireland, she sent him a telegram breaking the engagement. Distraught, George returned to Sewanee, where he remained for the next three years.

In 1916 George returned to Ireland for a visit. While there he was afflicted with a form of neuritis that left him blind for several weeks. He resigned from his post at Sewanee by cable and took up the duties of a curate at Booterstown, County Dublin.

In the winter of 1916, as he was recovering from his blindness, George received two or three pamphlets about the Bahá'í Faith from Louise Finley, the librarian at Sewanee. Interested, he wrote to the address on the pamphlet asking for books, and in July 1917 received the three volumes of *Tablets of Abdul Baha Abbas*. On the same day that the books arrived George met Anna Sarah (Nancy) Maxwell, who became his wife in 1918. They had two children, Brian, born in 1920, and Una, born in 1921. In March 1919 George became Rector of Ahascragh in County Galway and on 10 June he wrote his first letter to 'Abdu'l-Bahá:

> I want to acknowledge the light and uplift and happiness and exhilaration which are coming to me through the knowledge of your teachings, the reports of your life and through the writings of Bahaollah; and to offer my thanks, deep heartfelt and ever-growing for this extraordinary benefit.
>
> Recognizing that you are immersed in cares and important work, I should hardly have ventured to intrude upon you but that I read in Vol. ii of your Tablets the other day that it is necessary for every soul who believes in (his) Lord to send Abdul Baha a letter of acknowledgement in the Oneness of God.
>
> . . . I wished to thank you and to ask you for help that I might make the better speed out of the Valley of Search into the Valley of Love. I am not impatient; not a bit! I am quite willing to travel for the hundred thousand years, – but I am hungry and empty![3]

'Abdu'l-Bahá responded six weeks later, on 24 July 1919:

> I pray on thy behalf that the fire of love be set aglow in thy heart and spiritual sensations may stir and move thy soul, so that thou mayest be quickened, mayest fly and soar toward the Ideal Friend, mayest sacrifice thy soul to the Beloved of the World and consecrate thy life to the diffusion of the Divine Fragrances. If thou attainest unto such a bounty thou shalt become the sign of guidance, shalt become an enkindled candle in the gathering of men, shalt be baptized with the spirit of life and the fire of the Love of God, shalt be born again from the world of nature and shalt attain unto everlasting life.[4]

A few months after receiving this Tablet, in 1920, George sent his declaration of faith to 'Abdu'l-Bahá in the form of a poem, later published under the title 'Recognition', which begins:

Hail to Thee, Scion of Glory, Whose utterance poureth abroad
The joy of the heavenly knowledge and the light of the greatest of days!
Poet of mysteries chanting in rapture the beauty of God,
Unto Thee be thanksgiving and praise![5]

The Master replied on 19 December 1920:

> Thy letter has been received. Every word indicated the progress and upliftment of thy spirit and conscience. These heavenly susceptibilities of thine form a magnet which attracts the confirmation of the Kingdom of God; and so the doors of realities and meanings will be open unto thee, and the confirmations of the Kingdom of God will envelop thee . . .
>
> It is my hope that thy church will come under the Heavenly Jerusalem.[6]

From this time on George devoted all his energies to the attempt to acquaint his fellow clergymen in the Church of Ireland to an understanding of Bahá'u'lláh. The Bahá'í Faith had not yet reached the point in its development where Bahá'ís had to separate themselves from their previous religious affiliations and so George Townshend remained a clergyman, although clearly a Bahá'í.

On 16 November 1921 George wrote again to 'Abdu'l-Bahá:

> The Truth which thou hast spoken has enveloped and consumed me. I have no thought nor hope nor longing other than this . . .
>
> Freely, willingly, with a song of exultation in my heart and blessings on my lips, I make this surrender. I cannot live nor exist and do otherwise than thus yield myself. That from which I flee is no longer tolerable. That to which I turn is the reality, the inborn Truth of all men and of the world as of me . . .
>
> This one thing I ask: that I may have the wisdom to understand and the firmness to obey implicitly the command of God.[7]

The letter arrived in Haifa on 8 December 1921, less than two weeks after 'Abdu'l-Bahá had passed away.

After 'Abdu'l-Bahá's passing, George's life became a perpetual struggle to free himself from his ecclesiastical orders while he served Shoghi Effendi. The former he would not achieve for another 26 years; the latter he accomplished by assisting Shoghi Effendi in his translation work.

Shoghi Effendi had few helpers in the 1920s and 1930s and welcomed

George's offer of 27 February 1926 to assist in the work of translating the Holy Writings. Shoghi Effendi responded immediately to his 'dear fellow worker', sending him on 28 March the first part of his translation of the Hidden Words.

Three weeks later George returned the translations with his comments. The Guardian replied:

> I deeply appreciate your most valuable suggestions and am glad to learn that you will continue in the days to come to collaborate with me in such an important, arduous and delicate task.[8]

Thus was born a rare and wonderful relationship which would endure until George's passing in 1957. During this time Shoghi Effendi wrote 147 letters to George and George wrote over 200 letters to the Guardian. Hofman writes that during this 31-year period George assisted in the anglicization and editing of translations made by the Guardian and advised him on certain points of idiomatic English, reviewing such translations as the Hidden Words (1926–7); the Kitáb-i-Íqán (1930); *The Dawn-Breakers* (1930–1); *Gleanings from the Writings of Bahá'u'lláh* (1934–5); *Prayers and Meditations by Bahá'u'lláh* (1937); and Epistle to the Son of the Wolf (1940). In addition George assisted the Guardian with his history of the Faith, *God Passes By* (1943–4). He also wrote the introductions to *The Dawn-Breakers* and *God Passes By*, working in close collaboration with Shoghi Effendi, and, at the Guardian's bidding, chose the titles for these works.

Shoghi Effendi was, of course, as sole interpreter of the Word of God, the final arbiter of the translated text. Thus, while George provided advice as to syntax, idioms and questions of English literary style and the like, which the Guardian accepted or rejected at his discretion, the translations are Shoghi Effendi's own and are imbued with the authority of the Guardian.

No one, apart from Shoghi Effendi and George himself, and Ethel Rosenberg in the early days, knew of the collaboration between the two men, as George begged the Guardian not to publish his name on the title page of *The Hidden Words* or the Introduction to *The Dawn-Breakers*, as the Guardian wished to do. George felt such identification with the new revelation would damage his chances of bringing his church 'under the Heavenly Jerusalem', as the Master had hoped. Shoghi Effendi accepted his plea and thus the title page of *The Hidden Words* states that the translation was made 'with the assistance of some English friends'.[9] Later George changed his mind and the Guardian announced triumphantly on the title page of *God Passes By* that the Introduction was by George Townshend, M.A., Canon of St Patrick's Cathedral Dublin, Archdeacon of Clonfert.[10]

George wrote more than 60 books, pamphlets, poems and commentaries of his own. At Shoghi Effendi's request he contributed essays and poems to successive volumes of *The Bahá'í World* and prepared and presented a paper on 'Bahá'u'lláh's Groundplan for World Fellowship' for the first conference of the World Congress of Faiths in London in 1936. His best-known works are, perhaps, his trilogy on the Bible and the Bahá'í Faith: *The Promise of All Ages*, *The Heart of the Gospel* and *Christ and Bahá'u'lláh*.

The Guardian greatly appreciated and valued George's writing ability. In 1955 Shoghi Effendi told John Ferraby when he was in Haifa that George was 'the best writer we have. He must be taken care of. He is the best living Bahá'í writer'.[11] So strongly did Shoghi Effendi feel that George should concentrate his energies on writing that he had written to him around 1948:

> I strongly feel that you should concentrate in the years to come, on writing for the Cause, whose literature you can, more than anyone else throughout the Bahá'í world, enrich.[12]

After his services for Shoghi Effendi, George Townshend's second goal was to free himself from the Church of Ireland. In the early years of his service to the Church he held to 'Abdu'l-Bahá's admonition that 'the veil must in no wise be suddenly rent asunder',[13] feeling instead that the Faith would enrich, purify and rebuild Christianity. In his remote Galway parish, he remained for the most part and for many years ignorant of the profound changes rocking Christianity and the Church. He hoped and for some time believed that Christianity, as a whole, would be revitalized through the teachings of Bahá'u'lláh.

Gradually, however, he came to realize that materialism, agnosticism and atheism had hopelessly shattered the solidarity of Christianity. He longed, as early as 1926, to be by some means released from his clerical duties, which he felt were constricting his services to Bahá'u'lláh and separating him from his fellow believers. In 1933 he was elected, one of eight in all Ireland, a Canon of St Patrick's Cathedral, Dublin and was made Archdeacon of Clonfert.

Meanwhile he proclaimed, alone and unaided but with increasing brilliance and frankness, the Cause of Bahá'u'lláh. In *The Promise of All Ages* he announced the advent of Bahá'u'lláh, sending this work to his fellow clergymen. In his Bible classes he spoke openly about 'Abdu'l-Bahá. In the Church of Ireland *Gazette* he circulated his essay 'Reflection on the Hidden Words'. His scholarly work was greeted with utter apathy by his fellow churchmen.

While the Guardian applauded his courageous acts in proclaiming the Cause, George's determination to leave the Church was delayed repeatedly and indefinitely by his wife, who was unwilling to abandon a secure way of life for an uncertain future without a job and a pension. On more than one occasion, as George contemplated openly his wish to break with the Church, Nancy threatened to leave him or else simply to denounce him publicly. For George, the break-up of his home would be disastrous for the Cause and would undermine his prestige with those he hoped most to influence within the Church.

As a consequence of Nancy's opposition, George was unable, until 1947 and at the age of 70, to leave the Church. On 12 March of that year he wrote to Shoghi Effendi:

> After a business meeting on March 4th the Bishop showed me an air letter addressed by an Anglican missionary to the Archbishop of Canterbury complaining of *The Promise of All Ages*, a book which, he said, exalted Bahá'u'lláh at the expense of Christ and was otherwise objectionable . . . the Bishop said all he wanted to hear was if the book lowered Christ. I said certainly not; but that I had much more to tell him. I myself believed Bahá'u'lláh was Christ returned . . . I had said more in my Introduction to *God Passes By* than in *The Promise of All Ages*, and had sent it to him; I intended to say more still and was ready to leave the Church. I withdrew nothing and modified nothing I had written. He is *very* kind, and very narrow; and was utterly perplexed. He asked a number of questions . . . My departure is now certain and near.[14]

Many years before, Nancy had promised to support George should he be attacked over the publication of *The Promise of All Ages*. Now, though unhappy, she stood by her word. On 30 September 1947, in consultation with the National Spiritual Assembly of the British Isles, George renounced his orders, resigned all his clerical positions and, family unity preserved, moved with his wife and daughter into a small bungalow in a suburb of Dublin as a voting member of the Bahá'í community.

Shortly after his resignation from the Church George worked with the National Spiritual Assembly of the British Isles on 'Operation Townshend', a great effort to promote the Bahá'í Faith. In *The Old Churches and the New World Faith* George gave his reason for renouncing his Orders – 'to be loyal to Christ as I know Him' – and issued a challenge to all Christians to accept Christ in His new appearance 'in the glory of the Father'. This was sent to over eight thousand people in the British Isles, including all bishops, senior clergy, members of both Houses of Parliament and political leaders. In addition, at Shoghi Effendi's behest, similar campaigns were launched in Australia, Canada and the United States and several European Bahá'í communities translated the article for the same purpose. The response from the Church was, however, negligible.

George Townshend's modesty and unassuming nature and his occasional absent-mindedness often caused people initially to overlook the strength of his character and personality. Adib Taherzadeh described his own reaction when he first encountered George in Manchester in 1950:

> Frankly I wasn't really impressed at that stage. He was speaking at the Centre and I thought I was going to hear a great and forceful personality; but because of his wonderful meekness and humility . . . I could not believe this was the famous George Townshend I had heard about.
>
> Later on I came to realize that this was really the source of his greatness – his humility and modesty. I realized on looking back, that he never spoke of himself, of the things he had done for the Faith. He never said anything for instance about his work for Shoghi Effendi . . . It was Nancy who used to tell me all these things, and George would just listen and say very little.[15]

George was very lonely at his pioneer post in Dublin and suffered many hardships in his bungalow. He undertook much of the housework and dealt with the many problems and discomforts. His greatest hardship was, perhaps, being dependent on the Bahá'í Fund: the National Spiritual Assembly of the British Isles had, with the approval of the Guardian, provided him with a small income to supplement the meagre royalties he earned from his books. After George left the Church he put all of his energies into the Bahá'í Faith. He attended conferences and summer schools but, most of all, he wrote.

On 24 December 1951 George received a telephone call from the secretary of the National Spiritual Assembly in London, who read him the text of a cable from Shoghi Effendi:

> MOVED CONVEY GLADTIDINGS YOUR ELEVATION RANK HAND CAUSE. APPOINTMENT OFFICIALLY ANNOUNCED PUBLIC MESSAGE ADDRESSED ALL NATIONAL ASSEMBLIES. MAY SACRED FUNCTION ENABLE YOU ENRICH RECORD SERVICES ALREADY RENDERED FAITH BAHAULLAH.[16]

After 30 years of developing the Administrative Order, Shoghi Effendi had appointed the first contingent of 12 Hands of the Cause. George replied to his Guardian on 14 January 1952:

> From my inmost heart with deep humility I thank you for the bounty you have bestowed on me in appointing me a Hand of the Cause of God.
>
> In response I wish now to offer my entire submission to you as Guardian of the Cause and state my ardent desire to give all I am and all I have to the service of the Faith of Bahá'u'lláh. May He grant me an ever warmer love, and ever deeper wisdom, in following His will and bearing witness to His truth.[17]

George's appointment as a Hand of the Cause did not enable him to fulfil his inmost longings – to make a pilgrimage to the Holy Land and meet Shoghi Effendi, to rouse the Church of Ireland, to revisit America and to realize Nancy's wholehearted support for his work. His health did not permit him to travel and Shoghi Effendi encouraged him to complete his final work, *Christ and Bahá'u'lláh*, for which the Guardian waited anxiously.

In 1953 George made his only trip as a Hand of the Cause, to attend the Intercontinental Teaching Conference in Stockholm. In 1954 he appointed two Auxiliary Board members, Dorothy Ferraby and Marion Hofman, to assist him in his work as a Hand in 'fostering the spiritual welfare of the Bahá'ís in the entire area of the British Isles, including its islands, Norway, the Faroe islands and Iceland'.[18]

During the final years of his life George was periodically confined to nursing homes in Dublin. Nevertheless he continued to pour upon the believers his love and guidance. Unable to attend conferences and summer schools in Britain as his health declined, he was present at all of them through the messages he sent and received. His poor health made work on his book difficult, but he did not abandon it:

> By this time . . . he could speak and write only with difficulty, and this difficulty increased as the months went by. Near the end he seemed to be retaining and working out in his head whole portions of the book, or even the whole book, and then condensing it in his head into lengths he would be able dictate.[19]

On the last day of his life George Townshend received the published volume of *Christ and Bahá'u'lláh* in his hands. He died in Baggot Street Hospital, Dublin on 25 March 1957 and, following a Bahá'í service, was interred in the churchyard of Enniskerry, close to the graves of his mother and sister. Perhaps his supplication to Bahá'u'lláh came to the minds of those who mourned him:

> Only Beloved! With a heart on fire
> And all my longings set in one desire
> To make my soul a many-stringed lyre
>   For Thy dear hand to play.
> I bend beneath Thy mercy-seat and pray
> That in the strength of perfect love I may
> Tread with firm feet the red and mystic way
>   Whereto my hopes aspire.
>
> I have forgotten all for love of Thee
> And ask no other joy from destiny
> Than to be rapt within Thy unity
>   And – whatso'er befall –
> To hear no voice on earth but Thy sweet call,
> To walk among Thy people as Thy thrall
> And see Thy beauty breathing throughout all
>   Eternal ecstasy.
>
> Lead me forth, Lord, amid the wide world's ways,
> To bear to Thee my witness and to raise
> The dawn song of the breaking day of days.
>   Make my whole life one flame
> Of sacrificial deeds that shall proclaim
> The new-born glory of Thy ancient name;
> And let my death lift higher yet the same
>   Triumphal chant of praise![20]

The Guardian's cable summed up the heroic record of his life:

> DEEPLY MOURN PASSING DEARLY LOVED MUCH ADMIRED GREATLY GIFTED OUTSTANDING HAND CAUSE GEORGE TOWNSHEND. HIS DEATH MORROW PUBLICATION HIS CROWNING ACHIEVEMENT ROBS BRITISH FOLLOWERS BAHÁ'U'LLÁH THEIR MOST DISTINGUISHED COLLABORATOR AND FAITH ITSELF ONE ITS STOUTEST DEFENDERS. HIS STERLING QUALITIES HIS SCHOLARSHIP HIS CHALLENGING WRITINGS HIS HIGH ECCLESIASTICAL POSITION UNRIVALLED ANY BAHÁ'Í WESTERN WORLD ENTITLE HIM RANK WITH THOMAS BREAKWELL DR ESSLEMONT ONE OF THREE LUMINARIES SHEDDING BRILLIANT LUSTRE ANNALS IRISH ENGLISH SCOTTISH BAHÁ'Í COMMUNITIES. HIS FEARLESS CHAMPIONSHIP CAUSE HE LOVED SO DEARLY SERVED SO VALIANTLY CONSTITUTES SIGNIFICANT LANDMARK BRITISH BAHÁ'Í HISTORY. SO ENVIABLE POSITION CALLS FOR NATIONAL TRIBUTE HIS MEMORY BY ASSEMBLED DELEGATES VISITORS FORTHCOMING BRITISH BAHÁ'Í CONVENTION. ASSURE RELATIVES DEEPEST LOVING SYMPATHY GRIEVOUS LOSS. CONFIDENT HIS REWARD INESTIMABLE ABHÁ KINGDOM.[21]

George Townshend's grave is marked by a stone surmounted by an open book, its text 'and I saw a new heaven and new earth'.

# Valíyu'lláh Varqá
# 1884–1955

Valíyu'lláh Khán Varqá was the third son of Mírzá 'Alí-Muḥammad Varqá, who laid down his life for the Cause along with his son Rúḥu'lláh in 1896, and the grandson of Ḥájí Mullá Mihdí Yazdí. His mother was Fáṭimih, the daughter of Ḥájí Mírzá 'Abdu'lláh Khán Núrí of Mázindarán. Both of his grandfathers were staunch believers in the Cause of Bahá'u'lláh. Born in 1884 in Tabríz, Valíyu'lláh spent his early years with his family in Tabríz in the household of his maternal grandmother, a woman of the Sháhsavan tribe and a fanatical Muslim.

Mírzá 'Abdu'lláh Khán was a member of the court of the Prince Regent Muẓaffaru'd-Dín Mírzá, but fell out of favour when false reports were submitted to the Prince Regent by enemies of the Cause, stating that he had permitted Bahá'ís to gather in his home to conduct anti-government activities. He was therefore forced to leave Tabríz and go to Ṭihrán.

Mírzá 'Abdu'lláh Khán's wife, who was deeply hostile to the Faith, allowed Valíyu'lláh's father no peace at home and soon sought his death by hiring an assassin. He was therefore forced to flee Tabríz, which he did in the dead of night. Enraged that he should have escaped her clutches, the mother-in-law sought his death warrant through a local mujtahid related to her. As a result of her hostility and machinations, the breach between her and her husband and between 'Alí-Muḥammad Varqá and his wife so widened that no alternative remained but divorce.

Being very young, Valíyu'lláh and his brother Badí'u'lláh were left in the care of their mother and grandmother while the two older sons accompanied their father to Zanján. Badí'u'lláh died in childhood. The grandmother's hatred of the Cause was so deep and she vilified 'Alí-Muḥammad Varqá to such an extent that Valíyu'lláh wept for his father's apparent deviation from the true Faith.

When Valíyu'lláh was 16 his paternal uncle, Ḥájí Mír Ḥusayn, moved the youth from his grandmother's home to his own home in Míyanduáb. Under the influence of this devout Bahá'í, Valíyu'lláh himself became a believer some time before the age of 20.

A confirmed Bahá'í, Valíyu'lláh yearned to visit the Holy Shrines and the Centre of the Covenant. He left Míyanduáb for Tabríz, where he was to join another believer as a travelling companion on the road to 'Akká. However, the Local Spiritual Assembly of Tabríz consulted about young Valíyu'lláh and directed him to join his brother 'Azízu'lláh in Ṭihrán. 'To persuade them to revise their decision', Valíyu'lláh later wrote, 'was out of the question and I was therefore obliged to leave for Ṭihrán.'[1]

In Ṭihrán Valíyu'lláh entered the Tarbíyat School, where he took up his studies. In his spare time he began to study English and Arabic, later attending the American High School in the city.

Eventually, and with the permission of his brother, Valíyu'lláh made his pilgrimage to 'Akká and met 'Abdu'l-Bahá. From 'Akká he proceeded to Beirut, where he continued his studies. Every summer of his stay in Beirut 'Abdu'l-Bahá invited him to 'Akká, where he had the opportunity to study the Cause and take courses with other students under the tutorage of Ḥájí Mírzá Ḥaydar-'Alí.

Valíyu'lláh intended to continue his studies in England, but in 1909 'Abdu'l-Bahá instructed him to return to Ṭihrán. While in Ṭihrán, he married Bahíyyih <u>Kh</u>ánum, the daughter of Saní-us-Sulṭán. Together they had ten children, three of whom died in infancy. The remaining seven were all firm believers in the Cause of God.

For a time following his marriage Valíyu'lláh worked as a secretary in the Russian Legation. In 1912 he received permission to join 'Abdu'l-Bahá's entourage in America, where he acted as 'Abdu'l-Bahá's treasurer and occasionally as His interpreter. He also accompanied the Master on His journeys to London and Paris.

When Valíyu'lláh returned to Ṭihrán he found employment as First Secretary Translator at the Turkish Embassy, gaining the respect of his co-workers for the way he performed his duties. Many of his colleagues learned of the Bahá'í Faith from him and became friendly towards the Bahá'ís. During the Second World War, however, and after many years of service, he was asked to undertake a task that touched on politics and he immediately resigned his post.

In his youth Valíyu'lláh served on the Local Spiritual Assembly of Ṭihrán and on various Bahá'í committees. When the National Spiritual Assembly of Iran was established in 1934, he was elected to it, occasionally serving as chairman.

In 1938 the Trustee of the Ḥuqúqu'lláh, Ḥájí Ghulám Riḍá Iṣfahání, known as Amín-i-Amín, passed away. Shoghi Effendi then appointed Valíyu'lláh to be Trustee. As Trustee, Valíyu'lláh was in regular contact with Shoghi Effendi, from whom he earned frequent praise for his efficiency and faithfulness in carrying out his tasks.

Valíyu'lláh was among the first contingent of Hands of the Cause to be appointed by the Guardian, on 24 December 1951. At the request of Shoghi Effendi, in 1953 he attended the Intercontinental Conferences in Kampala and Chicago. The Guardian then asked him to travel to South America, where he visited Bahá'ís and taught the Faith for 46 days. In July he left for Europe to participate in the Stockholm Conference and to visit many cities in Germany.

While in Germany, he became ill and had an operation in Ulm. Not waiting to convalesce completely, he travelled first to India to participate in the New Delhi conference and then to Iraq, Egypt, Syria and Turkey to meet with the Bahá'í communities. While he was in Iraq he again fell ill and had to rest in the Baghdád Ḥaẓíratu'l-Quds before resuming his tour. The cold weather in Turkey also adversely affected his health and he returned to Iran for three months before going on pilgrimage and meeting Shoghi Effendi. His two-week visit in the Holy Land greatly inspired and revitalized him.

On leaving the Holy Land Valíyu'lláh, on the instructions of the Guardian, went to Germany, where he joined other Hands of the Cause and continued his medical treatment. He then travelled to Austria, staying in Vienna for some three months, giving public addresses to large crowds and teaching the Cause before returning to Iran.

In 1955 severe pains compelled him once again to seek medical treatment in Europe. He was admitted to hospital in Tübingen, where he died on 12 November. Shoghi Effendi instructed that a memorial be erected at his own expense at the grave of Mr Varqá in Stuttgart. On 15 November the Guardian cabled the Bahá'í world:

PROFOUNDLY GRIEVED LOSS OUTSTANDING HAND CAUSE GOD, EXEMPLARY TRUSTEE ḤUQÚQ, DISTINGUISHED REPRESENTATIVE MOST VENERABLE COM-

> MUNITY BAHÁ'Í WORLD, WORTHY SON BROTHER TWIN IMMORTAL MARTYRS FAITH, DEARLY BELOVED DISCIPLE CENTRE COVENANT. SHINING RECORD SERVICES EXTENDING OVER HALF CENTURY ENRICHED ANNALS HEROIC FORMATIVE AGES BAHÁ'Í DISPENSATION. HIS REWARD ABHÁ KINGDOM INESTIMABLE. ADVISE ERECT MY BEHALF BEFITTING MONUMENT HIS GRAVE. HIS MANTLE AS TRUSTEE FUNDS ḤUQÚQ NOW FALLS ON 'ALÍ MUḤAMMAD, HIS SON. INSTRUCT ROWḤÁNÍ ṬIHRÁN ARRANGE BEFITTING MEMORIAL GATHERINGS CAPITAL PROVINCES HONOUR MEMORY MIGHTY PILLAR CRADLE FAITH BAHÁ'U'LLÁH. NEWLY-APPOINTED TRUSTEE ḤUQÚQ NOW ELEVATED RANK HAND CAUSE.[2]

When asked why his father was named a Hand of the Cause, Dr 'Alí Muḥammad Varqá replied, 'Because Shoghi Effendi recognized in him this capacity, devotion and sincerity. From him there was a feeling of nothingness. He devoted his life, mind and health to the Faith. The Faith for him was above all.'[3]

Amelia Collins

Dorothy Baker

Dorothy Baker speaking at a meeting in India

Dorothy Baker at Kanpur, India

'Alí-Akbar Furútan

'Alí-Akbar Furútan with Bahá'ís in Leicester, England

'Alí-Akbar Furútan with the Spiritual Assembly of Moscow, 1990

'Alí-Akbar Furútan at a youth conference in Sheffield, England

Dr Ugo Giachery

Dr Ugo Giachery views the construction of the Samoan Temple near Apia, 1982

Dr Ugo Giachery with children during the Finnish Bahá'í Summer School, 1985

Dr Hermann Grossmann

Dr Hermann Grossmann,
Frankfurt, Germany, 1951

Horace Holley

Leroy Ioas

Leroy Ioas with Bahá'ís in Africa, 1953

Leroy Ioas with four African Bahá'ís who had invited Shoghi Effendi to Africa

Leroy Ioas visits Bahá'ís in Leicester, England

Sutherland Maxwell

May and Sutherland Maxwell

Charles Mason Remey

Ṭarázu'lláh Samandarí

George Townshend

Fourteen Hands of the Cause at the European Intercontinental Teaching Conference in Stockholm, 1953

Valíyu'lláh Varqá with 'Azízu'lláh Varqá, Ṭihrán, 1908

Valíyu'lláh Varqá

# V

# Hands of the Cause Appointed by Shoghi Effendi on 29 February 1952

CABLEGRAM, 29 FEBRUARY 1952

ANNOUNCE FRIENDS EAST AND WEST, THROUGH NATIONAL ASSEMBLIES, FOLLOWING NOMINATIONS RAISING THE NUMBER OF THE PRESENT HANDS OF THE CAUSE OF GOD TO NINETEEN. DOMINION CANADA AND UNITED STATES, FRED SCHOPFLOCHER AND CORINNE TRUE, RESPECTIVELY. CRADLE OF FAITH, DHIKRU'LLÁH KHÁDEM, SHU'Á'U'LLÁH ÁLÁ'Í. GERMANY, AFRICA, AUSTRALIA, ADELBERT MUHLSCHLEGEL, MÚSÁ BANÁNÍ, CLARA DUNN, RESPECTIVELY. MEMBERS AUGUST BODY INVESTED IN CONFORMITY WITH 'ABDU'L-BAHÁ'S TESTAMENT, TWOFOLD SACRED FUNCTION, THE PROPAGATION AND PRESERVATION OF THE UNITY OF THE FAITH OF BAHÁ'U'LLÁH, AND DESTINED TO ASSUME INDIVIDUALLY IN THE COURSE OF TIME THE DIRECTION OF INSTITUTIONS PARALLELING THOSE REVOLVING AROUND THE UNIVERSAL HOUSE OF JUSTICE, THE SUPREME LEGISLATIVE BODY OF THE BAHÁ'Í WORLD, ARE NOW RECRUITED FROM ALL FIVE CONTINENTS OF THE GLOBE AND REPRESENTATIVE OF THE THREE PRINCIPAL WORLD RELIGIONS OF MANKIND. . .

SHOGHI

# Shu'á'u'lláh 'Alá'í
## 1889–1984

When Shu'á'u'lláh 'Alá'í was seven, his father wrote to 'Abdu'l-Bahá and received a Tablet from Him in return. In this Tablet, 'Abdu'l-Bahá plays upon the meaning of Shu'á'u'lláh's name, 'ray of the sun of divinity', and commands him to radiate and illumine the horizons. Shu'á'u'lláh's father instructed his son to commit the precious words to memory:

> O flame of the love of God! The ray must shed light and the sun must rise; the full moon must shine and the star must gleam. Since thou art a ray, beseech thou the Lord to enable thee to give illumination and enlightenment, to brighten the horizons and to consume the world with the fire of the love of God. I hope that thou mayest attain such a station, nay surpass it. Upon thee be His glory.[1]

These words, Mr 'Alá'í said in an interview when he was 84 years old, became his 'guide and refuge in life'.[2]

Shu'á'u'lláh was born into a Bahá'í family in Ṭihrán on 16 November 1889. His father, Siyyid Muḥammad Náẓimu'l-Ḥukamá, held several degrees in theology and was supposed to become a cleric, following the tradition of his family. When his close friend 'Andalíb became a Bahá'í, Siyyid Muḥammad tried to bring him back to what he thought was the straight path. Instead, he became a believer himself, at the age of 19, and was subsequently confirmed when he received a Tablet addressed to him spontaneously by Bahá'u'lláh. Fearless in proclaiming the Bahá'í Cause, Siyyid Muḥammad was condemned to death as a heretic at his birthplace in Lahíjan (Gílán) but escaped to Ṭihrán, where he eventually became a physician to the guards and household of the Sháh.

Shu'á'u'lláh's mother, Khadíjih (known as 'Bíbí Ján'), was related to Mírzá Aḥmad Azghandí of Khurásán, one of the early believers referred to in *The Dawn-Breakers.*

Shu'á'u'lláh studied at home until the age of ten, when he was sent to the newly-opened Tarbíyat school in Ṭihrán. Later he attended medical school, but after a time he left to study accountancy at the Polytechnic of Ṭihrán.

Shu'á'u'lláh worked first for the Ministry of Customs in Ṭihrán. When he was 19 he served as financial officer of the Police Department. Finding the coffers empty, he raised a large sum from levies on vodka, tobacco and opium, and city-gate taxes on goods and produce entering the walled city from the countryside. From 1914 to 1919 he was treasurer of the Ministry of Justice, establishing such a high personal reputation for reliability that parties to lawsuits, litigation cases and arbitrations deposited and entrusted their funds to him while the courts decided to whom impounded money and property should go. He was chosen to go to the war fronts in the north to pay soldiers their arrears of salary. He carried out this task so well, in temperatures below freezing in the winter of 1921, that he was promoted to chief controller of army finances, a position he held for 25 years, rising to the rank of general.

General 'Alá'í left the army for a few years and served as Director-General of Finance to the Ministry of Post and Telegraph during the period when the whole service was being modernized. He returned to the army in 1930, but also served as head of the Carpet Company of Iran as well as on the boards of directors of the Bank Melli of Iran (the National and later the Central Bank) from its inception in 1927 and of Bank Sepah for 30 years. Often charged with the conduct of delicate commissions, he once supervised the inventory of the Crown jewels, which were valued at $7 billion.

When he was just 18 years old 'Alá'í was appointed a member of the 'Maḥfil-i-Muratib' committee, established by the Hands of the Cause as the embryonic Central Assembly of Ṭihrán. Its responsibility was to conduct Bahá'í meetings in Ṭihrán and to assume certain of the functions of a Local Spiritual Assembly. In 1913 'Alá'í was elected to the Local Spiritual Assembly of Ṭihrán, on which he served without interruption for 30 years.

'Alá'í married his cousin Furúghíyyih 'Alá'í when he was 23. She possessed wisdom, patience and common sense. Together they had a family of five children: Ḥishmat, Mihrangíz, Bihjat, Faraḥangíz and Amír.

In 1934 the National Spiritual Assembly of Iran was established and Shu'á'u'lláh was elected to it. He served on the body until 1952, when the Guardian called upon him to assume worldwide duties. In 1944 he pioneered with his family to Tajrísh, a village in the suburbs of Ṭihrán, and was soon elected to serve on its Local Spiritual Assembly.

On 29 February 1952 General 'Alá'í was appointed a Hand of the Cause. Almost immediately he began his international travels. In 1952 he and his wife went on pilgrimage to the Holy Land and afterwards 'Alá'í travelled through Egypt, Sudan and Iraq. He attended the four intercontinental conferences held in 1953 in Kampala, Wilmette, New Delhi and Stockholm, and visited Bahá'í centres in the United States, Germany, Italy, Switzerland, the Netherlands, India, Pakistan, Egypt, Lebanon, Syria and Turkey. In 1956 he travelled to India, Ceylon, Indonesia and Malaysia and then participated in the first Southeast Asia teaching conference in August. In April 1957 he represented Shoghi Effendi at the inaugural convention of the National Spiritual Assembly of Pakistan. In 1959–60 he visited India, Pakistan, Hong Kong, Macau, Japan, Vietnam and Malaysia. In April 1961 he represented the Bahá'í World Centre at the inaugural conventions of Colombia and Jamaica and in 1962 attended the formation of the National Spiritual Assembly of Sri Lanka. From April to November 1961 he visited the United States, France, Belgium, the Netherlands, Germany, Italy, Switzerland and Turkey. In the 1970s General 'Alá'í concentrated on the protection of the Faith in Iran, but he did continue to travel. In 1975, for example, he visited Europe and the United Kingdom, and he was able to leave Iran in 1977 and 1978 to consult with the International Teaching Centre in Haifa. Altogether he travelled to more than 35 countries, some of them on more than one occasion, and to all continents except Australia. In addition, General 'Alá'í helped to manage the Bahá'í properties in Iran, a service often involving important negotiations with the government. Because of his reputation as a financier, his rank of army general, his connections with diplomatic channels, as well as the sheer force of his personality, he could obtain appointments with high officials of government and negotiate for the recognition of the Bahá'í Faith and the protection of the Bahá'ís.

In 1978 General 'Alá'í left Iran and moved to France, where he lived until 1981, when he resettled in Scottsdale, Arizona. There, in 1984, on his ninety-sixth birthday, General 'Alá'í passed peacefully away in the presence of close family members and devoted friends.

The Universal House of Justice paid tribute to his remarkable life in a cable dated 18 November 1984:

> GRIEVED ANNOUNCE PASSING HANDCAUSE SHUAULLAH ALAI 16 NOVEMBER THUS ENDING MORE THAN SEVENTY YEARS UNINTERRUPTED DEDICATED SERVICES THRESHOLD BAHAULLAH. HE WAS TOWER STRENGTH CRADLE FAITH WHERE HE SERVED EMINENTLY DEVOTEDLY IN ITS EMERGING ADMINISTRATIVE INSTITUTIONS SINCE THEIR INCEPTION. HIS MEMBERSHIP MANY DECADES NATIONAL ASSEMBLY FREQUENTLY AS CHAIRMAN BEARS WITNESS TRUST BAHAIS IRAN PLACED HIS NOBLE PERSON. HIS EXEMPLARY COURAGE REPRESENTING INTERESTS FAITH HIGH PLACES HIS INTEGRITY PERFORMING OFFICIAL DUTIES ENHANCED PRESTIGE BELOVED FAITH HE SO DILIGENTLY SINCERELY CHAMPIONED ENTIRE LIFE. HIS MANIFOLD ACHIEVEMENTS CROWNED HONOUR APPOINTMENT HANDCAUSE 29 FEBRUARY 1952. THIS ENABLED HIM EXTEND SERVICES FAITH INTERNATIONAL ARENA. SUPPLICATING SACRED THRESHOLD PROGRESS RADIANT SOUL ABHA KINGDOM. ADVISE HOLD MEMORIAL GATHERINGS BAHAI WORLD INCLUDING ALL MASHRIQULADHKARS.[3]

# Músá Banání
# 1886–1971

Músá Banání was a man of remarkable exuberance, exceptional firmness, unhesitating obedience and utter humility. Born into a Jewish family in Baghdád, he suffered many privations as a child. His father died when Músá was only four years old and the struggle for survival that followed allowed the young boy no opportunity to go to school. 'To the end of his life he could only read and write Persian and Arabic in the Hebrew alphabet that he was taught as a small child.'[1] When he was 17 he left home alone, following his older brother 'Ishráq to Kirmánsháh in Iran.

'Ishráq became a Bahá'í in Iran but Músá, who was making his living in Kirmánsháh as a merchant, was not interested in the religion. However, in 1911 Fáḍil Mázindarání, a prominent Bahá'í teacher, and Siyyid 'Abdu'l-Ḥusayn Ardistání visited the town. They were photographed at a Bahá'í meeting together with members of the local Bahá'í community, including 'Ishráq. Later the authorities used this photograph to identify and arrest the believers. Músá Banání, who resembled his brother, was mistakenly detained.

At the prison, the authorities tried to force the Bahá'ís to recant their Faith. Mr Banání became an unwilling witness to the torture of Mr Abrár, a frail, elderly cell-mate who heroically refused to deny his beliefs. Músá secured his own release by telling his gaolers he was not a Bahá'í and reviling the Faith. Though glad to be free, Mr Banání 'was seized by a profound spiritual convulsion, a tumult of the soul. He reproached himself bitterly for having glibly denounced a Faith of which he knew so little.'[2] He began a study of the Cause, attending meetings for seekers, and eventually became a Bahá'í early in 1913.

The transformation of Mr Banání's life which followed his conversion astonished many who knew him. He resolved that he would marry only a Bahá'í, so that his children might be nurtured in the Cause of Bahá'u'lláh. When he married Samíḥih Rafí'í Ardistání in 1925, he became the son-in-law of Siyyid 'Abdu'l-Ḥusayn Ardistání, the same Bahá'í teacher whose visit in 1911 to Kirmán<u>sh</u>áh had resulted in Músá's arrest and subsequent conversion to the Faith. The Banánís had six children.

Mr Banání was an entrepreneur, and by the onset of the First World War had accumulated enough capital to profit from the opportunities brought about by the war economy. At the end of the war, however, the collapse of the economy led to his bankruptcy. In about 1920 he moved to Ṭihrán, where he rebuilt his fortune. Convinced that his bankruptcy was morally justified in light of his immoderate profiteering in war time, and although he had no legal obligation to do so, he sought out all his creditors and paid his debts. When his creditors realized he was acting on his principles as a Bahá'í, many of them became Bahá'ís themselves.

In 1934 Mr Banání travelled to the Holy Land, spending 26 days as a pilgrim in the presence of Shoghi Effendi. The experience

> created an intense flame of love and loyalty that melted and fused the essence of Músá Banání's being. His devotion to Shoghi Effendi remained the hallmark of his character to the end of his life. The Guardian, in turn, perceived the simplicity, directness, unbounded energy, and spiritual potential of Músá Banání and nurtured these qualities by showering a joyful love upon him.[3]

During the pilgrimage Shoghi Effendi told a group of pilgrims that Mr Banání was 'one equal to a thousand',[4] and he sent him to Egypt to meet with and encourage the Bahá'ís in Cairo, Alexandria, Port Said and Ismailiyyah.

When he returned to Persia, Mr Banání served as a member of the national committee responsible for identifying and acquiring historic sites associated with the Faith. The committee was able to purchase and restore the house in Ṭihrán in which Bahá'u'lláh had been born.

With the outbreak of war in 1939, at a time when most of Mr Banání's business associates were preparing to profit from the conflagration, Músá closed his business and lived on the income from his properties. He was scrupulous in the payment of his Ḥuqúqu'lláh obligations, insisting that they be paid immediately they fell due.

By 1950 Mr Banání was a man of considerable means. He had built and moved into a luxurious house and was looking forward to a comfortable retirement. Then 'Azíz Yazdí, a family friend, brought to the Banání home a cablegram from Shoghi Effendi that was to change Músá's life.

By the beginning of 1950 the Faith of Bahá'u'lláh had only touched the northern shores and southern tip of the vast continent of Africa. In April of that year the Guardian sent a cable to the annual Bahá'í convention of the British Isles, calling attention to Africa:

> HOUR PROPITIOUS GALVANIZED FIRMLY KNIT BODY BELIEVERS BRACE ITSELF EMBARK AFTER ONE YEAR RESPITE YET ANOTHER HISTORIC UNDERTAKING MARKING FORMAL INAUGURATION TWO YEAR PLAN CONSTITUTING PRELUDE INITIATION SYSTEMATIC CAMPAIGN DESIGNED CARRY TORCH FAITH TERRITORIES DARK CONTINENT . . . HOUR STRUCK UNDERTAKE PRELIMINARY STEPS IMPLANT BANNER FAITH AMIDST AFRICAN TRIBES MENTIONED TABLET CENTRE COVENANT.[5]

The Two Year Plan to which Shoghi Effendi referred came to be known as the 'Africa Campaign' and was placed under the direction of the National Spiritual Assembly of the British Isles. In August 1950 Shoghi Effendi called upon the American Bahá'í community to lend its assistance to the project which he described as

> marking a significant milestone in the world-unfoldment of the Faith, supplementing the work initiated fifty years ago on the North American continent . . . providing the prelude to the full-scale operations destined to be launched at a later period of the unfoldment of the Divine Plan aiming at the conversion of the backward, oppressed masses of the swiftly awakening continent.[6]

Before the year's end, the National Spiritual Assemblies of Iran, Egypt and India were also asked to participate.

It was this cablegram that 'Azíz Yazdí shared with Músá Banání. Mr Banání responded immediately. He put an end to all his business concerns, abandoned his comfortable life and left Iran. In 1951 he pioneered to Kampala, Uganda, with his wife, Samíḥih; his daughter, Violette; his son-in-law, 'Alí Nakhjavání; and his granddaughter, Bahíyyih. His resettlement in a land previously unopened to the Faith cheered the heart of the Guardian, who had sent this cable on 17 January 1951:

INFORM MUSA BANANI HIGHLY APPROVE PIONEERING AFRICA WITH NAKHJAVANI FERVENTLY PRAYING FOR HIS SUCCESS AND ENTIRE FAMILY.[7]

The Banání family arrived at its pioneering post just as the Africa Campaign was getting under way. Mr Banání bought a home at 3 Kitante Road in Kampala, where the warmth of the Persian household greatly attracted enquirers. Later that year the Banánís and Nakhjavánís were joined by Philip Hainsworth, a pioneer from England. Soon the first fruits of the teaching work were born: the first two Africans to enrol in the Faith, Crispian Kajubi of the Buganda tribe and Frederick Bigabwa of the Mtoro tribe, became Bahá'ís in Kampala.

In February 1952 Mr Banání went on his second pilgrimage, accompanied by his wife. The teaching work was moving forward in Africa and so the reunion with the Guardian was an especially joyous one. Every day Shoghi Effendi gave Mr Banání detailed instructions for the development of the Cause in Africa.

While the Banánís were at the World Centre, two significant events occurred. Before they had left Kampala it had been agreed that the pioneers would hold a special meeting for the African enquirers while the Banánís were in Haifa. The meeting was timed to coincide with the hour when Shoghi Effendi usually visited the Shrines. At the appointed time the Guardian and Mr Banání prayed together at the Shrines for the progress of the Faith. The next morning Enoch Olinga declared his belief in Bahá'u'lláh to the pioneers in Kampala. By 21 April 1952 the number of new believers was sufficient to elect Uganda's first Local Spiritual Assembly in Kampala. Enoch Olinga was among the members. By October there were 100 believers in Uganda.

The second significant event occurred on the final day of the Banánís' pilgrimage. As they were taking leave of the Guardian, he told them what he had already announced to the Bahá'í world on 29 February: that Mr Banání, 'the spiritual conqueror of Africa', had been elevated to the rank of Hand of the Cause.

> Announce friends East and West . . . following nominations raising the number of the present Hands of the Cause to nineteen . . . Germany, Africa, Australia Adelbert Mühlschlegel, Músá Banání, Clara Dunn, respectively.[8]

The ever-humble Músá protested:

> I am not worthy. I cannot read or write. My tongue is not eloquent. Give this mantle to 'Alí Nakhjavání who is doing the lion's share of teaching in Africa.[9]

Shoghi Effendi replied, 'It is your arising that has conquered the continent. 'Alí's turn will come.'[10]

Shoghi Effendi directed the Hands of the Cause to attend all of the four intercontinental teaching conferences called to launch the Ten Year Crusade. Mr Banání played a major role in organizing the first of the four, which took place in Kampala between 12 and 18 February 1953. In a large tent erected in the grounds of the Kampala Ḥaẓíratu'l-Quds, 232 Bahá'ís representing 30 ethnic groups and 19 countries gathered to hear the details of a plan destined to take the Bahá'í Faith to all corners of the globe.

After the Kampala conference Mr Banání travelled to the United States to attend the conference in Wilmette in April and May. He then spent the next two and a half months travelling in America and visiting Bahá'í communities before going on to the conferences in Stockholm and New Delhi in July and October.

Mr Banání also visited the Bahá'ís across Africa. One of his earliest journeys was with Hand of the Cause Mr Khadem and both of their wives in 1953. They visited nearly every country in sub-Saharan Africa where there were Bahá'ís, including Kenya, Ethiopia, Tanganyika, Rhodesia, South Africa, Angola, the Belgian Congo, Liberia, Sierra Leone, Morocco and Tunisia.

Mr Banání kept in touch with the Bahá'ís through the *Banání Bulletin*, a newsletter which he produced from time to time from about 1953 to about 1956. This newsletter was sent to every Local Assembly, pioneer and isolated Bahá'í in Africa, as well as to the Auxiliary Board members and National Assemblies who had responsibilities for Africa.

In 1954 the Guardian, in a cable to the Hands of the Cause and all National Spiritual Assemblies, called for the appointment of Auxiliary Boards in each continent of the world:

> HOUR RIPE FIFTEEN HANDS RESIDING OUTSIDE HOLY LAND PROCEED DURING RIḌVÁN APPOINTMENT, EACH CONTINENT SEPARATELY, FROM AMONG RESIDENT BAHÁ'ÍS THAT CONTINENT, AUXILIARY BOARDS, WHOSE MEMBERS, ACTING DEPUTIES, ASSISTANTS ADVISERS HANDS, MUST INCREASINGLY LEND ASSISTANCE PROMOTION INTERESTS TEN YEAR CRUSADE.[11]

Asked by Shoghi Effendi to appoint a Board of nine members to assist in the teaching campaign, Mr Banání named to the African Auxiliary Board John Allen, Elsie Austin, 'Alí Nakhjavání, Jalál Nakhjavání, John Robarts, William Sears, Muḥammad Mustafa Soleiman, Valerie Wilson and 'Azíz Yazdí.

In the spring of 1954 Músá Banání received a cable from the Guardian requesting that he purchase land for a Temple site. Although he had just undergone eye surgery, from which he was still recuperating, he immediately set out to search for a suitable property. Within a week he was able to cable the Guardian that a site had been selected and purchased.

The Faith expanded rapidly in Africa. In 1955 there were over 120 local spiritual assemblies on the continent, with 31 new assemblies having been formed in Central and East Africa alone. Uganda formed 17 new assemblies, increased the number of its African believers to nearly 900 and the number of centres to over 100. Kenya formed 8 new assemblies and Tanganyika 2; local assemblies were organized for the first time in the Belgian Congo, Ruanda-Urundi, Zanzibar, the Seychelles Islands, Ashanti, French Cameroon and the Canary Islands. British Cameroon, where Enoch Olinga had pioneered in October 1953, realized 8 new assemblies. Spanish Guinea, Comoro Islands and St Thomas Island were finally opened to the Faith. Shoghi Effendi cabled Músá Banání in April 1955:

> REJOICE GREATLY, ADMIRE DEEPLY, GRATEFUL MAGNIFICENT ACHIEVEMENTS VALIANT FRIENDS, COLOURED WHITE PIONEERS, TEACHERS, ADMINISTRATORS, FOUR AREAS AFRICAN CONTINENT. LOVING FERVENT PRAYERS SURROUNDING THEM.[12]

Shoghi Effendi was so pleased with the growth of the Faith that in August 1955 he called for the erection of the Mother Temple of Africa, as a 'supreme consolation to the masses of oppressed valiant brethren in the Cradle of the Faith'.[13] The following year four new Regional Spiritual Assemblies were elected at Riḍván: Central and East Africa with its seat in Kampala, South and West Africa with its seat in Johannesburg, North West Africa with its seat in Tunis and North East Africa with its seat in Cairo. The Hand of the Cause attended all four inaugural conventions as the Guardian's personal representative.

The passing of Shoghi Effendi in November 1957 was a great blow to Mr Banání, 'but it made him doubly resolute in fulfilling Shoghi Effendi's plans'.[14] A short time before his passing, in October 1957, Shoghi Effendi had called for the convocation of five successive intercontinental conferences to be held in Kampala, Sydney, Chicago, Frankfurt and Jakarta during 1958. Mr Banání attended the conferences in Kampala in January and Frankfurt in July. On the fourth day of the Kampala conference the Guardian's representative, Rúḥíyyih Khánum, and Músá Banání placed in the foundations of the Mother Temple of Africa two gifts from the Guardian: a silver box containing sacred earth from the Shrine of Bahá'u'lláh and a wooden box containing plaster from the Báb's prison cell at the castle fortress of Máh-Kú.

In 1958 a monument of white Carrara marble was erected over the resting place of Shoghi Effendi. 'A single marble column, crowned by a Corinthian capital is surmounted by a globe, the map of Africa facing forward . . .'[15] The victories in Africa had brought the beloved Guardian great joy in the final years of his life. The Faith continued to grow rapidly in Africa for the rest of the Ten Year Crusade. By its end in 1963 there were Bahá'ís in 2,655 localities across the continent and 1,076 local spiritual assemblies. More than half the assemblies were in Uganda. Over 40,000 new believers had been enrolled in Central and East Africa, over half of them living in the Congo.

During the last years of his life Músá Banání suffered increasingly from health problems. In August 1960 he suffered a stroke, which left him paralysed down one side of his body. Eventually one leg had to be amputated and he lost the sight in one eye. In 1961 the Custodians wrote to the Hands in the field of Mr Banání's 'delicate state of health . . . which prevents him from moving about'[16] and only a month later wrote that they 'had our dear Músá Banání much in mind, as the state of his health is still precluding him from actual participation in the affairs of the Cause'.[17]

In October 1967 six intercontinental conferences were held simultaneously to commemorate the centenary of Bahá'u'lláh's proclamation to the kings and rulers of the world. The Hand of the Cause of God Músá Banání was present at the conference in Kampala. On the final day of the conference,

> beloved Áqá Ján, our 'dear father' . . . was carried down the stairs and into the auditorium in the arms of a loving friend, was gently placed in his wheelchair and taken to the speakers' platform. Every believer rose to his feet in sponta-

> neous, deeply sincere love, respect and honour. Here was the hero of Africa, scarred but unbent and unwavering, Mr Banání, sixteen years a pioneer to Africa, and in the twilight of his life, ill and almost blind with diabetes, paralysed on his right side by a devastating stroke, and now straight from bed, his left leg amputated above the knee three weeks ago to arrest the angry thrust of gangrene. We sang *Alláh-u-Abhá* when he entered; we listened intently while his daughter, Violette Nakhjavání, translated his message; we admired his stern self-control as he sat in obvious physical discomfort throughout the talks of his fellow-Hands. An era seemed to have ended; we sensed it. Would he ever come amongst us like that again? Never mind – we have lived with the towering example of his dedication, loyalty, obedience, sacrifice, service and long-suffering; is this not blessing enough? Are these not the lessons which no eloquence can teach? How great the wisdom of God, that here amongst the simple, unlettered people of Africa He placed a giant who would, without the aid of words, teach all Africa the meaning of the word 'faithful'.[18]

In the remaining years of his life Músá Banání was unable to move about, yet 'his daily prayers were offered for those Bahá'í communities which were experiencing distress'.[19] He died on 4 September 1971 and, in fulfilment of his last wish, was buried 'in his favourite spot in the soil of Africa, within the shadow of the Mother Temple of that continent'.[20] Upon his passing the Universal House of Justice cabled the Bahá'í world:

> PROFOUNDLY MOURN PASSING DEARLY LOVED HANDCAUSE MUSA BANANI RECALL WITH DEEP AFFECTION HIS SELFLESS UNASSUMING PROLONGED SERVICES CRADLE FAITH HIS EXEMPLARY PIONEERING UGANDA CULMINATING HIS APPOINTMENT AS HAND CAUSE AFRICA AND PRAISE BELOVED GUARDIAN AS SPIRITUAL CONQUEROR THAT CONTINENT. INTERMENT HIS REMAINS AFRICAN SOIL UNDER SHADOW MOTHER TEMPLE ENHANCES SPIRITUAL LUSTRE THAT BLESSED SPOT. FERVENTLY PRAYING SHRINES PROGRESS HIS NOBLE SOUL. MAY AFRICA NOW ROBBED STAUNCH VENERABLE PROMOTER DEFENDER FAITH FOLLOW HIS EXAMPLE CHEER HIS HEART ABHA KINGDOM. CONVEY FAMILY MOST TENDER SYMPATHIES ADVISE HOLD MEMORIAL MEETINGS ALL COMMUNITIES BAHAI WORLD BEFITTING GATHERINGS MOTHER TEMPLES.[21]

# Clara Dunn
# 1869–1960

Clara Dunn cherished a prayer revealed by 'Abdu'l-Bahá. She memorized it and in old age could be seen with hands upraised, beseeching her Lord in the words of this prayer, so dear to her heart:

> O Lord, my God and my Haven in my distress! My Shield and my Shelter in my woes! My Asylum and Refuge in time of need and in my loneliness my Companion! In my anguish my Solace, and in my solitude a loving Friend! The Remover of the pangs of my sorrows and the Pardoner of my sins!
>
> Wholly unto Thee do I turn, fervently imploring Thee with all my heart, my mind and my tongue, to shield me from all that runs counter to Thy will in this, the cycle of Thy divine unity, and to cleanse me of all defilement that will hinder me from seeking, stainless and unsullied, the shade of the tree of Thy grace . . .
>
> Make my heart overflow with love for Thy creatures and grant that I may become the sign of Thy mercy, the token of Thy grace, the promoter of concord amongst Thy loved ones, devoted unto Thee, uttering Thy commemoration and forgetful of self but ever mindful of what is Thine . . .[1]

Many believers were moved by the sight of Mother Dunn reciting this prayer. The words she uttered, special in themselves, revealed something of the depth of her yearning after God and of her devotion to His Cause. For over 40 years she mothered the Bahá'í community of the Australian continent. And as her span on this earth entered its eventide, her precious life was cherished and honoured by those Bahá'ís who knew her and whose spiritual fortunes were for ever linked to hers.

Clara was a native of London. She was born on 12 May 1869,[2] the sixth child of Thomas and Maria Holder. Her father was a rigid Methodist, her attractive Irish mother a Catholic. The family moved to Allendale, Canada, when Clara was about a year old, but poverty and religious disputes between her parents made Clara's childhood an unhappy one.

Partly to escape family tensions, when she was about 16 years old Clara married William Allen Davis, three years her senior, in Toronto. About 15 months after their marriage, their only son, Allen Jr, was born on 8 April 1887. The couple were living in Ontario at the time. Tragically, Davis was killed in a railway accident a year later, leaving Clara with the young child to support.

Clara decided to support herself by becoming a nurse. Her eldest brother took care of Allen Jr. Clara was unhappy that she could not bring up her child herself and felt that she was to blame for his many problems.

Clara worked as a nurse, mainly among the poor, for a number of years. However, she contracted typhoid fever and left her post. At the age of 33 she moved to the United States, settling in Walla Walla, Washington. There she soon found employment again.

In 1907 Clara met Hyde Dunn. She was working at a medical centre when he came into her office to put up a notice about a Bahá'í meeting. He asked her if she was interested in spiritual matters.

'I would be', was her reply, 'if I knew of any spiritual things.'

Hyde told Clara that a gentleman at the hotel had a wonderful message to share.

'Oh,' she said. 'Are you the one who has this message that you speak about?'

'No,' he replied. 'A far better man than I. He has journeyed to 'Akká and visited this wonderful Person in the prison. Would you come and speak to him at the hotel?' Clara said she would come.[3]

Clara listened to Hyde's companion, Ward Fitzgerald, present the Bahá'í message at the hotel, but was quite unimpressed by him. He looked material. She asked if the Faith was 'for everybody in the world, for every kind and colour'.[4] Assured that it was, Clara became convinced of the truth of the Bahá'í Cause.

For the next five years Clara struggled unceasingly to spread the teachings. Though her efforts were determined and her faith firm, she was unable to enrol a single person. Her material circumstances began to deteriorate. One of the doctors in the medical centre called her a quack and she had to give up her nursing job. Her mental anguish was such that she had a nervous breakdown and had to be hospitalized. A kind woman brought Clara to live with her, allowing her to sleep in the attic. However, the woman warned all Clara's acquaintances that she 'belonged to a crazy religion' and was completely mad.[5]

Gradually Clara's health improved, but her material circumstances did not. Difficult as her situation was, when she heard that 'Abdu'l-Bahá was coming to San Francisco, she determined that somehow she would make the journey to meet Him.

Clara had met a young Bahá'í woman from Spokane whose father, Mr Bailey, was the mayor of a small town near Walla Walla. Miss Bailey had sent her father to Clara in the hopes that he would become a Bahá'í. Instead, he had come to Clara's flat three times, on the third visit proposing marriage to her. She had refused. Now, learning of 'Abdu'l-Bahá's visit to California, Clara decided to ask her suitor for a loan to cover the expenses of the trip.

She went to his home on the tram. When she rang the bell she was curtly received by the housekeeper, who had designs on Mr Bailey herself in order to lay hands on his money for the education of her daughters. She knew Clara as the focus of her employer's affections and a consequent threat to her own marital intentions.

Clara asked whether Mr Bailey was at home.

'Yes, but you can't see him, he's sick!' the housekeeper responded.

Clara demanded to know where his room was. Speaking of the episode 42 years later, she said that nothing on the face of the earth would have stopped her. When the housekeeper would not tell, Clara found him herself and asked for the loan. Mr Bailey began to roar with laughter.

'Mr Bailey', Clara said, 'this is no laughing matter.'

Mr Bailey replied, 'Well, excuse me, won't you? My daughter sent me a telegram this morning: Father, telegraph me money at once to go to San Francisco to see 'Abdu'l-Bahá. I said to my housekeeper, here's my daughter gone crazy. Now the woman that I adored comes and asks the same question.'[6]

Clara got the loan from Mr Bailey, and that very night caught a train south. At Portland she encountered George Latimer's father, also a Bahá'í, who ran the dining room. He told her that George and his mother were already in San Francisco visiting 'Abdu'l-Bahá. Clara caught a second train, the Shasta Limited, just as it was pulling out of the station. She was so excited that she was unable to eat.

When Clara arrived in San Francisco she was confused by the size and bustling activity of the city. Surrounded by ferry buildings and hotel jockeys calling out the names of their hotels, she knew only that 'Abdu'l-Bahá could be found on Market Street. She managed to find a Market Street tram and asked the conductor how she might find some Persians. He told her that the tram stopped in front of their house.

Clara reached the house but at first could not get in. She rang the bell repeatedly, but no one would answer the door. Hungry and feeling miserable after travelling for 24 hours without food, she began to cry. Then she became angry, thinking how she had travelled a thousand miles only to discover that no one would open the door for her. From where she stood she could see people inside the house, looking radiant. She rang and rang the bell again. Finally she tried the door. It was unlocked.

Clara was soon ushered into 'Abdu'l-Bahá's presence. He was exhausted and stooped and appeared to her to be black as ink. She learned later that He had just seen dozens of newspapermen. She realized that He had taken away their iniquities and filled them with His love. 'I am very weary,' He said to her. Clara's heart was deeply affected and she begged to be excused from His room.[7]

In less than half an hour, 'Abdu'l-Bahá recalled Clara with an invitation to dine with Him. Amazingly, He appeared fully restored, and, to her, seven feet high. 'Oh, His smile was so beautiful!' she later recalled. He was so 'radiant and glorious looking.'[8]

At the dinner table 'Abdu'l-Bahá told a story about an old lady who took a duck to market, proclaiming her duck to be exceptionally large and wonderful. As He told the story 'Abdu'l-Bahá looked at Clara all the while. She realized He was teaching her some lesson. When I tell a story, she thought, I exaggerate. If God'll forgive me, I'll never do it again.[9]

After a dinner of wonderful Persian rice, and much joy, 'Abdu'l-Bahá went up to His room. Hyde Dunn approached Clara and said, 'I was the one who should have opened the door.'

'Thank God you left it unlocked', Clara replied, 'so that I could get in.'[10]

Years later Clara gave her first impressions of the Master:

> There was something about His presence that is indescribable. When somebody asked Shoghi Effendi, when I was with the Guardian at Haifa, 'Abdu'l-Bahá's station, he said, 'If He was the Mystery of God, then who would know His station? Could any human, if He was the Mystery of God? What human could understand His station?'[11]

The next morning, Clara was present for 'Abdu'l-Bahá's departure:

> He had a large bottle of rose water. When He came down the stairs I felt a distinct breeze of the spirit blow in my face and He went among us and anointed everybody.[12]

Less than five years later, Clara and Hyde were married, on 9 July 1917. In 1919 they were on holiday in Santa Cruz, California, when they received a copy of the Tablets of the Divine Plan. Reading through the Tablets and 'Abdu'l-Bahá's call for pioneers, the couple, though nearing retirement age, decided to go to Australia.

Plans were set in motion. Clara, however, wondered whether they should both go. While they continued their preparations, Hyde wrote to the Master for advice. One day, after what seemed an infinite wait, a telegram arrived from 'Abdu'l-Bahá: 'HIGHLY COMMENDABLE.' Hyde and Clara were both delighted.[13] They set sail on the SS *Sonoma* in January 1920 and arrived in Sydney on 10 April.

Their pioneering venture was a success:

> Not young, they had given up everything and sailed to Australia, practically out of funds. They struggled against vicissitude, became successful in business, and were a model of love and unity. Wherever they went, they sowed the seeds of the oneness of humanity. There was an energy about them, and they were a powerful example to all they met. The Faith began to spread, not in vast numbers, but modestly and consistently.[14]

During the next 21 years Clara and Hyde Dunn raised up a widespread Bahá'í community and many spiritual assemblies. The numbers of believers grew steadily as they travelled from place to place, often setting up house for a time in order to facilitate the growth of the Faith in a locality. They were so well loved that they became known as Mother and Father Dunn.

Some time after their arrival in Australia, Clara received a letter from a believer who addressed her as 'Dear Mother'. When she read the letter Clara recalled a dream in which she learned that she would some day be called Mother by many people. Clara wrote back saying she and Hyde were pleased to be called Father and Mother, but she also asked the Guardian whether the believers should refer to them in this way. 'Yes,' he replied, 'you are as their parents.'[15]

Friends felt sure that the Dunns called upon the Holy Spirit for strength and guidance to serve the Cause of God. Father Dunn attracted people through the sweetness of his smile and his kind and gentle nature; he always had a good answer for a seeker's question. Mother Dunn possessed a magnetic personality, dressed almost regally, and reflected a wonderful light and sweetness of the Holy Spirit. Clara attracted people to Bahá'í meetings; Hyde confirmed those people who had been inspired by Clara. However they did it, it worked. Numerous people learned of the Faith through the Dunns. When someone asked the Guardian what the best method of teaching the Faith was, Shoghi Effendi said to follow the example of the Dunns and do what they did.[16]

In August 1931 Keith Ransom-Kehler arrived in Australia, travelling to Brisbane, Sydney, Melbourne and Adelaide, where the Dunns were making a visit. In Adelaide she gave many talks about the Cause. Father Dunn was impressed:

> While as yet, only a few days with us, she has given many interesting and attractive talks, holding her audiences in rapt attention, giving all an appetite or desire for more spiritual food. Many hearts have become thrilled and eager inquiry is being made for public lectures.[17]

After she left Australia Keith wrote to the *Bahá'í News*, saying that she had given a series of lectures in Adelaide and that 'Mr and Mrs Dunn professed themselves much pleased'.[18] She was evidently much pleased with them as well. In an essay about pioneers she wrote:

> Mr and Mrs Dunn (lovingly called Father and Mother by all Bahá'ís) are of singular beauty both of person and character. Mr Dunn has the rarest and most charming disposition: loving, forgiving, genial . . . She lives in the Presence of God with a kind of awe and candour that assure men of His Power and Benignity. [Even while seriously ill she was still] ministering and serving . . . until her very persistence in doing so carried its own great message.[19]

Not long after Keith's departure, Mother Dunn went on pilgrimage to the Holy Land. Hyde was unable to accompany her owing to his work. Her signature is recorded in the visitors' book at the Mansion of Bahjí on 15 January 1932. Her arrival was eagerly anticipated by Shoghi Effendi. In a letter dated 17 December 1931 and probably addressed to Amy Dewing of New Zealand, his secretary wrote:

> I believe Mrs Dunn is planning to come this spring for a visit to Haifa. Perhaps you will meet her before she starts. Shoghi Effendi is eagerly waiting to see this noble soul who introduced the Cause into Australia and has been so self-sacrificing in her services.[20]

While she was on pilgrimage, the Guardian expressed to her his desire that the Bahá'ís of Australia and New Zealand form their first National Spiritual Assembly as soon as possible. Graham Hassall notes that

> As early as 1925, with the Guardian's knowledge, plans had been made for the election of a National Assembly in 1926, however they were postponed following a letter from the Guardian; there was a need for more Assemblies working in unison.[21]

Now the Guardian felt the time was right for a National Assembly to be established. On her return to Sydney, Clara conveyed this message to the believers. The Local Spiritual Assembly of Sydney wrote to the other spiritual assemblies of Australia and New Zealand and a date was set for the first national convention, in May 1934.

The Guardian wrote to the convention and the new National Assembly on 15 May 1934:

> I rejoice to learn of the momentous step the Bahá'ís of Australia and New Zealand have taken. They will surely be reinforced by the hosts of the Kingdom, and deserve the praise and admiration of their fellow-believers throughout the world. Constancy, co-operation, unity and steadfast adherence to the spiritual and administrative principles of the Faith are essential during these days when the foundations of the Universal House of Justice are being laid through your devoted efforts in your own country. I will continue to pray for you from the depths of my heart.[22]

The Australian Bahá'í community continued to grow and develop. Stanley and Mariette Bolton purchased land at Yerrinbool to be developed as a Bahá'í summer school. Father Dunn laid the foundation stone of the first building on 11 October 1936.23 On 2 May 1937, following the national convention, an opening ceremony was held with prayers, addresses, tree planting and afternoon tea.[24] The first Yerrinbool Bahá'í Summer School was held from 8 to 23 January 1938.[25] The Hyde Dunn Memorial Hall was officially opened in January 1943[26] and an adjoining room was made available for Mother's use when she attended the school. As water had to be stored in tanks erected on hefty stands, the roof of this room formed the platform on which a water tank stood.

In 1941 Clara became a widow for a second time, when Hyde passed away on 17 February. She appeared wonderfully composed at his funeral service. Shortly after the funeral the Guardian praised her courage, saying that he was pleased she had accepted Father Dunn's passing in 'such a noble and exemplary Bahá'í spirit'.[27] In the same letter the Guardian asked that three good photographs of Hyde Dunn and some of his grave and tombstone be sent to him. Then, in his own hand, he addressed the Australian Bahá'ís:

> The community of the Most Great Name in those far-off islands has lost a great leader, a stalwart upholder of the New World Order of Bahá'u'lláh. The influence he has exercised will however continue to live, and the example he has set will inspire the rising generation to perform deeds as great and brilliant as those which will ever remain associated with his name. Our dear friend, Mr Hyde Dunn, will, from his exalted station intercede on your behalf, and you should, on your part strive to emulate one whom Bahá'í historians will recognize and acclaim as Australia's spiritual Conqueror. I will pray for his dear spiritual children from the depths of my heart.[28]

As the year 1941 drew to a close and the war threatened the Australian continent, Shoghi Effendi wrote to the believers in 'the most distant outpost of our beloved Faith', encouraging them 'not to allow any disturbance, suffering, or anxiety to dim the splendour of their faith, to deflect them from their high purpose, to cause any division in their ranks, to interfere with the steady consolidation and expansion of their activities and institutions'.[29]

As the war continued and times were so uncertain, Shoghi Effendi encouraged the Australian community to hurry the erection of Father Dunn's memorial and assured Mother Dunn that future believers of Australia would honour and cherish his grave. Shoghi Effendi appealed to the National Assembly to watch over Mother Dunn in her advancing years as she 'deserves the greatest love and consideration in view of the imperishable services she and Father Dunn rendered the Cause there'.[30]

On 21 May 1944 a national Ḥaẓíratu'l-Quds was officially dedicated in Sydney. Shoghi Effendi applauded the National Spiritual Assembly for its acquisition of the property, saying that the Centre would 'act as a powerful magnet and attract the manifold blessings of the Almighty and lend a tremendous impetus to the organized activities of the believers in Australia and New Zealand'.[31] Believers from various Australian communities and the press attended the dedication ceremony. In her dedication speech Clara recalled her meeting with 'Abdu'l-Bahá and said that the Ḥaẓíratu'l-Quds was the outcome of the labours of the believers. She was confident that they would carry the Cause forward.

Three years later the National Spiritual Assembly, at the request of the Guardian, launched a Six Year Plan to establish the administrative order throughout Australia and New Zealand. To help with the plan, Mother Dunn travelled to New South Wales and Tasmania, where much interest in the Cause was aroused.

The successful conclusion of this plan encouraged Shoghi Effendi to challenge the Australian and New Zealand believers to an even greater task:

> The victorious conclusion of the Plan formulated by your Assembly, which posterity will recognize as a landmark of the utmost significance in the development of the Faith of Bahá'u'lláh in the Antipodes, has filled my heart with joy and thanksgiving, has evoked profound admiration in the hearts of the followers of the Faith in both Hemispheres, and fully qualified the Bahá'í Communities in Australia, New Zealand and Tasmania to embark upon their Ten-Year Plan, which constitutes so important and vital a phase of the global Crusade launched by their sister Communities in every continent of the globe.[32]

On 29 February 1952 Clara Dunn was appointed a Hand of the Cause of God. Now in her mid-eighties, she was frail but possessed a vibrant personality and a remarkable memory.

The next year Clara attended the four-day National Jubilee Convention. There she counselled those present to love each other the same way as the Master attracted everyone with His love. Success, she said, depends on cultivating this love. Within a few weeks of this convention she pioneered to Newcastle, on the coast of New South Wales.

In October of the same year, Clara attended the New Delhi intercontinental teaching conference. Nearly 500 believers from 31 countries produced one of the first tangible proofs of emerging world unity – a universal gathering which must have thrilled Mother Dunn's heart. As one of the early pioneers to speak at this event, she said:

> this is the most wonderful occasion of my life. My late husband, John Henry Hyde Dunn, and I responded to the Divine Call. I want to tell those who have answered the call of the Guardian, to stand and go. It will be the greatest joy and pleasure of your lives, even if the tests come. We need them to prove us. Bahá'u'lláh paid the price, set the pace, and the Master gave us the path to follow. We have nothing to fear. If we have faith, we can conquer the whole world. The Supreme Concourse is waiting to help us.[33]

In 1954 Clara attended the Bahá'í summer school in New Zealand. The Guardian afterwards wrote to the National Assembly saying that to have done so at her age 'was surely a remarkable achievement'.[34] Yet, despite her advanced age, in the next three years Clara visited every Australian state, and at the 21st Annual Bahá'í Summer School in Yerrinbool, held at the end of 1956, she was present for every session. At Riḍván 1957 she attended, as the Guardian's representative, the election of the first National Spiritual Assembly of the Bahá'ís of New Zealand, held at the Ḥa. zíratu'l-Quds in Auckland.

Clara's son, Allen, whom she had left in the care of her brother so many years before, died in 1957. In a letter written on his behalf Shoghi Effendi sent his condolences to her:

> He was very sorry to hear that dear Mother Dunn's son had died. This, no doubt, in spite of her devotion and fortitude, must have been a severe blow to her at her age; and he hopes the friends will do all they can to comfort and take care of this precious soul – the Mother of their Community. Please assure her that he prays for the progress of the soul of her son in the Holy Shrines.[35]

Within four months, Shoghi Effendi himself had passed away, plunging the Bahá'í world into grief and consternation. Clara, now in her late eighties, travelled to the Holy Land in the company of Hand of the Cause Collis Featherstone, where she attended the sessions of the first Conclave of Hands. Mrs Marjory Bowes accompanied and cared for Mother Dunn on the journey, as Clara was very frail and suffering badly from the effects of the mandatory travel inoculations.[36]

A few months later Clara attended the second of five intercontinental conferences called by Shoghi Effendi, at Sydney, and recounted for those present her early pioneering experiences. Later that same day she attended the foundation ceremony of the Australian Mas͟hriqu'l-Ad͟hkár. Over 250 people participated in the historic event, at which Clara Dunn placed in the foundation of the Mother Temple some plaster from the prison cell in which the Báb had been confined at the fortress of Máh-Kú.

Clara spent her final years in a flat at the Ḥaẓíratu'l-Quds in Sydney. She watched as her own spiritual children left Australia as pioneers to open new lands within the Pacific islands. She witnessed the erection of the Mother Temple of Australia. And she lived to see the election of the Regional Spiritual Assembly of the South Pacific Islands. But, most of all, she witnessed the truth of 'Abdu'l-Bahá's words addressed to her and John Henry Hyde Dunn so long ago: 'Sow ye a pure seed – so that ere long an opulent harvest may be reaped.'[37]

Vibrant to the end of her days, she retained her Irish humour, delighting those around her. Many were the prayers she could recite from memory, but on the eve of her passing, she could be heard reciting the prayer dearest to her heart:

> O Lord, my God and my Haven in my distress! My Shield and my Shelter in my woes! . . . Stay not from me the gentle gales of Thy pardon and grace, and deprive me not of the wellsprings of Thine aid and favour.
>
> 'Neath the shade of Thy protecting wings let me nestle, and cast upon me the glance of Thine all-protecting eye.
>
> Loose my tongue to laud Thy name amidst Thy people, that my voice may be raised in great assemblies and from my lips may stream the flood of Thy praise.
>
> Thou art, in all truth, the Gracious, the Glorified, the Mighty, the Omnipotent![38]

Clara Dunn was laid to rest beside her husband at the Woronora Cemetery in Sydney. The Hands of the Cause in the Holy Land sent the following cable to all National Spiritual Assemblies:

> GRIEVE ANNOUNCE PASSING HAND CAUSE CLARA DUNN DISTINGUISHED MEMBER AMERICAN BAHÁ'Í COMMUNITY WHO WITH HYDE DUNN SPIRITUAL

CONQUEROR AUSTRALIA RESPONDED MASTERS APPEAL DIVINE PLAN AROSE CARRIED FAITH ANTIPODES RENDERED UNIQUE UNFORGETTABLE PIONEER SERVICE OVER FORTY YEAR PERIOD. ADVISE HOLD MEMORIAL GATHERING TEMPLE. SHARE MESSAGE HANDS NATIONAL ASSEMBLIES.[39]

# Zikrullah Khadem
## (D͟hikru'lláh K͟hádim)
## 1904–1986

He dreamed that the Greatest Name fell to the floor and that he was at a great funeral. In the dream, a sickness came over him. He felt grief-stricken and helpless. He awoke, convinced that some great personage in the Bahá'í world had passed away.

In the days ahead, he went about his responsibilities in a state of anguish and anxiety. Usually a source of joy and inspiration to the friends, Mr Khadem was unable to restrain the tears as he stood at the podium before gatherings of loving but anxious believers. They naturally asked, 'What is troubling you?' Alas, the 53-year-old Hand of the Cause was unable to explain.

Not many weeks after this disturbing dream, Mr Khadem was in Germany when he received the news: the Guardian had passed away that very morning. Mr Khadem rushed to the Bahá'í Centre and received confirmation of the report. He became ill and felt grief-stricken and helpless, just as in the dream.

Such is one of the great mysteries of God – the power to see events before they occur. Mr Khadem, whose love and devotion to his Guardian were a sterling example to the believers throughout his long and illustrious life, would render 28 more years of imperishable services before foreseeing in another dream his own pilgrimage to the worlds beyond.

Zikrullah Khadem was born in Ṭihrán in 1904, the second child of Mírzá Naṣru'lláh and Ráḍíyyih K͟hánum. 'Abdu'l-Bahá had bestowed the name 'K͟hádim', which means 'servant', on Mírzá Naṣru'lláh for his faithful service at the Pilgrim House for four years after the passing of Bahá'u'lláh.

In a Tablet addressed to Mírzá Naṣru'lláh's mother, 'Abdu'l-Bahá praised her son's services:

> Wert thou to know to what bounty he hath attained, and what great blessing he hath received, thou wouldst assuredly spread thy wings and soar in the heavens . . . Erelong the clear evidences of these favours will be apparent and manifest, like unto the sun shining from the horizon of existence, and the bright light of this grace will enkindle the lamp of that family. Soon thou shalt rejoice at that which he will offer in servitude, and thy heart shall be gladdened at meeting him.[1]

When Ráḍíyyih Khánum read this Tablet she felt that a great blessing would come to her family.

Zikrullah (meaning 'the mention of God') was a very unusual child and his father trained him to take advantage of his capacities. He had an excellent memory, so Mírzá Naṣru'lláh required his son to memorize passages from the Bahá'í writings daily and to recite these before breakfast. Steadfast in his own obedience to 'Abdu'l-Bahá, Mírzá Naṣru'lláh undoubtedly imparted this sense of loyalty as well as his strong faith to his son.

Once Zikrullah was not given a position he dearly wanted. His father, perceiving his son's disappointment, consoled him, saying,

> O my dear, my heart! Why are you agonized with what happens in this world? Does not the Lord know our heart? He knows. And whatever is good, He plans for you! 'It may happen that you will hate a thing which is better for you; and it may happen that you will love a thing which is worse for you; God knows, and you know not.' . . . Be happy with whatever God has planned for you.[2]

The Khadems lived at the Ḥayát-i-Bágh in Ṭihrán, an enclave of Bahá'í homes around a large garden, which had been purchased at the instruction of 'Abdu'l-Bahá. The neighbourhood was, however, particularly difficult and the Bahá'í children would be cursed and pelted with stones and often had to run away from their persecutors. One day Zikrullah ran home to his father with a bloody ear from having been struck by a sharp stone.

Zikrullah was educated at the Dáru'l-Funún and afterwards taught briefly at the Tarbíyat School, a Bahá'í secondary school in Ṭihrán. He then went to work in the south of the country as an interpreter and language tutor for the Anglo-Persian Oil Company. He taught Persian to the English-speaking employees, using an accelerated method of teaching which he developed, and opened a language school that used this method. He was eventually appointed personal assistant to the British general manager of the company.

Zikrullah made his first of six pilgrimages to the Holy Land in 1925. Before being given permission to go, he was so eager to be near the new Guardian, so filled with ardour and unquenchable longing, that he actively sought the company of anyone intending to make or returning from pilgrimage to ease his interminable wait. One such was Ḥájí Amín, the Trustee of Ḥuqúqu'lláh, who advised the young man not to write a strongly worded letter to the Guardian seeking permission, but a milder one, suggesting that 'the paradise of good pleasure is preferable to the paradise of pilgrimage'.[3] But Zikrullah could not wait; his patience had run out. Lacking permission, he journeyed via Ba_gh_dád to Haifa, arriving at the House of 'Abdu'l-Bahá, where he suddenly realized his rashness. Fortunately he received, at that moment, the prized letter of permission, which had been prepared that very day.

For Zikrullah, merely being in the presence of the Guardian was in itself sufficient to make the pilgrimage memorable. But there were many other highlights. It was during this pilgrimage that the Guardian laid out the additional three rooms to the Shrine of the Báb. Zikrullah was asked to hold one end of the string as the Guardian outlined the location of the new rooms. Shoghi Effendi asked Zikrullah to convey to the youth of Iran the Guardian's love and encouragement, his desire that they deepen themselves in the Faith and his hope that they would study English. When Zikrullah asked for a picture of the Guardian, Shoghi Effendi gave him a picture of 'Abdu'l-Bahá holding a rose, a photograph he cherished.

When he returned from pilgrimage Zikrullah was a changed man. His only desire was to please Shoghi Effendi. His only thought was to serve his Lord. In later years he often spoke of this first pilgrimage and the transforming effect it had on him.

In about 1930 Mr Khadem left his post at the oil company and returned to Ṭihrán, where he worked as a translator at the Iraqi Embassy until 1944. In 1933 Zikrullah was introduced to Jávídu_kh_t Jávíd at her parents' home, as was the custom. He was accompanied on this visit by Keith

Ransom-Kehler. Zikrullah and Jávídukht were married on 3 October 1933. They had five children: Mozhan, Jena, Riaz, Ramin and May.

During the late 1930s Mr Khadem travelled extensively throughout Iran. He and his wife – his constant travelling companion – journeyed by car over rough and dangerous roads every week to meet the believers and to carry out assignments for the Guardian. When they had visited every city in Iran, the Guardian asked them to visit them all a second time.

One journey was to Nayríz, where Mr Khadem was to take photographs of the graves of the martyrs. As he was taking the pictures he was arrested and taken to gaol:

> With the Bahá'ís' assistance, Mr Khadem was released. The camera and photographs were returned. In the Nayríz court, a long indictment of Mr Khadem's 'crimes' was drawn up and sent to Ṭihrán for a hearing. There the indictment led to extensive publicity for the Faith because Mr Khadem was able to give public testimony to the truths of the Faith while demonstrating his own innocence. He sent a complete report along with the court indictment to the beloved Guardian.[4]

On another occasion the Khadems were stopped on the road by a distinguished gentleman, who approached and greeted them. He explained that he had had a dream the night before that the occupants of a blue car would arrive the next morning with greetings from the beloved Guardian. So convinced was he that he had run to the road as soon as he had awakened and dressed. The Khadems were driving a blue car and did indeed bear greetings from the Guardian. Their meeting with the Bahá'ís that day 'created loving, spiritual bonds that linked our hearts forever'.[5]

Shoghi Effendi encouraged Mr Khadem to use his skills in English to translate Bahá'í works from English into Persian. In a letter dated 15 March 1932, Shoghi Effendi directed him to contact the National Spiritual Assembly of the United States to obtain the material. His translations were eventually distributed to the Iranian Bahá'ís through the East–West Committee of the National Spiritual Assembly of Iran. These included articles from *The Bahá'í World*, parts of *The Advent of Divine Justice* and *The Promised Day is Come*.

In 1938 Mr Khadem was elected to the National Spiritual Assembly of Iran, serving on that body until 1960. While he was in the Holy Land in 1940, Mr Khadem was asked by the Guardian to find ways for the

Iranian Bahá'ís to come on pilgrimage. He was also asked to encourage the Iranian Bahá'ís to pioneer. On his return to Iran, Mr Khadem was able to fulfil both these requests, finding a route for the pilgrims through Iraq to the Holy Land and facilitating the departure of numerous pioneers.

Between 1940 and 1957 Mr Khadem was entrusted with the responsibility for receiving mail and cablegrams from Shoghi Effendi addressed to institutions and individuals in Iran. One such message was an instruction to the National Spiritual Assembly to hold special celebrations for the centenary of the Declaration of the Báb in Shíráz. Another was the message of the Guardian to that commemoration. It was the middle of the Second World War and there was no postal service. The message had been sent as far as Baghdád but had not yet arrived in Ṭihrán. As time was getting short, Mr Khadem asked a Bahá'í pilot if he would fly to Baghdád and collect the letter. Despite the dangers of flying during the war, the pilot agreed. When Shoghi Effendi's message arrived in Ṭihrán, Mr Khadem took it by car to Shíráz, using four spare tyres borrowed from a friend. He arrived exactly two hours after sunset on the day of the commemoration, just in time to convey the special message of Shoghi Effendi to the assembled Bahá'ís.

One Friday morning during the fast of 1952 a cablegram arrived from the Guardian, dated 28 February and addressed to Mr Khadem himself:

> MOVED CONVEY GLAD TIDINGS YOUR ELEVATION RANK HAND CAUSE. APPOINTMENT OFFICIALLY ANNOUNCED PUBLIC MESSAGE ADDRESSED ALL NATIONAL ASSEMBLIES. MAY SACRED FUNCTION ENABLE YOU ENRICH RECORD SERVICES ALREADY RENDERED FAITH BAHÁ'U'LLÁH.[6]

Unbelieving at first, until the Bahá'í world was officially notified by Shoghi Effendi Mr Khadem told no one except his wife and mother of his appointment. He would spend the rest of his life praying fervently, night and day, to become worthy of it.

Not many days later, on 11 March 1952, the Khadems were scheduled to leave on pilgrimage. On this particular pilgrimage, Mr Khadem received a blessing for which he had yearned and prayed: that of carrying a very precious copy of the Kitáb-i-Íqán to the Holy Land. This volume was a copy in 'Abdu'l-Bahá's handwriting, with notations by Bahá'u'lláh in the margins. For many years it had been in the possession of Fátimih Khánum Afnán, but since 1948 the book had been kept in a safe in Ṭihrán by the National Spiritual Assembly of Iran. Two days before the Khadems' scheduled departure, the Guardian cabled with instructions to bring the volume to Haifa. Mr Khadem was ecstatic, and on the five-hour journey read the entire book which he was entrusted to deliver.

On this sixth and final pilgrimage in which Mr Khadem attained the presence of Shoghi Effendi, he was asked by the beloved Guardian to chant a passage from the Qayyúmu'l-Asmá'. Later Mr Khadem recalled that memorable occasion:

> Those pages written in the beloved Guardian's own handwriting were so very precious. I wished with all my heart that I could have them. How I would have treasured such a gift! But of course I didn't say anything. I begged Bahá'u'lláh to fulfil this fervent wish. Alas, it was not to be granted then. As I finished chanting, the beloved Guardian reached for those precious pages.[7]

On 25 March a second cable arrived from Shoghi Effendi, referring to Mr Khadem as the 'ITINERANT HAND'.[8] Shortly afterwards, Mr Khadem left his employment to be of service to Shoghi Effendi full time. He began to travel constantly. During the Ten Year Crusade he visited Bahá'í centres in Italy, Belgium, Switzerland, Germany, Austria, France, Spain, Portugal, England, Scotland, Ireland, Norway, Sweden, Denmark, the Netherlands, Luxembourg, Cuba, Jamaica, Haiti, Puerto Rico, Venezuela, Colombia, Panama, Costa Rica, Nicaragua, Honduras, El Salvador, Guatemala, Mexico, the United States, Cyprus, Lebanon, Pakistan, India, Thailand, Hong Kong, Japan, Taiwan, Macau, the Philippines, East and West Malaysia, Burma, Iraq, Iran, Japan, Canada, Finland, Indonesia, Yugoslavia and Africa. He attended teaching conferences in Brussels, Kampala, Chicago, Australia, Singapore and Panama City. From the time of his appointment as a Hand of the Cause, Mr Khadem visited more than one thousand Bahá'í centres, many more than once.

On 1 May 1953, on the Guardian's instructions, Mr Khadem attended the dedication of the Mother Temple of the West, together with 11 other Hands of the Cause. There he found instructions from Shoghi Effendi asking him to chant a selection from the writings of the Báb. This was the very same text he had yearned to possess on pilgrimage the year before! Overwhelmed at having so unexpectedly received those precious pages, he remembered in heightened awe Shoghi Effendi's promise 16 years earlier that he would chant at the dedication of the House of Worship in Wilmette.

In November 1957 came the tragic news of the passing of Shoghi Effendi. The dream which Mr Khadem had had some weeks before had come true. Mr Khadem later wrote about the devastating effect this had on him:

> For an entire year I was in a state of extreme agony and many times repeated to myself a poem of Nabíl-i-Zarandí alluding to a passage in the Qur'án: 'Those Egyptians, they saw a youth (Joseph) and cut their palms. Thou who had seen such a king hath not sacrificed thyself for him.'[9]

From October to December 1958 Mr Khadem acted as substitute member of the nine Hands of the Cause resident in the Holy Land. In 1959 he represented the Hands at the election of the National Spiritual Assembly of Turkey. Between July and September 1959 he travelled through Europe.

At the Conclave of the Hands of the Cause in 1959 it became clear that it would be useful for another Hand of the Cause to reside in the Western Hemisphere. Mr Khadem volunteered to do this. In the summer of 1960 the Khadems settled in the United States. The move brought many challenges: Mr Khadem had to resolve the family's affairs in Iran, accustom himself to a foreign culture and improve his English. He willingly accepted these difficulties to assist the Cause. For some time he served the whole of the Americas and the surrounding islands by himself. Eventually Dr Giachery served in Central America and Mr Kházeh assumed responsibility for South America.

In April 1963 Mr Khadem attended the first International Convention in Haifa, at which the Universal House of Justice was elected. He then travelled to London to attend the first Bahá'í World Congress, where seven thousand Bahá'ís from all over the world gathered to celebrate the centenary of the Declaration of Bahá'u'lláh. In the same way that he had served the Guardian, now Mr Khadem served the House of Justice. He was ever ready to respond to its wishes. Wherever he went, he emphasized the importance of obedience to this institution and reverence for it.

After the election of the Universal House of Justice Mr Khadem continued to travel, but he also spent more time studying the Bahá'í and other holy scriptures and historical documents. In 1972 the Universal House of Justice asked him to research and document the places associated with the lives of the Central Figures of the Faith. He immediately secured a modest office in Evanston, Illinois and, with the help of a part-time secretary, he started work on the project he called a 'Registry of Bahá'í Holy Places'. He read all the available sources about the history of the Faith and the early believers, studying accounts in Persian, Arabic, English and French. He corresponded with anyone he thought might help identify the various sites, as well as with National and Local Spiritual Assemblies and early believers.

He completed the 134-volume work in five years and sent it to the Universal House of Justice in 1977. The Universal House of Justice commended his services:

> on behalf of Bahá'í historians of the future, as well as the entire Bahá'í community, deepest gratitude for the meticulous research and thorough investigation you have made of historic sites hallowed by the sacred associations of the past.[10]

'My mind is now at rest,' Mr Khadem said.

Mr Khadem had long been interested in the financial affairs of the Faith. In the 1950s he had served as the treasurer of the National Spiritual Assembly of Iran and was personally aware of the benefits of paying Ḥuqúqu'lláh. He believed that if the Universal House of Justice made the law of Ḥuqúqu'lláh applicable to the American Bahá'ís all the financial needs of the Faith would be met. At the 75th Annual American National Convention, held in 1984, Mr Khadem energetically and persuasively encouraged the friends to petition the Universal House of Justice for permission to have the law of Ḥuqúqu'lláh apply to them. The Universal House of Justice replied in January 1985 that it would translate the text relating to Ḥuqúqu'lláh into English so that the rank and file of the believers could become familiar with the law.

In 1986 Mr Khadem began to suffer increasingly from back pain. Blessed throughout his life with excellent health, he was now afflicted with metastatic cancer. In July he was confined to bed. During the next months he exhorted the Bahá'ís to be 'encouraged, enthusiastic, united and self-sacrificing'.[11] In a letter to the National Spiritual Assembly of the Bahá'ís of the United States, he wrote:

> I wish to thank you from the bottom of my heart for all your kindnesses, as representatives of the American Bahá'í Community, that you've shown to me

> over the past 26 years. I am deeply indebted to our Beloved Guardian for having sent me to the West to witness the glorious victories of our Beloved Faith. As I look back over the years, I can only humbly supplicate: 'O Lord, increase my astonishment at Thee!'
>
> Please be assured of my deepest gratitude and love for each one of you and for the entire American Bahá'í community. I have been thinking of you and your heavy task in the years to come, especially these next crucial years of the Six Year Plan. I wish for you Bahá'u'lláh's blessings and assistance in continually promoting the unity of the friends and rising to your high destiny . . .
>
> May He continue to guide you to fulfil the glorious destiny of this wonderful community as foreseen by the Beloved Master. May He protect you and surround you with His bounties and blessings.[12]

Zikrullah Khadem died around four o'clock on the morning of 13 November 1986. His friends and acquaintances sent hundreds of messages of love to his family. The Universal House of Justice sent this message to Bahá'ís everywhere:

> WITH SORROWFUL HEARTS ANNOUNCE PASSING INDEFATIGABLE FEARLESS DEFENDER FAITH DEEPLY LOVED HAND CAUSE ZIKRULLAH KHADEM. HIS STERLING SERVICES TO THE CAUSE, HIS TOTAL CONSECRATION TO TASKS ASSIGNED TO HIM BY BELOVED GUARDIAN, HIS OUTSTANDING EFFORTS AS MEMBER NATIONAL SPIRITUAL ASSEMBLY CRADLE FAITH, HIS VALUABLE SOUL-UPLIFTING STIMULATION IMPARTED BODY BELIEVERS NORTH AMERICA, PARTICULARLY UNITED STATES BAHA'I COMMUNITY, HIS UNTIRING ENDEAVOURS THROUGH HIS TALKS AND WRITINGS IN SAFEGUARDING COVENANT AND IN INSTILLING APPRECIATION LOVE FOR SHOGHI EFFENDI SHED UNDYING LUSTRE OVER PERIOD HIS ADMIRABLE STEWARDSHIP CAUSE GOD. OFFERING PRAYERS HOLY SHRINES PROGRESS HIS RADIANT SOUL ABHA KINGDOM. URGE HOLD BEFITTING MEMORIAL GATHERINGS HIS NAME AT ALL HOUSES OF WORSHIP AS WELL AS IN ALL LOCAL BAHA'I COMMUNITIES.[13]

# Adelbert Mühlschlegel
# 1897–1980

Rúḥíyyih Khánum was overwhelmed with grief. On Monday morning, 4 November 1957, after passing two restless nights through which she had felt an unaccountable sadness, she entered the room of her beloved husband and found him dead. Within minutes had she contacted his doctor, who arrived quickly. Massaging the Guardian's heart proved useless. The cause of death was given: coronary thrombosis brought on by the Asiatic flu.

On that first catastrophic day Rúḥíyyih Khánum managed to contact Hands of the Cause Hasan Balyuzi, John Ferraby and Ugo Giachery, requesting that they join her. She sent two telegrams notifying the Bahá'í world, the first stating that Shoghi Effendi was ill, the second that he had passed away. Milly Collins arrived the next day from Haifa to be with Rúḥíyyih Khánum through this difficult time.

On Tuesday morning Rúḥíyyih Khánum spoke to Hand of the Cause Adelbert Mühlschlegel by telephone and asked him if he would prepare the Guardian's body for burial. As he was a physician and a man known for his spirituality, Rúḥíyyih Khánum felt that he could endure the sorrow of this last service, in the spirit of consecration and prayer necessary for such a sacred occasion. He arrived that night with Hand of the Cause Hermann Grossmann. With help of these six Hands, Rúḥíyyih Khánum made preparations for the funeral.

On Thursday afternoon Rúḥíyyih Khánum and Dr Mühlschlegel went together to wash the body of the Guardian in preparation for its burial. Leaving with Dr Mühlschlegel towels, cloths, soap and fine quality white silk in which to wrap the body, Rúḥíyyih Khánum waited in an ante-room for one and a half hours while her fellow Hand went about his sacred task. Adelbert Mühlschlegel recorded afterwards:

> Something new happened to me in that hour that I cannot, even after a few days, speak of, but I can mention the wisdom and love that I felt pour over me. In that room – which to worldly eyes would have appeared so different – there was a tremendous spiritual force such as I have only felt in my life in the holy Shrines. My first impression was the contrast between the body left behind and the majestic, transfigured face, a soul-stirring picture of the joyous victory of the eternal over the transient. My second impression, as I prayed and thought and carefully did what I had to do, was that in this degree of consecration to the work of God I should work all my life, and mankind should work a thousand years, in order to construct 'the Kingdom' on earth; and my third thought was, as I washed each member of his body and anointed it, that I thanked those beloved hands which had worked and written to establish the Covenant, those feet that had walked for us, that mouth that had spoken to us, that head that had thought for us, and I prayed and meditated and supplicated that in the short time left to me, the members of my body might hasten to follow in his path of service; and my last thought was of my own distress because I felt how unworthy my hands were to anoint that blessed brow with attar-of-rose as the Masters of old were wont to do to their pupils; and yet what privileges, what duties fall to us, the living, to watch over what is past and mortal, be it ever so exalted. A great deal of mercy, love, and wisdom were hidden in this hour.[1]

Adelbert Mühlschlegel was born on 16 June 1897 in Berlin. His father was a high-ranking army medical officer in the service of the king of Württemberg and his mother was the daughter of a Protestant priest. They both came from old families in the former imperial town of Biberach an der Riss, Upper Swabia. Adelbert's childhood, which he described as cheerful, was spent in Ludwigsburg and Stuttgart. His father, a disciplined man with a pragmatic attitude towards life, encouraged the young boy to play sports and influenced his choice of profession. From his radiant mother Adelbert received a longing for spiritual values. Both his parents gave him much love and attention.

Adelbert finished secondary school during the First World War and then served in the medical corps, but he increasingly longed for spiritual enlightenment. He was convinced that a new era was emerging. After the war he studied medicine at Freiburg im Breisgau, Greifswald and Tübingen. While at Greifswald in 1920 he received a letter from his mother telling him that she had found at Stuttgart a new and universal religion, the Bahá'í Faith. He studied the little material available at that time and realized that it was the truth for which he had been searching. He wrote a letter to 'Abdu'l-Bahá confirming his belief in Bahá'u'lláh. On 16 October 1920 he received a Tablet from the Master:

> O thou son of the Kingdom! Thy letter hath been received. It was like unto a bag of musk. When I opened it, the fragrance of the love of God was perceived. It is my hope that thy rivulet may develop into a sea and surge with the breezes of divine guidance, casting a wave to the East and another to the West.
>
> Be thou deeply thankful to thy teacher and show unto her heartfelt and spiritual gratitude, because it was she who caused thee to hear the divine call and it was through her that thou didst attain to eternal grace. Thou wert earthly and thou becamest heavenly; thou wert in darkness and thou didst attain illumination; thou wert of the world of matter and thou becamest divine, and thou didst obtain a portion and share of the eternal bestowal. Be filled with happiness and derive joy from the melody of the Supreme Concourse![2]

In 1922 Adelbert opened a medical practice in the working-class environment of eastern Stuttgart. He began immediately to participate in the teaching work of the small German Bahá'í community, giving talks and translating Bahá'í works into German. He wrote a melodrama for the third 'Bahá'í Congress', held in September 1924. In 1924 he was elected to the National Spiritual Assembly of Germany, serving on the body until it was disbanded in 1937.

In 1926 Adelbert married Herma Weidle, who had been born in Stuttgart in 1902. Herma had a cheerful disposition and a vivacious and fun-loving nature and was much loved. Adelbert's intimate co-worker in all his Bahá'í activities, she possessed a caring heart and soon the Mühlschlegel home became a centre for Bahá'í activity, hospitality and friendship. The Mühlschlegels had two girls and three boys, one of whom died in early childhood.

Around 1930 Adelbert began to translate the Kitáb-i-Íqán into German. He wrote to Shoghi Effendi about his translation in May 1930 and received a response in June:

> Concerning his translation of the Íqán, Shoghi Effendi has finished it, but it

needs going over and retyping, and this he cannot as before summer. By the next autumn he believes it will be ready for publication.

Shoghi Effendi would therefore advise you to wait until then before you take any decision as to your German translation.

Shoghi Effendi much appreciates the service you are rendering. The Íqán is the most important book written on the spiritual significance of the Cause. I do not believe any person can consider himself well versed in the teachings unless he has studied it thoroughly. To publish it therefore in a comprehensive German will be one of the greatest services rendered to the Cause in that land.[3]

At the end of 1931 the Guardian sent Adelbert his English translation of the Íqán, which he hoped would help Adelbert in revising his German translation. In February 1932 Shoghi Effendi again wrote to Adelbert about his translation of the Íqán, regretting that his lack of knowledge of Persian prevented Dr Mühlschlegel from going to the original text:

He sincerely hopes that before long we will have some of the younger members of the German Bahá'ís who would make translation their life-work, and with that object in mind make a thorough study of Persian and Arabic. They would surely be rendering a wonderful service to their nation as well as to the Faith as a whole.[4]

The Guardian did not know that Adelbert had already achieved some mastery of Persian.

To this letter Shoghi Effendi added in his own hand:

I wish to . . . assure you of my keen and heartfelt appreciation of your high and painstaking endeavours for the spread and consolidation of the Faith in that land. The German believers have undergone tests of unprecedented severity. They have weathered the storm in a marvellous spirit and with fine and praiseworthy determination. These tests were God-sent, and will serve to deepen the roots of the Faith in that promising country. Wishing you success in your devoted labours and assuring you of my prayers in your behalf.[5]

Some three and a half months after Adolf Hitler came to power in Germany, Shoghi Effendi, through his secretary, wrote to Adelbert Mühlschlegel on 16 May 1933:

> The Guardian . . . does sincerely hope that the reports we receive here about the sentiments rampant in Germany are untrue to fact, that it is a regeneration of the people rather than a retrogression towards a dead past. Because whatever we say of Germany, we have to admit that its people are endowed with a spiritual vitality quite superior to many other races. Being in the heart of that populated continent and being inspired by such a strong religious spirit, Germany can easily achieve a wonderful task in regenerating the world.[6]

As the political situation in Germany deteriorated, the Guardian, in a letter of 11 February 1934 written on his behalf to the German National Spiritual Assembly, outlined the believers' duties towards their government and their Faith:

> At the outset it should be made indubitably clear that the Bahá'í Cause being essentially a religious movement of a spiritual character stands above every political party or group, and thus cannot and should not act in contravention to the principles, laws, and doctrines of any government. Obedience to the regulations and orders of the state is indeed, the sacred obligation of every true and loyal Bahá'í. Both Bahá'u'lláh and 'Abdu'l-Bahá have urged us all to be submissive and loyal to the political authorities of our respective countries. It follows, therefore, that our German friends are under the sacred obligation to whole-heartedly obey the existing political regime, whatever be their personal views and criticisms of its actual working. There is nothing more contrary to the spirit of the Cause than open rebellion against the governmental authorities of a country . . .
>
> For whereas the friends should obey the government under which they live, even at the risk of sacrificing all their administrative affairs and interests, they should under no circumstances suffer their inner religious beliefs and convictions to be violated and transgressed by any authority whatever. A distinction of a fundamental importance must, therefore, be made between *spiritual* and *administrative* matters. Whereas the former are sacred and inviolable, and hence cannot be subject to compromise, the latter are secondary and can consequently be given up and even sacrificed for the sake of obedience to the laws and regulations of the government. Obedience to the state is so vital a principle of the Cause that should the authorities in Germany decide to-day to prevent the Bahá'ís from holding any meeting or publishing any literature they should obey and be as submissive as our Russian believers have thus far been under the Soviet regime. But, as already pointed out, such an allegiance is confined

merely to administrative matters which if checked can only retard the progress of the Faith for some time. In matters of belief, however, no compromise whatever should be allowed, even though the outcome of it be death or expulsion.[7]

Later that same month the Guardian asked Adelbert to write an article in German for *The Bahá'í World*. In April Dr Mühlschlegel replied to Shoghi Effendi, enclosing an article and poetry. His article 'Zwei Heilige Grabstätten' and poems 'Glaube', 'Gott, Prophet, Mensch' and 'Hymne' appeared in volume 6 (1934–1936). That same year Adelbert translated the Kitáb-i-'Ahd, Bahá'u'lláh's Book of the Covenant, into German. The Guardian wrote to him:

I greatly value these fresh evidences of your continued, your intelligent and most helpful labours for a better understanding and a wider diffusion of the essentials and fundamentals of our beloved Faith.

You are indeed a pillar of the Administrative Order, which, despite the storms and tests of recent years, is rearing its head in the heart of your beloved and promising country. Persevere, be happy and confident.[8]

Adelbert continued to provide German translations of Bahá'í literature, gradually acquiring a working knowledge of other European languages and also of Arabic. He was an ardent Esperantist, and as early as 1925 attended an Esperanto congress at which Martha Root was also present. She wrote, 'Adelbert Mühlschlegel, a fine Bahá'í Esperantist from Stuttgart, gave a beautiful address on the Teachings of Bahá'u'lláh about a universal auxiliary language.'[9]

In 1934 Dr Mühlschlegel wrote to the Guardian asking permission to come on pilgrimage. In November Shoghi Effendi, in a letter written on his behalf, welcomed the Mühlschlegels:

It is his sincere and much-cherished hope that this pilgrimage will, in addition to its manifold spiritual blessings, give you a full opportunity to discuss with him in detail about the conditions of the Cause in Germany, and particularly as to the ways and means whereby the friends can best extend and consolidate the foundations of the Administration throughout that country.[10]

After much delay, Dr Mühlschlegel and Herma made their pilgrimage to the Holy Land in 1936. Their meeting with Shoghi Effendi greatly increased their devotion to the Faith and gave them spiritual reserves for the long years of persecution and war that were to come. On one occasion Shoghi Effendi walked alone with Adelbert in the gardens for a quarter of an hour.

In 1937 all Bahá'í activities and institutions were banned in Germany by order of the Gestapo, owing to the Faith's 'international and pacifist teachings',[11] and a great part of Dr Mühlschlegel's library of Bahá'í books was confiscated. Later in the year, however, Herma Mühlschlegel, blessed with a beautiful voice, after some difficulty obtained the government's permission to travel regularly to Zürich for singing lessons. This opportunity enabled her to act as a channel of communication between the World Centre and the German Bahá'ís. In February 1938 Shoghi Effendi wrote, praising her services:

> The services you are rendering in these days of stress and turmoil are highly appreciated and deserve the highest praise.[12]

Three months later he wrote again:

> Wishing you and your dear and distinguished husband, the utmost success in your unceasing and noble endeavours for the promotion and protection of the Faith in these days of stress and trial, and assuring you of my abiding and loving gratitude.[13]

As a result of Herma Mühlschlegel's courage, much-needed guidance continued to flow from the Guardian to the beleaguered believers in Germany in the period before the Second World War.

With the onset of war in 1939, a blanket of obscurity settled over the German Bahá'í community. The administrative institutions were outlawed and did not meet. Believers were intimidated; Bahá'í meetings were stopped. Dr Mühlschlegel carried on his medical practice throughout the war, also serving as a medical attendant in the civil defence. In 1944 the family home was bombed. At the end of the war, Dr Mühlschlegel escaped the fate of thousands of German civilians forced to labour in France by leaping into a crowd in the city of Karlsruhe. He walked back to Stuttgart over the fields at night.

After 1945 Dr Mühlschlegel and Herma re-established a centre of Bahá'í activity in their new home and Herma used her talents as an administrator and teacher. During those difficult post-war years, Adelbert would compose songs and poems to lighten the burden of their material difficulties. Together he and Herma provided a home which enveloped everyone with warmth and humour, a place where many young Iranian Bahá'ís stayed upon their arrival for studies in Germany before they found accommodation in the ruined German cities.

In August 1945 the German Bahá'ís received permission from the government of occupation in Germany to organize, and in April 1946 the National Spiritual Assembly of Germany and Austria was re-established. Adelbert was elected to the body and served as a member until 1959, often as chairman.

On 29 February 1952 Shoghi Effendi cabled the Bahá'í world that the number of Hands of the Cause had been raised to 19 through the elevation of seven believers to this rank. Among them was Adelbert Mühlschlegel.

The next year Dr Mühlschlegel participated in the intercontinental conference in Stockholm and in 1957 he represented the Guardian at the convention to elect the first Regional Spiritual Assembly of Scandinavia and Finland.

Following the passing of the Guardian in 1957, the Hands of the Cause elected from among their number nine members to serve the interests of the Cause in the Holy Land. Dr Mühlschlegel was initially elected to the body but was unable to serve in this capacity, and Abu'l-Qásim Faizi was chosen to replace him. Dr Mühlschlegel did, however, act as substitute custodian, together with Ugo Giachery, John Ferraby, Shu'á'u'lláh 'Alá'í, 'Alí Muḥammad Varqá and William Sears. The Custodians wrote to all National Spiritual Assemblies on 8 August 1958:

> This arrangement has been most fortuitous as it has brought us first-hand reports of the status of the Faith in various areas and enabled these temporary Custodians to better sense the over-all needs of the Faith as seen from the World Centre.[14]

In 1958 Adelbert and Herma left Stuttgart and pioneered to various centres, eventually settling in Tübingen. In July 1958 Adelbert participated in the intercontinental conference in Frankfurt, and later in the year attended the Conference of European Hands. After the conference he planned to travel through Scandinavia, but on the eve of his departure he suffered a heart attack and had to cancel his trip. Near the beginning of 1959, he retired from his medical duties. From this time on he devoted his entire time to the service of the Faith.

In the years before the election of the Universal House of Justice Adelbert was busy. In 1960 he assisted the Regional Assembly of Scandinavia and Finland in its teaching and consolidation work. When Hand of the Cause Charles Mason Remey made his unfounded claim to be the second Guardian, Dr Mühlschlegel hastened to Germany to ensure the loyalty of the National Spiritual Assembly and believers to the Custodians. In 1962 he represented the World Centre at the inaugural conventions of the National Spiritual Assemblies of Finland and Sweden. In spite of ill health, he continued his travels to various parts of Europe, visiting almost every European summer school. Through his visits to European countries between 1953 and 1963, he assisted in increasing the number of national spiritual assemblies on the continent from 3 to 16.

In 1964 Herma passed away after a long and difficult illness, throughout which Adelbert cared for her. When she passed away he wrote:

> after intense suffering, she radiantly ascended to the eternal homeland, on the blessings of which she had so often reflected on earth.[15]

She was remembered by the Universal House of Justice in a cable sent on her passing:

> GRIEVED NEWS ASSURE PRAYERS HOLY SHRINES BEHALF NOBLE SOUL HERMA MUHLSCHLEGEL NOW PASSED TO ETERNAL WORLD HER SPIRIT SERENE SELF-SACRIFICE WORTHY EMULATION ALL BELIEVERS.[16]

Following his wife's death, Adelbert moved to Vienna to help strengthen the Austrian Bahá'í community. A year after his move he married Ursula Kohler, the secretary of the National Spiritual Assembly of Austria. She became his close companion and collaborator.

Dr Mühlschlegel continued his travels in Europe for much of the decade. When the Universal House of Justice established the Continental Boards of Counsellors in 1968 and the burden of work was taken in some measure from the shoulders of the Hands of the Cause, Dr Mühlschlegel was able to take his first journey to another continent to serve the Faith. In 1969–70, at the request of the Universal House of Justice, he travelled to Iran, India, Pakistan, Bangladesh, Sri Lanka, Sikkim and Nepal to help the believers in their teaching work.

In 1970 he and Ursula moved to Fribourg in Switzerland to assist the National Spiritual Assembly open one of its French-speaking cantons. To secure a residence permit, Adelbert enrolled in the University of Fribourg as a student of comparative religion. By 1974 a healthy community had been established and the Mühlschlegels were asked by the Universal House of Justice to resettle in Hofheim, Germany, near the Mother Temple of Europe. Again their home became a centre of Bahá'í activity and hospitality.

In 1971 Dr Mühlschlegel travelled to Africa, where he attended the conventions establishing the National Spiritual Assemblies of Lesotho and of Swaziland. In 1972 he attended the inaugural convention of the National Spiritual Assembly of the Seychelles. He spoke at the international Bahá'í youth conferences in Fiesch, Switzerland, in 1971 and in Salzburg, Austria; Padua, Italy; and Plon, Germany, in 1972. In 1975 he visited South America. In all of these activities he was accompanied by Ursula.

Although his heart was becoming weaker, Adelbert and his wife pioneered to Athens in 1977. Dr Mühlschlegel was now 80 years old, but still was able to attend the convention establishing the first National Spiritual Assembly of Greece that year.

After this Dr Mühlschlegel lived a more restricted life. The warmth and harmony of his home attracted many, and although he was confined first to his home, then to his chair and finally to his bed, many drew their inspiration from him. Over the years he had written many articles on Bahá'í subjects, some of which appeared in volumes of *The Bahá'í World* and other periodicals, and he had as his main intellectual task the writing of a world history in which all civilizations were treated equally. In 1977 a collection of his poems was published by Bahá'í-Verlag. Now he devoted himself to preparing a book on the personal development of one's Bahá'í characteristics and the achievement of maturity in the Cause. Before he could finish the work, however, he passed away, on 29 July 1980. He was buried on the shores of the Mediterranean in the Protestant sector of Athens' First Cemetery. His funeral was attended by friends from eight countries. The Universal House of Justice cabled the Bahá'í world:

WITH SORROWFUL HEARTS ANNOUNCE PASSING BELOVED HAND CAUSE ADELBERT MUHLSCHLEGEL. GRIEVOUS LOSS SUSTAINED ENTIRE BAHAI WORLD PARTICULARLY FELT EUROPE MAIN ARENA HIS DISTINGUISHED SERVICES CAUSE

GOD. SERVING FOR MANY YEARS NATIONAL SPIRITUAL ASSEMBLY GERMANY HE BECAME AFTER ELEVATION RANK HAND CAUSE ONE OF CHAMPION BUILDERS EMERGING EUROPEAN BAHAI COMMUNITY CONSTANTLY TRAVELLING ENCOURAGING RAISING SPIRITS FRIENDS RESIDING WHEREVER SERVICES MOST NEEDED FINALLY PIONEERING GREECE AND SURRENDERING HIS SOUL PIONEER POST. HIS CONSTANT WILLINGNESS SERVE HIS ABILITY ENDEAR HIMSELF BELIEVERS AND OTHERS ALIKE BY HIS LOVING GENTLENESS SERENE HUMILITY RADIANT CHEERFULNESS HIS NEVER CEASING PURSUIT KNOWLEDGE AND TOTAL DEDICATION BLESSED BEAUTY PROVIDE WONDERFUL EXAMPLE BAHAI LIFE. ADVISE FRIENDS COMMEMORATE HIS PASSING AND REQUEST BEFITTING MEMORIAL SERVICES ALL MOTHER TEMPLES.[17]

# Siegfried Schopflocher
## 1877–1953

Fred Schopflocher was born in Germany and raised as an orthodox Jew. When he finished school he became an agnostic, while at the same time searching for a more universal religious expression. At the turn of the 19th century he emigrated to Canada, where he became a successful businessman in Montreal. He was founder and president of the Canadian Bronze Powder Works Ltd, with offices in many parts of the globe, and held the world patent rights for bronze powder.

In 1918 Fred married Florence Evaline 'Lorol' Snyder at the Marble Collegiate Church in New York City. Born in 1886 of a Swiss father and a New Yorker mother, Lorol came from an affluent home with which she 'suddenly became bored'.[1] Her travels alleviated her boredom somewhat, but it was her contact with the Bahá'í Faith that put meaning into her life.

Lorol met May Maxwell, whose home was in Montreal, soon after her marriage. Mrs Maxwell invited her to Green Acre, where Lorol became a Bahá'í around 1920. Captivated by the charm of the future Bahá'í summer school, she invited her husband to visit and share her attraction both to Green Acre and to the Bahá'í Cause. During a visit there in the summer of 1921 Fred Schopflocher joined the Bahá'í Faith, the first Jew in Montreal to become a Bahá'í.

Green Acre had been created by Sarah Jane Farmer, who conceived the idea of establishing a summer school dedicated to the ideals of peace and religious unity. In 1894 she launched her dream, and at Green Acre raised the first known peace flag in the world. The success of Green Acre in attracting religionists, scholars and educators to the retreat exceeded her fondest hopes. After Miss Farmer became a Bahá'í in 1900, many of the programmes offered at Green Acre focused on the Bahá'í teachings. 'Abdu'l-Bahá visited the school for a week in 1912.

The school, however, suffered many financial difficulties over the years. By 1912 Sarah Farmer, whose health was poor, was unable to continue in her capacity as director. Green Acre passed into the possession and control of the Green Acre Fellowship. The Fellowship and a number of Trustees managed the affairs of the school until 1925. Fred spoke on behalf of the Trustees at the Annual Fellowship meeting held at Green Acre, at which the Board proposed that the school come directly under the control of the National Spiritual Assembly of the Bahá'ís of the United States and Canada:

> What has been done is only due to the cooperation of the members of this Fellowship without which the Board of Trustees cannot do anything. It is the spirit of cooperation and coordination which has brought about the material and physical improvements in the last few years – and an expression also of my gratitude toward Green Acre for here I have experienced real and loving friendships which I have never known before, and I tried to put into the work the spirit of love and service. There is no greater mysticism to be experienced I think than that which a man or woman finds for the first time when they really contact that true spirit of loving service which is selfless and ideal and promoted by the heart which has been touched with the love of God; only for the sake of God do they serve and for the advancement of His Cause; and this is my debt to Green Acre. When I first came here I was presented with a little booklet which told of the ideals of this centre, and I said: Is it possible? I thought to myself it is not possible for such a place to exist! . . . I came to the conclusion that it was not the outer Green Acre, even with its beautiful setting and surroundings, but that it was the deep meaning of Green Acre, its ideals, its universal platform, its deep spiritual significance, its standards of unity and human solidarity that I loved so much and which I have tried to follow, which many succeed in following, and all of us will succeed in this endeavour through cooperation and selfless service, and it will be our privilege to lift up others, and see that they also enjoy this happiness and the loving friendships. There is the mysticism of Green Acre, and there is true mysticism. There is the demonstration of the spirit of love in action. It was this Bahá'í spirit which attracted me . . . There is to come before you a resolution which the Board of Trustees has prepared in absolute unity with the greatest consideration realizing its importance. With the adoption of such a resolution, we will be able surely to have the support of all the Green Acre people of the world, and which will bring all of us definitely into relation with Green Acre.[2]

Over the years Fred donated several important properties to Green Acre and took an active part in its upkeep and the extension of its facilities.

Not long after he became a Bahá'í Fred was elected to the National Spiritual Assembly of the United States and Canada, serving on the body for 15 years at different times between 1924 and 1947. When Canada formed a separate National Spiritual Assembly in 1948, Fred was elected to it, serving until his death in 1953. It was largely through his efforts, and those of Horace Holley, that the National Spiritual Assembly of Canada was able to become incorporated by an Act of the Parliament of Canada.

Fred's business affairs took him to many parts of the world. He made his first of many trips to Haifa in 1922. There he met Shoghi Effendi and immediately became devoted to him. For his part, Shoghi Effendi found Fred a 'zealous and promising disciple of 'Abdu'l-Bahá'.[3] Shoghi Effendi often gave Fred specific tasks to carry out while on his international journeys, and encouraged him to visit the Bahá'í communities wherever he went. On these journeys Fred came to appreciate 'the extraordinary bond linking the believers throughout the world in their love for a common Cause'. Normally, he said, 'it would have been impossible for a Westerner to make contact with so wide a variety of peoples in East and West . . . but the world-wide community of the believers has destroyed all barriers'.[4]

One of the Bahá'ís Fred met in the course of his travels was Martha Root, who was in Port Said in 1925, waiting to sail to Europe. She had just left Haifa and felt renewed and restored, and Fred cheered her even further with news from home. When she boarded her ship Fred came aboard to see her off with presents of chocolates and a little money to be used for her 'comforts'. Martha wrote to the Wilhelms that the money 'will be such a big help in the publicity work I so long to do – my "comfort" is to promote the Cause. I will use it very carefully and I think I shall later write Mr Schopflocher and tell him just how every £ was spent. There is so much to do and everything costs so much.'[5]

In 1936 Fred travelled to Australia. The Guardian was anxious that the Bahá'í community there make the best use of Fred's tour, and in a letter of 25 September 1936, written on his behalf, asked them to enable him to visit every Bahá'í community in Australia and, if possible, New Zealand:

> Mr Schopflocher is surely known to you and to many friends in Australia. He is truly one of the most distinguished believers in the West. He has a deep

> knowledge of the Cause, and specially of the Administration, and has contributed a unique share towards its establishment and consolidation in the States. For many years a member of the American N.S.A., he revealed such great qualities of heart and mind as very few of his fellow-members were able to manifest. He supported valiantly and generously, and through both moral and financial means, the various institutions of the Cause . . . The friends owe him indeed a great debt, and can never be too grateful for what he has accomplished, and is still so splendidly accomplishing, for the Faith in the West.[6]

A little over four months later, the Guardian thanked the National Spiritual Assembly of Australia and New Zealand, in a letter of 4 February 1937 written through his secretary, for its warm welcome to Mr Schopflocher:

> It is his fervent hope that the spirit his visit has released will long serve to sustain the friends in their heavy task of expanding the foundations of the Administrative Order throughout that continent.[7]

As part as the same tour, Fred travelled to India. Shoghi Effendi wrote to the Indian National Spiritual Assembly on 7 January 1937 expressing his confidence

> that the steps you have taken to render his trip successful will greatly help in giving the Faith a wide and long needed publicity. The opportunity that has been offered you has been truly splendid, and you certainly deserve to be heartily congratulated for having fully availed yourselves of it.[8]

While Fred Schopflocher travelled and served the Cause, his wife was blazing her own amazing path of service. On behalf of the Cause of God, she travelled nine times around the world, visiting 86 countries, including Soviet Russia, many more than once. She was among the first travel teachers to Central and South America and to the African continent. Her teaching work in Hawaii, Japan and China was praised by Keith Ransom-Kehler, while Agnes Alexander mentioned Lorol's travels to Burma, India, Iran and Iraq. One account describes Lorol as 'venturing into regions difficult of access, dangerous even for travel. With brave heart and with a blazing enthusiasm for the Bahá'í Cause she has been enabled to reach many prominent men and women of the East and present her message to them.'[9]

One of Fred Schopflocher's greatest services to the Cause was the impetus he gave to the building of the Wilmette House of Worship. Although there was much interest in the Temple, the National Spiritual Assembly never had quite enough money to begin work on the superstructure. In December 1925 it devised a 'Plan of Unified Action' to accumulate $400,000 within three years, enough to construct the first unit of the superstructure. By the end of 1926, only $51,039 had been contributed and the contributions in 1927 proved just as disappointing.

At the 1928 National Convention the delegates heard Allen McDaniel, the chairman of the National Spiritual Assembly, report on a conversation he had recently had with the Guardian in the Holy Land. Shoghi Effendi believed that the Bahá'ís had lost confidence in the National Assembly. He stated that the new Assembly must assure the believers that it would not exceed its budget, as it had done in previous years, and would allocate all the monies received over its budgetary needs to the Temple Fund. On hearing this, Fred announced to the Convention that he would make a special contribution of $25,000. His unexpected generosity inspired the other delegates to pledge an additional $15,000. Elated, the National Assembly later decided to transfer $25,000 to the Temple Fund account. After this, contributions increased dramatically, such that by the beginning of March 1929 the Temple Fund showed a balance of $87,000.

Around this time, Lorol Schopflocher arrived in Haifa after an extended trip to India. As he greeted her, Shoghi Effendi handed her a cable from her husband, who reportedly wrote: 'Are you willing to contribute $50,000 to Temple which may mean you do not get a new Cadillac this year?' Recalling this incident three decades later, Lorol said:

> I laughed out loud and Shoghi Effendi grinned as he said, 'What do you think of this?' I laughed again and said 'Why not $100,000?' I scribbled a cable on a table napkin and sent Fugeta, the Master's old Japanese servant, off to the telegraph office . . . The reply came back, 'You win, love to Shoghi Effendi, love, Fred.'[10]

Thus, on 16 March the National Spiritual Assembly was able to add a further $110,000 to the Temple Fund.

In 1937 the first Seven Year Plan was launched. One goal of the Plan was to raise $350,000 to complete the exterior ornamentation of the House of Worship. The construction work was to be done in stages, as money became available. In the opening weeks of the Plan Fred Schopflocher pledged another $100,000 to the Temple project – no small sum in those times, particularly in the middle of the Great Depression.

Siegfried Schopflocher early understood the significance of the Temple and its potential to influence the growth of the Faith. Not only did he contribute financially to it, he also stimulated fresh enthusiasm for the completion of its exterior decoration at a time when many had lost interest. His dedication to the construction of the Temple was much appreciated by the Guardian, who called him the 'Chief Temple Builder'.[11] Shoghi Effendi felt that it was Fred's unfailing and generous assistance that was mainly responsible for the Temple's steady and efficient construction.

Fred learned of his appointment as a Hand of the Cause directly from the Guardian during one of his visits to Haifa. Rúḥíyyih Khánum was present at the Pilgrim House table when Shoghi Effendi told him of his decision: 'Freddie turned so white I thought he was going to faint!'[12] The Guardian officially announced his appointment, along with that of six others, on 29 February 1952.

One of three German-born Hands of the Cause, Siegfried Schopflocher's particular assignment was to assist the National Spiritual Assembly of Canada to establish its national Ḥaẓíratu'l-Quds. In 1953 he attended the Canadian National Convention and then the intercontinental conference in Chicago. He visited western Canada near the end of June, deepening the understanding of the Bahá'ís about the Hands of the Cause and informing them of the tremendous services of the Guardian. He planned to attend the New Delhi intercontinental conference, but fell ill a few days before his departure. He passed away on 27 July 1953 and was buried close to the grave of Sutherland Maxwell in the Mount Royal Cemetery in Montreal. On his passing the Guardian cabled:

> PROFOUNDLY GRIEVED PASSING DEARLY LOVED, OUTSTANDING STAUNCH HAND CAUSE FRED SCHOPFLOCHER. NUMEROUS, MAGNIFICENT SERVICES EXTENDING OVER THIRTY YEARS ADMINISTRATIVE TEACHING SPHERES UNITED STATES, CANADA, INSTITUTIONS BAHÁ'Í WORLD CENTRE GREATLY ENRICHED ANNALS FORMATIVE AGE FAITH. ABUNDANT REWARD ASSURED ABHÁ KINGDOM. ADVISING AMERICAN NATIONAL ASSEMBLY HOLD BEFITTING MEMORIAL GATHERING TEMPLE HE GENEROUSLY HELPED RAISE. ADVISE HOLD MEMORIAL GATHERING MAXWELL HOME COMMEMORATE HIS EMINENT PART RISE ADMINISTRATIVE ORDER FAITH CANADA. URGE ENSURE BURIAL

CLOSE NEIGHBOURHOOD RESTING PLACE DISTINGUISHED HAND CAUSE SUTHERLAND MAXWELL.[13]

# Corinne Knight True
## 1861–1961

When Corinne True was born in Oldham County, Kentucky on 1 November 1861 Abraham Lincoln was President of the United States. Only eleven years before Corinne's birth, the Báb, Forerunner of the Bahá'í Revelation, was martyred in far-off Persia. Bahá'u'lláh, the Supreme Manifestation of God, to Whom Corinne would devote more than 60 years of service, would not declare Himself to His followers for another 17 months. Another half century would pass before 'Abdu'l-Bahá would make His historic trip to America.

During her long and eventful life, Corinne would bear eight children in 27 years of marriage and outlive her husband by 52 years. She would see Civil War Union soldiers invade her parents' home, the end of slavery, Custer's 'Last Stand', the industrial revolution, the uproar over Jesse James and Billy the Kid, the erection of the Statue of Liberty, the coming of the electric light bulb, the transition from stagecoach to motor car, Teddy Roosevelt's Rough Riders, the Wright Brothers at Kitty Hawk, the toppling of kings from their thrones, Woodrow Wilson and the League of Nations, Prohibition, the Great Depression, the rise and fall of Hitler, the atom bomb, jet travel, Sputnik and the ascent of John F. Kennedy to the American presidency.

Corinne's parents, Moses and Martha Knight, were Kentucky plantation owners whose Southern aristocratic leanings ensured that, even when the family moved North, Corinne completed her education in a Southern finishing school. Exposed to the culture and charm associated with the South, Corinne, while doing well academically, loved attending balls, horse riding and accompanying her father around the plantation.

Moses had been a Presbyterian minister, but a throat ailment had forced his retirement from the ministry while he was still a young man. Nevertheless he read the Bible daily and lived by its code faithfully, and Corinne developed an extensive knowledge of scripture which would assist her as a Bahá'í teacher in later years. Meanwhile she surrendered her heart to Christ, but often remarked as a child, 'How wonderful it must have been to have lived in the days when Christ was on earth.'[1]

When Corinne was 14 the family moved first to Louisville and then, a year later, to Chicago. Corinne was away at finishing school when new neighbours from Maine moved in next door. Returning home on holiday, she met the neighbours' son, Moses Adams True. Soon the couple were in love and sought approval for their marriage. Mr Knight opposed Corinne's marriage to a Northerner and would not give his consent, so Moses True and Corinne eloped on 24 June 1882. Bewildered, Moses Knight, according to the Southern culture of male patriarchal dominance, reacted to his favourite child's disrespect by refusing to see her or speak to her for nine years and by cutting her out of his will. He even refused to see his first grandchild, Harriet, who was born in August 1883.

After Harriet's birth the Trues moved to Michigan, where they lived for eight years. During this period Corinne had four more children: Laurence, Charles (Davis), Edna and Arna. Moses Knight eventually forgave his daughter and she and her family returned to Chicago to live in a house he gave to her. The house was, however, to prove a source of tragedy when Harriet fell down the basement stairs in 1892 and died from her injuries. Corinne found her faith in God severely shaken; Harriet's death made no sense to her. Why would God take such a tender person away?

No one could comfort Corinne and she could find no solace in traditional Christianity. Moses and Corinne sought answers in Unity – a progressive movement within Christianity – in Christian Science and in Divine Science. Eventually, the pain of Harriet's death subsided, and 14 months after the accident Corinne gave birth to twins, Kenneth and Katherine. In 1896 Nathanael was born.

In late 1898 diphtheria swept through Chicago. Several of the True children contracted the disease, which can lead to suffocation and heart damage. The Trues spent many a sleepless and anxious night nursing the sick children. One night at the end of May 1899 little Nathanael, who was badly affected, was sitting on his mother's lap. 'He seemed to be staring into space, his face luminous. Suddenly he reached up his hands toward the ceiling and pleaded, "Oh, play with me."' The next moment he was dead. Grieved by this latest calamity, Corinne believed that in Nathanael's final moments he had been approached by souls from the next world.[2]

Answers from a merciful God often come in the midst of crisis and calamity, and several months after Nathanael's death, Corinne was invited by a friend to a lecture on religion given by three Persians. Almost immediately, she realized at the lecture that she had been exposed to the message of God for this age and committed herself to the Bahá'í Faith.

Thereafter Corinne regularly attended the weekly meetings where excerpts from The Book of Certitude, The Hidden Words and Tablets from 'Abdu'l-Bahá were read. As there were no Bahá'í books in English, such passages were copied on sheets of paper and circulated to those who wished to have them. Corinne obtained copies of some of these passages and studied them diligently. They helped broaden her love for and knowledge of God. She prayed that her husband might also embrace the new Revelation, but she did not tell her parents about it as she felt they would not understand.

Corinne became a Bahá'í some time late in 1899. As were all new believers, she was encouraged to write to 'Abdu'l-Bahá. Several months passed before she received a Tablet from Him, sent from the Holy Land through Lua Getsinger in October 1900. This Tablet helped her understand the death of three-year-old Nathanael:

> Be not grieved nor troubled because of the loss which hath befallen thee – a loss which caused the tears to flow, sighs to be produced, sorrow to exist and hearts to burn in great agony; but know, this hath reference only to the physical body, and if thou considerest this matter with a discerning and intelligent eye, thou wilt find that it hath no power whatsoever, for separation belongeth to the characteristics of the body. But concerning the spirit, know that thy pure son shall be with thee in the Kingdom of God and thou shalt witness his smiling face, illumined brow, handsome spirit and real happiness. Accordingly, thou wilt then be comforted and thank God for His favour upon thee.[3]

A few weeks after the arrival of 'Abdu'l-Bahá's Tablet seven-year-old Kenneth contracted diphtheria, and died on 14 January 1901. Once again, 'Abdu'l-Bahá comforted Corinne, in a Tablet sent in May 1901:

> Be not grieved at the calamity which hath unexpectedly come upon thee and for the misfortune which heavily weigheth upon thee. It behoveth one like thee to endure every trial, to be pleased with the decree and to commit all thy affairs to God so that thou mayest be a calm, approved and pleasing soul before God. Know thou, that thy beloved son hath soared, with the wing of soul, up to the loftiest height which is never-ending in the Kingdom of God. Rejoice at this great prosperity . . . Truly, I say unto thee, wert thou informed of the position in which is thy son, thy face would be illumined by the lights of happiness.[4]

In another Tablet from 'Abdu'l-Bahá, Corinne found a code for living which she would follow for the rest of her life:

> Believe thou in God, and keep thine eyes fixed upon the exalted Kingdom; be thou enamoured of the Abhá Beauty; stand thou firm in the Covenant; yearn thou to ascend into the Heaven of the Universal Light. Be thou severed from this world, and reborn through the sweet scents of holiness that blow from the realm of the All-Highest. Be thou a summoner to love, and be thou kind to all the human race. Love thou the children of men and share in their sorrows. Be thou of those who foster peace. Offer thy friendship, be worthy of trust. Be thou a balm to every sore, be thou a medicine for every ill. Bind thou the souls together. Recite thou the verses of guidance. Be engaged in the worship of thy Lord, and rise up to lead the people aright. Loose thy tongue and teach, and let thy face be bright with the fire of God's love. Rest thou not for a moment, seek thou to draw no easeful breath. Thus mayest thou become a sign and symbol of God's love, and a banner of His grace.[5]

Corinne's faith was reinforced by 'Abdu'l-Bahá's words and she became calm, patient and steadfast. Her husband was amazed at her new-found strength. He did not, however, share her faith. As Corinne became more involved in the affairs of her new religion she asked 'Abdu'l-Bahá for advice. He told her:

> As to thy respected husband: it is incumbent upon thee to treat him with great kindness, to consider his wishes and be conciliatory with him at all times, till he seeth that because thou hast directed thyself toward the Kingdom of God, thy tenderness for him and thy love for God have but increased, as well as thy concern for his wishes under all conditions.[6]

Yet Corinne longed for the two of them to work shoulder to shoulder in the Cause. 'Abdu'l-Bahá, realizing her concern, revealed for her the now well-known prayer for husbands:

> O God, my God! This Thy handmaid is calling upon Thee, trusting in Thee, turning her face unto Thee, imploring Thee to shed Thy heavenly bounties upon her, and to disclose unto her Thy spiritual mysteries, and to cast upon her the lights of Thy Godhead.
>
> O my Lord! Make the eyes of my husband to see. Rejoice Thou his heart with the light of the knowledge of Thee, draw Thou his mind unto Thy luminous beauty, cheer Thou his spirit by revealing unto him Thy manifest splendours.
>
> O my Lord! Lift Thou the veil from before his sight. Rain down Thy plenteous bounties upon him, intoxicate him with the wine of love for Thee, make him one of Thy angels whose feet walk upon this earth even as their souls are soaring through the high heavens. Cause him to become a brilliant lamp, shining out with the light of Thy wisdom in the midst of Thy people.
>
> Verily Thou art the Precious, the Ever-Bestowing, the Open of Hand.[7]

In the early days of the 20th century, women were still regarded as the inferior sex. They could not vote in elections, were limited in professional choices and often could not participate with men in business affairs. Thus, when some of the early believers such as Thornton Chase and Corinne True felt a need to establish an administrative organization for the Bahá'í Faith, they naturally followed the convention of the times and set up an institution with only men as members. The Chicago House of Justice (renamed to the House of Spirituality the next year) was established in 1901. Having no right of membership, the women eventually formed the Women's Assembly of Teaching after 'Abdu'l-Bahá wrote to Corinne:

> As to you, O ye other handmaids who are enamoured of the heavenly fragrances, arrange ye holy gatherings, and found ye Spiritual Assemblies, for these are the basis for spreading the sweet savours of God, exalting His Word, uplifting the lamp of His grace, promulgating His religion and promoting His Teachings, and what bounty is there greater than this?[8]

These two institutions worked in parallel. The House of Spirituality focused its energies on regulating community affairs. Its decisions were ratified in a weekly community meeting attended by both Bahá'ís and enquirers. The Assembly of Teaching concentrated more on teaching the Faith by organizing meetings, study groups and public gatherings.

In 1903, inspired by news of the House of Worship at 'Ishqábád, the House of Spirituality asked 'Abdu'l-Bahá for permission to build a Mashriqu'l-Adhkár in America. Approving the proposal, 'Abdu'l-Bahá charged Corinne with the responsibility for helping to raise it. Astonished, Corinne found herself confronted by perhaps the greatest challenge any one believer could have faced in the early 20th century. She lacked, she believed, many of the skills required for the task, being a housewife in a male-oriented society. Yet when 'Abdu'l-Bahá wrote giving her instructions about the Temple, as president of the Women's Assembly of Teaching she raised the subject before the members. They then raised some money, opened a bank account and appointed a treasurer.

Three years after the launching of the Temple Project, Corinne's eldest son, Laurence, had a sailing accident and died. His sudden death prompted Corinne to request permission to visit 'Akká. Welcoming Corinne to 'Akká as His daughter, 'Abdu'l-Bahá talked to her about the necessity for tests, His words touching the core of sorrow within her being.

> He likened tests to a ship laden with food, headed to a people dependent on the cargo, being tossed about by fierce winds and high waves. Those on board were uncomfortable. Yet the ship must proceed, for it carried food which would be the cause of life. So man must suffer the winds and waves of tests to bring life to the people.[9]

Corinne brought with her to the Holy Land a scroll on which she had collected nearly 800 signatures from Bahá'ís across America who petitioned 'Abdu'l-Bahá for permission to begin construction of the Temple. The petition, initiated by the Women's Assembly of Teaching, read: 'We, the undersigned, desire to arise for the erection of the first Mashrak-el-Azkar in America in compliance with the Tablets revealed in behalf of this great Spiritual Edifice.'[10] When Corinne presented 'Abdu'l-Bahá with the gifts sent by the American believers, He lit on the petition, held it high and exclaimed: 'This . . . this is what gives me great joy. Go back, . . . go back and work for the Temple; it is a great work, the best thing you could do, Mrs True.'[11]

When she returned to America, Corinne wrote a booklet entitled *Notes Taken at Acca* in which she told of her experiences on pilgrimage and noted 'Abdu'l-Bahá's enthusiasm for the Temple project, explaining how the Master had given her guidance about the location for the Temple – it was to be a spacious piece of land – and its general dimensions:

> He said it would take much to build the Temple, but we must have meetings about the work, labour hard and pray to God and He would bless our efforts . . . He said the Temple was the greatest matter today for the upbuilding of the Cause.[12]

On her return home Corinne, remembering the Master's remarkable capacity for work, rededicated herself to the Cause. She thought about the Temple Project every day and worked to increase the contributions to it. In addition to holding two offices on the Women's Assembly of Teaching, she hosted regular teaching meetings in her home.

What Corinne learned on pilgrimage helped her understand that the Temple was for America, not just Chicago. Thus, she believed, the responsibility for its erection belonged to every Bahá'í in the land. Noting that a person should strive to comprehend the service God wants him to perform, she declared:

> The Messengers bring us God's way and it is for man to completely sacrifice his will, his judgement, his reason and accept the commands of God's mouthpiece. The tablets reveal to us that '. . . the most important matter today is to establish a Mashrak-el-Azkar and to found a Temple . . .'[13]

No doubt Corinne's words were inspired by 'Abdu'l-Bahá's now famous statement about the Temple:

> Now the day has arrived in which the edifice of God, the divine sanctuary, the spiritual temple, shall be erected in America! I entreat God to assist the confirmed believers in accomplishing this great service and with entire zeal to rear this mighty structure which shall be renowned throughout the world. The support of God will be with those believers in that district that they may be successful in their undertaking, for the Cause is great and great; because this is the first Mashrak-el-Azcar in that country and from it the praise of God shall ascend to the Kingdom of Mystery and the tumult of His exaltation and greetings from the whole world shall be heard!
>
> Whosoever arises for the service of this building shall be assisted with a

great power from His Supreme Kingdom and upon him spiritual and heavenly blessings shall descend, which shall fill his heart with wonderful consolation and enlighten his eyes by beholding the glorious and eternal God![14]

Although the Temple was to become Corinne True's best-known service to the Bahá'í Cause, she was also a remarkable teacher. Reserved by nature, she tended to respect people's privacy. Overcoming feelings of inadequacy, she taught the Faith in the knowledge that only the Message of Bahá'u'lláh could save a drowning civilization. She introduced the Faith into Michigan, helping establish Bahá'í communities in Grand Rapids, Muskegon, Grand Haven and Fruitport. While she continued to teach in Chicago, she was instrumental in bringing the Faith to many areas in Milwaukee.

Corinne's children recalled their mother telling people about the Faith in the parlour. She would present the Message calmly, often using her extensive biblical knowledge to enhance her presentation. Her dynamic personality created a spiritual atmosphere where Bahá'í standards were upheld. People from all over the world and from different walks of life passed through her home. Whether travelling teachers, recuperating surgical patients, destitute persons or 'Abdu'l-Bahá Himself, Corinne's daughters often found their house full of unusual and fascinating people.

The House of Spirituality had formed teams to look for land for a Temple site. Corinne, who was in the forefront of the search, and another believer located the site at Grosse Point. In 1908 Corinne persuaded the House of Spirituality to buy the property, and two lots were purchased on a bluff overlooking Lake Michigan in the village of Wilmette. The House of Spirituality also took an option on twelve adjoining lots and eventually purchased them. Not everyone was pleased with the decision. Thornton Chase felt it 'rather lacking in wisdom to place the Temple away out in the country, where it not only requires from one and a half hour to two hours with the very best transportation to reach it, to say nothing of a long walk at the further end.'[15]

Nevertheless, the following year the Bahá'í Temple Unity was formed to coordinate all aspects of the building of the Temple. Elected at a convention held in the Trues' new home on Kenmore Avenue, the body would eventually evolve into the National Spiritual Assembly of the United States and Canada. Corinne, one of three women elected to the nine-member Executive Board, was made financial secretary.

During this hectic period Moses True was deeply involved in Bahá'í activities, although he was not himself an avowed believer. He missed Corinne when she was away from home and he never recovered from the blow he suffered at the death of his son Laurence. On 26 November 1909 he told Percy Woodcock, a Bahá'í from New York, 'If the Revelation is as you say it is, Mr Woodcock, then I am a Bahá'í.'[16] Fifteen days later, he died of a heart attack. He was 52 years old.

Corinne's response to Moses's passing was to throw herself into her Bahá'í work, keeping up her busy pace in service to the Cause as a reflection of her serenity and utter submission to the Will of God. She replied to one of the hundreds of people who wrote to her at this time:

> As this is the Springtime in the Cause great thunderstorms must attend to its establishment and each soul will be able to find just how deep down into the Work it has thrust the tendrils of his or her heart, and if they are deeply, firmly rooted, the storms will only make them stronger. Pray dear Sister that I may not be shaken by this catastrophe.[17]

In another letter, she declared:

> Bahá'u'lláh said that every destruction was followed by a construction. So although my earthly family is so rapidly devastated, yet through the Word of Bahá'u'lláh and 'Abdu'l-Bahá the spiritual family of Abhá is growing and growing and I find myself with brothers and sisters all over the world who love with that pure spiritual love.[18]

In 1910 Corinne's son Davis contracted tuberculosis while working in an Oregon logging camp. Worried for her son's health, Corinne nevertheless continued to work for the Temple Project. It was rumoured that 'Abdu'l-Bahá might come to America. Corinne longed for the Bahá'ís to have greater unity. In 1911 'Abdu'l-Bahá had written, telling them, 'If ye are yearning for my meeting, and if in reality ye are seeking my visit, ye must close the doors of difference and open the gates of affection, love and friendship. Ye must pulsate as one heart, and throb as one spirit.'[19] Corinne believed that the building of the Temple would bring the Bahá'ís together, so she continued to exhort them to greater effort. She found, however, that this often created more disunity, much to her dismay.

In April 1912 'Abdu'l-Bahá arrived in America. Corinne invited Him to visit her home, reasoning that she and Arna had been guests in His. He agreed, and arrived in Chicago on 29 April.

By this time Davis had been suffering with tuberculosis for some two years. When 'Abdu'l-Bahá came to the Trues' home, He asked to see the young man and spent a long time with him. Emerging from Davis's room, He cried out, 'The calamities in this house must cease.'[20] Corinne was overjoyed. She felt certain that her last remaining son would recover. Indeed, at the end of His visit the Master told Corinne that Davis was a wonderful young man and that He found him much better than expected. He asked Corinne to accompany Him to His lectures that day. While Corinne was away, however, Davis died. Only then did Corinne realize that 'Abdu'l-Bahá had been referring to Davis's spiritual condition, not his physical one.

The next day was the historic occasion on which 'Abdu'l-Bahá laid the cornerstone of the Temple. Standing among the nearly 400 people awaiting 'Abdu'l-Bahá's arrival, Corinne wondered whether the human tragedy so relentlessly stalking her would ever cease. Some time later she unburdened her heart to 'Abdu'l-Bahá, asking about her husband. 'Abdu'l-Bahá assured her that they would be reunited in the next world and that Moses had accepted Bahá'u'lláh. Corinne said to Him, 'I have had a great many sorrows . . . I have had a sad life – sad things to bear.' 'I know, I know, Mrs True', He replied, 'because I have sent them to you.'[21]

Over the next years Corinne worked hard to increase the contributions to the Temple Fund. Whenever a donation came in, she invariably wrote a personal letter of thanks and encouragement to the contributor. In May 1914 she addressed the American Bahá'ís through the magazine *Star of the West*:

> The followers of Baha'o'llah should not pause a moment in the great endeavour to complete the Mashrak-el-Azkar. Abdul-Baha says, '*the most important thing in this day is the SPEEDY ERECTION of the Edifice. Its mystery is great and cannot be unveiled as yet. In the future it will be made plain . . .*'
>
> A stated amount as a building fund has been named. Is not this in itself a call to the Bahais, singly and collectively, to make every effort possible to raise the fund? It is a call to activity. Work, work, work! – so that the 'Greatest Branch' of God may dedicate the foundation and lay the corner-stone of this Edifice and pronounce a blessing upon it that will give it a superlative degree of importance throughout countless ages.[22]

Corinne worked on the Temple Project and taught the Faith to the point of exhaustion. Construction of the Temple could not begin until $200,000 had been collected, and 'Abdu'l-Bahá had advised the Bahá'í Temple Unity not to contract any debts. In 1914 the First World War broke out and it became difficult to contact 'Abdu'l-Bahá. Disunity developed among members of the Chicago Bahá'í community and complaints were made about Corinne's work as finance secretary. Although she was completely vindicated, the incident deeply distressed Corinne and she was emotionally drained. Nevertheless, she continued to promote the Temple Fund, addressing a conference in Chicago in 1917, when the Fund was still some $67,000 short of its target:

> In this day the Sun of Spiritual Truth has again arisen in the Orient, and its radiance is seen in the Occident as well. Baha'o'llah has said that the human family was once one, dwelling together in the greatest state of harmony. Then differences crept in and racial and religious bias appeared until discord and hatred were found among the children of men. The great purpose of the Bahai Movement is to restore the foundation of human solidarity. The Mashrak-el-Azkar is the outward sign of the inward spiritual Reality which brings to pass this glorious work. Those who join with sincerity in the building of this unique and wonderful edifice share the bounty of God and are under His protection.[23]

Corinne's burning desire was to complete the edifice in 'Abdu'l-Bahá's lifetime and she must have suffered inwardly when construction of the foundations was delayed until 1920. In 1919 she went on her second pilgrimage to the Holy Land, meeting up with her daughter Edna in France en route. While they were in Italy, waiting to board the ship to Alexandria, they met John Esslemont, who was on his way to the Holy Land to consult 'Abdu'l-Bahá about his book on the Bahá'í Faith.

While Corinne was on pilgrimage 'Abdu'l-Bahá spoke to her about the Temple, but did not seem at all concerned about its slow progress. Before she left Haifa 'Abdu'l-Bahá entrusted her with a message for the American Bahá'ís. But it was nothing to do with the Temple; it was about firmness in the Covenant:

> My message to them is that they must be united, must remain firm and steadfast, must always be turning to the Kingdom and must be manifestations of truthfulness, of faith, of harmony and of self-sacrifice.[24]

When Corinne returned home she continued her work to promote the Temple Fund. At the Bahá'í Temple Unity Convention in 1920 the design for the Temple was decided and the architect chosen. The blueprints were sent to 'Abdu'l-Bahá for approval; He approved the concept but suggested that the proposed building be on a smaller scale so that it would not cost more than a million dollars. The necessary $200,000 was by this time in the bank and Corinne hoped that the edifice would be speedily erected.

About eight months after the Convention 'Abdu'l-Bahá wrote to Corinne telling her that 'all the affairs relative to the Mashreq'ul-Azkar are to be referred to the annual Convention'.[25] Corinne had for so long been the link between the Temple Project and 'Abdu'l-Bahá that she found this advice hard to follow. When new problems arose, she turned, as she had always done, to 'Abdu'l-Bahá for advice; but He responded by cable: 'ALL AFFAIRS CONCERNING UNIVERSAL TEMPLE REFERRED GENERAL CONVENTION. I CANNOT INTERFERE. SUBMIT EVERYTHING CONVENTION.'[26] This was the last message Corinne ever received from the Master. Nine months later He passed away.

After 'Abdu'l-Bahá's passing Corinne helped the Bahá'ís to understand the terms of His Will and Testament and to obey the new Guardian, Shoghi Effendi. A difficult time for many, 'Corinne worked hard at helping the friends cut through rumour and misinformation, anxiety and ignorance, to gain an accurate insight of the Guardianship.'[27]

In 1922 Shoghi Effendi invited a number of Bahá'ís, including Corinne, to Haifa to discuss the future of the Cause. She was now 60 years old and he was 25, but when she met the Guardian there was no doubt in her mind that he was able to lead the Faith.

In the years following this second pilgrimage the administration of the American Bahá'í community developed under the guidance of Shoghi Effendi, its national institution making the transition from the Bahá'í Temple Unity to the National Spiritual Assembly. By 1925 the transition was complete, with the new National Assembly being elected by secret ballot. Although she had served on the Bahá'í Temple Unity from its inception until 1923, Corinne was not elected to the new body; however, she continued in her role as financial secretary for the Temple Board.

Gradually the House of Worship took shape. The National Convention of 1928 was the first to be held in the Temple's Foundation Hall. Corinne felt she had to move closer to the Temple to watch its development. In 1930 she moved to Wilmette, only five blocks from the House of Worship.

Within a year, work began on the building's superstructure and Corinne travelled once again to Haifa.

As she grew older, Corinne developed in steadfastness and certitude. Writing to her on her return from pilgrimage in 1931, Shoghi Effendi said, 'Your staunch, unswerving faith, your boundless devotion, and assiduous care to preserve the integrity and extend the bounds of the Cause, are among the most richly valued assets that the Faith of Bahá'u'lláh has in that land.'[28]

When Corinne returned from her pilgrimage, the superstructure of the Temple was completed; she could see it from her home. The Guardian had asked Corinne to regard the Temple as her first and most sacred obligation, but she was busy with several other projects as well. She was chairman of a committee responsible for indexing and editing unpublished Tablets of 'Abdu'l-Bahá, while in 1933 she planned the devotional services in the Temple and spoke at weekly public meetings in Foundation Hall. She was a member of the Local Spiritual Assembly of Wilmette and she held classes and firesides in her home.

In time Corinne became known as Mother True. As her age became steadily more prodigious, this early believer, Mother of the Temple and renowned teacher and friend became like a mother to all who knew her.

In 1937 Shoghi Effendi launched the first Seven Year Plan and Corinne's thoughts focused on how to achieve its goals. In 1943 she was recognized as perhaps the only believer to have attended all 35 Annual Conventions.

The following year marked the centenary of the Bahá'í Faith. Corinne was asked to participate in the commemoration. Although 83 at the time, she spoke on 'The Universal House of Worship' and wrote a history of the development of the Temple from 1903 to 1915. A few months later she addressed a special centenary session for the Latin American believers.

In 1947, at the age of 86, Corinne sailed to Europe with her daughters Katherine and Edna. The three visited Bahá'í pioneer posts in the Netherlands, Belgium, Luxembourg and Switzerland. Three years later she spoke at the Unity Banquet of the European Teaching Conference in Copenhagen, being one of the few believers who had personally known the Master. Returning home, she busied herself revising *The Promulgation of Universal Peace* for the National Spiritual Assembly.

Shoghi Effendi deeply appreciated Corinne's devotion to the Cause:

> My heart is filled with gratitude for the fresh evidences of untiring activity, of exemplary loyalty, of steadfastness and devotion that you have so powerfully manifested in recent months. You are truly a tower of strength in these days of stress and trial, worthy of the unquestioning confidence reposed in you by 'Abdu'l-Bahá. Persevere in your meritorious work, and rest assured that my prayers will continue to be offered for you and for your dear daughters.[29]

Sixteen years later, on 26 March 1952, when Corinne was in her ninety-first year, Shoghi Effendi cabled:

> MOVED CONVEY GLAD TIDINGS YOUR ELEVATION RANK HAND CAUSE. APPOINTMENT OFFICIALLY ANNOUNCED PUBLIC MESSAGE ADDRESSED ALL NATIONAL ASSEMBLIES. MAY SACRED FUNCTION ENABLE YOU ENRICH RECORD SERVICES ALREADY RENDERED FAITH BAHAULLAH.[30]

Corinne True accepted her appointment without questioning it. Her concern was how she could serve the Cause most effectively in her new role. Later the same year she went on her last and most memorable pilgrimage.

When Corinne True arrived in the Holy Land, she found Shoghi Effendi enthusiastic and full of anticipation of the great victories to be won during the forthcoming Ten Year Crusade. The Guardian spent much time with Corinne, delighting in her memories of the early days of the Faith in America. Leroy Ioas, who lived at the time at the World Centre, remarked that he had never seen Shoghi Effendi respond to anyone as he did to Corinne.

Six months later Corinne was escorted by her daughters to the dedication ceremony of the House of Worship in Wilmette. Hailed by the press as an architectural wonder, the House of Worship attracted hundreds of people of diverse classes, countries and ages to the ceremony. What thoughts must Corinne True have had as she sat beneath the magnificent dome?

In 1957 came the terrible news of the passing of Shoghi Effendi. Fearful that the shock would kill her mother, Edna was amazed when Corinne, after a few moments of silence, said with assurance, 'You must know that this is the will of God.'[31]

Corinne was unable to attend the Conclave of the Hands of the Cause called in Haifa after the passing of Shoghi Effendi, owing to her frailty and health. The other Hands, however, kept in close touch with her, reporting on developments in the Faith. One personal letter especially appreciated was from Hand of the Cause William Sears:

> This is a letter of love, to send to you the deepest heartfelt appreciation for all your great services to our precious Faith. Your devotion and sacrifice in helping to raise up that most Holy House of Worship in Wilmette, is an immortal achievement. The beloved Master said that when the Temple was completed, from that point of light, the Faith of Bahá'u'lláh would be carried to all parts of the world. This prophecy came true in 1953, with the launching of the great World Crusade, and all the victories I have seen and thrilled to can be directly traced back to the building and raising up of that great edifice, with whose name, your own name, will be forever linked.[32]

During the final weeks of her life, Corinne was heard to recite in a strong voice passages she had memorized from the writings. Confined to bed most of the last months of her life, she passed quietly away on 3 April 1961 at the age of 99. From the Hands of the Cause in the Holy Land came this tribute:

> GRIEVED LOSS DISTINGUISHED DISCIPLE ABDU'L-BAHA HAND CAUSE CORINNE TRUE HER LONG ASSOCIATION EARLY HISTORY FAITH AMERICA RAISING MOTHER TEMPLE WEST STAUNCH UNFAILING CHAMPIONSHIP COVENANT STEADFAST SUPPORT BELOVED GUARDIAN EVERY STAGE UNFOLDMENT WORLD ORDER UNFORGETTABLE ENRICH ANNALS FAITH WESTERN WORLD. URGE HOLD BEFITTING MEMORIAL GATHERING MASHRIQU'L-ADHKAR.[33]

General Shu'a'u'll'áh 'Alá'í

General 'Alá'í, with Shamsi Navidi, in London

Músá Banání

Clara Dunn

Zikrullah Khadem and his wife, Javidukht

Zikrullah Khadem at a pioneer institute, United States, 1985

Zikrullah Khadem

Zikrullah Khadem with Bahá'ís during the Caribbean Conference, Kingston, Jamaica, May 1971

Adelbert Mühlschlegel

Hands of the Cause Adelbert Mühlschlegel and Hasan Balyuzi

Siegfried Schopflocher

Hands of the Cause in Africa

Corinne True

# VI

# Hands of the Cause Appointed Individually by Shoghi Effendi

# Amatu'l-Bahá Rúḥíyyih Khánum (Mary Sutherland Maxwell) 1910–2000

Amatu'l-Bahá Rúḥíyyih Khánum was the daughter of William Sutherland Maxwell and May Bolles Maxwell. Her father, from an old Scots-Canadian family, was a Hand of the Cause and the distinguished architect of the superstructure of the Shrine of the Báb. A saintly man, he was one of the few individuals to have a close personal relationship with the Guardian. Her mother, an American and the first Bahá'í in Europe and later in Montreal, was designated "Abdu'l-Bahá's beloved handmaid' and His 'distinguished disciple' by Shoghi Effendi. She achieved the 'priceless honour' of a 'martyr's death' at her passing in 1940.[1]

Amatu'l-Bahá Rúḥíyyih Khánum was born Mary Sutherland Maxwell eight years after her parents' marriage. Her birth on 8 August 1910 was the answer to their prayers at the Holy Shrine in 'Akká, where May and Sutherland Maxwell had gone on pilgrimage in February 1909. Munírih Khánum, the wife of 'Abdu'l-Bahá, had greeted May, who had been on pilgrimage in 1899, with the words, 'First as a young girl, now with your husband; on your next visit, you will come with your child!'[2] Already approaching their middle years when Mary was born, the Maxwells received a message from 'Abdu'l-Bahá in 1911:

> Thy utmost desire was to have a child for whom thou hast prayed and supplicated while in 'Akká. Praise be to God that the prayer is answered and thy desire realized. In the garden of existence a rose has blossomed with the utmost freshness, fragrance, and beauty.[3]

In 1913 He wrote to them, 'I beg God that this little child may become great and wonderful in the Divine Kingdom'.[4]

In 1912 'Abdu'l-Bahá visited Montreal, staying three nights at the Maxwell home. Mary was two years old at the time and 'Abdu'l-Bahá lavished much love upon her. Later the same year her mother took her to New York, where she once again met the Master.

As a child, Mary received much of her spiritual training from her mother. In about 1914, when Mary was still a very young child, Mrs Maxwell opened what was perhaps the first Montessori school in eastern, possibly all Canada, in their home for Mary and a few other children. Mary's education was largely undertaken at home with private tutors. 'Gifted with great energy and an intensely inquiring mind, she supplemented this basic curriculum with an eclectic range of studies that included subjects as diverse as economics, literature and German.'[5] When she was older Mary enrolled in McGill University as a part-time student.

Mary's parents influenced her greatly: 'Family bonds were unusually close, with the result that Mary was powerfully influenced by both the spirit of tolerance and universality that animated her mother and the creativity of her father.'[6] May Maxwell was independent, eager for truth, bold in her teaching work, sympathetic and held a special affection for the underprivileged. 'May Maxwell is really a Bahá'í,' 'Abdu'l-Bahá said. 'She breathed no breath and uttered no word save in service to the Cause of God.' 'Whosoever meets her feels from her association the susceptibilities of the Kingdom. Her company uplifts and develops the soul.'[7] Sutherland Maxwell was a man of good judgement, uprightness, truthfulness, courtesy, friendliness and graciousness[8] who passed his artistic appreciation and talent on to his daughter. 'Abdu'l-Bahá loved Sutherland very much and told May during His visit to Montreal that she should not neglect her husband now that she had a child.[9]

When she was eight Mary was among the Bahá'í children who participated in the ceremony to unveil the Tablets of the Divine Plan at the 11th Annual Bahá'í Convention in New York in 1919. She gave her first Bahá'í talk when she was 15. She was a member first of the Montreal Bahá'í Youth Committee and later of the Youth Committee of the United States and Canada, and was a founding member of the Fellowship of Canadian Youth for Peace.

Mary made three pilgrimages to the Holy Land. The first was in 1923 with her mother, who, never physically strong, had suffered a complete breakdown following the passing of 'Abdu'l-Bahá. Sutherland Maxwell felt the only hope of restoring his wife to health was for her to make a pilgrimage to see Shoghi Effendi. Thus, Mary and her mother arrived in Haifa in April 1923 to visit the new Guardian 'who literally resurrected a woman who was so ill she could still not walk a step'.[10] They stayed in the Holy Land and in Egypt for almost a year, and on two occasions spent many months in Haifa. Shoghi Effendi was burdened at the time with the machinations of the Covenant-breakers and the young Mary was much affected by his grief:

> I shall never forget how he looked when he called my mother and me to his bedroom, in 1923; we stood at the foot of his bed, where he lay, obviously prostrated and heart-broken, with great black shadows under his eyes, and he told us he could not stand it, he was going away.[11]

Mary made her second pilgrimage in 1926, when she was accompanied by Juliet Thompson and Daisy Smyth, two of her mother's friends. In 1937 she came to Haifa for a third time, arriving in January with her mother. On 24 March she married Shoghi Effendi in a simple ceremony in the room of the Greatest Holy Leaf in Haifa. Her mother later wrote:

> There was a time that I agonized with a mother's weakness and instinctive protection over the terrific deprivation in all her outer human ways, and the austere discipline of the life of my child. . . . And as I have witnessed, from year to year, the profound and mystic change in Rúḥíyyih Khánum . . . I have marvelled at the grace of God and His delicate and perfect handiwork.[12]

The marriage of Rúḥíyyih Khánum to Shoghi Effendi was unpretentious but nonetheless historic. No one except the couple, their parents and Shoghi Effendi's brother and two sisters knew that the wedding was to take place. For the occasion, Mary was dressed entirely in black – as was customary among oriental women of the time – with the exception of a white lace blouse. The couple went by car to Bahjí, where Shoghi Effendi took the ring he had previously given to Mary, and placed it on her finger. This ring was a simple gold one, engraved with the symbol of the Greatest Name, and had been given to Shoghi Effendi by the Greatest Holy Leaf. Shoghi Effendi then entered the inner Shrine of Bahá'u'lláh, gathered up petals and flowers from the threshold and chanted the Tablet of Visitation. Afterwards the couple returned to Haifa and went to the room of the Greatest Holy Leaf, where the wedding took place. 'There was no celebration, no flowers, no elaborate ceremony, no wedding dress, no reception.'[13] Mary, now Rúḥíyyih Khánum, Madam Rabbani, went to the Western Pilgrim House to join her parents and Shoghi Effendi went back to work.

Despite the simplicity of the wedding, Shoghi Effendi considered his marriage an important event. He showered his congratulations on Rúḥíyyih Khánum's parents at supper that evening and gave the handful of flowers he had gathered to May in commemoration of the occasion. The news of the marriage was sent by cable to the Bahá'í communities of America and Iran over the signature of Shoghi Effendi's mother:

> ANNOUNCE ASSEMBLIES CELEBRATION MARRIAGE BELOVED GUARDIAN. INESTIMABLE HONOUR CONFERRED UPON HANDMAID OF BAHÁ'U'LLÁH RÚḤÍYYIH KHÁNUM MISS MARY MAXWELL. UNION OF EAST AND WEST PROCLAIMED BY BAHÁ'Í FAITH CEMENTED.[14]

This announcement brought a flood of congratulations from Bahá'ís around the world.

Following his marriage, the work, triumphs and trials of Shoghi Effendi continued as before, except that he now had a devoted companion to share some of his load. Rúḥíyyih Khánum acted as Shoghi Effendi's secretary for 16 of the 20 years they had together. She was by his side when he addressed the Bahá'ís of the West in *The Advent of Divine Justice* and *The Promised Day is Come*, escaped capture in France by the invading Nazi forces, travelled the length of Africa as the safest route between London and Haifa in 1940, wrote *God Passes By*, remained in Haifa throughout the dangerous civil war, saw to the completion of the superstructure of the Shrine of the Báb, secured control of the Mansion of Mazra'ih, witnessed the disaffection of his family, launched the World Crusade destined to culminate in the election of the first Universal House of Justice, faced the worst crisis of the Faith in the land of its birth in 1955 and oversaw the spread of the Faith to 175 countries across the globe.

Rúḥíyyih Khánum was Shoghi Effendi's indefatigable helpmate. As his secretary she listened carefully when he dictated innumerable letters or summarized replies in response to an unceasing and increasing flood of incoming mail or read aloud his translations and letters. She worked with him for hours on *God Passes By*, reading the original manuscript, proof-reading and making corrections, and adding by hand the seemingly endless accent marks. She made travel arrangements, met prominent people, ran the household and acted as his representative. She helped in his map-making and nursed him through crises of sickness and exhaustion.

Even as Rúḥíyyih Khánum struggled to ease some of Shoghi Effendi's burdens, she agonized over his sufferings. He was, she said, like a barometer of the Cause of God, registering good news and bad with joy or despair. When some thoughtless individual or institution unloaded some care upon him, she was annoyed. When the pressures of having to have everything referred to him exhausted or depressed him, she worried. When, one by one, his entire family denied him, she shared his sorrow. When he lay prostrate or wept from the weight of his ordeals, she cried out to God. Again and again, as she suffered by his side, Rúḥíyyih Khánum watched and prayed, wondering whether Shoghi Effendi's life might be cut short by his cares.

Recalling 'Abdu'l-Bahá's admonition to let no dust of despondency stain Shoghi Effendi's radiant nature, Rúḥíyyih Khánum recorded in her diary:

> I wouldn't wish on the devil the sufferings Shoghi Effendi and I pass through. I could never describe them – mental and nervous anguish . . . alone . . . work, work, work, all day long. Buying land, problems, letters, questions, mischief, ill-will, suspicion, ad infinitum.[15]

> I suppose there are as many hells as there are people. But not many, I hope, live in the particular hell Shoghi Effendi and I do. [For those who may not understand . . . I mean agony, intense, burning suffering.][16]

Shoghi Effendi gave Rúḥíyyih Khánum the title 'Amatu'l-Bahá', 'Handmaiden of Bahá', and the tribute he paid to her is perhaps the greatest testimony to the role she played at his side:

> It was a member of that same community [Canada] who won the immortal distinction of being called upon to be my helpmate, my shield in warding off the darts of Covenant-breakers and my tireless collaborator in the arduous tasks I shoulder.[17]

Over the years, Rúḥíyyih Khánum and Shoghi Effendi made trips together to England, Europe and Africa. In the House of Commons they sat in the visitors' gallery during one of the sessions and Rúḥíyyih Khánum realized how this scene must have impressed Shoghi Effendi as a young man. Together they visited famous European museums and art galleries, she delighting in his love of symmetry and beauty. When they passed through Africa, Shoghi Effendi surprised her by wanting to see the Belgian Congo. They travelled many times to Switzerland, where she was happy to see him enjoy the natural beauty of the countryside.

In 1951 Shoghi Effendi established the International Bahá'í Council as the forerunner to the Universal House of Justice. On 8 March 1952 he enlarged it, adding, among others, Amatu'l-Bahá Rúḥíyyih Khánum as liaison between himself and the Council. Eighteen days later, Rúḥíyyih Khánum was appointed a Hand of the Cause of God in the place of her father, who had passed away on 25 March 1952. Of her appointment, and that of others, she later wrote:

> To try to describe with what feelings of stupefaction, of unworthiness and awe the news of this honour overwhelmed the recipients of it would be impossible. Each heart received it as a shaft that aroused an even greater love for and loyalty to the Guardian than that heart had ever held before.[18]

Five and a half years after her appointment, Rúḥíyyih Khánum suffered the agonizing shock and grief of the sudden and premature passing of Shoghi Effendi while in London. The near unbearable pain of the morning of 4 November 1957 she described as the 'depths of my agony that black and terrible day'.[19] Her first concern was the protection of the Faith, prompting her to break the news to the Bahá'í world in two telegrams, in the first asking the Bahá'ís for prayers for divine protection and in the second announcing Shoghi Effendi's passing:

> SHOGHI EFFENDI BELOVED OF ALL HEARTS SACRED TRUST GIVEN BELIEVERS BY MASTER PASSED AWAY SUDDEN HEART ATTACK IN SLEEP FOLLOWING ASIATIC FLU. URGE BELIEVERS REMAIN STEADFAST CLING INSTITUTION HANDS LOVINGLY REARED RECENTLY REINFORCED EMPHASIZED BY BELOVED GUARDIAN. ONLY ONENESS HEART ONENESS PURPOSE CAN BEFITTINGLY TESTIFY LOYALTY ALL NATIONAL ASSEMBLIES BELIEVERS DEPARTED GUARDIAN WHO SACRIFICED SELF UTTERLY FOR SERVICE FAITH.[20]

The death of Shoghi Effendi precipitated the worst crisis the nascent Faith of God had yet experienced. For the first time in its 113-year history, the Cause of Bahá'u'lláh was bereft of a divinely guided leader. None of the religious systems of the past had avoided schisms after the passing of its Founder, when matters of faith were left to the dictates of the followers. Now, however, the Bahá'ís rallied around the Hands of the Cause because Shoghi Effendi, drawing on the Will and Testament of 'Abdu'l-Bahá, had charged the Hands with the protection of the Faith and clarified their relationship with the National Spiritual Assemblies. Thus the potential danger of the Faith's fragmentation was met and overcome.

Just five months before his passing, on 4 June 1957, Shoghi Effendi had cabled:

> DIVINELY APPOINTED INSTITUTION HANDS CAUSE, INVESTED VIRTUE AUTHORITY CONFERRED TESTAMENT CENTRE COVENANT TWIN FUNCTIONS PROTECTING PROPAGATING FAITH BAHÁ'U'LLÁH, NOW ENTERING NEW PHASE PROCESS UNFOLDMENT ITS SACRED MISSION. TO ITS NEWLY ASSUMED RESPONSIBILITY ASSIST NATIONAL SPIRITUAL ASSEMBLIES BAHÁ'Í WORLD SPECIFIC PURPOSE EFFECTIVELY PROSECUTING WORLD SPIRITUAL CRUSADE, PRIMARY OBLIGATION WATCH OVER, INSURE PROTECTION BAHÁ'Í WORLD COMMUNITY, IN CLOSE COLLABORATION THESE SAME NATIONAL ASSEMBLIES, NOW ADDED.[21]

In this remarkable cable the Guardian went on to describe the dangers to which the Faith was exposed and restated the importance of the National Assemblies' close association with the Hands. In his final message to the Bahá'í world, in October 1957, Shoghi Effendi described the Hands of the Cause as 'the Chief Stewards of Bahá'u'lláh's embryonic World Commonwealth, who have been invested by the unerring Pen of the Centre of His Covenant with the dual function of guarding over the security, and of insuring the propagation, of His Father's Faith'.[22]

These highly significant messages assured that the National and Regional Assemblies, together with the body of believers, would cling to the institution of the Hands of the Cause. Nevertheless, as the Hands gathered in London for Shoghi Effendi's funeral service, Rúḥíyyih Khánum, in the midst of near incapacitating grief, took precautions to protect the Faith against any possible attack. On the very day of Shoghi Effendi's passing she telephoned the International Bahá'í Council in Haifa, speaking to its Secretary-General, Leroy Ioas, and arranged that the door to the Guardian's apartment be sealed so that no one could enter until the Hands could take the appropriate action. She further arranged for Mr Ioas to notify the State of Israel of Shoghi Effendi's passing. Her private grief was recorded in heart-rending poems, the first written less than a month after the Guardian's death, kept among her personal papers until their publication nearly 30 years later.[23]

During the funeral of Shoghi Effendi on 9 November, Rúḥíyyih Khánum was supported by her fellow Hands, particularly Amelia Collins. Devastated, she returned to Haifa shortly after the funeral. On 15 November she and four other Hands of the Cause entered the apartment of the Guardian and sealed with tape and wax his safe and desk. On 19 November Rúḥíyyih Khánum and eight other Hands of the Cause, chosen by her, re-entered the room, examined the seals for signs of tampering and then examined the contents of the safe and desk. No will or testament of the Guardian was found. The Hands of the Cause gathered at their first Conclave at the Mansion of Bahá'u'lláh at Bahjí issued a Proclamation on 25 November stating that the Guardian had left no will and had not appointed an heir.

The Will and Testament of 'Abdu'l-Bahá stated that the Hands of the Cause should choose from among themselves nine Hands 'that shall at all times be occupied in the important services in the work of the Guardian of the Cause of God'.[24] Now that the Guardian had passed away, Rúḥíyyih Khánum later wrote, the Hands were 'faced with the inescapable obligation of voting from amongst the membership of the Hands of the Cause for who would . . . accept to live and serve at the World Centre as one of the nine legal Custodians'.[25] Rúḥíyyih Khánum, already a Hand resident in the Holy Land, was appointed one of the Custodians.

Rúḥíyyih Khánum participated in each of the Conclaves of the Hands and represented the World Centre at several conferences, national conventions and events between 1958 and the election of the Universal House of Justice in 1963: the intercontinental conference in Kampala in 1958 (where she represented the Guardian); the conference of European Hands in Copenhagen in 1959; the conventions of the United States and Canada in 1960; the dedication of the Mother Temple of Africa in January 1961 and of Australia in September 1961; and the conference of European Hands in Luxembourg in 1962. She also visited Bahá'í centres in Uganda, Kenya, Tanganyika, Australia, Malaya, Indonesia, Vietnam, Cambodia, Thailand and Burma.

In April 1963 the Universal House of Justice was elected. Immediately following the election, Bahá'ís from all over the world gathered in London for the first Bahá'í World Congress, to mark the centenary of the Declaration of Bahá'u'lláh and the successful conclusion of the Ten Year Crusade. Rúḥíyyih Khánum was the first speaker at the opening session and concluded with these words:

> I am sure that the believers in this room and their fellow-believers all over the world are going to face the future now with a fresh determination to win even more marvellous victories than have been won in the past. This is the way we show our love for Bahá'u'lláh, our love for 'Abdu'l-Bahá and our gratitude for the bounty of the Divine Plan; and this is how we demonstrate our love for our Guardian, who wore himself out and burned himself up in leading the way and showing us how we could go forward and what we must do. I am sure that every Bahá'í is going to do his utmost in the years to come.[26]

Only once had Shoghi Effendi intimated what Rúḥíyyih Khánum might do after his passing: he supposed she would travel and visit and encourage the friends in different countries. Following the election of the Universal House of Justice, Rúḥíyyih Khánum, setting an example for Bahá'ís everywhere of the possibilities for promoting the Faith, embarked on truly prodigious world travels. At the age of 53 she set out on a series of journeys which, over the next 30 years, would take her more than 100,000 miles overland and some half a million miles by air. During the course of her life she visited some 185 countries, major islands and territories.

In 1964 Rúḥíyyih Khánum spent nine months in the Indian subcontinent, seven of them in India itself, travelling over 50,000 miles by air, rail, car and cart to visit Bahá'ís in villages and towns throughout the country.[27] In 1967 she travelled for seven months in Panama and nine South American countries. On 5 August 1969 she and her companion, Violette Nakhjavání, arrived in Kampala at the start of the 'Great African Safari', undertaken in four stages ending in February 1973. During the Safari Rúḥíyyih Khánum drove her Land-Rover some 36,000 miles through 34 African countries and was received by 17 heads of state. This remarkable journey brought the praise of the Universal House of Justice:

> YOUR TRAVELS AFRICAN CONTINENT UNIQUE UNPARALLELED IN NUMBER COUNTRIES VISITED HEADS STATE INTERVIEWED EXTENSIVE PUBLICITY

OBTAINING LOVING ENCOURAGEMENT SPIRITUAL STIMULATION IMPARTED STANDARD HEROISM EXAMPLE SELFSACRIFICE EVINCED OVER SUCH LONG PERIOD UNDER SUCH ARDUOUS CONDITIONS. FEEL ASSURED GLORIOUS SPIRIT BELOVED GUARDIAN IN COMPANY RADIANT SOULS YOUR DISTINGUISHED PARENTS HIGHLY ELATED SINGULARLY PROUD OVER RANGE QUALITY RESULTS YOUR SPLENDID ENDEAVOURS. LOVING THOUGHTS TENDERLY WITH YOU THIS DAY FERVENTLY PRAYING SHRINES BLESSINGS BAHAULLAH MAY INCREASINGLY SURROUND YOU GUIDE YOUR STEPS REINFORCE PRODIGIOUS EFFORTS. SPIRIT YOUR LOVE FIDELITY DEDICATION SO BRILLIANTLY DEMONSTRATED SETS SHINING EXAMPLE HIS ARDENT LOVERS LABOURING ALL CONTINENTS AND COUNTLESS GENERATIONS YET UNBORN.[28]

In 1973 Rúḥíyyih Khánum toured Alaska and in 1974 she paid her first visit to China, also visiting India, Sikkim and Nepal. In 1975 she embarked on the seven-month 'Green Light Expedition', journeying mostly by boat over 8,000 miles through the Amazon river basin. In 1977 she undertook her third trip to India and went on to Thailand, Burma, Hong Kong, Japan and Australia before returning to India in October to lay the foundation stone for the House of Worship in New Delhi. In 1978 she visited several European countries, spent nine weeks in Japan, then travelled on to Taiwan, Hong Kong and Macau. She also spent ten weeks in the Pacific, following the conference inaugurating the construction of the House of Worship in Samoa. In 1981 she visited twelve Central American countries as well as Scotland, the islands of the North Sea and Cyprus. In 1982 she spent five weeks in Haiti before travelling to Canada, the United States, Greenland, Iceland and the United Kingdom. In 1983 she visited Turkey and countries in Europe, while in 1984–5, she toured 26 countries in the Pacific and Asia, including India, Thailand, Korea, Guam, Papua New Guinea, Samoa, Micronesia, Melanesia, Polynesia and Japan. In 1988 she travelled extensively throughout China, visiting the country again in 1989, when she also spent a week in Mongolia. In 1990 she went to Argentina to attend a special conference commemorating the 50th anniversary of her mother's passing there, before travelling to Europe, the Far East, China and Tibet. In 1992 she represented the Universal House of Justice at the second Bahá'í World Congress, in New York. In 1993 she undertook an arduous journey to 13 countries and territories of the former Soviet Union, travelling for four months and covering territory from Yakutsk in Siberia to the Baltic states in the west, most of the Central Asian Republics and central Russia. The year 1994 saw Rúḥíyyih Khánum in Mongolia for a second time, as well as Turkey and London. On many of her journeys Rúḥíyyih Khánum visited the primitive peoples of these far-flung regions of the planet, saying of the simple villagers she met:

> I've had such wonderful experiences with tribal people and villagers . . . and so many times I've said, 'Oh! If only the Bahá'ís could see this. If they could know what it is like to be in these places, if they could meet these people, see how wonderful they are, they would feel a more personal response to the Tablets of the Divine Plan, and to the appeals so repeatedly made by the Master, by Shoghi Effendi, and now by the Universal House of Justice.'[29]

Wherever she travelled, Amatu'l-Bahá encouraged the believers to teach the Faith and attract increasing numbers of new souls to the Cause of God.

Amatu'l-Bahá once told the story of how Shoghi Effendi said the believers can address their prayers to holy souls who have passed away – to members of their family, to those they love and of course to Bahá'u'lláh and 'Abdu'l-Bahá – so long as they understand their stations. She said she had often turned her heart in prayer to her father or mother for help. After the passing of Shoghi Effendi, when she was trying to complete his work on the International Archives, she often turned to her father because he was a great artist and architect and she felt he was helping her from the invisible world. On her long and arduous journey through Africa, whenever she had trouble with the car, she would call out to the Supreme Concourse and exclaim that there must be someone up there who knew about cars! This always worked, she said.

Violette Nakhjavání, Rúḥíyyih Khánum's travelling companion, described how Amatu'l-Bahá taught the Faith:

> [Rúḥíyyih Khánum] never uses words which offend people or insult other people's beliefs. She brings out points of similarity and encourages everyone. I can never remember in these many years of having the privilege of being present at her meetings, ever hearing a word of criticism of other religions or their leaders, or a word of argument or dispute. As a result of this attitude, at the end of her meetings people are drawn to her and to the Cause of Bahá'u'lláh, no matter in what spirit they may have come. Often, with deep sincerity, she has praised in her speeches and on television and radio interviews the services

of Christian missionaries in Africa, reminding people of the great deal of good they have done in the past and still continue to do.[30]

Rúḥíyyih Khánum mastered four languages – English, Persian, German and French – and wrote five books: *Prescription for Living, The Priceless Pearl, A Manual for Pioneers, The Desire of the World* and *The Guardian of the Bahá'í Faith.* In 1996 she published a collection of her poems written in the months following the death of Shoghi Effendi, *Poems of the Passing.* She compiled, and wrote the introduction to, *The Ministry of the Custodians 1957–1963* and made two full-length (two-hour) documentary films, *The Green Light Expedition* and *The Pilgrimage.* She also wrote many articles and plays.

Rúḥíyyih Khánum laid the cornerstones of the Bahá'í Houses of Worship in Kampala (1958), Panama (1967), New Delhi (1977) and Samoa (1979) and represented the World Centre at the dedication ceremonies of the Houses of Worship in Wilmette (1953), Kampala and Sydney (1961), Frankfurt (1964), Panama (1972), Samoa (1984) and New Delhi (1986).

In 1996 Amatu'l-Bahá attended the 75th anniversary of the founding of the Bahá'í community in Brazil. On 7–8 August that year, following her visit to Brazil, she was present at the 50th anniversary commemoration of the opening of Portugal to the Bahá'í Faith. In attendance were 300 believers, representing over eight countries and including members of the Gypsy race.

Her last trip took place in the summer of 1997, when she attended a conference marking the 50th anniversary of the Faith's establishment in Spain. On that historic occasion 1,500 believers from 44 countries were present at the new Palace of Congresses in Madrid. The conference received excellent press and television coverage. From Madrid, Amatu'l-Bahá attended a conference in the Basque country of northern Spain, followed by a gathering at Alicante in the south, organized primarily for the Gypsy Bahá'ís. In August she visited Luxembourg, where she addressed 230 friends, urging them particularly to teach the principles of the Faith, and in September she visited Landegg Academy in Switzerland for the dedication of the Rabbani chair for Bahá'í History. There she spoke on the life of her mother and participated in handing out diplomas to the first graduates of the academy's Master's degree. In Haifa in April 1998, for the last time, she opened the International Bahá'í Convention – every one of which she had opened since the holding of the first convention in 1963.

A courageous and indefatigable Hand of the Cause of God, her poem 'This is Faith', composed in 1953, gives an insight into the ennobling influence behind her long and remarkable life:

To walk where there is no path
To breathe where there is no air
To see where there is no light –
This is Faith.

To cry out in the silence,
The silence of the night,
And hearing no echo believe
And believe again and again –
This is Faith.

To hold pebbles and see jewels
To raise sticks and see forests
To smile with weeping eyes –
This is Faith.

To say: 'God, I believe' when others deny,
'I hear' when there is no answer,
'I see' though naught is seen –
This is Faith.

And the fierce love in the heart,
The savage love that cries
Hidden Thou art yet there!
Veil Thy face and mute Thy tongue
Yet I see and hear Thee, Love,
Beat me down to the bare earth,
Yet I rise and love Thee, Love!
This is Faith.[31]

On 19 January 2000 Amatu'l-Bahá Rúḥíyyih Khánum departed this earthly life, leaving behind her many admirers and lovers from around the globe whose anguished hearts could only be assuaged by pondering these words from the Universal House of Justice:

To the Bahá'ís of the World,

In the early hours of this morning, the soul of Amatu'l-Bahá Rúḥíyyih Khánum, beloved consort of Shoghi Effendi and the Bahá'í world's last remaining link with the family of 'Abdu'l-Bahá, was released from the limitations of this earthly existence. In the midst of our grief, we are sustained by our confidence that she has been gathered to the glory of the Concourse on High in the presence of the Abhá Beauty.

For all whose hearts she touched so deeply, the sorrow that this irreparable loss brings will, in God's good time, be assuaged in awareness of the joy that is hers through her reunion with the Guardian and with the Master, Who had Himself prayed in the Most Holy Shrine that her parents be blessed with a child. Down the centuries to come, the followers of Bahá'u'lláh will contemplate with wonder and gratitude the quality of the services – ardent, indomitable, resourceful – that she brought to the protection and promotion of the Cause.

In her youth, Amatu'l-Bahá had already distinguished herself through her activities in North America, and later, both with her dear mother and on her own, she had rendered valuable service to the Cause in Europe. Her twenty years of intimate association with Shoghi Effendi evoked from his pen such accolades as 'my helpmate,' 'my shield,' 'my tireless collaborator in the arduous tasks I shoulder.' To these tributes he added in 1952 his decision to elevate her to the rank of Hand of the Cause of God, after the death of her illustrious father.

The devastating shock of the beloved Guardian's passing steeled her resolve to lend her share, with the other Hands of the Cause, to the triumph of the Ten Year Crusade, and subsequently to undertake, with characteristic intrepidity, her historic worldwide travels.

A life so noble in its provenance, so crucial to the preservation of the Faith's integrity, and so rich in its dedicated, uninterrupted and selfless service, moves us to call for befitting commemorations by Bahá'í communities on both national and local levels, as well as for special gatherings in her memory in all Houses of Worship.

With yearning hearts, we supplicate at the Holy Threshold for infinite heavenly bounties to surround her soul, as she assumes her rightful and well-earned position among the exalted company in the Abhá Kingdom.

The Universal House of Justice[32]

A funeral service was held at the House of the Master in Haifa, which had been her home for over 60 years, in the presence of the members of the Universal House of Justice and of the International Teaching Centre, family members, the assembled pilgrims, invited guests and the staff serving at the World Centre. Following the service, the body of Amatu'l-Bahá Rúḥíyyih Khánum was laid to rest in the garden opposite the House of the Master and situated between the two historic Pilgrim Houses where she had stayed during her pilgrimages to the Holy Land.

# Jalál Kházeh
# (Jalál'ulláh Kháḍi')
# 1897–1990

Jalál Kházeh was the recipient of many messages of praise and encouragement from his beloved Guardian: 'PROUD YOUR SERVICES ENCOURAGE FRIENDS CENTRES ARISE PARTICIPATE CRUSADE'; 'urge [Kházeh] to continue his travels and assure him how deeply the Guardian values his wonderful services'; 'I profoundly appreciate his continuous services . . . his trips to different communities and localities have had a long-lasting impression on the friends'.[1] Mr Kházeh, whose example of service to the Cause illumines the meanings of 'heroic fortitude' and 'steadfast endeavour', revealed in his autobiography many years later his astonished reaction to such loving kindness: 'if we take one step sincerely in His exalted path, He comes towards us one thousand steps through His goodness and grace'.[2]

Jalálu'lláh Khazeh was born on 24 February 1897 in Ṭihrán. His father, Ghulám-Riḍá, was a native of the village of Sidih near Iṣfahán, from where he had been forced to flee owing to persecutions. Ghulám-Riḍá's first wife had left him to marry a Muslim, after which he had married Jamálíyyih Ṭihrání, the daughter of Karbalá'í Mihdí Ṭihrání, who had at one time been imprisoned for three years in the Síyáh Chál in Ṭihrán for his Faith. The children of Ghulám-Riḍá and Jamálíyyih's marriage were Jalálu'lláh and Farkhundih.

Ghulám-Riḍá suffered from poor health and died at the age of 35. Jalál was then just seven years old, and his sister five. Their mother brought up the two children and saw to their education. Jalál received his primary schooling at the Tarbíyat School in Ṭihrán and in the weekly Bahá'í classes of Áqá Muḥammad Ḥusayn Ulfat and 'Alí-Akbar Rafsanjání. With his mother's guidance and the instruction of these two great scholars, Jalál grew up with his faith in the Cause of the Blessed Beauty firmly established.

From the age of 17 Jalál studied and practised veterinary medicine, working mostly as an officer in the army. At the age of 19 he was awarded the rank of lieutenant. During his years of army service he was stationed in many towns, including Qazvín, Hamadán, Kirmánsháh, Sanandaj, Khurramábád, Burújird and Ahváz, and in each place he served on the Local Assembly and on Bahá'í committees. He retired from the army with the rank of colonel in 1943.

When Jalál was 19 years old he married Jamálíyyih, the daughter of Ustád Ḥasan 'Alí Mi'márbáshí Kashání. They had two sons and three daughters.

Within a year of his retirement from the army Jalál Kh※ázeh was elected to the National Spiritual Assembly of Iran. That year's National Convention was a special one, held in Shíráz on the 100th anniversary of the Declaration of the Báb, and Mr Kházeh attended it as a delegate. He served on the National Assembly for five years, and subsequently he was elected to the Local Spiritual Assembly of Ṭihrán, and served as its secretary for three years. In addition to his administrative duties, Mr Kházeh travelled extensively in Iran to teach the Faith and to encourage the believers – services which brought him much praise and encouragement from the Guardian. Eventually, at the end of 1951 he resigned from his Assembly work so as to devote his time to travel-teaching.

Around this time he received permission from the Guardian to go on pilgrimage, and in March 1952 he travelled to the Holy Land to visit the Holy Places in Haifa and 'Akká and to meet Shoghi Effendi. This meeting changed Jalál's life and he thereafter often described himself as a 'new creation'. Shoghi Effendi charged his disciple with serving the Cause throughout Persia, and especially with familiarizing and enthusing the friends with the goals of the Ten Year Crusade. The Guardian emphasized that he should give preference to the isolated centres rather than group centres because 'if we do not visit the friends who are isolated in a place as pioneers or for some other reason, their tree of being will wither'.[3]

He went to the National Spiritual Assembly and asked to know the number of Bahá'í centres in Persia. They gave him a list of one thousand centres, which included Spiritual Assemblies, groups and isolated believers. Subsequently Mr Kházeh found that each centre required a three-day commitment of time due to poor road conditions. He would have to travel by foot, bicycle, horse-back, donkey and car to complete the task set him by the Guardian. This task, he realized, would require eight years of continuous travel.[4]

Ever mindful of the importance of visiting isolated believers, Mr Kházeh once travelled a distance of 50 kilometres, riding for two days by mule through forests and mountains, to meet the only believer in Dilmán. At the end of his exhausting journey he had to be carried into a room of the believer's home, where he collapsed on the floor, unable to utter a word. After he had rested, his host, upon learning that Mr Kházeh had been sent by the beloved Guardian, was so overcome with emotion that he insisted on circumambulating his guest. 'He began to walk around me in circles,' Jalál Kházeh wrote years later, 'intoning Holy Tablets and prayers, shedding tears . . . I felt that this man exerted a strength and power which made me sit down.'[5]

At the bidding of the Guardian, Jalál Kházeh attended the intercontinental conference in Kampala, Uganda, in 1953, afterwards visiting Bahá'í communities in Kenya, Ethiopia, Eritrea, Aden, Muscat, Bahrain and Kuwait.

During the course of his travels in Iran, Jalál Khazeh was awakened by Bahá'í friends at four o'clock one morning in late December 1953. A telegram had arrived appointing him a Hand of the Cause, and the friends wished to congratulate him. Overwhelmed by the news, he retired to commune with his Lord. Mr Kházeh recalled of his appointment: 'God knows the state I entered when I read this cable. On the one hand, I saw my weakness, and on the other hand, I saw the arduousness of my future task, and the fire of hopelessness began to consume me.'[6]

At Riḍván 1954, Jalál Kházeh was re-elected to the National Spiritual Assembly. Nevertheless he continued his extensive travels in Iran, prompting the Guardian to comment in a letter written on his behalf, 'your services and travels set an example for the friends in Iran.'[7]

So far, Mr Kházeh's arena of service had been more or less confined to Iran, but now he was set to work on the worldwide stage. In April 1957 he represented the Guardian at the first election of the Regional Spiritual Assembly of North-East Asia, held in Tokyo. From there, he travelled to Korea, Taiwan, Hong Kong, Burma and Pakistan, where he visited and encouraged the Bahá'ís.

The passing of the Guardian interrupted Mr Kházeh's goal of visiting all the Bahá'í centres in Iran. As one of the nine Hands of the Cause acting as Custodians during the interregnum, he lived, with his wife, in the Holy Land from November 1957 until September 1963.

During those years he travelled internationally, as well as serving the Faith in the Holy Land. The Hands of the Cause asked him to visit all the important Bahá'í centres in Iran to explain to the friends why there was no Guardian and to reassure them concerning the situation of the Faith. In 1958 he attended the intercontinental conference in Frankfurt, afterwards visiting Bahá'í communities in the Netherlands, Belgium, France, Germany, Austria, the United Kingdom and Turkey. In 1960 he spent five months in India and Sri Lanka.

When the newly elected Universal House of Justice decided in 1963 that five Hands of the Cause should remain in the Holy Land, Mr Kházeh chose South America as his field of service. He and his wife settled in Campinas, in São Paulo state, Brazil, and from this base he served ten National Spiritual Assemblies and their Bahá'í centres. Over the next six years he made extensive travels throughout the continent. He also helped to develop a Latin American Bahá'í newsletter, visited North America, Central America and Europe, and in 1968 attended the opening session in Bolivia of the first Continental Board of Counsellors of South America.

In 1969 Mr Kházeh returned briefly to Iran before embarking on a six-month trip through 16 European countries. Eventually, suffering from the effects of a weakened heart, he entered hospital. Nevertheless, at Riḍván 1970 he attended the inaugural national conventions of Dahomey, Togo and Niger in Cotonou and of Ghana in Accra, and four months later he attended the Oceanic Conference in Mauritius. He then returned to Iran, where he inspired successful teaching in the provinces. In 1972 he represented the Universal House of Justice at the inaugural conventions of Singapore, Eastern Malaysia and Brunei. Despite continuing poor health, he travelled around the world in 1973, visiting India, Japan, Alaska, Canada, the United States and Switzerland. The following year he returned to South America for an extended tour, which was followed by visits to many localities in the islands of the Caribbean.

While he was in Alaska, some of the native believers present at a large gathering which was also attended by American believers explained to Mr Kházeh that the Americans did not give them a chance in the consultations to give their opinions. Because they were well-educated the Americans perceived issues very quickly and then took decisions, whereas, the Indians explained, they must think about the same issues before reaching a conclusion. Through his loving presence and wise counsels Mr Kházeh was so successful in bringing the Indians and Americans together that the former adopted him as their grandfather and entitled him 'Keeyalhwe', which means 'Peacemaker'. The Americans embraced the Indian friends as brothers and asked their forgiveness.[8]

Over the next year and a half Jalál Kházeh compiled a very valuable manual for the Spiritual Assemblies in Iran. In 1976, from his home in Bábulsar, he visited Bahá'ís in virtually all localities in the provinces of Mázindarán and Gilán. Although his health was poor, he attended the International Convention in Haifa in 1978. On his return to Iran he suffered the passing of his beloved wife. Soon he found himself in grave danger, when Revolutionary Guards of the Islamic Republic entered his house, interrogated him and confiscated all his Bahá'í correspondence, documents and books. On the advice of the Local Spiritual Assembly, he left Bábulsar for Ṭihrán and went into hiding, changing his residence from time to time. When orders were issued for his arrest in 1984, his daughter Núrániyyih and the Bahá'ís helped him to flee the country. In declining health, and with his eyesight deteriorating, he was taken out of Iran over a very difficult and dangerous route and eventually reached Pakistan, where he stayed as a refugee, first in Quetta and then in Karachi, for about four months.

On receiving permission to emigrate to Canada, Mr Kházeh and his daughter made their way to Toronto. By this time he was 87 years old and very frail, and in his remaining years he could only serve the Cause by offering advice to the friends. News of the imprisonment and martyrdom of Iranian Bahá'ís worsened his condition and he passed away on 21 February 1990.

Around 250 people attended the funeral service on the afternoon of 27 February. That evening, a memorial service was held in a large auditorium at the Ontario Science Centre, with approximately 500 people present. Two months later a memorial service arranged on behalf of the National Spiritual Assembly of the United Kingdom was held in London. Member of the Auxiliary Board Mrs Shamsi Navidi shared with those present glimpses into the character of Mr Kházeh, highlighting both his handsome stature and his warm personality.

Mr Kházeh spoke English well, and some Spanish, and he had a mastery of both Persian and Arabic. As a public speaker he was eloquent and impressed people with his knowledge of the Faith.

The word *kházi‘* means ‘humble’ in both Arabic and Persian. In his presence, people were affected by Mr Kházeh’s humility. Years earlier, when he had been honoured by the Guardian’s appointing him a Hand of the Cause, Jalálu’lláh Kházeh had sent this tender supplication to his beloved in a telegram:

> THE FUTURE LIES IN THE HANDS OF THIS SERVANT. I WILL EITHER FIND A SPOT IN THE PARADISE OF NEARNESS TO HIM BY ATTRACTING THE BOUNTY OF THE INCOMPARABLE PROTECTOR, OR I WILL BE NEGLECTFUL AND CARELESS AND FALL INTO THE FIRE OF REMOTENESS FROM HIM. THUS, I ASK YOU FOR YOUR SUPPORT AND HELP, SO THAT THE FEEBLE BACK OF THIS NONENTITY WILL BE ENABLED TO CARRY THIS HEAVY LOAD AND WILL COME TO A GOOD END IN THIS PASSING WORLD.[9]

His beloved Shoghi Effendi, foreseeing the future, knew that Mr Kházeh would indeed come to a good end, for he replied: ‘REST ASSURED CONFIDENT GREAT SUCCESS. SHOGHI.’[10]

The Universal House of Justice announced his passing in these words:

> DEEPLY GRIEVED ANNOUNCE PASSING STAUNCH TIRELESS PROMOTER FAITH HAND CAUSE GOD JALÁL KHÁZEH. HIS STRENUOUS ENDEAVOURS CRADLE FAITH HOLY LAND LATIN AMERICA AND WORLDWIDE TRAVELS AFTER PASSING GUARDIAN SET SHINING EXAMPLE OF UNSHAKABLE DEDICATION AND COURAGE, OF UNDEVIATING LOYALTY AND PERSEVERANCE. IMPERISHABLE RECORD HIS STERLING SERVICES AS GIFTED TEACHER DEFENDER CAUSE NEVER TO BE FORGOTTEN. HIS NOBLE SPIRIT NOW ABHÁ KINGDOM WILL UNDOUBTEDLY INTERCEDE BEHALF PERSIAN BAHÁ’Í COMMUNITY WHOSE VITAL INTERESTS HE SERVED WITH SUCH HIGH DISTINCTION OVER SEVERAL DECADES. FERVENTLY PRAYING HOLY SHRINES FOR PROGRESS HIS ILLUMINED SOUL IN REALMS ON HIGH. ADVISE FRIENDS EVERYWHERE HOLD BEFITTING MEMORIAL GATHERINGS HIS HONOUR PARTICULARLY ALL HOUSES OF WORSHIP.[11]

# Paul Edmond Haney
# 1909–1982

Paul Haney's paternal grandfather, the Rev Richard Haney, a well-known Methodist minister, was one of six founders of Northwestern University in Evanston, Illinois. Paul's father, Charles Freeborn Haney, was one of the Rev Haney's seven children. He was an attorney and successful in several businesses. In 1893 he married Mary Ida Parkhurst of New York City. As a young girl she had begun a spiritual quest for truth, going from church to church.

Restless spiritually, the Haneys searched persistently for satisfying answers. In January 1900 they noticed a young married couple meeting with a group of men dressed in oriental clothes. Attracted to the group, the Haneys introduced themselves to Charles and Elizabeth Greenleaf, who gave them the Message of Bahá'u'lláh. Almost immediately the Haneys became Bahá'ís.

Early in her Bahá'í life Mary was given the name 'Mariam' by 'Abdu'l-Bahá. In 1909 Charles and Mariam made their pilgrimage to the Holy Land, basking in the presence of 'Abdu'l-Bahá for nine days as guests in His home. Mariam later published her pilgrim's notes as 'A Heavenly Feast'. One day the Master said to the Haneys:

> Conveying the Message is accomplished to-day by the Confirmation of the Holy Spirit, and not by any fund of knowledge or by the possession of facts. The confirmations of the Holy Spirit are obtained by attractions of the heart. Without these attractions, the former is unobtainable. The proof of this is evident. The disciples of Christ, with the exception of St Paul, were not learned men, but they taught the world. By the power of attraction, zeal and conflagration, as well as severance from the world and by the giving of life,

> they taught. And this proved the magnet attracting the confirmations of the Holy Spirit.[1]

Mariam was expecting a baby at the time of the pilgrimage and 'Abdu'l-Bahá bestowed His blessing on the unborn child. Six months after the pilgrimage Mariam gave birth to a son in Los Angeles. The Haneys wrote immediately to 'Abdu'l-Bahá, who replied giving the boy his own name – 'Abdu'l-Bahá – as well as the name Paul. Some time later Corinne True asked the Master if He had indeed given the name 'Abdu'l-Bahá to Paul Haney. In a letter to Mariam Haney, Corinne wrote, 'He confirmed what you were given. Paul for the outside world. His real name is 'Abdu'l-Bahá.'[2]

Mariam received several Tablets from 'Abdu'l-Bahá, many of them mentioning her son: 'The newly born babe is blessed, and acceptable in the Divine Kingdom. He is a servant of the Blessed Perfection and belongeth to Him. Thank God for having been confirmed to attain such a blessing . . . I ask God that my namesake, 'Abdu'l-Bahá, may grow and develop day by day and that his radiant face may be illumined with the light of the greatest bestowal.'[3]

Charles Haney died in 1919, when Paul was ten years old. Mariam wrote to 'Abdu'l-Bahá asking what He wished her to do. 'Abdu'l-Bahá directed her to Washington DC. Growing up in the American capital, Paul became known for his charm and his unusual height. He had blue eyes and red hair, a 'frank and open countenance and cheerful disposition'.[4] Mariam had a profound influence on her son. When he entered Central High School Paul reassured his mother that he was not interested in the wild life apparently enjoyed by so many of the other youth. 'He enjoyed being decent and spiritually-minded and concerned with others.'[5]

As he grew up, Paul attended Green Acre Summer School and many Bahá'í activities. His mother was appointed to the newly-established National Teaching Committee when he was 11 and Paul accompanied her to a number of Bahá'í conventions and conferences. Over the years Paul formed a close friendship with Mary Maxwell and gained the admiration of May Maxwell. As his 15th birthday approached, May wrote to Mariam: 'I have a peculiar love for that dear, blessed boy'.6 Seven years later, when Paul was appointed to the National Teaching Committee at the age of 22, May wrote:

> As for you dear Paul I feel that you bring to the National field of teaching not only the steadfast faith, the spirit of devotion and sacrifice which so characterized the older generation of Bahá'ís and on which foundation our beloved Cause has been established in America, but the forward vision, the world-wide horizon, the thrilling life and motion of which our youthful Guardian is the Head and Source.[7]

Paul attended Northwestern University, taking advantage of the scholarships provided in perpetuity for the descendants of the University's founders to study economics and earn his MBA. His first article, 'The Economic Organization of Society in the New World Order', appeared in *The Bahá'í Magazine* of January 1934.

By now Paul was a professional economist, and his life centred on his career and on his service to the Bahá'í Faith. As well as being a member of the National Teaching Committee, he was a member of the first National Youth Committee of the United States. In 1940 he met Helen Margery Wheeler at Green Acre and in 1942 they married, residing in Washington DC, near Mariam. In 1946 Paul was elected to the National Spiritual Assembly of the United States and Canada. In 1948 Canada elected its own National Spiritual Assembly and Paul represented the United States at its formation. He served as chairman of the National Spiritual Assembly of the United States from 1950 to 1957. He also served as chairman of the Temple Trustees Construction Committee and represented the American National Assembly at the formation of the Regional Spiritual Assembly of South America in 1951 and of the Regional Spiritual Assembly of Italy and Switzerland in 1953.

In January 1954 Hand of the Cause Dorothy Baker died in a plane crash near the island of Elba. In March Paul received a cable from the Guardian:

> ANNOUNCE YOUR ELEVATION HAND CAUSE CONFIDENT DIVINE BLESSINGS FUTURE SERVICES.[8]

Paul cabled a reply:

> OVERWHELMED OUTPOURING BELOVED GUARDIAN'S BOUNTY BESEECH PRAYERS DIVINE ASSISTANCE RENDER ACCEPTABLE SERVICES RISE ABOVE FEELING COMPLETE UNWORTHINESS DEVOTED LOVE PAUL HANEY.[9]

On 19 March the Guardian cabled the National Spiritual Assembly of the United States:

> ANNOUNCE ALL NATIONAL ASSEMBLIES ELEVATION PAUL HANEY RANK HAND OF THE CAUSE.[10]

Shortly after Paul's appointment, Mariam Haney received a letter written on behalf of Shoghi Effendi:

> He hopes that dear Paul will ever-increasingly be able to render the Cause important services. Surely you and his father in the Abhá Kingdom must rejoice to see how your cherished hopes are being fulfilled in this beloved son, who is so devoted, and has the interests of the Faith so completely at heart.[11]

Although now a Hand of the Cause, Paul remained a member of the National Spiritual Assembly of the United States for a further three years, representing it at the first annual convention of South and West Africa in 1956. The next year he represented the Guardian at the first Alaskan convention, in Anchorage, and anointed all those present with attar of rose.

The shock of the sudden passing of Shoghi Effendi in London in November 1957 was followed by the weight of added responsibilities for the Hands of the Cause, who gathered in the Holy Land after the Guardian's funeral to discuss the future of the Cause. A main task was to elect from among their number a body of nine members who would continue the work of the Guardian at the World Centre. Rúḥíyyih Khánum later described this first Conclave of the Hands of the Cause:

> we were faced with the inescapable obligation of voting from amongst the membership of the Hands of the Cause for who would, if chosen by all of us, accept to live and serve at the World Centre as one of the nine legal Custodians. For those who were not already part of the body of the Hands in Haifa this meant literally burning all their bridges behind them. I can remember the words of Paul Haney, an economist just promoted in the prominent investment firm to which he had belonged for some years, with the assurance of financial increases and a substantial pension on retirement, as he bowed his head and said, 'You are only called once.'[12]

This sacrifice was made doubly difficult for Paul, who would henceforth be separated from his beloved mother. Mariam, who was now 85, wrote to Rúḥíyyih Khánum in April 1958:

> The beloved Paul is so pure-hearted, so conscientious, so noble a soul that when this great blessing and honour came to him – that is, of being one of the nine Hands of the Bahá'í Cause to abide in Haifa – he said he could not live with himself had he not accepted this tremendous spiritual bounty . . . naturally I miss Paul – the pure-hearted – but I believe I am with him daily in his service. Distance is no real separation when there is understanding and love.[13]

Paul's life was now fully oriented towards serving the Cause of God. He represented the Hands of the Cause at several national conventions, including those of Mexico and the United States in 1961 and of Spain and Portugal in 1962. He helped his fellow Hands work through the agonizing problems brought about by Charles Mason Remey's defection, for him a very bitter and tragic experience, as he and Remey had been friends. In 1963 Paul was present in Haifa for the election of the first Universal House of Justice, and at the World Congress that followed in London he had the honour of announcing the results of the election to the assembled Bahá'ís. He also gave an outstanding address on the importance of the Bahá'í World Centre.

Paul composed the definitive statement on the Hands of the Cause and their activities in the period between the passing of the Guardian and the election of the Universal House of Justice, entitled 'The Institution of the Hands of the Cause of God'.[14] In 1963 the Universal House of Justice asked Paul to be one of five Hands of the Cause to remain in the Holy Land. He was appointed to the Editorial Committee which gathered information from the whole Bahá'í world, compiled and edited it and then distributed it to all National Spiritual Assemblies. At Riḍván 1965 he represented the Universal House of Justice at the 56th Annual Convention of the United States.

In September 1965 Paul's mother Mariam passed away. The Universal House of Justice sent a cable to the National Spiritual Assembly of the United States:

> GRIEVED ANNOUNCE PASSING MARIAM HANEY DEVOTED SERVANT BAHAULLAH MOTHER BELOVED HAND CAUSE PAUL HANEY. HER TOTAL DEDICATION FAITH

SPANNING PERIOD MORE THAN SIXTY FIVE YEARS STAUNCH UPHOLDER COVENANT EARLIEST DAYS TESTING TIRELESS ACTIVITIES CIRCULATING TABLETS MASTER SERVICES NATIONAL AND INTERNATIONAL LEVEL WHOLEHEARTED LOYALTY STEADFASTNESS ASSURE LOVING WELCOME ABHA KINGDOM.[15]

From this time on Paul travelled extensively. In 1967 he represented the House of Justice at the intercontinental conference in Frankfurt, one of six marking the centenary of the proclamation of Bahá'u'lláh to the kings and rulers. Before the conference, Paul and five other Hands of the Cause visited the House of Bahá'u'lláh in Edirne to pray; afterwards he visited all of the Scandinavian countries, Austria, Spain, Belgium, Switzerland and the United Kingdom.

The next year in August, 1968, he was the featured speaker at the First Bahá'í Oceanic Conference in Palermo, Sicily. The conference was held to commemorate the 100th anniversary of Bahá'u'lláh's departure from Adrianople to 'Akká. Paul was at the podium addressing thousands of Bahá'ís attending from 67 countries. In a country that is normally void of rain in August, a storm of Biblical proportions deluged Palermo. On four separate occasions when the Hand of the Cause concluded some moving passage, the storm would erupt and force him to pause each time in his presentation. Finally Mr Haney regarded the phenomenon as the Lord God's way of emphasizing his points. Hearing this the audience broke out into laughter and applause.

In 1970 Paul represented the House of Justice at the inaugural national convention of Botswana and Malawi, and travelled through Uganda, Kenya, Tanzania, Rhodesia and South Africa. He participated in the North Atlantic Oceanic Conference in Reykjavik, Iceland, in 1971. He travelled in the United Kingdom in 1973 and in the United States in 1974. He attended Youth Conferences in the Netherlands and Switzerland in 1975. In 1977 he attended the international teaching conferences in Bahia, Brazil, and Merida, Mexico, and travelled in Panama and the Caribbean. He attended a youth conference in Germany in 1980, visited centres in Switzerland and participated in the conference in Malaysia. In 1981 he represented the Universal House of Justice at the inaugural meeting of the Continental Board of Counsellors in Asia, travelling through India and Pakistan afterwards. He attended the international conference in Quito, Ecuador, in 1982, and the subsequent satellite conferences in Costa Rica and Panama.

Paul also represented the World Centre at diplomatic functions in Jerusalem. In 1967, during the Vietnam conflict, he was asked by the Universal House of Justice to consult with the National Spiritual Assembly of Vietnam about the future development of the Faith in that country.

Paul was an enthusiastic golfer and a founding member of the Caesaria Golf Club, near Haifa. He often acted as a judge at the competitions and tournaments and would say, with a twinkle in his eye, that golf was 'his second religion'.

On 3 December 1982 Paul was killed instantly in an automobile accident. The Universal House of Justice sent the following cable to the Bahá'í world:

> WITH STRICKEN HEARTS ANNOUNCE SUDDEN IRREPARABLE LOSS THROUGH AUTOMOBILE ACCIDENT 3 DECEMBER HIGHLY DISTINGUISHED GREATLY PRIZED HAND CAUSE GOD STAUNCH DEFENDER COVENANT PAUL HANEY. THIS DISTINGUISHED SERVANT BAHAULLAH WAS BLESSED CHILDHOOD THROUGH ATTAINMENT PRESENCE ABDUL-BAHA. HIS NATURAL GENTLENESS GENUINE HUMILITY UNAFFECTED UNBOUNDED LOVE HIS UPRIGHTNESS INTEGRITY HIS SINGLE-MINDED DEVOTION CAUSE SINCE YOUTHFUL YEARS HIS UNFAILING RELIABILITY METICULOUS ATTENTION DETAIL CHARACTERIZED HIS HISTORIC SERVICES BOTH NATIONAL AND INTERNATIONAL LEVELS. SPANNING MORE THAN HALF CENTURY HIS TIRELESS LABOURS INCLUDED LONG-TIME MEMBERSHIP AMERICAN NATIONAL ASSEMBLY. SINCE 1954 HE CONSECRATED HIS ENERGIES AS MEMBER UNIQUE COMPANY CHIEF STEWARDS FAITH AND LATER AS MEMBER BODY HANDS CAUSE RESIDING HOLY LAND AT ONE OF MOST CRITICAL PERIODS BAHAI HISTORY. LAST DECADE HIS EARTHLY LIFE WAS FULLY DEDICATED DEVELOPMENT NEWLY FORMED INTERNATIONAL TEACHING CENTRE. GENERATIONS YET UNBORN WILL GLORY IN HIS IMPERISHABLE ACHIEVEMENTS AND BE INSPIRED BY HIS UNIQUE FORTITUDE. ARDENTLY SUPPLICATING HOLY THRESHOLD PROGRESS HIS NOBLE SOUL ABHA KINGDOM. ADVISE HOLD THROUGHOUT BAHAI WORLD INCLUDING ALL MASHRIQUL-ADHKARS MEMORIAL GATHERINGS BEFITTING HIS HIGH RANK AND HIS MERITORIOUS SERVICES.[16]

# Dr 'Alí Muḥammad Varqá
# 1912–2007

'Alí Muḥammad Varqá was born during 'Abdu'l-Bahá's historic journeys to the West, in 1912. His father, Valíyu'lláh, was a member of 'Abdu'l-Bahá's entourage. At the time of his birth in Ṭihrán his uncle, 'Azízu'lláh, took his photograph and sent it to Valíyu'lláh. One of the believers showed the picture to 'Abdu'l-Bahá, who wrote on the two arms of the infant 'Yad-i-Mu'ayyad' (Confirmed Hand) and gave the child the name 'Alí Muḥammad after his martyred grandfather.

'Alí Muḥammad Varqá took degrees in economics and history from the University of Ṭihrán and the Teachers' Training College. In 1935 he married Rawḥáníyyih Muhtadí and they had three daughters, Elahe, Nadieh and Faraneh. In 1946 he was given a government grant to study in Paris and in 1950 earned his doctorate from the faculty of literature and human sciences at the Sorbonne with his thesis *Problèmes de l'hydrolique agricole et de l'irrigation en l'Iran.*

When he returned to Iran in 1950, he was appointed assistant professor at the University of Tabríz. Later he became professor of physical geography and geomorphology at Ṭihrán University. During this period he was very active on local and national Bahá'í committees until the death of his father.

In 1938 Valíyu'lláh was appointed Trustee of the Ḥuqúqu'lláh and in 1951 a Hand of the Cause. When he passed away in November 1955, Shoghi Effendi appointed Dr Varqá to replace his father:

> PROFOUNDLY GRIEVED LOSS OUTSTANDING HAND CAUSE GOD, EXEMPLARY TRUSTEE ḤUQÚQ . . . HIS MANTLE AS TRUSTEE FUNDS ḤUQÚQ NOW FALLS ON 'ALÍ MUḤAMMAD, HIS SON . . . NEWLY-APPOINTED TRUSTEE ḤUQÚQ NOW ELEVATED RANK HAND CAUSE.[1]

After being appointed a Hand, the beloved Guardian chanced to come across 'Azízu'lláh's photograph of the infant 'Alí Muḥammad Varqá with 'Abdu'l-Bahá's notation 'Confirmed Hand.' A divine mystery, Shoghi Effendi had been unaware of the existence of the photograph.

As a Hand of the Cause, Dr Varqá and fellow Hands of the Cause Mr Furútan, General 'Alá'í and Mr Samandarí travelled in 1957 to Iraq to pay homage on behalf of the Guardian to the memory of Bahá'u'lláh's father, Mírzá Buzurg – that 'blessed and highly revered personage'[2] – whose remains had been identified and reinterred in a Bahá'í cemetery there.

After Shoghi Effendi's passing in November 1957, Dr Varqá attended the Conclave of the Hands of the Cause in the Holy Land. He was among the nine Hands who, on 19 November, entered the Guardian's sealed room to search the contents of his safe and desk for a will and testament. Finding no such document, these Custodial Hands certified the following:

> That the safe and desk have been opened and searched and the non-existence of a Will and Testament executed by Shoghi Effendi was definitely established.[3]

Dr Varqá lived in Iran, but would spend his summer months in Haifa, acting as a substitute Custodian to relieve the Hands resident in the Holy Land for other duties.

In 1958 Dr Varqá participated in the intercontinental conference held in Djakarta–Singapore and in 1962 he represented the World Centre at the inaugural elections of the National Spiritual Assemblies of Belgium and of Luxembourg.

The same year he was sent by the Custodians to France for 15 days 'to help strengthen that Community and to consult with the National Spiritual Assembly'[4] following the disaffection of a senior Hand of the Cause, Charles Mason Remey. The National Spiritual Assembly had opted to follow his claim as second Guardian, a consequence of which was that the estranged institution had to be re-elected.

In 1963 Dr Varqá travelled to the Holy Land to be present at the election of the first Universal House of Justice. Following this, he participated in the first Bahá'í World Congress in London and afterwards visited the British community.

As representative of the Universal House of Justice in the years following 1963, he attended the inaugural elections of many National

Spiritual Assemblies: Congo-Brazzaville and Central African Republic in 1971; Jordan in 1975; French Antilles in 1977; Mauritania in 1978; the Windward Islands in 1981; Martinique and French Guiana in 1984; Czechoslovakia in 1991; Greenland and the Regional Spiritual Assembly of Ukraine, Moldova and Belarus in 1992; the Regional Assembly of Slovenia and Croatia in 1994; and Sicily in 1995. In 1968 he attended the establishment of the first Board of Counsellors in Northwest Africa.

Dr Varqá, being fluent in French, the Universal House of Justice often asked him to visit French-speaking countries and over the years he visited Bahá'í communities in North Africa, Zaire, Cameroon, Chad, Central African Republic, Senegal, Mauritania, France, French Guiana, Martinique, Guadeloupe and other Francophone countries.

He also travelled to Latin America, the United States, South America, India, Canada, Europe, South-East Asia and the Caribbean. He attended numerous conferences, including Persian-speaking conferences, international youth conferences, international teaching conferences and Bahá'í summer schools.

In the 1970s the Universal House of Justice assigned Dr Varqá the special task of assembling reliable accounts of the early days of the development of the Faith in various parts of the world. He had to acquire narratives, documents, tapes and other materials from early believers and pioneers.

While Dr Varqá was visiting Bahá'í communities in Europe in 1978, he received a message from the National Spiritual Assembly of Iran advising him to delay his return home, as the government had determined to impose a heavy duty on the Bahá'í properties and endowments that had been held in the name of Shoghi Effendi. The National Assembly believed that if Dr Varqá, who was the representative of the owners of Bahá'í property and the Trustee of Ḥuqúqu'lláh, was not in the country, the Assembly might better negotiate with the government to reduce the tax. Thus, with the approval of the Universal House of Justice, he remained in Europe to perform other services. When the Iranian Revolution occurred in 1979, the situation for the Bahá'ís worsened and Dr Varqá never returned to Iran. He was accepted as a refugee in Canada, where he lived for a number of years before being called to service in the Holy Land by the Universal House of Justice.

As Trustee of Ḥuqúqu'lláh from 1955, the institution under his remarkable stewardship expanded from its narrow base among the Iranian believers to include every Bahá'í on the planet. Regional and national boards were established. Conferences for deputies and representatives began in 1987. The Office of Ḥuqúqu'lláh was established in the Holy Land in 1991. The law of Ḥuqúq became universally applicable in 1992. And the International Board of Trustees with branches throughout the world to promote continued widespread application the Ḥuqúq was established in 2005. As knowledge of this great law spread widely among the believers, Dr Varqá was thus able to shape this great Institution in his 52 year Trusteeship and finally oversee its transition two years before his passing.

Speaking on the importance and application of the law of Ḥuqúq at the Sixth International Convention, held in 1988, Dr Varqá elucidated:

> . . . we cannot expect to comprehend the essence and the wisdom hidden in this sacred law. They are kept in the treasury of God's knowledge and are related to the evolution and progress of the human soul in the world of God. What we can conceive by our human understanding is that the payment of Ḥuqúqu'lláh is the sign of our love and obedience, a proof of our firmness and steadfastness and a symbol of our trustworthiness in the Covenant of Bahá'u'lláh. It creates and develops our spiritual quality which leads us towards perfection; it harmonizes and balances our material endeavour, protects us from excessive desire which is born in our human nature, and when unleashed turns into a preventive element for our spiritual growth. When man realizes that a part of his income will be honoured by the acceptance of the Lord, the presence of God is felt in all his endeavours, and undoubtedly he will strive to live his life in a just and legitimate manner in order that his offering may deserve to be spent in the path of God.[5]

In 1997 Dr Varqá was the guest of honour at a series of conferences in New York, Dallas, Chicago and Los Angeles where at least 5,000 of the Bahá'í friends were able to learn more about the Ḥuqúqu'lláh. Intending to rest in Vancouver, British Columbia, Dr Varqá instead ended up addressing 1,100 eager believers who gathered to hear him.

Dr Varqá spoke on the victories which come with self-discipline and advised the youth on the crucial role they can play in the work of pioneering, teaching and child education. But it is in his role as the fifth and longest serving Trustee of Ḥuqúqu'lláh that he centred his work, inspiring the Bahá'í world with the words of Bahá'u'lláh:

> Beseech ye God that He may enable everyone to discharge the obligation of

> Ḥuqúq, inasmuch as the progress and promotion of the Cause of God depend on material means. If His faithful servants could realize how meritorious are benevolent deeds in these days, they would all arise to do that which is meet and seemly. In His hand is the source of authority and He ordaineth as He willeth. He is the Supreme Ruler, the Bountiful, the Equitable, the Revealer, the All-Wise.[6]

Upon the passing of this last surviving Hand of the Cause on 22 September 2007 at his home in Haifa, the Universal House of Justice addressed to the Bahá'ís of the World:

> . . . In the early hours of last night, revered, greatly admired, well-loved Hand of the Cause of God Dr. 'Alí-Muḥammad Varqá departed this earthly plane after a period of outstanding consecrated service to the Blessed Beauty that spanned many decades.
>
> With grieving hearts we bid farewell to the last of that noble company, the Chief Stewards of Bahá'u'lláh's embryonic World Commonwealth, into which he is now gathered in realms of deathless delight and joy. The fervour of his love for the teaching work inspired countless believers across the globe, whether at the events he attended as the representative of the Guardian or of the Universal House of Justice, or in his extensive travels to promote the goals of the Master's Divine Plan. In such activities he contributed mightily to the progress of the Ten Year Crusade and subsequent global teaching plans. Until his final days, he was leonine in his determination to protect the Faith. He wore with marked distinction the mantle of Trustee of Ḥuqúqu'lláh that fell to him from the shoulders of his illustrious father, impressing a record of imperishable achievement on the annals of the Formative Age – achievement which he set a pattern that secures important features for the operation into the future of that divinely ordained institution. Throughout the many years of his valiant endeavor to maintain the integrity of the two offices of so high a rank to which he was simultaneously elevated, his manner was imbued with a luminous gentleness, a genuine kindliness and a natural dignity which combined to reflect the character of a saintly personality. For these exemplary traits he will ever be remembered. Our heartfelt sympathy reaches out to the members of his dear family in their sad loss, which is shared by the entire Bahá'í community. With deeply held trust in the bounties of the Gracious Lord, we pray at the Sacred Threshold for the progress of his resplendent soul throughout the divine worlds. . .
>
> Universal House of Justice, 23 September 2007

# Agnes Baldwin Alexander
# 1875–1971

Among Agnes Alexander's outstanding qualities were her reliance on what she called her 'guidance' and her complete submission to the Will of God. Her intuition never failed her, nor did her courage to follow that guidance. Often she would feel so strongly that she should follow some course of action that she would immediately proceed with her plans, shortly afterwards receiving directions from the Holy Land to do exactly that. Indeed, even the story of how she encountered the Bahá'í Faith and became a believer is a story of mysterious spiritual forces at work.

Descended from distinguished Christian missionaries who braved hardships and sacrifices to Christianize the Sandwich Islands, Agnes was born in Honolulu on 21 July 1875. Her maternal grandparents were the Rev and Mrs Dwight Baldwin, who sailed from New Bedford, Massachusetts, with the fourth company of missionaries sent by the American Board of Missions in 1831. They arrived in Hawaii after a voyage of 161 days. For a time, Rev Baldwin was the only doctor on the islands of Molokai, Maui and Lanai. Caring for the physical as well as the spiritual needs of the indigenous people, he laboured for 36 years until his health failed.

Agnes's paternal grandparents, the Rev and Mrs William Patterson Alexander, arrived the following year. Their voyage, aboard a whaling ship, lasted 186 days. Once in Hawaii, Rev Alexander became widely known as an eloquent preacher. The young people at the mission admired and loved him. When he passed away, a lament in Hawaiian was sent to Agnes's grandmother:

Alas, alas, Father William is dead!
Dead is the missionary and friend;
Our friend who stood fast for the right;
Our friend in the rain and the wind;
Our friend in the heat of the sun;
Our friend in the cold of the mountain;
Our friend on the Eight Seas;
Alas, alas, our friend has departed!
Gone to the glorious heaven of Christ,
He will return no more.[1]

Agnes attended Oahu College, graduating in 1895. She then studied education at the University of California at Berkeley and at Oberlin College but did not complete a degree. She returned to Hawaii, where she taught elementary school.

When Agnes was 25, her chronic ill-health prompted her father to suggest that she travel with a group of Hawaiians touring the United States and Europe. Gentle and timid by nature, Agnes was forced, in the event, to travel across the Atlantic alone. En route to Rome, she suddenly felt that she was nearing her goal.

Settled in a pension in Rome, she was irresistibly drawn to Mrs Charlotte Dixon and her two daughters, who seemed to exude happiness. Agnes overcame her shyness and gathered her courage to ask Mrs Dixon what was the source of her joy.

Just exactly what Mrs Dixon said to Agnes is not known but her words made Agnes weep. Mrs Dixon gave Agnes a handwritten copy of a Bahá'í prayer which, Agnes later said 'answered all the longings' of her heart.[2] Retiring to her room one night three days later, Agnes found she was unable to sleep. During the night she became 'overwhelmingly aware' that Christ had returned. The next morning, she met Mrs Dixon and immediately exclaimed, 'Christ is on this earth!' 'Yes, I can see by your face that you know it.'[3]

Agnes declared her belief in Bahá'u'lláh on 26 November 1900 and, as was usual at the time, wrote a letter of acceptance to 'Abdu'l-Bahá. 'Until one has been awakened by the Breath of the Holy Spirit,' she later said, 'one is asleep, for the only reality is that of the spirit. For twenty-five years I was asleep.'[4]

Agnes remained in Italy for about three months, contemplating her new Faith and studying afresh the Bible, the one Bahá'í prayer Mrs Dixon had given her and a copy of the Hidden Words. Mrs Dixon had also given her the addresses of some believers. The nearest to her was May Ellis Bolles and it was to her that Agnes wrote requesting more information about the Faith. She was in Milan when she received a reply from May dated 28 January 1901:

> My precious Sister!
>
> Praise be to God that He has enlightened your heart in these wonderful days of the Coming of His Kingdom, and that He has in His Mercy guided you to the Truth.
>
> Please God we may soon welcome you in our midst in Paris and that you may then receive the full Revelation, and much help and instruction. In the meantime, I send you the enclosed pamphlets, Tablets and prayers, which by the Grace of God will illumine your understanding and fill you with the Breath of Life. I also enclose my photograph of our Great and Glorious Lord, which was given to me when I made the pilgrimage to 'Akká . . .
>
> My Lord appeared to me in a vision twice, two years before I heard the Great Message, and when, by the great bounty of God, and without regard to my unworthiness, I was permitted to be among the first Americans to visit 'Akká – I beheld my dear Lord, I knew Him by my visions . . .
>
> One thing, dearest spiritual sister, I would say to you. Although the fire of love of God is burning in your heart, and you are longing to spread the glad tidings, be very careful – for every soul is not ripe – and our dear Lord has told us never to give to drink of this pure water of life, but to the thirsty . . . [5]

In the spring of 1901 Agnes set out for Paris. There she met many of the early French, English and American believers, including May Bolles, Monsieur Henri, Emogene Hoagg, Laura Barney, Lua and Edward Getsinger, Ethel Rosenberg and Charles Mason Remey, as well as Mírzá Abu'l-Faḍl and Ali Kuli Khan. May Bolles became Agnes's spiritual mother and her guiding star.

Agnes remained in Paris for three and a half months and then felt it was time to return home to proclaim her newly-found Faith to the people of the Hawaiian Islands. She had packed her bags and was about to proceed to London when a messenger arrived with a Tablet from 'Abdu'l-Bahá, in which He told her 'to be like a divine bird, return to Hawaii, spread the wings of sanctity over the island, warble melodies in praise of God, gladden thereby the Supreme Concourse, cause seeking souls to be attracted as moths to a lighted lamp, and be the means of making Hawaii illumined by the Light of God'.[6] After spending the summer at Green Acre in Maine, Agnes arrived home on 26 December 1901, the first Bahá'í to set foot in Hawaii. What thoughts must have accompanied this descendant of Christian missionaries as she sought to fulfil Christ's promise, 'Thy kingdom come. Thy will be done'? Although many whispered that Agnes had joined some strange cult, her father said that the trip had been Agnes's salvation and her sister said simply that if her newly-found Faith made her happy, it must have some merit. No one in her family, however, was moved to investigate the new religion and for eight years Agnes taught the Bahá'í Faith covertly.

The first Hawaiian after Agnes to become a Bahá'í was Clarence Hobron Smith, to whom Agnes had taught the Faith while in Paris. The first to become a Bahá'í in Hawaii was Elizabeth Muther, who enrolled in 1902. By 1909 there were 11 Bahá'ís in Hawaii and on 6 January 1911 Agnes was elected chairman of the Honolulu Bahá'í Assembly.

In 1905 Agnes travelled to Alaska, the first Bahá'í to visit the territory. In 1913 both of her beloved parents died. Her sister sailed for California and Agnes was left alone. She now felt it was time to travel to other parts of the world and teach the Faith. First, however, she wished to visit her spiritual mother, May Bolles Maxwell. She spent a blissful month at the Maxwell home in Montreal before proceeding to New York. During this period she received a Tablet from the Master dated 13 October 1913 encouraging her to travel to Japan.

Hoping to visit relatives in Italy and the Master in the Holy Land en route to Japan, Agnes was delayed in Switzerland by the outbreak of World War I. In August 1914 she received another Tablet from 'Abdu'l-Bahá urging her to go directly to Japan and 'be like unto a realm-conquering army and a farmer'[7] but saying that still she was free to choose to come to the Holy Land. Completely submitting to the Will of God, Agnes sailed to Japan. She boarded the *Mayazaki Maru* at Marseilles and, on 1 November 1914, she disembarked at Kobe, Japan, the second Bahá'í to settle in the country, George Augur having arrived in June. Agnes lived in Japan for the next 23 years, although she made several trips home to Hawaii; she never did meet 'Abdu'l-Bahá.

'Consider ye,' 'Abdu'l-Bahá wrote in 1916 in one of the Tablets of the Divine Plan,

> that Miss Agnes Alexander, the daughter of the Kingdom, the beloved maidservant of the Blessed Perfection, travelled alone to the Hawaiian Islands, to the Island of Honolulu, and now she is gaining spiritual victories in Japan! Reflect ye how this daughter was confirmed in the Hawaiian Islands. She became the cause of the guidance of a gathering of people.
>
> . . . in the Hawaiian Islands, through the efforts of Miss Alexander, a number of souls have reached the shore of the sea of faith! Consider ye, what happiness, what joy is this! I declare by the Lord of Hosts that had this respected daughter founded an empire, that empire would not have been so great! For this sovereignty is eternal sovereignty and this glory is everlasting glory.[8]

The first person to become a Bahá'í in Japan was an 18-year-old student, Kikutaro Fukuta, who accepted the Faith in the spring of 1915. However, Agnes's greatest successes came from her contacts with the blind and with Esperantists. Through her interest in Esperanto, she met Vasily Eroshenko, a blind Russian who taught her Braille in English and Esperanto. Agnes wrote 'A letter to the Blind Women of Japan' in Braille, which was translated into Japanese Braille. This was Japan's first Bahá'í publication for the blind and the first Bahá'í work to be translated into Japanese.

In 1918 Agnes visited the United States and spent some time with Martha Root, whom she had met in Japan in 1915. Martha was anxious to improve her Esperanto so that she would be prepared for an Esperanto conference to be held at Green Acre in July. Ignoring signals from Agnes that she wished to remain asleep, every morning at 6:30 Martha would rouse Agnes from her bed so that her visitor could teach her Esperanto.[9]

Three years later, Agnes travelled to Korea, becoming the first Bahá'í to teach the Faith in that country. She later wrote:

> During the month spent in Seoul, God's power had been triumphant. All doors had been opened. Japanese and Koreans, both Buddhist and Christians, had heard the Bahá'í Message and were now free to search themselves. It could not be said they had been forgotten in God's great plan for the New Day.[10]

When she returned to Tokyo she forwarded to the Master the brief expressions of faith some of the Koreans had written. The Master's reply to the 15 Korean 'heavenly sons' arrived in February 1922, several months after His passing:

> Praise be to God, that celestial light guided and led you to the Sun of Reality, bestowed everlasting life and granted heavenly illumination. Ye are like seedlings which have been planted by the hand of Bestowal in His Spiritual Rose-Garden. It is my hope that through the warmth of the Sun of Reality, the pouring down of the showers of mercy and the wafting of the breezes of bestowal, ye may progress day by day so that each one may become a blessed tree, full of leaves and flowers and throw your shade over great multitudes.[11]

On 1 September 1923 a major earthquake shook Japan. Two-thirds of Tokyo burned, thousands lost their lives and over a million people were left homeless. Agnes was talking to Ida Finch, an American Bahá'í who lived in Japan for four years, when the earthquake struck:

> Miss Alexander escaped to the street . . . We read the prayer of protection and remained on the street most of the afternoon for the quaking and shaking continued at intervals all day and for many days after.[12]

Agnes later recalled:

> . . . after the great quake and fire masses of humanity passed along the broad roadway near home, coming, coming, coming from the burning district below . . . scarcely anything to be found to eat . . . food was brought in from the outer provinces . . . there was no running water and the fires could not be put out; the trains and tramways, the gas, electric lights and telephones all ceased operating . . . with the help of a kind student friend I found my way to what had been the American Embassy; but only a few pillars remained. The only centre remaining at Tokyo was the New Imperial Hotel.[13]

Although none of the Bahá'ís was injured, Agnes's house was unsafe and she was persuaded by Martha Root to spend some time with her in China. There they contacted Sun Yat Sen, presented a message of peace to a school for children of army officers, gave out several hundred of Roy Wilhelm's blue booklets about the Bahá'í Faith, visited four Chinese cities, spoke at numerous schools and reached many prominent people. Later that year, Agnes returned to Hawaii, becoming the first to teach the Bahá'í Faith on the island of Kauai and the first Bahá'í travel teacher to the Big Island.

Over the years Agnes visited Taiwan, Hong Kong, the Philippines, the United States, Canada and Europe. She used her knowledge of Esperanto to make contacts for the Faith and was able to obtain much publicity.

In the late 1920s Shoghi Effendi wrote to her:

> I long to hear of your determination to return to Japan and pick up the thread of your unsparing efforts and activities for the promotion of the Cause of God. I feel that your destiny lies in that far-off and promising country where your noble and pioneer services future generations will befittingly glorify and thankfully remember. May the Beloved remove every obstacle from your path and enable you to resume your active work in that land.[14]

After four years in Hawaii, Agnes returned to Japan, where she focused her efforts on reaching people in professional and intellectual circles. In October 1930 Martha Root joined Agnes in Tokyo, speaking at universities and high schools and to clubs and religious groups. One of Japan's great newspapers arranged a conference on the Faith, held on 20 December, with Martha and three other distinguished speakers. Over two thousand people attended. For Agnes, the highlight of Martha's visit was the broadcast of a talk over the Tokyo Central Broadcasting Station. Martha's presentation was heard all over Japan and the text of the talk was published on the front page of the *Japan Times*. Much to Agnes's distress, Martha's ultimate goal was to contact the Imperial Household. After numerous rebuffs, Martha succeeded in meeting with the Minister of the Imperial Household, to whom she presented gifts for His Imperial Majesty.

In 1931 Keith Ransom-Kehler, a Bahá'í scholar and speaker, visited Japan for six weeks. Both she and Martha Root were able to move in the intellectual circles which had been carefully cultivated by Agnes.

In 1932 Agnes supervised the translation of Esslemont's *Bahá'u'lláh and the New Era* into Japanese. On 21 March 1932 she participated in the formation of the first Local Spiritual Assembly of Tokyo. Unfortunately, owing to the situation in Japan, it was disbanded two years later.

In March 1937 Agnes set sail for Haifa where she at last met the Guardian. She offered him the same love and devotion she had given his grandfather. Shoghi Effendi, for his part, appreciated the services Agnes had rendered the Cause of Bahá'u'lláh and treated her as an honoured guest. At Shoghi Effendi's request, Agnes wrote her two histories of the Bahá'í Faith, on Hawaii and Japan.

Japan's involvement in World War II prevented Agnes's return to that country until 1950. Shortly after returning to Tokyo she moved to a tiny room in Kyoto, living modestly and spending her resources on the Faith rather than on herself. Although Hawaii was always 'home' to her, she loved Japan and the Japanese people. After a visit to Hiroshima she wrote to a friend:

> I feel an especial love for these people . . . Our beloved Guardian wrote that the people of this city who had suffered so cruelly had a right to hear of the teachings of Bahá'u'lláh for peace and brotherhood, so you can imagine I feel a deep interest and love here.[15]

Agnes cherished the words of the Guardian in his first letter to the Japanese Bahá'ís, written 26 January 1922:

> What promises He ['Abdu'l-Bahá] gave us all regarding the future of the Cause in that Land . . . 'Japan will turn ablaze! Japan is endowed with a most remarkable capacity for the spread of the Cause of God! Japan . . . will take the lead in the spiritual reawakening of the peoples and nations that the world shall soon witness! . . . the Hand of the Unseen is ever active and triumphant in lands, even as distant as Japan!'[16]

Once someone asked Agnes when she would leave Japan. 'Why dearie', she replied, "Abdu'l-Bahá told me to go to Japan. He never told me to leave it!'[17]

In 1954 Agnes was among the first contingent of those appointed to the Auxiliary Board for Asia. Three years later, on 27 March 1957, she was elevated to the rank of Hand of the Cause of God, replacing George Townshend, who had passed away on 25 March:

> AGNES ALEXANDER DISTINGUISHED PIONEER FAITH ELEVATED RANK HAND CAUSE CONFIDENT APPOINTMENT WILL SPIRITUALLY REINFORCE TEACHING CAMPAIGN NORTH SOUTH HEART PACIFIC OCEAN.[18]

Agnes was elected to the National Spiritual Assembly of North-East Asia in 1957 and served until 1963. When the Guardian passed away in November 1957, she travelled to his funeral in London and then on to Haifa for the first Conclave of the Hands of the Cause. She attended the Intercontinental Conferences in Sydney and Djakarta-Singapore in

1958 and afterwards travelled through the United States and Europe in September and October. She visited Korea again in July 1961. In 1963 she attended the International Convention in Haifa at which the first Universal House of Justice was elected, afterwards joining thousands of Bahá'ís in London for the first Bahá'í World Congress. In the early 1960s she assisted with the process of mass conversion in the Philippines and in 1964 represented the Universal House of Justice at the formation of the National Spiritual Assembly of the Hawaiian Islands.

Agnes planned to attend the World Congress of Esperantists in Tokyo in 1965 but fell and broke her hip. For two years she was confined to a hospital in Tokyo but never complained, telling her friend, 'Dearie, nothing happens by chance.'[19]

In 1967, at the age of 92 and unable to walk or write, Agnes decided it was time to go home to Hawaii. She returned to Kyoto to dispose of her books and mementos before leaving. She spent the final years of her life in Honolulu. On 1 January 1971 she slipped quietly away to the Abhá Kingdom. She was buried in the family plot behind Kawaiahao Church in Honolulu.

A member of the National Spiritual Assembly of the Hawaiian Islands was closely associated with Agnes for ten years. He remembers that 'her steadfastness, her faith, her absolute certitude in the Cause, her strict obedience and loyalty to the Covenant have been a high standard to emulate . . . It is difficult to capture the balance between, on the one hand, her continual childlike wonderment, purity and innocence, and, on the other hand, her formidable, audacious and persevering teaching qualities.'[20]

On 4 January 1971, the Universal House of Justice cabled the Bahá'í world:

> PROFOUNDLY GRIEVE PASSING ILLUMINED SOUL HAND CAUSE AGNES ALEXANDER LONG-STANDING PILLAR CAUSE FAR EAST FIRST BRING FAITH HAWAIIAN ISLANDS. HER LONG DEDICATED EXEMPLARY LIFE SERVICE DEVOTION CAUSE GOD ANTICIPATED BY CENTRE COVENANT SELECTING HER SHARE MAY MAXWELL IMPERISHABLE HONOUR MENTION TABLETS DIVINE PLAN. HER UNRESTRAINED UNCEASING PURSUIT TEACHING OBEDIENCE COMMAND BAHAULLAH EXHORTATIONS MASTER GUIDANCE BELOVED GUARDIAN SHINING EXAMPLE ALL FOLLOWERS FAITH. HER PASSING SEVERS ONE MORE LINK HEROIC AGE. ASSURE FAMILY FRIENDS ARDENT PRAYERS HOLIEST SHRINE PROGRESS RADIANT SOUL REQUEST ALL NATIONAL SPIRITUAL ASSEMBLIES HOLD MEMORIAL MEETINGS AND THOSE RESPONSIBLE HOLD SERVICES MOTHER TEMPLES.[21]

Agnes Alexander

Bahá'ís of Honolulu on the occasion of the visit of Charles Mason Remey and Howard Struven, December 1909. *Standing left to right*: Howard Struven, Japanese maid, Mrs Coombs, Mrs Fletcher, Charles Mason Remey, Mrs Sutherland, Mrs Rowland, George Augur. *Seated, left to right*: Mrs Augur, Agnes Alexander, Virginia Rowland (child), Mrs Johnson, Miss Muther

Paul Haney

Paul Haney with his wife, Margery

Corinne True and Paul Haney

Paul Haney with pioneers at the International Teaching Conference, Mérida, Mexico, February 1977

Amatu'l-Bahá and Paul Haney assist at the election of
the first Universal House of Justice, 1963

Jalál Kházeh

Hands of the Cause William Sears, Zikrullah Khadem, ‘Alí-Akbar Furútan, General Shu‘a‘u’ll’áh ‘Alá’í, Raḥmatu’lláh Muhájir, Ṭarázu’lláh Samandarí, Collis Featherstone, Abul-Qásim Faizi, Dr Hermann Grossmann, Jalál Kházeh at Bahjí

Amatu'l-Bahá Rúḥíyyih <u>Kh</u>ánum

Amatu'l-Bahá and Músá Banání at the laying of the foundation stone of the House of Worship at Kampala, Uganda, 26 January 1958

Amatu'l-Bahá with chiefs and sub-chiefs in Ishamba, Zaire, January 1972

Amatu'l-Bahá Rúḥíyyih Khánum with the first National Spiritual Assembly of the Andaman and Nicobar Islands

Amatu'l-Bahá with Princess Gcenaphi and Chief Johannes Diamini of Swaziland at the Master's House, March 1984

Amatu'l-Bahá presents The Promise of World Peace to Pérez de Cúellar, Secretary-General of the United Nations, 1985

Amatu'l-Bahá Rúḥíyyih Khánum with the first National Spiritual Assembly of Romania, Riḍván 1991

'Alí Muḥammad Varqá

‘Alí Muḥammad Varqá at a conference for Deputies of Ḥuqúqu’lláh, Landegg Academy, August 1991

# VII

# Hands of the Cause Appointed by Shoghi Effendi on 2 October 1957

OCTOBER 1957

SO MARVELLOUS A PROGRESS, EMBRACING SO VAST A FIELD, ACHIEVED IN SO SHORT A TIME, BY SO SMALL A BAND OF HEROIC SOULS, WELL DESERVES, AT THIS JUNCTURE IN THE EVOLUTION OF A DECADE-LONG CRUSADE, TO BE SIGNALIZED BY, AND INDEED NECESSITATES, THE ANNOUNCEMENT OF YET ANOTHER STEP IN THE PROGRESSIVE UNFOLDMENT OF ONE OF THE CARDINAL AND PIVOTAL INSTITUTIONS ORDAINED BY BAHÁ'U'LLÁH, AND CONFIRMED IN THE WILL AND TESTAMENT OF 'ABDU'L-BAHÁ, INVOLVING THE DESIGNATION OF YET ANOTHER CONTINGENT OF THE HANDS OF THE CAUSE OF GOD, RAISING THEREBY TO THRICE NINE THE TOTAL NUMBER OF THE CHIEF STEWARDS OF BAHÁ'U'LLÁH'S EMBRYONIC WORLD COMMONWEALTH, WHO HAVE BEEN INVESTED BY THE UNERRING PEN OF THE CENTRE OF HIS COVENANT WITH THE DUAL FUNCTION OF GUARDING OVER THE SECURITY, AND OF INSURING THE PROPAGATION, OF HIS FATHER'S FAITH.

THE EIGHT NOW ELEVATED TO THIS EXALTED RANK ARE: ENOCH OLINGA, WILLIAM SEARS, AND JOHN ROBARTS, IN WEST AND SOUTH AFRICA; HASAN BALYUZI AND JOHN FERRABY IN THE BRITISH ISLES; COLLIS FEATHERSTONE AND RAHMATU'LLÁH MUHÁJIR, IN THE PACIFIC AREA; AND ABU'L-QÁSIM FAIZÍ IN THE ARABIAN PENINSULA – A GROUP CHOSEN FROM FOUR CONTINENTS OF THE GLOBE, AND REPRESENTING THE AFNÁN, AS WELL AS THE BLACK AND WHITE RACES AND WHOSE MEMBERS ARE DERIVED FROM CHRISTIAN, MUSLIM, JEWISH AND PAGAN BACKGROUNDS.

SHOGHI

# Hasan Balyuzi
# (Ḥasan Muvaqqar Balyúzí)
# 1908–1980

Hasan Balyuzi, an Afnán, was the only Hand of the Cause related to the Guardian, sharing with him a great-grandfather, Ḥájí Mírzá Abu'l-Qásim. This ancestor was one of two brothers of Khadíjih-Bagum, the wife of the Báb. His daughter, Fáṭimih-Sulṭán-Bagum, married Muḥammad-Ḥasan, a merchant whom Bahá'u'lláh accepted as a member of the Báb's family. Their son was Mírzá 'Alí Muḥammad Áqá, Muvaqqaru'd-Dawlih, Hasan's father. He was very knowledgeable and thought highly of education, having received part of his own in England. Hasan's mother, Munavvar Khánum, could trace her lineage from both brothers of Khadíjih-Bagum. Thus Hasan Muvaqqar Balyuzi had a noble lineage and a long connection with the Bábí and Bahá'í Faiths.

Born in Shíráz on 7 September 1908, Hasan had an eventful childhood. Most of his early years were spent in Búshihr, where his father was governor of the Persian Gulf Ports and Islands. During the First World War the family's house was pillaged, and when the British occupied Búshihr in 1915 the family was forced to resettle in India, spending the next four years in Bombay and Poona. Although their financial circumstances became strained, they were highly respected, and they were sustained by Tablets and news from 'Abdu'l-Bahá that reached them through Bahá'í pilgrims. Their home became a gathering place for the learned.

At the age of four, Hasan began to study English. Later, in India, he studied Persian, Arabic and history before entering the English high school known as Bishop's College, where he continued to perfect his

English. In the future he would apply his mastery of that language in scholarly works, translations from the Persian, administrative tasks and public speaking.

After the war, the family returned to Iran and settled in Ṭihrán. Muvaqqaru'd-Dawlih became a member of the Cabinet (Vazír) as Minister of the Interior. Hasan was enrolled in the Cyrus School and completed his middle school education. Four months before his 13th birthday, however, in 1921, his beloved father died. Within a year or so of this sad event, Hasan moved with his mother to Shíráz.

As there were no senior high schools in Shíráz, a paternal uncle contacted Professor E. G. Browne in 1925 and asked whether the professor could take charge of his nephew's education. Browne, who had recently suffered a severe heart attack, and was to die in the first week of 1926, declined the request. Hasan decided to pursue his studies at the Preparatory School of the American University in Beirut. This decision would profoundly alter his life.

At this time Hasan Balyuzi did not count himself a Bahá'í. He knew of the Cause only through the family relationships with 'Abdu'l-Bahá and Shoghi Effendi, visits of distinguished Bahá'ís and Bahá'í social events in Shíráz. Although both his parents were believers, Hasan had learned little of the Faith from them, owing to restrictions preventing the discussion of the Faith in the household. Lacking knowledge of the Cause, he could not accept that there could be another Prophet after Muḥammad.

Hasan's journey to Beirut took him through the Red Sea, Port Said and Haifa. He spent one night on Mount Carmel. This was the same night that the Guardian remained at John Esslemont's bedside in the old Pilgrim House as the latter passed his last hours on earth. While this crisis was unfolding, Hasan was placed in a drawing room in the house of 'Abdu'l-Bahá and was unexpectedly visited by Shoghi Effendi. The Guardian talked with him for over an hour with such kindness and patience that the 17-year-old Balyuzi was confirmed in the Faith. Many years later, Mr Balyuzi wrote of this event:

> It was that bounty of meeting Shoghi Effendi and all that I saw in him, which confirmed me in the Faith of Bahá'u'lláh. The course of my life was changed.[1]

Following this eventful meeting in Haifa, Hasan became an outstanding Bahá'í and student. He began to correspond with believers in Europe and America, sharing with them news of Bahá'í activities. At the time Shoghi Effendi was encouraging Iranian Bahá'í students to study in Beirut before going to Europe. As one of the first Bahá'í students at the university, Hasan provided leadership by bringing Bahá'í students together, arranging weekly programmes, encouraging them to prepare talks, seeking from the Guardian permission for these students to visit Haifa and writing articles about the Faith. When a pamphlet he wrote, entitled *Bahá'u'lláh*, was presented to the Guardian, Shoghi Effendi said that Mr Balyuzi should write three volumes, on the lives of Bahá'u'lláh, the Báb and 'Abdu'l-Bahá.[2] Hasan's friend and fellow student Abu'l-Qásim Faizi said, reflecting on those days, 'That was the happiest period of our lives when dear Hasan put all of us on a path conducive to the approval and appreciation of the beloved Guardian.'[3]

One of the top students at the American University, Hasan also played football and tennis and participated in the Drama and Debating Societies, as well as the Bahá'í Society. His early studies were in chemistry, but for his postgraduate studies he took history, receiving in 1932 a Master's degree in Diplomatic History.

In February 1932, in the company of Mr Faizi, he made a final pilgrimage to Haifa, which included a visit to the newly-restored Mansion of Bahjí. This marked the last time he ever saw Shoghi Effendi. Seven months later he left Beirut for England, where he played a central role in the history of the Cause over the next 48 years.

Hasan continued his education in Diplomatic History at the London School of Economics, studying history, political science and diplomacy, concentrating on the relations of the European powers to the Persian Gulf States. He received his M.Sc. (Econ) in 1935. He then began work on a doctorate, studying the effect of 'British Public Opinion on Franco-German Relations after World War I'. However his university career was interrupted by the outbreak of the Second World War.

At Riḍván 1933, soon after his arrival in London, Hasan was elected to the National Spiritual Assembly of the British Isles, as well as to the Local Spiritual Assembly of London. Meanwhile he became an able assistant to Lady Blomfield and a source of comfort and encouragement to Iranians living in London. As there was no Bahá'í centre in the city, he rented a place that soon became a focal point of Bahá'í activities.

Hasan had been in England less than 18 months when he published in an Iranian newspaper an article on the current political situation in

Europe. On 8 February 1934 the Guardian, in a letter written on his behalf, expressed astonishment at Mr Balyuzi after his own 'repeated and emphatic warnings to the friends that they should refrain from participating whether directly or indirectly in any political activity'.[4]

Poised on the threshold of a possibly brilliant career in the diplomatic service, Mr Balyuzi nevertheless replied promptly to the Guardian. In a letter through his secretary, dated 2 March 1934, Shoghi Effendi responded to Hasan, remarking on his difficult but courageous decision:

> He was much impressed by your immediate response . . . and he has deeply appreciated the firm decision you have taken not to enter any political or diplomatic career. He is fully conscious of the sacrifices you have accepted to undergo for the sake of maintaining the integrity of the Teachings. For the field of work which your parents wanted you to enter was one in which you had great possibilities of progress, and you might have even had a chance to attain the position which your father had occupied in the ministry. But you can be certain that the example you have set before the friends by refusing to meddle in any sort of political activity is one which all of them will appreciate and through which they will be encouraged to suffer even greater sacrifices. The Cause, indeed, can progress only through the continued and whole-hearted sacrifices of the believers. And it is on young, intelligent and well-educated Bahá'ís like yourself that has been laid the chief responsibility of demonstrating to the friends and to the non-believers alike, that the spirit of heroism, of loyalty and of unqualified devotion to the Faith is more than ever animating the faithful and is moulding and shaping their lives.[5]

The next year the Guardian praised Hasan Balyuzi for having already contributed a valuable share to the development of the Cause in Britain. Together with David Hofman, an English Bahá'í who returned to Britain from America in 1936, Hasan revitalized the British Bahá'í community. During the next four years he helped launch a nationwide teaching campaign, organized the first British summer school, participated in the annual mid-winter teaching conferences, contributed to the monthly magazine *New World Order* and helped the National Spiritual Assembly achieve legal incorporation. He was also be a member of the London Bahá'í Youth Group and an active spokesperson for the Faith.

When Hasan decided to return to Iran prior to the Second World War, a believer who prized his contributions to the Cause in England appealed to the Guardian to intercede. His departure, she strongly felt, would harm the institutions of the Cause and their activities. Shoghi Effendi replied that Mr Balyuzi would receive further bounty and assistance in service to the Cause if he remained in England, but he did not direct Hasan to stay. However, on reading the Guardian's comments Mr Balyuzi decided to remain in London.

As the war approached, the British Bahá'í community was encouraged by a letter from the Guardian, who was 'delighted with the work which is being so energetically conducted . . . particularly by their national elected representatives whose magnificent efforts, courage and perseverance deserve the highest praise'.[6] During the war, Shoghi Effendi expressed his love and concern for the British Bahá'ís in over 60 messages. The believers responded with increased activity in prosecuting the teaching work, in spite of 'the unprecedented calamities and confusion that now afflict their country'.[7]

In 1940 Mr Balyuzi accepted an appointment with the newly formed Persian Service of the British Broadcasting Corporation (BBC). This appointment assured his continued residence in England when war began. His broadcasts included talks on Iranian culture, western history and culture, translations into Persian of many classics of English prose and poetry,[8] features on current affairs and interviews with Iranian personalities. His talks were greatly admired by an Iranian audience during more than 20 years. He also wrote special features, wrote and performed plays and assisted in Shakespeare productions.

At Riḍván 1940 Hasan was elected vice-chairman of the National Spiritual Assembly. The next year he wrote *A Guide to the Administrative Order* and provided invaluable assistance to David Hofman, who edited Lady Blomfield's *The Chosen Highway*, to which Hasan wrote the preface.[9]

In June 1941 Hasan married Molly (Mary) Brown at the Bahá'í Centre in Torquay. She was a ballet dancer and the daughter of Kathleen Brown (later Lady Hornell), one of England's most steadfast and active Bahá'ís. Hasan and Molly had together attended many Bahá'í firesides and meetings. The couple lived temporarily in Evesham, where the BBC moved for the duration of the war. They had five sons, perhaps explaining Hasan's comment some years later that 'a girl has not been born into our family for two hundred years'.[10]

In 1942 Hasan was elected chairman of the National Spiritual Assembly, a post he would hold for 17 years. He was described as bringing loving patience, deep sympathy, profound wisdom and lovable hilarity to the meetings. One member recalled the joy, eagerness and excitement of the meetings. Another remembered him as gentle and influential, and still another recalled his anecdotes, light-hearted stories and perfect chairmanship.

Indeed Hasan Balyuzi possessed an easy yet dignified bearing, an appreciation for every effort made by others to serve the Faith, a sympathy towards the apparent frailties of human conduct, an understanding for the longings of human souls, a quiet persevering in fulfilling his own responsibilities, an untarnished steadfastness in his loyalty to the Covenant, a complete and heartfelt obedience to the Central Figures of the Faith, and a staunch support for all the institutions of the Administrative Order.

Hand of the Cause Ugo Giachery, himself an aristocrat, provided a pen-portrait of Mr Balyuzi at the time of their first encounter in 1953:

> he was young, elegant, soft-spoken, gentle and graceful. His luxuriant black hair enhanced the handsomeness of his countenance; to me he appeared the embodiment of the perfect Persian aristocrat. His linguistic ability was truly superb.[11]

Hand of the Cause Mr Furútan told Marion Hofman that he had never met a man as modest and humble as Mr Balyuzi.[12] Farhang Afnán, a young relative whom Mr Balyuzi looked after for almost 17 years, said, 'I was enraptured by his kindness, gentleness and understanding. As time passed, I came to realize more and more what a unique person he was . . . He was like a many faceted precious jewel.'[13]

Given such marvellous descriptions of Hasan Balyuzi, little wonder those who gathered around him were inspired by and attracted to his person.

In addition to his work on the National Spiritual Assembly, Hasan Balyuzi was often chairman of the annual convention and of the London Spiritual Assembly and was a member or secretary of numerous committees, including those for *New World Order*, literature, reviewing Bahá'í literature, archives, assembly development, Persians, consolidation, summer school management and programme, the national centenary, public relations, visual aids, European and Asian teaching and a number of committees connected with the London Ḥaẓíratu'l-Quds. His committee work involved, among many other things, helping to formulate publishing policy, planning press publicity for the completion of the exterior of the Wilmette House of Worship, preparing a history of the Faith in the British Isles for the 1944 centenary and promoting the first British Six Year Plan.

At the same time he addressed and dispatched the *Bahá'í Journal* to the British Bahá'ís and spoke at summer schools, the annual teaching conferences, public meetings and firesides.

Asked how he could attend to so many demanding tasks, Hasan Balyuzi replied, 'Whenever I think of what our beloved Guardian is doing for us I am ashamed of how little we are doing in response and sleep escapes my eyes.'[14] Many evenings he would sit through the night at his desk, engaged in his work.

Molly Balyuzi was highly gifted herself. She assisted her husband in producing dramatic and distinctive scripts about the Faith. Her presence with Hasan at summer school created a joyous atmosphere. Because she preferred a background role and devoted herself to their children, Hasan was able to focus on his herculean tasks. When O. Z. Whitehead visited them in 1979 he was 'much touched by the love and consideration which they showed for each other'. He realized, he said, that Hasan 'could not do his vastly important work without her devoted care'.[15]

It was partly owing to Mr Balyuzi's intensive administrative work that the British Bahá'í community was so successful in winning the goals of the Six Year Plan (1944–50). At the outset of the Plan, George Townshend, who lived in Ireland, was the only member of the Bahá'í community of the British Isles residing outside of England. The Plan called for the formation of 19 new spiritual assemblies in England, Wales, Scotland, Northern Ireland and Eire. The British Bahá'í community rose to the challenge and, having accepted the assistance of John Robarts in the Plan's closing weeks, the National Spiritual Assembly was able to cable the Guardian on 17 April 1950 that total victory was assured. At the Annual Convention in 1950, Hasan Balyuzi read to a triumphant assemblage the Guardian's cable:

> HEART FLOODED JOY STRIKING EVIDENCE BOUNTIFUL GRACE BAHÁ'U'LLÁH ENABLING VALOROUS DEARLY LOVED BAHÁ'Í COMMUNITY BRITISH ISLES TRIUMPHANTLY CONCLUDE FIRST HISTORIC PLAN HALF CENTURY BRITISH BAHÁ'Í HISTORY.[16]

In the same message Shoghi Effendi called upon the British Bahá'í community to ready itself, after a year's respite, for yet another historic undertaking. Referred to as the Africa Campaign,[17] this challenging enterprise required the British National Spiritual Assembly to be the consultative body for all African territories, as various national Bahá'í bodies worked in concert to expand the Cause in that continent.

Largely untouched by the teachings of Bahá'u'lláh at the outset of the campaign, at its close the African continent celebrated the enrolment of more than 600 Bahá'ís living in over 190 localities and representing over 60 tribes. The Kampala conference in 1953, attended by Hands of the Cause and 123 representatives of some 30 African tribes, was presided over by Hasan Balyuzi. In his first mission overseas, Mr Balyuzi convened the meeting, presided over all its sessions, spoke at the public meeting in Makerere University College and participated in consultations between National Spiritual Assembly representatives and the Hands of the Cause in attendance.

Listening to Shoghi Effendi's message to the British National Convention a few months later, the delegates could bask in the glow of their Guardian's praises, reflect upon the historic significance of the victories so recently won and ponder the challenges of the World Spiritual Crusade upon which they were about to embark:

> WARMLY CONGRATULATE ASSEMBLED DELEGATES BAHÁ'Í COMMUNITY BRITISH ISLES CELEBRATING MOST GREAT FESTIVAL HOLY YEAR ON MAGNIFICENT VICTORIES ACHIEVED AFRICAN CONTINENT EXCEEDING HIGHEST HOPES PLAN FORMULATED TWO YEARS AGO ORIGINALLY CONCEIVED MERE PRELUDE AFRICAN CAMPAIGN ASSUMED SUCH PROPORTIONS YIELDED SUCH FRUIT DESERVE BE REGARDED DISTINCT STAGE CAMPAIGN LAUNCHED BRITISH BAHÁ'Í COMMUNITY BEYOND BORDERS HOMELAND SIX YEAR PLAN FIRST COLLECTIVE UNDERTAKING BRITISH BAHÁ'Í HISTORY LAID BROADENED FOUNDATIONS ADMINISTRATIVE INSTITUTIONS DESTINED DIRECT OPERATION FUTURE OVERSEAS ENTERPRISES BRITISH BAHÁ'Í COMMUNITY TWO YEAR PLAN INAUGURATED WITHIN AFRICAN CONTINENT GLORIOUS MISSION SAME COMMUNITY CALLED UPON ACCOMPLISH THROUGHOUT BRITISH DEPENDENCIES EASTERN WESTERN HEMISPHERES HOUR PROPITIOUS TRIUMPHANT RICHLY BLESSED BRITISH NATIONAL SPIRITUAL ASSEMBLY PARTICIPATE ELEVEN SISTER NATIONAL ASSEMBLIES EAST WEST IMPENDING WORLD SPIRITUAL CRUSADE THROUGH LAUNCHING TEN YEAR PLAN EMBRACING THREE CONTINENTS GLOBE CALCULATED CARRY STAGE FURTHER THEIR OWN PARTICULAR CRUSADE THROUGHOUT NUMEROUS WIDELY SCATTERED HIGHLY DIVERSIFIED COLONIES PROTECTORATES BRITISH EMPIRE HASTEN DAY BE ABLE ASSUME PREPONDERATING SHARE SUCH VAST HIGHLY MERITORIOUS PIONEERING ENTERPRISE.[18]

In the face of such wide-ranging goals, Hasan Balyuzi's work increased. During the first seven years of the World Crusade he served on five national committees and chaired the European and Asian Teaching Committee. This committee was concerned with opening seven European goal countries and consolidating the Faith in Eire and Hong Kong.

In January 1955 Mr Balyuzi and Hands of the Cause Dr Grossmann and Mr Ioas spoke at the ceremony to dedicate the National Ḥaẓíratu'l-Quds in London. The next year, only five years after the launching of the Africa Campaign, he was in Kampala to convene the first convention of the Bahá'ís of Central and East Africa, called to elect the first Regional Spiritual Assembly of the area.

In October 1957 the Guardian named two British Bahá'ís, Hasan Balyuzi and John Ferraby, as Hands of Cause. The British National Assembly sent a cable to Shoghi Effendi expressing its gratitude for these appointments, and in reply came the Guardian's final message to the British Bahá'ís, dated 11 October 1957: 'CONFIDENT BRITISH COMMUNITY RICHLY DESERVES NEW HONOUR. SHOGHI.'[19]

When Shoghi Effendi passed away less than a month later, it was to Hasan Balyuzi, the Guardian's Afnán cousin, that Rúḥíyyih Khánum first turned. By the evening of 4 November Hands of the Cause John Ferraby and Ugo Giachery were also at her side. Together these Hands attended to the pressing matters precipitated by the Guardian's ascension. Rúḥíyyih Khánum, Hasan Balyuzi and Ugo Giachery selected an appropriate grave site and suitable casket. At the funeral service on 9 November mournful believers filed past the casket for two hours to pay their respects. Beside the grave, a prayer was chanted in Persian, after which Hand of the Cause Hasan Balyuzi read a final prayer in English.

Nine days after the funeral, 26 Hands of the Cause assembled in the Holy Land to consult on the situation facing the worldwide Bahá'í community. During their deliberations at this first Conclave, the assembled Hands, in accordance with the provisions of the Will and Testament of 'Abdu'l-Bahá, elected a body of nine from among their number to serve continuously at the Bahá'í World Centre. Mr Balyuzi was elected among the original nine, and when he was later unable to serve in that capacity, he was designated an alternate Hand in the Holy Land.

As an alternate Hand, Mr Balyuzi spent weeks or even months in Haifa. There he provided invaluable services in preparing the archives for transfer to the International Archives building. His broad knowledge enabled him to identify Tablets and other materials. At the end of long work days, he brought much-needed humour to the Hands in the Eastern Pilgrim House. He attended all the Conclaves of the Hands from 1957 to 1963, undertaking the translation of deliberations in the sessions.

Dr Giachery described Mr Balyuzi as never having recovered from the blow of Shoghi Effendi's death.[20] Nevertheless, in addition to his work at the World Centre, he devoted all the rest of his energies to the successful completion of the Guardian's World Crusade. Within a week of Britain's receipt of the Proclamation of the Hands, he was meeting with representatives of local assemblies and national committees in the Ḥaẓíratu'l-Quds to explain the situation of the Faith. He performed the same service at a teaching conference in Leeds early in 1958, where his talk greatly moved his audience.

Hasan attended British teaching conferences in 1959, 1960 and 1962 and ten conferences of the European Hands between 1958 and 1964. He was present at the Frankfurt international teaching conference in 1958 and at the laying of the cornerstone of the European Temple in 1960. He visited various Bahá'í communities in Britain, including Bangor, Edinburgh and Manchester. He provided a stirring review of British Bahá'í history at the 1960 convention and gave a course on the Covenant that same year at the Harlech summer school. In 1961 he travelled to Ecuador and Peru, representing the World Centre at the first national conventions of these countries. The same year he headed north to Canada, where he visited Indian reservations and was honoured with a pow-wow. At the national commemoration of 'Abdu'l-Bahá's journeys in Britain, Hasan shared the platform with Leroy Ioas as they recalled the Master's visit to England, and in January 1963 he and Dr Mühlschlegel addressed the believers in Edinburgh on the 50th anniversary of 'Abdu'l-Bahá's visit to Scotland. In 1962 Mr Balyuzi attended the first national conventions of the Netherlands and Denmark, representing the World Centre.

Owing to his increased work as a Hand of the Cause, Mr Balyuzi resigned from the National Spiritual Assembly in February 1960. Many believers felt the British Bahá'í community suffered a great loss. However, Hasan continued to consult with the National Assembly as a Hand of the Cause whenever he was in England and as his health permitted. At such meetings he might discuss a dozen subjects. When he could not attend, he sent suggestions, and he advised Assembly officers between meetings.

The first World Congress in 1963 was the last time many Bahá'ís saw

Mr Balyuzi. His stirring closing address at the first session recalling the history of the Faith and providing a vision of the future would be long remembered. Exhausted by years of overwork, he would henceforth devote his ebbing strength to scholarship and to completing the task Shoghi Effendi had set him so many years before, writing the trilogy on the Central Figures of the Faith.

According to Moojan Momen, in the 1960s three major deficiencies existed in the literature of the Faith: almost nothing of an academic nature had appeared for more than 50 years, the history of the Faith was limited to a few books and very little good material had been published since the death of George Townshend in 1957. Mr Balyuzi's work began the process of correcting these deficiencies.

In 1963 an enlarged version of his earlier essay on Bahá'u'lláh was published as *Bahá'u'lláh: The Word Made Flesh.* Mr Balyuzi then set about writing the first of his trilogy. He re-started work on a book about 'Abdu'l-Bahá begun in the 1940s, but soon discovered he needed a separate work on the relationship between E. G. Browne and the Bahá'í Faith. He consequently published *Edward Granville Browne and the Bahá'í Faith* in 1970, delaying publication of *'Abdu'l-Bahá: The Centre of the Covenant of Bahá'u'lláh* until 1971. His writing of the book *The Báb: The Herald of the Day of Days*, published in 1973, was greatly assisted by the work done on his behalf by Moojan Momen in the British Public Record Office and was the first Bahá'í book to make use of official documents from government archives. Three years later, in 1976, he completed *Muḥammad and the Course of Islám*, written because he felt no history of Islám was available that combined accuracy and scholarship with a sympathetic approach to the religion of Muḥammad.

Then, feeling that his short work on Bahá'u'lláh was too brief in comparison to his other books, Mr Balyuzi once again turned his attention to the life of Bahá'u'lláh. Anticipating a work of more than one volume, he painstakingly researched every source, coming across more and more material as he wrote. He had completed one volume, *Bahá'u'lláh, The King of Glory*, and had nearly finished a second when he suddenly passed away. *Bahá'u'lláh* was published shortly after his death, in 1980. His second volume on Bahá'u'lláh, *Eminent Bahá'ís in the Time of Bahá'u'lláh*, was completed by his publisher, Marion Hofman and research assistant, Dr Momen and eventually published in 1985.

Mr Balyuzi intended to publish a series of booklets on the lives of prominent members of the Afnán, family but only one short volume was completed, *Khadíjih-Bagum: The Wife of the Báb*, which was published a year after his death.[21]

In his sketch of Mr Balyuzi in *Studies in Honor of the Late Hasan M. Balyuzi*, Dr Momen commented on Mr Balyuzi's research skills:

> Much of his writing ran counter to present-day styles of scholarly prose. But his work is imbued with two qualities which will cause it to be remembered long after much other material written to such standards has been forgotten. First, was his assiduous pursuit of truth. He would take endless trouble to track down even the most minor fact or date. He would write several letters in pursuit of just one piece of information which might take up only one line in his book. He did not hesitate to discard large sections of his manuscript if his researches left any doubt as to the truth of what he had written . . . Second, was his integrity . . . He wrote nothing for fame or self-advancement. He wrote only what he thought correct after due consideration . . . He always maintained that it was best to tell it 'warts and all'.[22]

Mr Balyuzi would work on several books at once, which helped relieve the fatigue of concentrating on a single manuscript. Marion Hofman remarked:

> Often it was his habit to continue far into the night, and so he would turn for refreshment from writing, to research, to reading for background. It is probable that his mind dwelt on the work in hand almost constantly. He was meticulous in assembling his materials . . . All his books were submitted in his own handwriting, and even quotations were copied by hand to ensure that his choice of deletions would be followed.[23]

The fruit of Mr Balyuzi's indefatigable labours was works described by Dr Giachery as 'gem-like', which 'will remain among the most outstanding writings to enlighten the paths of seekers for centuries to come'.[24]

In October 1979 Mr Balyuzi had a heart attack. He seemed, however, to recover well and visited the Guardian's resting place on 4 November, his first visit for a long time. On 26 November he spoke to the Bahá'ís at the London Ḥaẓíratu'l-Quds on a favourite theme, 'The Power of the Covenant', saying to the friends that he hoped to be with them more often.

He longed to carry to 'Akká and lay at the threshold of the Shrine of Bahá'u'lláh a copy of *Bahá'u'lláh, The King of Glory*. The first copy of his book reached England in February 1980, but rather than see it himself, he asked that it be delivered for special leather binding. Before he could realize his longing, Hasan Balyuzi passed away quietly in his sleep in the early morning hours of 12 February 1980. The volume is now preserved in the International Bahá'í Library.

On 15 February 1980, in the New Southgate Cemetery, Hasan Muvaqqar Balyuzi was buried near the grave of his beloved Guardian in the presence of family and many friends. On the day of his passing, the Universal House of Justice cabled to the Bahá'í world a fitting tribute to the Hand of the Cause of God who had stood so eminently among both the learned and the rulers:

> WITH BROKEN HEARTS ANNOUNCE PASSING DEARLY LOVED HAND CAUSE HASAN BALYUZI. ENTIRE BAHAI WORLD ROBBED ONE OF ITS MOST POWERFUL DEFENDERS MOST RESOURCEFUL HISTORIANS. HIS ILLUSTRIOUS LINEAGE HIS DEVOTED LABOURS DIVINE VINEYARD HIS OUTSTANDING LITERARY WORKS COMBINE IN IMMORTALIZING HIS HONOURED NAME IN ANNALS BELOVED FAITH. CALL ON FRIENDS EVERYWHERE HOLD MEMORIAL GATHERINGS. PRAYING SHRINES HIS EXEMPLARY ACHIEVEMENTS HIS STEADFASTNESS PATIENCE HUMILITY HIS OUTSTANDING SCHOLARLY PURSUITS WILL INSPIRE MANY DEVOTED WORKERS AMONG RISING GENERATIONS FOLLOW HIS GLORIOUS FOOTSTEPS.[25]

# Abu'l-Qásim Faizi
# (Abu'l-Qásim Fayḍí)
# c. 1906–1980

Abu'l-Qásim Faizi. It is a name that rolls magically off the tongue, a name that attracts, whether or not one ever knew the beloved Hand of the Cause. He once told a pilgrim to the Holy Land that each of the Hands possessed some quality of the Guardian, which he then enumerated, concluding that only he lacked this blessing. The pilgrim replied, 'You have the quality of love.'[1]

Mr Faizi carried on a prodigious correspondence with Bahá'ís around the world. Those who were privileged to receive his letters tell of his encouragement, his inspiration and his love. When he was once asked why he kept up such a volume of correspondence, often staying up until very late to do so, he replied that as the Guardian had done this, he could attempt to do no less.

Faizi, as he liked to be called, was born in Qum, Iran, probably in 1906. He did not like the celebration of birthdays apart from those of the Manifestations and did not know the exact date of his own birth.[2]

Faizi's parents were first cousins, and descendants of the eminent Shí'í scholar Mullá Muḥsin-i-Fayḍ. His father was a Bahá'í at heart and his mother a devout follower of Muḥammad. Faizi's early education was in Qum, where he grew up among fanatical Muslims. As a result, he often spoke of Qum with a note of sadness. He enjoyed attending the local gymnasium there, the *zúr-khánih*, a traditional Persian establishment providing both physical exercise and spiritual training. Faizi took every opportunity to slip away from home to watch the sportsmen exercising.

When Faizi was about 14 or 15 years old, the family moved to Ṭihrán, where his life underwent a dramatic change for the better. His father enrolled him in the Bahá'í Tarbíyat School. Here he excelled in both sports and academic studies; in later years he spoke with reverence about his teachers.

In time, Faizi's Bahá'í classmates took him to the character training classes held every Friday. Though he at first did not realize the connection between the classes and the Faith, he was eventually attracted to the Bahá'í teachings and became a believer. When his mother realized that he had converted, she encouraged him to observe the Bahá'í laws, even arising at dawn during the Bahá'í Fast to prepare his breakfast.

After completing his studies at the Tarbíyat School, Faizi spent some time at the American College in Ṭihrán before proceeding, at the age of 19, to the American University at Beirut. Bahá'í students at the university were permitted to make their pilgrimage and visit the Guardian in the Holy Land during their holidays and Faizi, together with fellow student Hasan Balyuzi, travelled to Haifa at every opportunity.

From the moment Faizi met Shoghi Effendi until the end of his life, he was possessed with but one desire: to serve the Guardian. For from that first encounter, he laid his whole heart at his beloved's feet instantly, completely and for ever.

Abu'l-Qásim Faizi and Hasan Balyuzi were kindred souls upon whom Shoghi Effendi poured his favours. Once the Guardian sent them to visit the Mansion of Bahá'u'lláh in Bahjí when it was still occupied by Covenant-breakers. The Mansion and the rooms once occupied by Bahá'u'lláh were, at that time, in terrible condition. The two friends were the first believers permitted to sleep in the Mansion after its restoration. On another occasion, just before Faizi's return to Iran, Shoghi Effendi gave him a small bouquet of flowers to lay at the grave of Keith Ransom-Kehler on his behalf. Faizi also had the privilege of meeting the Greatest Holy Leaf, then in the evening of her life, and was greatly inspired by her.

His studies in Beirut completed, and his degree in English Literature and Education obtained, Faizi made plans to return to Ṭihrán. His intention was to serve at the Tarbíyat School, thus fulfilling the Guardian's wish that Bahá'í youth would consecrate their lives to the service of the Cause. When asked by the Guardian whether the Bahá'í schools in Iran were closed for the nine Bahá'í Holy Days, Faizi replied that he did not believe so. Shoghi Effendi commented that the schools should be closed for the Holy Days even if the government permanently closed them for doing so.

On returning to Iran Faizi undertook a period of compulsory military service. Three weeks before he was due to finish, in 1934, the government of Iran permanently closed all Bahá'í schools after they refused to remain open on Bahá'í Holy Days.

Reluctantly, Faizi accepted a position with the Anglo-Iranian Oil Company in Ṭihrán. He enjoyed a good salary and there were many opportunities to excel in his career, but he was not satisfied. Recalling that Shoghi Effendi had advised him not to defile himself with this world, and assured of his Guardian's prayers, Faizi seized an opportunity to teach the Bahá'í children of the village of Najafábád near Iṣfahán, where the Bahá'í school had also been closed. Surprising his friends and associates, he gave up his position with the oil company and, accompanied by his widowed mother, went to Najafábád, where he spent the next five years teaching some 400 Bahá'í children.

When Shoghi Effendi received a report from the National Spiritual Assembly about Faizi's move, he wrote:

> This spontaneous decision will attract divine confirmation and is a clear proof of the high endeavour, the pure motive, and the self-sacrifice of that favoured servant of the divine Threshold. I am extremely pleased and grateful to him and I pray from the depths of my heart for the success of that active, radiant youth.[3]

In Najafábád Faizi organized classes in the homes of the Bahá'ís, travelling from house to house from dawn through the afternoon. Faizi's mother helped him in many ways. She loved the children and supported her son financially with the little money left by her husband. At about this time, she dreamed of the Báb and became a Bahá'í.

In 1939 Faizi married Gloria 'Alá'í of Ṭihrán, whom he had known for many years. They had two children, May and Naysan.

In Najafábád Faizi regularly attended Bahá'í meetings and visited the Bahá'í friends, inspiring them with stories. He loved to listen to the older generation talking about the days of Bahá'u'lláh and the courage of the believers. This was perhaps the beginning of his lifelong penchant for collecting stories, which he then shared with Bahá'ís around the world.

From Najafábád Faizi went to Qazvín, where he organized Bahá'í classes for all ages, particularly youth.

In 1941 Shoghi Effendi called upon the Iranian Bahá'ís to pioneer to neighbouring countries. Faizi responded immediately, setting out with his wife for Baghdád, where they hoped to obtain a visa to one of the countries in the Arabian Peninsula. Forced to remain in the Iraqi capital for a year before the visa was granted, Faizi brought a new spirit to the Bahá'í community. He began regular study classes for their youth, encouraged new believers and made friends among the Bahá'í families.

Near the end of their year in Baghdád, and with their money running out, Mr Faizi was offered a job teaching at a secondary school in Bahrain. When he arrived on the island in December 1942 to take up the position, the authorities learned he was a Bahá'í and withdrew their offer of employment. Fortunately, the Faizis were not deported. Despite this setback, the terrible heat, lack of water, malnourishment, discomfort and hostility, the Faizis, knowing that Shoghi Effendi had asked pioneers to remain at their posts, remained in Bahrain.

They were not permitted to mention the Faith, so strange rumours circulated about their beliefs. Slowly and painstakingly, Faizi, in his sweet, gentle manner, began to win the hearts of the people. After some seven years other pioneers arrived in the countries along the coast of Arabia. When they encountered difficulties, Mr Faizi was able to strengthen them through his wonderful letters, encouraging them to remain at their posts.

The pioneers in Arabia loved Mr Faizi. To them he was a father and a close friend, and they looked to him as their example. The Guardian called him 'the Spiritual Conqueror of Arabia', writing that 'The unceasing meritorious services of that radiant youth in these past years illumine the annals of the Cause of God and set an example for all to follow.'[4]

Faizi had a natural gift for healing the ills that afflict souls. For instance, he befriended a notorious thief in Bahrain who had spent much of his time in prison. Whenever he met the man on the street, Faizi would send purchases he had made with the man and give him some money for his trouble. Once the items entrusted to the thief were expensive. Nevertheless, without fail, the man always delivered Faizi's goods, never once stealing a single item.

Mr Faizi attended the intercontinental conference in New Delhi in 1953 and afterwards travelled to Australia and New Zealand with Hand of the Cause Mr Furútan to translate for him. He was in Europe in October 1957 when he learned the news that he had been appointed a Hand of the Cause by the Guardian. Only a few weeks later, the Guardian passed away in England. Grief-stricken, Mr Faizi travelled to London to attend the funeral, at which he chanted the Prayer for the Dead.

He then attended the first Conclave of the Hands of the Cause, doing much of the translation between English and Persian. He was elected one of the nine Custodians – Hands of the Cause resident in the Holy Land. He and his family then moved to Haifa, where Mr Faizi served as a link between the Hands from the East and those from the West, owing to his knowledge of both Persian and English.

From this time, Mr Faizi began to travel widely, his knowledge of Persian, Arabic, French and English, his warm personality, humour and engaging public-speaking ability enabling him to serve Bahá'í communities in all parts of the globe. He was a frequent visitor to Bahá'í summer and winter schools in Europe and elsewhere, teaching classes on subjects such as The Book of Certitude.

In 1960 Charles Mason Remey claimed to be the second Guardian, a baseless claim that was, nonetheless, accepted by several members of the National Spiritual Assembly of France. Mr Faizi was sent to France by the Custodians to deal with the situation. As a result of his efforts, three members repented their actions, but five others did not, causing the National Spiritual Assembly to be disbanded by the Custodians. Under his guidance, the Local Spiritual Assembly of Paris acted as the central Assembly for France until the new National Spiritual Assembly could be established.[5]

A revealing expression of the spirit of Mr Faizi was his admiration of the Universal House of Justice, elected for the first time in April 1963. Six months after its formation he wrote:

> The first and foremost news that I must share with you is the health, unity and the enthusiasm of the members of the Universal House of Justice. It is simply miraculous that a group of people never knowing each other before, never working with each other and every one belonging to a special kind of work and interest become so amalgamated together that today they are one body and one soul. Such unity attracts the light of guidance and that is the sole reason why we witness the light of confirmation, strength and God's wishes and desires even in every word they utter. This makes every Bahá'í happy and determined to do more.[6]

Mr Faizi travelled extensively, often representing the Universal House of

Justice at Bahá'í conferences and events. He advised National Spiritual Assemblies, met heads of state and world dignitaries, gave public addresses and private talks, conducted study classes for the Bahá'ís, visited the pioneers at their posts, encouraged the youth to serve the Cause, inspired the friends through his writings and translations and continued his voluminous correspondence. In 1968 he visited Malaysia, Thailand, Vietnam, Indonesia, the Philippines, Taiwan, Korea, Japan, Hawaii, the United States mainland, Canada and the British Isles and attended the oceanic conference in Sicily and the commemoration in Haifa of the centenary of Bahá'u'lláh's arrival in the Holy Land. In 1969 he visited India, Sri Lanka, Malaysia, Laos, Hong Kong, the Philippines, Australia and New Zealand, and attended the first youth conference of the South Pacific, in Western Samoa. In 1970 he travelled to Hawaii, Guam, the Philippines, Singapore, India, Ghana and Cameroon. In 1972 he visited most of the countries of western Europe, attending the Bahá'í youth conferences at Padua and Plön. In 1974 he travelled throughout the Americas and on to Europe. In 1977 he travelled to Malaysia, Singapore, Australia, New Zealand, Tonga, Papua New Guinea, Fiji, the New Hebrides and Samoa.

In his later years Mr Faizi suffered from diabetes and heart problems. As his health gradually deteriorated, he was confined to bed more than once during his travels. Once he had to be rushed to hospital in the middle of a lecture. Eventually he was unable to travel, but he continued to keep up his correspondence and to receive pilgrims in his home.

In addition to writing to his many friends, Mr Faizi published a number of books and articles. Some of his best-known works in Persian and English are *Payám-i-Dúst va Bahár-i-Ṣad-u-Bíst* (1963–64); *Dástán-i-Dústán* (1964–65); the translation into Persian of *The Priceless Pearl* (1969); *Three Meditations on the Eve of November the Fourth* (1970); *Explanation of the Emblem of the Greatest Name* (1970–71); *Our Precious Trusts* (1973); *The Wonder Lamp* (1975); and the translation into English of *Stories from the Delight of Hearts* (1980).

Near the end of his life, Mr Faizi was described as having an aura of pure light about him. When he passed away on 19 November 1980 he left behind on his desk some gifts for the pilgrims – quotations from the writings in his own calligraphy.

On his passing the Universal House of Justice cabled to the Bahá'í world:

HEARTS FILLED WITH SORROW PASSING INDEFATIGABLE SELF-SACRIFICING DEARLY LOVED HAND CAUSE GOD ABUL-QASIM FAIZI. ENTIRE BAHAI WORLD MOURNS HIS LOSS. HIS EARLY OUTSTANDING ACHIEVEMENTS IN CRADLE FAITH THROUGH EDUCATION CHILDREN YOUTH STIMULATION FRIENDS PROMOTION TEACHING WORK PROMPTED BELOVED GUARDIAN DESCRIBE HIM AS LUMINOUS DISTINGUISHED ACTIVE YOUTH. HIS SUBSEQUENT PIONEERING WORK IN LANDS BORDERING IRAN WON HIM APPELLATION SPIRITUAL CONQUEROR THOSE LANDS. FOLLOWING HIS APPOINTMENT HAND CAUSE HE PLAYED INVALUABLE PART WORK HANDS HOLY LAND TRAVELLED WIDELY PENNED HIS LITERARY WORKS CONTINUED HIS EXTENSIVE INSPIRING CORRESPONDENCE WITH HIGH AND LOW YOUNG AND OLD UNTIL AFTER LONG ILLNESS HIS SOUL WAS RELEASED AND WINGED ITS FLIGHT ABHA KINGDOM. CALL ON FRIENDS EVERYWHERE HOLD BEFITTING MEMORIAL GATHERINGS HIS HONOUR, INCLUDING SPECIAL COMMEMORATIVE MEETINGS HIS NAME IN HOUSES WORSHIP ALL CONTINENTS. MAY HIS SHINING EXAMPLE CONSECRATION CONTINUE INSPIRE HIS ADMIRERS EVERY LAND. PRAYING HOLY SHRINES HIS NOBLE RADIANT SOUL MAY BE IMMERSED IN OCEAN DIVINE MERCY CONTINUE ITS UNINTERRUPTED PROGRESS IN INFINITE WORLDS BEYOND.[7]

# Harold Collis Featherstone
## 1913–1990

An event early in Collis Featherstone's life was to influence his spiritual destiny. One day he was travelling home by train. Deeply involved in reading, he did not notice that the train had reached his station. As the train pulled out, he started to jump onto the sand between the two sets of tracks. Although he was hurrying, something warned him to exit from the other side of the train. He immediately turned and jumped from the other side. At that exact moment an express train came roaring through on the side he had decided so instantaneously to avoid. Afterwards he would wonder what had caused him to change his mind so that his life was saved.

Collis was born 15 months before the start of the First World War, on 5 May 1913, in the historic town of Quorn in the state of South Australia. At the time of his birth, 'Abdu'l-Bahá was concluding His Western tour with a third visit to Paris. Shoghi Effendi, under whose guidance Collis would serve upon becoming a Bahá'í, was attending school in Beirut.

The son of a railway station master who worked for the South Australian Railways, the boy was named Harold Collis, but was known as Col or Collis. His father's job took the family to several towns, but Collis's most memorable years were spent in Smithfield. Between 1925 and 1928 he daily travelled the 28 kilometres to Adelaide, where he attended Adelaide High School. His school report said he was 'diligent, well-behaved and polite, thoroughly reliable and straightforward'.[1] His handwriting was neat and controlled, a skill that would attract comment throughout his life. He enjoyed cycling and played cricket, batting with his left hand, and tennis, with his right hand. He was in all other respects right-handed.

Collis's search into spiritual matters began in earnest during his youth in Smithfield. He was confirmed in the Church of England at 15 years of age. Since he had not been baptized in the church before his confirmation, church authorities were wont to remind him of the error. This unforgiving attitude caused him some uneasiness, while one event confirmed his misgivings about the church's teaching on the resurrection of the body: a violent storm exposed the decomposing remains of his pet dog. These incidents influenced Collis's spiritual search.

Collis moved to Adelaide in the 1930s, where he attended up to three church services of different denominations nearly every Sunday. He was impressed by the Rev. G. E. Hale, a Unitarian minister who included quotations from the scriptures of other great religions in his sermons. This inspired him to visit the public library to investigate other religions.

Meanwhile Collis was developing his professional career by studying accounting at night school and working in an office. For the four years from 1932 he worked for a large engineering firm where he learned the fitting, turning and die-making trade, specializing in metal die construction and design, and in the mass production of components. This experience enabled him to set up in 1938 a precision engineering partnership and factory making pressed metal parts, a business which he owned for over 35 years. He became recognized in the industry for his excellent workmanship and for his fairness and integrity in the conduct of his business. He bought out his partner in the 1950s.

Collis formed another partnership in 1938: he married Madge Green on 5 March. They lived at Albert Park in the Port Adelaide area. Between 1939 and 1954 they had five children – four girls and one boy.

One day two intrepid Bahá'ís passed their way. Bertha Dobbins and Katherine Harcus had left Adelaide in the spirit of the Dawn-Breakers on foot in order to teach the Faith in the Port Adelaide area, a distance of some 14 kilometres. On their return trek, the two exhausted women paused and rested against the posting at a railway and road intersection at Albert Park in the Woodville area. There they called on the Greatest Name for a home to be opened to the Faith. The Featherstones' home was the nearest one to them.

Some time later a friend of Madge invited her to hear something important from a former school teacher. Madge looked forward to this outing with the children, eagerly anticipating what her friend's former teacher had to say. Thus it was that in 1944 Madge heard the Message of

Bahá'u'lláh for the first time, from Bertha Dobbins.

Madge began to attend afternoon Bahá'í meetings with her three small children. When she told Collis about them and showed him the Bahá'í literature she had received, he was instantly attracted. When he learned that the Faith was for all the peoples of the earth, he asked for a good book on the Faith to read. Bertha responded by lending Madge a copy of *The Dawn-Breakers*. Collis proceeded to study it that very night. When he reached page 92, he read the Báb's address to the Letters of the Living:

> O My beloved friends! You are the bearers of the name of God in this Day. You have been chosen as the repositories of His mystery. It behoves each one of you to manifest the attributes of God, and to exemplify by your deeds and words the signs of His righteousness, His power and glory. The very members of your body must bear witness to the loftiness of your purpose, the integrity of your life, the reality of your faith, and the exalted character of your devotion . . . O My Letters! Verily I say, immensely exalted is this Day above the days of the Apostles of old. Nay, immeasurable is the difference! You are the witnesses of the Dawn of the promised Day of God. You are the partakers of the mystic chalice of His Revelation. Gird up the loins of endeavour . . . Purge your hearts of worldly desires, and let angelic virtues be your adorning . . . The time is come when naught but the purest motive, supported by deeds of stainless purity, can ascend to the throne of the Most High and be acceptable unto Him . . . Beseech the Lord your God to grant that no earthly entanglements, no worldly affections, no ephemeral pursuits, may tarnish the purity, or embitter the sweetness, of that grace which flows through you . . . Scatter throughout the length and breadth of this land, and, with steadfast feet and sanctified hearts, prepare the way for His coming. Heed not your weaknesses and frailty; fix your gaze upon the invincible power of the Lord, your God, the Almighty . . . Arise in His name, put your trust wholly in Him, and be assured of ultimate victory.[2]

Collis realized this Message was from God. His search had yielded the fairest fruit. Meanwhile the Featherstones opened their home for evening Bahá'í meetings, fulfilling the prayer of Bertha Dobbins and Katherine Harcus when they had called on the Greatest Name across from the Featherstones' home. The firesides continued for several months, with Collis studying books of the writings of Bahá'u'lláh. In December 1944 he and Madge became members of the Bahá'í Faith, among the first 'young' people in the area.

The firesides continued. Although the greater Adelaide community consisted of only 30 to 40 believers, lavish suppers and genuine dedication accompanied the meetings. Usually a speaker gave a short address on some aspect of the Faith. The Featherstones brought their own brand of enthusiasm into the activities of the community, and the numbers of believers grew.

At the time that Collis and Madge became Bahá'ís, the national Bahá'í community comprised three Local Spiritual Assemblies; the National Spiritual Assembly of Australia and New Zealand had been established only ten years previously. Yet the Featherstones had the impression that there were many believers throughout Australia, owing, no doubt, to the positive energy the friends generated. In years to come, whenever Collis reflected on his early days as a believer, he would recall the joy and excitement that prevailed among the Bahá'ís.

In 1945 Collis and Madge met Clara 'Mother' Dunn, who arrived in Adelaide in May for a visit organized by Bertha Dobbins. In July that year she stayed for a week at the Featherstones' home. Mother Dunn, together with her husband, had established the Cause in Australia in 1920. Hyde Dunn had passed away in 1941, much to Collis's regret.[3]

Often when he was not satisfied with the answers he received from individuals or institutions to questions about the Faith, Collis would write to Shoghi Effendi for advice. When he wrote in 1945 with a list of questions he had been unable to resolve, the following message in Shoghi Effendi's own hand was penned on the reply: 'May the Spirit of Bahá'u'lláh bless and reinforce your efforts, and may He aid you to obtain a clearer understanding of the essentials of His Faith, and to advance its best interests, and contribute to the consolidation of its God-given institutions.'[4]

In the same letter, writing on his behalf, the Guardian's secretary gave these guidelines to Collis: 'The Guardian hopes you, your wife, and the other young people who are so active in the Cause in your neighbourhood will render it many services, promote unity and love in the community, strengthen the administrative foundations of the Faith, and attract many new souls to it.'[5]

As well as receiving these inspiring messages from the Sign of God on earth, Collis and Madge were encouraged by Bertha and Joe Dobbins to be bold in their service to the Cause of God – to establish an assembly in their area, to teach actively, to travel for the Faith and to attend Bahá'í summer schools. The Featherstones embraced all of these challenges.

They attended their first Bahá'í summer school in 1947. In later years they took the whole family, travelling the 3,000 kilometres by car and caravan to economize. Madge made almost all her own and the children's clothes, just so the family could afford such involvement in Bahá'í activities.

In 1947 the Six Year Plan for the Australian and New Zealand Bahá'ís was launched. This plan provided an impetus for sustained teaching activities and the expansion of the Faith. In 1948 the Woodville Assembly was established, which included Albert Park. The community invited the National Assembly members as well as Mother Dunn to attend a public meeting announcing the Assembly's formation. Approximately 100 people attended the function, which attracted much publicity.

In 1946 Collis and Harold Fitzner initiated monthly teaching trips to Kingston, a community south of Adelaide, which required them to travel several hours by bus. Eventually Collis was able to buy a car, enabling him to take other Bahá'ís, including Mother Dunn, to Kingston. The Featherstones continued to teach in Kingston until 1953, but they concentrated on consolidating the Woodville community and on establishing a Local Spiritual Assembly in Port Adelaide. During this period Collis served for several years on the Regional Teaching Committee in South Australia.

Although he had attended the National Convention as an observer twice before, Collis did not attend as a delegate until 1949, when he was elected to the National Spiritual Assembly. He served on the body, often as chairman, until 1962.

In the mean time the Featherstones exerted an ever-widening and beneficial influence on the believers in South Australia. They gave deepening classes, hosted firesides, supported teaching activities, attended committee meetings and set up public meetings. In 1953, at the end of the Six Year Plan, they helped form the Local Spiritual Assembly of Port Adelaide by selling their house in Albert Park and moving as homefront pioneers. Thus was the Six Year Plan completed with last-minute effort.

Collis got things done. When Bahá'í books were unobtainable in Australia, he simply obtained a license and bought many books from the United States. Later, when the government experienced a difficulty with its balance of payments, it only allowed an import quota to those who had purchased books in the previous year. As the National Spiritual Assembly needed to buy books and could not get an import licence, Collis allowed it to use his quota. When his cigarette smoking interfered with his desire to fast, he gave up the habit. When he desired to present the Bahá'í teachings more effectively, he took a course in public speaking. Little wonder that Collis was once described as 'spirit in action'.[6]

In addition to their many Bahá'í activities, Collis and Madge helped European and English migrants to settle in Australia and to be reunited with their loved ones. They assisted the Bahá'ís of the Philippines by sending books and clothing after the Second World War. Collis also served on the committee of the District and Bush Nursing Society (DBNS) until their move to Port Adelaide.

The Featherstones' ninth year as Bahá'ís was especially significant. Having already achieved many victories, they joyously marked the commencement of the Ten Year Crusade by attending the interconti-nental conference in New Delhi and going on pilgrimage.

The New Delhi conference focused on the goals of the Ten Year Crusade, those attending deliberating on the steps needed to open the Asiatic and South Pacific areas to the Faith. The Featherstones were overwhelmed by their first experience of the coming together of so many believers of different racial, religious and cultural backgrounds.

From New Delhi, Collis and Madge travelled to the Holy Land for their pilgrimage to the Holy Shrines. They also had the privilege of meeting Shoghi Effendi, by whom they were further overwhelmed. As Madge was to later record:

> If we needed any further confirmation of the power of Bahá'u'lláh's words to transform and bring about peace on earth, we saw it demonstrated by the Guardian, who inspired the Bahá'ís the world over and guided the establish-ment of Bahá'í Institutions around the world. We were unbelievably happy and uplifted.[7]

During the Featherstones' pilgrimage, the Guardian praised Hyde and Clara Dunn as true conquerors because they remained at their posts. He spoke in great detail to the pilgrims about the Hands of the Cause and their work in teaching and protecting the Faith. Only two years before, he had appointed the first living Hands and had recently announced that Auxiliary Boards would be appointed for the first time at Riḍván 1954. Collis asked the Guardian to elaborate on this subject, which was a new development in the Cause; he 'was keen to understand how the Guardian saw it all working'.[8] Shoghi Effendi therefore elucidated such themes as the role of the Hands and their Auxiliary Boards; God's plan and the divine plan; the relationship between individual Bahá'ís and government; the need for Assembly members to be frank, wise and uncompromising in their relationship with the authorities and to demonstrate that Bahá'ís are patriotic but apolitical; the role and responsibilities of the pioneers; and the role of Australia and Japan, through which runs a 'spiritual axis' whose 'northern and southern poles will act as powerful magnets'.[9] Madge and Collis returned from their pilgrimage renewed and full of energy and enthusiasm.

In 1953 six members of the National Spiritual Assembly left Australia as pioneers. Owing to family and business commitments, Collis was not among them, but he and Madge offered to support Bertha Dobbins in pioneering to the New Hebrides, for which she was named a Knight of Bahá'u'lláh. The Featherstones' financial support to her continued for many years.

In 1952 Clara Dunn was appointed a Hand of the Cause by Shoghi Effendi. In 1954 Shoghi Effendi established the Auxiliary Boards to assist the Hands. At the Australian National Convention in 1954 Clara appointed Collis Featherstone and Thelma Perks the first Auxiliary Board members for the 'Australian Continent', which included New Zealand and the Pacific region. Feeling quite unworthy of his new role, Collis also found himself secretary of the Asian Teaching Committee, established to assist in the settlement of pioneers mainly in the Pacific region.

It was as a Board member that Collis took the first of his many overseas trips when he visited New Zealand and Fiji at the end of 1954. On this occasion his task was to inspire and encourage isolated pioneers and to deepen the new islander Bahá'ís. The next year he travelled more extensively in Papua New Guinea and the Solomon Islands, while in 1956 he visited Indonesia. As a member and as secretary of the Asian Teaching Committee, Collis was very involved in the production of a regular newsletter for the pioneers called *Koala News*. The newsletter became a lifeline of support and news to the pioneers and Collis often worked late into the night to bring it out on time. When an important message arrived from Shoghi Effendi during the day, Madge would type it out and duplicate it so that Collis could rush it to the post office before midnight.

As a National Assembly member, Collis was deeply involved during the early years of the Crusade in various legal matters, such as securing the Assembly's by-laws, the incorporation of local spiritual assemblies and the recognition of the Bahá'í marriage ceremony. When the Guardian advised Collis in 1955 that he 'attached the utmost importance to the Incorporation of the Local Assemblies',[10] he determinedly pursued this objective. Whatever the goals of the Crusade, Collis was systematic and relentless in following them.

On Monday morning 7 October 1957 Collis received a phone call from the secretary of the National Spiritual Assembly, Noel Walker, about a cable that had just been received from the Guardian. Whenever a letter or cable came from Shoghi Effendi, the believers would eagerly anticipate its contents. Collis in particular would get very excited. This time, however, the cable shocked him. Madge recalled that it 'hit him like a bombshell'.[11] Informing his business partner that he'd just received some disturbing news, Collis took the remainder of the day off. The cable which so disturbed Collis read:

> ANNOUNCE YOUR ELEVATION RANK HAND CAUSE CONFIDENT NEW HONOUR WILL ENABLE YOU RISE GREATER HEIGHTS SERVICE BELOVED FAITH.[12]

Less than a month later the Guardian passed away. Collis's life underwent dramatic changes. Not only was he now one of the Chief Stewards upon whose shoulders the fate of the entire Bahá'í world depended but he would also travel extensively throughout the Australasian region and beyond as a Hand of the Cause. He rearranged the management of his business in such a way that he was able to attend to his new responsibilities, maintain a growing correspondence with his Auxiliary Board members, individuals and institutions, and look after his family.

Following Shoghi Effendi's passing, Collis travelled with Clara Dunn to Haifa for the first Conclave of the Hands of the Cause. There they learned the devastating news that the Guardian had left no will and hence no heir. The Hands of the Cause thus took responsibility for completing the goals of the Ten Year Crusade.

Initially Collis's responsibilities continued to be mainly in the Australasian region, where the establishment of a Regional Spiritual Assembly for the Pacific was pressing. After the formation of the Assembly in Suva in 1959, Collis was able to direct his efforts further afield. During the remainder of the World Crusade he made 29 visits to 14 countries in Australasia and Asia, travelled to 9 countries in Europe and 5 in Central America, and went six times to the Holy Land, mostly to attend the Conclaves of the Hands of the Cause. He had the good fortune on his way to the fifth Conclave in 1961 to pass near the Most Great House of Bahá'u'lláh in Baghdád and to visit the most Hallowed Spot where Bahá'u'lláh had declared His mission 98 years before, in the Garden of Riḍván.

Ever self-sacrificing, Collis used his annual Christmas holiday period in 1958–59 to visit the Maoris, at the request of the National Spiritual Assembly of New Zealand. In 1961 he took the place of Hand of the Cause John Robarts, who had fallen ill, on an extensive trip through Central America. The gruelling itinerary exhausted Collis and he required six months to recover.

Collis was very conscious of the importance of each moment. He used to tell the believers with whom he met that they were making history now. He collected and bound copies of early Bahá'í magazines, *Star of the West*, the *Australian Bahá'í Quarterly* (later called the *Australian Bahá'í Bulletin*), the American *Bahá'í News* and the *Herald of the South*. He kept detailed records of correspondence, programmes, itineraries and reports of all his travels, which he later put together in volumes and bound. He collected photographs and became himself a photographer and film developer. When he travelled to India and to the Holy Land, he made two 16mm silent colour movie films entitled *East Meets West* and *Bahá'í Holy Places in Israel*, which he later used extensively and effectively in teaching. Shoghi Effendi provided the title for the second of these. Collis made a tape recording of Mother Dunn relating her experience of meeting 'Abdu'l-Bahá in San Francisco in 1912, and he made a 16mm colour film at the November 1958 Conclave showing the 25 Hands of the Cause in attendance.

Collis resigned from the National Spiritual Assembly of Australia in 1962 in order to devote more time to his duties as a Hand of the Cause. In 1963 the first Universal House of Justice was elected by the members of 56 National Spiritual Assemblies. Collis would later fondly recall the meetings of the newly elected House of Justice with the Hands of the Cause at the London Bahá'í Centre at 27 Rutland Gate and the sense of relief the Hands felt that God was at last enthroned in this living institution.

Following the first World Congress in 1963, Collis travelled extensively during the next five years, making 66 visits to 42 countries in all continents. When his Auxiliary Board was expanded from four to nine members in 1964 and his territory of responsibility extended to include north-east and south-east Asia, Collis arose to his herculean tasks with such vigour that he knew all the Bahá'ís, their strengths, problems and needs in this vast region of the world.

The believers were overjoyed to meet Collis when he came to their countries. His love and radiance instilled in them a new confidence and vision. He was described as the 'essence of detachment' and 'in harmony with the spiritual side of life'. He, on the other hand, often lamented and agonized over his keenly felt inability to fulfil his obligations to his children as a result of his extended travels and the paperwork connected with his business. He was known to fret about his business and the end-of-month figures. Nevertheless, he dearly loved his children and he had no cause to worry about his business affairs.

Between 1968 and 1976 Collis made 126 visits to 49 countries in all but one continent of the globe. He attended three of eight oceanic and continental conferences, in Singapore, Suva and Sapporo, during 1971. In 1976 he was present at the international teaching conferences in Anchorage and Paris.

In 1976 the Universal House of Justice asked Collis to make himself totally free to travel. This meant selling his engineering firm. The next year he and Madge moved from Adelaide to Rockhampton, central Queensland. During the 36 years of his international travels, Collis made 529 visits to 108 countries, visiting many of them more than once and averaging more than 14 journeys a year. He also made innumerable visits to all parts of Australia, many by car and caravan. He officially represented the Universal House of Justice at several conferences and at the inaugural conventions of a number of national spiritual assemblies.

An example of Collis's extremely busy schedule is provided by his itinerary for 1981–82, when he was approaching his seventieth year:

1981

January: Conference at Australian House of Worship on functioning of Boards of Counsellors. National Teaching Conference in New South Wales.

February–May: A 72-day journey to nine National Spiritual Assembly areas and scores of islands and communities in the Pacific.

June: Visited all major towns and adjacent areas in North Queensland, approximately 3,000 km by road, giving many firesides and public meetings.

July: Attended Teaching Conference in South Queensland and then on to Toowoomba and Brisbane, giving firesides and press, radio and TV interviews, visiting sick Bahá'ís in hospital and concluding with a Counsellors' conference.

August: Attended an Institute on the Seven Year Plan in Wollongong, met with the National Spiritual Assembly in Sydney and participated in a conference for Auxiliary Board Members in Australia.

September: Visited 18 Australian cities covering four states.

October: Attended Counsellors' conference in Adelaide, South Australia, spoke at public meetings and visited innumerable Bahá'í communities.

November–December: Travelled to Malaysia, Thailand, Burma, Sri Lanka, Singapore and Indonesia.

1982

February: Special Auxiliary Board Member Conference for Assistants in Australia, at Yerrinbool Bahá'í School.

April–August: Four-month round the world trip of 19 countries. Highlights included the International Conference in Manila in May and the International Conference in Dublin in June where he represented the Universal House of Justice.

September: International Conference at Canberra.

October: Conference for Auxiliary Board Members and their Assistants at Yerrinbool.

December: Two-month visit to the Philippines, Japan, Korea, Taiwan, Hong Kong, Thailand, Malaysia, Singapore and Australia.[13]

Madge accompanied Collis on most of his travels. His knowledge of travel routes and sectors was invaluable. Often he showed travel agents the most economical way of travelling across the complex island chains of the Pacific, thus getting good value for money.

Collis suffered two heart attacks in 1986 and one in 1988. Nevertheless, he persevered with his travels, visiting Bahá'ís in remote villages and islands where access was possible only by foot, bicycle or dugout canoe. Howard Harwood, one of the Counsellors who travelled in the island areas of Australasia, wrote of Collis's travels: 'One thing I soon discovered was that wherever I went, no matter how remote, Collis had been there ahead of me. He was very well known and respected everywhere.'[14]

On all his travels Collis shared the message of Bahá'u'lláh whenever the opportunity arose or could be arranged. He strove to protect the believers by making government authorities fully aware of the Faith and its principles. This meant that he met many people of influence, including heads of state, chiefs and prime ministers. He believed in the importance of making friends for the Faith.

As a speaker, Collis liked to relax his audiences with funny stories which illustrated spiritual principles. He would exhort the believers constantly to deepen themselves in the holy writings as well as to study the letters and writings of the Guardian and the Universal House of Justice. The writings were to him a mine, whose gems he shared with all the friends. He carried with him his own book of selected quotations, together with well-worn and highlighted copies of the Wills of both Bahá'u'lláh and 'Abdu'l-Bahá, from which he often quoted.

Collis believed that only the best would do for the Cause of God. Himself conscious and disciplined towards the value of money, he lived frugally but spent willingly for the Faith. At the same time, he was sensitive to the spirit of the Faith and the power of the words of Bahá'u'lláh to move himself and others. A practical man, Collis kept up with world events over a short wave radio to which he often listened until late at night.

On 14 September 1990 Collis and Madge journeyed to Asia, where they planned to visit Lahore, Pakistan, for an international youth conference, passing through New Delhi, Rawalpindi and Karachi. In Kathmandu, Nepal, Collis suffered a fatal heart attack on 29 September. He was laid to rest in the Bahá'í cemetery, which overlooks the beautiful valley of Kathmandu, under the snow-capped peaks of the Himalayas.

The Universal House of Justice remembered Collis's sterling qualities and services in a cable to the Bahá'í world of 1 October 1990:

> DEEPLY GRIEVED ANNOUNCE PASSING VALIANT HAND CAUSE GOD COLLIS FEATHERSTONE WHILE VISITING KATHMANDU, NEPAL, COURSE EXTENSIVE JOURNEY ASIA. HIS NOTABLE ACCOMPLISHMENTS AS STAUNCH, FEARLESS DEFENDER COVENANT, HIS UNCEASING COMMITMENT PROPAGATION CAUSE ALL PARTS WORLD, ESPECIALLY PACIFIC REGION, HIS UNREMITTING PERSEVERANCE FOSTERING ESTABLISHMENT LOCAL, NATIONAL INSTITUTIONS ADMINISTRATIVE ORDER, HIS EXEMPLARY DEVOTION TO WRITINGS FAITH, HIS OUTSTANDING PERSONAL QUALITIES UNSWERVING LOYALTY, ENTHUSIASM, ZEAL AND DEDICATION, DISTINGUISH HIS MANIFOLD SERVICES THROUGHOUT MANY DECADES. OFFERING PRAYERS

HOLY SHRINES BOUNTIFUL REWARD HIS RADIANT SOUL ABHA KINGDOM. ADVISE FRIENDS EVERYWHERE HOLD BEFITTING MEMORIAL GATHERINGS, PARTICULARLY IN MASHRIQU'L-ADHKARS, RECOGNITION HIS MAGNIFICENT ACHIEVEMENTS.[15]

# John Graham Ferraby
# 1914–1973

John Ferraby was an Englishman from a liberal Jewish family whose ancestors had migrated from the Netherlands to England in the early 1800s. He was the son of Ida Oppenheim and Harry Friedeberg. John's father was connected with naval outfitting at Portsmouth, England. After the Nazis came to power, the family changed its name from the German-sounding Friedeberg to Ferraby.

Born just eight months before the outset of the First World War, on 9 January 1914, John was brought up in Southsea, Hampshire, where he lived until his father died in 1936. The family then moved to London. John was educated at Malvern College, an English public school, and won a major scholarship to King's College, Cambridge, where he studied mathematics and experimental psychology.

After leaving university, John fell ill for a time and was thus exempted from conscription into the armed forces, which was introduced in the 1930s. He worked for a company called Mass Observation that was involved with research into public opinion, largely on the statistical side, and he later joined the British Export Trade Organization.

When he was 27 years old John learned about the Bahá'í Faith from a friend, Victor Cofman. He went to the library and found John Esslemont's book, *Bahá'u'lláh and the New Era*. His curiosity piqued, he tried to find out more from the publisher, and when this avenue failed he located the London Bahá'ís through the telephone directory. He wished to talk to some Bahá'ís but found it difficult to meet them, as the Bahá'í centre was often closed owing to the 'blitz'. Eventually he succeeded in contacting the Bahá'ís, including Hasan Balyuzi. He spent every evening talking with them and after two weeks decided to become a Bahá'í himself. From this time on the Bahá'í Faith took precedence over everything else in his life:

> John's whole life as a Bahá'í was one of activity and intense devotion. From the moment of his declaration the Faith came absolutely first with him and nothing else mattered, and this was true until the end of his life, whatever his circumstances and condition.[1]

The following Riḍván, 1942, John was elected to both the National Spiritual Assembly of the British Isles and the London Spiritual Assembly. In 1943 he married Dorothy Cansdale, who had become a Bahá'í in 1934 and whom he had met at the Bahá'í centre in 1941. She had been active in the London Bahá'í youth group in the 1930s and in 1941 had been elected to the National Spiritual Assembly. In 1945 the couple's daughter, Bridget (Brigitte), was born.

In 1946 John was elected secretary of the National Spiritual Assembly. At first he worked in his spare time, using a room in his home as an office, but within four years his responsibilities required his full attention. In 1950 the National Spiritual Assembly resolved to pay him for his services. Shoghi Effendi agreed with this decision:

> The Guardian approves your resolution to keep Mr Ferraby as paid secretary of the Assembly. He deeply appreciates Mr Ferraby's devoted services.[2]

In the early 1950s the National Spiritual Assembly of the British Isles began to look for a suitable building to purchase as a national Ḥaẓíratu'l-Quds in London. A large, several-storey house was eventually found in the fashionable Knightsbridge district and was purchased in 1954. John handled the negotiations, surveys and planning applications and persuaded the Westminster City Council to approve 27 Rutland Gate as a Bahá'í centre. The Ferraby family moved into the top floor flat in December 1954, and lived there until the end of 1959.

In addition to his work as secretary of the National Assembly, John managed the British Bahá'í Publishing Trust. In 1951 the two-year 'Africa Campaign' was launched, designed to open the African continent to the Bahá'í Faith. From 1951 to 1956 John was a member of the Africa Committee, which was charged with settling Bahá'í pioneers on the continent. Many of the African territories were British colonies or protectorates, and John used his status as the secretary of the National Assembly to establish a good relationship with the British Colonial Office and thereby assist Bahá'ís to settle in many parts of Africa. The Africa Campaign also called for the translation of a simple introductory booklet about the Bahá'í Faith into twelve African languages. John wrote the booklet, found translators and oversaw the printing and publication of the translations. In 1953 he attended the intercontinental conferences in Kampala and Stockholm.

Like many Bahá'ís inspired by the Guardian's call in 1953 to take the Faith to every corner of the globe, the Ferrabys arose to pioneer at the beginning of the Ten Year Crusade. However, Shoghi Effendi cabled on 22 July 1953:

> ADVISE FERRABYS REMAIN ENGLAND MORE MERITORIOUS.[3]

In June 1954, in a letter written on his behalf, he elaborated on this advice:

> He greatly appreciated the desire of John and Dorothy Ferraby to go out as pioneers, but considered that it would weaken the work of the National Assembly altogether too much. Important as the pioneer field is, if all the most able workers go out, the campaigns carried on from different national bases will become absolutely unwieldy for lack of adequate able management.[4]

In the early 1950s John wrote two small booklets on the Bahá'í teachings, published in 1954 under the titles *Progressive Revelation* and *Bahá'í Teachings on Economics.*

In 1955 John went on pilgrimage to the Holy Land and met Shoghi Effendi. This experience deepened his devotion to the Head of the Faith. The Guardian praised John's work for the Cause, especially his role in developing the administration in the British Isles, and called him a 'pillar of the Administrative Order'. He suggested that John write more for the Faith.

After his pilgrimage John began to write, as a man inspired, *All Things Made New*, working early in the morning, late at night and at weekends until the book was completed. The book is divided into an introduction and three parts. John began by directing his readers' attention to the revolutionary changes of the previous 150 years and their causes, and presenting an overview of the Central Figures of the Bahá'í Faith and of its growth. In Part I he described the teachings of Bahá'u'lláh, examining such subjects as the oneness of God and religion, the unity of humankind, economics, personal conduct and the relationship between science and religion. In Part II he discussed the Central Figures of the Faith. In Part III he wrote about the Bahá'í community, including the Administrative Order, the Covenant and the laws and obligations binding upon Bahá'ís. *All Things Made New* was widely used and was published in the British Isles, the United States and India. When he received a copy, the Guardian praised the book to pilgrims, saying it would assist the Faith for a long time.

In 1957 John was appointed a Hand of the Cause of God. He was one five Hands of the Cause born in the British Isles (the others being Hyde and Clara Dunn, John Esslemont and George Townshend) and one of three of Jewish origin (Músá Banání and Siegfried Schopflocher being the other two). He had barely had time to come to terms with his new status when he was badly unsettled by the passing, on 4 November 1957, of Shoghi Effendi, to whom he had a deep devotion. As the Guardian passed away in London, John was called upon to shoulder many of the responsibilities for the funeral. Both he and Hasan Balyuzi were asked by Rúḥíyyih Khánum to make the arrangements for the burial. Afterwards he travelled to Haifa for the first Conclave of the Hands of the Cause, staying on for some three months to assist in the work until the nine Hands chosen to reside in the Holy Land were able to settle there. Returning to the United Kingdom, he continued his work as secretary of the National Assembly as well as carrying out his functions as a Hand of the Cause. In 1959 he was chosen to be one of the Hands of the Cause resident in the Holy Land and moved to Haifa, remaining there until the election of the Universal House of Justice at Riḍván 1963.

In 1958 John attended the intercontinental conference in Frankfurt, Germany, and in 1962 he represented the Hands of the Cause at the formation of the first Norwegian National Spiritual Assembly. In 1963 he returned to Britain, where he attended the first Bahá'í World Congress in London. He and his family then moved to Cambridge, where he settled for the remainder of his life.

During this period John worked as one of the Hands of the Cause in Europe, acting as their secretary. He travelled extensively in Europe, attending conventions and conferences and consulting with National Assemblies. He attended the Mediterranean conference in Palermo, Sicily, in 1968 and summer schools in Belgium, Luxembourg, France, Germany, the Netherlands and Denmark as well as the British Isles. He was also present at the International Conventions in Haifa in 1968 and 1973.

Near the end of the 1960s John's health deteriorated, limiting his activities. He worked from time to time on a book about comparative religion but was unable to complete it. On 5 September 1973 he died in his sleep in Cambridge, where he is buried.

The National Spiritual Assembly of the United Kingdom wrote on John's passing:

> With deep sorrow we have to announce the sudden passing of Mr John Ferraby, at his home in Cambridge. The funeral was held at the City Cemetery, Newmarket Road, Cambridge at 12 noon on Tuesday, 11 September, and a memorial service in the Ḥaẓíratu'l-Quds on Sunday, 7 October at 3 p.m.
>
> The sad news was immediately conveyed to Haifa and we received this cable [from the Universal House of Justice]:
>
> REGRET SUDDEN PASSING HAND CAUSE JOHN FERRABY. RECALL LONG SERVICES FAITH BRITISH ISLES CROWNED ELEVATION RANK HAND CAUSE VALUABLE CONTRIBUTION BAHA’I LITERATURE THROUGH HIS BOOK ALL THINGS MADE NEW. REQUESTING BEFITTING GATHERINGS MASHRIQULADHHKARS MEMORIAL MEETINGS ALL COMMUNITIES BAHA’I WORLD.[5]

# Raḥmatu'lláh Muhájir
# 1923–1979

*by Iran Furútan Muhájir*

Raḥmatu'lláh Muhájir was born on 4 April 1923 in the town of Sháh 'Abdu'l-'Aẓím in Iran. He was a fourth generation Bahá'í whose distinguished ancestors had suffered banishment and severe persecution at the hands of the Muslims. 'Abdu'l-Bahá had written to the family, addressing them as 'Ay Muhájirán' ('O Pioneers') and they adopted this as the family name.[1]

When Raḥmat was about nine years old the family moved to Ṭihrán. The Muhájir home became a centre of Bahá'í activities and many meetings were held there at which prominent Bahá'ís would often speak. Raḥmat regularly attended these meetings, which imbued him with the knowledge of the Faith of Bahá'u'lláh at an early age.

When Raḥmat was 15 years old the Muhájir family left Ṭihrán to pioneer to Kalár-Dasht, where they remained for three years. When the family was forced to return to Ṭihrán, Raḥmat continued to be an active member of the community, serving as a member of both the local and the national Bahá'í youth committees and participating in most of the Bahá'í youth teaching activities. Raḥmat was by nature very sociable and had a good sense of humour, and he was thus popular with his peers. These characteristics were to continue throughout his life and would serve him well in his travels and contacts with the peoples of the world.

In the autumn of 1944 Raḥmat was accepted as a student at the School of Medicine at the University of Ṭihrán. Nevertheless, he postponed his studies and went to Riḍá'iyyih, a city in the northern province of Ádhirbáyján. There he taught youth and children's classes during the day and adult literacy classes in the afternoons. He dedicated his evenings to Bahá'í meetings and firesides. These activities marked his first venture into the field of social development. After two years Raḥmat returned to Ṭihrán to take up his medical studies.

These studies did not stop Raḥmat from participating in Bahá'í activities. In 1948 he was appointed to serve on the National Pioneering Committee and, to the astonishment of family and friends, just a few months before his graduation he suspended his studies for three months in order to assist in the achievement of the goals of the 45-Month Teaching Plan. After the successful completion of the Plan, he returned to his studies, graduating with honours in 1952.

In October 1951 Raḥmat married Írán Furútan, the daughter of 'Alí-Akbar Furútan, who was appointed a Hand of the Cause in December 1951. The couple moved to Iṣfahán, where Raḥmat worked at a hospital administered by the American Point Four Marshal Plan. In 1953 Dr Muhájir, accompanied by his wife and mother, went on pilgrimage to the Holy Land. The Ten Year Crusade had just begun, and during the pilgrimage Shoghi Effendi talked to Raḥmat about the Plan, particularly about the Pacific region and specifically about the Indonesian archipelago.

Shortly after this pilgrimage, Dr Muhájir – whose love for service had increased a thousandfold in the presence of Shoghi Effendi – and his wife decided to pioneer to the Mentawai Islands off Indonesia. Without knowing anything about the islands, Raḥmat resigned from his position at the hospital, sold nearly all of the couple's belongings, bought one-way tickets to Jakarta and left Iran in January 1954.

In February the Muhájirs arrived at Muara Siberut, on the island of Siberut Selatan, one of the four islands of Mentawai. Dr Muhájir was employed by the Ministry of Health of Indonesia as the doctor for the community. In March 1954 Shoghi Effendi designated the Muhájirs Knights of Bahá'u'lláh.

The Mentawai Islands had been used as a penal colony during the time of Dutch colonization. Hardened criminals had been exiled there and more or less forgotten. Malaria, tuberculosis and skin disease were endemic. The mortality rate was very high, owing to lack of medical attention.

The indigenous Mentawais lived in scattered hamlets far from Muara Siberut. Despite the lack of facilities and means of transport, Raḥmat set to work with a determination and zeal which only his strong faith in Bahá'u'lláh could induce. He combined teaching the Faith with a programme of preventative health care and social development which, in a few years, transformed the lives of the inhabitants of Siberut Selatan.

Raḥmat quickly learned the Mentawai language and began to teach the local elders about the Bahá'í Faith. By the middle of 1954, 25 elders had become Bahá'ís, forming the nucleus of the thousands who accepted the Faith in the years to come.

As the number of Bahá'ís grew, Raḥmat spent more time in the villages, teaching the Faith in a simple language which everyone could understand. By the middle of 1955 there were four hundred Bahá'ís on the island and by 1956 more than a thousand. In April 1957 the Guardian, recognizing this achievement, wrote to the Bahá'í world:

> A special tribute, I feel, should be paid in this survey of worldwide Bahá'í achievements, to the heroic band of pioneers, and particularly to the company of the Knights of Bahá'u'lláh, who, as a result of their indomitable spirit, courage, steadfastness, and self-abnegation, have achieved in the course of four brief years, in so many of the virgin territories newly opened to His Faith, a measure of success far exceeding the most sanguine expectations . . .
>
> To Uganda, opened on the eve of the Global Crusade, where the number of the avowed adherents of the Faith has now passed the eleven hundred mark, and the number of Bahá'í centres exceeds one hundred and eighty, to the Gilbert and Ellice Islands and Gambia where the number of the believers has reached five hundred and three hundred respectively, must be added Mentawai Islands, where adult Bahá'ís now number over eleven hundred . . .[2]

In April 1957 Raḥmat was elected to the Regional Spiritual Assembly of South-East Asia. This meant having to leave the islands from time to time for meetings. While he was in Jakarta in October 1957 he received a cable from the National Spiritual Assembly of Iran, relaying a telegram from the Guardian:

> INFORM RAHMATULLAH MUHAJIR ABULQASIM FAIZI THEIR ELEVATION RANK HAND CAUSE CONFIDENT NEW HONOUR WILL ENHANCE RECORD THEIR HISTORIC SERVICES.[3]

Raḥmat's wife relates that 'His first reaction was absolute perplexity. He shut himself in a room for hours and wept constantly. It took two days of continuous prayer before he could emerge, pale and wan, to cable his obedience to the beloved Guardian.'[4]

A year after the passing of Shoghi Effendi the Muhájirs sadly left the Mentawai Islands to enable Raḥmat to carry out his duties as a Hand of the Cause more effectively. By this time, however, there were some four thousand Bahá'ís on Siberut Island, 12 Bahá'í schools and 33 Local Spiritual Assemblies. Dr Muhájir had launched a vigorous and successful campaign to eradicate malaria and many of the other diseases were now encountered much less frequently. The children of Mentawai had all been examined and inoculated by Raḥmat and the rate of mortality had fallen significantly. So important was the work undertaken by Raḥmat in the Mentawai Islands that in 1960 a delegation of Indonesian government officials who visited the islands wrote in their 115-page report entitled 'Research News':

> The progress of the Bahá'í religion in Siberut can be explained as follows: In the year 1955 [sic] a Persian doctor came to Siberut. His name was Muhájir, Raḥmatu'lláh, a government doctor who assisted and worked for the health of the people. At the same time he was very active in spreading the Bahá'í Faith. He went to different villages deep into the island, going through very difficult and dangerous circumstances. Facing death he distributed medicine and other things . . . This work brought in great results . . .
>
> The Bahá'í way of teaching is very special, unique and interesting . . . They meet at the houses of the people, drink and eat with them, and live months and months in the middle of the jungle with the people. In short there is no movement that can compare itself with the Bahá'ís in Siberut, specially in their courage, perseverance and purity of motive.[5]

Raḥmat's international Bahá'í activities and worldwide travels on behalf of the Bahá'í Faith started in 1957 and continued for 22 years. He travelled on five continents, visiting virtually every country in the world, some of them many times. For example, in the first three years of the Five Year Plan he visited more than 50 countries.[6] He was instrumental in teaching thousands of the indigenous peoples of Africa, Central and South America, Australia and Asia. Although his main purpose was to teach the Bahá'í Faith and carry out his duties as a Hand of the Cause of God, he continued to assist the Bahá'ís to create social development projects.

His skills as a physician and public health educator helped many Bahá'í communities establish schools, develop educational programmes and aid the indigenous and needy people of the world in their everyday lives.

It is perhaps as the initiator of mass teaching projects that Dr Muhájir is best remembered. He had a talent for enthusing Bahá'í communities to take forward his recommendations to teach on a scale never before attempted. Several times he travelled to India, where the progress of the Cause was very slow. In 1961 he met with the National Spiritual Assembly and emphasized the need to teach the masses. Such was his effect on the Bahá'ís that the number of believers grew from 850 at the time of his visit to 65,000 in 1963.

Raḥmat made 22 trips to the countries of Asia, initiating mass teaching not only in India but in the Philippines, Korea, Laos, Malaysia, Indonesia and Taiwan. He also assisted in the establishment of a firm foundation for Bahá'í administration in these and other Asian countries.

Dr Muhájir visited Africa 13 times, travelling through every country and many cities and villages. Here he helped the Bahá'ís to formulate plans for teaching, training children and furthering the advancement of women. Many Bahá'í institutes and schools were established as a result, several of which were named in his memory.

He made over 10 visits to the Bahá'ís of the North American continent, with the primary objective of reaching the Indian and African-American peoples. He also appeared on television, gave press interviews and visited prominent people. He made 13 visits to the European continent, travelling to every country and stimulating teaching activities wherever he went. He travelled seven times to the Islands of the Pacific, Australia and New Zealand and nine times to the countries of Central and South America, where he was instrumental in starting mass teaching in Ecuador and other countries.

Hundreds of Ḥaẓíratu'l-Quds, Bahá'í institutes and schools around the world were found and purchased through his assistance. He participated in countless conferences, Bahá'í summer schools and conventions, attending some as representative of the Universal House of Justice. Although he met with many heads of state and was interviewed by newspapers and appeared on television programmes, his main love was for the indigenous peoples of the world. He was happiest when he was in a remote village in Africa or the Pacific, or trekking the mountains of South America to visit the Indians of Bolivia or Chile.

Raḥmatu'lláh Muhájir suffered a heart attack while participating in a teaching conference in Quito, Ecuador, and passed away on 29 December 1979. On the occasion of his passing, the Universal House of Justice sent the following cablegram to the Bahá'í world:

PROFOUNDLY LAMENT UNTIMELY PASSING IN QUITO ECUADOR BELOVED HAND CAUSE RAHMATULLAH MUHAJIR FOLLOWING HEART ATTACK COURSE HIS LATEST SOUTH AMERICAN TOUR. UNSTINTED UNRESTRAINED OUTPOURING OF PHYSICAL SPIRITUAL ENERGIES BY ONE WHO OFFERED HIS ALL PATH SERVICE HAS NOW CEASED. POSTERITY WILL RECORD HIS DEVOTED SERVICES YOUTHFUL YEARS CRADLE FAITH HIS SUBSEQUENT UNIQUE EXPLOITS PIONEERING FIELD SOUTHEAST ASIA WHERE HE WON ACCOLADE KNIGHTHOOD BAHAULLAH HIS CEASELESS EFFORTS OVER TWO DECADES SINCE HIS APPOINTMENT HAND CAUSE STIMULATING IN MANY LANDS EAST WEST PROCESS ENTRY BY TROOPS. FRIENDS ALL CONTINENTS WHO MOURN THIS TRAGIC LOSS NOW SUDDENLY DEPRIVED COLLABORATION ONE WHO ENDEARED HIMSELF TO THEM THROUGH HIS GENTLENESS HIS LUMINOUS PERSONALITY HIS EXEMPLARY UNFLAGGING ZEAL HIS CREATIVE ENTHUSIASTIC APPROACH TO FULFILMENT ASSIGNED GOALS. URGE FRIENDS EVERYWHERE HOLD MEMORIAL GATHERINGS BEFITTING HIS HIGH STATION UNIQUE ACHIEVEMENTS. MAY HIS RADIANT SOUL ABHA KINGDOM REAP RICH HARVEST HIS DEDICATED SELF-SACRIFICING SERVICES CAUSE GOD.[7]

# Enoch Olinga
## 1926–1979

> . . . I very humbly beg to assure my dearly loved Guardian of my unreserved loving devotion to the Cause of Bahá'u'lláh, and my submissiveness to every one of the Guardian's admonitions in the way of promoting the fundamental interests of our Faith . . .[1]

The purity of devotion demonstrated in this excerpt of a letter to Shoghi Effendi from the only African Hand of the Cause is typical of the eagerness with which Enoch Olinga served his beloved Cause and Guardian for more than a quarter of a century.

Born on 24 June 1926, the second son of a family of Christian converts whose home was in the Teso north-eastern part of Uganda, Enoch received his early education at Tilling, where the family moved in 1927. He later went to school at Ngora, a small town near his home, and to high school in Mbale District. In 1941, when he was 15, Enoch was drafted into the British Army Education Corps and went to Nairobi. He later served in the East African King's Rifles Corps in south-east Asia, travelling in Burma, East Pakistan, Ceylon and India. After the war, in 1946, Enoch returned to Uganda, where he began work with the government Department of Public Relations and Welfare, stationed in Soroti and Mbale. In the next few years he married his first wife, Eunice, had the first of his six children by her, and wrote two books in his own language, Ateso, as well as *Social and Economic Problems – Their Solution*. He trained as an economist and worked for the government as a translator.

In 1951 Enoch heard about the Bahá'í Faith from a friend. At this time there were virtually no Bahá'ís in Africa. The British National Spiritual Assembly, at the behest of Shoghi Effendi, had launched the two-year

Africa Campaign in 1950 to take the Bahá'í teachings to the whole continent, and in 1951 Mr and Mrs Músá Banání, their daughter Violette, her husband 'Alí Nakhjavání and their daughter Bahíyyih settled in Kampala. Enoch was introduced to 'Alí Nakhjavání and a friendship began.

Enoch was, at the time, a heavy drinker, which led to his dismissal from his government post as he was unable to discharge his duties. Somewhat disillusioned with his life, he began to attend the evening meetings held in the Banání home, attracted by the warmth of the Persian household.

Mr and Mrs Banání went to the Holy Land on pilgrimage in February 1952. While they were away the pioneers in Kampala – the Nakhjavánís and Philip Hainsworth – held a meeting for all the Africans interested in the Faith. The meeting coincided with the time when Shoghi Effendi usually visited the Shrines, and he and Mr Banání said special prayers there together. A large number of people attended the meeting, including Enoch, but, much to the dismay of the pioneers, nothing happened. Later that night, however, Enoch returned and asked many questions, particularly on biblical subjects and about the return of Christ. His last question was 'How does one become a Bahá'í?' Early the next morning, he appeared with a letter asking that he be accepted as a Bahá'í. Enoch was the third Ugandan, and the first of the Teso tribe, to accept the Faith.

When he became a Bahá'í, Enoch gave up all alcohol immediately. So remarkable was the change in his conduct and attitude that his wife also accepted the Faith. Soon after, several of Enoch's fellow Teso tribesmen followed his lead in embracing the Faith of Bahá'u'lláh. Two months after Enoch's enrolment, Kampala formed its first Local Spiritual Assembly.

In July and August 1952, Enoch returned to Tilling to teach the Bahá'í Faith and 17 people became Bahá'ís. People wanted to see 'Alí Nakhjavání, the 'white man' who had converted Enoch, so 'Alí taught the Teso for several weeks, with Enoch and later another Bahá'í translating for him. Over 90 people accepted the Faith as a result, including Enoch's own father. At the beginning of January 1953, eight months after the Local Spiritual Assembly of Kampala was formed, Shoghi Effendi wrote to the Bahá'í world:

> Rejoice to share with Bahá'í communities East and West thrilling reports of feats achieved by the heroic band of Bahá'í pioneers labouring in divers widely scattered African territories, particularly in Uganda, in the heart of the continent, reminiscent alike of episodes related in the Book of Acts

> and the rapid, dramatic propagation of the Faith through the instrumentality of the dawn-breakers in the Heroic Age of the Bahá'í Dispensation. The marvellous accomplishments signalizing the rise and establishment of the Administrative Order of the Faith in Latin America have been eclipsed. The exploits immortalizing the recently launched crusade in the European continent have been surpassed. The goal of the seven-month plan, initiated by the Kampala Assembly, aiming at doubling the twelve enrolled believers, has been outstripped. The number of Africans converted in the course of the last fifteen months, residing in Kampala and outlying districts, with Protestant, Catholic and pagan backgrounds, lettered and unlettered, of both sexes, representative of no less than sixteen tribes, has passed the two hundred mark.[2]

Eighteen months after his conversion, Enoch responded to the Guardian's appeal for pioneers to open new African territories to the Faith. Setting out in a small Peugeot station-wagon on 27 August 1953, Enoch, together with his friends 'Alí and Violette Nakhjavání and two other new African Bahá'ís, embarked on a long and tortuous journey across Africa on uncharted and poorly maintained roads. Their goal was British Cameroon, more than 3,000 kilometres away. On the eve of their departure the Guardian cabled them: 'LOVING, FERVENT PRAYERS ACCOMPANYING YOU.'[3]

The first stop on the two-month journey was Kamina, in what was then the Belgian Congo, where Samson Mungono was dropped off. The party then pressed on to Brazzaville in French Equatorial Africa and established Max Kenyerezi at his pioneer post. The worst part of the journey was through Gabon, where the car frequently had to be lifted out of the mud. On one day they made only 100 kilometres in 16 hours; on another, only 25 in 14 hours. The car finally broke down in elephant country, and Enoch volunteered to walk the 80 kilometres to a town to get help.

A city-bred and educated African, this act required much courage on Enoch's part. He had done little travelling in the bush. He feared strange African tribes, dangerous jungle animals and deadly snakes. He faced these fears bravely and walked through mud, weathered a severe rain storm and avoided elephants crashing into the jungle. Sick, feverish, exhausted, caked with mud and frightened, Enoch, at the end of 55 kilometres, cried out, 'You fool! Why are you doing this?'[4]

Shaken and weeping, he fell asleep, as he later recalled, and dreamed of his beloved Guardian. In the dream, Shoghi Effendi lifted Enoch to him, set him on his feet and gave him consolation and assurance. Enoch awoke a different person, refreshed, calmed and determined.

Nevertheless, he could not avoid the gnawing concern for the Nakhjavánís' safety. Left behind with the broken car on a near impassable road, had they been robbed or, worse, killed? Enoch agonized over how he would break the news to the Banánís. Later, when the Nakhjavánís, who had somehow managed to repair the car, caught up with him, Enoch could only stare unbelievingly at them as though they were apparitions. On reaching the town, Enoch was so ill that he had to be hospitalized for two days, and could not travel for a week.

In the early evening of 15 October 1953, the three Bahá'ís entered British Cameroon and Enoch immediately cabled Shoghi Effendi of his safe arrival. This was the last day of the Holy Year which Shoghi Effendi had set in commemoration of the centenary of the declaration of Bahá'u'lláh. Shoghi Effendi named Enoch a Knight of Bahá'u'lláh, a title given the first Bahá'ís to settle in the virgin territories designated to be opened to the Faith during the Ten Year Crusade. The Nakhjavánís moved on to neighbouring French Cameroon, while Enoch became a lodger in the home of David Tanyi, who became the first believer to declare in Cameroon and later a Knight of Bahá'u'lláh himself for French Togoland.

Enoch lived for ten years in Cameroon before returning to Uganda. He was instrumental in the establishment of the Faith in West Africa, principally Cameroon, Nigeria and Ghana. In addition to sowing the seeds that brought into the Faith the thousands of his own people who formed the majority of believers in Uganda before its civil war, Enoch raised up within six months of his arrival in Cameroon a number of pioneers who opened other virgin territories to the Faith.

The Guardian was deeply moved by Enoch's reports of these new believers:

> The manner in which the Faith has spread in Africa is truly remarkable, and overshadows the manner it has spread in other parts of the world. It indicates how glorious will be the future of the Faith in that great continent.[5]

In 1956 Shoghi Effendi brought into being several Regional Spiritual Assemblies in Africa, each covering a number of territories. The

Assembly serving the largest area was that of North-West Africa, comprising 25 territories, including British Cameroon, and having its seat in Tunis. Despite the vastness of the area, there were only about one thousand Bahá'ís and 38 Local Spiritual Assemblies in the region. Enoch was elected chairman of the Regional Spiritual Assembly.

In 1957 Enoch Olinga received permission from the Guardian to make his pilgrimage to the Holy Land. Arriving on 3 February, he was the first black African to make the pilgrimage. Shoghi Effendi accommodated him in the Eastern Pilgrim House, which is situated near the Shrine of the Báb, and treated him as one of the oriental pilgrims. This meant Enoch was able to spend time walking in the gardens with his beloved Guardian and to visit the Shrines with him. During these days the Guardian spoke of the exalted rank of the Hands of the Cause and paid tribute to the greatness of Músá Banání. Uganda, he said, was the heart of Africa and Mr Banání was the heart of the heart.

Years later Enoch told Hooper Dunbar that the Guardian 'taught me all things'. Mr Dunbar believed that while Enoch was on pilgrimage the Guardian must have covered the whole range of divine and human knowledge with him in outline form.[6] Soon after Enoch left the Holy Land Shoghi Effendi named him 'Abu'l-Futúḥ', the 'Father of Victories' for his work in Uganda, his pioneering to British Cameroon and becoming a Knight of Bahá'u'lláh, his raising of pioneers from among recent converts and his teaching of 300 souls. The Guardian considered these feats 'unique in the history of the Crusade'.[7]

Soon after his pilgrimage, Enoch returned to Uganda to fetch his wife and children now that he seemed to be permanently established in West Africa. Summoned to the Banánís' home in October 1957, he was handed a cable from the Guardian notifying him of his elevation to the rank of a Hand of the Cause. When he read the message, Enoch prostrated himself flat on the floor, a mark in Africa of deep submission to one's lord. Only four years a Bahá'í at the time of his appointment, he was, at 31, the youngest Hand of the Cause.[8] Two days later, on 4 October, Enoch cabled Shoghi Effendi:

> BELOVED'S HOLY MESSAGE JUST RECEIVED BENUMBED MY FACULTIES. WITH MUCH SUBMISSIVENESS AND HUMBLENESS I ACCEPT DIVINE FAVOUR, FEEL DEEPLY GRATEFUL BELOVED'S SACRED WISHES FOR OUR PROGRESS. BESEECH HIS PRAYERS FOR CONFIRMATION GUIDANCE AND SPIRITUAL DEVELOPMENT.[9]

A month later the Guardian passed away in London. Unable to attend the funeral service, Enoch was, however, present at every Conclave of the Hands of the Cause. By this time a gifted speaker, Enoch possessed the endearing quality of laughter, which so cheered his fellow Hands. His laugh was joyous and contagious and brought welcome relief from the otherwise serious drama unfolding at the World Centre between November 1957 and April 1963. Weighed down with crushing responsibilities, Enoch's fellow Hands saved up funny stories to tell him at the annual Conclave. Enoch would chuckle and then convulse with a laughter which would spread, affect and lighten the hearts of his fellow Hands of the Cause.

Sadly, Enoch's reunion with his wife in West Africa was not successful, and after about three years Eunice returned to East Africa, leaving the children with Enoch. In 1961 the Olingas were divorced, and two years later Enoch and his second wife, Elizabeth, went to Nairobi. Enoch and Elizabeth had two children. Eventually the family returned to Tilling in Uganda.

The Hands of the Cause asked Enoch to be the chairman of the opening session of the Bahá'í World Congress held in the Albert Hall in London in April 1963. Six months later Enoch wrote to Rúḥíyyih Khánum and asked for prayers for his 'weak, frail and helpless self'.[10]

As a Hand of the Cause, Enoch Olinga travelled widely, journeying to all parts of Africa, India, South-East Asia, Australasia, the Pacific Islands, the Americas and Europe. He attended three of the 1958 continental conferences: in Kampala, Frankfurt and Singapore. In 1960 he visited many localities in West and North Africa as well as Sicily and Italy. The following year, he travelled to the Greater Antilles and Central America. In 1962 he was in East Africa, the Sudan, Ethiopia and the Congo. He represented the Hands of the Cause at the inaugural conventions of the National Spiritual Assemblies of Jamaica, the Dominican Republic and Cuba, and represented the Universal House of Justice at many inaugural conventions of National Spiritual Assemblies, including those of the Indian Ocean; South Central Africa; Swaziland, Lesotho and Mozambique; Burundi and Rwanda; Upper West Africa; Chad; Sierra Leone; Liberia and Guinea; Upper West Africa; Upper Volta; and Iceland. He attended the oceanic conferences held in Sicily in 1968 and in Singapore in 1971. As problems in Africa steadily mounted, he made significant tours across the continent from the mid 1970s, taking time also to attend the international teaching conferences in Bahia, Mérida and Nairobi in 1976 and 1977.

During his lengthy travels, Enoch was received by many heads of state and notables, including President Jomo Kenyatta of Kenya, President Ahmadou Ahidjo of the Cameroon Republic, President Hastings Kamuzu Banda of Malawi, President William Tubman of Liberia, His Highness Malietoa Tanumafili II of Western Samoa, the Dalai Lama and President Zalman Shazar of Israel.

Enoch touched and inspired the hearts of the countless people he met. Following a visit by him to Brazil, the National Spiritual Assembly stated that 'It was as if a dear, long expected friend had come.' At a public meeting, Mr Olinga spoke 'with such love and good will that many present were overcome by emotion, applauded and some were unable to withhold their tears'.[11] In Argentina 'his presence ignited the love of God in some hearts and blew on the flame of others'.[12] In Africa Enoch was referred to as 'an ideal teacher, a pioneer whom all could emulate'.[13] As a result of his visit to Chile, nearly a tenth of the country's ten million people heard the name Bahá'u'lláh. Speaking of his travels in South America, Enoch said:

> the friends are wonderful! . . . It is a source of real joy and happiness to witness the zeal, the devotion and determination of the dear friends, veteran and new; old and young; pioneers and native believers. I am so impressed by what they are able to accomplish for the Cause of God, and it is my very sincere hope that the heavenly spirit which is animating and assisting them may enable them to be victorious over the dark forces of unbelief. They are wonderful and highly consecrated.[14]

Enoch wanted the believers to be happy. 'Are you happy?' he would ask. In a recorded talk he spoke about how to be happy. The believers should be happy, he said, because they had been enabled by Bahá'u'lláh to recognize Him as the Lord of this Day. In the whole world, the beloved Guardian had told Enoch when he was in Haifa, very few people are happy. Only those who know and love God in this Day, and bear the Holy Name of the Manifestation of God for today, can be happy. When we love Him, we receive His bounties, graces and favours. And one of His heavenly bestowals is happiness.

Enoch said that there is a higher station than that of happiness. The Guardian, he said, stated that the Bahá'ís must be joyful; to become so the believers must become familiar with the Will of God revealed through Bahá'u'lláh. Jesus Christ had said that the day would come when the Will of

God would be revealed to the world. Once the Bahá'ís had become familiar with the Will of God, they must obey it. It is obedience to the Will or Law of God which makes us joyful.[15] Thus the twin inseparable duties required of human beings – recognition and obedience[16] – bring happiness and joy.

On another occasion Enoch spoke of the assistance available to every believer. Citing the Guardian, he said that the Holy Spirit is hovering, ready to enter the hearts. Meetings are always encompassed by this Spirit, which is why the Bahá'ís must have conferences and gatherings to enjoy fellowship, love and unity. These gatherings, he said, would attract divine confirmations, so that when people left they would be guided and helped in their work.

He said that the difference between the Faith and other ideologies is that Bahá'u'lláh has released enormous amounts of divine love. This is why it is possible to unite the world. This unity will lead to peace. This is the power that is assisting the Bahá'ís to teach. It is a divine power. If one could see the inner world, he would see that this power is luminous and dynamic. Mortals cannot stop it. No one can extinguish it.[17]

After the death of Músá Banání in 1971, Enoch bought the Banání–Nakhjavání home in Kampala in which he had accepted the Faith. However, the political situation in Uganda deteriorated throughout the 1970s, culminating in a terrible civil war, and Enoch spent much time protecting and comforting the endangered Bahá'í community. In September 1977 the Faith was banned, its administrative bodies and activities suspended and the House of Worship closed. Enoch was shocked by this development, saying, 'No! No one can ban the Faith of God.'[18] He wrote to the president outlining the nature and status of the Faith, but without effect.

By March 1979 the civil war was well under way. Enoch's son Badi was kidnapped by soldiers and disappeared for a week. Enoch himself was in a motor accident with an army lorry and robbed of a large amount of money. By April thousands of Ugandans were fleeing Kampala. Enoch sent his family back to Tilling for safety. He was persuaded to take refuge on the Temple property, but refused to leave the capital himself. One night a fierce artillery battle raged around the hill on which the Temple stands and Enoch spent the whole night praying. The next day he found that the Temple had not been damaged but that the government had been defeated. Immediately, he went to the Temple and opened all the doors, offering prayers of thanks.

Although the government had been overthrown, chaos still reigned in the city, with both soldiers and townspeople looting and fighting. Enoch returned to his home in Kampala to find it being stripped bare by looters. As his family was eager to rejoin him, Enoch decided to restore the house.

The ban on the Faith was not lifted for some months after the fall of the government, but the situation had changed so significantly that the Universal House of Justice decided to appoint an interim committee to oversee Bahá'í activities in Uganda and to manage the Bahá'í properties. The committee met for the first time on 25 and 26 August 1979, with Enoch chairing the meeting.

Having other matters to see to, Enoch did not attend the second meeting of the committee on 15 September. His wife and three of the children were at home, anticipating a family reunion. On 16 September the family went to the Temple grounds where Enoch briefed the Bahá'ís about the situation of the believers in Iran. Later in the day some of the youth provided music while Enoch and Elizabeth joined in the dancing.

Later that evening, at about 8:30, the Olingas' houseboy heard someone shaking the gate to the family compound. Looking through the window, he saw five armed men walking towards the back door which led to the kitchen of the Olinga house. The men shouted, 'Open!' and banged on the door. Lennie, Enoch's youngest son, opened the door and there was the sound of gun shots. The houseboy fled in terror.

The next morning the houseboy found Enoch's body lying in the courtyard and a trail of blood leading from the kitchen to a bedroom. Here the pitiful mangled remains of Enoch's wife and three of his children were found heaped on the floor.

It is thought that Enoch was in the sitting room when he heard cries and shooting. He came immediately into the compound at the back. From there, he was either taken in to see his family shot or saw them lying dead. He was heard to be weeping and sobbing out loud but then he was shot from behind in the chest and hips and fell in front of the garage.

The tragedy shocked the Bahá'í world. Was it an attack on a well-known leader of the Faith or one of many acts of terrorism occurring in that troubled land? The truth may never be known.

Enoch and his family were buried on 24 September on Kikaya Hill, next to Hand of the Cause Músá Banání.

To the stunned followers of Bahá'u'lláh worldwide, the Universal House of Justice cabled:

WITH GRIEF-STRICKEN HEARTS ANNOUNCE TRAGIC NEWS BRUTAL MURDER DEARLY LOVED GREATLY ADMIRED HAND CAUSE GOD ENOCH OLINGA BY UNKNOWN GUNMEN COURTYARD HIS KAMPALA HOME. HIS WIFE ELIZABETH AND THREE CHILDREN BADI, LENNIE AND TAHIRIH HAVE ALSO FALLEN INNOCENT VICTIMS THIS CRUEL ACT. MOTIVE ATTACK NOT YET ASCERTAINED. HIS RADIANT SPIRIT HIS UNWAVERING FAITH HIS ALL-EMBRACING LOVE HIS LEONINE AUDACITY IN THE TEACHING FIELD HIS TITLES KNIGHT BAHAULLAH FATHER VICTORIES CONFERRED BELOVED GUARDIAN ALL COMBINE DISTINGUISH HIM AS PREEMINENT MEMBER HIS RACE IN ANNALS FAITH AFRICAN CONTINENT. URGE FRIENDS EVERYWHERE HOLD MEMORIAL GATHERINGS BEFITTING TRIBUTE HIS IMPERISHABLE MEMORY. FERVENTLY PRAYING HOLY SHRINES PROGRESS HIS NOBLE SOUL AND SOULS FOUR MEMBERS HIS PRECIOUS FAMILY.[19]

# John Aldham Robarts
# 1901–1991

When the physical garment is laid aside and the soul ascends to the spiritual world, the life of the departed one is remembered in both worlds. In the spiritual world, his works are judged, his understanding is enlightened and his consciousness heightened. In the physical world, he may be remembered for his titles, his affluence and his prestige. He may be remembered for his business acumen, leadership talent or problem-solving ability. Or he may be remembered for the force of his influence, the standards he upheld and the fruits he produced.

Those who knew and loved John Aldham Robarts cherish in their memories and hearts a life of distinction. His children remember his encouragement, his fun-loving nature, his wise counsels and his caring nature. Business colleagues valued his leadership, respected his faith and sought his companionship. His fellow Bahá'ís treasured his steadfast service, keen perceptiveness, inspiring challenges, disarming humour, reliance upon prayer, genuine warmth and indefatigable devotion. Seekers were drawn to his spirit of love, voice of encouragement and clarity of vision. And Audrey, his dear wife of 63 years, recalled many more absorbing details of his remarkable life, ennobling still further his memory and attesting to the eternal love she cherishes for her consort in all the worlds of God.

A genuinely modest human being, John Robarts, in his manifold accomplishments, lived naturally and unpretentiously the kind of life 'Abdu'l-Bahá desired for the Bahá'ís:

> I desire distinction for you . . . In the love of God you must become distinguished from all else. You must become distinguished for loving humanity,

> for unity and accord, for love and justice. In brief, you must become distinguished in all the virtues of the human world – for faithfulness and sincerity, for justice and fidelity, for firmness and steadfastness, for philanthropic deeds and service to the human world, for love toward every human being, for unity and accord with all people, for removing prejudices and promoting international peace. Finally, you must become distinguished for heavenly illumination and for acquiring the bestowals of God. I desire this distinction for you.[1]

John Robarts's progenitors also distinguished themselves in their own times for their love of God and their service to humanity. In the 19th century, during a hurricane in Barbados, his great-grandmother gave birth to her son in an old bake oven half underground – a harrowing experience. She vowed to dedicate her child, whom she named Tempest, to God, if he were spared. The infant grew up to be the Reverend Thomas Tempest Robarts, a canon in the Anglican Church.

Thomas Tempest had five children. Ernest, the eldest, joined a fundamentalist denomination known as the Plymouth Brethren. Henry joined the Knights of Pithias, an organization which may date back to the Crusades. The third child, Aldham, John's father, remained an Anglican and was manager of the Canadian Imperial Bank of Commerce in Port Arthur (now Thunder Bay) on the north shore of Lake Superior. His death at the age of 49 was mourned by a vast concourse of people who assembled for his funeral. Ella, Thomas's fourth child, became a devoted Bahá'í teacher. Her summer home at the end of the lane leading to Green Acre Bahá'í School was a centre of Bahá'í hospitality. Thomas's youngest child, Grace Robarts Ober, was dedicated to the service of God by her parents. For 32 years she served the Bahá'í Cause and at her death the Guardian described her as a distinguished worker in the teaching field. A grandson of Thomas's brother was prime minister of Ontario for ten years. Upon the announcement of his death, he was lauded in the Ontario legislature for his trustworthiness and fairness.

John Robarts was born on 2 November 1901 in Waterloo, Ontario. His parents, Aldham Wilson Robarts and Rachel Mary Montgomery Campbell, were of English and Scottish descent, respected for the quality of loyalty. When John was six he began a newspaper delivery round in the neighbourhood and, like his two older sisters, attended elementary school in Port Arthur. Around this time his Aunt Grace became a Bahá'í.

From his boyhood John was known for his competence, reliability, integrity and enthusiasm, with the result that he never had to apply for any position he ever held. While attending the renowned Bishop Ridley College in St Catharines, Ontario, during his youth, he was offered a position as secretary to a Canadian National Railways superintendent. In 1918 the World War had just ended and jobs were scarce. Nearing the end of his schooling, John consulted with his father about the offer and decided to leave school and accept the job. Applying himself, he promptly acquired secretarial skills, including shorthand and typing.

Later, just as his secretarial post came to an end, John was invited to work in the grain exchange in Winnipeg. His job was to shovel grain into boxcars. He had to travel in the summer, generally living in small country boarding houses and commuting to and from Winnipeg over unpaved roads, either muddy or dusty depending on the weather. After this onerous job he worked selling farm supplies, still travelling over country roads. The dust of those boxcars and roads, as well as some family susceptibility, caused John to suffer from asthma, bronchitis and emphysema for much of his life.

In the mid 1920s John met Audrey FitzGerald. Born on 20 December 1904, Audrey was the daughter of Edward FitzGerald and Kate Bulmer. Her father could boast ancestry among the ancient Irish, Welsh, English and Spanish. Her mother's ancestors were English, French and Cree. A great-great-grandfather in the time of the British American colonies had carried on a fur trade in Canada, while Audrey's maternal grandmother was a Cree. Audrey's maiden name, FitzGerald, originated with a family in the vale of the Arno in Florence during feudal times.

For a time John and Audrey went out together, although road conditions made it difficult for them to meet. The Roaring Twenties lured many of the youth of that generation, but not John or Audrey – who did, however, enjoy dancing and listening to music. In 1926 John formed a partnership with James Graham and the two men launched a domestic heating business, which proved to be very troublesome. The next year they established The Overhead Door Company of Canada in Toronto. John was its president and general manager for Eastern Canada. Meanwhile, Audrey went off to France to study music with a director of the Fontainebleau Academy. During their three-year engagement John and Audrey were often separated, having to endure not only an ocean between them but a tedious over-the-seas correspondence, before they were able to celebrate their marriage on 3 March 1928 at St George's Anglican Church in Winnipeg.

About six months before his marriage John finally met his aunt Grace Robarts Ober. In a letter John wrote years later, he recalled this meeting and his early exposure to the Bahá'í Faith:

> In 1927 I lived in Toronto and the Obers lived in Buffalo, some one hundred and twenty-five miles away. One day in the autumn [my Aunt Grace] telephoned me. She had come to Toronto on a visit and she asked me to have lunch with her. I was delighted and we sat over the lunch table all afternoon, right through dinner. Then I thought it was too late to let her drive home alone, so I offered to drive with her and return to Toronto by bus the following day. But upon our arrival at the bus terminal in Buffalo she suggested that as we were having such a lovely time together she would drive me back to Toronto, which she did. She helped me to choose my diamond engagement ring for my fiancée, Audrey FitzGerald. We were married the following year, and a few months later we visited the Obers, met Harlan, and at our request learned something about the Bahá'í Faith for the first time.[2]

Harlan and Grace Ober had become Bahá'ís independently in 1906. Six years later Grace served 'Abdu'l-Bahá by securing and readying apartments for Him and then acting as housekeeper and hostess during His travels on the East Coast of America.

> She kept the [home] immaculate, and always ready for the constant stream of guests from morning to night, Bahá'ís and inquirers and souls in difficulty to whom 'Abdu'l-Bahá was always a loving Father. It was during one of the New York City visits of 'Abdu'l-Bahá that He suggested her marriage to Harlan Ober. Gaining the consent of these two devoted believers, who in His consummate wisdom He had drawn together, He, on the following day, July 17, 1912, married them in the morning according to the Bahá'í marriage.
>
> This infinite bounty of being chosen for each other and joined in marriage by the Centre of the Covenant Himself was a unique favour bestowed upon these two souls alone, out of all America.[3]

Over the next ten years, John and Audrey were exposed to the Bahá'í Cause. Harlan and Grace came often to Toronto in order to visit a Bahá'í and further the teaching work. The Robartses would meet the Obers and drive them to firesides, collecting them later for dinner at their home. Some time later Grace rented a place in Toronto, wishing to establish a local spiritual assembly there. John and Audrey would occasionally attend Grace's meetings, where they were no doubt stirred by what they heard. But they remained uncommitted because, as Audrey said, they were a team and wanted to be sure they would be in the Cause together.

In the early years of their marriage John and Audrey were very in involved raising their family. Aldham Edward was born in 1929, followed 14 months later by John FitzGerald (Gerald) in 1930. In 1934 Patrick Tempest was born. Meanwhile John was busy with his work. His mother, now a widow, visited every weekend. Audrey gave up her music. Life was hectic.

The Overhead Door Company turned out many hundreds of doors annually and filled many large orders. By 1934, however, the Depression caused demand for doors to decline and the partners decided to sell the business. A competitor bought the company and then mothballed the Graham–Robarts product in favour of an inferior door. Although economic times were precarious, John found a job for each of their 20 factory employees.

Only after his former employees had been relocated did John accept an invitation urged on him to join the Manufacturer's Life Insurance Company. He then completed the Alexander Hamilton Business Courses, qualifying as a Chartered Life Underwriter (CLU). Working in the insurance business, John was a sincere and responsible planner for couples' estates and their financial security. In 1938 he joined the London Life Insurance Company as district manager of its Toronto King Street Agency. As the manager, John gave the men close personal attention, understanding the balance between support that would build confidence and pressure that could destroy it.

In 1937 Howard Colby Ives and his wife, Mabel, came to Toronto to help establish the local assembly. John and Howard discussed the Faith during lunches and Howard was able to answer some of John's questions. Confronted by John's uncertainty, Howard encouraged him to ask God for a sign. John decided to give God a sign by giving up smoking. This he did immediately and permanently, even though he smoked up to two packs of cigarettes a day at the time. Later, when his new telephone was installed, he was amazed to find that his telephone number was Waverley 1844.

Eventually John became a Bahá'í. He recalled, 'One evening in November 1937, after Audrey and I had dined with the Obers, I realized, while we were praying, that I had accepted the station of Bahá'u'lláh.'[4] A few months later he and Audrey together declared, in the presence of Harlan, that they were Bahá'ís. Sadly, Grace, John's beloved aunt who had first told him about the Faith and who had inflamed his heart with her contagious love for the Cause, had recently died in dramatic circumstances at the 1938 annual Bahá'í convention, shortly after delivering a report of her teaching activities to the assembled delegates.

After John and Audrey became Bahá'ís, the sons of Ernest Robarts and their families severed all ties with them. Years before, Ernest had disassociated himself from Grace and Ella, convinced that Bahá'u'lláh was the anti-Christ. Although their decision to separate themselves from John and Audrey must have been painful, Audrey, in her loving way, later wrote simply: 'In their own way they were faithful to the Covenant of God as they saw it.'[5]

In the 1920s and 1930s a strong element of Christian orthodoxy prevailed in Canada. This attitude, mixed with the conviction that the League of Nations meant an end to all war, caused the generality of people, including Bahá'ís, to lapse into a lethargic state underpinned by the illusion of peace. The handful of scattered believers did not always possess the courage to differentiate themselves from the society in which they lived. Even the Guardian's frequent appeals seemed to do little to inspire the believers to arise. In 1936 Canada had only two Assemblies, one in Montreal and another in Vancouver, and there were fewer than 50 Bahá'ís scattered across other towns and cities.[6] The Canadian believers needed a practical, efficient and inspired organizer. John was able to fulfil this role. According to Audrey:

> John was the right person at the right time in the right place. His ability to speak with warmth and good humour and his talent for organizing and administering the follow-up of all teaching activity brought excellent results.[7]

Together John and Audrey plunged into the teaching work. The second year of Shoghi Effendi's first Seven Year Plan was under way. They helped form the first Spiritual Assembly of Toronto in April 1938 and then proceeded to help win the other goals of the Plan, which called for the establishment of a local assembly in every Canadian province by 1944. Thus John made many teaching trips to Halifax, Charlottetown, Moncton and other localities in the Maritime provinces.

John's dedication to the strengthening of Bahá'í communities and the establishment of assemblies continued in Hamilton and Ottawa in the 1940s. For a year he travelled to Hamilton one night each week by train. There he would dine with someone, attend the fireside and, afterwards, meet over coffee at a restaurant with 10 or 20 people. He would then stay the night in a hotel and return to Toronto early the next morning in time for work. After the Assembly was established in Hamilton, John focused on Ottawa. Travelling there on Friday night, he would spend Saturday and Sunday at various firesides and meetings, returning home on Sunday night. In 1948 Ottawa elected its first Local Spiritual Assembly. In 1950 John and Audrey helped establish an Assembly in Forest Hill Village, a Toronto suburb where they were then living.

Ever conscious of the value of time, John would treasure, act upon and frequently quote these words of Shoghi Effendi:

> The field is indeed so immense, the period so critical, the Cause so great, the workers so few, the time so short, the privilege so priceless, that no follower of the Faith of Bahá'u'lláh, worthy to bear His name, can afford a moment's hesitation.[8]

In response, John created teaching opportunities. He hired a private dining room near his office and began weekly lunchtime firesides in Toronto. Business associates would gather, invite their friends and hear different speakers. He constantly arranged other meetings, brought people together, involved individuals in teaching, widened the field of friendships, generated exciting news and encouraged people to give talks.

At the same time John and Audrey began to host firesides in their home. At first no one attended, but gradually numbers grew, with many young people and visiting teachers coming. Of these firesides Nina Grace Robarts Tinnion, the Robartses' fourth child, has written:

> The warmth of Audrey and John's informal hospitality was in itself an eloquent teacher. Every Wednesday evening for years they held a lively fireside in their home. When there was not an invited a speaker John gave the talk himself, frequently tailoring his words and aiming them, with uncanny perception and utmost love, at one unidentified, sometimes identifiable, individual present. One never knew who might be the next focus of his attention. Far from humiliating anyone, the effect was to electrify the people there by drawing

> every individual into a kind of loving complicity that at any moment could erupt into waves of laughter or nods of enlightenment.[9]

Another spiritual mentor from the early days, George Spendlove, said about teaching others: 'Awaken their interest before arousing their prejudices.'[10] John and Audrey, whose marriage was a good example of teaching, naturally followed this wise counsel. Nina has written about the quality of her parents' firesides:

> The Robarts's firesides and teaching activities are legendary. To them can be traced the spiritual ancestry of innumerable Bahá'ís, some of whom pioneered, several became Knights of Bahá'u'lláh, others went on to serve the Faith with distinction in arenas of Bahá'í activity ranging from the private home to the Universal House of Justice. Inexhaustible through all eternity must be the harvest for Bahá'u'lláh of such constancy in teaching.[11]

In 1940 the National Spiritual Assembly of the Bahá'ís of the United States and Canada appointed John to the first Ontario Regional Teaching Committee. He served as secretary, its only officer, from 1941 until 1944, and then as chairman for the next two years. Audrey was a member in 1943 and 1944. John and Lloyd Gardner organized the first Ontario Summer School at Rice Lake in 1941 and John was, for some years, chairman of the Ontario Summer School Committee.

John's chairmanship of these and other administrative bodies undoubtedly resulted from his ability to create unity among the consulting members, instil in them confidence and focus their deliberations on each situation's underlying principle. Shoghi Effendi had said that one should seek the principle and act upon it. Under John's leadership and because he had faith in the power of consultation, decisions could be efficiently reached and carried out. The members were comfortable with his modest manner, the atmosphere of warmth he created and his ability to turn a difficult situation around with his humour.

In 1946, following a two-year respite, the second Seven Year Plan was launched. Shoghi Effendi, in a letter to the delegates at the American Bahá'í Convention, wrote that the third objective of the new Plan included the establishment of a National Spiritual Assembly in Canada, separate from that of the United States. In the same year the National Teaching Committee of Canada was formed, with John as its chairman.

This committee was instrumental in achieving the goal: Canada's first National Spiritual Assembly was formed in 1948. The election was held at the Maxwell home in Montreal. John was elected chairman, a post he held until 1953, when he, Audrey, Patrick and Nina pioneered to Africa.

The fourth objective of the second Seven Year Plan was to carry the Plan across the ocean to the shores of the Old World: to initiate systematic teaching activity on the European continent, with the aim of establishing spiritual assemblies in the Low Countries, Scandinavia, the Iberian Peninsula and Italy.[12] To Canada specifically, on the formation of its National Spiritual Assembly in 1948, Shoghi Effendi assigned the difficult goal of opening Greenland.[13]

In 1949 John travelled to Europe, where he attended the Brussels conference and then visited seven of North America's ten European goal countries, including the Netherlands, Belgium, Luxembourg, Sweden, Norway and Denmark. During this trip he met with government officials for Greenland, winning their good will. Two years later a Bahá'í pioneer was able to enter Greenland and open it to the Faith.

In 1950 the British Bahá'ís had reached the final weeks of their Six Year Plan and were behind schedule in securing its final objectives. Despair hung heavy on the believers. John readily volunteered his services and the Canadian National Assembly offered to cover his expenses. Overjoyed, the National Teaching Committee of the British Isles eagerly routed John through ten cities, where he was able to witness 18 declarations in 13 days. Sacrificing a well-earned holiday to make this historic trip, he wrote to Audrey that he 'didn't do it – it just happened when I was there'.[14] Nevertheless the Committee wrote, in part:

> Our gratitude to Canada is eclipsed only by our deeply felt debt to John himself. His tour was magnificent, his work unforgettable, and his contribution to the Plan invaluable.[15]

Though John was busy with the Faith and his work, his children had many special times with 'Dad'. Often he would invite one or the other son or daughter to his office and take him or her out to a meal. When the boys did not want to attend birthday parties because there might be dancing, John gathered them together after dinner, turned on a familiar and rhythmic record and showed them how to dance. He loved music of the big bands, had enjoyed playing the harmonica in his youth, and liked to sing around the piano with family and friends. Following their father's lead, the boys quickly caught the rhythm of the music. John also helped his sons and their friends learn how to speak in public. And he could be seen outside among the youngsters (his and the neighbours') skipping rope, playing ball or bicycle riding.

In 1953 Hand of the Cause Siegfried Schopflocher was scheduled to represent Canada at the New Delhi intercontinental conference, one of four conferences planned to launch the Ten Year Crusade. Sadly, he passed away before the conference. John offered to go in his stead. Shoghi Effendi accepted his offer with loving appreciation.

At the conference in October, John addressed a public meeting on the subject 'Towards a World Federation' and gave a eulogy at a memorial meeting in honour of Hand of the Cause William S. Maxwell. He was also inspired to pioneer. Cabling Audrey to meet him in New York, John offered their pioneering services to Shoghi Effendi. Within four days of the New Delhi conference, John had sent a message to the World Centre saying that he and Audrey would pioneer anywhere in the world. Shortly afterwards Shoghi Effendi replied by cable: 'BECHUANALAND HIGHLY MERITORIOUS. LOVE, SHOGHI.'[16]

The cable came to John's office. As neither he nor Audrey knew the whereabouts of their new pioneer post, Audrey consulted an encyclopedia. Located between South Africa to the south and Southern Rhodesia to the north, Bechuanaland (now Botswana and formerly Bophuthatswana) was a land-locked country the size of France, embracing seven tribes. Comprised mostly of the Kalahari desert and without tarred roads, the country was a British protectorate with an extra-territorial capital 14 miles beyond its southern border, in South Africa. There, in the city of Mafeking (later Mafikeng), four members of the Robarts family settled for the next three years. For opening Bechuanaland to the Bahá'í Faith John, Audrey and Patrick were named Knights of Bahá'u'lláh. Nina, still a child of 13, was not able to have this honour.

The men of the Toronto King Street Agency of London Life were astonished by the decision of John and Audrey to abandon John's highly successful career and comfortable lifestyle to go as self-supporting pioneers with their two younger children to such a remote and surely uninviting part of the world. Under John's direction, the Agency had, over the last 15 years, become widely known throughout Canada and parts of the United States. Although the Agency was small, with only nine agents, the productivity of these men was very likely the highest in the country. Moreover, every agent belonged to the prestigious Million Dollar Round Table. An outstanding model branch, Toronto King was very close-knit, with many activities involving the agents and their wives. Some of these men had become Bahá'ís. Hosting a special farewell meeting for John, they presented him with a gold Omega wristwatch with the following inscription:

> To John A. Robarts c.l.u.
> whose faith comes first
> from the men of Toronto King
> Dec. 21st, 1953[17]

Nearly 40 years later, at the close of John's earthly life, these men were still in touch with their highly esteemed manager.

On Christmas Day 1953 the Robartses had a farewell gathering with John's sister and husband in Port Hope, Ontario, John's mother having passed away in July. Bookings had been made on the first ship to sail to South Africa. This turned out to be a small Norwegian cargo liner, called the *Thorshall.* Following their Christmas dinner, John, Patrick, Nina and Audrey set out for Montreal on the first leg of their African adventure. Aldham and Gerald headed in the opposite direction, to Toronto. Aldham would pioneer to Nigeria while Gerald would pioneer on the homefront. This departure marked the last time the six Robartses were to be together as a family for 36½ years.

After a three-week ocean journey on the *Thorshall*, the four Robartses reached Cape Town. John was approached by representatives of two South African life insurance companies with job offers even before he and his family had a chance to disembark!

Such was their joy at the Guardian's approval of their move to Bechuanaland that the Robartses arrived in Mafeking only 16 weeks after receiving Shoghi Effendi's cable. No sooner had they settled into their house in Mafeking than they began to receive visitors, among them Bill, Marguerite and Billy Sears, who stayed for several days. Bill and John would serve together in the years ahead as Auxiliary Board members, Regional Spiritual Assembly members and Hands of the Cause.

In 1954 John was appointed to the newly-established Auxiliary Board by Hand of the Cause Músá Banání. There were nine such Board members who served on the African continent.

In the same year John drew a prominent medical practitioner into the Cause. Dr Modiri Molema was the first Bahá'í in Bechuanaland. Since the authorities sometimes raided his office and home, owing to his former participation in the then banned African National Congress, Dr Molema did not register his membership in the Faith. Some of his African friends whom he introduced to John and Audrey were also under surveillance. When Dr Molema asked to have weekly firesides, Audrey made 125 yards of curtains to cover the windows so no one could see in.

*The Bahá'í World* for 1954–1963 highlights the difficulties faced by the first pioneers to southern Africa:

> The pioneers who opened this area to the Faith were, as the Guardian testified, 'a singularly distinguished and devoted group of pioneers' and more than most, they needed heroic qualities and wisdom to deal with the manifold problems confronting them in this part of the world. One day their story will be told freely, and their glorious deeds will be cherished by generations to come.[18]

Dr Molema gave the Robartses letters introducing them to six chiefs of tribes in the Protectorate. As a result of this gesture of courtesy, the Robartses were received by the chiefs and were invited to return. By presenting his friends and certain family members to John, Audrey and Nina, Dr Molema opened Bechuanaland to the Bahá'í Faith.

A year after their arrival in Mafeking the four Robartses received the bounty of a nine day pilgrimage. On their first evening in Haifa they entered the dining room of the Pilgrim House and met Shoghi Effendi. He placed them at the table: Audrey at the head and John opposite Shoghi Effendi, where he was able to look right into the Guardian's face. As Rúḥíyyih Khánum was seated on Shoghi Effendi's right and they occupied those same seats for seven days, John had a wonderful opportunity to see them both.

Asked years later in the film *Retrospective* about the impression the Guardian made on him, John replied: 'He made an impression on me that seized my heart. I loved him so much.'[19] John often said that to know Shoghi Effendi was to want to make him happy, to serve him in any way possible and to arise wholeheartedly to expedite his wishes. John's reverence for the Guardian touched the heart and his service to him set a standard to be emulated. Later John would arise to execute the directions of the Hands of the Cause and the Universal House of Justice with similar loyalty and zeal.

John was permitted to take notes of Shoghi Effendi's words during the pilgrimage, which he did at a fair speed. Shoghi Effendi unveiled the future of Canada, recommended an approach to prayer, instructed the Robartses on their work in Africa, spoke about the stages of evolution in the Faith, warned that Bahá'ís must not dishonour the Faith, shared the drawing of the new Archives building, pointed out the characteristics of the British, disclosed the future suffering of the United States, showed John and Audrey the scroll of the Knights of Bahá'u'lláh, clarified the Bahá'í position on the Communist system, elaborated on the Formative and Golden Ages of the Faith, contrasted the Administrative Order with the World Order, and shared with them his plans for the laying out of the Arc and the locations of the future administrative buildings, including the seat of the Universal House of Justice.

Shoghi Effendi asked John not to cut his ties with Canada and said he hoped he would be on the Regional Spiritual Assembly to be formed in southern African in 1956. John knew at that moment that he would be on that Assembly! Perhaps not surprisingly, Shoghi Effendi told Audrey, 'You must vie with him spiritually.'[20] Finally, Shoghi Effendi said that he wanted

> '. . . a mass of black African Bahá'ís' on that continent. He said we were there to teach the blacks, to associate with the whites only as much as was necessary. We would teach whites another time. He said to select one African, teach him or her thoroughly and encourage him or her to teach his or her own people. One good African teacher would be more effective than one hundred pioneers. We should remain on the sidelines and encourage Africans; never let them lose confidence in us, as it would be very hard to regain lost confidence, if ever. He said that in the past whites had gone to take something from Africa, but we had something to give.[21]

In 1956 three Regional Spiritual Assemblies were elected in Africa for the first time. John was elected to the Regional Spiritual Assembly of the Bahá'ís of South and West Africa, which had its seat in Johannesburg. In February of the following year and after forming the first Spiritual Assembly of Mafeking (the Assembly was black African; the Guardian instructed the Bahá'ís to form all-black assemblies so as not to arouse the suspicion of the authorities), the Robartses moved to Southern Rhodesia (Zimbabwe), from where they continued their work in Bechuanaland. Then, on the morning of the launching of the first Sputnik, 5 October 1957, the Robartses received the following telegram:

> LOVING CONGRATULATIONS ELEVATION HAND CAUSE GOD. FERVENT PRAYERS DIVINE GUIDANCE ALWAYS.[22]

John thought the cable was for Audrey. Handing it to her he exclaimed, 'Audrey, you are a Hand of the Cause!' She retorted immediately, 'I certainly am not!'[23] Two hours later a cable arrived from Hand of the Cause Mr Banání asking John to come to Kampala for the first meeting of the Hands for Africa on 15 October, thus clarifying the matter. The Hands of the Cause in Africa at that time were Músá Banání, Enoch Olinga, William Sears and John Robarts.

As a Hand of the Cause, John continued to travel internationally. On these occasions Audrey carried on the pioneer work alone, despite occasional riots and other troubles in their area. Not infrequently she drove hundreds of miles alone on rough roads in Southern Rhodesia and Bechuanaland, gathering people together for meetings despite many dangers. Nevertheless, she felt that she was really not alone because Shoghi Effendi knew their whereabouts and always prayed for the pioneers. Moreover, she felt she had been spared from a life-threatening illness in 1941 for a purpose: 'It gave me an extraordinary feeling of security and a realization that we would all receive the promised assistance.'[24]

When the Guardian died in November 1957 John and Audrey were devastated. John was unable to arrive in London in time to attend the funeral but he was present for the first historic Conclave (and subsequent Conclaves) of the Hands of the Cause in Haifa. While he was gone Audrey set out overland for Salisbury, 300 miles away, where a memorial service was being held for the Guardian. She had no one to whom she could turn in her grief. On the way to Salisbury, she kept turning on the windscreen wipers when she couldn't see the road for her tears.

During the historic yet agonizing years of the ministry of the Custodians, John often roomed with Enoch Olinga at the annual Conclaves. The two of them would sometimes laugh long into the night, keeping other the Hands awake. Enoch delighted his fellow Hands as he used literally to roll on the floor when something tickled him. John used to save up humorous stories during the year just for Enoch. Humour brought welcome relief to the Hands.

An example of the spontaneity of John's sense of humour occurred when he was attending a banquet at which a new Auxiliary Board member was seated to his left. To her left sat William Sears. She was quite nervous to find herself seated between two Hands of the Cause and excitedly whispered to John that she was afraid she would spill her dinner. John instantly replied, 'Spill to the left!'[25]

Between 1958 and 1966 John participated in three intercontinental Bahá'í conferences, made two extended visits to Bahá'í centres in Canada and travelled extensively throughout the African continent. Audrey accompanied her husband on his African travels and to French-speaking areas, where she translated for him. John addressed the Bahá'í World Congress in London on the subject 'Our Sacred Duty, Our Glorious Challenge'. He visited and encouraged Bahá'ís imprisoned in Morocco for their Faith. He represented the Universal House of Justice at the inaugural conventions for the Regional Spiritual Assemblies of West Africa and West Central Africa. Between 1961 and 1966 he was Trustee of the Continental Fund for Africa.

Following his second Canadian trip, of nearly seven months, in 1960, John wrote a letter to the Bahá'ís in Canada from his home in Southern Rhodesia.* This letter included excerpts from letters believers had written to him about the amazing results they had achieved after hearing him speak about the importance and power of prayer. In it John recorded a conviction fundamental to his faith: Divine inspiration and assistance are obtainable 'by developing a greater intensity of devotion to God and a determination to arise to serve Him'. He wrote that we achieve this 'through intensive and loving prayer, through reading some of the Teachings morning and evening, and through arising to teach.'[26] Further, he repeatedly stressed the power of the Long Obligatory Prayer, the Tablet of Aḥmad, the Remover of Difficulties, a teaching prayer and the repetition of the Greatest Name 95 times a day. Many individuals and communities, he said, experienced miraculous results when they recited these prayers often and asked God to guide them in greater service to the Cause.

'One thing', he emphasized, 'is that wherever there are Bahá'ís there are

* He also wrote the Introduction to *Messages to Canada*, a compilation of Shoghi Effendi's letters to Canada written between 1923 and 1957.

people waiting, ready to accept Bahá'u'lláh, to give their love and life to Him. We are surrounded by these devoted seekers. God will guide us to them, or them to us, if we will turn to Him in that greater intensity of devotion.'[27]

In 1966 John was assigned to Canada so that he could serve North America as a Hand of the Cause. The Robartses left Africa, having established an Assembly in Bulawayo and opened many localities to the Cause during their pioneering years. Henceforth they would keep in close touch with Africa and return to visit and encourage the believers.

In 1992, Audrey, in her eighty-eighth year, undertook a nine-week teaching trip in southern Africa before travelling to Haifa for the historic commemoration of the centenary of the ascension of Bahá'u'lláh. While she was in Bophuthatswana to address a major conference in Mmabatho (Mafikeng), the National Spiritual Assembly addressed her as the 'beloved mother of our country'. Four years later she reminisced about the years in Africa: 'How anyone could not love those dear people I will never understand. It was the greatest thing to have had those thirteen years among those people. How I missed the black faces when [we returned to Canada]'.[28] By 1995 the firm foundation John and Audrey laid in former Bechuanaland had yielded 67 local spiritual assemblies, 81 groups and over seven thousand Bahá'ís.

A letter from two of the early African believers conveys something of the impact the Robartses had in the region:

> I recall back in the fifties when the Prophet Bahá'u'lláh was first mentioned in Mafikeng on Botswana land in the late Dr Molema's home by you, Audrey and John. It was not mentioned boldly as is said today but was whispered because of security reasons.
>
> I remember getting to your house creeping in the dark to be taught the teachings of Bahá'u'lláh. I recollect those spiritual moments we enjoyed – the spiritual love, harmony to hear of the good tidings of Bahá'u'lláh which were said to us. We had lost hope – I was very desperate, did not have the future and your pioneering changed our attitudes to the white man and humanity at large. We are a balanced people today because of the Teachings of Bahá'u'lláh.[29]

John possessed a remarkable ability to communicate. Not only did he inspire audiences with his love for the teachings through marvellous stories but he also wrote straight from the heart, as though the recipient were present. Before preparing some of his letters he would consult with Audrey, on whose prudence, wisdom and knowledge of the teachings he could rely utterly.

In his early years John was often sought as a speaker for life insurance conferences and for the Boy Scouts. Because he could concentrate for long and uninterrupted periods, he developed a keenness of mind which permitted extraordinary accomplishments. Not easily distracted, he was known to have dictated as many as 52 beautiful letters in a single day.

As a former sales manager, John was fond of telling the Bahá'ís that 'we have the world's most difficult product to sell. But we have what no other "salesman" or product has: the promised assistance of God!'[30] He continually encouraged the believers to attract confirmations by teaching. This way, he said, others will join in, even the disaffected. The one remedy for all our ills, he said, is teaching.

John advised one community to pray to God for guidance as to what to say to comfort people. He said to watch the time spent in the local spiritual assembly meetings and how that time is spent, as every member sacrifices to attend. He suggested that the Nineteen Day Feasts be made so happy that no one would want to miss them. He recommended that the Bahá'ís prepare talks on the life of Bahá'u'lláh as this would increase their love for Him, inspiring and preparing them to teach.

During the last quarter century of his life John continued into an advanced age carrying the glad tidings of Bahá'u'lláh's revelation around the globe. Whether dedicating Bahá'í properties, visiting Australasia for six months, being present at international teaching conferences, attending the five-yearly international conventions in Haifa, representing the Universal House of Justice at Bahá'í conferences or convening the first meeting of the Continental Board of Counsellors for Northeast Asia, John, in spite of impaired health, just kept on and on and on.

In his eighty-third year John was adopted as an elder by the Tlingit people of the Yukon and honoured with the name 'Wolf Teeth'. In addition, he served as a member of the incorporated Local Spiritual Assembly of Rawdon, Quebec, in order to save it from lapsing. Two years later he made his last international teaching trip, to 11 cities in Ireland, while in 1990 he had to be restrained from participating in a Soviet travel teaching project, owing to his frailty.

Recalling John Robarts's most endearing qualities, his daughter wrote:

> Among John's most endearing qualities were his quick sense of humour and infectious laugh. He was a brilliant story teller. He often recounted real-life stories interspersed with pertinent quotations from Bahá'í scriptures. These stories conveyed a powerful spiritual message, and could move his listeners from tears or helpless laughter to renewed dedication to the Cause of God, and promptly to action, the goal for which they were intended. His calls for pioneers, his appeals on behalf of the Funds, his exhortations to heartfelt prayer, to 'planning our work and working our plan', raised innumerable individuals, families and communities to new spiritual levels of daily living, service and happiness.
>
> He continually invited, urged and guided the Bahá'ís to connect with that Source of all light that guided him, that was ever-present to him, that he so clearly saw lovingly surrounding us all, ready to rush to our assistance if we would but take the first step. He never doubted the capacity of the believers to win every goal. John seemed to walk the mystical path with practical feet and a penetrating eye. It was as though his vision extended beyond this material world and into the spiritual realm, enabling him to see straight to the heart of matters, to answer the unspoken question, to respond quickly and appropriately to the unuttered need.[31]

When the luminous soul of John Aldham Robarts passed out of this world on 18 June 1991, he was remembered by his distraught loved ones around the world in hundreds of tributes, in quiet contemplation and in renewed dedication. Some 400 people attended his beautiful funeral service where, in close proximity that day to the reposing form wherein the essence of John sojourned for well-nigh 90 years, they could pay homage. As his body was being laid to rest in the Ecumenical Cemetery at Rawdon, some would have pondered the constancy with which he laboured all his life in God's vineyard, others the excellence of his rank, his works and his servitude.

Perhaps John Aldham Robarts's legacy to those who would follow in the footsteps of this cherished Standard-bearer is that steadfastness begets distinction:

> All the virtues of humankind are summed up in the one word 'steadfastness', if we but act according to its laws. It draws to us as by a magnet the blessings and bestowals of Heaven, if we but rise up according to the obligations it implies.

> God be praised, the house of the heart is lit by the light of unswerving constancy, and the soul's lodging is bedecked with the ornament of faithfulness.
>
> Steadfastness is a treasure that makes a man so rich as to have no need of the world or any person or any thing that is therein. Constancy is a special joy, that leads us mortals on to lofty heights, great progress, and the winning of the perfections of Heaven. All praise be to the Beloved's holy court, for granting this most wondrous grace to His faithful people, and to His favoured ones, this best of gifts.[32]

On John's passing the Universal House of Justice sent a message to the Bahá'ís of the world:

> WITH SADDENED HEARTS ANNOUNCE PASSING MUCH-LOVED STAUNCH PROMOTER FAITH, KNIGHT BAHÁ'U'LLÁH, HAND CAUSE GOD JOHN ROBARTS. HIS DISTINGUISHED ADMINISTRATIVE TEACHING PIONEERING ACTIVITIES IN HIS NATIVE CANADA, IN AFRICA AND EUROPE, DURING MINISTRY BELOVED GUARDIAN AND SUBSEQUENTLY ON WORLD SCALE THROUGH HIS INTERNATIONAL TRAVELS WERE SOURCE ABUNDANT INSPIRATION COUNTLESS FRIENDS MANY LANDS. HIS RELIANCE AND EMPHASIS ON PRAYER IN ALL EFFORTS PROMOTION CAUSE AND HIS SUSTAINED SERVICES PATH LOVE FOR BLESSED BEAUTY WERE CHARACTERIZED BY SPIRIT CERTITUDE, SELF-EFFACEMENT AND VIGOUR WHICH SET A STANDARD OF STEWARDSHIP THAT HAS ENRICHED ANNALS FAITH. HE HAS ASSUREDLY EARNED BOUNTIFUL REWARD ABHÁ KINGDOM. PRAYING HOLY SHRINES PROGRESS HIS RADIANT SOUL. ADVISE HOLD BEFITTING MEMORIAL GATHERINGS IN HIS HONOUR THROUGHOUT WORLD INCLUDING ALL HOUSES WORSHIP. CONVEY DEAR AUDREY, BELOVED CHILDREN AND THEIR FAMILIES MOST LOVING SYMPATHY.[33]

# William Sears
# 1911–1992

William Bernard Patrick Michael Terence Sears VII was born to Catholic parents in Duluth, Minnesota on 28 March 1911. There, on 20 September 1912, at the age of almost 18 months, he had the first of a succession of dreams in which he saw a beautiful, shining white figure who brought indescribable peace and rapture. Not understanding the apparition, he described his unusual visions to his mother in his childhood language. The 'man in light' '. . . called me Peter. He told me not to follow in their footsteps.' On another occasion he reported that the 'shiny white figure' '. . . beckoned to me with his finger. He said, "I'm waiting for you. Search for me. Be like Peter. Fish."'[1]

From his early years, William Sears possessed an unusual interest in God. He would ask his parents, his grandfather, the preacher, the local people and even the mayor such questions as: 'Did God have a wife? . . . Where was His house? . . . Could He speak Chippewa Indian? . . . Did He really love everybody? . . . Why did He make mosquitoes?'[2]

Soon, young William found in his grandfather a spiritual mentor from whom he received satisfying answers and loving encouragement. 'Don't you quit asking questions and searching for what's in your heart,' Grandfather would tell young William, 'or your dream will never come true.'[3] 'If you find the light,' he told his grandson, 'never stumble or let it go.'[4]

With his grandfather's advice, William started studying the Bible. He studied keenly the history of biblical events, prophecies of the last days, the coming of the Son of Man in the glory of the Father, and the return of the Spirit of Truth. 'Someday I'm going to go all over the world and tell people about God,'[5] he told his parents. For this reason, he yearned to study and to understand what was in the Bible.

Whenever William could spend time with his grandfather, he learned much about the ways of people and of the world. When hearts are turned towards material things of this world, the old man would say, they become dark. But when they're turned to God and forget the things of the earth, they become bright and shiny inside. God, he said, doesn't cause suffering; people do that. The shepherds of the world are more interested in the wool than in the lambs. God knows what's going to happen, but He doesn't make it happen. Everyone is born with free will and a soul and chooses between right and wrong. 'If we were all a little busier trying to know what God wants instead of what we want, there wouldn't be so much trouble down here,' he told his grandson. 'And if they spent a little more time thinking about the inside part that lasts forever and a little less about the outside part that rots, they'd be better off when they get born into the next world.'[6]

William was a good listener. 'When I grow up I'm going to find out all about everything, then I'm going all over the world and tell people so that they won't hurt each other any more.'[7] A precocious lad, William Sears already understood his destiny.

When William did 'grow up', he enrolled at the University of Wisconsin and attended classes for a year. However, the harsh economic realities of the Great Depression eventually found him struggling for a living instead of studying for Alma Mater. He wrote his grandfather an apparently unhappy letter, the tone of which angered the old man, who replied: 'Nobody loves the William Sears that has a job and money and fine clothes. Nobody. Neither your mother nor father nor friends – not even your old grandfather. They love the qualities you possess. The kindness, the gentleness, the justice, the courage, the generosity – this is what they love. And as these things grow in you, their love for you becomes greater. And if you lose these qualities their love begins to wither and die. Anybody can be happy when everything is going fine, but it takes nobility to be happy when things are difficult.'[8]

Encouraged by his grandfather to stop worrying and to try writing about the Depression, William found some success in the next few years, writing and publishing nine one-act plays, two of which won awards. During this period he married, and he and his wife had two children, Bill, Jr and Michael. Following the birth of their second child, his wife was seriously ill in hospital for some months, and then passed away. Their infant son was placed in a sanatorium, where doctors said he would have to remain for several years.

Perhaps to assuage his heart-ache, William worked at his writing 12 to 18 hours a day. However, he found himself being 'pushed farther and farther away from [his] dream each day, and more and more into a world that cared very little about the things of the spirit'.[9] Not surprisingly, when he sent his grandfather a copy of an accolade recognizing the excellence of one of his plays, the older gentleman replied with a telegram: 'Look out! You may drop the torch.'[10]

Out of the blue, William was offered a job as a radio announcer at WOMT in Manitowoc, Wisconsin. He was hired as news editor and newscaster, and handled 15 minutes of news every hour, on the hour, 12 hours a day. The job did not last, but it marked the beginning of the rise of Mr Sears's professional star. The post at WOMT was followed by positions at WHBL in Sheboygan, WKBB in Dubuque, KFBK in Sacramento, KUTA in Salt Lake City, KPO in San Francisco, WPEN and WCAU in Philadelphia, and WCAU-Television and CBS.

While at WKBB, Bill Sears met Marguerite Reimer. She had come in to the radio station for an interview, and he was smitten. She had 'ripe-wheat hair, robin's-egg blue eyes, perfect teeth, a head-turning figure, and a smile that completely took away all your noble ideas about not becoming interested.'[11] On their first date he told her about his dream, and she told him about 'Abdu'l-Bahá.

Bill really did not want to discuss religion, but that night he accepted a book from Marguerite which she said would surprise him. The book was a record of 'Abdu'l-Bahá's public talks in America: *The Promulgation of Universal Peace*. Back home, Bill experienced a stab-like thrill of wonder when he came across the date of one of 'Abdu'l-Bahá's talks: 20 September 1912. He had spoken in Minneapolis, Minnesota, a short distance from where William had lived and dreamed as a child. In His talk, He had warned people to investigate the truth for themselves and not to follow in the footsteps of those who blindly accept things.

Bill was startled by this revelation, but remained unconvinced. However, his relationship with Marguerite blossomed. He proposed marriage to her, and she accepted.

In 1940, they had not been married long when Bill dreamed again of that wonderful figure from his childhood. In the dream, he was seated on a rock while the familiar figure came rushing towards him on a pair of skis, his white beard blowing in the breeze. 'Come with me,' the mystery person said. Then they were racing together down the mountain and onto a wide ledge, where they stood and looked out into a valley in which a city twinkled with flickering lights. The air became warm and was permeated with the fragrance of roses. Pointing towards the city, the wonderful figure smiled and said, 'This is the city,' and then vanished.[12]

Bill shared this dream with Marguerite. 'Where is this city?' she asked, after he had recounted the dream. He replied that he had never seen it before but would not fail to recognize it if he saw it again.[13]

They lived for a short time in Sacramento, before heading to Salt Lake City where Marguerite was a homefront pioneer. Marguerite promptly found their 'dream house', and told the real estate agent to hold the property for a few days even though they had no money for the down payment. Whether she acted on strong faith or on strong hunch, they had the money within an hour of the deadline, from an unexpected source – a maturing insurance policy. Bill was sceptical, but he learned quickly to respect this remarkable lady when she decided that she wanted something.

Just before Christmas they went for a drive high above the city, to City Creek Canyon. At that time of the year the city was beautifully lit by outdoor Christmas displays. As they were returning down the canyon, in the direction of the city, they stopped the car at Lookout Point. A premonition seized Bill as he approached a ledge. 'I stepped to the ledge,' Bill later wrote, 'and there lying below me was the magic city I had seen so clearly in my dream.' He turned to Marguerite, and said, 'This is the city.'[14]

Back home, Marguerite asked Bill many questions about his dream. He described the bearded figure who had stood on the ledge with him and promised that Bill would see the city. After a while, Marguerite showed Bill a picture of a man. Bill saw the 'white beard, soft as silk, the flowing white robes, the smile of eternal kindness', and was deeply moved.

'This', he said, 'is the man.'

'That', Marguerite said, 'is 'Abdu'l-Bahá.'[15]

There was no escaping it. Bill could no longer ignore such remarkable coincidences in his life. Some day he was going to find out all about God and tell the world about Him. Had the day of reckoning dawned? Launching into an earnest investigation of the Bahá'í Faith, Bill became convinced of the truth of the Cause through reading *The Dawn-Breakers*. Christ had indeed returned, but as a 'thief in the night'. It was a hundred-year-old mystery that no one had been able to solve.

One evening, Bill retired to the privacy of their den, where he pondered *The Book of Proofs* for three hours and then knelt before God in prayer until dawn. 'What went on during those hours', he later wrote, 'is between God and myself.' When he emerged the next morning, he embraced Marguerite and said, 'I am a Bahá'í.' 'I know,' she replied. 'I've always known.'[16]

During the years immediately following, Mr Sears became a very visible media personality. He was Radio Director for the Gillham Advertising Agency in Salt Lake City, and Radio Director for the Knox-Reeves Agency in San Francisco. For two years he was the narrator of a day-time soap on NBC. He won the first TV-Guide Magazine Award for the most popular 15-minute television sports programme at WCAU, and had the highest rated two-hour night-time humour programme in Philadelphia. His sports programme, *The Bill Sears Show*, aired for 15 minutes five days a week and was awarded an Emmy as the best sports series of 1951. He appeared twice on the *Ed Sullivan Show* with episodes from *In the Park*, the comedy drama he had created with Paul Ritts. And he was the only media personality to be listed in Edward R. Murrow's *This I Believe* for his exemplary life. He was earning a huge salary and was well on his way to becoming one of the media giants of the era. But he gave it all up to pioneer to Africa.

In some 40 pages of his book *All Flags Flying*, Mr Sears explained why: 'Bahá'í pioneers', he wrote, 'are preparing the way so that every person on earth, in every part of the planet, can have his or her chance to enter into . . . the Kingdom of God on earth . . .'[17]

The Sears family arrived in South Africa in 1953, at the outset of the Ten Year Crusade, in response to the Guardian's appeal for pioneers, and began what Bill later described as the most exciting and happiest years of their Bahá'í pioneering lives. Tick fever, broken ribs, a coronary, Asian flu, malaria, hepatitis and deadly cobras could not dampen his enthusiasm. Settling on a farm 25 kilometres outside Johannesburg, they raised peacocks and grew a wide variety of fruits and vegetables. From their ample harvest they prepared foods and baked cakes. Baking-day invariably coincided with deepening classes, study classes and firesides, attracting people in droves from neighbouring communities. According to Bill, Marguerite conducted a permanent open house at their farm.

Bill's creative talent was soon in evidence again. He launched the radio programme *That Man Sears*, which became so popular that it was heard from the Atlantic Ocean to the Indian Ocean, from Cape Town in South Africa to Lorenço Marques (Maputo) in Mozambique

In April 1954 William Sears made his first pilgrimage to the Holy Land.

His deepest longing was to meet the Guardian, but his heart was filled with trepidation. Hand of the Cause of God Ugo Giachery had told him in Rome how he felt shivers down his spine every time he approached the door to the Pilgrim House dining room, like a little boy who had been caught with jam on his face. Bill recalled later that Dr Giachery had not told him that it was such a cold shiver and that there was so much jam!

Filled with trepidation as he anticipated meeting the Guardian, he felt both misgivings for his shortcomings and the yearnings of his devotion. On Bill's first night the Guardian was absent from Haifa, staying at Bahjí. When the pilgrims were gathered in the Pilgrim House for dinner on the second night, Bill felt himself revealed in all his unworthiness as Shoghi Effendi came towards him, held out his arms and embraced him. Bill found that his throat was constricted and his eyes were misty.

'I had made my living by words,' he wrote later. But when the Guardian 'asked me about my journey . . . [I] could think of nothing to say in his presence. My words were feeble, clumsy and uncertain. It was as though a glib tongue had been made fearful that it might try to say something witty or clever.'[18] William Sears recorded that memorable first meeting for posterity:

> I felt only a transcendent happiness. I watched the Guardian with rapt attention and ever increasing devotion. This was as close, in our day, as man could come to the direct source of the power of God, His Majesty, His Justice, His Mercy, His Love. I felt them all flowing from the Guardian . . .
>
> This Guardian could be impressed by only one thing, service to the Faith. Nothing could ever influence his judgement; not wealth, position, power, or friendship . . .
>
> One thing was apparent to me at once. My life was changing. My concept of the Faith, of teaching, of service, none of these would ever be the same again . . .
>
> The Guardian calls you to a higher service. He lifts you up to heights of limitless joy, then sets you gently down. Having revealed the treasure, he requests the payment, which is service to the Faith of God . . . Not big projects planned, but small projects completed. He does not interest himself in what you are going to do, but in what you have done.[19]

William Sears described the Guardian as being short in stature, with dark hair, greying at the sides, a medium to dark complexion, and dark eyes that became lighter when animated, as though burning with some inner fire. Shoghi Effendi had small, slender, expressive hands. He was smooth shaven, with a dark moustache. He had an energetic quality and was very sturdy.

As a pioneer himself, Bill naturally remembered what Shoghi Effendi had to say about pioneering:

> The Guardian said that the friends feel that it is difficult to leave their homes and pioneer, even to move to the goals inside their own countries. They do not see that he is not asking them to sacrifice. He is protecting them from themselves. He is protecting them not only from the calamity that is rushing toward them outwardly, but he is protecting them from the calamity that is rushing toward them inwardly.[20]

Five days after Mr Sears arrived for his pilgrimage, on 1 April 1954, the Guardian sent his historic cable directing the Hands of the Cause of God to appoint Auxiliary Boards, whose members would assist them in their work of the propagation and protection of the Faith.[21]

The final moments before his parting from his beloved Guardian brought heart-ache to William:

> The Guardian came around the head of the table to take my hands in parting. I clung to him, trying to drain courage from him. He said he would pray for the success of the work in South Africa. Then he embraced me! He kissed me upon the cheeks. I pressed him to my heart. He smiled lovingly to me. 'I hope when you make your next pilgrimage,' he said, 'that you will bring some of your African children with you.' Then he was gone![22]

Mr Músá Banání, the Hand of the Cause in Africa, appointed William Sears as a member of his Auxiliary Board. The area for which Mr Sears was responsible included 14 countries and 4 islands in the region that came under the jurisdiction of the Regional Spiritual Assembly of South and West Africa when it was formed two years later.

In 1956 Mr Sears was elected to first Regional Spiritual Assembly, and served as its chairman. Marguerite, who was also elected to the Assembly, served as its secretary. Then, in October 1957, Mr Sears received the message from Shoghi Effendi that he had been appointed a Hand of the Cause of God.

As a Hand of the Cause, Mr Sears travelled the equivalent of 20 times around the world. The list of places he visited would fill pages, and includes such far-flung destinations as Lagos, Kyoto, Canberra, San Jose, Addis Ababa, Port au Prince, Jakarta, Adrianople, Anchorage, Ṭihrán, West Berlin, New Delhi, Reunion Island, Buenos Aires, Pearl Harbor, Canton, Brussels, Cyprus, the list goes on and on.

During 1958, and again from 1961 to 1963, he served as one of the Custodians of the Faith in the Holy Land. In 1958 he attended the intercontinental conference in Kampala, Uganda and the first National Convention in France. Between 1959 and 1961 he visited all the National Spiritual Assemblies in North, Central and South America.

Following the first election of the Universal House of Justice, William and Marguerite resettled in the United States. There, his first major project was the 1965–66 California Victory campaign, which served as a model for mass teaching in other parts of the world. With Dr Amín Banání he produced four cassette tapes of *Stories from the Children's Dawn-Breakers*, and with his friend Robert Quigley he helped to create the first series of quality Bahá'í television programmes, and co-authored *The Flame*. In 1984, his labours enabled the Bahá'í radio station WLGI, at the Louis Gregory Institute, to go on air.

Whether travelling the world or at home, William Sears embodied 'Abdu'l-Bahá's instructions to the Hands of the Cause:

> The obligations of the Hands of the Cause of God are to diffuse the Divine Fragrances, to edify the souls of men, to promote learning, to improve the character of all men and to be, at all times and under all conditions, sanctified and detached from earthly things. They must manifest the fear of God by their conduct, their manners, their deeds and their words.[23]

Well versed in the writings of the Faith, William spoke with clarity, force and love from the teachings, while reminding the believers that his own words were 'ashes'. When invited to give a talk, Mr Sears might spend weeks in preparation, rather than merely expecting to stand before an audience and be inspired. His Bahá'í library of the major works of the Central Figures of the Faith was literally worn out through use. His ability to quote from scripture often moved his audience and he inspired both young and old to strive to embody a more noble style of life and to reach for a loftier standard of service to the Holy Threshold.

A man of concentrated energy, intense devotion, and prodigious accomplishments, Mr Sears launched many teaching campaigns around the world in which he emphasized the greatness of this day, the urgency of the hour and the capacity of the Bahá'ís to fulfil any task they set themselves. He was always on the look-out for a soul who could set a continent ablaze. He longed to see the believers arise to their high calling. He often quoted from the writings passages asserting humanity's greatness and potential:

> Say, verily any one follower of this Faith can, by the leave of God, prevail over all who dwell in heaven and earth . . .[24]

> He that summoneth men in My Name is, verily, of Me, and he will show forth that which is beyond the power of all that are on earth.[25]

Mr Sears urged the believers to rely on the assistance of the Supreme Concourse, a resource so under-used, he said, that the accumulation of power waiting to come to our aid was awesome. Asked how Bill drew on this power himself, Marguerite replied:

> Firstly, earnest daily prayer. Not only morning and night – but frequently during the day.
>
> His complete reliance on the creative Word and his 'pondering' to get more and more answers from every Word.
>
> His work, whatever he was doing at the time, was always in the forefront of his mind. He carried a very small notebook always in case an idea came when [he was] away from his desk so he could write it down to transfer where needed later.
>
> His concentration was complete when he was working.
>
> Nothing else existed – there were no half-way measures. This was intensified when he became a Bahá'í.
>
> It was like an acetylene torch in its intensity – and as a result of this, I'm sure attracted help constantly from the Supreme Concourse.[26]

A brilliant educator, Mr Sears was able to translate his own knowledge of the Faith into terms everyone could understand. He often used physical examples to demonstrate spiritual concepts. Once, for example, he set out mirrors to reflect the sun, indicating how God is mirrored in His Manifestations. Another time he turned a glass upside down before pouring water onto it, showing how earth-bound people cannot receive the waters of Bahá'u'lláh's teachings.

Eleven of Mr Sears's books were published during his lifetime. He used a variety of writing techniques to make his points and address different audiences. Perhaps his best known work is *Thief in the Night*, which has inspired thousands of readers around the world since its first publication in 1961. Demonstrating how the Bahá'í Faith fulfils biblical prophecy, *Thief in the Night* is one of the best-selling Bahá'í books. It has been reprinted more than 20 times in English and translated into 12 languages. His other published works include *The Wine of Astonishment*, *Release the Sun*, *God Loves Laughter*, *A Cry from the Heart*, *The Prisoner and the Kings*, *Prince of Peace*, *All Flags Flying*, and *The Flame*. Since his passing, *In Grandfather's Barn* and *The Half-Inch Prophecy* have also been published.

In the evening of his life, though he suffered from diabetes, failing eyesight, arthritis and general debility and had to be driven everywhere, carried or wheeled from car to meeting place and continually shielded by his wife from well-meaning offers of assistance by Bahá'ís and friends, and though he appeared exhausted before and after meetings, he nevertheless possessed an amazing ability to speak to the believers with the power of a much younger man and to stir the friends to greater heights. Such was the love of this indefatigable Hand of the Cause whose body wore out but whose spirit shone with brilliance and power.

When his final moments on this earthly plane inevitably arrived, William Sears simply fell down, too exhausted to rise again, and then his noble soul abandoned its earthly temple.

On his passing on 25 March 1992, the Universal House of Justice cabled:

> OUR HEARTS DEEPLY SADDENED, BAHÁ'Í WORLD GREATLY DEPRIVED, BY PASSING HAND CAUSE GOD WILLIAM SEARS, VIBRANT, CONSECRATED, STOUT-HEARTED STANDARD-BEARER FAITH BAHÁ'U'LLÁH. HIS MORE THAN HALF-CENTURY UNBROKEN SERVICE MARKED BY UNFLINCHING DEVOTION TO BELOVED GUARDIAN, INFECTIOUS ENTHUSIASM FOR TEACHING, GALVANIZING SENSE DRAMA, DISARMING HUMOUR, SPECIAL LOVE FOR CHILDREN, UNFLAGGING DETERMINATION IN FACE DIFFICULTIES. HE WILL EVER BE REMEMBERED FOR DEDICATING FULL RANGE HIS CREATIVE AND ENERGETIC CAPACITIES AS WRITER, EDITOR, LECTURER, RADIO AND TELE-

VISION PROGRAMME DIRECTOR, TO HIS VARIED SERVICES AS TRAVELLING TEACHER TO NUMEROUS COUNTRIES, PARTICULARLY IN THE AMERICAS, AND AS PIONEER TO AFRICA WHERE HE WAS MEMBER OF AUXILIARY BOARD AND THE NATIONAL SPIRITUAL ASSEMBLY SOUTH AND WEST AFRICA WHEN IN 1957 HE WAS ELEVATED RANK HAND CAUSE. HE LATER SERVED AS MEMBER BODY HANDS HOLY LAND. HIS LOSS ACUTELY FELT IN NORTH AMERICA WHERE HE EXPENDED LAST MEASURE HIS EBBING STRENGTH PROMOTION TEACHING ACTIVITIES. DYNAMIC EFFECTS HIS WORK ENDURE THROUGH HIS MANY BOOKS AND RECORDINGS. GENERATIONS TO COME WILL REJOICE IN RICH LEGACY LEFT THEM THROUGH HIS HISTORIC ACCOMPLISHMENTS. FERVENTLY PRAYING HOLY SHRINES PROGRESS HIS ILLUSTRIOUS SOUL ABHÁ KINGDOM. ADVISE FRIENDS THROUGHOUT WORLD COMMEMORATE HIS PASSING. REQUEST BEFITTING MEMORIAL SERVICES IN HIS HONOUR ALL HOUSES WORSHIP.[27]

Hasan Balyuzi

Hasan Balyuzi and three of his five sons

Abu'l-Qásim Faizi speaks to Bahá'ís in London

Abu'l-Qásim Faizi

Abu'l-Qásim Faizi with Hushmand Fatheazam

Collis Featherstone

Collis Featherstone
with his wife,
Madge, and Golbang
in Thailand, 1988

John Ferraby

John Ferraby with his wife, Dorothy, and daughter, Brigitte

Dr Raḥmatu'lláh Muhájir

Enoch Olinga

Enoch Olinga looks on as a transcontinental telephone call is made between the Oceanic Conference of the South China Seas, Singapore, and the Continental Conference for West and central Africa, 1–3 January 1971

John Robarts

John Robarts with Counsellors at the Counsellors/Auxiliary Board Conference in Manitoba, Canada, 1984

William Sears

Hands of the Cause Zikrullah Khadem and William Sears

# Appendix I

The Universal House of Justice

26 November 2007

To the Bahá'ís of the World

Dearly loved Friends,

We are moved on the occasion of this Day of the Covenant to reflect on the august Institution of the Hands of the Cause of God in the aftermath of the decease only two months ago of the last remaining Hand of the Cause, Dr. 'Alí-Muḥammad Varqá. It was just a few weeks before the fiftieth anniversary of the passing of Shoghi Effendi that our world community suffered this grievous loss. How sobering, indeed, it is to realize that Dr. Varqá's departure brought to an end the remarkable stewardship of an institution whose legacy is unparalleled in religious history! At so significant a juncture in the Formative Age of the Faith, it is only fitting that an effort be made to understand more deeply than before the significance of the achievements of so outstanding an organ of the Administrative Order – one that proved to be so integral to the evolution of our world community during its nascent years.

We trace the origins of the Institution to Bahá'u'lláh Himself, Who designated four renowned promoters of His teachings as Hands of the

Cause of God. In a period before the administrative system of the Faith was inaugurated, they became rallying points for the friends, as much because of the virtuous character of their personal lives as for their unceasing endeavours in proclaiming the Teachings and defending the Faith against its detractors. They remained resolute in such activities despite the severe persecution, including imprisonment in some instances, to which they were subjected by the authorities. These distinguished personages remained active during the ministry of 'Abdu'l-Bahá, Who, in 1899, instructed them to take steps to form the Local Spiritual Assembly of Ṭihrán, on which they all served. The focus of these first Hands on propagation and protection of the Faith, as well as their efforts to edify believers as to the importance of the new Laws, intimated even then the pattern of functioning the Institution would adopt at a later stage in the advancement of the Bahá'í community.

The Master did not Himself appoint Hands of the Cause, but referred to four believers posthumously as such. However, His Will and Testament confirmed the Institution and extended it by authorizing the Guardian of the Faith to appoint consecrated souls to it. At first, over a period of three decades, Shoghi Effendi named ten such souls posthumously; all were distinguished for the constancy, vigour and impact of their efforts to propagate the Cause and promote its best interests. The Guardian's designation in December 1951 of twelve living believers as Hands of the Cause introduced the Bahá'í world to a wholly new dynamic in the operation of the Order of Bahá'u'lláh; through it the Hands exerted an unusual vitality during the Ten Year Crusade, particularly after the sudden passing of the Sign of God. His subsequent appointment of seven more in February 1952 and replacement thereafter of five of those deceased kept the number of living Hands at nineteen until less than a month before his departure, when in his last message to the Bahá'í world he identified an additional eight, bringing the total to twenty-seven. Shoghi Effendi's description of them as the 'Chief Stewards of Bahá'u'lláh's embryonic World Commonwealth' prefigured the world-shaking reality of the unexpected responsibilities that would be thrust upon them on the morrow of his passing.

The Guardian now forever gone, the Hands' first task, despite the sorrow that overwhelmed them, was to restore the composure of a grief-stricken community. A vital aspect of that task was, of course, to settle the minds of the friends about the direction that the Faith would take. The Hands acted with dispatch. Only sixteen days after the burial of the Guardian, they issued from the Holy Land a proclamation to the Bahá'ís of East and West. Declaring that, after a thorough search, no will or instruction of Shoghi Effendi had been found, they set forth in this message the procedures they would follow in meeting the daunting challenge they faced. It announced that a body of nine Hands, designated 'Custodians', was constituted to function at the Bahá'í World Centre to protect the Faith, maintain communications with National Spiritual Assemblies in connection with the prosecution of the Ten Year Plan and on administrative matters, and attend to all issues related to the preservation of the World Centre of the Faith. The friends everywhere derived from this first communication assurance that the ship of the Cause would safely traverse the waters severely troubled by the Guardian's passing. Subsequent messages issued from conclaves of the Hands held in the Holy Land further infused confidence in the believers who arose to meet the goals set before them in the Plan.

The Hands residing outside the Holy Land, in addition to giving close attention to the progress of the Plan in their own regions, undertook extensive journeys to visit and encourage the believers in every clime. Their travels covered the entire surface of the planet as they pursued every opportunity to advance the work of the Plan left by Shoghi Effendi. The obligations of the Hands spelled out in the Will and Testament of 'Abdu'l-Bahá were carried out with the selflessness, fearlessness and zeal characteristic of their activity. To 'diffuse the Divine Fragrances, to edify the souls of men, to promote learning, to improve the character of all men' – all these they undertook with outstanding, sometimes astonishing, results. Such travels did not cease with the conclusion of the Ten Year Plan but continued with unabated intensity, the legendary journeys of Amatu'l-Bahá Rúḥíyyih Khánum generating immeasurable stimulus. Thus the activities of the Hands demonstrated to a superlative degree the efficacy of Bahá'u'lláh's assertion that the 'movement itself from place to place, when undertaken for the sake of God, hath always exerted, and can now exert, its influence in the world.'

Among the principal results of their combined labours, these stand out: maintenance of the stature of the Faith as an independent and indivisible Order; protection of the Cause against schism, despite the disloyalty to the Covenant of one among their exalted company, Mason Remey, whom they were obliged to cast out; preservation of the properties and maintenance of the Holy Places and gardens at the World Centre; success in the vast expansion of the Faith. All these hard-won accomplishments prepared the path to the smooth transition that the Hands effected from the ministry of Shoghi Effendi, as head of the Faith, to that of the Universal House of Justice, for whose first election they meticulously prepared the Bahá'í world, especially the fifty-six National Spiritual Assemblies that participated in it. The Hands of the Cause delivered to the House of Justice a community that was so greatly transformed during the Ten Year Plan as to place the Faith of Bahá'u'lláh on the map as a world religion in every legitimate sense. The grand celebration at the World Congress in London attended by Bahá'ís from countries of every continent demonstrated the validity of that claim.

Beyond the World Crusade, the Hands of the Cause threw the full weight of their support behind the newly formed Universal House of Justice, whose creation their valiant efforts ensured. They undertook many missions on its behalf and pursued tasks befitting their continuing obligation to propagate and protect the Faith. As in the absence of the Guardian there was no way further to appoint Hands of the Cause, the Hands in the Holy Land in particular performed what may well be viewed as a distinct and final mark of service: they assisted the House of Justice to extend into the future the functions of propagation and protection in the special character of their institution. Hence, in 1968 Continental Boards of Counsellors were raised up and then in 1973 was created the International Teaching Centre foreshadowed in the writings of Shoghi Effendi. In their tireless support of the House of Justice in the design of these institutions and in the guidance they lent to their development, the Hands left to the Bahá'í world a further legacy that only future generations will be able adequately to appreciate. A shining value of their ultimate exertions is evident in the stature to which the International Teaching Centre has risen in such a short time and the permeating influence of the institution of the Counsellors which reaches every nook and cranny of our worldwide community.

It is highly worthy of note that the body of the Hands, with one exception, remained unbeguiled by the allurements of power that commonly corrupt those who are suddenly thrust by force of circumstances into positions of elevated rank and authority. In this instance, all of creation cannot but bear witness to the integrity of their stewardship, the unblemished virtue of their faithfulness to principle.

A point to ponder as well is the survival to the last of the one who was simultaneously appointed in 1955 to the two offices of Hand of the Cause and Trustee of Ḥuqúqu'lláh. That he was able to shape the latter institution and finally to see to its administrative transition in the formation in 2005 of the International Board of Trustees of Ḥuqúqu'lláh, with branches spread throughout the globe, is yet another sign of the constancy and abundance of the providential confirmations which have attended the evolution of the Administrative Order. Clearly, then, the work of the divinely ordained Institution of the Hands of the Cause of God was indispensable to the progress of the Faith from the Heroic Age to an early period of the Formative Age; its effects are certain to endure as an integral part of the Order of Bahá'u'lláh. The passing of Dr. Varqá marks both the end of a chapter of Bahá'í history and the beginning of a new stage in the unfolding of that Order.

With such thoughts astir in our minds, we recognize with increasing wonder and appreciation the magnitude of the contributions of the Hands of the Cause of God to the growth and consolidation of the Faith in all parts of the world. In our grateful hearts we recite with deep emotion the benediction so eloquently exclaimed by the Lord of Hosts: 'Light and glory, greeting and praise be upon the Hands of His Cause, through whom the light of fortitude hath shone forth and the truth hath been established that the authority to choose rests with God, the Powerful, the Mighty, the Unconstrained, through whom the ocean of bounty hath surged and the fragrance of the gracious favours of God, the Lord of mankind, hath been diffused.'

[signed: The Universal House of Justice][1]

# Bibliography

'Abdu'l-Bahá. *Memorials of the Faithful.* Wilmette, Ill.: Bahá'í Publishing Trust, 1971.

— *The Promulgation of Universal Peace.* Wilmette, Ill.: Bahá'í Publishing Trust, 1982.

— *Selections from the Writings of 'Abdu'l-Bahá.* Haifa: Bahá'í World Centre, 1978.

— *Tablets of Abdul Baha Abbas.* New York: Bahá'í Publishing Committee, vol. 2, 1940.

— *Tablets of the Divine Plan.* Wilmette, Ill.: Bahá'í Publishing Trust, 1993.

— *The Will and Testament of 'Abdu'l-Bahá.* Wilmette, Ill.: Bahá'í Publishing Trust, 1971.

'Alá'í, 'Abdu'l-'Alí. *Mu'assisiy-i-Ayádíy-i-Amru'lláh.* Ṭihrán: Bahá'í Publishing Trust, 130 BE (AD 1973).

The Báb. *Selections from the Writings of the Báb.* Haifa: Bahá'í World Centre, 1976.

*Bahá'í International News Service*, 1970, July 1989, March 1990, March 1992.

*Bahá'í Journal.* National Spiritual Assembly of the United Kingdom, October 1973, October 1992.

*Bahá'í News.* National Spiritual Assembly of the United States, February 1938, September 1968, June 1973, January 1976, February 1976, April 1976, June 1980, May 1984, December 1986, October 1990.

*Bahá'í Prayers: A Selection of Prayers revealed by Bahá'u'lláh, the Báb and 'Abdu'l-Bahá.* Wilmette, Ill.: Bahá'í Publishing Trust, 2002.

*Bahá'í World, The.* vols. 1–12, 1925–54. Rpt. Wilmette, Ill.: Bahá'í Publishing Trust, 1980.

*Bahá'í World, The*, vol. 13. Haifa: The Universal House of Justice, 1970.

*Bahá'í World, The*, vol. 14. Haifa: The Universal House of Justice, 1974.

*Bahá'í World, The*, vol. 15. Haifa: Bahá'í World Centre, 1976.

*Bahá'í World, The*, vol. 16. Haifa: Bahá'í World Centre, 1978.

*Bahá'í World, The*, vol. 18. Haifa: Bahá'í World Centre, 1986.

*Bahá'í World, The*, vol. 19. Haifa: Bahá'í World Centre, 1997.

*Bahá'í World, The*, vol. 20. Haifa: Bahá'í World Centre, 1998.

*Bahá'í World 1999–2000, The*. Haifa: Bahá'í World Centre, 2001.

*Bahá'í World 2003–2004, The*. Haifa: Bahá'í World Centre, 2005.

Bahá'u'lláh. *Epistle to the Son of the Wolf*. Wilmette, Ill.: Bahá'í Publishing Trust, 1988.

— *The Hidden Words*. Wilmette, Ill.: Bahá'í Publishing Trust, 1990.

— *The Kitáb-i-Aqdas*. Haifa: Bahá'í World Centre, 1992.

— *The Kitáb-i-Íqán*. Wilmette, Ill.: Bahá'í Publishing Trust, 1989.

— *Tablets of Bahá'u'lláh revealed after the Kitáb-i-Aqdas*. Haifa: Bahá'í World Centre, 1978.

*Bahíyyih Khánum, the Greatest Holy Leaf: A Compilation from Bahá'í Sacred Texts and Writings of the Guardian of the Faith and Bahíyyih Khánum's Own Letters*. Haifa: Bahá'í World Centre, 1982.

Balyuzi, H. M. *'Abdu'l-Bahá*. Oxford: George Ronald, 1971.

— *The Báb*. Oxford: George Ronald, 1973.

— *Bahá'u'lláh, The King of Glory*. Oxford: George Ronald, 1980.

— *Edward Granville Browne and the Bahá'í Faith*. Oxford: George Ronald, 1970.

— *Eminent Bahá'ís in the Time of Bahá'u'lláh: With Some Historical Background*. Oxford: George Ronald, 1985.

Brown, Ramona Allen. *Memories of 'Abdu'l-Bahá*. Wilmette, Ill.: Bahá'í Publishing Trust, 1980.

Cameron, Glenn, and Momen, Wendi. *A Basic Bahá'í Chronology*. Oxford: George Ronald, 1996.

*Canadian Bahá'í News*, March 1990, June 1990, special memorial section to the July 1991 issue.

Chapman, Anita. *Leroy Ioas*. Oxford: George Ronald, 1998.

Collins, William. *Bibliography of English-Language Works on the Bábí and Bahá'í Faiths, 1844–1985*. Oxford: George Ronald, 1990.

*Compilation of Compilations, The*. Prepared by the Universal House of Justice 1963–1990. 2 vols. [Sydney]: Bahá'í Publications Australia, 1991.

*Diary of Juliet Thompson, The*. Los Angeles: Kalimát Press, 1983.

Dunbar, Hooper. *Forces of Light and Darkness*. A deepening class presented and recorded over several days at Louhelen Bahá'í School.

Dunn, Clara. *Recalls Becoming a Bahá'í and Meeting 'Abdu'l-Bahá*. A taped recording by Victor Richards in the home of H. Collis Featherstone, 1954.

Faizi, A. Q. *Milly: A Tribute to Amelia E. Collins.* Oxford: George Ronald, 1977.
Ferraby, John. *All Things Made New.* London: George Allen and Unwin, 1957.
Freeman, Dorothy. *From Copper to Gold.* Oxford: George Ronald, 1984.
Furútan, 'Alí-Akbar. *The Story of My Heart.* Oxford: George Ronald, 1984.
Garis, M. R. *Martha Root: Lioness at the Threshold.* Wilmette, Ill.: Bahá'í Publishing Trust, 1983.
Giachery, Ugo. *Shoghi Effendi: Recollections.* Oxford: George Ronald, 1973.
*Green Acre on the Piscataqua.* Eliot, Maine: Green Acre Bahá'í School Council, 1991.
Hassall, Graham. *The Bahá'í Faith in Australia 1920–34.* Yerrinbool: Bahá'í Studies Conference, April 1983.
— *Yerrinbool Bahá'í School 1938–1988.*
Ḥaydar-'Alí, Ḥájí Mírzá. *Stories from the Delight of Hearts: The Memoirs of Ḥájí Mírzá Ḥaydar-'Alí.* Los Angeles: Kalimát Press, 1980.
Hofman, David. *George Townshend.* Oxford: George Ronald, 1983.
Holley, Horace. *Bahai, the Spirit of the Age.* London: Kegan Paul Trench Trubner, 1921.
— *Bahaism: The Modern Social religion.* London: Sidgwick and Jackson, 1913.
— *A Pilgrim to Thonon.* Letchworth: Garden City Press, 1911.
— *Present-Day Administration of the Bahá'í Faith.* Wilmette, Ill.: Bahá'í Publishing Committee, 1947.
— *Religion for Mankind.* London: George Ronald, 1956.
— *The Social Principle.* New York: L. J. Gomme, 1915.
*Holy Bible.* King James Authorized Version. Cleveland and New York: The World Publishing Company.
Honnold, Annamarie. *Why They became Bahá'ís.* New Delhi: Bahá'í Publishing Trust, 1994.
*Ḥuqúqu'lláh, The Right of God.* Compiled by the Research Department of the Universal House of Justice. Oakham: Bahá'í Publishing Trust, 1986.
Ioas, Leroy. *In the Days of the Guardian.* Wilmette, Ill.: Bahá'í Publishing Trust, 1977.
*Japan Will Turn Ablaze.* Japan: Bahá'í Publishing Trust, 1974.
Khadem, Javidukht. *Zikrullah Khadem, The Itinerant Hand of the Cause of God.* Wilmette, Ill.: Bahá'í Publishing Trust, 1990.
*The Ministry of the Custodians, 1957–1963: An Account of the Stewardship of the Hands of the Cause.* Haifa: Bahá'í World Centre, 1992.
Momen, Moojan. *Dr. John E. Esslemont Hand of the Cause of God.* London: Bahá'í Publishing Trust, 1975.

— , ed. *Studies in the Bábí and Bahá'í Religions: Studies in Honor of the Late Hasan M. Balyuzi*. Los Angeles: Kalimát Press, 1988.

Morrison, Gary. 'Hand of the Cause, Agnes Alexander: A Eulogy'. *Bahá'í News*, 1971.

Morrison, Gayle. *To Move the World*. Wilmette, Ill.: Bahá'í Publishing Trust, 1982.

Muhájir, Irán Furútan. *Dr Muhájir, Hand of the Cause of God, Knight of Bahá'u'lláh*. London: Bahá'í Publishing Trust, 1992.

Nabíl-i-A'ẓam. *The Dawn-Breakers: Nabíl's Narrative of the Early Days of the Bahá'í Revelation*. Wilmette, Ill.: Bahá'í Publishing Trust, 1970.

Nakhjavání, Violette. *Amatu'l-Bahá Visits India*. New Delhi: Bahá'í Publishing Trust, 1984.

— *The Great African Safari: The Travels of Amatu'l-Bahá Rúḥíyyih Khánum in Africa, 1969–73*. Oxford: George Ronald, 2002.

Olinga, Enoch. *Are You Happy?* A recorded talk by Mr Olinga. Wilmette, Ill.: Bahá'í Publishing Trust, 1980.

Périgord, Emily McBride. *Translation of French Foot-Notes of the Dawn-Breakers*. Wilmette, Ill.: Bahá'í Publishing Trust, 1970.

Rabbaní, Rúḥíyyih. *The Guardian of the Bahá'í Faith*. London: Bahá'í Publishing Trust, 1988.

— *Poems of the Passing*. Oxford: George Ronald, 1998.

— *The Priceless Pearl*. London, Bahá'í Publishing Trust, 1969.

— 'This is Faith'. A poem written in 1953. By permission of the author.

Ransom-Kehler, Keith. *Presenting Keith Ransom-Kehler*. A résumé, circa 1922, provided to the author by the Bahá'í World Centre.

Robarts, Audrey. A recording of Mrs Robarts speaking about John Robarts. January–February 1995. Tapes 1 and 2.

Robarts, John A. *Letter to Bahá'ís*. Provided to the author by Mrs Audrey Robarts, 1995.

Rutstein, Nathan. *Corinne True: Faithful Handmaid of 'Abdu'l-Bahá*. Oxford: George Ronald, 1987.

— *He Loved and Served: The Story of Curtis Kelsey*. Oxford: George Ronald, 1982.

Samandarí, Ṭarázu'lláh. *In His Presence*. A talk by Hand of the Cause Mr Samandarí at the Bahá'í World Congress, London, 1963.

Schoen, Janet. 'A Love Which Does Not Wait'. *Bahá'í News*, no. 541, April 1976.

Sears, William. *A Cry from the Heart: The Bahá'ís in Iran*. Oxford: George Ronald, 1982.

— *All Flags Flying*. Goodwood: National Spiritual Assembly of the Bahá'ís of South and West Africa, 1985.

— *God Loves Laughter*. Oxford: George Ronald, 1984.

— *In Grandfather's Barn*. Wilmette, Ill.: Bahá'í Publishing Trust, 1997.
— *The Half-Inch Prophecy*. South Africa: Bahá'í Publishing Trust, 2000.
— *Pilgrimage to Haifa*. Bahá'í National Archives of Hawaii.
— *Prince of Peace*. India: Bahá'í Publishing Trust.
— *The Prisoner and the Kings*. Toronto, Ont.: General Publishing Company, Ltd, 1971.
— *Release the Sun*. Wilmette, Ill.: Bahá'í Publishing Trust, 1995.
— *Thief in the Night*. Oxford: George Ronald, 1961, 1980.
— *The Wine of Astonishment*. Oxford: George Ronald, 1983.
— and Quigley, Robert. *The Flame*. Oxford: George Ronald, 1973.
Shoghi Effendi. *The Advent of Divine Justice*. Wilmette, Ill.: Bahá'í Publishing Trust, 1990.
— *Citadel of Faith: Messages to America 1947–1957*. Wilmette, Ill.: Bahá'í Publishing Trust, 1965.
— *God Passes By*. Wilmette, Ill.: Bahá'í Publishing Trust, rev. edn. 1974.
— *The Light of Divine Guidance: The Messages from the Guardian of the Bahá'í Faith to the Bahá'ís of Germany and Austria*. 2 vols. Hofheim-Langenhain: Bahá'í-Verlag, 1982.
— *Messages to America*. Wilmette, Ill.: Bahá'í Publishing Trust, 1947.
— *Messages to the Antipodes*. Mona Vale NSW: Bahá'í Publications Australia, 1997.
— *Messages to the Bahá'í World*. Wilmette, Ill.: Bahá'í Publishing Trust, 1971.
— *Messages of Shoghi Effendi to the Indian Subcontinent, 1923–1957*. New Delhi: Bahá'í Publishing Trust, 1995.
— *This Decisive Hour*. Wilmette, Ill.: Bahá'í Publishing Trust, 2002.
— *The Unfolding Destiny of the British Bahá'í Community: The Messages of the Guardian of the Bahá'í Faith to the Bahá'ís of the British Isles*. London: Bahá'í Publishing Trust, 1981.
*Star of the West*. Rpt. Oxford: George Ronald, 1984.
Stockman, Robert. *The Bahá'í Faith In America*, vol. 1. Wilmette, Ill.: Bahá'í Publishing Trust, 1985.
— *The Bahá'í Faith in America, Early Expansion, 1900–1912*, vol. 2. Oxford; George Ronald, 1995.
Sulaymání, 'Azízu'lláh. *Maṣábiḥ-i-Hidáyat*. Ṭihrán: Bahá'í Publishing Trust, 121 BE.
Taherzadeh, Adib. *The Covenant of Bahá'u'lláh*. Oxford: George Ronald, 1992.
— *The Revelation of Bahá'u'lláh*, vol. 1. Oxford: George Ronald, 1974.
— *The Revelation of Bahá'u'lláh*, vol. 2. Oxford: George Ronald, 1977.
— *The Revelation of Bahá'u'lláh*, vol. 3. Oxford: George Ronald, 1983.

— *The Revelation of Bahá'u'lláh*, vol. 4. Oxford: George Ronald, 1987.

Tinnion, Nina Robarts. *John A. Robarts Memorial Article and Endnotes*, unpublished, 1995.

*To Follow a Dreamtime, 'Father' and 'Mother' Dunn, The Spiritual Conquerors of a Continent.* Commemorating the Fiftieth Anniversary of the Arrival of the Bahá'í Faith in Australia, 18 April 1970. Paddington, New South Wales: The National Spiritual Assembly of the Bahá'ís of Australia, Inc., 1970.

Townshend, George. *The Old Churches and the New World Faith.* London: National Spiritual Assembly of the British Isles, 1949.

Troxel, Duane. Talk to Bahá'ís of Santa Fe, New Mexico, circa 1989.

True, Corinne. *Notes Taken at Acca.* Chicago: Bahá'í Publishing Society, 1907.

The Universal House of Justice. *Messages from the Universal House of Justice 1963–1986.* Wilmette, Ill.: Bahá'í Publishing Trust, 1996.

van den Hoonaard, Will C. *The Origins of the Bahá'í Community of Canada, 1899–1948.* Waterloo, Ontario: Wilfrid Laurier University Press, 1996.

Varqá, Mehdi. *Varqá, 'Alí Muḥammad, the Martyr.* An article prepared for *The Bahá'í Encyclopedia.*

*Victory Promises.* A compilation by the National Spiritual Assembly of the Bahá'ís of the Hawaiian Islands, 1978.

*The Vision of Shoghi Effendi.* Ottawa: Bahá'í Studies Publications, 1993.

Waterman, Graham and Kaye. *H. Collis Featherstone.* An In Memoriam article, 1994.

Weinberg, Robert. *Ethel Jenner Rosenberg.* Oxford: George Ronald, 1995.

Whitehead, O. Z. *Portraits of Some Bahá'í Women.* Oxford: George Ronald, 1996.

— *Some Bahá'ís to Remember.* Oxford: George Ronald, 1983.

— *Some Early Bahá'ís of the West.* Oxford: George Ronald, 1976.

Whitmore, Bruce W. *The Dawning Place.* Wilmette, Ill.: Bahá'í Publishing Trust, 1984.

Zinky, Kay, comp. *Martha Root, Herald of the Kingdom.* New Delhi: Bahá'í Publishing Trust, 1983.

# References and Notes

## Introduction

1. Bahá'u'lláh, *Kitáb-i-Aqdas*, para. 173.
2. Bahá'u'lláh, *Tablets of Bahá'u'lláh*, p. 221.
3. Shoghi Effendi, quoted in Bahá'u'lláh, *Kitáb-i-Aqdas*, note 183.
4. 'Abdu'l-Bahá, *Will and Testament*, p. 13.
5. ibid. p. 12.
6. *Kitáb-i-Aqdas*, note 183.
7. Shoghi Effendi, *Messages to the Bahá'í World*, p. 127.
8. 'Abdu'l-Bahá, *Will and Testament*, p. 12.
9. The Universal House of Justice, *Messages from the Universal House of Justice*, p. 6.
10. ibid. p. 14.
11. ibid. p. 44.
12. The Universal House of Justice, quoted in *Ministry of the Custodians*, p. 2.

I

## Ḥájí Ákhúnd

1. 'Abdu'l-Bahá, *Memorials of the Faithful*, p. 9.
2. ibid. p. 10.
3. Balyuzi, *Eminent Bahá'ís*, p. 266.
4. Taherzadeh, *Revelation of Bahá'u'lláh*, vol. 4, p. 298.
5. 'Abdu'l-Bahá, *Memorials of the Faithful*, p. 11.
6. Taherzadeh, *Revelation of Bahá'u'lláh*, vol. 4, p. 297.
7. ibid.
8. ibid. p. 322.
9. 'Abdu'l-Bahá, *Memorials of the Faithful*, p. 11.
10. ibid. pp. 11–12.

## Ibn-i-Aṣdaq

1. Balyuzi, *Eminent Bahá'ís*, p. 171.
2. Taherzadeh, *Revelation of Bahá'u'lláh*, vol. 4, p. 302.

3. Balyuzi, *Eminent Bahá'ís*, p. 172.
4. ibid. p. 173.
5. ibid. p. 174.
6. Bahá'u'lláh, quoted in Shoghi Effendi, *Advent of Divine Justice*, p. 84.
7. Bahá'u'lláh had occasionally used the term 'Hands' in His earlier Tablets (e.g. Súriy-i-Haykal) but no particular individual had been so designated.
8. Balyuzi, *Eminent Bahá'ís*, p. 173.
9. Bahá'u'lláh, quoted in Shoghi Effendi, *Advent of Divine Justice*, pp. 83–4.

**Ibn-i-Abhar**

1. Taherzadeh, *Revelation of Bahá'u'lláh*, vol. 4, p. 306.
2. ibid.
3. ibid. pp. 308–10.
4. ibid. p. 311.
5. ibid. p. 307.

**Ḥasan-i-Adíb**

1. 'Alá'í, *Mu'assisiy-i-Ayádíy-i-Amru'lláh*. pp. 450–64. Provisional translation provided by the Bahá'í World Centre.

II

**Mullá Riḍá**

1. Balyuzi, *Eminent Bahá'ís*, p. 98.
2. Taherzadeh, *Revelation of Bahá'u'lláh*, vol. 1, p. 86.
3. ibid. p. 89.
4. ibid. p. 86.
5. Ḥaydar-'Alí, *Delight of Hearts*, p. 92.
6. Balyuzi, *Eminent Bahá'ís*, pp. 100–1.
7. Quoted in ibid. pp. 102–3.
8. ibid. pp. 105–6.
9. Taherzadeh, *Revelation of Bahá'u'lláh*, vol. 1, p. 87.
10. Balyuzi, *Eminent Bahá'ís*, pp. 107–8.
11. Taherzadeh, *Revelation of Bahá'u'lláh*, vol. 1, p. 88.
12. Balyuzi, *Eminent Bahá'ís*, p. 111.
13. Sulaymání, *Maṣábiḥ-i-Hidáyat*. Provisional translation provided by the Bahá'í World Centre.

**Nabíl-i-Akbar**

1. 'Abdu'l-Bahá, *Memorials of the Faithful*, p. 1.
2. ibid.
3. ibid. p. 2.
4. ibid. p. 3.
5. See Taherzadeh, *Revelation of Bahá'u'lláh*, vol. 4, pp. 33–49.
6. ibid. pp. 48–49.
7. Taherzadeh, *Revelation of Bahá'u'lláh*, vol. 2, p. 42.
8. ibid. p. 48.

9. 'Abdu'l-Bahá, *Memorials of the Faithful*, p. 3.
10. ibid. pp. 4–5.

**Mullá Ṣádiq**

1. 'Abdu'l-Bahá, *Memorials of the Faithful*, p. 5.
2. ibid. p. 6.
3. ibid.
4. Nabíl-i-A'ẓam, *Dawn-Breakers*, pp. 100–1.
5. Balyuzi, *Eminent Bahá'ís*, p. 11.
6. Nabíl-i-A'ẓam, *Dawn-Breakers*, p. 145.
7. ibid. p. 146.
8. ibid.
9. ibid. p. 147. It is reckoned that Mullá Ṣádiq was about 45 years old at this time, although there are no records of his birth. If he was thought to be old and frail in 1845, one can only speculate on how advanced his age was when he died in 1889.
10. ibid. pp. 147–8.
11. 'Abdu'l-Bahá, *Memorials of the Faithful*, p. 6.
12. Nabíl-i-A'ẓam, *Dawn-Breakers*, p. 381.
13. ibid. p. 416.
14. 'Abdu'l-Bahá, *Memorials to the Faithful*, p. 7.
15. Upon learning of his conversion, Bahá'u'lláh revealed a Tablet in his honour. He was the grandfather of the former member of the Universal House of Justice Luṭfu'lláh Ḥakím.
16. 'Abdu'l-Bahá, *Memorials of the Faithful*, p. 7.
17. Balyuzi, *Eminent Bahá'ís*, p. 22–3.
18. Taherzadeh, *Revelation of Bahá'u'lláh*, vol. 3, pp. 258–9.
19. 'Abdu'l-Bahá, *Memorials of the Faithful*, p. 8.
20. Balyuzi, *Eminent Bahá'ís*, p. 23.

**Mírzá 'Alí-Muḥammad Varqá**

1. Mírzá 'Alí-Muḥammad Varqá, quoted in Balyuzi, *Eminent Bahá'ís*, p. 75.
2. ibid. p. 84.
3. ibid. pp. 94–6.
4. 'Abdu'l-Bahá, *Memorials of the Faithful*, pp. 84–5.
5. ibid. pp. 85–6.
6. Balyuzi, *Eminent Bahá'ís*, p. 77.
7. Taherzadeh, *Revelation of Bahá'u'lláh*, vol. 4, p. 54.
8. ibid. p. 55.
9. Later 'she was honoured by a Tablet revealed by 'Abdu'l-Bahá, and she received the title of Amatu'l-Hagh (the maidservant of God) by Him. I [Hand of the Cause Dr Varqá] remember her helping me in my childhood to memorize Bahá'í prayers. She passed away in our home when I was 8 or 9 years old, and she was buried in our family grave yard and finally was transferred to the Bahá'í cemetery in Ṭihrán before its destruction by the mob during the revolution.' From a letter to the writer from Hand of the Cause Dr 'Alí-Muḥammad Varqá.
10. Taherzadeh, *Revelation of Bahá'u'lláh*, vol. 4, p. 60.

11. Balyuzi, *Eminent Bahá'ís*, pp. 90–1.
12. ibid. p. 95.

III

**Ḥájí Amín**

1. Taherzadeh, *Revelation of Bahá'u'lláh*, vol. 3, pp. 77–8.
2. Bahá'u'lláh, in *Compilation of Compilations*, vol. 1, p. 489.
3. From a letter written by Shoghi Effendi to the second Bahá'í National Convention in Iran, dated July 1928. Provisional translation provided by the Bahá'í World Centre.

**'Abdu'l-Jalíl Bey Sa'ad**

1. *Bahá'í World*, vol. 9, p. 598.
2. Shoghi Effendi, *This Decisive Hour*, p. 20.
3. Letter written on behalf of Shoghi Effendi, in *Messages to the Indian Subcontinent*, p. 224.
4. Shoghi Effendi, *This Decisive Hour*, p. 75.

**John Henry Hyde Dunn**

1. Shoghi Effendi, *Messages to America*, p. 45.
2. Shoghi Effendi, *God Passes By*, p. 308.
3. *To Follow A Dreamtime*, p. 1.
4. Dunn, *Recalls Becoming a Bahá'í and Meeting 'Abdu'l-Bahá.*
5. ibid.
6. Brown, *Memories of 'Abdu'l-Bahá*, p. 33.
7. Dunn, *Recalls Becoming a Bahá'í and Meeting 'Abdu'l-Bahá.*
8. *Star of the West*, vol. 7, no. 4, p. 30.
9. *Bahá'í World*, vol. 9, pp. 594–5.
10. ibid. p. 595.
11. ibid.
12. ibid.
13. *To Follow a Dreamtime*, p. 5.
14. Shoghi Effendi, *Messages to the Antipodes*, p. 16.
15. *Bahá'í World*, vol. 9, p. 595.
16. Cited in Whitehead, *Some Bahá'ís To Remember*, p. 162.
17. Garis, *Martha Root*, p. 187.
18. Notes of Harold and Florence Fitzner, 4 September 1995.
19. Garis, *Martha Root*, p. 188.
20. Cited in Whitehead, *Some Bahá'ís To Remember*, p. 161.
21. *To Follow a Dreamtime*, p. 9.
22. *To Follow a Dreamtime*, pp. 4–5.
23. *To Follow a Dreamtime*, pp. 10–11.
24. Shoghi Effendi, *Messages to the Antipodes*, p. 108.
25. *To Follow a Dreamtime*, p. 11.
26. ibid. pp. 11–12.

27. ibid. p. 12.
28. Notes of Harold and Florence Fitzner.
29. *Bahá'í World*, vol. 9, pp. 595–6.
30. ibid. p. 596.
31. Keith Ransom-Kehler, Martha Root and May Maxwell.
32. *Bahá'í World*, vol. 9, p. 597.
33. *To Follow a Dreamtime*, p. 17.

**John Ebenezer Esslemont**

1. Momen, *Dr. John E. Esslemont*, p. 2.
2. ibid. p. 8.
3. ibid. pp. 8–9.
4. *Bahá'í World*, vol. 1, p. 134.
5. Cited in Momen, *Dr. John E. Esslemont*, p. 33.
6. Weinberg, *Ethel Jenner Rosenberg*, p. 172.
7. Cited in Momen, *Dr. John E. Esslemont*, p. 10.
8. ibid. p. 11.
9. ibid. p. 13.
10. ibid. p. 16.
11. ibid. p. 21.
12. Weinberg, *Ethel Jenner Rosenberg*, p. 174.
13. ibid. p. 175.
14. Rabbani, *Priceless Pearl*, p. 40.
15. Momen, *Dr. John E. Esslemont*, p. 25.
16. Cited in Weinberg, *Ethel Jenner Rosenberg*, p. 213.
17. Momen, *Dr. John E. Esslemont*, p. 27.
18. Rabbani, *Priceless Pearl*, p. 91.
19. Garis, *Martha Root*, p. 214.
20. Whitehead, *Some Early Bahá'ís of the West*, p. 178.
21. Garis, *Martha Root*, p. 210.
22. Momen, *Dr. John E. Esslemont*, p. 36.
23. *Bahá'í World*, vol. 8, pp. 934–5.
24. ibid.

**Louis George Gregory**

1. Elaine Snider Eilers, quoted in Morrison, *To Move The World*, p. 314.
2. ibid. p. 24.
3. ibid. p. 4.
4. Quoted in ibid. p. 7.
5. Quoted in ibid. pp. 45–6.
6. 'Abdu'l-Bahá, in *Star of the West*, vol. 12, no. 6, p. 121.
7. Quoted in Morrison, *To Move the World*, p. 59.
8. Shoghi Effendi, *Advent of Divine Justice*, p. 33.
9. *Bahá'í World*, vol. 12, p. 668.
10. Quoted in Morrison, *To Move the World*, pp. 66–7.
11. ibid. p. 72.
12. ibid. p. 89.
13. ibid. p. 70.

14. ibid. p. 116.
15. Quoted in ibid. p. 117.
16. *Bahá'í World*, vol. 12, p. 669.
17. *Bahá'í World*, vol. 4, p. 487.
18. *Bahá'í World*, vol. 2, p. 282.
19. ibid.
20. Morrison, *To Move The World*, p. 154.
21. *Bahá'í World*, vol. 4, p. 488.
22. *Bahá'í World*, vol. 12, p. 666.

**Keith Ransom-Kehler**

1. *Bahá'í News*, April 1976, pp. 9–10.
2. 'Presenting Keith Ransom-Kehler', p. 1.
3. Khadem, *Zikrullah Khadem*, p. 26.
4. *Bahá'í News*, April 1976, p. 10.
5. *Bahá'í World*, vol. 5, pp. 57–8.
6. ibid. p. 391.
7. Rabbani, *Priceless Pearl*, p. 306.
8. ibid.
9. *Bahá'í World*, vol. 5, p. 391.
10 ibid.
11. ibid. p. 392.
12. ibid. p. 391.
13. ibid. p. 393.
14. Khadem, *Zikrullah Khadem*, p. 25.
15. *Bahá'í World*, vol. 5, p. 402.
16. ibid. p. 397.
17. ibid. p. 398.
18. ibid. p. 409.
19. Khadem, *Zikrullah Khadem*, p. 26.
20. ibid. pp. 24–5.
21. Shoghi Effendi, *This Decisive Hour*, pp. 6–7.
22. *Bahá'í World*, vol. 5, p. 398.
23. ibid. p. 409.

**Muḥammad Taqí Iṣfahání**

1. *Bahá'í World*, vol. 11, p. 500.
2. ibid.
3. ibid. p. 501.
4. ibid. p. 502.
5. ibid.

**Martha Louise Root**

1. From a talk by Dr Duane Troxel to Bahá'ís of Santa Fe, New Mexico, circa 1989.
2. Rabbani, *Priceless Pearl*, p. 105.
3. ibid. p. 103.

4. Shoghi Effendi, *God Passes By*, p. 386.
5. ibid.
6. ibid. pp. 386–7.
7. Garis, *Martha Root*, p. 12.
8. The name of Pittsburgh was temporarily changed to Pittsburg between 1894 and 1911.
9. Garis, *Martha Root*, p. 43.
10. Zinky, *Martha Root, Herald of the Kingdom*, pp. 9–10.
11. Garis, *Martha Root*, p. 106.
12. Rabbani, *Priceless Pearl*, p. 100.
13. ibid. p. 101.
14. ibid. p. 103.
15. ibid. p. 101.
16. Garis, *Martha Root*, pp. 481–2.
17. Rabbani, *Priceless Pearl*, p. 106.
18. Shoghi Effendi, *This Decisive Hour*, p. 42.
19. *Bahá'í World*, vol. 8, pp. 646–7.
20. Schoen, 'A Love Which Does Not Wait', *Bahá'í News*, no. 541, April 1976, p. 4.
21. Shoghi Effendi, *God Passes By*, p. 388.

**Muṣṭafá Rúmí**

1. Shoghi Effendi, *Messages to the Indian Subcontinent*, p. 143.
2. ibid. p. 260.
3. ibid. p. 261.
4. ibid. p. 264.
5. Shoghi Effendi, *Messages to the Antipodes*, p. 257.

**Roy C. Wilhelm**

1. Rutstein, *He Loved and Served*, p. 25.
2. Whitehead, *Some Early Bahá'ís of the West*, p. 88.
3. 'Abdu'l-Bahá, quoted in *Bahá'í World*, vol. 12, p. 663.
4. Rutstein, *He Loved and Served*, p. 26.
5. 'Abdu'l-Bahá, quoted in *Bahá'í World*, vol. 7, p. 806.
6. See *Bahá'í World*, vol. 9, p. 803 for a reproduction of this photograph.
7. *Bahá'í World*, vol. 7, pp. 802–7.
8. Garis, *Martha Root*, p. 47.
9. *Bahá'í World*, vol. 7, p. 540.
10. *Bahá'í World*, vol. 12, p. 664.
11. 'Abdu'l-Bahá, *Promulgation of Universal Peace*, pp. 213–14.
12. Thompson, *Diary of Juliet Thompson*, p. 324.
13. ibid. pp. 324–5.
14. *Bahá'í World*, vol. 12, p. 662.
15. Rutstein, *He Loved and Served*, p. 27.
16. Garis, *Martha Root*, pp. 57–8.
17. Quoted in Whitehead, *Some Early Bahá'ís of the West*, p. 94.
18. The Báb, *Selections from the Writings of the Báb*, p. 87.
19. Quoted in Whitehead, *Some Early Bahá'ís of the West*, p. 95.

20. Rabbani, *Priceless Pearl*, p. 49.
21. ibid.
22. ibid.
23. ibid. p. 56.
24. Rutstein, *He Loved and Served*, p. 113.
25. Garis, *Martha Root*, p. 226.
26. ibid. p. 302.
27. ibid. pp. 382–3.
28. ibid. p. 494.
29. Morrison, *To Move the World*, p. 93.
30. *Bahá'í World*, vol. 7, p. 541.
31. *Bahá'í World*, vol. 12, p. 664.
32. ibid. p. 662.

IV

**Dorothy Beecher Baker**

1. From Jean M. Minney, 1970.
2. Bahá'u'lláh, *Kitáb-i-Íqán*, p. 236.
3. Freeman, *From Copper to Gold*, p. 313.
4. ibid. p. 7.
5. ibid. pp. 79–80.
6. On several occasions Dorothy remarked that 'this is always to be God's home'. The house was used freely by the Lima Bahá'í community while the Bakers lived there and became the Bahá'í Centre. The house passed to the Bahá'í community in 1963 after the death of Frank Baker, who left it to the community in his will. Letter from Mary Keubler with compilation by Mae L. Vaughn, September 1966.
7. Freeman, *From Copper to Gold*, p. 83.
8. ibid. p. 87.
9. Quoted in ibid. p. 114.
10. Morrison, *To Move The World*, p. 276.
11. Freeman, *From Copper to Gold*, p. 131.
12. ibid. p. 213.
13. ibid. pp. 245–6.
14. ibid. p. 313.
15. ibid. p. 171.
16. ibid. p. 147.
17. *Bahá'í World*, vol. 13, p. 333.
18. Freeman, *From Copper to Gold*, p. 276.
19. ibid. p. 298.
20. ibid.
21. ibid. p. 300.
22. *Bahá'í World*, vol. 12, p. 670.
23. Freeman, *From Copper to Gold*, p. 308.

## Amelia Collins

1. Shoghi Effendi, *Messages to the Bahá'í World*, p. 79.
2. Whitehead, *Portraits*, p. 74.
3. Faizi, *Milly*, p. 18.
4. ibid. p. 8.
5. ibid. p. 7.
6. *Bahá'í World*, vol. 13, p. 836.
7. Faizi, *Milly*, p. 9.
8. Shoghi Effendi, quoted in Rabbani, *Priceless Pearl*, pp. 258–9.
9. Shoghi Effendi, *Messages to the Bahá'í World*, pp. 8–9.
10. *Bahá'í World*, vol. 13, p. 839.
11. Faizi, *Milly*, p. 10.
12. ibid.
13. Quoted in *Bahá'í World*, vol. 13, p. 837.
14. ibid.
15. Faizi, *Milly*, p. 20.
16. ibid. p. 38.
17. ibid. p. 39.
18. Abdu'l-Bahá, quoted in *Bahá'í World*, vol. 13, p. 834.
19. *Ministry of the Custodians*, p. 333.

## 'Alí-Akbar Furútan

1. Quoted in Furútan, *Story of My Heart*, pp. 22–3, as revised by Mr Furútan in his review of this article.
2. Cited in ibid. pp. 37–8, as revised by Mr Furútan in his review of this article.
3. Cited in ibid. pp. 44–5, as revised by Mr Furútan in his review of this article.
4. ibid. pp. 58–9.
5. ibid. p. 82.
6. ibid. p. 127.
7. Shoghi Effendi, *Messages to the Bahá'í World*, p. 123.
8. ibid. pp. 127–8.
9. Furútan, *Story of My Heart*, p. 142.
10. ibid. pp. 145–6.
11. Letter to the author.
12. *Bahá'í World 2003–2004*, p. 229–30.

## Ugo Giachery

1. Giachery, *Shoghi Effendi*, p. 111.
2. *Bahá'í World*, vol. 18, p. 718.
3. Giachery, *Shoghi Effendi*, p. 6.
4. ibid. p. 31.
5. ibid.
6. ibid. p. 8.
7. ibid.
8. ibid. p. 1.
9. Shoghi Effendi, *God Passes By*, p. 275.
10. ibid. p. 276.

11. Rabbani, *Priceless Pearl*, p. 235.
12. Giachery, *Shoghi Effendi*, p. 75.
13. ibid. pp. 69, 77–8.
14. Giachery, 'An Account of the Preparatory Work in Italy', *Bahá'í World*, vol. 12, p. 243.
15. ibid. p. 245; Giachery, *Shoghi Effendi*, p. 105.
16. Giachery, *Shoghi Effendi*, p. 78.
17. ibid. p. 79.
18. ibid. p. 20.
19. ibid. p. 24.
20. ibid. p. 56.
21. ibid. p. 25.
22. ibid. p. 81.
23. Agnes Ghaznavi-Fischer, letter to the author, 19 September 1995.
24. Giachery, *Shoghi Effendi*, p. 32.
25. *Bahá'í World*, vol. 12, p. 239.
26. Giachery, *Shoghi Effendi*, p. 126.
27. ibid. p. 127.
28. ibid. p. 136.
29. ibid. p. 17.
30. ibid. p. 123.
31. Rabbani, *Priceless Pearl*, p. 291.
32. Shoghi Effendi, *Messages to the Bahá'í World*, p. 46.
33. Giachery, *Shoghi Effendi*, p. 167.
34. ibid. pp. 175–81.
35. *Bahá'í World*, vol. 13, p. 385.
36. *Bahá'í World*, vol. 15, pp. 180–3.
37. Giachery, 'One God, One Truth, One People', *Bahá'í World*, vol. 14, pp. 612–19.
38. Ghaznavi-Fischer, letter to the author, 19 September 1995.
39. *Bahá'í World*, vol. 18, p. 717.
40. *Bahá'í International News Service*, July 1989, p. 1.

**Hermann Grossman**

1. *Bahá'í World*, vol. 15, pp. 417–18.
2. Shoghi Effendi, *Light of Divine Guidance*, vol. 1, p. 25.
3. ibid. p. 78.
4. ibid. pp. 79–80.
5. *Bahá'í World*, vol. 15, p. 419.
6. ibid.
7. *Bahá'í World*, vol. 10, p. 21.
8. ibid. p. 22.
9. ibid.
10. Shoghi Effendi, *Light of Divine Guidance*, vol. 1, pp. 101–2.
11. *Bahá'í News*, September 1968, p. 3.
12. ibid. p. 1.

**Horace Hotchkiss Holley**

1. His birth certificate reads Horace Alfred Holley. Apparently he preferred Hotchkiss, a name prominent in his family. Letter to the author from Claire Vreeland.
2. See Blomfield, *Chosen Highway*, pp. 1–2.
3. ibid.
4. *Bahá'í World*, vol. 13, p. 850.
5. ibid. p. 851.
6. Holley, *A Pilgrim to Thonon*, Letchworth: Garden City Press, 1911.
7. Holley, *Bahaism: The Modern Social Religion*, London: Sidgwick and Jackson; New York: Mitchell Kennerly, 1913.
8. *Bahá'í World*, vol. 13, pp. 251–2.
9. Holley, *The Social Principle*, New York: L. J. Gomme, 1915.
10. *Bahá'í World*, vol. 13, p. 852.
11. Holley, *Bahai, the Spirit of the Age,* London: Kegan Paul Trench Trubner, 1921.
12. *Bahá'í World*, vol. 13, p. 853.
13. ibid.
14. ibid.
15. ibid. pp. 853–4.
16. Whitehead, *Some Bahá'ís to Remember*, p. 247.
17. *Bahá'í World*, vol. 13, p. 855.
18. ibid. p. 853.
19. ibid. p. 855.
20. Shoghi Effendi, *Bahá'í Administration*, p. 157.
21. Rabbani, *Priceless Pearl*, p. 210.
22. Holley, *Religion for Mankind*, London: George Ronald, 1956.
23. *Bahá'í World*, vol. 13, p. 855.
24. ibid.
25. ibid.
26. ibid. p. 856.
27. *Bahá'í World*, vol. 12, p. 935.
28. *Ministry of the Custodians*, p. 227.
29. ibid. pp. 217–18.

**Leroy C. Ioas**

1. *Bahá'í World*, vol. 14, p. 291.
2. ibid.
3. Stockman, *The Bahá'í Faith in America*, vol. 1, p. 78.
4. *Bahá'í World*, vol. 14, p. 292.
5. ibid.
6. ibid.
7. ibid.
8. ibid.
9. ibid. p. 293.
10. ibid.
11. ibid. p. 294.
12. ibid.

13. ibid. p. 295.
14. Chapman, *Leroy Ioas*, p. 157.
15. *Bahá'í World*, vol. 14, p. 295.
16. Chapman, *Leroy Ioas*, p. 157.
17. *Bahá'í World*, vol. 14, p. 296.
18. ibid. p. 297.
19. Universal House of Justice, *Messages from the Universal House of Justice*, p. 66.

**William Sutherland Maxwell**

1. Shoghi Effendi, *Messages to the Indian Subcontinent*, p. 357.
2. *Bahá'í World*, vol. 12, p. 658.
3. ibid.
4. Shoghi Effendi, *God Passes By*, p. 275.
5. Shoghi Effendi, *Unfolding Destiny*, p. 166.
6. Rabbani, *Priceless Pearl*, p. 241.
7. Shoghi Effendi, *Citadel of Faith*, pp. 95–6.
8. Ugo Giachery, *Shoghi Effendi*, p. 93.
9. *Bahá'í World*, vol. 12, p. 661.
10. Shoghi Effendi, Research Department, Bahá'í World Centre.
11. Shoghi Effendi, *Messages to the Indian Subcontinent*, p. 357.

**Charles Mason Remey**

1. Stockman, *Bahá'í Faith in America*, vol. 1, ch. 6.
2. Stockman, *Bahá'í Faith in America*, vol. 2, p. 152.
3. ibid.
4. 'Abdu'l-Bahá, *Selections*, pp. 196–9.
5. Stockman, *Bahá'í Faith in America*, vol. 2, p. 232.
6. Collins, *Bibliography of English-Language Works*, p. 135.
7. ibid. pp. 133–5.
8. Stockman, *Bahá'í Faith in America*, vol. 2, p. 222.
9. 'Abdu'l-Bahá, *Tablets of Abdul Baha Abbas*, vol. 2, p. 458 (identified by Stockman, ibid. p. 463).
10. ibid. p. 466. (identified by Stockman, *Bahá'í Faith in America*, vol. 2, p. 463).
11. ibid. p. 459–60.
12. Letter to the author from the Archives Office, Bahá'í World Centre, 3 January 1997.
13. *Bahá'í World*, vol. 2, pp. 121–2.
14. Stockman, *Bahá'í Faith in America*, vol. 2, p. 291.
15. *Japan Will Turn Ablaze*, p. 11.
16. Letter to the author from Nell Golden, secretary to Amatu'l-Bahá Rúḥíyyih Khánum.
17. Stockman, *Bahá'í Faith in America*, vol. 2, p. 319.
18. For the designs of Mr Maxwell and Mr Remey see *Bahá'í World*, vol. 8, pp. 511–12; another view of Mr Remey's design, as well as his description of it, can be found in *Star of the West*, vol. 11, no. 5, pp. 85–7.
19. Whitmore, *Dawning Place*, p. 88.
20. *Star of the West*, vol. 11, no. 4, p. 67.

21. Whitmore, *Dawning Place*, p. 94.
22. Shoghi Effendi, *Messages to the Bahá'í World*, pp. 7–8.
23. Rabbani, *Priceless Pearl*, p. 252.
24. Shoghi Effendi, *Messages to the Bahá'í World*, p. 20.
25. ibid. pp. 8–9.
26. Rabbani, *Priceless Pearl*, p. 141.
27. Giachery, *Shoghi Effendi*, pp. 178–9.
28. *Bahá'í World*, vol. 13, p. 341.
29. *Ministry of the Custodians*, p. 29.
30. ibid. p. 35.
31. ibid. pp. 35–6.
32. Shoghi Effendi, *Messages to the Bahá'í World*, p. 127.
33. Shoghi Effendi, quoted in *Bahá'í World*, vol. 13, p. 315.
34. *Ministry of the Custodians*, p. 168.
35. ibid. p. 165.
36. Rúḥíyyih Khánum, Introduction, *Ministry of the Custodians*, p. 16.
37. ibid.
38. *Ministry of the Custodians*, pp. 196–7.
39. ibid. p. 224.
40. ibid. p. 208.
41. ibid. p. 223.
42. The Universal House of Justice, *Wellspring of Guidance*, p. 2.
43. The Universal House of Justice, *Messages from the Universal House of Justice*, p. 271.

**Ṭarázu'lláh Samandarí**

1. *Bahá'í World*, vol. 15, p. 410–11.
2. Samandarí family papers.
3. ibid.
4. *Bahá'í World*, vol. 15, p. 411.
5. Ṭarázu'lláh Samandarí, *In His Presence*.
6. ibid.
7. *Bahá'í World*, vol. 15, p. 412.
8. Samandarí family papers.
9. Bahá'u'lláh, *Kitáb-i-Aqdas*, para. 38.
10. Shoghi Effendi, *God Passes By*, p. 247.
11. Taherzadeh, *Covenant of Bahá'u'lláh*, p. 185n and Balyuzi, *Eminent Bahá'ís*, pp. 209–10.
12. *Bahá'í World*, vol. 15, p. 413.
13. ibid.
14. ibid. p. 414.
15. Samandarí family papers.
16. Muhájir, *Dr Muhájir*, p. 659.
17. *Bahá'í News*, April 1968, p. 3.
18. From a talk given by Mr Samandarí in Fort Worth, Texas, 1968.
19. *Bahá'í World*, vol. 15, p. 416.
20. ibid. p. 414.
21. ibid. p. 416.

**George Townshend**

1. Hofman, *George Townshend*, p. 14.
2. ibid. p. 39.
3. Quoted in ibid. p. 45.
4. Quoted in ibid. p. 47.
5. Quoted in ibid. p. 49.
6. Quoted in ibid. p. 50.
7. Quoted in ibid. p. 52.
8. ibid. p. 57.
9. Bahá'u'lláh, *Hidden Words*, title page. Ethel Rosenberg also assisted in the translation.
10. Letter to the author from David Hofman, 1992.
11. Hofman, *George Townshend*, p. 241.
12. ibid. p. 334.
13. 'Abdu'l-Bahá, *Will and Testament*, p. 25.
14. Hofman, *George Townshend*, pp. 186–7.
15. ibid. pp. 335–6.
16. ibid. p. 348.
17. ibid. p. 349.
18. ibid. p. 355.
19. *Bahá'í World*, vol. 13, p. 844.
20. Hofman, *George Townshend*, p. 318.
21. ibid. p. 365.

**Valíyu'lláh Varqá**

1. *Bahá'í World*, vol. 13, p. 832.
2. ibid. p. 831.
3. An interview with Hand of the Cause Dr 'Alí Muḥammad Varqá, 1990.

V

**Shu'á'u'lláh 'Alá'í**

1. *Bahá'í World*, vol. 19, p. 593.
2. ibid.
3. ibid. pp. 594–5.

**Músá Banání**

1. *Bahá'í World*, vol. 15, p. 421.
2. ibid. p. 422.
3. ibid.
4. ibid.
5. Shoghi Effendi, *Unfolding Destiny*, p. 245.
6. Shoghi Effendi, *Citadel of Faith*, pp. 87–8.
7. Shoghi Effendi, *Unfolding Destiny*, p. 257.
8. Shoghi Effendi, *Messages to the Bahá'í World*, pp. 20–1.
9. *Bahá'í World*, vol. 15, p. 423.

10. ibid.
11. Shoghi Effendi, quoted in *Bahá'í World*, vol. 12, p. 377.
12. *Bahá'í World*, vol. 13, p. 285.
13. Shoghi Effendi, *Messages to the Bahá'í World*, p. 90.
14. *Bahá'í World*, vol. 15, p. 423.
15. Rabbani, *Guardian of the Bahá'í Faith*, p. 238.
16. *Ministry of the Custodians*, p. 320.
17. ibid. p. 328.
18. *Bahá'í World*, vol. 14, p. 248.
19. *Bahá'í World*, vol. 15, p. 423.
20. ibid.
21. ibid. p. 421.

**Clara Dunn**

1. 'Abdu'l-Bahá, *Bahá'í Prayers*, pp. 132–3.
2. Mrs Madge Featherstone states that this date has not been verified. Letter to author from Mrs Featherstone.
3. Dunn, *Recalls Becoming a Bahá'í.*
4. Whitehead, *Some Bahá'ís to Remember*, p. 155.
5. ibid.
6. Dunn, *Recalls Becoming a Bahá'í.*
7. ibid.
8. *Bahá'í World*, vol. 13, p. 859.
9. Dunn, *Recalls Becoming a Bahá'í.*
10. Whitehead, *Some Bahá'ís to Remember*, p. 156.
11. Dunn, *Recalls Becoming a Bahá'í.*
12. Whitehead, *Some Bahá'ís to Remember*, p. 157.
13. *Bahá'í World*, vol. 13, p. 860.
14. Garis, *Martha Root*, p. 188.
15. *To Follow a Dreamtime*, p. 4.
16. Harold and Florence Fitzner, from notes provided to the author by Mrs Madge Featherstone.
17. Whitehead, *Some Bahá'ís to Remember*, p. 164.
18. ibid.
19. ibid.
20. Shoghi Effendi, *Messages to the Antipodes*, p. 63.
21. Hassall, *Bahá'í Faith in Australia 1920–34*, pp. 12–13.
22. Shoghi Effendi, *Messages to the Antipodes*, p. 95.
23. *Bahá'í World*, vol. 7, p. 514.
24. *Bahá'í News*, no. 114, February 1938, p. 8.
25. *To Follow a Dreamtime*, p. 14.
26. Hassall, *Yerrinbool Bahá'í School 1938–1988.*
27. Shoghi Effendi, *Messages to the Antipodes*, p. 167.
28. ibid. p. 168.
29. ibid. p. 180.
30. ibid. p. 220.
31. ibid. p. 209.
32. ibid. p. 342.

33. Whitehead, *Some Bahá'ís to Remember*, p. 171.
34. Shoghi Effendi, *Messages to the Antipodes*, p. 364.
35. ibid. p. 440.
36. Letter to the author from Mrs Madge Featherstone, 19 December 1995.
37. *To Follow a Dreamtime*, p. 4.
38. *Bahá'í Prayers*, pp. 132–3.
39. *Ministry of the Custodians*, p. 245.

**Zikrullah Khadem**

1. Khadem, *Zikrullah Khadem*, p. 4.
2. Quoted in ibid. p. 7.
3. ibid. p. 9.
4. ibid. p. 30.
5. ibid. p. 31.
6. ibid. p. 47.
7. ibid. p. 93.
8. ibid. p. 52.
9. ibid. p. 119.
10. ibid. p. 144.
11. ibid. p. 149.
12. ibid. p. 150.
13. *Bahá'í News*, December 1986, p. 2.

**Adelbert Mühlschlegel**

1. *Bahá'í World*, vol. 13, pp. 218–20.
2. *Bahá'í World*, vol. 18, p. 611.
3. Shoghi Effendi, *Light of Divine Guidance*, vol. 1, p. 37.
4. ibid. p. 40.
5. ibid. pp. 40–1.
6. ibid. p. 47.
7. ibid. pp. 54–5.
8. ibid. pp. 62–3.
9. Garis, *Martha Root*, p. 232.
10. Shoghi Effendi, *Light of Divine Guidance*, vol. 1, p. 63.
11. Cameron and Momen, *Basic Bahá'í Chronology*, p. 250.
12. Shoghi Effendi, *Light of Divine Guidance*, vol. 1, p. 91.
13. ibid. pp. 95–6.
14. *Ministry of the Custodians*, p. 108.
15. *Bahá'í World*, vol. 14, p. 368.
16. ibid. p. 367.
17. *Bahá'í World*, vol. 18, p. 613.

**Siegfried Schopflocher**

1. van den Hoonaard, *Origins of the Bahá'í Community of Canada*, p. 75.
2. *Bahá'í Year Book*, p. 93.
3. Shoghi Effendi, *Messages to Canada*, p. 12.
4. *Bahá'í World*, vol. 12, p. 665.

5. Garis, *Martha Root*, p. 217.
6. Shoghi Effendi, *Messages to the Antipodes*, pp. 118–19.
7. ibid. p. 125.
8. Shoghi Effendi, *Messages to the Indian Subcontinent*, p. 153.
9. *Bahá'í World*, vol. 15, p. 488.
10. Quoted in Whitmore, *Dawning Place*, p. 132.
11. *Bahá'í World*, vol. 12, p. 664.
12. Rúḥíyyih K͟hánum, Introduction, *Ministry of the Custodians*, p. 4.
13. *Bahá'í World*, vol. 12, p. 664.

**Corinne Knight True**

1. *Bahá'í World*, vol. 13, p. 846.
2. Rutstein, *Corinne True*, p. 22.
3. 'Abdu'l-Bahá, *Tablets of Abdul Baha Abbas*, pp. 85–6.
4. ibid. p. 86.
5. 'Abdu'l-Bahá, *Selections*, pp. 26–7.
6. ibid. p. 122.
7. ibid. pp. 121–2.
8. ibid. p. 80.
9. Rutstein, *Corinne True*, p. 59.
10. 'Mother of the Temple', *Bahá'í News*, January 1976, p. 6.
11. ibid. p. 7.
12. True, *Notes Taken at Acca*, p. 21.
13. 'Mother of the Temple', *Bahá'í News*, January 1976, p. 5.
14. 'Abdu'l-Bahá, *Tablets of Abdul Baha Abbas*, pp. 96–7.
15. Cited in Rutstein, *Corinne True*, p. 80.
16. ibid. p. 87.
17. 'Mother of the Temple', *Bahá'í News*, February 1976, p. 16.
18. ibid.
19. Cited in Rutstein, *Corinne True*, p. 95.
20. ibid. p. 99.
21. ibid. p. 109.
22. *Star of the West*, vol. 5, no. 4, p. 56.
23. *Star of the West*, vol. 8, no. 14, pp. 202–3.
24. *Star of the West*, vol. 10, no. 17, p. 306.
25. Cited in Rutstein, *Corinne True*, p. 149.
26. ibid.
27. ibid. p. 152.
28. ibid. p. 177.
29. ibid. p. 200.
30. 'Mother of the Temple', *Bahá'í News*, January 1976, p. 23.
31. ibid. p. 24.
32. Cited in Rutstein, *Corinne True*, p. 213.
33. *Ministry of the Custodians*, p. 257.

VI

**Amatu'l-Bahá Rúḥíyyih Khánum**

1. *Bahá'í World*, vol. 8, p. 631.
2. ibid. p. 637.
3. ibid.
4. ibid.
5. Douglas Martin, in Rabbani, *Poems of the Passing*, p. x.
6. ibid.
7. *Bahá'í World*, vol. 8, p. 638.
8. *Bahá'í World*, vol. 12, p. 658.
9. ibid.
10. Rabbani, *Priceless Pearl*, p. 150.
11. ibid. pp. 118–19.
12. *Bahá'í World*, vol. 8, p. 641.
13. Rabbani, *Priceless Pearl*, p. 151.
14. ibid. p. 152.
15. ibid. p. 167.
16. ibid. p. 176.
17. Shoghi Effendi, *Messages to Canada*, p. 141.
18. Rabbani, *Priceless Pearl*, p. 259.
19. ibid. p. 447.
20. ibid.
21. *Bahá'í World*, vol. 13, p. 338.
22 Shoghi Effendi, *Messages to the Bahá'í World*, p. 127.
23. See Rabbani, *Poems of the Passing*.
24. 'Abdu'l-Bahá, *Will and Testament*, p. 12.
25. Rúḥíyyih Khánum, Introduction to *Ministry of the Custodians*, p. 10.
26. *Bahá'í World*, vol. 14, pp. 62–3.
27. This journey is documented in Nakhjavání, *Amatu'l-Bahá Visits India.*
28. This journey is documented in Nakhjavání, *The Great African Safari.*
29. *Bahá'í World*, vol. 15, p. 588.
30. *Bahá'í News*, January 1976, p. 20.
31. *Bahá'í News*, June 1973, pp. 18–19.
32. Rabbani, 'This is Faith', 1953.
33. *Bahá'í World 1999–2000*, p. 194–5.

**Jalál Kházeh**

1. *Bahá'í World*, vol. 20, pp. 790, 789, 791.
2. ibid. p. 790.
3. ibid.
4. Khazeh, Talk by Jalál Kházeh.
5. *Bahá'í World*, vol. 20, p. 791.
6. ibid. p. 792.
7. ibid. p. 790.
8. Khazeh, Talk by Jalál Kházeh.

9. *Bahá'í World*, vol. 20, p. 792.
10. ibid.
11. ibid. p. 788.

**Paul Edmond Haney**

1. Whitehead, *Some Early Bahá'ís of the West*, p. 158.
2. *Bahá'í World*, vol. 18, p. 614.
3. ibid.
4. ibid.
5. ibid. p. 615.
6. ibid. p. 614.
7. ibid. p. 615.
8. ibid. p. 616.
9. ibid.
10. ibid.
11. From a letter written on behalf of Shoghi Effendi, 8 May 1954, cited in Whitehead, *Some Early Bahá'ís of the West*, p. 168.
12. Rúḥíyyih Khánum, Introduction to *Ministry of the Custodians*, p. 10.
13. *Bahá'í World*, vol. 18, p. 617.
14. See *Bahá'í World*, vol. 13, pp. 333–79.
15. *Bahá'í World*, vol. 14, p. 346.
16. *Bahá'í World*, vol. 18, pp. 617–18.

**'Alí Muḥammad Varqá**

1. *Bahá'í World*, vol. 13, p. 831.
2. ibid. p. 297.
3. *Ministry of the Custodians*, pp. 27–8.
4. ibid. p. 371.
5. Dr 'Alí Muḥammad Varqá, a talk given by the Hand of the Cause and Trustee of Ḥuqúqu'lláh at the Sixth International Convention, pp. 4–5.
6. Bahá'u'lláh, quoted in *Ḥuqúqu'lláh, The Right of God*, p. 1.

**Agnes Baldwin Alexander**

1. Honnold, *Why They Became Bahá'ís*, p. 5.
2. *Bahá'í World*, vol. 15, p. 424.
3. ibid. pp. 424–5.
4. ibid.
5. Honnold, *Why They Became Bahá'ís*, pp. 8–9.
6. *Bahá'í World*, vol. 15, pp. 425–6.
7. Morrison, *Hand of the Cause, Agnes Alexander: A Eulogy*, p. 7.
8. 'Abdu'l-Bahá, *Tablets of the Divine Plan*, pp. 41–2.
9. Garis, *Martha Root*, pp. 82–3.
10. *Bahá'í World*, vol. 15, p. 427.
11. *Japan Will Turn Ablaze*, p. 32.
12. Garis, *Martha Root*, p. 174.
13. ibid. pp. 174–5.

14. *Bahá'í World*, vol. 15, p. 427.
15. ibid. p. 428.
16. *Japan Will Turn Ablaze*, p. 58.
17. *Bahá'í World*, vol. 15, p. 428.
18. ibid.
19. ibid. p. 429.
20. Morrison, *Hand of the Cause, Agnes Alexander: A Eulogy*, p. 7.
21. *Bahá'í World*, vol. 15, p. 430.

VII

**Hasan Balyuzi**

1. *Bahá'í World*, vol. 18, p. 637.
2. An account by Abu'l-Qásim Afnán appearing in the *Bahá'í News* of June 1980 states that Mr Balyuzi wrote a pamphlet entitled *Bahá'u'lláh* during his years in Beirut. Dr Moojan Momen, Mr Balyuzi's research assistant, writes that the work was published in 1938, while Mr Balyuzi was in London. Momen states that Shoghi Effendi encouraged Mr Balyuzi to 'continue this work by adding essays on the lives of the Báb and 'Abdu'l-Bahá' (Momen, ed., *Studies in Honor of the Late Hasan M. Balyuzi*, p. xiv).
3. *Bahá'í World*, vol. 18, p. 638.
4. ibid. p. 639.
5. ibid.
6. Shoghi Effendi, *Unfolding Destiny*, p. 125.
7. ibid. p. 141.
8. His translations of literary works into Persian were done with such mastery as to astound well-read contemporaries. So impressed was one great Persian scholar with Mr Balyuzi's translations that he 'felt that the original writers were Persian-speaking . . . and, without a doubt, one of the best ways to determine a good translation is for the reader to feel that the script was originally written in that same language' ('Hasan M. Balyuzi: Scholar, author, historian, devoted servant of the Cause of God', *Bahá'í News*, June 1980, pp. 7–8).
9. Lady Blomfield asked Mr Balyuzi to write the preface to her book. In it he praises the author and her work as the repository of a wealth of material essential to the study of Bahá'í history.
10. *Bahá'í World*, vol. 18, p. 641.
11. ibid. p. 643.
12. ibid. p. 645.
13. ibid. p. 644.
14. ibid. p. 642.
15. ibid. p. 640.
16. Shoghi Effendi, *Unfolding Destiny*, p. 245.
17. See the chapters on Músá Banání and Enoch Olinga for more details regarding the Africa Campaign.

18. Shoghi Effendi, *Unfolding Destiny*, p. 297.
19. ibid. p. 387.
20. *Bahá'í World*, vol. 18, p. 645.
21. Mr Balyuzi's other works include three books in Persian entitled *The Story of Three Sisters* (the Brontës), *Half-Brothers*, and *Words in English Derived from Persian* (in which he traced the roots of over 700 English words).
22. Momen, ed., *Studies in Honor of the Late Hasan M. Balyuzi*, p. xvii.
23. *Bahá'í World*, vol. 18, pp. 649–50.
24. ibid. p. 651.
25. ibid. p. 635.

### Abu'l-Qásim Faizi (Abu'l Qásim Fayḍí)

1. Letter to author from Shirley Macias, Bahá'í World Centre, 1988.
2. Gloria Faizi stated: 'The year 1906 is given in Mr Faizi's passport. He did not pick it himself. The day on which he was born, as well as the month, are not known and Faizi never attempted to pick a date.' Letter to author from Gloria Faizi.
3. *Bahá'í World*, vol. 18, p. 661.
4. ibid. p. 664.
5. *Ministry of the Custodians*, pp. 203–4.
6. Quoted in letter to author from Shirley Macias.
7. *Bahá'í World*, vol. 18, p. 659.

### Harold Collis Featherstone

1. Waterman, *H. Collis Featherstone*, p. 2.
2. Nabíl-i-A'ẓam, *The Dawn-Breakers*, pp. 92–4.
3. From the diary of H. Collis Featherstone, with details provided by Madge L. Featherstone.
4. Shoghi Effendi, *Messages to the Antipodes*, p. 234.
5. ibid.
6. Letter from the National Spiritual Assembly of the Bahá'ís of Australia, quoted in Waterman, *H. Collis Featherstone*, p. 13.
7. Waterman, *H. Collis Featherstone*, p. 6.
8. Letter to author from Mrs Madge Featherstone.
9. Shoghi Effendi, *Messages to the Antipodes*, p. 442.
10. ibid. p. 382.
11. Letter to author from Mrs Madge Featherstone.
12. Shoghi Effendi, *Messages to the Antipodes*, p. 446.
13. Letter to author from Mrs Madge Featherstone.
14. Waterman, *H. Collis Featherstone*, p. 12.
15. *Bahá'í World*, vol. 20, pp. 817–18.

### John Graham Ferraby

1. *Bahá'í World*, vol. 16, p. 512.
2. Shoghi Effendi, *Unfolding Destiny*, p. 250.
3. ibid. p. 320.

4. ibid. pp. 332–3.
5. *Bahá'í Journal*, October 1973, p. 2.

**Raḥmatu'lláh Muhájir, by Iran Furútan Muhájir**

1. *Bahá'í World*, vol. 18. p. 652.
2. Shoghi Effendi, *Messages to the Bahá'í World*, p. 113.
3. Muhájir, *Dr Muhájir*, p. 80.
4. ibid.
5. ibid. pp. 87–8.
6. *Bahá'í World*, vol. 18, p. 655.
7. ibid. pp. 651–2.

**Enoch Olinga**

1. *Bahá'í World*, vol. 18, p. 623.
2. Shoghi Effendi, *Messages to the Bahá'í World*, pp. 133–4.
3. *Bahá'í World*, vol. 18, p. 621.
4. Notes of Florence Mayberry, 2 June 1981.
5. *Bahá'í World*, vol. 18, p. 623.
6. Dunbar, *Forces of Light and Darkness.*
7. *Bahá'í World*, vol. 18, p. 625.
8. Mírzá 'Alí-Muḥammad Varqá was 38 when he was martyred and made a Hand of the Cause by 'Abdu'l-Bahá; Raḥmatu'lláh Muhájir was 34 at the time of his appointment, while Zikru'llah Khádem was 33.
9. *Bahá'í World*, vol. 18, p. 626.
10. ibid. p. 627.
11. *Bahá'í International News Service*, circa 1970, p. 4.
12. ibid.
13. *Bahá'í News*, May 1984, p. 6.
14. *Bahá'í International News Service*, circa 1970, p. 6.
15. Olinga, *Are You Happy?*
16. See Bahá'u'lláh, *Kitáb-i-Aqdas*, para. 1.
17. Dunbar, *Forces of Light and Darkness.*
18. *Bahá'í World*, vol. 18, p. 630.
19. ibid. p. 634.

**John Aldham Robarts**

1. 'Abdu'l-Bahá, *Promulgation*, p. 190.
2. Whitehead, *Some Bahá'ís To Remember*, pp. 137–8.
3. *Bahá'í World*, vol. 8, p. 658.
4. Whitehead, *Some Bahá'ís To Remember*, p. 138.
5. Letter to author from Audrey Robarts.
6. van den Hoonaard, *Origins of the Bahá'í Community of Canada*, pp. 302–5.
7. Letter to author from Audrey Robarts.
8. Shoghi Effendi, *Advent of Divine Justice*, p. 46.
9. *Bahá'í World*, vol. 20, p. 402.
10. Robarts, *Audrey Robarts Speaking about John A. Robarts.*

11. Tinnion, *John A. Robarts Memorial Article*, p. 7.
12. Shoghi Effendi, *This Decisive Hour*, p. 113.
13. Shoghi Effendi, *Messages to Canada*, p. 104.
14. Tinnion, *John A. Robarts Memorial Article*, p. 15.
15. ibid. p. 43.
16. *Bahá'í World*, vol. 20, p. 804.
17. Tinnion, *John A. Robarts Memorial Article*, p. 30.
18. *Bahá'í World*, vol. 13, p. 289.
19. *Vision of Shoghi Effendi*, p. 171.
20. ibid. p. 168.
21. ibid.
22. ibid. p. 176.
23. ibid.
24. ibid. p. 167.
25. Tinnion, *John A. Robarts Memorial Article*, p. 11.
26. Robarts, *Letter to Bahá'ís.*
27. ibid.
28. Robarts, *Audrey Robarts Speaking about John A. Robarts.*
29. Tinnion, *John A. Robarts Memorial Article*, p. 52.
30. Robarts, *Letter to Bahá'ís.*
31. *Bahá'í World*, vol. 20, p. 803.
32. *Bahíyyih Khánum, The Greatest Holy Leaf*, p. 148.
33. *Bahá'í World*, vol. 20, p. 809.


**William Sears**


1. Sears, *God Loves Laughter*, pp. 13 and 23.
2. ibid. p. 17.
3. ibid. p. 32.
4. ibid. p. 34.
5. ibid. p. 41.
6. ibid. pp. 65–6.
7. ibid. p. 66.
8. ibid. p. 90.
9. ibid. p. 94.
10. ibid.
11. ibid. p. 103.
12. ibid. p. 127.
13. ibid. pp. 127–8.
14. ibid. p. 141.
15. ibid. p. 142.
16. ibid. p. 163.
17. Sears, *All Flags Flying*, p. 190.
18. Sears, *Pilgrimage to Haifa*, p. 3.
19. ibid. pp. 3 and 5.
20. ibid. p. 5.
21. Shoghi Effendi, *Messages to the Bahá'í World*, pp. 58–9.
22. Sears, *Pilgrimage to Haifa*, p. 7.
23. 'Abdu'l-Bahá, *Will and Testament*, p. 13.

24. The Báb, *Selections from the Writings of the Báb*, p. 153.
25. Bahá'u'lláh, *Tablets of Bahá'u'lláh*, p. 13.
26. Marguerite Sears, letter to the author, 1992.
27. *Bahá'í World*, vol. 20, p. 800.

## Appendix I

1. This document has been downloaded from the *Bahá'í Reference Library*. https://www.bahai.org/library/authoritative-texts/the-universal-house-of-justice/messages/20071126_001/1#441668222 'Abbás, Mullá, 3

# Index

The entries are indexed letter by letter, thus 'Tablets of the Divine Plan' precedes 'Tablet to the Hague'. Hyphens are treated as spaces; connection letters -i- and y-i- are ignored.


'Abdu'l-'Azíz, Sulṭán, 154
'Abdu'l-Bahá, ii, xiii-xiv, 5, 6-7, 10-12, 14, 19n, 25-6, 28, 29, 34, 36-7, 39, 40, 47, 49, 54-5, 60, 68-70, 78-82, 84, 88, 92, 97, 99, 116-17, 122, 123, 129, 145, 147, 161-2, 205, 207, 209-10, 214, 217, 233, 250, 267, 270-1, 277, 280, 283, 311, 316-17, 323-4, 336, 369, 377, 387, 442-3
  advocates racial harmony, 77-80, 83-4
  ascension of, 70, 81, 97, 122, 195, 241
  Divine Plan of, 188, 198, 331, *see also* Tablets of the Divine Plan
  in Egypt, 97, 186
  home of, 49, 69, 116-17, 121, 193, 236, 315, 336-7, 344, 368
  mentions names of Hands of the Cause, 3, 6-7, 14, 16, 19n, 24, 25-6, 27, 29, 34, 36-7, 39, 40, 49
  station of, 41, 214, 216, 231, 271
  Tablets of, 10, 14, 16, 24, 60, 68, 78-9, 81, 98, 102-3, 112, 120, 125, 140, 145, 176, 178-9, 186, 210, 214, 215-6, 218, 220, 229-30, 233, 234, 240-1, 255, 280, 290, 308-10, 312, 318, 345, 349, 358-60, 360-1, 367, 405, 422, *see also* Tablets of the Divine Plan
  travels in North America and Europe, 54-5, 66, 79-80, 101-2, 118-20, 129, 185, 195, 196, 205-6, 218, 250, 269-71, 300, 314-15, 324, 351, 376, 395, 424, 442
  Will and Testament of *see* Will and Testament of 'Abdu'l-Bahá
'Abdu'l-Ḥusayn Ardistání, 259-60
'Abdu'l-Ḥusayn Iṣfahání, 98
'Abdu'lláh K͟hán-i-Núrí, Mírzá, 39-40, 41-2, 249
Abrár, Mr, 259
Abu'l-Faḍl Gulpáygání, Mírzá, 21, 28, 50, 52, 97, 358
Abu'l-Ḥasan-i-Ardikání, Ḥájí *see* Amín, Ḥájí
Abu'l-Qásim, Ḥájí Mírzá, 367
Adíbu'l-'Ulamá *see* Ḥasan-i-Adíb, Ḥájí Mírzá
Administrative Order, 153, 157, 188-9, 193, 221, 222, 246, 293, 302, 305, 317, 372, 398, 402, 403, 413, 433
*Advent of Divine Justice, The,* 282, 326
Afnán, Farhang, 372
Afnán family, 36, 109, 284, 367, 378
Africa Campaign, 261-2, 374, 401-2, 412
Aḥmad Azg͟handí, Mírzá, 256
Aḥmad Yazdání, 10
Aḥmad-i-Yazdí, 35
Ák͟húnd, Ḥájí ('Alí-Akbar-i-S͟hahmírzádí), 3-7, 14, 22, 49
'Ala'i, Counsellor, 174
'Alá'í, Furúg͟híyyih, 256
'Alá'í, General S͟hu'á'u'lláh, 255-8, 295, 352
  family of, 255-7
'Alá'u'd-Dawlih, 41, 42
Alexander, Agnes Baldwin, 89, 102, 218, 302, 356-64
Alexander, Rev. and Mrs William Patterson, 356-7
'Alí, Mullá (Jináb-i-Mu'allim), 230
'Alí-Akbar Ardistání, Mullá, 32
'Alí-Akbar-i-S͟hahmírzádí, Mullá *see* Ák͟húnd, Ḥájí

'Alíy-i-Kaní, Ḥájí Mullá, 4
'Alí-Muḥammad, Mírzá *see* Ibn-i-Aṣdaq
'Alí-Muḥammad, Siyyid *see* Báb, the
'Alí-Muḥammad Áqá, Mírzá, Muvaqqaru'd-Dawlih, 367-8
Allen, John, 264
All-England Bahá'í Council, 71
Almond, Percy and Maysie, 58
Amatu'l-Bahá Rúḥíyyih Khánum (Mary Maxwell), xvi, 104, 144, 145, 152, 162, 170, 201, 205-6, 208-9, 211-2, 218, 221, 222, 223, 224, 226, 288-9, 304, 323-37, 345, 348-9, 375, 403, 416
Amín, Ḥájí (Ḥájí Abu'l-Ḥasan-i-Ardikání, Amín-i-Iláhi), 6, 47-9, 281
'Andalíb, 231, 232, 255
Apostles of Bahá'u'lláh, 7, 11, 14, 16, 28, 38, 49
Aqá Ján, Mírzá, 9
Arnadóttir, Hólmfridur, 141
Asadu'lláh, Áqá Siyyid, 21, 22, 23
Asadu'lláh-i-Iṣfahání, Mírzá, 207
Augur, George, 359
Austin, Elsie, 83, 264
Australian Bahá'í Bulletin, 395
Auxiliary Boards, 153, 263-4, 363, 393, 394, 396, 431, 435, 446

Báb, the, 4, 29-31, 111, 121, 161, 169, 171, 207, 209-10, 226, 229, 236, 265, 277, 306, 367, 369, 377, 389
Shrine of *see* Shrine of the Báb
Bábí Faith, 3, 12
Badí', 99
Bahá'í Council (England), 69-70
Bahá'í Faith, teaching the *see* Teaching the Bahá'í Faith
*Bahá'í Magazine, The*, 346, *see also Star of the West*
*Bahá'í Nachrichten*, 181
*Bahá'í News*, 86, 152, 187, 272, 395
*Bahá'í Prayers*, 112
Bahá'í Publishing Trust (Committee, Society)
British, 401
of Egypt, 98
of Germany (Bahá'í-Verlag), 297
of Persia, 90
of United States, 120, 187, 215
*Bahá'í Quarterly*, 60
*Bahá'í Revelation, The*, 215
*Bahá'í Scriptures*, 187
Bahá'í Temple Unity, 83, 118, 219-20, 313, 316, 317
*Bahá'í World, The*, xxiii, 83, 84, 86, 88, 105-6, 117, 141, 187, 189, 190, 192, 242, 282, 293, 297, 432
Bahá'í World Centre, 156, 157, 165, 167, 170, 207-8, 212, 222, 223, 294, 295, 330, 334, 347, 348, 349, 352, 375-6, 416
*Bahá'í World Faith*, 187, 190
Bahá'u'lláh, xiii, xxiii, 4, 8, 21, 25-6, 30-1, 36, 40-1, 48, 109, 116, 117, 161, 171, 195, 205, 207, 214, 225, 229, 230-3, 283, 306, 369, 377, 395, 436
appointment of Hands of the Cause by, 1-15, 458
ascension of, 6, 231-3
Declaration of, 35, 47
proclamation of to kings and rulers, 154, 265, 349
Shrine of *see* Shrine of Bahá'u'lláh
Tablets of, 5, 9, 10, 12, 13, 27, 36, 48, 98, 99, 110, 156, 215, 230, 234, 255, 459
*Bahá'u'lláh and the New Era* (Esslemont), 67-72, 74, 105, 160, 362, 400
Bahíyyih Khánum *see* Greatest Holy Leaf
Bailey, Mr, 269
Baker, Dorothy Beecher, 129-38, 191, 192, 346
family of, 367-8
Baker, Effie, 57-8, 150
Baker, Frank, 130-1, 136, 465
Baker, Louise *see* Mathias, Louise Baker
Baker, Sally, 130-1
Baker, William, 130
Baldwin, Rev. and Mrs Dwight, 356
Balyuzi, Hasan, 170, 224, 226, 288, 367-79, 381, 401, 403, 477
family of, 367-8
Balyuzi, Mary (Molly) Brown, 371, 373
Banání, 'Ishraq, 259
Banání, Músá, 224, 259-66, 403, 412, 415, 418, 419, 431, 434, 446
Banání, Samíḥih Rafí'í Ardistání, 260, 261, 412
Barney, Laura Clifford *see* Dreyfus-Barney, Laura
Bayán, 12
Beecher, Ellen Tuller 'Mother', 129, 131, 132
Beecher, Henry and Luella, 130
Benes, President Eduard, 105
Benke, Lina, 176
Bíbí Ṭúbá, 41
'Big Ben' and 'Little Ben', 103, 120-1, 361
Bigabwa, Frederick, 262
Blomfield, Lady, 123, 184, 369, 371, 478
Blundell, Sarah, 57
Bolles, May Ellis *see* Maxwell, May Bolles
Bolles, Randolph, 205, 213

Bolton, Stanley and Mariette, 273
Boman, Shirin, 137
Book of His Covenant *see* Kitáb-i-'Ahd
Bosch, John and Louise, 197, 203
Bourgeois, Louis, 220
Bowes, Marjory, 276
Braille, 360
Brauns-Forel, Marta, 180
Breakwell, Thomas, 214, 248
Browne, Professor Edward Granville, 11, 101, 368, 377
Buzurg, Mírzá, 352

Calamity, 236, 309, 314, 315, 371
Carver, George Washington, 78
Central Assembly of Ṭihrán, 6, 10, 14, 15, 234, 256
Central Organization for a Durable Peace, 10
Chase, Thornton, 54, 101, 117-18, 215, 310, 313
Christ, 41, 117, 122, 158, 194, 235-6, 244-5, 307, 357, 359, 412, 417, 443
Christianity, Christians, 243, 307, 333, 344-5, 356
Coffee, Rabbi Rudolf I., 197
Cofman, Victor, 400
Collins, Amelia Engelder, 139-46, 199, 201, 221, 223, 224, 288, 330
Collins, Thomas H., 139, 140-1
Conclaves, *see* Hands of the Cause, Conclaves of the
Consultation, 149, 341-2
Continental Boards of Counsellors, xvi, 296, 341, 349, 352, 437
Cooper, Ella Goodall, 54, 195, 197
Covenant, the, 6, 82, 122, 168, 181-2, 216, 228, 232, 289, 309, 316, 349, 354, 372, 378, 398, 403
Covenant-breakers, 6, 10, 98, 112, 122, 161, 168-9, 182, 200, 201, 224, 232-3, 325, 327, 381
Covenant-breaking, 181, 216, 226-8
Custodians *see* Hands of the Cause, Custodians

Daidanaw, 111-13, 218
Dargan, George Washington, 75-6
Davis Jr, Allen, 268, 276
*Dawn-Breakers, The (Nabíl's Narrative)*, 51, 58, 72, 150, 242, 256, 389, 443
Dealy, Paul, 194
Dewing, Amy, 273
Dickens, Charles, 53
Dixon, Charlotte, 357
Ḍíyá'u'lláh, Mírzá, 232
Dobbins, Bertha, 388-90, 391, 393
Dobbins, Joe, 391
Dreyfus-Barney, Hippolyte, 123, 214
Dreyfus-Barney, Laura, 123, 214, 358
DuBois, W E B, 77
Dunbar, Hooper, 415
Dunn, Clara, 53, 54-6, 225-6, 262, 267-78, 390, 391, 392-5, 403
Dunn, Fanny, 53, 55
Dunn, John Henry Hyde, 53-63, 268, 270, 271-4, 276, 277-8, 390, 392

Eroshenko, Vasily, 360
Esperanto, Esperantists, 64, 66, 72, 293, 360, 362, 364
Esslemont, John Ebenezer, 64-74, 187, 193, 248, 368, 403
  family of, 64, 65

Fáḍil Mázandarání, 259
Fá'iq, 98
Faisal, King, 105
Faizi, Abu'l-Qásim, 145, 295, 369, 380-6, 478
  family of, 380-81, 382
Faizi, Gloria 'Alá'í, 382, 478
Farhád Mírzá, Prince, 21
Farmer, Sarah Jane, 299-300
Fatḥ-'Alí Sháh, 9
Fáṭimih Bagum, 5
Fáṭimih-Sulṭán-Bagum, 367
Featherstone, Harold Collis, 276, 387-99
  family of, 387-8, 396
Featherstone, Madge Green, 388-94, 397
Ferraby, Dorothy Cansdale, 246, 401, 402
Ferraby, John, 170, 183, 226, 288, 295, 375, 400-4
  family of, 400-1
Finch, Ida, 361
Finley, Louise, 240
Fitzgerald, Ward, 53-4, 268
Fitzners, Harold and Florence, 61, 391
Four Year Plan, 355
Frankland, Kathryn, 197
Franz Joseph II, Prince of Liechtenstein, 172
French, Nellie Stevison, 139
Fukuta, Kikutaro, 360
Furútan, 'Alí-Akbar, xvi, 147-57, 352, 372, 383, 406
  family of, 147, 151, 157
Furútan, 'Aṭá'iyyih (Ataieh) Khánum, 150
Gardner, Lloyd, 428
George, Florence, 66, 70
Getsinger, Edward, 358
Getsinger, Lua, 54, 77, 97, 118, 308, 358

Geyserville Bahá'í School, 197, 202-3
Ghulám-Riḍá, 338
Ghulám-Riḍá Iṣfahání, Ḥájí (Amín-i-Amín), 251
Ghulám-Riḍá Khán, 23
Giachery, Angeline Westergren, 159, 160, 170, 172, 173, 209
Giachery, Ugo, 81, 158-74, 201, 208-10, 223, 224, 285, 288, 295, 372, 375, 376, 378, 445
*God Passes By*, 53, 107, 190, 242-3, 326
Goodall, Helen, 54, 122
Great African Safari, 331-2
Greatest Holy Leaf (Bahíyyih Khánum), 42, 122, 325-6, 381
Green Acre, 86, 133, 206, 214, 299-301, 345, 359, 360, 422
Greenleaf, Charles and Elizabeth, 344
Green Light Expedition, 332
Gregory, George, 76
Gregory, Louis George, 75-86, 125, 133
Gregory, Louisa 'Louise' Mathew, 78, 80-1, 82, 86
Grossmann, Anna Hartmuth, 177, 180, 182
Grossmann, Elsa Maria, 180
Grossmann family, 177, 181
Grossmann, Hermann, 137, 175-83, 288, 375
Guardian *see* Shoghi Effendi
Guthrie, Dr William Norman, 187

Haakon, King, 105
Haddad, Anton, 215
Hádí, Ḥájí Mullá, 25
Hádí Najmábádí, Shaykh, 15
Hainsworth, Philip, 262, 412
Ḥájibu'd-Dawlih, 38-9, 43-4
Hale, Rev. G. E., 388
Ḥakím, Dr Luṭfu'lláh, 66, 67, 68, 69, 71, 221, 223, 459
Ḥakím Masíḥ, 8, 35, 459
Hall, Edward, 71
Hands of the Cause,
- appointed by Bahá'u'lláh, 1-16
- appointed individually by Shoghi Effendi, 321-64
- appointed posthumously by Shoghi Effendi, 45-126
- 'Chief Stewards', xiv, 225, 228, 329, 350, 394
- Conclaves of the, 145, 153, 157, 182, 193, 226, 234, 276, 285, 319, 330, 347, 352, 363, 375-6, 384, 394, 395, 403, 416, 434
- Custodians, xiv, 145, 153, 157, 193, 202, 225-6, 265, 277, 285, 295, 296, 330, 341, 347, 352, 375, 384, 403, 434, 447
- first contingent appointed by Shoghi Effendi, 127-252, 392
- first mention of by Bahá'u'lláh, 10
- following defection of Charles Mason Remey, 226-8
- following passing of Shoghi Effendi, 201-2, 224, 319-20, 330, 341, 352, 403
- functions of, xiii-xiv, 153, 329, 392-3, 447
- institution of, xiii-xiv, xv, 153, 348
- named by 'Abdu'l-Bahá, 19-44
- no way to appoint further, xv, 341
- Proclamation of the, 193, 224, 225, 330, 376
- resident in the Holy Land, 200, 201, 330, 347, 348, 354 *see also* Hands of the Cause, Custodians
- second contingent appointed by Shoghi Effendi, 253-320
- third contingent appointed by Shoghi Effendi, 365-450
- tributes to, ii, xv, xvi-xvii, 3, 6, 7, 12, 24, 28, 29, 36-7, 49, 52, 53, 59, 61-3, 73-4, 86, 94-5, 99, 106, 107-8, 113, 126, 137-8, 145-6, 156-7, 174, 183, 193, 203, 228, 236-7, 248, 251-2, 258, 266, 277, 287, 297, 304-5, 320, 336, 343, 350, 364, 379, 386, 398-9, 404, 410, 439

Haney, Charles Freeborn, 344-5
Haney, Helen Margery (Helen Margery Wheeler), 346
Haney, Mariam (Mary Ida Parkhurst), 82, 344-5, 347, 348-9
Haney, Paul Edmond, 183, 199, 344-50
Haney, Rev. Richard, 344
Hannen, Joseph and Pauline, 77
Happiness, 140, 417, 441
Harcus, Katherine, 388, 390
Harding, President, 84
Harris, Hooper, 14
Harwood, Howard, 397
Ḥasan-i-Adíb, Ḥájí Mírzá (Adíbu'l-'Ulamá), 15-16
Ḥasan 'Alí Mi'márbáshí Kashání, 339
Ḥasan-'Amú, Ḥájí Mírzá, 26
Ḥasan Vazir, Mírzá, 4
Hassall, Graham, 273
Hatch, Willard, 54-5
Ḥaydar-'Alí, Ḥájí Mírzá, 20, 27, 117, 236, 250
Healing, 58, 64-5, 67
Hearst, Phoebe, 213
Henderson, George W., 83
Henri, Monsieur, 358
*Herald of the South*, 395
Hidden Words, 66, 72, 112, 116, 242-3, 244, 308, 357

Himmler, Heinrich, 179
Ḥisámu's-Salṭanih, 35
Hitler, Adolf, 291
Hoagg, Emogene, 123, 358
Hofman, David, 239, 370, 371
Hofman, Marion, 246, 372, 377-8
Holley, Bertha Herbert, 184-6
Holley, Doris Pascal, 186, 191
Holley, Hertha, 185
Holley, Horace Hotchkiss, 118, 184-93, 212, 224, 226, 301
Holley, Marcia, 186
Hopper, Herbert, 213
Hornell, Lady (Kathleen Brown), 371
Houses of Worship (Mas͟hriqu'l-Ad͟hkár), 10, 20, 142, 157, 237
  Australia, 63, 223, 225-6, 277, 334, 396
  Germany, 145, 182, 201, 297, 334, 376
  India, 332, 334
  Iran, 142, 223
  'Is͟hqábád, 73, 147, 217
  Italy, 171
  Mount Carmel, 145, 169-70, 221, 223
  North America, 66, 70, 131-2, 142, 152, 189, 195, 198-9, 203, 217, 218-20, 221, 284-5, 303-4, 311-18, 319, 320, 334, 373
  Panama, 334
  Samoa, 332, 334
  Uganda, 223, 225, 264, 265, 266, 330, 334, 418-19
Ḥuqúqu'lláh, 48-9, 251, 252, 261, 286, 351-2, 354-5
Ḥusayn, Imám, 22, 29, 30
Ḥusayn, Mírzá, 42-3
Ḥusayn, Siyyid, 32
Ḥusayn Bus͟hrú'í, Mullá, 8, 30, 33-4
Ḥusayn K͟hán, 34
Ḥusayn Khán-i-Íraváni, 31

Ibn-i-Abhar (Mírzá Muḥammad-Taqí), 12-14
Ibn-i-Aṣdaq (Mírzá 'Alí-Muḥammad, S͟hahíd Ibn-i-S͟hahíd), 8-11, 35
Ibráhím-i-Abharí, Mírzá, 12
Ímán, Ḥájí, 42-3
Intercontinental Teaching Conferences, 234, 263, 265
  1953
    Chicago, 152, 169, 192, 211, 223, 251, 257, 263, 304
    Kampala, 136, 152, 192, 201, 223, 251, 257, 263, 340, 374, 402
    New Delhi, 136, 152, 167, 169, 171, 192, 212, 223, 251, 257, 263, 276, 304, 383, 392, 430
    Stockholm, 152, 169, 171, 182, 192, 223, 246, 251, 257, 263, 295, 402
  1958
    Frankfurt, 144, 171, 225, 265, 295, 341, 376, 403, 416
    Jakarta and Singapore, 201, 235, 265, 352, 363
    Kampala, 225, 235, 265, 330, 416, 447
    Sydney, 224, 225, 265, 277, 363
    Wilmette, 171, 201, 226, 265
  1967, 154, 265-6, 349
    Frankfurt, 183, 349
Intermarriage, 79-80
International Archives, 142, 166, 169, 200, 223, 234, 333, 375-6
International Bahá'í Council, 142, 167, 171, 199-200, 203, 221-2, 223, 226, 227, 328, 329
International Teaching Centre, xvi, 257, 350
Ioas, Charles and Maria, 194-5
Ioas, Leroy, 167, 192, 194-203, 223, 224, 319, 329-30, 375, 376
Ioas, Sylvia Kuhlman, 195, 199, 223
Ioas family, 194, 195-6, 202
Iranian Revolution, 342, 354
'Isá, Mírzá, 4
Ismu'lláhu'l-Aṣdaq *see* Ṣádiq-i-Muqaddas-i-K͟hurásání, Mullá
Ives, Howard Colby and Mabel, 425

Jack, Marion, 214
Jamál Burújirdí, Siyyid, 4
Jamál Effendi (Sulaymán K͟hán), 109-10
Jordan, David Starr, 197

Kajubi, Crispian, 262
Kámrán Mírzá, 20, 21, 49
Káẓim-i-Ras͟htí, Ḥájí Siyyid, 29-30
Kehler, James, 87-8
Kelsey, Curtis, 121-2
Kempton, Honor, 58
Kenyerezi, Max, 413
Khadem, Jávídu͟kht Jávíd, 281-2
Khadem, Zikrullah, xvi, 88, 92, 263, 279-87, 479
  family of, 279, 282, 285
K͟hadíjih-Bagum, 367, 378
K͟hádim, Mírzá Naṣru'lláh, 279-80
Khan, Ali Kuli, 79-80, 118, 130, 358
K͟hayru'lláh, Ibráhím, 213-14, 215
K͟házeh, Fark͟hundih, 338
K͟házeh, Jalál, 338-43
K͟házeh, Jamáliyyih, 339
K͟házeh, Núráníyyih, 342

Kinney family, 186
Kitáb-i-'Ahd, xiii, 233, 293
Kitáb-i-Aqdas, xiii, 154, 156, 215, 232
Kitáb-i-Íqán, 3, 98, 112, 190, 242, 283-4, 290-1, 308, 384
Knight, Moses and Martha, 306-7
Knights of Bahá'u'lláh, 393, 406, 407, 414, 420, 427, 430, 433
Knobloch, Alma, 176
Kohler, Paul, 180
Krug, Grace, 118
Ku Klux Klan, 76

Lamprill, Gretta, 59
Latimer, George, 190, 197, 218, 269
Lawḥ-i-Aḥbáb, 36
Lawḥ-i-Dunyá, 6
Lawḥ-i-Ḥikmat, 27
Lawḥ-i-Ra'ís, 110
Letters of the Living, 30, 236
Lincoln, Abraham, 306
Liqá'íyyih Khánum, 42
Louhelen Summer School, 132
Love, 240, 247, 260, 309, 320, 363, 380, 418, 441

Malietoa Tanumafili II, 171-2, 173, 417
Marie, Queen of Romania, 105-6, 221
Martyrdom, 9, 12, 38-9, 43-4, 87, 94-5, 206, 233, 236, 252
Marzotto, Count Paolo, 172
Mashhadí 'Alí, 23
Mashriqu'l-Adhkár *see* Houses of Worship
Mas'úd Mírzá, Ẓillu's-Sulṭán, 41
Mathew, Louisa *see* Gregory, Louisa
Mathews, Loulie and Wanden, 159
Mathias, Louise Baker, 134
Maxwell, Edward, 204-5, 206
Maxwell, Mary *see* Amatu'l-Bahá Rúḥíyyih Khánum
Maxwell, May Bolles, 88, 142, 205-6, 211, 213-14, 218, 299, 323-5, 326, 332, 336, 345-6, 358, 364
Maxwell, William Sutherland, 162-3, 167, 204-12, 218, 220, 304, 305, 323-5, 333, 336, 430, 469
McDaniel, Allen, 303
Mihdí, Ḥájí Siyyid, 110
Mihdí, Siyyid, 20
Mihdíy-i-Yazdí, Ḥájí Mullá, 39-40
Mills, Mountfort, 123, 189, 190
Miṣbáh, 'Azízu'lláh, 151
Molema, Dr Modiri, 432, 436
Molyneux, Dr, 106
Momen, Moojan, xxiii, 377-8, 477
Morten, Marjorie, 118
Muhájir, Írán Furútan, 406
Muhájir, Dr Raḥmatu'lláh, 137, 235, 405-10, 479
family of, 405-6
Muḥammad-'Alí, Mírzá, 6, 42, 233
Muḥammad-'Alíy-i-Sabzivárí, Karbalá'í, 147
Muḥammad-'Alíy-i-Zunúzí, Mírzá, (Anís), 161
Muḥammad-Báqir, Mírzá, 33
Muḥammad-i-Furúghí, 33
Muḥammad-Ḥasan, 367
Muḥammad-Ḥasan, Mírzá (King of Martyrs), 87, 95, 97
Muḥammad-Ḥasan-i-Sabzivárí, Shaykh, 39
Muḥammad-Ḥusayn, Mírzá (Beloved of Martyrs), 87, 97
Muḥammad Ḥusayn Ulfat, Áqá, 339

Muḥammad-Káẓim-Samandar, 229
Muḥammad Mustafa Soleiman, 264
Muḥammad Náẓimu'l-Ḥukamá, Siyyid, 255-6
Muḥammad-i-Qá'iní *see* Nabíl-i-Akbar
Muḥammad-Riḍá, Ḥájí Mírzá, 36
Muḥammad-i-Riḍáy-i-Muḥammad-Ábádí, Mullá *see* Riḍá, Mullá
Muḥammad Sháh, 31
Muḥammad-Taqí, Ḥájí Mírzá *see* Vakílu'd-Dawlih
Muḥammad-Taqí, Mírzá *see* Ibn-i-Abhar
Muḥammad-Taqí, Shaykh (Son of the Wolf), 16
Muḥammad Taqí Iṣfahání, 97-8
Mühlschlegel, Adelbert, 183, 262, 288-98, 376
Mühlschlegel, Herma Weidle, 290, 294-5, 296
Mühlschlegel, Ursula Kohler, 296-7
Muḥsin-i-Fayḍ, Mullá, 380
Munavvar Khánum, 367
Mungono, Samson, 413
Munírih Khánum, daughter of Mullá 'Alí-Akbar, 14
Munírih Khánum, wife of 'Abdu'l-Bahá, 323
Murtaḍáy-i-Anṣárí, Shaykh, 25
Muther, Elizabeth, 359
Muẓaffari'd-Dín Sháh, 23, 41
Nabíl-i-Akbar (Muḥammad-i-Qá'iní), 15, 25-8
Nabíl-i-Zarandí, 231, 285
*Nabíl's Narrative* see *Dawn-Breakers*
Nakhjavání, 'Alí, 261-2, 263, 264, 412-14
Nakhjavání, Bahiyyih, 261-2, 412
Nakhjavání, Jalál, 264
Nakhjavání, Violette Banání, 261-2, 266, 331, 333, 412-14

Náṣiri'd-Dín Sháh, 20, 26, 35, 49, 99
  assassination of, 22, 38
Naṣru'lláh, Mírzá, 279-80
National Spiritual Assemblies (also Regional NSAs), 144, 152, 153, 182, 189, 200, 222, 225, 227, 263, 277, 295, 296, 329, 341, 348, 385, 395, 396, 433, 447
  Alaska, 347
  Arabia, 234
  Argentina, Chile, Uruguay, Paraguay and Bolivia (Regional), 352
  Australia, 171, 395
  Australia and New Zealand, 57, 59-60, 61, 63, 113, 273, 274-5, 302, 390, 391, 392, 393-4
  Austria, 296
  Baltic Republics, 155
  Belgium, 352
  Belize, 171
  Benelux (Regional), 182
  Bophuthatswana, 436
  Botswana and Malawi, 349
  Brazil, 417
  Brazil, Peru, Colombia, Ecuador and Venezuela, Republics of (Regional), 193
  British Isles, 123, 244-5, 246, 261, 369, 370, 371-2, 373, 374, 375, 376, 401, 402, 412
  Brunei, 341
  Burma, 235
  Burundi and Rwanda, 416
  Canada, 191, 301, 304, 346, 428-9
  Central African Republic, 352
  Central America and the Antilles (Regional), 191
  Central and East Africa (Regional), 264, 375
  Chad, 416
  Colombia, 257
  Congo-Brazzaville, 352
  Cuba, 416
  Czechoslovakia, 352
  Denmark, 376
  Dominican Republic, 416
  Eastern Malaysia, 341
  Ecuador, 376
  Egypt, 50-1, 98, 261
  Finland, 296
  France, 228, 352, 384, 447
  French Antilles, 352
  Germany, 296, 297
  Germany and Austria, 177, 180, 181, 201, 290, 292, 295
  Greece, 297
  Greenland, 352
  Haiti, 171
  Hawaiian Islands, 364
  Hungary, 155
  Iberian Peninsula (Regional), 171
  Iceland, 416
  India and Burma, 112
  India, Pakistan and Burma, 261, 302
  Indian Ocean, 416
  Iran, 90, 94-5, 151, 152, 153, 234, 251, 257, 261, 282, 284, 286, 339-40, 354, 382, 407
  Italy, 171
  Italy and Switzerland, 171, 346
  Jamaica, 257, 416
  Jordan, 352
  Leeward, Windward and Virgin Islands, 171
  Lesotho, 297
  Liberia and Guinea, 416
  Luxembourg, 352
  Martinique and French Guiana, 352
  Mauritania, 352
  Netherlands, 376
  New Zealand, 276, 395
  North East Africa (Regional), 264, 415
  North East Asia (Regional), 340, 363
  North West Africa (Regional), 264, 415
  Norway, 403
  Pacific (Regional), 394
  Pakistan, 257
  Peru, 135, 376
  Scandinavia and Finland (Regional), 295, 296
  Seychelles, 297
  Sicily, 352
  Sierra Leone, 416
  Singapore, 341
  Slovakia, 355
  Slovenia and Croatia (Regional), 352
  South America (Regional), 346
  South and West Africa (Regional), 264, 347, 433, 446
  South Central Africa (Regional), 416
  South East Asia (Regional), 152, 407
  South Pacific Islands (Regional), 277
  Soviet Union, 155
  Sri Lanka, 257
  Swaziland, 297
  Swaziland, Lesotho and Mozambique, 416
  Sweden, 296
  Switzerland, 171, 296-7
  Turkey, 285

Ukraine, Moldova and Belarus (Regional), 352
United Kingdom, 342
United States, 136, 184, 193, 199, 346, 347, 348
United States and Canada, 52, 83, 86, 89-93, 118, 123, 133, 134, 141, 184, 188, 189, 191, 197, 198, 282, 286-7, 300, 301, 303, 313, 317, 346, 428
Upper Volta, 416
Upper West Africa (Regional), 416
Venezuela, 171
Vietnam, 349
West Africa (Regional), 435
West Central Africa (Regional), 435
Windward Islands, 352
Náyibu's-Salṭanih, 5
Nine Year Plan, 153, 202
*Nova Tago, La*, 177, 179

Obedience to government, 292-3, 393
Ober, Grace Robarts, 118, 176, 422-3, 424-6
Ober, Harlan, 14, 82, 176, 424-6
Olga, Princess, 105
Olinga, Elizabeth, 416, 419-20
Olinga, Enoch, xvi, 154, 262, 411-20, 434
Olinga, Eunice, 411, 416
Olinga family, 411, 416, 418-20

Palermo Conference, 154, 172, 403, 416
Parker, Katherine, 66
Parkhurst, Mary Ida *see* Haney, Mariam
Parsons, Agnes, 84, 122
Paul, Prince, 105
Perks, Thelma, 393
Perseverance, 165-6
Pioneering, 60-1, 113, 136, 160, 234, 236, 261-2, 266, 271, 275-6, 277, 278, 283, 298, 359, 374, 383, 386, 393, 402, 405, 406-7, 413-14, 415, 429, 430-2, 433-4, 444, 446
Political activity, 370, 393
Prayer, 135, 141, 145, 333, 357, 434, 435, 448
*Priceless Pearl, The*, 104
*Proclamation of Bahá'u'lláh, The*, 171, 172
*Promised Day Is Come, The*,190, 282, 326
*Promulgation of Universal Peace, The*, 318, 442
Psychology, 156

Qá'im, 20
Qaṣidiy-i-Varqá'íyyih, 19
Qayyúmu'l-Asmá', 31, 284
Quddús, 8, 30-4, 96
Quigley, Robert, 447

Rabbani, Madame *see* Amatu'l-Bahá Rúḥíyyih Khánum (Mary Maxwell),
Race amity conferences, 84-5
Racial issues, 75-86, 134, 154-5
Rafsanjání, 'Alí-Akbar, 233, 339
Ransom, Julia, 87
Ransom, Ralph (Guy), 87
Ransom-Kehler, Keith, 59, 87-96, 272, 281, 302, 362, 381
Rasúl, Ḥájí, 229
Regional (National) Spiritual Assemblies *see* National Spiritual Assemblies
Remey, Charles Mason, 79, 123, 143, 193, 210, 213-38, 296, 348, 352, 358, 384, 469
Revell, Jessie and Ethel, 221, 223
Rexford, Orcella, 196
Reza Sháh Pahlaví, 190
Rice Lake, 428
Riḍá, Mullá (Mullá Muḥammad-i-Riḍáy-i-Muḥammad-Ábádí), 19-24
Risáliy-i-Siyásíyyih, 11
Robarts, Audrey FitzGerald, 421, 423-36
Robarts, Grace *see* Ober, Grace Robarts
Robarts, John Aldham, xvi, 264, 373, 395, 412-39
Robarts family, 422, 425, 429-32
Roche, Nellie Jennings, 239
Root, Martha Louise, 58, 72-3, 99-108, 117-18, 120, 121, 123-5, 221, 293, 301, 360-2
Root, Nancy Hart, 99, 103
Root, Timothy T., 99, 103
Rosenberg, Ethel, 67, 70, 71, 123, 358
Rúḥíyyih Khánum *see* Amatu'l-Bahá Rúḥíyyih Khánum
Rúmí, Muṣṭafáy-i-, 109-14

Sa'ad, 'Abdu'l-Jalíl Bey, 50-2
Sacrifice, 95-6, 125, 160, 446
Ṣádiq-Muqaddas-i-Khurásání, Mullá (Ismu'lláhu'l-Aṣdaq), 3, 8, 29-37, 459
Samandarí, Ṭarázíyyih, 229, 233, 234
Samandarí, Ṭarázu'lláh, xvi, 229-37, 352
Samandarí, Thurayyá, 232-3
Samandarí family, 229
Schopflocher, Florence Evaline 'Lorol' Snyder, 299, 302-3
Schopflocher, Siegfried (Fred) 59, 212, 299-305, 403, 430
Schwarz, Consul and Alice, 123
Sears, Marguerite Reimer, 431, 442-4, 446-9
Sears, William, xvi, 264, 295, 320, 431, 434, 435, 440-50
Sears family, 431, 440-2

Sethji, Narayan Rao (Vakíl), 111
Seven Valleys, 130, 178
Seven Year Plan (North America),
first, 85, 196, 198, 304, 318, 426
second, 160, 428-9
Shahíd Ibn-i-Shahíd *see* Ibn-i-Aṣdaq
Sháh-Muḥammad Manshádí, Ḥájí, 4, 48
Shaw, George Bernard, 238
Shaykhís, 3, 25
Shoghi Effendi, 51, 59, 60, 62-3, 67-74, 79, 96, 98, 99, 106-7, 122-3, 126, 132, 134, 136, 139, 140-4, 158, 168-70, 179, 184, 194, 234, 245, 246, 251, 260, 262, 272, 273, 281-5, 301, 303, 325-30, 331, 336, 338, 339-40, 343, 352, 354, 362-3, 368-9, 370, 377, 380-4, 387, 392-4, 402-3, 406, 411, 412, 414-15, 417-18, 430, 432-3, 434, 445-6
appointed Guardian, 71, 82, 98
appoints Hands of the Cause, 49, 52, 63, 74, 86, 94, 98, 107, 113, 126, 128, 142, 254, 328, 340, 346-7, 351-2, 363, 366, 434
builds superstructure of the Shrine of the Báb, 160-6, 204, 206-12, 326
family of, 224, 326-7
funeral of, 144, 153, 170, 201, 224, 288-9, 329-30, 363, 375, 384, 403
Hands of the Cause appointed posthumously by, 45-126
letters of, 105, 106, 133, 143, 148-9, 150, 153, 159-60, 166, 177, 178, 181, 187-9, 190, 191, 197, 199, 243, 274, 283, 291-4, 302, 318, 319, 347, 352, 362, 363, 370, 371, 373, 382, 383, 390, 398, 401, 402, 406, 414, 415, 427, 428-9, 435n
literary style of, 159-60, 242
marriage of, 206, 325-6
passing of, xiv, 144, 152, 170, 193, 201, 224, 226, 234, 265, 276, 279, 285, 288-9, 319, 328-9, 375, 403
resting place of, 265, 378-9
sufferings of, 88-9, 104, 199, 325, 327
summons prominent Bahá'ís to Haifa (1922), 122-3, 220-1, 317
translations by, 69, 72, 242, 291
tributes by *see* Hands of the Cause, tributes to
work of, 187-9, 190, 199, 207, 326-7, 373
Shrine of the Báb, 121, 126, 152, 161-6, 200, 204, 206-12, 221, 223, 281, 323, 326
doors of, named for Hands of the Cause, 49, 167, 200, 203, 212
Shrine of Bahá'u'lláh, 121, 142, 143-4, 145, 167-8, 200, 201, 224, 225, 233, 265, 379
Síyáh-Chál, 8, 22, 35
Six Year Plan (Australia and New Zealand), 275, 391
Six Year Plan (British Isles), 373, 374, 429
Six Year Plan, International (1986-92), 287
Smith, Clarence Hobron, 359
Smyth, Daisy, 325
*Some Answered Questions*, 98, 112
Spendlove, George, 428
Spiritual Assemblies, 61, 71, 86, 88, 89, 130, 142, 151, 155, 159, 160, 171, 195, 196-7, 198, 202, 205, 215, 217, 234, 251, 257, 262, 263, 264, 265, 271, 273, 286, 310-11, 339, 340, 342, 359, 362, 369, 373, 390, 391, 393, 394, 401, 408, 412-13, 425, 426-7, 429, 433, 436, 437
*see also* Central Assembly of Ṭihrán, National Spiritual Assemblies
Sprague, Sidney, 16, 217
*Star of the West*, 83, 187, 218, 219, 315, 395
Steadfastness, 438
Stevenson, Margaret, 57
Stowe, Harriet Beecher, 129
Struven, Howard, 217-18
Ṣubḥ-i-Azal *see* Yaḥyá, Mírzá
Sulaymán Khán *see* Jamál Effendi
Sun Yat Sen, 361

Ṭabarsí, Fort Shaykh, 3, 8, 33-4
Tablet of Aḥmad, 35, 72, 131, 134, 435
Tablets of the Divine Plan, 55-6, 60, 81, 99, 103, 172, 271, 324, 333, 364
Tablet to the Hague, 69
Taherzadeh, Adib, 19n, 245
Ṭáhirih, 105, 107, 229
Tanyi, David, 414
Tarbíyat Schools, 14, 15, 151, 250, 256, 281, 339, 381-2
Tash, Tamur, 91
Teaching the Bahá'í Faith, 9, 12, 19, 27, 102, 135, 137, 148, 155, 272, 313, 333-4, 344-5, 346, 388, 409, 427-8, 437, 448
Ten Year Crusade, xiv, 136, 152, 169, 171, 179, 182, 201, 263, 265, 275, 284, 319, 326, 331, 336, 339, 374-5, 392, 394-5, 402, 406, 414, 415, 444
Thompson, Juliet, 118-19, 218, 325
Ṭihrání, Jamálíyyih, 338
Ṭihrání, Karbalá'í Mihdí, 338
Tinnion, Nina Grace Robarts, 427-8
Tolstoy, Leo, 106, 149
Townshend, Anna Sarah (Nancy) Maxwell, 240, 244-5

Townshend, George, 238-48, 363, 373, 377, 403
Townshend family, 238
True, Corinne Knight, 68, 201, 219, 220, 224, 306-20, 345
True, Edna, 68, 136, 307, 316, 318, 319
True, Moses Adam, 307, 309-10, 314, 315
True family, 307-8
Truman, President Harry S., 190
Tudor Pole, Major Wellesley, 67, 70, 123

'Udhrá Khánum, Ḍiyá'u'l-Ḥájiyyih (Aghá Ján), 9
United Nations, 182, 199, 221
Universal House of Justice, xiv-xvi, 153-4, 156-7, 220-1, 222, 228, 273, 286, 296-7, 326, 332, 336-7, 341, 343, 349, 353-4, 384, 386, 396, 420, 449
  election of, 183, 202, 225, 226, 285, 330, 348, 353, 364, 379
  Seat of, 172-3, 433

Vail, Albert, 131
Vakíl (Narayan Rao Sethji), 111
Vakílu'd-Dawlih (Ḥájí Mírzá Muḥammad-Taqí), 73, 145, 193
Varqá, Dr 'Alí Muḥammad, 224, 252, 295, 351-5
Varqá, Mírzá 'Alí-Muḥammad, 38-44, 102, 249-50, 351, 479
Varqá, 'Azizu'lláh, 40, 41, 42, 250, 351
Varqá, Badí'u'lláh, 40, 42, 249-50
Varqá, Rawḥáníyyih Muhtadí, 351
Varqá, Rúḥu'lláh, 38-9, 42-4, 102, 249
Varqá, Valíyu'lláh, 40, 42, 102, 249-52, 351
Varqá family, 39-40, 41, 42, 102, 249-50, 351, 460
Vatican, 172
Victoria, Queen of England, 106

Weeden, Ben, 208-9, 221
Weeden, Gladys, 221
Wheeler, Helen Margery *see* Haney, Helen Margery
Whitaker, Oswald, 57
Whitehead, O Z, 373
Wilhelm, J O, 123-4
Wilhelm, Laurie, 115-17, 120, 125
Wilhelm, Roy, 101, 105, 106, 115-26, 190, 301, 361
Wilhelm II, Kaiser, 175
Will and Testament of 'Abdu'l-Bahá, xiii, xiv, 97, 112, 140, 202, 222, 224, 225, 226, 235, 317, 329, 330, 375, 398
Wilson, Valerie, 264
Women, 10, 14, 150, 217, 310-11, 409
Woodcock, Percy, 314
World Congress
  First Bahá'í, xiv-xv, 183, 202, 285, 331, 352, 364, 377, 395, 403, 416, 435
  Second Bahá'í, 332
World Order of Bahá'u'lláh, 141, 153, 178, 182, 433
*World Order of Bahá'u'lláh, The*, 190
*World Order Magazine*, 83
*World Unity Magazine*, 187

Yaḥyá, Mírzá, 12, 24
Yazdí, 'Aziz, 261, 264
Yerrinbool Bahá'í School, 273-4
Youth, 15, 149, 291, 297, 324, 349, 355, 368-9, 381, 385, 386, 390, 405-6

Zaynu'l-'Ábidín Khán, 26
Ẓillu's-Sulṭán (Mas'úd Mírzá), 41

www.ingramcontent.com/pod-product-compliance
Lightning Source LLC
Chambersburg PA
CBHW071231300426
44116CB00008B/989
*9780853984139*